Total Quality Control

THIRD EDITION, Revised

Fortieth Anniversary Edition

A. V. Feigenbaum
President, General Systems Company, Inc.
Pittsfield, Massachusetts

McGraw-Hill, Inc.

New York · St. Louis · San Francisco · Auckland · Bogotá
Caracas · Hamburg · Lisbon · London · Madrid
Mexico · Milan · Montreal · New Delhi · Paris
San Juan · São Paulo · Singapore
Sydney · Tokyo · Toronto

046949

TO THE MEMORY OF H.S.F., J.V. AND I.V.

TOTAL QUALITY CONTROL, 3/e Revised
INTERNATIONAL EDITION 1991

Certain technical terms and usages in this book, although
reflecting only the masculine gender, are in fact the parlance of
the fields and should be interpreted to apply to both sexes.

Exclusive rights by McGraw-Hill Book Co. - Singapore
for manufacture and export. This book cannot be re-exported
from the country to which it is consigned by McGraw-Hill.

4 5 6 7 8 9 0 CMO SW 9 5 4 3

The sponsoring editor for this book was Gail Nalven, the
editing supervisor was Kimberly A. Goff, and the production
supervisor was Suzanne W. Babeuf.

This book was set in Baskerville. It was composed by ComCom.

Library of Congress Cataloging-in-Publication Data

Feigenbaum, A. V. (Armand Vallin)
Total quality control / A.V. Feigenbaum—3rd ed., rev.
p. cm.
Includes bibliographical references and index.
ISBN 0-07-020354-7:
1. Quality control. I. Title
TS156.F44 1991
658.5'62—dc20   90-48438
                                                      CIP

When ordering this title use ISBN 0-07-112612-0

Printed in Singapore

CONTENTS

PART SIX   **APPLYING TOTAL QUALITY CONTROL IN THE COMPANY**   613

18.   New-Design Control 615

PREFACE TO
FORTIETH ANNIVERSARY EDITION

Quality leadership is the key to business success in the 1990s. Since its original presentation in this book, total quality has become increasingly widely recognized as the basis for achievement of this quality result by companies both large and small.

The lifestyles of consumers and the business effectiveness of companies now depend upon the reliable, consistent performance of products and services with no tolerance for the lost time and costs of any failures. Quality has become the fundamental strategy for competitiveness today.

Moreover, quality has gone global. It has become the key for effectively focusing any company, anywhere, for market growth and profitability through quality leadership. The General Systems Company experience in installing total quality control in hundreds of companies throughout the world is that it is the best return-on-investment opportunity for both manufacturing and service organizations.

The key is recognition that quality is what the customer—not the company—says it is. It results from strong customer-driven work and teamwork processes throughout all areas of the organization. These are processes which people understand, believe in and are part of, and which must be systematically developed in terms of the best quality practices that are available in the world.

There is a staggering difference between such total quality control and the partial approach of those companies in which quality, while given attention, is characterized by a collection of technical projects and motivational initiatives. Quality has become the most powerful corporate change agent of our time and perhaps the single most important managerial demand facing many companies today.

The several editions of *Total Quality Control* over the past four decades have been directed to providing the basis for converting a company from a partial quality control past to a total quality control future. *Total Quality Control* has consistently confronted the depiction of quality as a narrow technical specialty or a promotional device with a very different principle. The principle presented here is, in its essence, that quality is a fundamental way of managing an organization. It improves the basic business, management, and technical activities so as simultaneously to achieve customer satisfaction, human resource effectiveness, and lower costs.

Awareness of the importance of quality is everywhere today. One of the major reasons for the importance of an initiative such as the Malcolm Baldrige National Quality Award program to the enhancement of the competitiveness of the United States manufacturing and service organizations is that for the first time it establishes guidelines which establish the total quality basis for competitive quality leadership. And such international standards as the ISO 9000 series, while minimum total quality entry level in concept, nonetheless point toward a broad and systematic, rather than narrow, approach to quality achievement. However, the successful implementation of customer-perceived quality results still varies widely among companies.

The creation of this edition began with a question to me by a journalist about my evaluation, as its originator, of the thoroughness and depth of the understanding of total quality in the face of the widespread attention it is now receiving. I told him that the positive factor is the prevalent business recognition today that quality must be defined in customer and not producer terms, and that its achievement depends upon a clear and effective organization-wide program rather than upon a single department or a few specialists. The negative side has been the failure to emphasize strongly enough that accomplishing this is very, very hard work, that it doesn't depend merely upon attention to single quality techniques nor episodic motivational programs, and that it requires relentless, long-term detailed total quality execution.

One of the keys to total quality control is the personal leadership of managers who have acquired the know-how in depth for establishing their organization's quality program and for mobilizing the knowledge, skills, and attitudes of everyone at all levels in its implementation. The objective of this Fortieth Anniversary Edition is to provide the basis for such total quality control understanding by management readers as well as by those with quality professional interest, and indeed by men and women in all the occupations in which quality is of major importance today. This Fortieth Anniversary Edition focuses upon meeting the quality imperative of the 1990s, through the iteration of the fundamental principles and practices of total quality control that have been proven in many companies over a period of many years, together now with the addition of a concise discussion and review of why application of these practices is essential to meeting competitive demands in the 1990s.

Part One through Part Six are, therefore, essentially the same in the presentation of these fundamentals as described in the **Preface to Third Edition.** For this new edition, the book includes the addition of Part Seven, **The Total Quality Imperative for the 1990s,** which reviews the marketplace demands for quality today, the benchmarks of total quality control for meeting these demands, and the management principles that are key to its application. The book concludes with the principles of total quality control: **A Summary.**

The book is organized so that each chapter, as well as each part, can be read as a unit in itself, thereby permitting easy use by the manager, the quality professional, the analyst, and by other readers in terms of their particular quality application. This also permits the ready use of the book in the class-room as well as in other education and training situations.

It is my hope that this Fortieth Anniversary Edition will serve the readers of this book in the pursuit of the quality excellence that is the motivator that drives us all.

I want to express my deep gratitude to Donald S. Feigenbaum, whose practical judgment, creative insights, and constant encouragement have provided an essential foundation and guideline for all of this work. Without his help and support, neither this nor any other edition of *Total Quality Control* would have been possible. Thanks must also be given to Ms. Leslie Warren for her careful attention to many aspects of the book.

It should be remembered that this edition draws heavily on prior editions of *Total Quality Control*. The many men and women who contributed to those previous editions continue to play an important role in the success of this edition.

Dr. Armand V. Feigenbaum
General Systems Company, Inc.
Pittsfield, Massachusetts

PREFACE TO THIRD EDITION

Quality is the basic customer decision factor for an explosively growing number of products and services today—whether the buyer is a housewife, an industrial corporation, a government agency, a department store chain, or a military defense program.

Quality has become the single most important force leading to organizational success and company growth in national and international markets. The return-on-investment from strong and effective quality programs is providing excellent profitability results in firms with effective quality strategies. This is demonstrated by substantial increases in market penetration, by major improvements in total productivity, by much lower costs of quality, and by stronger competitive leadership.

Success in the implementation of this business strategy varies widely, however, among the organizations of the world. More than at any time in memory, buyers perceive that the products of certain companies are significantly higher in quality than those of their competition and they buy accordingly.

A wider variation of effectiveness than ever before also exists among the quality programs of companies. Some are strong in depth and in commitment. Others deal in half measures and try to meet fundamental quality requirements with the fireworks display of one-time quality encouragement programs or through dusting off the application of a few traditional quality-control techniques.

Because of the wide variation in quality results, the search for the genuine keys to success in quality has become a matter of deep concern to management of companies the world over. And experience is disclosing a fundamental basis for achieving this success.

Quality is in its essence a way of managing the organization. Like finance and marketing, quality has now become an essential element of modern management. And effectiveness in the management of quality has become a necessary condition for effectiveness in industrial management itself.

Industrial experience throughout the United States, the Far East, Europe, and Latin America has shown that Total Quality Control (TQC) whose original presentation was made in earlier editions of this book, provides the foundation for this successful management of quality to assure customer satisfaction. The purpose of *Total Quality Control,* Third Edition, is to explain the modern management of quality in practical terms and in depth.

The field of total quality control provides the structure and tools for managing quality so that there is continuous emphasis throughout the organization on quality leadership; genuine investment in, and implementation of, modern technology for quality throughout sales, engineering, and production; and top-to-bottom human commitment to quality and productivity. In effect, quality and its cost are managed and engineered and motivated throughout the organization with the same thoroughness and depth with which successful products and services are themselves managed and engineered and produced and sold and serviced. This makes quality-control programs as important to the success of the organization as capital investment programs, product development programs, and productive efficiency programs—and, in fact, essential to the success of these programs.

Quality control is thus much more than merely a grouping of technical projects and motivational activities, without any clearly articulated managerial focus. Nor does modern quality control have any single regional or geographic identity, nor does it travel under any exclusive national passport. Indeed, one major characteristic of modern quality control is its worldwide character.

The Third Edition of *Total Quality Control* is thus designed and written to present the modern field of quality control as a body of managerial, technological, behavioral, and economic knowledge—together with the organized application of this knowledge to the practical improvement of industrial operations for national as well as international markets. It has greatly extended the foundations of the earlier editions of the book by integrating with them the developments and experience of recent years, as the field of quality control has continued to mature managerially and to deepen technically in response to the wealth of industrial experience.

Quality control is discussed from a business point of view in terms of the economics of profitability, of market leadership and of productivity and cost control. It is considered in the managerial terms of organization, participative management, and strategic planning as well as of the systems approach to quality. It is reviewed with regard to marketing and sales activities from market quality identification and product planning to the determination of customer quality attitudes and of buyer quality expectations. It is explained from the point of view of engineering activities, including the design and quality-oriented development of products, reliability determination, manufacturing-engineering quality coordination, liability control, and safety assurance.

Quality control is examined with regard to the necessary purchasing actions from vendor selection to the ongoing maintenance of supplier quality. It is discussed over the range of activities which bear upon production quality, from manufacturing planning, process control, and automation to equipment capability evaluation and final product assurance.

The book provides a sharp focus upon new approaches to and measurement of total productivity—in the office as well as the factory. It reviews product service and installation actions in quality. It considers both national and international quality operations. And, throughout, thorough attention is paid to the human behavioral and employee-management-relations aspects of modern quality, from recognition of today's worker attitudes to motivation, employee involvement, and the development of genuine and widespread quality commitment.

Moreover, because new product developments, changing buyer demands and technological growth, and continuing competitive pressures make quality a moving target—one that is never static—the future is always placing its thumbprint on quality control. As was the case with the earlier editions, *Total Quality Control,* third edition, is designed to provide the reader—in its tools and activities that deal effectively with the present—with a foundation for also planning successfully to meet the requirements of this future.

I

Total Quality Control is directed to those men and women in industry, commerce, services, and government who are responsible for the successful operation of an organization or some part of it. They may have such responsibilities as chief executive, general manager, manufacturing director, marketing head, chief engineer, quality manager, manufacturing engineering director, quality-engineer, process-control engineer, market and sales planner, reliability engineer, purchasing agent-buyer, development and design engineer, production supervisor, statistician, education and training director, computer systems analyst, merchandise manager, customer service specialist, liability-loss-control attorney, and many others.

It is important to recognize that, once the interest of a few technical people, quality control today is the primary concern of an increasingly large number of managers, engineers, statisticians, and men and women working in many occupations and throughout many organizations in many nations of the world. The problems to which these men and women direct their attention exist in a wide range of forms: the establishment of the right quality objectives in organization plans; the assurance of a positive customer reaction to products; the development of appropriate levels of reliability in a company's components and assemblies; the maintenance of the maximum control of process in the factory; the performance of the right kind of job of preproduction testing; the establishment of meaningful relations between vendor and purchaser; and the improvement of expenditures on quality costs and the corresponding improvement in business results.

The book is designed to help the men and women with these responsibilities and in these occupations to meet successfully the challenging problems they face daily in assuring customer satisfaction by improving product quality and by reducing its related costs. The book may be used in the following ways:

1. As a means to obtain an effective understanding of modern quality management
2. As a guide to the modern practices of quality control
3. As a basis for appraising the organizational, cost-management, and behavioral principles of quality control
4. As a way to learn about the engineering technologies and the statistical approaches of modern quality control
5. As a text for use in management education
6. As a fundamental, comprehensive textbook for quality-control educational programs and courses
7. As a methodological review, refresher, and up-dating for currently operating quality personnel—whether in quality control, marketing, product engineering, manufacturing, or product service
8. As a reference for men and women interested in a wide range of techniques such as preproduction engineering methods, purchasing procedures, quality engineering practices, inspection and testing routines, quality equipment concepts, and quality administration activities

II

The book contains 21 chapters, consolidated in six parts, and concludes with a summary of the principles of total quality control. The book is organized so that each chapter, as well as each part, can be read as a unit in itself, thereby permitting the easy use of the book by the manager, the engineer, the analyst, and other readers in terms of their quality application; it also permits the ready use of the book in classroom as well as in other education and training situations.

The contents of *Total Quality Control* are best described by a summary of its six parts:

Part One—"Business Quality Management." This section presents, in Chapters One through Four, the overall scope of total quality control and the major benefits its application brings to a modern organization. It discusses the management of quality with emphasis upon companywide and plantwide activities; strategic planning that makes quality an integral factor in business planning; competitive market leadership through strong customer quality assurance; and profitability improvement, cost reduction, and return-on-investment performance from quality programs.

It profiles today's buyer—consumer, industrial corporation, government body—and the quality requirements they bring to the marketplace. It profiles today's producers and the new quality demands they face, including such forces as increasingly strong quality competition, strict product liability, safety assurance, and consumerism—and the new business opportunities represented by these forces. It profiles today's worker—white collar and blue collar—and the new workplace environment that is evolving.

Part One considers the range of modern issues dealt with by total quality programs, including major productivity improvements; new and more rapid product development and introduction; automation and changing process technology; computer application and software control; new approaches to vendor and supplier relationships; and the internationalization of operations. It relates this range of quality pressures to today's marketplace, technology, production, and service organizational environment and identifies the total quality factors for meeting customer, market leadership, profitability, and productivity objectives.

Part Two—"The Total Quality System." The purpose of this section is to review, in Chapters Five through Seven, the systems approach to quality and the economics that govern cost-effective systems management.

The section reviews the range of workforce, machine, and information considerations that are involved in the assurance of quality. It outlines the details of the costs of quality including operating quality costs—both of control and failure of control; and other costs of quality such as use-oriented and life-cycle costs, indirect costs, vendor costs, and equipment investment costs.

Part Three—"Management Strategies for Quality." This section presents, in Chapters Eight and Nine, the operating management foundations for quality. It discusses how quality is organized today, and it considers the fundamental issues involved in organizing successfully.

It reviews the development and achievement of total commitment to quality throughout the organization, including education and training; employee-participation programs from round tables and quality circles to quality of working life activities; and the range of management-employee-involvement activities which are essential to the assurance of quality.

Part Four—"Engineering Technology of Quality." The objective of this section is to present, in Chapters Ten through Twelve, the three basic engineering technology areas of total quality control. Quality engineering is discussed with regard to the identification of customer quality requirements and the establishment of quality policy; the development of quality in new products; the analysis of quality activities; and the planning of quality activities.

Process-control engineering is explained in terms of technical steps through which these quality requirements are met in vendor material, in production, and in customer service. Quality-information equipment engineering is reviewed to cover equipment for inspection and testing as well as for computer-aided quality information processing and control.

Part Five—"Statistical Technology of Quality." This section presents, in Chapters Thirteen through Seventeen, five principal areas of statistical methodology in total quality control: frequency distributions; control charts; sampling tables; special methods; and product reliability.

These statistical procedures have often been presented in a fashion requiring advanced mathematical training for their interpretation. Instead, this section provides the point of view represented by these methods in basic algebra and arithmetic.

Formulas, charts, and tables are furnished to the extent that they seem required. Reference material is suggested in footnotes for those readers whose interests and background make further detail about statistics and reliability desirable.

Part Six—"Applying Total Quality Control in the Company." The purpose of this section is the discussion, in Chapters Eighteen through Twenty One, of applications of quality control to company problems, with emphasis on four basic areas: new-design control; incoming material control; product control; and special-process studies.

New-design control is reviewed with regard to the quality of new-product designs and the improvement of the design quality of existing products. Incoming material control is presented in terms of closely integrated control activities with vendors where the cost-effective burden of quality proof rests with the supplier. The examination of product control covers preproduction, in-process, final assembly, shipment, and field product service activities. Special-process studies emphasize programs for both systematic quality improvement and permanent corrective action to eliminate quality deficiencies.

Throughout this presentation of applications, examples are discussed and representative tabular forms and plans outlined.

The book concludes with a summary of the basic principles of total quality. These principles are reviewed as key factors in managing an organization to assure the achievement of the right customer quality at the right quality cost.

III

For the author to include his individual debt to those who have influenced this book, he would have to list associates in his own company as well as scores of colleagues—unfortunately too numerous to mention—in other companies and professional associations in the United States and throughout the world.

A fundamental and unique debt is owed to Donald S. Feigenbaum, who has been deeply involved in all aspects of the planning, development, and review of this book. Donald Feigenbaum's original and pioneering work in systems engineering and systems management, as well as in executive and general management, has provided the foundation and guidelines for the discussions in these areas. With respect to a number of the concepts discussed, the author is acting much as a recorder of the work of Mr. Feigenbaum.

Appreciation must be expressed to Mrs. Nancy Way, who worked with the author in the full development of the book and who provided thoroughness and care throughout.

Particular appreciation must be given to Professor Mason Wescott, who reviewed in detail the statistical chapters and made a number of incisive recommendations and several improvements in the text.

Personal appreciation is owed Professor Leo Aroian, who read the section on statistical technology and gave valuable suggestions which benefited the text.

Deep gratitude must be expressed to Mrs. Marjorie Steele for overseeing the secretarial completion of the manuscript and for personally handling important parts.

Thanks must also be given to Miss Linda Sambel for graphic art for the book.

It should be recalled that this book draws heavily upon previous editions of *Total Quality Control.* The many persons who contributed to those earlier volumes thus have played a significant part in this book.

Armand V. Feigenbaum

PART ONE
Business Quality Management

CHAPTER 1

The Quality of Products and Services and Total Quality Control

Recent years have seen the growth of an unprecedented new kind of world marketplace of volume, of variation, and of quality. It is a marketplace in which the rising expectations of buyers—whether consumers or industrial corporations—coupled with the changing role of government have greatly intensified the demands upon business management.

The breadth and complexity of these demands embrace a whole spectrum of management problems—price structure and cost reduction, industrial relations and organizational development, technological change and mechanization, or selling and new product introduction. And all this is taking place within a framework in which business and government—not only at federal but at state and municipal levels—are moving into entirely new types of relationships.

Moreover, in a turbulent process which amounts to redefining "standards of living" in terms acceptable to all of us in our dual roles as consumers and producers, debates about pollution and economic growth and consumerism and energy and worker participation and team manufacturing are leading to changes in our industrial concepts so massive that some people have begun to say the changes constitute a second Industrial Revolution. The concepts have been evolving major new dimensions for both products and services as well as for the engineering and manufacturing processes that will produce them.

Effective solutions to many current problems are no longer matters of traditional management and engineering methodology. They are, instead, matters of critically important new management and engineering substance, such as:

Managing to assure *total company* productivity, rather than only that of the factory direct workers

3

- Managing to make the businessperson, the scientist, and the engineer a *sum* rather than a *difference*
- Managing to approach product consumerism positively rather than negatively
- Managing to confront the necessity for energy and materials conservation and waste reduction and improved resource utilization
- Managing in international terms rather than only as national managements looking outward to other markets

Nowhere is this need for improvement more clearly evident than in the area of the *quality* of products and services. This is a situation with which industry is vitally concerned and one calling for the new systems and technologies of total quality control.

The role of total quality control in attaining the necessary major improvements in both quality and quality costs is discussed in Chapter 1. Chapter 2 considers today's buyer and producer and the unique marketplace they share. Chapter 3 then examines the impact of today's changing conditions upon management in industry, commerce, and government. With this background, Chapter 4 then addresses the need to make quality control operational in plants and companies, identifying first the key factors that must be dealt with and then the key jobs necessary to achieve specific quality goals.

1.1 What Is the New Impact of Quality?

Today, our daily lives and schedules depend totally upon the satisfactory performance and operation of products and services—whether of a metropolitan electric network, a pharmaceutical in an intensive care ward, an automatic clothes washer for a growing young family, or the automobile which will be used as a family bus for 14 hours a day. This no-alternative situation—or "zero redundancy" in more technical terms—is basically something new for society, and it has explosively increased customer demand for greater durability and reliability in products and services.

While today's buyers continue to purchase with strong attention to price, unlike the buyers of only a few years ago, they place increasingly high emphasis upon quality, expecting acceptable products at *any* price level. It is quality as well as price that sells today, and quality that brings customers back for the second, third, and fifteenth time.

Indeed, industry's outstanding quality accomplishments in fulfilling these requirements during the past decades are familiar history. The major challenge that has resulted from more complex consumer products with increased functions and performance requirements is being met with growing effectiveness from consumer electronics and household durables to "miracle" fibers and home-heating and -cooling products. The high degree of reliability required for complex equipment systems, from long-range transportation to space vehicles, has made very great progress. While much more remains to be done, the results side of the quality picture shows some improvement.

Less improved, however, is the picture revealed when the behind-the-scenes effort to assure these high-quality standards is examined. For every dollar spent in planned engineering, production, and product service, a great number of industries today are losing many additional cents because of poor quality practices during engineering and manufacture or after a product is in the field.

Although most quality failures continue to be discovered in the factory instead of after shipment, the techniques for finding them often are excessively costly and wasteful. Moreover, in some cases, products which may fail soon after being placed in service have not always been detected in the factory. These conditions cannot be tolerated by any industry striving to maintain and improve its competitive position.

The costs of quality and safety today account for an increasingly significant proportion of the Gross National Product (GNP). The burden of expense falls heavily upon the manufacturer in the form of costs for quality, which may amount from 7 to 10 percent—and even more—of total sales billed. It also strongly affects the buyer, whose maintenance and operation costs may be comparable to the original purchase price, as well as the merchant, whose rate of product returns may equal or exceed the profit margin.

Product quality and safety thus have quite properly become a major concern of government and a political force with which to be reckoned. As the quality subject spills into the courts in the form of a growing avalanche of strict product-liability claims, it is altering 2000 years of "consumer beware" law into "producer beware" judgments. And the increasing public concern with quality has become so vocal that it is changing economic, legal, and political patterns of long standing.

The attainment and maintenance of satisfactory levels of customer satisfaction with the quality of products and services are today fundamental determinants for business health, growth, and economic viability. Correspondingly, quality is becoming a principal guidepost in the development and successful implementation of the managerial and engineering programs for realizing major business goals. And quality control—the managerial objectives, the tools, the techniques—must be fully effectively structured today to satisfy the demands of this new market and business framework.

1.2 What Is Total Quality Control and What Is Its Purpose?

The goal of competitive industry, as far as product quality is concerned, can be clearly stated: It is to provide a product and service into which quality is designed, built, marketed, and maintained at the most economical costs which allow for full customer satisfaction.

It is to the comprehensive, companywide system for achieving that goal which this book refers when it uses the phrase "total quality control." Or, as a definition:

Total quality control is an effective system for integrating the quality-development, quality-maintenance, and quality-improvement efforts of the various groups in an organization so as to enable marketing, engineering, production, and service at the most economical levels which allow for full customer satisfaction.

Its breadth and its essentiality to the achievement of business results make total quality control a new and important area of management. As a focus of managerial and technical leadership, total quality control has produced outstanding improvements in product quality and reliability for many organizations throughout the world.[1] Moreover, total quality control has achieved progressive and substantial reductions in quality costs. Through total quality control, company managements have been able to deal from strength and confidence in the quality of their products and services, permitting them to move forward in market volume and product mix expansion with a high degree of customer acceptance and profit stability and growth.

Total quality control provides the fundamental basis of positive quality motivation for all company employees and representatives, from top management through assembly workers, office personnel, dealers, and servicepeople. And a powerful total-quality-control capability is one of the principal company strengths for achieving vastly improved total productivity.

Effective human relations is basic to quality control.[2] A major feature of this activity is its positive effect in building up employee responsibility for, and interest in, product quality. In the final analysis it is a pair of human hands which performs the important operations affecting product quality. It is of utmost importance to successful quality-control work that these hands be guided in a skilled, conscientious, and quality-minded fashion.

Sound technological methods are also basic. A variety of these methods is now being used. Included are activities for specifying engineering tolerances in user-oriented terms, accelerated test methods for evaluating component and systems reliability, classifying quality characteristics, vendor rating methods, sampling-inspection techniques, process-control techniques, design of quality-control measuring equipment, computer-based quality data processing, gaging systems, standards establishment, product-quality evaluation and rating schemes, application of statistical techniques from $\overline{X}$ and R charts to designed experiments, and many others.

It is interesting to note that these individual methods have themselves been used as definitions for quality control over the years. The written and spoken word often finds quality control defined as some form of sampling inspection, as a portion of industrial statistics, as reliability work, or as simply inspection or testing. These several definitions have described only individual parts of, or methods in, an overall quality-control program. They may have contributed to the confusion with which the term is sometimes associated in industry.

The terms "quality control" and "quality assurance" have come to have different meanings in some organizations—each term referring to different aspects of customer quality-satisfaction activity. Total-quality-control programs in their operation include and integrate the actions involved in the work covered by both terms.

1.3 The Meaning of "Quality"

Quality is a customer determination, not an engineer's determination, not a marketing determination or a general management determination. It is based upon the customer's actual experience with the product or service, measured against his or her *requirements*—stated or unstated, conscious or merely sensed, technically operational or entirely subjective—and always representing a moving target in a competitive market.

Product and service quality can be defined as:

> The total composite product and service characteristics of marketing, engineering, manufacture, and maintenance through which the product and service in use will meet the expectations of the customer.

The purpose of most quality measurements is to determine and evaluate the *degree* or *level* to which the product or service approaches this total composite.

Some other terms, such as *reliability, serviceability,* and *maintainability,* have sometimes been used as definitions for product quality. These terms are of course individual *characteristics* which make up the composite of product and service quality.

It is important to recognize this fact because the key requirement for establishing what is to be the "quality" of a given product requires the economic balancing-off of these various individual quality characteristics. For example, the product must perform its intended function repeatedly as called upon, over its stipulated *life cycle* under intended environments and conditions of use—in other words, it must have good *reliability.* Of overriding importance, the produce must be *safe.* The reasonable degree of product service and maintainability must be established, so the product must have proper *serviceability* and *maintainability* over its life cycle. The product must have appearance suitable to customer requirements, so it must have *attractability.* When all the other product characteristics are balanced in, the "right" quality becomes that composite which provides the intended functions with the greatest overall economy, considering among other things product and service obsolescence—and it is the *total customer-satisfaction*-oriented concept of "quality" that must be controlled.

Moreover, this balance can change as the product or service itself changes. For example, each of the four stages of the maturity cycle through which many products pass demands a somewhat different quality balance—whether the first radial tires to the new more sophisticated radial products or the original wide-bodied aircraft to the ultimately more efficient and more comfortable passenger aircraft. Consumer television sets are one example. At the first stage, product quality was heavily dominated by *innovation* of the then-new function, which itself sold the product. Buyers of television sets, for instance, were first attracted to the then-new product's novelty and newness. Rough quality edges, such as unclear and wavy pictures, incessant static, and intermittent operation, were not primary deterrents to the consumer, who was pleased and interested to see for the first time "visual pictures."

As market acceptance increased, the television set entered the second stage —*conspicuous consumption*—and the tube was placed inside a handsome piece of furniture, with the black-and-white picture replaced by color. Attractability and appearance now also became big factors in the consumer's definition of quality.

At the third stage—*widespread use*—television has become built into the consumer's lifestyle. The adult uses the set for pictures of special events; the 13-year-old follows the programs featuring popular singers. Consistent product performance and serviceability are primary factors in quality, and purchase decisions are based on them.

The product enters the fourth stage of maturation when it becomes taken for granted; this is the *commodity* stage. The consumer depends on the television for the news, and the 13-year-old, now a critical and aware audience, demands fidelity of picture quality to see favorite performers. Reliability and product economy are essential to quality acceptance.

A crucial quality role of top management is to recognize this evolution in the customer's definition of quality at different stages of product growth. The necessary changes in company quality operations must be implemented on a leadership basis because trying to play "catch-up" when other firms have made the necessary quality changes is always too late. No matter how conscientiously it may be operated, a quality-control program which is managed as if a product is still in the conspicuous consumption or appearance stage—when the product is in fact in the widespread use or commodity stage—is likely to be unsuccessful in meeting consumer-satisfaction demands.

A significant factor in modern quality today is that this maturity cycle of many products has become rapid, particularly as a result of the increasing pace of new technology in some areas as well as growing customer demands and competitive pressures.

1.4 The Meaning of "Quality"—Orientation to Customer Satisfaction

Explicit as possible identification of all customer requirements is a fundamental initial basing point for effective quality control. When this has not taken place, it can create an inherent problem which none of the subsequent control activities can fully meet.

There has been a tendency in some industries to consider certain basic customer quality requirements as something "extra," whereas the customers assume them to be part of *any* product they purchase. This creates the situation where, for example, the seller offers a home-cooling unit for a certain price and then later qualifies this price by saying that a product which thoroughly cools and is also quiet has a higher price. But no customer knowingly selects any home-cooling product that does not cool and can keep her or him awake at night.

In the phrase "quality control," then, the word "quality" does not have the popular meaning of "best" in any abstract sense. To industry, it means "best for satisfying certain customer conditions," whether the product is tangible (an automobile, a refrigerator, a microwave oven) or intangible (bus route schedule, restaurant service, hospital care).[3]

Important among these customer conditions are (1) the actual end use and (2) the selling price of the product or service. In turn, these two conditions are reflected in 10 additional product and service conditions:

1. The specification of dimensions and operating characteristics
2. The life and reliability objectives
3. The safety requirements
4. The relevant standards
5. The engineering, manufacturing, and quality costs
6. The production conditions under which the article is manufactured
7. The field installation and maintenance and service objectives
8. The energy-utilization and material conservation factors
9. The environmental and other "side" effects considerations
10. The costs of customer operation and use and product service

The aim of these conditions is that quality which establishes the proper balance between the cost of the product and service and the customer value it renders, including essential requirements such as safety. As an example, a punch-press manufacturer in upstate New York was faced with two alternatives in the manufacture of a 4-inch washer. On the one hand, the company might use a stock die and standard materials to produce a washer that would sell for ¼ cent but whose quality could not be guaranteed for any conditions of excessive load or temperature. On the other hand, the company might purchase a special die and special materials to produce a washer which would sell for 2 cents and which could be guaranteed for high-load and elevated-temperature conditions.

The customer for the washers, who was contacted by the manufacturer's sales department, had an application where load and temperature conditions were of no consequence but where price was very important. The manufacturer's decision, therefore, was in favor of the ¼-cent washer, made from standard materials, which became the company's "quality" product and whose requirements were reflected back into the product conditions for the factory.

1.5 The Meaning of "Control" in Industry

Control in industrial terminology can be defined as:

> A process for delegating responsibility and authority for a management activity while retaining the means of assuring satisfactory results.

The procedure for meeting the industrial quality goal is therefore termed quality "control," just as the procedures for meeting production and cost goals are termed, respectively, production "control" and cost "control." There are normally four steps in such control:

1. *Setting standards.* Determining the required cost-quality, performance-quality, safety-quality, and reliability-quality standards for the product.
2. *Appraising conformance.* Comparing the conformance of the manufactured product, or the offered service, to these standards.
3. *Acting when necessary.* Correcting problems and their causes throughout the full range of those marketing, design, engineering, production, and maintenance factors which influence user satisfaction.
4. *Planning for improvements.* Developing a continuing effort to improve the cost, performance, safety, and reliability standards.

Effective control is today a central requirement for successful management. Where this control has failed, it has been a principal cause of increases in company cost and reductions in company income. And its failure has also been a principal contributor to the product-liability, -safety, and -recall developments which have added new dimensions to the problems of management.

As earlier mentioned, the pace of technology is increasing more and more rapidly for many products and services. This places an equally increasing demand for the economic and practical integration of this new technology into the operational practices of a company.

A major planning study stated the conclusion this way: "The significant changes over the next decade will take place in the way operational activities are structured (for control) in companies, as well as in new developments in operational technologies themselves."

This return to control as a central emphasis of management is a major balancing factor to the primary emphasis of the recent past, with its heavy orientation to growth in sales and production. However, for the quality field, it is a reaffirmation of basic principles. These principles are those of control in the positive, self-steering sense of establishing the preventively oriented control standards; evaluating product performance and conformance results against these standards; and then assuring the necessary adjustment actions throughout the entire marketing, design engineering, production, and maintenance cycle.

1.6 What Is the Scope of Total Quality Control?

The underlying principle of the total quality view, and its basic difference from all other concepts, is that to provide genuine effectiveness, control must start with identification of customer quality requirements and end only when the product has been placed in the hands of a customer who remains satisfied. Total quality control guides the coordinated actions of people, machines, and information to achieve this goal.

The reason for this breadth of scope is that the quality of any product is affected at many stages of the industrial cycle (Fig. 1.1):

1. Marketing evaluates the level of quality which customers want and for which they are willing to pay.
2. Engineering reduces this marketing evaluation to exact specifications.
3. Purchasing chooses, contracts with, and retains vendors for parts and materials.
4. Manufacturing Engineering selects the jigs, tools, and processes for production.

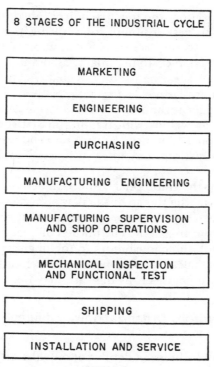

FIG. 1.1

5. Manufacturing Supervision and shop operators exert a major quality influence during parts making, subassembly, and final assembly.
6. Mechanical inspection and functional test check conformance to specifications.
7. Shipping influences the caliber of the packaging and transportation.
8. Installation and Product Service help ensure proper operation by installing the product according to proper instructions and maintaining it through service.

The determination of both quality and quality costs actually takes place throughout the entire industrial cycle. This is why real quality control cannot be accomplished by concentrating on inspection alone, or product design alone, or reject troubleshooting alone, or operator education alone, or supplier control alone, or statistical analysis alone, or reliability studies alone—important as each individual element is.

Total quality activities must exist in *all* the main-line operations: Marketing, Design Engineering, Production, Industrial Relations, Service, and similar key areas. Each quality-improvement and quality-maintenance effort—be it a change in equipment and work force, in interrelationship structure, in information flow, or in the management and control of these functions—must qualify *both* for its own contribution and its contribution toward total quality effectiveness.

Like traditional inspection, the quality-control function in this total quality view is still oriented to responsibility for assuring the quality of products shipped, but its broader scope places a major addition on this function. Quality control becomes oriented to customer quality assurance *at optimum quality costs.*

The total quality view sees the prototype quality-control person not as an inspector but as a quality *engineer and manager,* with an adequate background in the applicable product technology and modern systems engineering and systems management as well as with training in statistical methods, human behavior and motivational approaches, inspection and testing techniques, reliability studies, safety practices, and other such useful tools for improving and controlling quality.

Just as the theme of the traditional inspection activity was "bad parts and products shall not pass," the theme of the new approach is "make them right the first time." Emphasis is on defect *prevention* so that routine inspection will not be needed to as large an extent. The burden of quality proof thus rests not with inspection but with the contributors to the quality of the parts and products: design engineer, sales planner, manager, machinist, assembly foreman, vendor, product service engineer, as the case may be.

1.7 Total Quality Control's Organizationwide Impact—Total Quality Management

Total quality control includes in depth not only the activities of the quality-control function, but most importantly the interdependent multifunctional quality activities throughout the organization. Or, as a definition:

Total quality control's organizationwide impact involves the managerial and technical implementation of customer-oriented quality activities as a prime responsibility of general management and of the main-line operations of marketing, engineering, production, industrial relations, finance, and service as well as of the quality-control function itself.

The importance of this organizationwide impact is that for many organizations much of the quality-improvement demand today lies outside the work of the traditional inspection-and-test-oriented quality-control function. Traditional quality-control programs have been too limited in the face of some production processes that, in their present form and concept, simply will not produce the needed consistency of quality; in the face of some product designs that were created in overly narrow functional engineering terms and are just not sufficiently reliable in actual customer use; and in the face of product service programs that were developed in Band-Aid terms and cannot provide the necessary levels of product maintenance.

Truly effective total-quality-control programs enter deeply into the fundamental concept of such product designs, into the basic setup of such production processes, and into the scope of such product service because there is no other way to achieve the necessary levels of quality in today's market.

For example, the quality-definition activity of the marketing function, which is intended to determine the quality that users want, often has had an extremely low effectiveness prior to the institution of total-quality-control programs. Moreover, the design engineering function's quality and reliability definition, in the form of quantifiably meaningful specifications and drawings, sometimes has been only marginally effective. And when marketing and engineering specifications are not as clear as they should be, the customer-satisfaction impact of such activities as factory quality control and vendor control will be limited no matter how much individual emphasis they receive.

One essential contribution of total-quality programs today is the establishment of customer-oriented quality disciplines in the marketing and engineering functions as well as in production. Thus, every employee of an organization, from top management to the production-line worker, will be personally involved in quality control.

This is vital to establish the basic attitudes required for a positive approach to business quality achievement. Indeed, many people have been conditioned by experience and education to think primarily of business as price and production and sales, with quality perhaps sometimes more in the background. This conditioning begins in certain aspects of the more traditional forms of business training, which have sometimes dealt with price as the principal determinant of economic activity, with quality normally touched on as a more incidental business interest.

Similar attitudinal establishment can also be important throughout much of what might be thought of as the infrastructure of modern business organization. For example, the product planning activities of the marketing function were sometimes likely to treat quality requirements in only a general way. And, even that most important of technical components—product and design engineering—was sometimes likely to make technology and newness its overriding product-development target, with quality thought to be a perhaps less-challenging and less-interesting technical demand.

A powerful total-quality-control capability is one of the principal managerial and engineering strengths for a company today, providing a central hinge for economic viability. The institution of total quality control significantly broadens and deepens the work and the very concept of quality control in a modern company. It permits what might be called *total quality management* to cover the full scope of the product and service "life cycle" from product conception through production and customer service.

1.8 Systems Engineering and Management—Foundation for Total Quality Control

Total-quality-control work requires effective ways to integrate the efforts of large numbers of *people* with large numbers of *machines* and huge quantities of *information*. Hence, it involves systems questions of significant proportions, and a systems approach is inherent in total quality control.[4]

Historically, the meaning of the word "systems" has varied over a complete spectrum—from a "paperwork" office procedure at one extreme through a "software" computer program to a "hardware" equipment system at the other extreme. In quality control, the term "systems" has meant anything from factory troubleshooting procedures to a shelf of operating "manuals" and "handbooks" covering all product inspection and test routines.

Experience has shown that these approaches have been too narrow. Effective quality control requires the strong coordination of all the relevant paperwork and software and hardware and handbook activities. It requires the integration of the quality actions of the people, the machines, and the information into strong total quality systems. This book refers to this comprehensive systems approach when it uses the phrase "quality system." Or, as a definition:

> A quality system is the agreed on, companywide and plantwide operating work structure, documented in effective, integrated technical and managerial procedures, for guiding the coordinated actions of the people, the machines, and the information of the company and plant in the best and most practical ways to assure customer quality satisfaction and economical costs of quality.

A clearly defined and thoroughly installed total quality system is a powerful foundation for total quality control, organizationwide, and for total quality management. Without such systematic integration in a company, "quality management by anticipation" may remain the slogan and the conversation piece, but the actual condition can be quality management by crises and reaction to complaints. Quality can be a consequence rather than the result of carefully planned objectives and activities; it can be the end product of individual, sometimes unlinked actions throughout the entire marketing-engineering-production-service-quality process. It can be based upon sincere intentions but not guided by firm, quantitative customer quality targets implemented by clear organizationwide programs.

In contrast to this, strong quality systems provide a management and engineering basis for effective prevention-oriented control which deals economically and soundly with the present levels of human, machine, and informational complexity that characterize today's company and plant operations.

The new technologies of systems engineering and systems management are important bases for the establishment and the continuing operation and administration of quality systems. That this is so has fundamental technical and managerial impacts upon the work of the quality-control function as follows:

- *Systems engineering* is likely to provide what might be thought of as the fundamental "design technology" of the modern quality engineer.
- *Systems management* is likely to become a fundamental management guide for the quality manager.
- *Systems economics,* particularly with respect to formalized total quality cost accounting, is likely to provide a major business guide-control point for the general manager.

1.9 The Evolution of Total Quality Control

The development of quality control, as we know it today, has spanned this entire century. From a historical viewpoint, major changes in the approach to quality-control work have occurred approximately every 20 years (Fig. 1.2) and can be summarized as follows.

The first step in the development of the quality field, *operator quality control,* was inherent in the manufacturing job up to the end of the nineteenth century. Under that system, one worker, or at least a very small number of workers, was responsible for the manufacture of the entire product, and therefore each worker could totally control the quality of personal work.

In the early 1900s we progressed to *foreman quality control.* This period saw the large-scale advent of our modern factory concept, in which many individuals performing a similar task were grouped so that they could be directed by a foreman who then assumed responsibility for the quality of their work.

The manufacturing system became more complex during World War I, involving large numbers of workers reporting to each production foreman. As a result, the first full-time inspectors appeared on the scene, initiating the third step, which we can call *inspection quality control.*

This step peaked in the large inspection organizations of the 1920s and 1930s, separately organized from production and big enough to be headed by superintendents. This program remained in vogue until the tremendous mass-production requirements of World War II necessitated the fourth step of quality control, which we now identify as *statistical quality control.* In effect, this

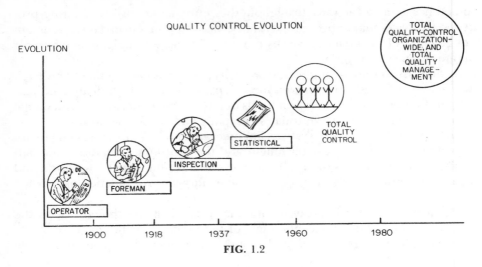

QUALITY CONTROL EVOLUTION

EVOLUTION

TOTAL QUALITY-CONTROL ORGANIZATION-WIDE, AND TOTAL QUALITY MANAGEMENT

TOTAL QUALITY CONTROL

STATISTICAL

INSPECTION

FOREMAN

OPERATOR

1900   1918   1937   1960   1980

FIG. 1.2

phase was an extension of the inspection phase and boiled down to making the big inspection organizations more efficient. Inspectors were provided with a few statistical tools, such as sampling and control charts. The most significant contribution of statistical quality control was that it provided sampling inspection rather than 100 percent inspection. The work of quality control, however, remained restricted to production areas and grew rather slowly.

The slowness of quality-control growth had little to do with problems of development of the technical and statistical ideas. The growth of such concepts as the control chart and the fundamental sampling plans was established very early. The stumbling block was the willingness or the ability of business and governmental organizations to take adequate steps concerning the findings of the technical and statistical work—as examples, to rebuild a lathe to improve its process capability, to reject a lot of incoming material and so shut down production, to suggest to the design engineer that a new device should be developed and evaluated with designed experiments before it was released to production.

Recommendations resulting from the statistical techniques often could not be handled by existing decision-making structures. Certainly, they were not effectively handled by the existing inspection groups, or by what evolved as the one-person statistical quality-control coordinators, or by the individual design engineers who were given part-time duties to evangelize the quality-control subject. The job being done was still basically the shop-floor inspection job, which could never get its arms around the really big quality problems as business management itself saw them.

This need brought us to the fifth step, *total quality control.* Only when firms began to develop a specific decision-making and operating framework for product quality which was effective enough to take suitable action on the quality-control findings did the firms obtain genuine results in better quality and lower costs. This total quality framework made it possible to review designs regularly rather than occasionally, to analyze in-process results and take control action at the manufacturing or the supplier source, and, finally, to stop production when necessary. Moreover, it provided the structure into which the early statistical quality-control tools could later be joined by the many additional techniques of metrology, reliability, quality information equipment, quality motivation, and the numerous other techniques now associated with the field of modern quality control and with the overall quality functional framework of a business.

As total quality control has come to have a major impact upon management and engineering practices, it has provided the foundation for the evolution in the decade of the 1980s and beyond of *total quality control organizationwide* (see Sec. 1.7), *total quality management,* and *quality as a major new business strategy,* next discussed in Section 1.10.

1.10 Quality—A Major Business Management Strategy

Because quality is a crucial hinge for business success or failure in today's quality-performance-oriented markets, it has become a major business strategic area in itself and a significant factor in what has come to be called "business strategic planning." The key is that quality control must be structured explicitly and measurably so as to contribute to business profitability and positive cash flow.

The principal characteristic of orienting quality as a primary business strategy is that the quality-control program must foster sound business growth strongly and positively. It must provide major competitive advantage to the company.

Quality leadership for a firm means a commitment to the engineering, production, and sale of products which consistently will perform correctly for buyers when first purchased and which, with reasonable maintenance, will continue to perform with very high reliability and safety over the product life. This is a much more basic and much more demanding business goal than traditional policy, termed "customer quality satisfaction," which in some firms has primarily meant that product service and technical assistance will be readily available to customers. The policy that a firm "will always fix the product so that it will work again for the buyer" is honorable and important. However, it represents a policy of customer service to deal with after-sales aspects of product problems; it does not represent modern quality strategic leadership in the marketplaces served by the company.

Two basic general management steps are required to establish quality as the necessarily strong business strategic area it must be in a company today:

· The total-customer-satisfaction-oriented concept of quality, together with reasonable costs of quality, must be established as one of the primary

business and product planning and implementation goals and performance measurements of the marketing, engineering, production, industrial
relations, and service functions of the company.

Assuring this customer-satisfaction quality and cost result must be established as a primary business goal of the quality program of the company
and of the quality-control function itself—not some narrower technical
goal restricted to a limited technical or production-oriented quality result.

A case in point is the development and introduction of new products so as
better to serve old and new markets. In the past, quality-control programs
usually directed their attention to assuring that unsatisfactory new products
would *not* be shipped to customers—even though this meant schedule delays
and inability to meet new markets on time and at a given price—and these
continue to be vital and necessary quality-control objectives. But quality-control programs now must also be much more effective in assisting the company
to assure that these new products *will* be shipped without the likelihood of
these delays and costs.

From a technical point of view, this means that the emphasis of quality-
control programs must expand from the concentration upon feed*back*—so that
unsatisfactory product does not go to market—to concentration also upon feed-
forward—so that both the unsatisfactory product is not likely to proceed very
far in the first place and that a *satisfactory* product will be the concentration of
product development.

Moreover, while improvements that are directly quality-oriented are the
major targets of such strategic planning, many other company activities are
favorably impacted by strong quality control because often what improves
quality also simultaneously improves many other areas of the company. Indeed, quality-control programs have a positive impact that is very broad and
very deep. Quality therefore provides a major "focus" and a managerial
"handle" for getting at major improvement areas throughout the company.

Figure 1.3 illustrates the business strategic impact areas of the quality program of a large consumer durable manufacturing corporation with regard to
the major business requirements of:

- Profit strategy
- Reduced cycle times
- Marketplace response
- Resource utilization

The quality program is thus specifically established as one of the principal
areas in the business strategic planning and policy of the company and a major
area in the modern business management concept (Secs. 1.11 through 1.14).

PROFIT STRATEGY	REDUCED CYCLE TIMES	MARKETPLACE RESPONSE	RESOURCE UTILIZATION	PLANNED BUSINESS CONTRIBUTIONS
	X	X		Much higher quality levels in new product introduction
X	X		X	Reduced new product introduction time cycles. Quicker response to market changes.
X		X		Greater effectiveness in meeting increasing quality competition.
X				Substantial improvements in quality costs as an aid to profitability.
X				Indirect labor reductions. Many fewer people can maintain quality.
			X	Much improved opportunities in employee work structuring, self-steering, and motivation.
	X	X		Much better control over product design modifications and performance.
		X		Stronger, more visible posture for meeting regulatory standards, safety and consumerist requirements.
		X		Stronger, more visible quality programs as marketing and technical aids
X			X	Greater opportunities for improved manageability and management control of operations.
	X		X	Even more systematic basis for delegation of authority.
		X		Improved assurance in product service in the dealer situation.
X		X	X	Reduced frequency and expense of field quality problems

BUSINESS STRATEGIC AREAS OF QUALITY PROGRAMS

FIG. 1.3

1.11 The Place of Total Quality Control in the Modern Business Management Concept: Profitability and Positive Cash Flow

The major new business strategic importance of quality has made it a central area of direct and explicit management attention today. Business managers are aware of the axiom that salability plus producibility plus productivity equals profitability. It takes but a moment's reflection to realize that total quality control contributes substantially to each element in this business formula.

Salability is enhanced through total quality control in that the balancing of various quality levels and the cost of maintaining them are market-planned in an organized manner. The result is that the manufactured product really can meet the customer's wants *both* in the satisfactory function of the product and the price that must be paid for it.

Producibility is improved because quality control offers guidance, based on quality experience, to the designing engineer while new products are being developed and to the manufacturing engineer while their production is being planned. Such guidance takes many forms, for example, consideration of the relationship between new design standards and the quality capabilities of the manufacturing plant.

Productivity is increased by emphasizing the positive control of quality rather than after-the-fact detection and rework of failures. The amount of salable production that comes off the assembly line becomes much higher than it would otherwise, be, without increasing a penny in the cost of production or increasing a single unit in the rate of production. Furthermore, positive action taken in the incoming-materials area frequently increases the production rate of the manufacturing equipment itself because defective purchased material is prevented from reaching the assembly line, where it will waste the efforts of skilled workers and expensive machines.

Thus, note that total quality control has a vigorous impact upon each of the three factors which influence profitability. Through careful analysis of customer wants and needs, the product can be provided with those qualities which motivate purchase by the customer and thus increase *salability.* When the quality of the product design and production process is established with *producibility* in mind, manufacturing costs can be substantially reduced and the possibility minimized of negative cost offsets such as costly product-recall action or very expensive product-liability suits. With the balanced manufacturing capability for quality production in place, *productivity* rises as costs per unit decrease. Thus, the industrial manager finds in total quality control a powerful new tool to increase the *profitability* and the positive cash flow of the business.

1.12 The Place of Total Quality Control in the Modern Business Management Concept: Some Examples

To make these points more specific, let us look at the performance of three companies whose general managers failed to include in their business management plans the contribution of total quality control to salability, producibility, productivity, and profitability as compared to a company which did include this contribution. Refer to these companies as A, B, C, and D (Fig. 1.4).

In company A, the basic business strategy was to increase product volume in an effort to climb above the break-even point. Company B's strategy was to market a new product, seeking much wider customer coverage. Company C's business technique was to obtain substantial cost reduction by moving from its old company location to a new plant. Here are the results in each case.

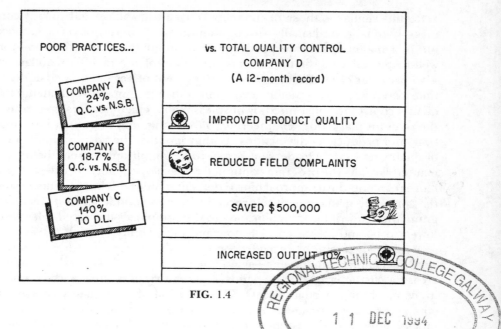

FIG. 1.4

Company A never made its planned production volume. Product rejects in process saw to that. One measure of the resulting lack of effective utilization of capacity is company A's quality costs of 24 percent of net sales billed.

Company B, with a new product, was unable to develop any real element of customer acceptance in the marketplace. One reason is shown in its quality costs of 18.7 percent of net sales billed.

Company C has not obtained the cost reduction sought from its new location. In this company, quality costs of 6.4 percent of net sales billed are most significantly compared with its direct labor base and come to 140 percent of direct labor.

As you might suspect, companies A, B, and C are not very profitable. Total quality control would have substantially helped each company to meet its particular objectives.

In contrast, let us examine company D, whose general management did include total quality control in its business management plans. Company D is a moderate-sized manufacturer of electronic devices with a business volume of approximately $10 million a year. Its total quality activity in 12 months improved product quality substantially, reduced field complaints severalfold, and reduced the going level of quality costs from an annual rate of about $1 million a year to a new annual rate of less than $500,000, a total savings of more than $500,000. This resulted in a more than one-third increase in the profitability of company D. In the process, company D's output increased 10 percent.

Results similar to those of company D have been achieved by many companies—both large and small—throughout the world in recent years. One example is a major worldwide producer of a broad range of products—long a well-respected leader in the field and with sales of several billion dollars a year —whose costs of quality had risen to 10 percent of net sales billed at the same time its reputation as a quality leader faced strong competitive challenge. Total quality control was instituted by business management leadership throughout the relevant marketing, engineering, purchasing, employee relations, inspection, and product service actions. Within months, the corporation's position of quality and safety leadership began to be significantly strengthened in the marketplace. As the program continued to develop, quality costs were reduced more than one-third, approaching 6 percent of net sales billed. This permitted the corporate management to proceed with new confidence in its quality program, thus contributing significantly to the company's increased sales volume, lower costs, and increased cash flow and profitability.

A further example is provided by a worldwide manufacturer of medium-sized mechanical equipment—again a leader in its field—faced by rapidly increasing customer quality demands, competitive pressures, and, correspondingly, much higher quality costs. The inclusion of total quality control in the company's business management plans significantly contributed to a new and much higher level of customer quality satisfaction and a rise in sales from \$90 million to \$160 million in a 2- to 3-year period—accompanied by a reduction in quality costs to net sales billed from approximately 12 percent to approximately 4 percent.

Many similar applications can be cited extending throughout industry. For example, Figure 1.5 illustrates the very favorable cumulative cash flow and return on investment of the quality-systems program of a medium-sized electronics manufacturing company over a several-year period.

These examples emphasize the tremendous potential profit that lies hidden and often untapped in the quality area for greater salability, producibility, and productivity. Total quality control provides managers with a significantly important means to acquire such profit.

1.13 The Place of Total Quality Control in the Modern Business Management Concept: The Range and Timing of Results and Benefits

Major improvements in levels of customer satisfaction—and the maintenance of those levels that are suitable—are principal objectives of total quality control. The customer-satisfaction-oriented benefits that may be expected from a total-quality-control program are:

· Improvement in product quality
· Improvement in product design
· Improvement in production flow
· Improvement in employee morale and quality-consciousness

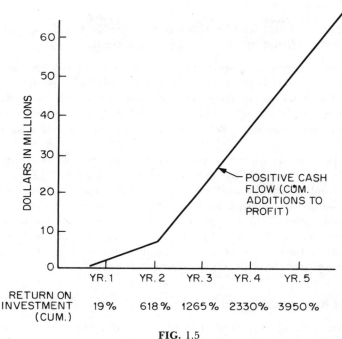

QUALITY SYSTEM PROGRAM
CUMULATIVE CASH FLOW AND RETURN ON INVESTMENT

FIG. 1.5

- Improvement in product service
- Improvement in marketplace acceptance

Moreover, there are major economic improvements that result, including:

- Reductions in operating costs
- Reductions in operating losses
- Reductions in field service costs
- Reductions in liability exposure

Experience has shown that when an improved quality level is attained by controlling product quality within the company, operating costs are generally reduced. This reduction in operating costs is possible because, in its past efforts to reach a balance between the cost of a product and the service it renders, industry has tilted the scales considerably in the direction of product costs that are too high. Many of the "costs of quality" are spent either to correct mistakes or to police them. These high costs in quality appraisal, internal failure due to rejections, and other similar categories have been substantially reduced by an effective program of quality control in many companies.

1.14 The Place of Total Quality Control in the Modern Business Management Concept: Return on Investment

Probably the single most important program performance economic indicator for industry today is the return on investment made. Return-on-investment results for firms which have instituted strong total quality-systems programs consistently have been excellent and may exceed the return on investment results from most other, usual economic investments made by these firms.

Indeed, experience in recent years has demonstrated that total-quality-control programs may often pay for themselves essentially from their beginnings and that the total return is many, many times the initial cost outlays to begin the program—making total-quality-control programs one of the most important "return-on-investment"[5] opportunities open to business management today. As compared to the initial cost outlays, they provide not only a very attractive payback time, but, even more significantly, they provide lasting and self-sustaining rather than merely temporary benefits.

1.15 Quality: Responsibility to Society

The benefits to be derived from a quality-control program are by no means confined to industry's profit-and-loss ledgers. A number of contributions to the social and public welfare result from such an activity, such as the availability of products which are not only more reliable but safer, both for the user and the environment. The activity of establishing proper balances between the cost of an industrial product and the service it renders is important in the effort to produce more goods at less cost and to sell them at lower prices. The right levels of quality mean better use of resources—not only of raw materials and energy supplies but of personnel and equipment. The importance of quality control to conservation and to waste reduction makes it a worthwhile program for achieving the improvements in resource utilization that today are so necessary to society throughout the world.

1.16 The Quality Challenge Facing Industry

There are thus three distinct trends that must be faced squarely by the company which designs, processes, and sells products and services in today's competitive marketplace:

1. *Customers have been increasing their quality requirements very sharply.* This tendency is likely to be amplified by intense competition in the period ahead.

Several underlying causes are responsible. New technology has made possible product offerings that provide more functions and higher performance. The trend has been made significant because products continue to grow more complex. This means that there is greater opportunity for failures to occur; hence, maintaining product quality, even at old levels, requires progressive increases in component-quality levels. Complexity also sometimes makes it difficult for the individual customer to judge accurately the quality of certain products at the time of purchase. Increasingly, customers expect a product that will provide its functions satisfactorily and reliably over its intended life and expect the producer to ensure that this is, in fact, the case.

2. *As a result of this increased customer demand for higher-quality products, present quality practices and techniques are now, or soon will be, outmoded.* The rapid development of new product technology and demands for increased product performance have made design reliability essential. Moreover, in production, the machined part that could once be checked with a factory gage must now be carefully measured with a temperature-controlled electronic device; material that could once be visually accepted if it were "reddish brown and shiny" must now be carefully analyzed, both chemically and physically, to ensure that it is beryllium copper instead of phosphor bronze. At the same time, automation, in which rapid quality evaluation is pivotal, has magnified the need for mechanization of inspection and test equipment, much of which is still basically in the manual stage. Indeed, the quality-control content of the manufacturing equipment investment dollar, already 15 to 25 percent in some companies, may well double in the next decade to purchase the benefit of this mechanization.

Likewise, improvements in labor-management relations are reemphasizing the operator's responsibility for controlling quality at its source rather than overemphasizing inspection of the product upon completion.

3. *Quality costs have become very high. For many companies they may be much too high if these companies are to maintain and improve their competitive position over the long run.* In fact, quality costs (inspection, testing, laboratory checks, scrap, rework, customer complaints, and similar expenses) have crept up to become a multimillion-dollar item. For many businesses the costs are comparable in degree with total direct labor dollars, distribution dollars, or purchased-material dollars.

Together, these three problems spell out the twin quality challenge that competitive conditions present to management: (1) considerable improvement in the quality of many products and many quality practices and, at the same time, (2) substantial reductions in the overall costs of maintaining quality.

These conditions involve a clear understanding of the many forces affecting quality, discussed next in Chapter 2.

Notes

[1]For the original presentations of the total quality approach, see A. V. Feigenbaum, *Total Quality Control; Engineering and Management,* McGraw-Hill Book Company, New York, 1961; "Total Quality Control," *Harvard Business Review,* vol. 34, no. 6, November–December 1956; and *Quality Control: Principles, Practice and Administration*, McGraw-Hill Book Company, New York, 1951.

[2]"Quality control" and "total quality control" will be used interchangeably through the balance of the book.

[3]For further discussion of the meaning of quality, the reader is referred to the following articles: B. P. Shapiro, "The Psychology of Pricing," *Harvard Business Review,* vol. 46, July–August, 1968, p. 20; D. M. Gardner, "Is There a Generalized Price-Quality Relationship?", *Journal of Marketing Research,* vol. 8, May 1971, pp. 241–243; and Z. V. Lambert, "Price and Choice Behaviour," *Journal of Marketing Research,* vol. 9, February 1972, pp. 35–40.

[4]The discussion closely follows the work of Donald S. Feigenbaum. See particularly "Systems Engineering—A Major New Technology," *Industrial Quality Control,* vol. xx, no. 3, September 1963; and "Managing Profitable Operations Through Engineered Systems," *Proceedings, 19th Conference of the European Organization For Quality Control,* Venice, Italy, September 1975.

[5]This "investment" is often in "expense" categories rather than only "investment" in the more usual accounting sense of primarily equipment and facilities outlays.

CHAPTER **2**

The Buyer, the Producer, and the New Marketplace Demands for Quality

The breadth and complexity of new demands for quality are reflected in the realities of today's marketplace. While our rate of achieved improvements in product quality and in quality programs has been substantial, the growth of user expectations for quality performance has grown at a far greater rate for many products and services, resulting in what might be thought of as a quality gap. As an economic corollary, and where strong quality programs have been absent, the costs of quality as a percent of sales also continue to grow from already high levels for these products and services.

Key objectives of modern total quality programs are to provide much more effective control of this complexity and, correspondingly, both to eliminate this quality gap where it exists and to reduce these quality costs. It is important, therefore, to identify the conditions which have contributed to the complexities that affect the control of quality today. Chapter 2 reviews several of these buyer, producer, and marketplace conditions which represent new demands upon quality.

2.1 The Buyer: A Profile

A major buying principle is increasingly dominating national and international markets: Buyers, whether individual consumers, industrial corporations, or government agencies, are now more and more emphasizing that the customer satisfaction they seek in their purchases is a *total value* concept of quality per unit of the price paid, with a new concentration upon greater product and service economy, safety, serviceability, and reliability. Care in purchasing has improved more than almost any other skill—particularly for industrial firms and increasingly for consumers.

This development has created a significant number of upward quality pressures upon today's products and services. Some of the key sources of these pressures are as follows.

Higher Performance Expectations

Not only have modern buyers grown to depend increasingly upon the availability and efficient operation of products and services, they have come to expect improvements in goods and services which demand higher and higher levels of scientific, technical, and economic achievement. They look, for example, toward much better health protection and more efficacious health-giving pharmaceuticals; increasingly high nutrient-content foods; more efficient refrigeration and storage of these foods; improved labor saving in the preparation and cooking of foods, in the washing of clothes, and across the whole range of human manually oriented tasks. They also expect, among many other things, greater effectiveness in the means of transportation to work and to school; much more economical home heating; more reliable communications, whether by mail, telephone, or other means; consistently reliable delivery of electric and other power sources.

Life Cycle and Service Costs

The products and services which buyers want to fulfill their expectations are likely to be different from those of the past; they are likely to be more functional and more basic. The products and services are thus broadening for buyers the scope of what they consider to be satisfactory quality.

Today's buyers recognize that the price paid is only the beginning of the product's cost to the user and that product life cycle cost must be a major buyer consideration in an era of higher prices.

For many products and services, this takes the form of buyer attention to what might be thought of as life cycle product value, with emphasis that product is fully satisfactory when first purchased and that it can be satisfactorily used for a reasonable length of time. Service and maintenance during product use are prominent examples of such quality concentration.

For instance, maintenance costs of some complex industrial and defense products were, in the past, higher than the original price of the equipment. Moreover, the service expense of some consumer products accounted for a significant proportion of the product life cycle cost. This was much too expensive for buyers and so led to much greater emphasis upon in-use quality factors.

2.2 The Buyer: A Profile (Cont'd.)

The Quality of Energy and the Environment

Energy utilization has always been a principal quality dimension for the buyers of many industrial products. Steam turbines for generating electricity have been evaluated for their consumption of fuel for many decades. Aircraft engines have long been designed, manufactured, and marketed with lowest possible energy use as a principal factor.

Public concern about energy costs and energy-resource availability—together with the environmental issues related to energy production—have now made energy an increasingly important quality factor for the buyers of consumer products. Fuel-consumption identification for automobiles has been the most prominent forerunner of this trend. Similar attention increasingly exists for other consumer products such as energy-utilization results for major household appliances. Moreover, the impact of the quality of energy utilization is having an increasingly major effect on the basic concepts of many products and services.

One example is refrigeration devices to keep food cold and safe. Since their introduction many years ago, they have been recognized as one of the consistently highest quality and most reliable of all consumer products as well as one of the most stable, in both design and market trends. But, this is now subject to major change. Studies have suggested that some refrigeration devices may cost significantly more in operating costs over their life cycle than the original purchase price itself. Reliability, safety, serviceability, and the conventional areas of quality attention represent a relatively small proportion of this additional cost. Instead, it is power that may account for much of the total life cycle cost, illustrating that by far the major element of total "user" costs is the energy consumed. This is causing major changes in some of these products, where appropriate, and a significant new dimension of quality measurement for this product.

Indeed, it is very clear that a long-term and growing factor in the quality of products and services increasingly will be the major attention to energy conservation by consumers, producers, and government. We are coming to recognize the need to evaluate the environmental effects of production processes as well as products themselves, so that new product development increasingly is held accountable not only for technical expertise and value but for raw-material consumption, energy consumption, and other direct and indirect environmental effects.

Price Inflation: For most buyers, higher-priced products have almost always meant higher-quality products, and to put it very simply, when inflation has had an effect, there will be progressively higher-priced products.

One of the least well-understood effects of inflation, when it has occurred in world markets, has been the corresponding growth of far greater buyer and consumer insistence upon basic quality. The producers may view higher product prices principally as a result of their own higher costs. The buyers, however, are more likely to remember the quality they have long associated with such a higher price and are likely to view the higher price as payment for what they expect to be higher quality.

The Developing Countries and World Markets

It was common in the past to view world business in the form of neat stereotypes—merchandise from some regions as usually low-priced articles, crafted articles from other regions as generally superior, productivity of developed industrial countries as invariably untouchable, and above all, the great masses of people throughout the world as happy if only they could attain *minimum* standards of life. But if there is any stereotype today, it is that there is no stereotype, and buyer quality concentration and total technological and management superiority are now becoming widely diffuse *throughout* the world, with a competitive impact only now beginning to be felt.

Former "have-not" consumers not only want merchandise they never had before, they want *good* merchandise for their money—not junk or shoddy— they are rapidly developing the discrimination to select the good from the shoddy and to be proud of the difference. Thus, the control of quality is assuming more and more importance in world markets.

2.3 The Buyer: Consumerism

Because they are likely to be more conscious of value than their predecessors, and perhaps better educated, today's consumers are more vocal and demanding. They insist that producer quality and safety functions be performed properly and that they be heard if, in their opinion, product quality and safety are not satisfactory. Thus, for the relevant products, there is established the groundwork for some of the mechanisms of what has come to be called "consumerism."

In some of its product-value-oriented characteristics, consumerism may be one of the long line of steps marking the rising expectations of consumers for what they receive in the marketplace. Such expectations have always been a major propelling force toward increasing economic growth and employment for producer companies and, indeed, for the nations of the world.

A key to business success in consumer marketplaces has been an ability to understand the character of these consumer expectations—including those for quality—to respond effectively and rapidly to them, and as often as possible to anticipate these expectations and act upon them before the consumer has even verbalized them. This is an essential producer function, because when consumers cannot find anyone to listen and with the understanding and authority to act that they feel is necessary, they may unburden their complaints to whoever will listen with attention and concern. Thus can begin the transfer to some other body of the quality-listening-post and action-initiating portion of the quality function historically belonging to the producer and the merchandising dealers. Thus can also begin the loss of the quality initiative and perhaps the business leadership position in their markets for the producer companies thus affected.

2.4 The Buyer and the Service Industries

The quality demands of buyers have been growing at a rapid rate for the increasing number of services that are being purchased in today's marketplace —fully as much as they have been growing for manufactured products.

These services can range from medical assistance and specialized education and urban transit through mail-order supplies and fast-food restaurants and recreational facilities. Today, they can account for almost two-thirds of the private, nongovernmental work force.

What have come to be called the service industries represent one of the fastest growing aspects of national economies. Correspondingly, the satisfaction of the buyers of services represents one of the most important quality determinants in today's national and international marketplaces, and the degree of this satisfaction has progressively more important crosseffects with the quality satisfaction and quality attitudes of the buyers of manufactured products.

Service activities represent an increasingly major area of the attention of total-quality-control programs. The principles, approach, and technologies of total quality control have been successfully applied to a broad spectrum of services. Traditionally, a principal characteristic of service activities has been that they are likely to be heavily dependent upon human skills, attitudes, and training, and the emphasis on the relevant total-quality-control applications has reflected this. Moreover, as services have become organized on a wider scale, becoming more professionalized and more mechanized, total-quality-control applications for services have become more and more similar in many respects to those for manufactured products.

Restaurants represent one example. Once an industry of small, personal service-oriented, individual proprietorships, today's restaurants are likely to be large chains whose integrated activities are central to the quality of the services provided to buyers. Food may be purchased under quality standards that are measured and controlled throughout the entire chain; food preparation may take place according to plans and schedules that are carefully organized; store managers and counter clerks may be trained for full customer service; and customers may be regularly queried about the quality of service they have received.

A representative example of such quality-control attention is the approach taken by an international hotel corporation.[1] In this well-managed company, a quality program has been developed to ensure uniformly high service standards at all the several hundred member inns and hotels. Working closely with the headquarters office, management at each location solicits customer reactions to their stay at the hotel. All guest comments, from letters and question-naires as well as from a special "hotline" complaint telephone installed in each room, are carefully measured and analyzed to determine if a negative trend is developing in any area of activity, such as housekeeping, front desk, engineer-ing, security, and restaurant service. In addition to corrective action, the qual-ity program is explicitly geared toward preventive action. For example, a rolling workbench—fully outfitted for minor repairs and with an 80-item checklist—regularly travels through each hotel, visiting each guest room once every 3 months. This simple but effective innovation has greatly reduced the number of guest calls to engineering because the repairs are made before guests can complain about them.

Similar approaches to the assurance of quality of services—recognizing the intensive quality demands of the service buyer—are becoming characteristic of successful enterprises throughout the service industries.

2.5 The Producer: A Profile

The increasing emphasis by the buyers of products and services upon a basic concept of quality as true value is being strongly felt by producers today. For the manufacturer and seller, as well as for the buyer, long-accepted quality ground rules are changing in the following basic areas.

Quality Responsibility

A fundamental and powerful concept of quality responsibility is being more and more widely recognized today. According to this concept, it is the primary obligation of the producer and the seller to satisfy to the buyer the perform-ance and economy of products and services in an effective way—and when this has not taken place, it is the obligation of the producer and the seller, not the buyer, to set matters right and to bear the cost of doing so.

Many strong producers and merchandising dealers have always emphasized their responsibility and leadership for the quality of the products they sell. They have built widespread marketplace growth and acceptance of their pro-ducts and services upon their obligation and commitment to quality and its maintenance. Within such companies there has been a strong emphasis of the workers' responsibility for their own quality and the vendors' responsibility for the parts supplied—all on a preplanned basis by the concern and with controls to ensure that the quality results are, in fact, satisfactory. Indeed, bad product quality has often occurred and has usually persisted where those producing and selling it have not borne the responsibility for the quality failures or the costs but instead have inflicted the costs upon the buyer.

Now the burden of these quality-failure costs has begun largely to move to *all* producers and sellers. Such trends as strict product liability in the courts, rigorous product-safety requirements, and the consumerist movement—sig-nificant as they have been in themselves—have been only the first outcomes as this producer-quality-responsibility concept has increasingly major economic effects throughout our business, governmental, and industrial institutions.

Quality Demands

All this is taking place at a time when producers must operate in a faster moving, more complex business climate than ever before. For many companies, sales billed today are probably well above 10 times or more what they were in the 1960s. Products and product features are more numerous; the number of models has been expanded greatly, and there is far greater intricacy of product designs, manufacturing processes, and field product service. This product and process explosion has greatly increased the quality demands upon producers.

Progressively Higher Quality Levels

One aspect of quality control which may not always have been clearly understood is this: The more successful a product becomes, the higher quality levels it is likely to have to achieve if the company is to grow profitably. This seeming paradox is very important to recognize because it is fundamental to a thorough understanding of the true nature of quality requirements facing today's producers.

Simple arithmetic sums up the experience in this matter: A 1 percent field failure rate for a consumer appliance product with a production-volume rate of 50,000 units per year means 500 failing units in customers' hands. Marketing success, and a 10-times production increase for the product, up to a 500,000-unit production rate with the same 1 percent field failure rate, means 5000 failing units in customers' hands each year (Fig. 2.1). This is equivalent, in the actual total number of dissatisfied customers, to what would have been the highly unacceptable failure rate of 10 percent at the earlier and lower production rate. This degree of negative product exposure can mean a far more damaging customer quality problem than would seem to be the case with maintenance of a constant failure rate for a successful product.

Indeed, experience demonstrates that this is the kind of product profile which represents a very high risk of product-liability claims and even of product recall today. Such products are not necessarily those with high failure rate *percentages.* They can be, instead, products with exposure to a large *total* number of dissatisfied customers.

It is clear, as identified in Section 1.4 and further explained in Chapter 13, that perfection in production is unfeasible both economically and statistically. However, it is not so easy to make much headway with such proof face to face with a customer whose new purchase is back in the repair shop for the fourth time in a month and who will not accept being a statistic on the wrong, even though small, percentage side of the economic averages, or with a governmental body or a court of law to which simple cause and effect may be that unsatisfactory products would not be shipped had they been properly inspected.

CONSUMER APPLIANCE PRODUCT ONE PERCENT FAILURE RATE

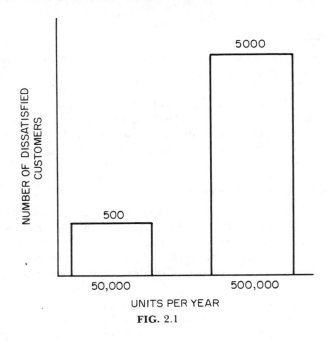

FIG. 2.1

For every product produced in increasing quantity, there is a numerical range of total negative customer exposure which the product business cannot tolerate. For producers, a strong quality-improvement program is essential to ensure that the failure rates for these products are progressively brought to levels whose total exposure will remain within the necessary range. Anything less invites producer risk of costly legal liability, undue warranty expenses, or widespread and very expensive product recall, discussed next in Sections 2.6 to 2.8.

2.6 Product and Service Liability and the Producer

A common denominator for many of the present social and market place forces bearing upon today's producers is the area which has come to be designated as product and service liability. Its impact upon quality control can be seen in buyer markets throughout the world.

The legal obligation of producers and sellers to compensate for injury or damage caused by defective products is in no respect a recent phenomenon. Indeed, the concept of liability has been with us a very long time, and only its emphasis has changed in recent years (Fig. 2.2). The first so-called landmark case of product liability came before the American courts in 1916. In what is now known as the MacPherson Case, tried before the New York Court of Appeals, Justice Kellogg ruled that an automobile manufacturer had a product-liability obligation to a car buyer (whose car wheels were defective) even though the sales contract was between the buyer and a car dealer. In one of his summary paragraphs (see Fig. 2.2), Justice Kellogg ruled as follows:

Landmark Cases in Product Liability

MacPherson vs. Buick Motor Co., New York, 1916: A manufacturer is liable for negligently built products that are "reasonably certain to place life and limb in peril," even though consumers do not buy directly from the manufacturer.

Greenman vs. Yuba Power Products Inc., California, 1963: A manufacturer is strictly liable when he sells a product that proves to have a defect that causes injury.

Larson vs. General Motors Corp., U.S. Court of Appeals, 8th Circuit, 1968: When faulty design of a product worsens an injury, a plaintiff may recover damages for the worsened part of the injury, even if the design defect did not cause the injury in the first place.

Cunningham vs. MacNeal Memorial Hospital, Illinois, 1970: It is not a defense to claim that a product (in this case blood infected by hepatitis) could not be made safer by any known technology. This ruling of the Illinois Supreme Court, the only case in which judges squarely refused to consider "state of the art," was reversed by a state statute defining the selling of blood as a service.

Cronin vs. J. B. E. Olson Corp., California, 1972: A product need not be "unreasonably dangerous" to make its manufacturer strictly liable for defective design.

Bexigs vs. Havir Mfg. Co., New Jersey, 1972: If an injury is attributable to the lack of any safety device on a product, the manufacturer cannot base a defense on the contributory negligence of the plaintiff.

Berkabile vs. Brantly Helicopter Corp., Pennsylvania, 1975: Whether the seller could have foreseen a particular injury is irrelevant in a case of strict liability for design defect.

Ault vs. International Harvester Co., California, 1975: Evidence that a manufacturer changed or improved its product line after the manufacture and sale of the particular product that caused an injury may be used to prove design defect.

Micallef vs. Miehle Co., New York, 1976: Evidence that an injured plaintiff obviously knew of a danger inherent in using a product will not defeat his claim if the manufacturer could reasonably have guarded against the danger when designing the product.

Barker vs. Lull Engineering Co., California, 1978: A manufacturer must show that the usefulness of a product involved in an accident outweighs the risks inherent in its design. In this radical ruling, the court shifted the burden of proof in design-defect cases from plaintiff to defendant.

FIG. 2.2

> We hold that under the circumstances the defendant owed a duty to all purchasers of its automobiles to make a reasonable inspection and test to ascertain whether the wheels purchased and put in use by it were reasonably fit for the purposes for which it used them, and, if it fails to exercise care in that respect, that it is responsible for any defect which would have been discovered by any such reasonable inspection and test.

Justice Kellogg then continued with this further portion of his opinion:

> The evidence indicates quite clearly that many other automobile manufacturers, prior to 1909, exercised no greater care as to wheels bought by them than the defendant exercised with reference to its wheels and that no accident had resulted therefrom. This evidence indicated, not that the defendant was careful, but that the manufacturer had been very lucky.

This is and has been the direction of the law for many years. However, recent years have dramatically further changed Justice Kellogg's older product-liability rules, which had been that manufacturers or sellers are likely to have liability primarily when they are unreasonably careless, or negligent, in what they have produced or how they have produced it. Instead, the courts have put in its place a more stringent rule termed "strict liability," which had some of its origins with products like explosives.

Two basic principles evolved as characteristic of strict liability. These principles, which today are becoming central guideposts for the modern product-liability point of view and which might be thought of as putting the *product* and *service itself* before the court, are as follows: *First*, what could be called a strong "product paternity responsibility" in the law for both manufacturer and merchandiser, requiring immediate responsiveness to unsatisfactory quality through product service or replacement, and second, full and completely accurate and truthful product life, safety, and quality reporting in advertising.

Basically, the principle of strong product paternity responsibility extends the producer's and merchant's responsibility for the product far beyond the factory door and the store shelf and well into the period of actual use by the consumer. By the act of "fathering" a product, the producer and merchant must be prepared to accept a substantial responsibility for that product in use, not only for performance, but environmental effects, safety, and so forth— under the circumstances of how the consumer actually uses the product rather than how the manufacturer instructs that it be used. Court cases under the new doctrine of strict product liability now suggest that the character of this product responsibility cannot be unilaterally determined by the producer or merchant in warranties but must also be multilaterally influenced by consumer considerations and public interest factors.

The *second* principle toward a full product reporting basis for advertising represents the basic issue of how frank advertisements must be in representing the product, covering not only its sales features but its possible life, safety, fabric durability, environmental side effects, and other qualities as well as instruction in the proper use of the product. Under strict product liability, *all* advertised statements are likely to require supportability by valid company quality-identification data very comparable to that now maintained for product identification under regulations for such products as automobiles.

These two strict product-liability principles place increasingly heavy pressure upon development and assurance of a very high degree of factually based evidence by the manufacturers and merchants in the performance and safety of their own products. This evidence must be in the quality of the product as first received by the consumer; in its durable and properly sized performance under the stress of wear as well as its protection from major possible side effects like fire; in the ability to help instruct the consumer in the proper use of the product; and in the factual information that will make credible and visible to consumers, public bodies, and the courts the basis for this product confidence. Only a strong and carefully structured program for total quality control can ensure that these goals will be met.

2.7 The Warranty and the Producer

Nowhere has the doctrine of product paternity had greater impact than in the producer's warranty to the consumer of the performance and reliability of goods and services. Increasingly, the producer's responsibility has come to extend into the circumstances of how the customer actually uses the product rather than how the manufacturer has instructed that it be used.

Indeed, the trend of recent court opinion indicates that today's producers and merchants in fact may in some instances assume a warranty obligation whether that obligation is so stated on the typical warranty card (Fig. 2.3). Moreover, the relatively short time limitations of many warranties may tend to be questionable under the current law. Thus, there is a forcing action upon manufacturers and service vendors to give guarantees that are explicit and that do not contain conditions or qualifications which may be ambiguous or unfair to the purchaser. A principal aim of total-quality-control programs is to strengthen the company's ability to support its warranties and to reduce their cost, through improved product and service safety and reliability.

2.8 Product Recall and the Producer

Another effect of today's product paternity doctrines is seen in the increasingly common and widespread programs known as "product recall." Even well-managed companies today find themselves obligated to prepare for the possibility of having to call back quantities of product from the field to correct problems which they have been unable, for a variety of reasons, to anticipate. Two such examples would be the breakdown or failure of a component and the improper servicing of a product after purchase.

Recent years have seen voluntary recall of products as diverse as automobiles and adhesives, bicycles and chemical sprays, paint removers and pace-

Important Notice to Consumer

This warranty has been drafted to comply with the new Federal Law applicable to products manufactured after July 4, 1975.

Full One-Year Warranty

XYZ COMPANY WARRANTS THIS PRODUCT TO BE FREE OF MANUFACTUR-ING DEFECTS FOR A ONE-YEAR PERIOD AFTER THE ORIGINAL DATE OF CONSUMER PURCHASE OR RECEIPT AS A GIFT. THIS WARRANTY DOES NOT INCLUDE DAMAGE TO THE PRODUCT RESULTING FROM ACCIDENT OR MISUSE.

IF THE PRODUCT SHOULD BECOME DEFECTIVE WITHIN THE WARRANTY PERIOD, WE SHALL ELECT TO REPAIR OR REPLACE IT FREE OF CHARGE, INCLUDING FREE RETURN TRANSPORTATION, PROVIDED IT IS DELIVERED PREPAID TO ANY XYZ-AUTHORIZED SERVICE FACILITY. THERE IS A NATION-WIDE NETWORK OF AUTHORIZED SERVICE FACILITIES WHOSE NAMES AND ADDRESSES ARE INCLUDED WITH THIS PRODUCT. ANY QUESTIONS REGARDING WARRANTY SERVICE CAN BE DIRECTED TO MANAGER–CONSUMER COUNSELING, XYZ COMPANY, NOTION UNIT DIVISION, 12345 MAIN STREET, U.S.A.

THIS WARRANTY GIVES YOU SPECIFIC LEGAL RIGHTS, AND YOU MAY ALSO HAVE OTHER RIGHTS WHICH VARY FROM STATE TO STATE.

FIG. 2.3 **A typical consumer warranty.**

makers, to name but a very few. Nor are mandated recalls uncommon today. Recent consumer legislation specifically requires that household products declared unsafe must be recalled from the market and that all affected parties in the distribution chain (purchasers, retailers, distributors, and so forth) may, in some circumstances, be reimbursed by the manufacturer in the event of a recall. Furthermore, if a manufacturer is unable to recall products effectively, the government is empowered to publicize the potential hazard.

Such trends underscore for producers the urgent need for quality programs which not only will enhance the likelihood of turning out products of high initial quality but will provide the necessary records and logs and product-tracking mechanisms that are vitally important in the event of product recall.[2]

2.9 The Marketplace: An Overview

Buyer expectations for trouble-free products and services have created a new and more demanding character of quality determination in today's national and international marketplace.

Industrial and governmental purchasers often have an objective basis for this determination in the form of their own specifications—or the specifications they require from the producer for this purpose. They can evaluate the degree to which the product and service, as purchased, meets these specifications. Moreover, they usually have a direct channel to the producer when failures occur.

Most consumers have a far more casual basis for their purchases and almost none of this control apparatus. Historically, they have depended upon the producer and merchandising dealer to set up and perform the necessary quality activities of specification, control, record keeping, responsiveness, and service.

In the past, there was an attitude in a few industries that, because of the less sophisticated buyer, products for the consumer market—while they must be produced with equally good quality—often require less sophisticated and less structured quality-control practices than those for industrial and governmental markets. Nothing could be further from the case. Because of the unique degree of consumer dependence upon the producer's quality- and safety-control programs, in the modern economic climate the less sophisticated the buyer, the greater the obligation as well as the competitive marketplace opportunity of the producer for a strongly structured quality program.

In sum, public expectations concerning the standard bearer of quality and safety leadership have swung to focus on consumer-product markets fully as much as upon industrial and government markets. Today's buyers expect consumer products to be among the leaders in the quality parade.

2.10 The Marketplace: An Example

The importance of attention to this new marketplace emphasis upon quality is illustrated by the experience of a major manufacturer of computer peripheral products.

As total quality programs have expanded throughout many companies of the world, they have consistently emphasized that one of the major keys in marketplace acceptance is the clear specification and the full achievement of the basic customer quality use-oriented characteristics of a product, such as its reliability and its serviceability. However, in the development and introduction of a major new product, the computer peripheral manufacturer primarily concentrated attention upon improved product performance and unique product features.

After initial rapid buyer acceptance, the marketplace growth of this product dropped sharply and company income fell off. Economic factors provide the basic reasons for the marketplace decline of the computer peripheral product. The initial production model, which sold at the average price of $4000, had after-sale costs of approximately $3250 over the product life—amounting to a total life cycle cost of $7250. Of this life cycle cost, $2500 was for service to maintain the product—representing a high 35 percent of total life cycle cost.

The poor economic value of this product gradually became understood by buyers and gradually became quantitatively determined by the producing company—who together shared the payment of these service costs in one form or another. One impact of the huge product service cost was a strong and negative effect on product sales to buyers—whose attitudes toward what were reasonable service costs had been conditioned by products with much lower total life cycle service cost.

The original marketing and product engineering documentation of this product had concentrated almost entirely upon specifying speed and accuracy on the marketing premise that these were the basic buyer demands and the features that would sell the product. However, these specifications had not been thorough in quantifying quality requirements for reliability and serviceability. And, this is what the buyers also really wanted.

Therefore, when a new model of this product was planned, the company took an entirely new approach. The newly established total quality program developed for the company entered strongly into the introduction of the new product and in the establishment and maintenance of customer quality requirements.

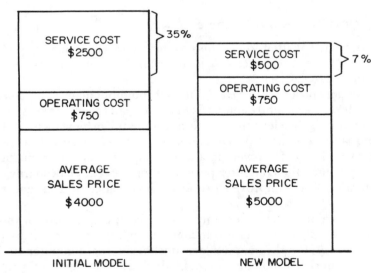

COMPUTER PERIPHERAL PRODUCT
LIFE CYCLE COST

FIG. 2.4

The results have been outstandingly successful, and the economic factors for the new model have proved very different than for the older one (Fig. 2.4). While the average selling price is $5000, the after-sale costs are only $1250—amounting to a total life cycle cost of $6250. Of this life cycle cost, $500 has been for service to maintain the product—representing 7 percent of total life cycle cost and one-fifth of the service cost of the earlier model. Even though the selling price of this newer model is higher, sales results have been four times greater than for the older model (Fig. 2.5), and they continue to increase; moreover, company income for the product is greatly improved. The reason for the product success is, to put it very simply, that the quality of the new model has been planned to fit today's market conditions and is correspondingly recognized by buyers as providing high value.

Moreover, as compared to the uptrend in quality costs in the absence of strong customer-oriented quality programs, the quality-cost/percent of sales results for the computer peripheral firm show a far more profitable situation. The quality-systems payoff for this firm can be seen also in a significant reduction in quality costs. And this result is reflected in the quality-cost improvements documented by company after company with modern total-quality-control programs.

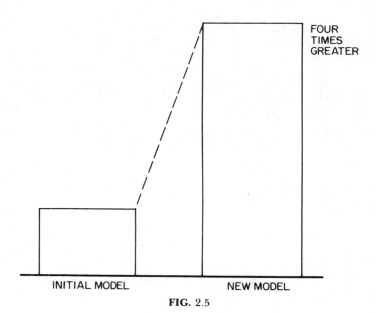

COMPUTER PERIPHERAL PRODUCT
SALES RESULTS

FOUR
TIMES
GREATER

INITIAL MODEL   NEW MODEL

FIG. 2.5

2.11 The Marketplace: Opportunity from Quality Leadership

Producer and merchandising dealer quality programs geared to meet today's marketplace thus not only must be technically and managerially sound, they must also be clear, understandable, and visible in a way that can be articulated to, thoroughly discussed and reviewed with, and accepted by buyers, the public, and the relevant governmental bodies where appropriate.

Such total quality control gives a producer major and unique competitive power in modern national and international marketplaces. Moreover, it provides the company with the basis upon which to take suitable market leadership initiative, as opposed to reacting defensively only to so-called consumerist pressures. Indeed, an increasing number of companies—some from abroad successfully developing new markets for the first time, others continuing their domestic growth with strong product performance—have made total quality control a principal foundation for their marketplace growth and profitability.

Never before has there been a greater marketplace demand for products of consistently high quality; never before have competitive opportunities been greater for the design, manufacture, and sale of products of truly superior quality; and never before has there been so deep a foundation of quality technology to guide the development of new quality strategies to provide leadership in meeting the current heavy buyer demands for quality.

Notes

[1] Barbara J. Mellin, "Sheraton's Quality Improvement Program," *Quality Progress,* vol. X, no. 12, December 1977, pp. 12–14. The interested reader can refer to a growing body of literature on quality control in service industries. Some examples include Joseph R. Troxell, "Standards for Quality Control in Service Industries," *Quality Progress,* vol. XII, no. 1, January 1979, pp. 32–34; R. J. Eilers, "Total Quality Control for the Medical Laboratory," *Proceedings of the International Symposium on Hematology and Clinical Pathology,* Italy, 1971, pp. 148–160; George Rosenzweig, "Cost of Quality in the Service Industries," *32nd Annual Technical Conference Transactions,* American Society for Quality Control, Chicago, 1978, pp. 321–325; and André Van Borredam, "L'assurance de la qualité de service dans le transport aerien," *Bulletin of the French Association for Industrial Quality Control,* vol. XIV, no. 4, December 1978, pp. 31–35.

[2] Product "traceability" is discussed in Sec. 20.22.

CHAPTER 3

Productivity, Technology, and the Internationalization of Quality

Explosive new social and economic demands for much more effective utilization of the materials and processes which make up today's increasingly technologically based products and services, together with new working patterns in factories and offices and the internationalization of markets, have become major influences upon what quality-control programs must be today.

Such areas as productivity, conservation, and safety represent basic forces upon quality control similar in importance to such forces as product liability and consumerism discussed in Chapter 2. The need for improved resource utilization—of energy, equipment, materials, the work force, indeed of such elements as water—is likely to have increasingly powerful impacts upon product marketing, design, and production over the next several years. Correspondingly, quality-control programs are being oriented with similar emphasis in companies and in national economies.

Chapter 3 discusses some of the principal productivity, technology, and international conditions that are affecting quality today.

3.1 The Worker: A Profile

The quality of products and services is, in essence, the result of human action and human work. And, an increasing number of all of us today, whether in a factory or in an office, want our work much more broadly to utilize our motivation, our education, and our minds as well as to recognize our economic, technical, and social awareness. Moreover, this social trend has been developing at the same time that economic trends are causing us to reexamine deeply, from engineering and management points of view, the conventional concepts of production.

A traditional, widely applied and widely accepted industrial concept has been that mechanization, combined with a high degree of job specialization, will result in high productivity, low costs, satisfied workers, and good quality. However, this is becoming less and less supported by the actual facts of operating experience. The almost complete correlation that once existed between higher levels of production-equipment investment alone and the resulting higher levels of worker productivity has begun to break down very badly. We are finding that many of the operations which have been the most advanced in the application of these traditional industrial concepts today are among those with the greatest problem in achieving productivity, quality, and motivational results.

Perhaps this should not be too surprising because the standard approaches to some factory practices have changed very little from the basic production-line concepts of the 1920s—where product quality was quite a different demand than from what it is today. Indeed, the total cost of quality was not even an identified factor in the cost control equation (as compared to today, where quality costs can be of the same magnitude as total factory labor costs), and employee quality motivation existed in an industrial climate not at all the same as today's.

In these standard production-line concepts, for example, station 8 is laid out to rough-tighten panel bolts A, C, and E; station 14 is laid out to torque-wrench-tighten bolts A and E; station 16 torque-wrench-tightens bolt C to achieve what is called line balance timing; station 22 welds down all bolts. It becomes anybody's guess as to where to place the responsibility for the high costs and the lost time when the panel opens up during use and a major quality and safety complaint results.

The rapidly increasing pressures for fundamental new work patterns confront us with the requirement to make sweeping changes in conventional production and work-place concepts not only in the factory but in the office. We shall, of course, have to maintain the power of the mechanization and specialization techniques, but we now also have to key them to recognizing that the skills and motivation of people and the clarity and efficiency of information are today as important to productivity, and certainly to quality, as the machines and regimens with which they work.

3.2 Total Quality and Total Productivity

These new work patterns in today's offices and factories, together with today's marketplace demands for quality, are broadening the concentration of productivity from the traditional primarily factory-oriented attention to "more product and service output per unit of resource input." The patterns are instead progressing toward a market-oriented business productivity concept measured by "more *saleable, good-quality* product and service output per unit of input"—which is a fundamentally different management objective, managerial performance measurement, and productivity program focus.

No company is likely to be profitable today with a bad product. The product that cannot be sold because it does not have adequate consumer value, or one that must be recalled from the field because it is unreliable or unsafe, or one that must be too often returned for service—these are unproductive outputs of negative business value to the company that offered them, no matter how so-called productively efficient the manufacturing process may have been in the traditional sense. The economically meaningful business indicator of productive input-output efficiency for company management in today's markets is the degree to which product and service output provide customer quality satisfaction, with the corresponding positive impact upon product saleability.

This customer-oriented business productivity measure changes the focus of program planning attention. No longer is the emphasis solely upon techniques to improve factory work efficiency, as has been the case for more than 50 years and as important as this remains; it is now also focused upon the fact that achieving customer-oriented productivity requires the strong use of modern quality programs. These programs help to bring about fundamental changes in marketing and product planning actions, in conventional production practices, in traditional industrial engineering approaches, and in the practice of management itself.

This is an important part of the new approach increasingly being widely used by major companies throughout the world: Industrial productivity must focus upon the input-output effectiveness across the *entire* scope of the company organization. Economists call the approach "total resource-factor productivity," or, simply, "total productivity."

3.3 Total Quality and Total Productivity: An Example

The result of this change in productivity approach and measurement is very significant. One example is the experience of a very large international manufacturer of mechanical and electromechanical products for industrial users.

In the plants of the company, some production operations, which were reported as 85 to 90 percent productively efficient in the old non-quality-oriented measurement concept (Fig. 3.1) were shown to be only 60 to 65 percent productively efficient when evaluated by more accurate and more realistic customer- and market-oriented productivity measurements. This one-third productivity deficiency demonstrated to the company one of the major causes of the persistent upward trends in its costs and expenses, and eliminating this productivity deficiency represented one of the biggest single cost control requirements for the company.

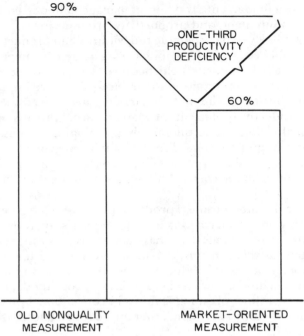

PRODUCTIVE EFFICIENCY

FIG. 3.1

A major key to accomplishing this result was recognizing the following: Even in many highly organized factories, there now exists what might be called a "hidden plant"—amounting to 15 percent to as much as 40 percent of produc-

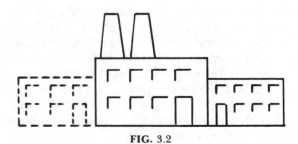

... THERE NOW EXISTS EVEN IN MANY HIGHLY ORGANIZED FACTORIES

"A HIDDEN PLANT"

FIG. 3.2

tive capacity, depending upon the particular circumstances (Fig. 3.2). This is the proportion of plant capacity that exists to rework unsatisfactory parts, to replace products recalled from the field, or to retest and reinspect rejected units. There is no better way to improve productivity than to convert this hidden plant to productive use, and modern quality programs provide one of the most important and most practical ways to accomplish this today.

In the case of the manufacturer just discussed, a total quality program directed to productive utilization of this wasted capacity was able to achieve great new improvements in productivity (Fig. 3.3). In many of the company's production operations, a significant proportion of the productivity increases required to close the one-third gap that had been found in true productive efficiency is now targeted and budgeted to come from quality programs and is being achieved by these programs.

3.4 Total Quality and Product Development

Until recently, many companies were largely dependent upon what has been called the "sequential" or "series" method for developing and making new

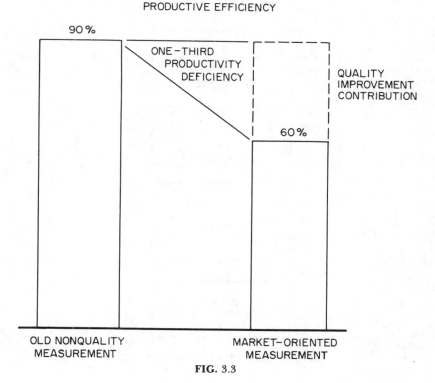

FIG. 3.3

equipment and products (Fig. 3.4). This approach begins with the initial time to research and develop the new product concept, followed by prototype production and thorough testing to everyone's satisfaction. After that, drawings are developed, production processes are installed, and production is started. Product-quality problems can be isolated readily in this kind of approach because, at least in principle, proceeding from one step to the next is dependent upon satisfactory product performance at each preceding "gate" in the development process.

Today, major product-development programs often do not have time to complete this sequential system of operation; the marketplace moves too fast. Instead, we increasingly are seeing what might be called the "parallel" approach to product development (Fig. 3.5). Research and development begins and carries forward while prototypes are being made and tested; as prototypes are being tested, unit production is begun. The parallel approach imposes more demanding operating requirements to assure trouble-free quality at the right cost, and it represents to a producer a quality problem of far greater

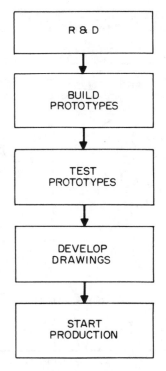

"SERIES" NEW PRODUCT DEVELOPMENT

FIG. 3.4

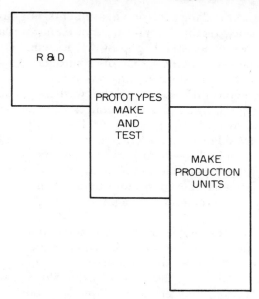

"PARALLEL" NEW PRODUCT DEVELOPMENT
FIG. 3.5

magnitude than experienced in earlier years and the basic need for much higher initial quality. It demands a strong total quality capability to assure development success.

3.5 Quality, Mechanization, and Automation

Modern production equipment—such as automatically controlled machine tools in the factory, integrated data processors in the office, large-scale computers to expedite managerial decision-making—is having a profound impact on the operation of business today. The lesson has been sharply taught that major technological changes cannot be simply overlaid upon old manufacturing or logistics or managerial foundations with any confident anticipation of sound and effective improvements. Where such superimposition has taken place, it has been the basic reason why some factory automation programs have not paid off and why some office computer programs occasionally end up requiring more personnel than there were prior to the machines' installation.

Indeed, with automation there can be *more* quality problems instead of fewer; there can be even *more intense* upward pressures on quality costs than exist today; there can be *much greater,* rather than less, need for high-level quality-control work.

These points can be illustrated by an example from the plant of a New

England manufacturer making precision instruments. For most hand-assembly lines, a 1 percent reject quality level for hardware once was a respectable goal and achieved only with consistently good work. Examination shows what this 1 percent level means for one of the factory's automated subassembly operations, the magnetic bearing support, for example.

This operation requires the use of two thin washers per subassembly, to be used as magnet spacers. The machine produces 720 subassemblies per hour, thus using 1440 washers. If 1 percent of the 1440 washers have a small burr or a slightly rounded edge, on the average there will be 14 machine stoppages per hour—1 every 4 minutes—due to washers jamming the track feeding the machine. Thus, with a respectable 1 percent level for hardware, the automated equipment will be out of operation more than it is in operation. Obviously, such a 1 percent reject level does not begin to be good enough for instrument automation.[1]

If one multiplies this example manyfold and adds a liberal sprinkling of other examples which reflect much greater quality complexities, one will find the true nature of the quality problem under automation emerging: Unless the "make-it-right-the-first-time" total-quality-control principle is *really* made to work, there will *be* no economically efficient automatic production because down time will see to that.

Compared with *hand* operations, automation will require far *better* procedures for determining the quality ability of new designs prior to the start of production; it will require far *tighter* controls over incoming-material quality and over in-process quality; it will require the development of far more *effective* inspection and test, measuring, and feedback control devices; it will also require the creation and use of far *higher* levels of total-quality-control engineering technology.

3.6 Quality Information Processing, Computer Technology, and Software Quality Control

One of the major recent improvement forces in many companies has been the development of strong, computer-based information programs to provide clear and timely measurements and data. However, the earlier forms of these programs often overlooked the systematic inclusion of key quality information, either in the computer data base or in routine data processing itself.

Total-quality-control programs have fostered the steps to structure these management information programs so that they also provide the precise, relevant quality data so essential today as guidelines to managerial and technical actions.

Three examples of the several major information areas that are important are:

· Economic data in the form of quality costs
· Customer data about product satisfaction
· Engineering, production, inspection, and test data about quality levels

With the great information-processing power provided by modern computers, both centrally as well as on an in-plant-distributed and interactive data form, an essential factor in strong modern quality control is the establishment of effective quality information processing at all relevant levels of organizational operations. Such quality information programs employ the data as a fundamental factor in the company and the plant informational system, gearing the information to the measurement and control of the important areas that impact quality control and to permanent corrective action.

Software Quality Control

With this great growth of the importance of quality information processing has come the comparable growth of the importance of what might be thought of as the quality control of computer information. This relates, in part, to the assurance of the quality of the computer hardware itself. While vitally important, the quality-control practices that are effective here are similar in principle and approach to the practices that have been generally developed for other forms of electronic equipment.

The quality of the software that drives the computer—and of the programming which creates the software—has also become of primary quality importance. A very high proportion of computer "crashes," that is, failure of operation, today may be caused by the unsatisfactory quality of software.

Software quality control has therefore become an essential part of company total-quality-control programs. Attention to the unique requirements of software quality is an activity that is integrated throughout the quality information-processing program. It begins in development and continues throughout computer hardware and software operation and maintenance both in office and in factory and testing installations.

3.7 Total Quality, Standards, and Specifications

As buyer quality requirements have intensified, and as producer programs to satisfy these requirements have grown more demanding, the establishment of clear standards—the first step in the control process as noted in Section 1.5 —has become more and more important to the achievement of quality.

While standards and their setting are a very old field of activity, many modern considerations have greatly affected the nature of what will be an effective standard for quality-control application under today's marketplace and production conditions. Among these are the following: The determination of what quality-related considerations—for product, process, system, terminology, or similar factors—should be covered by standards and specifications. How these standards and specifications should be evolved and documented. Which bodies should develop, approve, and maintain these standards —industry associations, professional bodies, buyer groups, governmental institutions, producing companies themselves? What should be the evaluation criteria for standards; how should standards be enforced; and what place do standards have in the legal and product-liability evaluation process? A key factor in total quality control is clear awareness of these considerations as background for the identification and application of the relevant product and service standards that must be integrated into the quality-program activities[2].

One of the principal complexities in the evolution and application of effective modern quality-control standards has been the need to consider in these standards the relevant aspects of certain new quality-oriented technologies and methodologies which have evolved over the past several decades, such as reliability techniques, statistical sampling, and modern test practices.[3] The formalization of standards and specification concepts—and of the organizational processes for their determination—had crystallized long before the appearance of these new areas. Consequently, achieving their integration into modern standards and specifications has represented a major area for quality-control attention.

Quality control of the past concentrated almost exclusively upon the internal production activities of the firm. Modern quality-control programs, in contrast, are moving also toward very strong and direct external connections with the customers of the concern. They emphasize product specifications and standards that clearly and fully define the service and reliability parameters of the product as well as the more usual design dimensions and manufacturing-process parameters. This is because quality is, as earlier discussed in Section 1.3, an evaluation made by users of the product, not by the producers. It is a judgment based upon the users' needs and desires, their reliability and service-ability demands, their particular product applications, and other conditions. These factors today can be important elements of product specifications and standards.

3.8 Total Quality and Safety

Always a matter of central attention, safety today has become an area of primary social as well as technical emphasis throughout world marketplaces. The safety of automobiles, pharmaceuticals, energy-generating plants, household appliances, toys, paints, health care, clothing and fabrics, construction, and a very broad spectrum of products and services is under close scrutiny.

Standards, programs, and measurements by producers and buyers and by governments strongly emphasize the prevention of product- or service-induced accidents which may threaten human life, welfare, or property. The attention is both to the direct effect of the product and service in terms of its accident-free operation and to the indirect impact upon safety—the so-called side effect result, such as of a hospital-administered test or drug or of a fabric in clothing or household furnishings.[4]

It was established earlier that safety is an overriding parameter of quality. Therefore, product and service safety represents a central and integral focus throughout total-quality-control programs. Safety considerations exist across what some have called the entire "cradle-to-grave" scope of total quality control. They can no longer be dealt with effectively by narrow approaches confined to the work of a single functional group in the company, as was the case in more traditional safety-oriented activities of an earlier and less demanding era.

An example of this earlier, narrower approach to product quality and safety is the case of a successful and well-managed consumer electronics products company. In this firm, product safety had historically been handled as a design engineering matter supported by a dedicated and competent safety review committee. The system was considered "foolproof" until an order for 10,000 power amplifiers was processed in accordance with a design that had been reviewed and determined "safe."

The amplifiers had a metallized on-off knob linked with a shaft that passed very close in the chassis to the power supply transformer that generated very high voltage and current. Four of the shafts used in the 10,000 amplifiers passed through sampling incoming inspection with a burr because the inspection plan had not been designed to screen out the passage of all burrs. When the metallized knob was turned to the On position, the burr in these four shafts bridged the power supply and therefore made the knob electrically "hot." The narrow approach to product safety in this company was a failure and was replaced by a modern, organizationwide, total-quality-control program.

A principal aim of quality programs in today's companies must be to assure total product-safety confidence before any product is released to the marketplace. The strong total quality system will be structured to explore all reasonable design alternatives, question whether any aspect of a product's design may contribute to its misuse or abuse, assess the effect of a failure or defect in any component, part, and predict the likelihood of failure and the degree of severity of possible consequences should it occur.

3.9 Total Quality and Liability Loss Prevention

Because of the emphasis upon product safety, and the major penalties of failure to assure safe product operation, product-liability loss control programs are a major requirement today for producers, merchandising dealers, and insurers. The central demand is to make product-liability loss control a continuous program instead of an occasional fireworks display in response to periodic crises, to weave in product loss control as an inherent, built-in factor within the basic control structure of a company rather than as an isolated matter turned to when crises arise. Anything less encourages risks that simply will not meet today's demand.

However, there has been a curious attitude prevalent in some companies which has represented one of the basic product-liability traps for these companies. This attitude is that the product-liability area is so specialized and requires such disciplined attention that it should be carefully confined to one area of the company only. Such a treatment has handled liability subjects as a self-contained legal or an insurance claims area, complete with the related specialized paperwork. Thus, it has been cut off from the mainstream of the marketing-engineering-production elements of the company that are deeply involved in the actions which can beneficially or negatively influence product-liability claims. Moreover, this has created a long-term insulation, walling off product-liability loss control programs from quality-control programs.

When the MacPherson opinion was being rendered in 1916 (see Sec. 2.6), both the concept and the organizational function of quality control were virtually unknown in industry. By the time quality control had become a major activity following World War II, product-liability loss control had long since become a specialized entity in many companies. Its language and quality control's language were different. Product-liability specialists and quality-control specialists in the same company sometimes did not know who the other was and had only a dim awareness of each other's programs.

Since there was very little dialogue, there was very little real recognition that each dealt with aspects of the same problem. Indeed, while there was much personal goodwill among the specialities, there was also some skepticism concerning the extent to which quality control, with its percent-defective concepts, and product-liability control, with its claims-control approach, could be of very much real mutual assistance. This remains the situation in many organizations today in the face of the obvious need for far greater coordination.

Precisely because this separation of product liability has been built into the long-term organizational evolution of many companies, it requires carefully developed programs to change this beneficially. The necessary coordination will not be made effective simply by establishing a management policy that states the *existing* product-liability control and the *existing* quality-control programs should find improved ways to cooperate. The new strict liability developments require, instead, changes in the company control concept itself. Total quality control is today the fundamental baseline upon which product-liability control must be built.

The fact is that errors which lead to product-liability problems, whether errors of omission or commission, frequently can be traced to routine and relatively minor decisions made in nearly all areas of a company's operation and at all levels of responsibility. The magnitude of an error often bears little relationship to the magnitude of potential loss resulting from it. Indeed, the cause may not be the result of an outright error at all but, for example, of well-intentioned production-line decisions[5].

The thoroughness and effectiveness of product-liability loss prevention are completely linked with the integration of liability-prevention activities at each stage of the industrial product cycle. Correspondingly, strong total-quality-control programs and strong liability-prevention programs are a sum—not a difference. A sound modern quality-control program is also a sound liability-prevention program[6].

3.10 Total Quality and Internationalism

Quality operations in an increasing number of companies and governmental programs today are becoming international in their outlook and scope. That this is so represents a major and extremely important broadening of the geographic boundaries of quality control.

Three principal trends now make internationalization an increasingly important dimension of total quality practice:

1. Growing worldwide scope and character of industrial corporations and of governmental programs
2. Demonstrable new importance of quality to success in international markets
3. Developing significance of quality control in governmental policy and negotiations on international trade

Broadening of industrial activity has taken many forms. Parts and materials are now routinely sourced worldwide, rather than as an occasional purchasing foray. Production policy planning and manufacturing facilities are integrated on an international scale. Engineering programs are becoming coordinated intercontinentally. Marketing and product services are organized throughout many countries.

An increasing number of companies correspondingly are becoming genuinely worldwide in their scope and operations. They are no longer national companies periodically looking abroad for new markets; they are instead international companies with worldwide interests. Moreover, government procurements and programs—especially paced by defense equipments such as aerospace and mobile ordnance—are becoming international as the rule rather than the exception. And products such as electricity-generating installations are today almost entirely worldwide in their planning and control.

The impact of all this upon quality control is very great. When a company designs a product in one country, procures its materials from another country, manufactures the product in still another country, and then markets and services that product throughout the world, the establishment of really strong international as well as national quality systems becomes essential for profitable operations.

The *second* trend toward internationalization is the demonstrable new importance of quality to success in international markets.

For a long time, deeply ingrained stereotypes have strongly influenced business policy thinking on trade—for example, technically innovative products, or very cheap products, or otherwise comletely unavailable products represent the keys to export success in the international consumer marketplace. But, many of the major recent successes in international trade have not been any of these.

These products have been neither highly technically innovative nor extremely cheap—indeed, with recognizable quality, they have sold at higher prices—and they have moved into markets already well-stocked with similar goods. They have been successful not because they fit into old stereotypes but because they have represented what has clearly become the real key to success in this new marketplace: product and service value in the eyes of the consumer.

The ability to achieve this result on an international scale has been the key to the success of companies that have become the export leaders. The lesson from this is that a major amount of their technological and managerial emphasis has been placed directly upon the areas which really have current quality meaning in today's value-oriented world markets.

This means international product planning to determine and act upon those product and service features representing real value to consumers of different countries, rather than merely exporting products with the *existing* features that suit home markets. It means fast-response international information networks, where changing consumer buying patterns or product service and spare parts requirements can be very quickly communicated and acted upon. It means the successful internationalizing of quick and reliable deliveries of products thousands of miles to their markets. Such major innovations as large-scale new logistics systems over land, sea, and air bring an overseas factory almost next door to the markets it services when the establishment of a domestic plant has not been possible or economical.

Thus, there is a need for worldwide quality and reliability systems to assure the satisfaction of consumers with the products in use, wherever in the world these products are bought and sold.

These areas comprise what economists call the "worldwide infrastructure" of a company, and internationalizing it effectively is fundamental to success in today's quality-oriented markets.

3.11 Total Quality and Internationalism: The Role of Government

The *third* trend in the internationalization of quality is the developing significance of quality control in governmental policy and negotiations on international trade.

In today's competitive world, a very important factor in governmental economic policy is the maintenance of world trade patterns that are as free as possible consistent with restrictions on such inequitable practices as "dumping," or the unfair pricing of comparable products in international versus national markets. However, products are comparable only if their quality is comparable, and this requires clear and measurable quality and quality practices. The increasingly intense governmental emphasis upon the maintenance of fairness in export and import practices will inevitably place equally increasing emphasis upon the quality-control programs that will maintain these requirements.

This is a major new force toward the internationalization of quality control throughout many countries. It is likely to add an import-oriented complement to the emphasis upon quality as a major export-oriented tool that some governments have been encouraging for many years as a major element of their economic policy.

Together, the trends toward internationalism—the growing worldwide scope of business, the new importance of quality, and the impact of quality upon government policy—reflect the shrinking boundaries of today's world. This has profoundly affected the policies, the attitudes, and the quality operation of companies.

Notes

[1]Section 12.22 discusses how modern quality technology is applied to meet the necessary quality requirements.

[2]Among the many bodies involved in the standards-setting process, the American National Standards Institute (ANSI), the American Society for Quality Control (ASQC), and the American Society for Testing and Materials (ASTM) play particularly significant roles related to broad impacts upon quality control. Many other institutions, associations, and federal, state, and governmental entities also play major roles in quality-oriented standards setting that must be clearly understood and carefully considered both for particular products and services as well as more broadly. The International Organization for Standardization (ISO) is a principal body playing a major standards role on an international scale; other international bodies, especially the International Electrotechnical Commission (IEC), also play important roles. On a national as well as an international basis, organizations such as the American Society of Mechanical Engineers (ASME) and the Electronics Industry Association (EIA) have significant activities.

[3]The development of consumer standards and specifications is reviewed in a paper by the author: A. V. Feigenbaum, "Integrating Specifications, Quality and Consumer Satisfaction," *Standardization News*, vol. 1, no. 10, 1973.

[4]The prevention of safety hazards to the user is a central goal for products and services. For a thorough discussion see R. P. Kytle, Jr., *Proceedings, 20th Conference of the European Organization for Quality Control*, Copenhagen, June 1976, pp. 107–115. However, the subject of to what degree it is possible for the product and service itself to carry the total accident-free burden remains an issue of discussion. See for example Walter Guzzardi, Jr., "The Mindless Pursuit of Safety," *Fortune*, Apr. 9, 1979, pp. 54–65.

[5]For an in-depth discussion of the spectrum of product safety, see D. S. Feigenbaum, "Wanted, New Strategies for Product Safety," *The National Underwriter*, Sept. 10, 1971.

[6]Liability loss prevention is further discussed in Sec. 10.28.

CHAPTER 4

What Are the Factors in Controlling Quality and What Are the Jobs of Quality Control?

During the past several years, there has been an extremely pronounced growth of competition in product quality. This competition has been apparent both in consumer lines and in the heavy industries.

A natural result of these circumstances has been for many companies to place a premium upon the establishment and maintenance of a good quality reputation. Such a reputation can be emphasized among customers by marketing and sales departments, and it can be the keynote of advertising policies. A poor-quality reputation, on the other hand, presents one of the most difficult points of sales resistance that a company has to overcome.

For example, a dip in consumer-goods sales during an interval in our national economy was attributed by marketing analysts in significant measure to what was termed a "consumer quality strike." Concerted buying resistance was in evidence as a result of quality deficiencies in a variety of products. Major factors in restoring purchases on these products were significant quality improvements by the manufacturers.

A reputation for quality, whether good or bad, is not a thing of chance. It is the direct result of the policies of a company related to the establishment and maintenance of strong and well-planned quality programs. To make such programs fully operational in plants and companies requires, as a starting point, a clear understanding of the many key factors that must be dealt with. These factors must then be related to the key jobs that must be accomplished within companies to achieve quality goals.

Chapter 4 is therefore operationally oriented, identifying first the broad areas where action toward quality is necessary and then classifying the actual jobs of quality control. The role of statistics and other quality-control technical methodology is also considered.

4.1 The 9 M's: Fundamental Factors Affecting Quality

The quality of products and services is directly influenced in nine basic areas, or what might be thought of as the "9 M's": markets, money, management, men, motivation, materials, machines and mechanization, modern information methods, and mounting product requirements. In each area, industry today is subject to a great number of conditions which bear upon production in a manner never experienced in any previous period.

1. **Markets.** The number of new and improved products offered in the marketplace continues to grow at an explosive rate. Many of these products are an outgrowth of new technologies involving not only the product itself but the materials and methods by which it is manufactured. Consumer wants and needs are carefully identified by today's businesses as a basis for developing new products. The consumer has been led to believe that there is a product to fill almost every need. Customers are demanding and getting more and better products today to fill these needs. Markets are becoming broader in scope and yet more functionally specialized in the goods and services offered. For an increasing number of companies, markets are international and even worldwide. As a result, businesses must be highly flexible and able to change direction rapidly.

2. **Money.** The increase of competition in many fields coupled with worldwide economic fluctuations has shaved profit margins. At the same time, the need for automation and mechanization has forced large outlays for new equipments and processes. The resulting increase in plant investment, which must be paid for through increased productivity, has made any major losses in production, due to scrap and rework, extremely serious. Quality costs associated with the maintenance and improvement of quality have reached unprecedented heights. This fact has focused the attention of managers on the quality-cost area as one of the "soft spots" in which its operating costs and losses can be decreased to improve profits.

3. **Management.** Responsibility for quality has been distributed among several specialized groups. Once the foreman and the product engineer had sole responsibility for product quality. Now Marketing, through its product planning function, must establish the product requirements. Engineering has responsibility for designing a product that will fulfill these requirements. Manufacturing must develop and refine the process to provide a capability adequate to make the product to the engineering specification. Quality Control must plan the quality measurements

throughout the process flow which will ensure that the end result will meet quality requirements. And quality of service, after the product has reached the customer, has become an increasingly important part of the total "product package." This has increased the load upon top management, particularly in view of the increased difficulty of allocating proper responsibility for correcting departure from quality standards.

4. **Men.** The rapid growth in technical knowledge and the origination of whole new fields such as computer electronics have created a great demand for workers with specialized knowledge. Specialization has become necessary as the fields of knowledge have increased not only in numbers but in breadth. Although specialization has its advantages, its disadvantage is breaking the responsibility for product quality into a number of pieces. At the same time, this situation has created a demand for the systems engineer who can bring together all these fields of specialization to plan, create, and operate various systems that will assure a desired result. The numerous aspects of business operating systems have become the focus of modern management.

5. **Motivation.** The increased complexity of getting a quality product to market has magnified the importance of the quality contribution of every employee. Human motivational research has shown that in addition to monetary reward, today's workers require reinforcement of a sense of accomplishment in their jobs and the positive recognition that they are personally contributing to achievement of company goals. This has led to an unprecedented need for quality education and for improved communication of quality-consciousness.

6. **Materials.** Owing to production costs and quality requirements, engineers are working materials to closer limits than ever before and using many new, so-called exotic metals and alloys for special applications. As a result, material specifications have become tighter and diversity of materials greater. The visual inspection and thickness check of a few years ago no longer is acceptable. Instead, rapid, precise, chemical, and physical measurements must be made, using highly specialized laboratory machines such as the spectrophotometer, lasers, ultrasonic devices, and machinability test equipment.

7. **Machines and mechanization.** The demand of companies to get cost reductions and production volume to satisfy the customer in intensely competitive markets has forced the use of manufacturing equipment which is steadily becoming more complex and much more dependent upon the quality of material fed into it. Good quality is becoming a critical factor in maintaining machine up time for full utilization of facilities. This is true for the entire span of manufacturing equipment, from deep-draw dies to automatic subassembly machines. The more companies mechanize and automate to get cost reductions, the more critical good quality will become, both to make these reductions real and to raise worker and machine utilization to satisfactory values.

8. **Modern information methods.** The rapid evolution of computer technology has made possible the collection, storage, retrieval, and manipulation of information on a scale never before imaginable. This powerful new information technology has provided the means for an unprecedented level of control of machines and processes during manufacture and of products and services even after they have reached the customer. And the new and constantly improving methods of data processing have made available to management far more useful, accurate, timely, and predictive information upon which to base the decisions that guide the future of a business.

9. **Mounting product requirements.** Great advances in the intricacy of engineering designs, demanding much closer control over manufacturing processes, have made the formerly ignored "little things" of great potential importance. Dust in an electronic assembly area, floor vibration transmitted to a numerically controlled machine tool, or room-temperature variation during adjustments to aerospace guidance systems are hazards to modern production.

Increased complexity and higher performance requirements for products have emphasized the importance of product safety and reliability. Constant attention must be given to make certain that no factors, known or unknown, enter the process to decrease the reliability of components or systems. Inherently reliable designs can deliver such reliability only as a result of such vigilance.

Thus, we see that many of these factors affecting quality are continually undergoing change. These, in turn, must be met with correspondingly strong programs for quality control.

4.2 How Complicated Are Modern Quality Problems?

Entwined within many company problems of product quality are several combinations of the nine technological and human factors.

As far as the technological factors are concerned, it is often difficult to trace a quality problem back to a single cause. The failure of an instrument assembly to pass a final preshipment inspection may be caused by earlier acceptance of faulty purchased materials, improper machining or processing of certain components, faulty assembly jigs, or any of a dozen other possibilities.

When these technological conditions have been traced, it is equally difficult to pin down the human factors. The faulty machining of a part may be due to carelessness of the machine operator, incorrect instruction by the foreman, to defective methods set up by the job planner, or a poor design by the engineer. Curtly blaming a foreman, operator, or engineer on a superficial basis may have little bearing on the true problem.

The situation was vividly illustrated in the experience of a northeastern factory which manufactures permanent magnets. One of the factory's small magnets was subject to very high rejects because of poor magnetic quality at the final electrical test, where each magnet was checked individually. This magnet type was produced in a process that had five major steps:

1. *Material mixing,* involving the bringing together of the necessary raw materials—aluminum, nickel, cobalt, and others—in the correct proportions
2. *Pressing,* involving the pressing into the desired shapes of the mix, which had been impregnated with certain hydrocarbons
3. *Sintering,* involving the subjection of the pressed mix to a temperature and an atmosphere in which the mix fused
4. *Grinding,* involving the machining of the magnet to the desired dimensions
5. *Inspection and test,* involving the 100 percent mechanical check of the magnets to assure their having the proper physical dimensions and the 100 percent electrical check to assure their magnetic quality

A member of the factory's planning and methods group took it upon himself to help the foreman reduce the high rejects on the small magnet line. After an analysis of the nature of the test rejects and at the completion of several process checks, the planner concluded that the defects were being caused by unsatisfactory furnace conditions during the sintering process.

The planner attempted, therefore, to adjust the furnace conditions so that satisfactory magnets could be produced continuously without an appreciable number of rejects. After several furnace changes, which seemed to have little success, he came to the conclusion that although the furnace might be the most important factor affecting magnetic quality, there were undoubtedly other contributing conditions, one or more of which had to be adjusted along with the furnace.

Where to allocate the responsibility for further study and corrective action of these other factors was a question the planner found difficult to answer with the sketchy information at his disposal. There were at least six groups that might have been responsible:

1. *The manufacturing personnel,* from the standpoint of operator care and skill, proper instruction, and adequate care of and attention to the furnace and its controls
2. *The planning and methods group,* in the selection of the furnace process and the design of the jigs and fixtures in connection with it
3. *The design engineers,* from the viewpoint of the original design, the selection of tolerances and operating characteristics, and the selection of materials
4. *The materials-ordering section,* in the choice of vendors and the quality guarantees it had required from these vendors
5. *The laboratory engineers,* in the standards they had set for the materials and the furnace atmosphere and annealing conditions they had recommended
6. *The mechanical-inspection and electrical-test activities,* from the standpoint of their judging the quality of the incoming materials and the results of the processes previous to the annealing operation

The planner took into account only the persons immediately concerned with the problem. He did not, therefore, include on his list the sales department, whose original contract with the customer had set up the specifications that were causing the magnet rejects.

No immediate action was taken by any of these groups except the planner's own. In fact, attention was soon drawn completely from the reject problem because, 3 days after the planner's apparently unsuccessful furnace trials, the rejects mysteriously dropped to a negligible percentage, and it seemed that they would remain low.

The planner uneasily shared credit with the foreman for the elimination of the rejects, doubtful in his own mind that the minor furnace adjustments he had made were actually causing the improvement. As he had feared and almost expected, the rejects suddenly soared a few weeks later, and the furor was again on.

The problem was finally solved when the factory management, recognizing this situation and other similar ones, completely and effectively reorganized its controls over product quality. It is interesting to note that this new program, after a month of hard work, had suggested not one but three major changes in the small magnet. These suggestions, which were put into effect, called for a tolerance change by Engineering, a closer control over furnace temperature by Manufacturing, and a different means of gaging by Inspection. These changes largely eliminated the high rejects at a savings of several thousand dollars annually, with a corresponding improvement in the quality of the magnet.

A member of the management group of the magnet company was asked to express his ideas about what he had learned from this experience concerning what an effective quality-control program should do. "Well, that's an easy one," he told his questioner. "It ought to find out what quality troubles there are and then see that the troubles are fixed so that they don't happen again."

He was asked how this situation could be brought about. "Why, by making it so that they pay some attention to quality ahead of time instead of waiting until everybody is all excited because a batch of bad parts is winged at final inspection or in the field. They all start blaming the factory for the whole business, when maybe it was because of a buildup of mistakes by the engineers, the production team, the purchasing people, the planners, and the inspectors."

There have been many glossier and more diplomatic descriptions of the jobs a quality-control program should do than this one. But none has pointed up more clearly the fact that to have any real control over the conditions affecting product quality, it is necessary to have controls at all important stages of the production process, from the inception of the engineering design through the final assembly and packaging of the product. Nor has it been better illustrated that preventive rather than corrective thinking must be at the core of the entire quality-control program.

4.3 Where Is Quality Control Used?

Since the fundamentals are basic, quality control has been and can be used in product-oriented industries ranging from consumer electronics, computers, and electric generators to bakery, pharmaceutical, and brewery products and in service-oriented industries from department stores, public transportation, and mail-order houses to medical care and hotel administration. Although the details of the approach may differ among industries and companies, the same fundamentals still obtain.

A major source of confusion in the question "Where is quality control used?" is that quality control is often defined in the questioner's mind as one of the individual quality-control methods rather than as a broad integrated program. Three analogies are: thinking only of screw machines when the phrase "manufacturing processes" is used, considering electronics engineering as the study of only semiconductors and circuits, and expecting that hotel administration is the work of only front desk guest receiving.

Quality control refers to the broad administrative and technical area of developing, maintaining, and improving product and service quality. It does not mean simply any single technical method for accomplishing these purposes because such a definition would be too restrictive.

The answer to the question "Where are quality-control *methods* used?" will, of course, depend upon the circumstances. The several methods available are not all satisfactory for every application but must be carefully selected to meet the conditions of each job.

4.4 What Are the Jobs of Quality Control?

The *jobs* of quality control gear right in with the production and service processes, and one means of distinguishing among them shows that there are four natural classifications into which they fall.

The first job of quality control may be termed *new-design control.* Included here is the quality-control effort on a new product while its marketable characteristics are being selected, design and reliability parameters are being established and proved by prototype tests, the manufacturing process is being planned and initially costed, and the quality standards are being specified. Both product and process designs are reviewed to eliminate possible sources of quality troubles before the start of formal production in order to improve maintainability and to eliminate threats to product reliability. In the case of quantity production, new-design control ends when pilot runs have proved satisfactory production performance, and with job-shop production the routine ends as work is being started on production of the components.

The second job of quality control is *incoming-material control.* Involved here are the procedures for actual acceptance of materials, parts, and components purchased from other companies or, perhaps, from other operating units of the same company. Occasionally, incoming-material control applies to parts produced in one area of the same factory for use in another area.

Specifications and standards are established as criteria for acceptance of raw materials, parts, and components. A number of quality-control techniques are applied to provide acceptance at most economical levels. These techniques include vendor-quality evaluations, certification of material and components by the vendor, acceptance sampling techniques, and laboratory tests.

When the design has been released for production, tools have been procured, and materials, parts, and components have been received, *product control,* the third job of quality control, comes into play. Product control involves the control of products at the source of production so that departures from quality specifications can be corrected before defective or nonconforming products are manufactured. It not only involves the materials and parts themselves but control of the processes that contribute the quality characteristics during the manufacturing operation. It seeks to deliver a reliable product that will perform satisfactorily during its expected life and under the conditions of use. It therefore also involves quality activities after production and in the field and product service, which assures the consumer recourse in obtaining the intended product function, should recourse be necessary for any reason.

The fourth job of total quality control is *special process studies,* which is concerned with investigations and tests to locate the causes of defective and nonconforming products and provide permanent corrective action. It is geared toward product and process improvement, not only in improving quality characteristics but in reducing costs.

Figure 4.1 shows how the quality-control jobs gear in with the production process.

4.5 What Is New-Design Control?

As a definition:

> New-design control involves the establishment and specification of the necessary cost-quality, performance-quality, safety-quality, and reliability-quality for the product required for the intended customer satisfaction, including the elimination or location of possible sources of quality troubles before the start of formal production.

Techniques used in new-design control include analysis of product function, quality research, environmental and end-use tests, classification of quality characteristics, establishment of quality levels and quality standards, process-capability studies, tolerance analysis, quality-ability analysis, failure mode and effect analysis, design review, log of prototype inputs, prototype tests, establishment of process parameters, product evaluation, safety studies, manufacturing-process review, establishment of reliability standards, development of

QUALITY CONTROL ACTIVITIES DURING THE PRODUCTION CYCLE

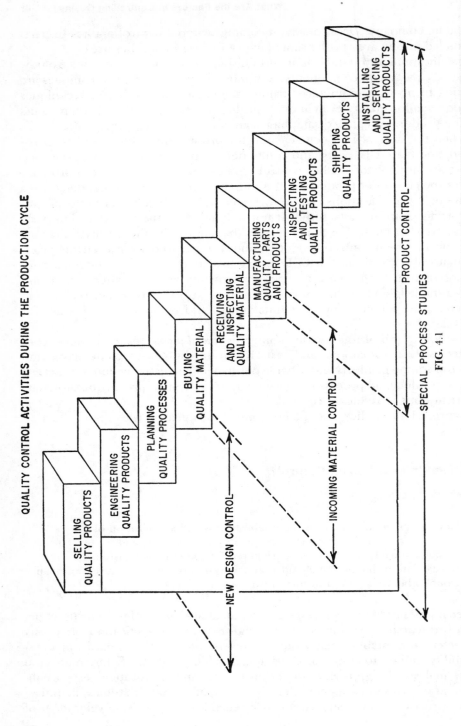

SELLING QUALITY PRODUCTS

ENGINEERING QUALITY PRODUCTS

PLANNING QUALITY PROCESSES

BUYING QUALITY MATERIAL

RECEIVING AND INSPECTING QUALITY MATERIAL

MANUFACTURING QUALITY PARTS AND PRODUCTS

INSPECTING AND TESTING QUALITY PRODUCTS

SHIPPING QUALITY PRODUCTS

INSTALLING AND SERVICING QUALITY PRODUCTS

NEW DESIGN CONTROL

INCOMING MATERIAL CONTROL

PRODUCT CONTROL

SPECIAL PROCESS STUDIES

FIG. 4.1

maintainability and service-ability standards, and pilot runs. New design control is treated in detail in Chapter 18.

4.6 What Is Incoming-Material Control?

As a definition:

> Incoming-material control involves the receiving and stocking, at the most economical levels of quality, of only those parts whose quality conforms to the specification requirements, with emphasis upon the fullest practical vendor responsibility.

There are three phases in incoming-material control:

1. Establishment of vendor-oriented survey, responsibility, and surveillance
2. Control on materials and parts received from outside sources
3. Control on materials and parts processed by other plants of the same company or other divisions of the plant

Techniques used in incoming-material control include vendor-capability evaluations; vendor rating plans; vendor certification of material, parts, and component quality; clear delineation of quality requirements; inspection and test procedures, including use of gages, standards, and specialized quality information equipment; selection of economical sampling plans for use at specified levels of quality; and measurement of inspection performance. Incoming-material control is treated in detail in Chapter 19.

4.7 What Is Product Control?

As a definition:

> Product control involves the control of products at the source of production and through field service so that departures from the quality specification can be corrected before defective or nonconforming products are manufactured and the proper service can be maintained in the field to assure full provision of the intended customer quality.

There are three phases in product control:

1. Control of machining or processing of components
2. Control of assemblies and packaging of batches
3. Control of customer product service

Techniques used in product control include implementation of a complete quality plan for in-process quality control and final product acceptance; process-capability studies; process sampling; nondestructive testing; control chart technique; tool, jig, and fixture control; calibration of quality information equipment; quality audit; operator instructions and training; analysis of complaints; and analysis of quality costs for their optimization and field service quality techniques. Product control is treated in detail in Chapter 20.

4.8 What Are Special Process Studies?

As a definition:

> Special process studies involve investigations and tests to locate the causes of nonconforming products, to determine the possibility of improving quality characteristics, and to ensure that improvement and corrective action are permanent and complete.

Techniques used in special process studies consist largely of special applications of the standard methods used in the other *jobs* of quality control together with the use of special methods. Special process studies are treated in detail in Chapter 21.

4.9 Does a Quality-Control Program Always Include These Four Jobs?

In a particular company, the actual details of the jobs of the quality-control program will depend upon the production circumstances. A company that purchases parts and materials and then machines and processes some of them, after which it assembles the various components, will probably include all four jobs of quality control in its program.

A producer of studs, nuts, and bolts, whose only mechanical facilities are screw machines, will very likely use only *product control* on machines and, possibly, *special process studies* in the quality-control program. The mail-order house may use chiefly *incoming-material control,* and the textile manufacturer both *incoming-material control* and *product control.* The chemical manufacturer, with "batch" production, may depend upon *new-design control* and *special process studies* together with *product control* and *incoming material control.*

All four jobs of a total-quality-control program were successively used by a device manufacturer during the design and production of an electronic controller. The controller was a device with two coils that provided electric force against which the mechanical force of spring-loaded contacts operated. It was produced in an area in which the following sequence of operations prevailed:

1. *Incoming materials.* Parts and materials from outside vendors were received, checked for conformance to specification, and then stocked.
2. *Processing parts.* These materials and parts were worked by a variety of manufacturing equipments, ranging from welders and punch presses to varnish dip tanks and wire strippers.

3. *Assembly.* The various components converged on an assembly line and were assembled to form the final product, which was mechanically and electrically checked.

This controller was an improved version of an earlier device which had been subject both to poor quality within the factory and excessive quality costs. Neither condition could be tolerated on the new design. The objective of the quality-control program on the controller was, therefore, to set up controls at each important stage of the design and manufacturing process so as to provide and maintain a high level of quality at a minimum of cost. The procedures that were used to accomplish this goal were classified as follows.

New-Design Control

While the controller was still in the design and planning stage, special reliability tests and pilot runs were used to analyze the design to make possible adequate guarantees to the customer, to provide reasonable specifications to the shop, and to make available sufficient advance information to the mechanical-inspection and electrical-test supervisors. Experience with previous similar designs; studies on the accuracies of the machines, tools, and processes to be used; and the full utilization of purchasing information were integrated to anticipate and minimize sources of possible quality troubles before production started.

Incoming-Material Control

Information gained from the new-design control procedures showed, with respect to the parts and materials purchased from vendors, those parts and those dimensions which were critical. Based upon these data, careful checks were made on the first lots of parts shipped in by the vendors to determine their quality and workmanship. Where parts were unsatisfactory, immediate contact was made with the vendor. This contact was followed up until the parts were satisfactory or the vendor in question was replaced.

As soon as there was assurance of the quality of a vendor's workmanship, reliable, cost-saving sampling schedules were set up to serve as controls. These sampling checks formed the basis for vendor ratings and, after production had started, for a continuing review of where and how specifications could be so controlled that it becomes possible to place primary responsibility for quality assurance upon the vendor.

Product Control

As the controller started into active production, each operator was carefully instructed in his or her part of the job. Similar instruction was given to new and replacement operators. A preventive maintenance program on the manufacturing equipment largely limited factors that previously had been problems, such as use of undersize machine-tool fixtures, taps, drills, and reamers and the gradual working down of the consistency of the varnish in the dip tanks used to impregnate the controller coils.

On the parts and subassemblies being machined and processed, suitable gaging equipments were made available to each operator. Patrol inspection, on a definite time schedule, gave additional assurance that any nonconforming or defective work would be located at its source. At the important points in the assembly cycle for the device, control charts and nonconformity breakdowns were set up to "telegraph" to the shop supervisors the magnitude and location of the quality troubles. Packaging and shipping were closely controlled. Formal corrective-action programs were closely emphasized to assure quick, permanent conclusions to nonconformity problems.

Special Process Studies

When control charts, patrol inspection checks, and reject breakdowns registered the presence of quality troubles that shop supervisors could not clear up, aid was furnished to them by those of the functional groups which could be most helpful in analyzing and taking corrective action on the problem. In cases of this sort, the quality-control organization had the responsibility of seeing that there was no duplication of effort in these studies and that the talent of the entire organization was effectively utilized.

Many of these studies involved straightforward problems that were solved by bringing together the proper individuals or groups to agree on specification improvements or fixture and tool redesign. Generally, tests were made to determine the nature of this corrective action. In a few instances, on complicated problems where several variables were involved, some of the statistical special methods were found useful in setting up and in interpreting the test runs.

Compared with the previous design, considerable improvements in quality and reduction in losses and costs were noted on this controller. One interesting sidelight is that these improvements were obtained at the same time that inspection and testing expenses were reduced about 40 percent below similar costs on the previous design.

4.10 What Part Does Statistics Play in the Quality-Control Job?

In light of the considerable publicity accorded the use of statistics in quality-control activity, a natural question is "What is the application of statistical methods in the four jobs of quality control?"

Statistics is used in a total-quality-control program whenever and wherever it may be useful. But statistics is only one tool to be used as a part of the total-quality-control pattern; it is not the pattern itself.

The *point of view* represented by these statistical methods has, however, had a profound effect upon the entire area of quality control. This point of view is represented by the following four statistical tools which may be used separately or in combination in the four quality-control jobs:

1. The *frequency distribution*, which is a tabulation or tally of the number of times a given quality characteristic occurs within the samples of product being checked. As a picture of the quality of the sample, it may be used to show at a glance (a) the average quality, (b) the spread of the quality, and (c) the comparison of the quality with specification requirements. This tool is used in the analysis of the quality of a given process or product.
2. The *control chart*, which is a graphical method for evaluating whether a process is or is not in a state of "statistical control." When the curve of the graph approaches or exceeds the limits, some change is suggested in the process that may require investigation. This tool may be used to maintain control over a process after the frequency distribution has shown that the process is "in control."
3. *Sampling tables*, which are a specific set of procedures that usually consist of acceptance sampling plans in which lot sizes, sample sizes, and acceptance criteria, or the amount of 100 percent inspection, are related. This tool is used when assurance is desired for the quality of material either produced or received.
4. *Special methods*, which include such techniques as the analysis of tolerances, correlation, and the analysis of variance. These methods have been hewn, for industrial quality-control use, out of the general body of statistics. This tool is used for special analyses of engineering designs or process troubles.

For general factory use, the frequency distribution, the control chart, and the sampling tables have been reduced to simple shop mathematics. Moreover, these statistical techniques are increasingly being built into modern manufacturing and data processing equipments, to increase greatly their utilization and effectiveness.

A general survey of the point of view represented by statistical methods is contained in the five chapters of Part 5: Chapter 13, "Frequency Distributions"; Chapter 14, "Control Charts"; Chapter 15, "Sampling Tables"; Chapter 16, "Special Methods"; Chapter 17, "Product Reliability."

4.11 What Part Does Other Methodology Play in the Quality-Control Job?

Statistics is essentially one of several techniques that may be applied in total quality control. What are some of the other techniques that can be used?

There are many of an engineering character that have developed in recent years. The technology of quality information equipment design affords solution for the measurement of quality characteristics and for their rapid analysis. The technique of reliability evaluation and analysis is a basis for predicting the reliability of a product under end-use conditions. The techniques of simulation also facilitate reliability prediction for various environmental conditions.

A general review of the engineering technology of quality control is contained in the three chapters of Part 4: Chapter 10, "Quality-Engineering Technology"; Chapter 11, "Process-Control-Engineering Technology"; Chapter 12, "Quality Information Equipment Engineering Technology."

4.12 Do These Jobs Apply to Job Lot As Well As to High-Quantity Production?

Much of the original quality-control publicity accorded the spectacular accomplishments of statistical sampling was in millions of articles. An unfortunate carry-over from this early publicity is the attitude still prevalent in some factories that the quality-control jobs are essentially tools for mass production.

Both practical experience and common sense show that this is not the case. The quality-control jobs are as applicable to job-lot production as to high-quantity production.

It is fully as necessary and useful to control the quality of the design of a new generator when only one unit is to be built as it is to carry on similar activity for a semiconductor device whose production rate will reach the hundreds of thousands. It is fully as important to control the materials and parts for this generator as it is to superintend them for the semiconductor. It is fully as basic to oversee the machining of parts and their assembly into a complete generator as it is to control this work for the semiconductor.

The methods used in the quality-control jobs may differ between the two products. Certain types of sampling methods will be better applicable in the quality-control jobs for the semiconductor. Process-capability studies will probably be relatively more useful in the generator program. The type of control chart that is ideal for the semiconductor will require considerable adaptation for use with the generator.

The administration of an overall, integrated quality-control program will be of equal value for both products in place of a sprawling, disjointed series of activities. It is likely that the administration and organization of this program will not differ very widely between high-quantity and job-lot production.

Another way of describing the basic differences between job-lot and high-quantity quality-control programs is as follows:

In mass-production operations, product quality can be effectively controlled by types of parts because all parts will be manufactured to the same drawings and specifications. However, in job-lot manufacture, the parts differ from job to job and only the process by which they are produced is common to all types of products.

Therefore, in mass-production manufacturing quality-control activities center on product and process, whereas job-lot manufacturing is a matter of controlling the process. For example, in the mass-production manufacture of coils, the emphasis of quality-control activities is on the coil type itself: its dimensions, fiber wrappings, and so on. But where varying types and sizes of coils are produced on a job-lot basis, the quality-control activities center on the common manufacturing process for producing the coils.

4.13 How Are the Jobs of Quality Control Accomplished?

Section 1.5 showed that the four steps in the overall control of quality are:

1. Setting standards
2. Appraising conformance
3. Taking corrective action
4. Planning for improvement

Although, to different degrees, these four steps are combined in each of the jobs of quality control, they appear to tie together effectively with these jobs in one-two-three-four order: A major portion of new-design control is setting standards; incoming-material control is largely a question of appraising conformance; product control is, in part, the procedure for taking corrective action; and special process studies have planning for improvement as one of their major aims.

From this breakdown of an overall quality-control program into its component parts, it can be readily seen that there are several by-product benefits over and above the major improvements which result from such a program. Successful prosecution of the jobs of quality control makes possible greatly increased knowledge about the accuracies and capabilities of machines and processes. It makes factual material about product quality available for market planning and merchandising activities. It stimulates better engineering designs by promoting reliability studies of new products before they have been placed in active production. It promotes improved inspection methods and relieves inspection monotony by substituting careful checks of samples for mass sorting of the 100 percent variety. It enables sounder setting of time-studied standards for labor by establishing quality standards for shop operations.

An important by-product of quality control is the provision of a reasonable and definite schedule for preventive maintenance to replace the hit-or-miss type of schedule that often leads to trouble. When product quality is to be emphasized in company advertising, quality control makes available powerful information for trade journals, magazines, and catalogs. It also furnishes a factual basis for cost accounting on such standard quality costs as prevention, appraisal, and failure.

To secure successfully these major and by-product benefits from the four jobs of quality control requires integrated, organized action by the various individuals and groups involved in the industrial cycle or, in other words, the creation of a quality system. Part 2 discusses the approach and implementation of a total quality system. Part 3 then reviews from a management viewpoint the various strategies necessary and available to set a quality program in motion.

PART TWO

The Total Quality System

CHAPTER **5**

The Systems Approach
to Quality

With so many factors involved in the managing of quality to meet present marketplace demands—and with the very broad scope of the four jobs of modern quality control required to satisfy these demands—it is essential that a company and a plant have a clear and well-structured system which identifies, documents, coordinates, and maintains all the key activities needed to assure the necessary quality actions throughout all relevant company and plant operations.

Without such systematic integration, many companies can lose in what might be thought of as their *internal company competition* between, on the one hand, their explosively increasing technological, organizational and marketing *complexity* and, on the other hand, the ability of their management and engineering functions to plan and control effectively and economically the product- and service-quality aspects of this complexity.

The hallmark of modern total quality systems is their effectiveness in providing a strong foundation for the economic control of this complexity, to the benefit of both improved customer quality satisfaction and lower quality costs.

Part 2 reviews the total quality system. Chapter 5 deals with this new systems perspective of quality. Key operating activities upon which a system is built and maintained are considered in Chapter 6. Chapter 7 then examines quality costs, one of the major indices of systems effectiveness.

5.1 What Is Today's Systems Requirement?

In its simplest terms, the keystone concept of modern quality thinking may be described as follows: *Quality must be designed and built into a product; it can not be exhorted or inspected into it.* In systems terms, however, giving operational meaning to this concept by applying the many powerful new techniques of quality and reliability in truly effective ways has come to represent a massive challenge.

The systems challenge that must be met is massive, in part, because quality achievement—as a thread that runs from product conception to satisfied customer use—is dependent upon people-machine-information interactions across all the functional areas of a company. It is massive, in part, because product quality—the sharpness of whose definition is the bricks and mortar of a quality system—is a very demanding concept to structure for complex products and services, one that is constantly shifting for most products and services. It is massive, in part, because the managerial approaches that are needed to operate these systems are not yet widely enough practiced in industry and government. It is massive, in part, because while it is possible to *communicate* the *ideas* of prevention and coordinated quality programs, their *application* faces individual prejudices and organizational patterns that often have been based upon lifetimes of policing habits and compartmentalized engineering, manufacturing, and quality control.

Too often, the magnitude of the systems requirement of *implementing* technically sound quality principles and techniques has been underestimated. There has been a tendency to funnel quality-systems problems into traditional functional channels too narrow to handle them adequately. And, in a number of companies, the introduction of quality *techniques* has been largely uncoordinated with the managerial *decision-making* process, with the result that the two quite unexpectedly have ended up in conflict with each other. In these situations, the missing catalyst has been the total quality system.

5.2 Defining the Total Quality System

As a definition:

> A total quality system is the agreed companywide and plantwide operating work structure, documented in effective, integrated technical and managerial procedures, for guiding the coordinated actions of the work force, the machines, and the information of the company and plant in the best and most practical ways to assure customer quality satisfaction and economical costs of quality.

The systems approach to quality begins with the basic principle of total quality control that customer satisfaction cannot be achieved by concentrating upon any one area of the plant or company alone—design engineering, reliability analysis, inspection quality equipment, reject troubleshooting, operator education, or maintainability studies—important as each phase is in its own right. Its achievement depends, instead, *both upon how well and how thoroughly these quality actions in the several areas of the business work individually and upon how well and how thoroughly they work together.* The creation and control of the proper product and service quality for the plant and company require that the many quality activities in its product and service cycle be integrated and measured —from market identification and product development and design through shipment and product service—on an organized, technically effective, and economically sound basis.

The total quality system is the foundation of total quality control, always providing the proper channels through which the stream of essential product-quality-related activities must flow. Together with other systems, it makes up the main-line flow of the total business system. Quality requirements and product-quality parameters change, but the quality system remains fundamentally the same.

5.3 The Total Quality System and the Engineering Technology of Quality Control

Experience in company after company demonstrates that while the development of modern quality control began with the introduction of new and very significant quality technical activities—which today comprise the engineering technology of quality control and which are reviewed in Chapters 10 through 12—it did not become real and effective until companies had established clear, powerful, and structured operating quality systems employing these technical results for improved customer quality satisfaction and lower quality costs.

This experience demonstrates that, to produce the most positive results from these technical activities, their introduction must be accompanied by the creation of equally powerful managerial and engineering decision making and operating total quality systems to put the techniques to work on a continuous basis and get payoff from them. Reliability studies of new products and reinspection of products found nonconforming have been two typical examples of the need for systems.[1]

Reliability Studies of New Products

A large worldwide electronics corporation had established a reliability program and a specialized reliability engineering component to make reliability and maintainability studies on new products. However, this work became an illustration to the company of the ineffectiveness of the employment of quality techniques when they operate in isolation from the mainstream of managerial decision making.

In the case of one new electronic home-appliance product, the results from a reliability and maintainability study confronted the design engineers and the marketing specialists in the company with the recommendation to hold up the new product in the face of a preagreed customer release plan that had been already scheduled throughout the dealer chain. But, in the absence of a clearly defined quality system, the company's product introduction program had not been adequately prethought as to how to handle reliability-analysis recommendations of this sort, so the recommendation went into an inadequate technical and managerial decision-making process.

What developed was a debate among the design engineers and the marketing specialists as to just what kinds of failure rates from which types of testing programs constituted the basis for talking about schedule holdups and product and process redesigns.

The reliability evidence was simply not well enough structured with respect to the management decision-making base, and so the new product introduction program went forward as scheduled—in spite of the negative recommendation—although much more uncomfortably—and with very uncertain customer quality-satisfaction risks and potentially hazardous product-liability consequences.

Reinspection of Product

An international automotive equipment corporation had a very rigorous procedure for final inspection of all outgoing products, with excellent measurement facilities, trained inspectors, and careful standards. However, when defects were identified at final inspection, the procedure for *re*inspection after the defects were corrected was considerably less rigorous. This reinspection could, under certain circumstances, be vague and not very visible and therefore represented a high quality-risk area to the company.

For example, early one Monday morning, the production superintendent of Machining Department A of the largest plant of the corporation received a phone call from the foreman of the plant's Final Inspection Department. It appeared that the latest shipment of automotive castings intended for shipment to a brake assembly plant contained burrs on one side of a machined surface.

Because of delivery pressure, the Machining Department superintendent's reaction was to ask for the entire lot to be brought back to the department for quick rework on the milling machines and what amounted to direct shipment of the castings to the customer with brief reinspection because of the time shortage. The ultimate result of this vital business decision was that the customer's incoming inspection department rejected 13 percent of the castings because they were not within the specified tolerance. What had happened was that the remachining had removed not only the troublesome burrs but some additional metal—and the reinspection had not been sufficiently thorough. The brake assembly plant customer reacted against "this obvious lack of attention to quality."

Thus, under the stress of production demands, and under certain conditions, this company had a gaping hole in its quality program which permitted the unintentional passing of unsatisfactory products. The company could be potentially open in these production situations to customer quality dissatisfaction and product-liability risks.

5.4 The Systems Engineering and Systems Management Approach

In quality control, it can be the single activity that is missed which creates the quality problem. The total quality system provides a company with integrated and continuous control attention to all key activities.

This is true whether the problem is one of reliability, appearance, serviceability, fit, performance, or any of the other major factors that customers add up when they decide about the quality of a product. Thorough analysis of the root causes of quality problems have usually shown that these problems exist in many, rather than a few, areas of the product. Figure 5.1 shows the broad spectrum of such a typical product-fault-cause analysis, in this instance the returns of a small consumer appliance for quality and safety reasons.

Since the effectiveness of each key quality activity in a plant or company can thus substantially increase—or decrease—overall quality effectiveness, the key to the modern systems engineering approach in quality control can be readily stated: *A modern total quality system must be structured and maintained so that all key activities—quality equipment, work force, information flow, standards, controls, and simi-*

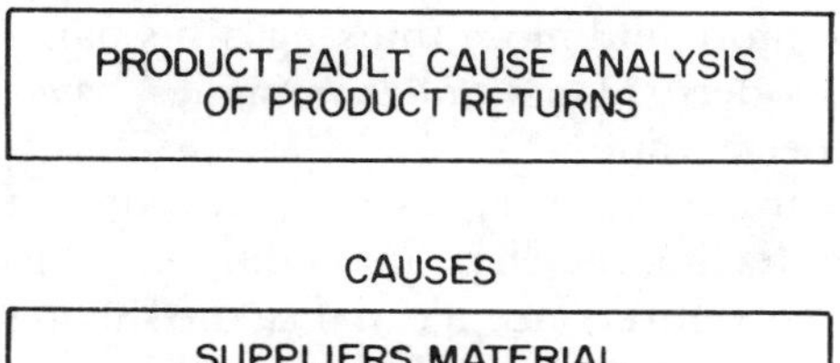

```
┌─────────────────────────────────┐
│   PRODUCT FAULT CAUSE ANALYSIS   │
│        OF PRODUCT RETURNS         │
└─────────────────────────────────┘

              CAUSES

┌─────────────────────────────────┐
│      SUPPLIERS MATERIAL           │
│        DEFICIENCIES               │
├─────────────────────────────────┤
│      DESIGN ENGINEERING           │
│           ERRORS                  │
├─────────────────────────────────┤
│      FACTORY PROCESS              │
│       INCONSISTENCIES             │
├─────────────────────────────────┤
│      FACTORY OPERATOR             │
│         MISTAKES                  │
├─────────────────────────────────┤
│      INSPECTION ERRORS            │
├─────────────────────────────────┤
│      MISAPPLICATION               │
│      AND MISLABELING              │
├─────────────────────────────────┤
│      PRODUCT SERVICE              │
│         MISTAKES                  │
└─────────────────────────────────┘
```

FIG. 5.1

lar major activities—must be established not only for their own effectiveness but for their interrelated impact on total quality effectiveness.

As a management and engineering concept, this interrelationship approach is basically different from the scientific management approach which characterized industrial operations for more than the first half of this century.

This earlier approach was that only by what might be called improvement through specialized *division of effort* could large enterprises be intelligently operated and managed. Correspondingly, the development of individual specialties began. In the early history of most companies, there really was no counterpart for the present-day design engineer. There was, of course, no production control, and only a rudimentary accounting specialty, which did not really flourish in industry until World War I. The same evolution may be traced for most other functions in industry today.

It is clear now, of course, that individualized specialization is not an unmixed blessing, despite the many outstanding advances it has brought to industry. Carried beyond a certain point, the theory of division of effort begins to create more problems than it solves, because it promotes narrowness of perspective, duplication of effort, and fuzziness of communication. Specialized terms, specialized concepts, specialized ways of approaching problems, fewer and fewer individuals of the plant and company realistically thinking of the total customer objectives of quality, more and more thinking of its parts—these are some of the problems that modern plants and companies have inherited from the earlier theories of specialization.

These problems represent the very ancient case, duplicated in modern guise, of the four blind men feeling the elephant at different areas. The difficulty has been that the division of effort concept can turn the solving of quality problems not into terms of the plant or company whole and its major activities but into terms which sometimes merely strengthen individual specialties within the plant.

The significance of the modern systems approach is that it adds to the older principle of improvement through division of effort the complementary principle of *improvement through integration of effort.* Indeed, *the hallmark of modern systems is the fundamental concept of integrated people-machine-information structures to economically and effectively control technical complexity.* The bases are cooperation and coordination.

5.5 The Organizationwide Scope of the Total Quality System and the Role of General Management

With the casually evolved quality systems that were characteristic of the past, the systems responsibility of management was equally casual and unlikely to be exercised very often. But experience indicates that the modern engineered quality-system structures are so new and so broad and so intensive that they will downgrade and come apart unless, from their beginnings, they are managed on a systems basis that is equally new and broad and intensive enough to ensure that the system will produce the intended results in operation. The basic responsibility for leading in the creation, improvement, and operation of quality systems must now rest in the hands of company management itself, rather than only in the hands of its functional components.

Because the scope of the integration of quality effort extends from initial consumer quality definition to assurance of actual consumer-product satisfaction, it might be thought of as "horizontal," in an organization-chart sense (Fig. 5.2). This is in sharp contrast to the responsibility assignment in traditional quality-control components, which might be thought of as organizationally "vertical," i.e., in one functional work segment only of the customer-definition-to-customer-satisfaction process, usually in inspection and test. In such traditional vertical functional setups, the many important and interrelated elements of quality work and decisions that exist throughout the various functions of the company were only vaguely (if at all) identified. The all-important interrelationships among these functions were likely to be equally vague when it came to resolving multifunctional quality problems, which usually represented the major product-quality demand.

The organizational approach for implementing the total quality system in a plant or company involves two parallel steps. The first step is clear establishment throughout all relevant company functions of the major quality actions and decision making—as well as interrelationships—within the plant and com-

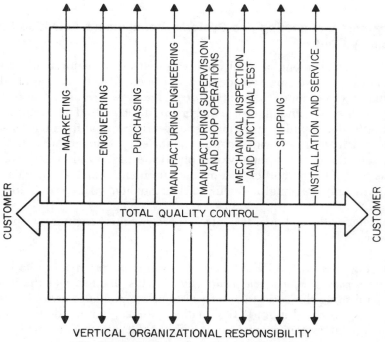

FIG. 5.2 Horizontal scope of total quality control.

pany and externally of dealer and customer and governmental and public body relationships. The second step is the addition of a major horizontal work scope —of policy and systems development and control—to the company's quality function (and, of course, correspondingly upgrading its capabilities as needed).[2]

From a general management point of view, the quality system must be approached as a major company resource fully as important as capital investment equipment programs, product-development programs, or new process technology programs—and, indeed, recognized as an essential condition for the effective utilization of these other programs. It requires fundamental leadership by company and plant management, whose commitment to quality must be thoroughly communicated to and understood by all members of the organization.

In principle, general managers must become the chief architects or designers of the quality system, just as they have the ultimate responsibility for structuring systems for cost control, production control, or any other of the systems which together make up the total business system for the company (see Sec. 1.8). As in all these systems, the general manager will, of course, delegate actual operating responsibilities, relying upon the modern quality function to play a major role in establishment of the operating quality system and to see, in cooperation with the functions throughout the company, that the system works.

5.6 Systems Engineering and Systems Management Activities for Quality Control[3]

For the achievement of total quality systems, the major field of systems engineering and systems management has been adapted and applied to the particular needs of modern quality control. It is now a center point of effective quality engineering and quality management directed to the development and on-going leadership of a strong, integrated—rather than fragmented—quality system which operates with economy, efficiency, and enthusiastic support throughout the entire company and plantwide organization. It is guided by systems economics and other systems measurements which are foundations for continuous and meaningful evaluations of quality, quality cost, and quality activities.

As applied with total quality control, these systems activities may be defined as follows:

1. *Systems engineering is the technological process of creating and structuring effective people-machine-information quality systems.* This also includes the process of establishing the audit to assure systems maintenance as well as the continuing work to upgrade the quality system, when needed, by matching the quality-system requirements with the most up-to-date quality technology.

As earlier introduced in Section 1.8, *systems engineering* is likely to provide what might be thought of as the fundamental "design technology" of the modern quality engineer.

2. *Systems management is the administrative process of assuring effective operation of the quality system.* This also includes administering the system so that its disciplines are, in fact, followed and enhance the system, when needed, by carefully adding to its improvements as they have been engineered.

   Systems management is likely to become a fundamental managerial guide for quality managers in their activities to guide and lead integrated quality activities throughout the organization.

3. *Systems economics, especially including quality cost, is the measurement and control process for guiding the most effective resource allocation of the people-machine-information content of the quality system.* The objective is that the lowest quality costs are achieved, consistent with full customer quality satisfaction, including guidance so that investments or other expenditures planned for the quality system will be based upon net economic improvements to be obtained throughout the system rather than in only a self-contained portion of that system.

4. *Systems measurements, particularly with respect to systems audits and customer quality determinations, are the process of the evaluation of the effectiveness with which the quality system meets its objectives and fulfills its goals.* Systems measurements are likely to provide key bench marks for quality-control personnel as well as for functional and general management.

5.7 Characteristics of the Total Quality System

There are four characteristics of the engineered total quality system that are of particular importance:

First, and most important, it represents a *point of view* for thinking about the way quality really works in a modern business company or governmental agency and how quality decisions can best be made. This point of view is of the major quality activities as continuous work processes. They start with the customer's requirements and end successfully only when the customer is satisfied with the way the product or service of the enterprise meets these requirements.

These are processes in which it is important for quality *both* how well each person, each machine, and each organization component *works individually* and how well they *all work together.* In these processes in a manufacturing business, for example, the best quality-control decision is not merely the historically usual one which is based upon conformance of the product with certain engineering specifications—important as this is in itself. It is, more fully, also the decision which is based upon the satisfactory quality of the product with reference to *total* customer expectations.

The *second characteristic* of the engineered quality system is that it represents the basis for the deeply thought-through *documentation,* not merely of a thick book of details but the identification of the key, enduring quality activities and the integrated people-machine-information relationships which make a particular activity viable and communicable throughout the firm. It is the specific way in which the manager, the engineer, and the analyst can visualize the who, what, where, when, why and how of his and her quality work and decision making as it affects the total scope of plant or company quality.

Each person can visualize her and his own work assignments and decision-making responsibilities in a quality activity, the quality work and decisions to which he or she has a relationship, the relevant quality work and decisions made by others, the machine interfaces, and the information inputs and outputs. The systems approach thus represents the way in which quality becomes a reality for the work force of the plant or company as a living part of their working life.

Third, the quality system is the *foundation* for making the broader scope quality activities of the company realistically *manageable* because it permits the management and employees of the plant and company to get their arms firmly around their customer-requirements-to-customer-satisfaction quality activities. Moreover, quality systems provide alternatives, under given quality situations, which provide a management base designed to be highly flexible in the face of the unexpected, to be the beneficiary of the full participation of the human resources of the company, to be measurable, and to be responsive to the feedback of actual results throughout the activity.

All too often, in the past, these customer-to-customer quality activities have been unmanageable because they have been fragmented and, hence, not effectively controllable. Individuals well down in the organization chart realistically have sometimes had far more impact on these activities than has the management itself.

The *fourth* characteristic of a total quality system is that it is the basis for the systematic *engineering of order-of-magnitude improvements* throughout the major quality activities of the company. Since a change in a key portion of quality work anywhere in the customer-to-customer activities of the company will have an effect—either good or bad—both upon all other portions of work and upon the *overall effectiveness* of the activity, the total quality system provides the framework and discipline so that these individual changes may practically be engineered for their degree of improvement of the total quality activity itself.

5.8 The Meaning of the Total Quality System

The modern total quality system is therefore far different in meaning, objective, implementation, actual operation, achieved results, and continuous maintenance from what, in some past usage, may have been termed the quality "system" of some plants or companies. This system was likely to be a rather general statement of the concern's good quality intentions, a narrowly oriented documentation of inspection and testing instructions, a manual of procedural statements drawn up as a showpiece response to customer demands that there be a quality program in the plant or company, a brave attempt by a quality-control component unilaterally to reach out to other plant or company functions, or a document to cover some outline for a quality system provided by some "systems" requirement from an outside source. Too often these documents were not implemented in the actual quality actions within the plant or company, were too superficial in the actions they did recommend, or were concentrated in only a restricted area of quality operations.

Today, the tightness or looseness of the quality system of a company or plant can be the sheer make-or-break test as to whether the organization achieves its goals of much improved product quality at much reduced quality costs. Industrial experience throughout the world has clearly demonstrated that a manufactured product or an offered service that is poor in quality and reliability is almost always a product or service that has been controlled by an equally poor quality system.

When considering the offerings of a firm, buyers today—particularly those from industrial concerns and governmental bodies—carefully examine the quality of the products themselves *and* the thoroughness, depth, and effectiveness of the assurance system behind the quality and value of the products. Consumers—particularly through groups and associations and increasingly as individuals—have been moving in the same direction.

5.9 Why a Total Quality System Is Necessary—An Example

As an illustration of the needs for effective, structured total quality systems, it is useful to consider the casually evolved system of a large international corporation which produces a very wide range of electronic, electromechanical, propulsion-mechanical, and process-oriented products. The markets for this corporation include industrial companies, government agencies, and individual consumers.

The corporation faced quality demands throughout the world that were literally expanding by the month, including potential product-liability and product-recall problems. Particularly deep concerns were that the company did not feel it "had its arms firmly around quality" and that it did not have effective managerial "handles" to get direct and positive action on its quality results. Especially frustrating in this well-managed company was the contrast between the situation regarding quality and what took place in areas like production flow and control of cost budgets, where firmly based management systems provided the intended results to management-initiated actions in reasonable periods of time.

The company had grown very substantially in both sales and number of products and services. However, quality programs—while also expanded and with the addition of many new techniques—were still pretty much structured upon the basis they had been during earlier and easier days for product quality. For example, the quality-control concept in the company was a traditional one, with such characteristics as these:

· A purely engineering design-based and a purely factory-based program with organizational walls between each and a program keyed to trying to assure conformance to engineering specifications that were neither clear enough nor sufficiently customer-use directed
· A program without a sufficient budgetary base to permit preventive effort to get quality and reliability engineering in during the engineering and manufacturing planning stage, where it can do the most good

The corporation believed it had a quality system because a thick quality-control manual had been prepared to include some of the long-existing quality-control instructions and some new ones. But, the manual primarily sat on bookcase shelves and had limited impact on actual day-to-day plant and company quality operations.

A central quality director had been appointed, reporting directly to upper management with the assignment of "assuring quality." However, his responsibilities were stated in general terms only, and, while his accountability was high, his actual authorities were vague as to actual detailed quality activities.

The control realities in the corporation were that quality responsibilities were fragmented throughout the entire organization: Design engineering tried to do what it could in preproduction reliability studies on a few products. Purchasing discussed the importance of quality with some suppliers but made no systematic measures of incoming quality performance to be discussed with these suppliers. Production, with large numbers of new employees and high turnover, was doing its best to impress the importance of quality work on these employees, but it had no systematic process-control programming to make this effective. Inspection ran an extensive receiving-material toll gate and an end-of-production-line conformance checking program, but the leakage of unsatisfactory products to the field was increasing. A quality-control component did quality planning for as many products as possible but was unable to provide very satisfactory coverage.

There was no common focus or coordination of this quality work—and its collective cost was very high, although with very limited prevention activity. Quality problems and major customer complaints periodically descended directly upon general management, which too often found itself frustrated both from quick quality improvements and from any real confidence that the improvements would stick after they had been achieved.

5.10 Why a Total Quality System Is Necessary—An Example (Cont'd.)

These fragmented quality activities in the international corporation generated many quality problems that were often self-created by the looseness of the corporation's quality actions. For this reason the corporation determined that it was necessary to establish a total quality system.

As the system was put into operation, step by step, its very major differences and benefits became clear, as compared to the traditional, casually evolved system. For some examples of the contributions of the quality system:

In Policy: The company's quality objectives were clearly and crisply identified.

In New Product Introduction: Quality-related activities were organized and structured to assure the quality ability and producibility of the product, to assure initial customer satisfaction, to minimize product service problems and reduce product-liability risks.

In Production: The corporation had traditionally reacted to important quality difficulty with what is usually termed "firefighting"—attempts to reduce or minimize the problem immediately. There had been procedures which called for developing permanent correction of such defects, but, unfortunately, these procedures contained loopholes that made the corrective action a temporary step. The loopholes permitted ready avoidance of the responsibility for carrying out this essential corrective action on a permanent basis through decisions made even at very low levels of management.

As a result, the company wasted resources regularly refighting the same or allied quality "fires" and customers frequently got poorer products than they should have—at a higher quality cost. The total quality system provided control activities to plug these loopholes and to require and measure the achievement of permanent corrective action.

In the Area of Spare Parts: Occasionally products of quality lower than that specified for original equipment had moved into replacement parts channels for the corporation. The total quality system spelled out practices so that this was properly controlled.

In Marketing and Advertising: Earlier there had been no insistence upon a systematic review of advertising to eliminate improper quality claims. The quality-systems approach plugged this potentially very damaging loophole, which could change completely the warranty picture of the company. Moreover, in the traditional approach, almost no one in the corporation had deliberately and consistently provided to marketing and advertising the feedback necessary for them to capitalize on successes and advances in the quality-related field. The systems approach demanded it.

These examples, together with many others across the whole range of operations for this company, are typical of the very major improvements brought about by the creation of a strong, documented total quality system.

The quality and reliability improvements from the total quality system provided the corporation with significant reductions in scrap (58 percent) and rework (61 percent), inspection and test costs (37 percent), and customer complaints (51 percent) (Fig. 5.3). Total quality costs, which had been running at 9 percent of sales billed before introduction of the total quality system, were reduced to 5.9 percent as the systems operation began to be effective. As the quality system became fully operational, quality costs for the corporation dropped to 4.7 percent of sales billed.

Similar dramatic improvement results from strong total quality programs can be found in companies and plants in a whole range of industries throughout the world. Basic to the development of these strong quality programs is the establishment of necessary strong total quality-systems activities such as are discussed next in Chapter 6.

Notes

[1]The key systems activities of the quality system are reviewed more broadly in Sec. 6.3.

[2]The major new business and systems responsibilities which have been added to the technical responsibilities of the quality function are more fully discussed in Chap. 8.

[3]The discussion is after "Systems Technology," an address by Donald S. Feigenbaum to the Joint Engineering Conference, Santa Barbara, Calif., October 1974.

QUALITY SYSTEM CONTRIBUTIONS

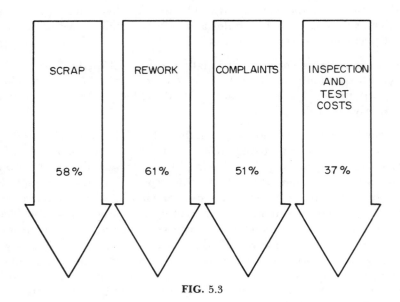

FIG. 5.3

CHAPTER **6**

Establishing the Quality System

Most companies inspect and test their products today; some carry on reliability and other technical investigations; many place attention to assuring the quality of parts and materials received from vendors; a number of companies emphasize product service. However, what basically distinguishes companies and plants with strong and effective quality programs today are the strength and effectiveness of the total quality system underpinning the total quality control of the company.

The modern total quality system is the result of the disciplined and structured design, installation, and maintenance of the complete range of the quality actions by the people, machines, and information which will genuinely assure quality to the customer and low quality costs to the plant and company. In operation, it requires the full and detailed implementation of these activities in the actual quality actions of the company and plant—and the conscientious and regular determination of the effectiveness of these actions.

Chapter 6 examines first the necessary quality actions and then in more detail certain systems activities and key areas of systems measurement which are important for a working and dependable total quality system.

6.1 Controlling the Quality-Systems Activity[1]

There are many quality actions that must be brought together in proper relationship to provide the single major function of getting a quality product to market. The starting point is recognition that, in companies today, most of the major operations—particularly including quality control—typically consist of a broad range of mutually related people, machines, material, and information activities.

These activities can usefully be regarded as systems[2]. As a definition:

91

A system is a group or work pattern of interacting human and/or machine activities, directed by information, which operate on and/or direct material, information, energy, and/or humans to achieve a common specific purpose or objective.

Many plants and companies have always had some form of an overall work pattern for quality—no matter how well or how poorly it has been documented—which has served as their quality system. In the past, most of these have merely grown up on a bits-and-pieces basis: The control activities have evolved over a period; the equipment has been installed from time to time; the job descriptions of people have been written as separate elements; information processing has not always been considered an explicit matter; planning and controlling of the complete system have almost never been established; quality costs have not been under direct management control.

In these essentially casually evolved quality systems, customer quality satisfaction and quality cost can be an unplanned, perhaps not fully motivated, consequence of sometimes unclear quality goals and sometimes unbalanced organizationwide quality actions.

Experience throughout industry demonstrates that when casually evolved systems—whose results, either good or poor, have been more a matter of circumstance than of management intent—can be effectively systems engineered and systems managed into total quality systems, they will provide major improvements in company quality and quality costs results needed to meet today's marketplace and competitive requirements. Indeed, such total systems structuring gives the company far greater quality effectiveness than its several quality activities individually considered. The structured quality system is far more than just the interacting activities which are characteristic of any system. It is, instead, *an integrated system to produce full customer quality satisfaction and minimum quality costs with most effective use of plant and company resources and with optimum speed, human harmony and motivation, economy, and overall control of action.*

Quality-improvement planning with a quality system is like planning the maintenance and improvement of the electrical system of a city with a complete distribution network plan of the existing situation available; improvement planning in the absence of a framework is like trying to do such electrical system planning in the absence of network diagrams upon which anyone can agree.

The systems engineering and systems management objective is to make the quality system for the plant and company *the most effective work pattern of people, machines, and information for assuring customer quality satisfaction and minimum quality costs throughout the entire customer-order to customer-delivery scope of the key quality activities of the plant or company.* This quality system serves as the *natural* basis for major management and engineering attention to these activities, leading to the total quality system as defined in Section 5.2.

6.2 Total Quality-System Principles

There are several principles which are fundamental to quality-systems engineering and which can be readily stated:

1. *Quality-systems engineering relates quality technology to quality requirements.* On the one hand, it provides the "feedforward" basis for identifying the total product- and service-quality requirements that will provide full effectiveness and economy in customer quality satisfaction. On the other hand, it provides the basis for identifying the quality technology that is available to meet these requirements—including quality engineering, process-control engineering, and quality information engineering. This includes what might be termed "hardware" technologies—that is, those bearing upon quality information equipment—in relevant areas such as electronic and electrical, mechanical, nuclear, chemical, and metallurgical subjects. It also includes what might be termed planning and control technologies—that is, those bearing upon human and procedural quality engineering and process-control engineering matters—in such relevant areas as quality research, design review, process-control audit, training, and similar subjects.

2. *Quality-systems engineering relates this quality technology to quality requirements in an organized form of necessary specific procedures and controls.* Moreover, because there is always a constant influx both of new requirements and new technology which bear upon system activities, the work of quality-systems engineering is the basis for this balancing-off of requirements and technology by guiding the introduction of practical improvements in the system as well.

3. *Quality-systems engineering considers the total range of relevant human, informational, and equipment factors needed for these procedures and controls.* It considers and integrates a spectrum of human, materiel, procedural, equipment, information, and financial factors. This type of many-factor consideration is in sharp contrast to the almost exclusive concentration upon one or another of these factors that has been typical of other, narrower approaches to quality work—such as emphasis upon either purely paperwork procedures or purely technical product designing.

4. *Quality-systems engineering specifically establishes the "feedback" measurements against which the quality system will be evaluated when in operation.* It explicitly establishes the *several,* overall quality economic and effectiveness measurements which will be used.

5. *Quality-systems engineering then structures the necessary quality system objectively and provides for audits of the system.*

6. *Quality-systems engineering and management provides for the ongoing control of the quality system in use.*

Thus, the quality-systems engineering process involves technical effort of the most rigorous sort. Moreover, in this era of increasing specialization, thinking in these systems terms cannot be confined to those men and women who happen to be termed "quality-systems engineers." Particularly, the modern systems engineering concepts provide a point of view so that all key individuals in the plant and company—factory employee, product engineer, test technician, serviceperson, or manager—can develop this understanding of the interrelationships of the various quality activities in the plant and company quality. The concepts also enable these individuals to understand their important quality contribution as related to all other contributions and to develop an awareness of the end purpose the quality actions serve together. Quality-systems engineering is thus the foundation for true *total quality management*.

6.3 Key Systems Activities for Total Quality Control

A quality system that has been engineered and is being managed—as compared to one that has merely casually grown—is structured to meet such objectives as the following:

· Defined and specific quality policies and objectives
· Strong customer orientation
· All the activities necessary to achieve these quality policies and objectives
· Organizationwide integration of the activities
· Clear personnel assignments for quality achievement
· Specific vendor-control activities
· Thorough quality-equipment identification
· Defined and effective quality information flow, processing, and control
· Strong quality-mindedness and organizationwide positive quality motivation and training
· Quality cost and other measurements and standards of quality performance
· Positive corrective-action effectiveness
· Continuous control of the system, including the feedforward and feedback of information and the analysis of results, and comparison with the present standards.
· Periodic audit of system activities

The key systems activities which will best meet the objectives of a specific company will, of course, be tailored to that company's requirements, resources, and goals. The systems engineering task for the company will involve documentation of the various systems and subsystems that make up the total quality system which "works" for the particular company. While the activity emphasis in portions of specific company quality systems vary, certain subsystems can be basic in programs for total quality control. These subsystems, which are examined in Sections 6.4 through 6.13, are as follows:

1. Preproduction quality evaluation, discussed in Section 6.4
2. Product- and process-quality planning, discussed in Section 6.5
3. Purchased-material quality planning, evaluation, and control, discussed in Section 6.6
4. Product- and process-quality evaluation and control, discussed in Section 6.7
5. Quality information feedback, discussed in section 6.8
6. Quality information equipment, discussed in Section 6.9
7. Quality training, orientation, and work force development, discussed in Section 6.10
8. Postproduction quality service, discussed in Section 6.11
9. Management of the quality-control function, discussed in Section 6.12
10. Special quality studies, discussed in Section 6.13

Figure 6.1 illustrates the contribution made by each subsystem to implementation of the four basic jobs of total quality control.

The key areas of systems measurement are examined in Section 6.14. Section 6.15 reviews certain systems activities that may be introduced and imple-

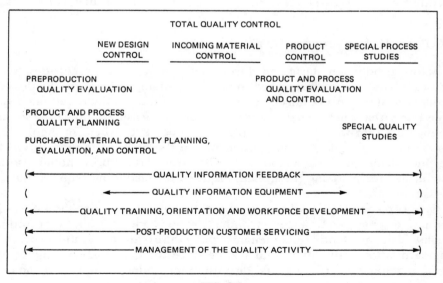

FIG. 6.1

mented in company operation, resulting in a documented, working quality system (Sec. 6.16). Section 6.17 reviews the essential work in ongoing management of the quality system. Section 6.18 then summarizes the hallmarks of an effective quality system.

6.4 Preproduction Quality Evaluation

Procedures are established to analyze formally both the product design and the process design to ascertain that the resultant product will fulfill the customer's requirements. Product Engineering should review its own designs, with appropriate assistance from analyses made by other functions. A fresh point of view often contributes valuable suggestions. The same review of process is required by Manufacturing Engineering.

Product evaluation should be done, where feasible, under actual end-use conditions. Environments should be duplicated, even to the extent of matching the skill of the person expected to understand and operate the device. Such an operator should be given the instructions that will be supplied. During the course of the evaluation, any unsatisfactory experiences that might result should be noted and corrective action taken.

During the preproduction quality evaluation, other important tasks are accomplished, such as the identification of important quality characteristics and their classification as to importance; review of specifications for clarity, compatibility, and economy; location and elimination of sources of manufacturing troubles and out-of-control quality problems before start of manufacture; and identification of adjustments to design or process to make them compatible.[3]

6.5 Product- and Process-Quality Planning

Before production starts and during the product- and process-designing phases, plans must be formalized to measure, attain, and control the desired product quality. This requires an analysis of product-quality requirements to determine what quality characteristics should be measured, how they should be measured, to what extent (sample or 100 percent), where in the process flow, who should take the measurement, and the limits of the measurement beyond which corrective action should be taken. Procedures should also be established for planning the devices required for taking the required quality measurements.

Quality planning also includes determination of numbers, qualifications, and training of quality-assurance personnel; methods and formats for recording quality data; preventive maintenance procedures for tools and processes; standardization, calibration, and maintenance for quality-measuring equipment; material flow, routing, and disposition procedures; in-process and outgoing quality audits; and issuance of detailed instructions covering quality-assurance activities.

6.6 Purchased-Material Quality Planning, Evaluation, and Control

This subsystem of the system provides the procedures necessary to the control of a very important quality input: purchased material. Such procedures ensure the means for clear delineation of quality requirements to vendors and for communicating to them the classification of quality characteristics by their relative importance. Procedures also provide for appraising the vendor's quality capability, facilities, and quality system prior to placement of the order. Establishment of procedures is made whereby vendors certify the quality of the lots they ship by means of objective quality measurements accompanying each lot. Other procedures include quality evaluation of purchased materials and feedback of quality information to vendors; correlation of vendor quality-measurement methods and equipment with purchased-material inspection; servicing of vendors to assure scheduled quality output; conducting incoming test, inspection, and laboratory examinations.

All these procedures, when established and followed, permit accomplishment of incoming-material control. This calls for close integration with the purchasing unit. Usually buyers have the responsibility for making all agreements and arrangements with vendors. Hence, quality information flow should take place through the buyer, or at least the buyer should be kept advised of any information flowing back and forth.

The important point is that the vendor fully understands what is important to the purchaser from a quality standpoint. The purchaser gets a measure of input quality and feeds back any information needed to correct or adjust the vendor's processes.

6.7 Product- and Process-Quality Evaluation and Control

The procedures established under this quality-system component provide for *implementing* the product- and process-quality planning. Those procedures having to do with service to the shop operator include the following:

1. Formally delineate relative importance of quality characteristics to shop personnel
2. Formally establish quality checks by shop personnel and monitor performance
3. Assure adequate measuring means to operators
4. Calibrate and maintain measuring devices used by operators

A number of procedures identify necessary measurement activities to be carried out by members of the quality-control organization:

1. Perform in-process quality evaluation to assure parts conformance to specification
2. Perform in-process tests on components and subassemblies to assure function in final assembly and under end-use conditions

3. Perform audits; audit adherence to in-process quality procedures
4. Perform end-of-line quality evaluations and inspections
5. Perform end-of-line quality-performance evaluations and tests
6. Make customer-centered, outgoing quality audits and life-testing, environmental, and reliability evaluations
7. Establish index of outgoing quality based upon audit results
8. Provide quality-measurement service
9. Evaluate material not fully acceptable and determine disposition
10. Measure overall productivity, effectiveness, and timeliness of product and process control, obtaining needed corrective action

Still other procedures are concerned with the work done in maintaining measuring equipment and quality ability of tools:

1. Operate and monitor system for preventive maintenance on tools, jigs, and fixtures
2. Calibrate and maintain quality-assurance measuring devices

A number of analytical procedures are identified in this quality-system component, such as those which:

1. Establish manufacturing-analysis; establish cost-reduction programs
2. Analyze quality-generated production delays
3. Make analyses of productivity, effectiveness, and timeliness of action of quality-assurance personnel
4. Correlate factory and field performance data to permit prediction of field failure and service-call rates
5. Establish complaint-analysis and reduction programs

Provision must be made for temporary and short-range planning to be carried on, such as to:

1. Perform quality-assurance operational planning
2. Maintain physical quality standards for use of shop

The establishment and maintenance of various types of quality standards are concerns in product control, such as:

1. Establish process-control limits
2. Maintain physical-quality standards for use of shop
3. Periodically review specifications, drawings, and so on for currency and accuracy

Other procedures required concern carrying out certain work assignments, as follows:

1. Perform disposition and routing of defective or nonconforming material
2. Obtain corrective action by appropriate position; follow up and determine effectiveness of action taken
3. Develop and establish customer quality-certification programs
4. Operate safety programs
5. Maintain quality records

As can be seen from the nature of these activities, this group forms the part of the quality system that is used in the shop or on the factory floor for the day-to-day control of quality. Note that some of the work is done by production operators, some is done by inspectors, and some would be the responsibility of the process-control engineer, as is shown in Chapter 11.

6.8 Quality Information Feedback

This, in effect, is the information system which forms a part of the quality system. It supplies the quality information needs of key personnel in the various functional areas. Procedures are established to analyze the quality information needs of all positions: vendors, purchasers, production-control people, shop supervisors, shop personnel, manufacturing planners and engineers, quality-control engineers and equipment designers, quality-assurance supervisors, quality-assurance personnel, product-design engineers, product planners, salespeople, product-service supervisors and personnel, customers, and general and functional managers. When analyzing needs, criteria are established for content, frequency, and permissible time delay. This is done for each position to provide timely decisions for effective action in quality areas.

Specific procedures are established which implement data collection, tabulation, analysis, and distribution. Included here are formats that will be concise with respect to responsibility for corrective action and sound with respect to measurements and their comparison bases. Formats for the following kinds of reports should be developed: incoming-material quality evaluations, in-process quality evaluations, end-of-line quality evaluations, product-reliability and -life evaluations, manufacturing losses, in-process quality audits, outgoing product-quality audits, field failure and service-call rates, complaint expenditures, special studies reports, various quality costs, and quality-system-measurements reports.

Periodic review of the quality information system is necessary to keep it current in meeting the changing needs of the company. Besides identifying new positions that require certain quality information, attention should be given to eliminating distributions currently serving no useful purpose.

The development and use of automatic quality-level-indicating devices are also considered factors in the quality information system. The past few years have seen a rapid growth of instrumentation which provides the means for communicating quality information to a control center. The chemical industry has some especially noteworthy installations for petroleum refining and other continuous-process operations.

6.9 Quality Information Equipment

Quality measurements that are necessary for the control of quality are identified during product- and process-quality planning. Planning also includes identification of measurement methods and the type of measuring and control equipment that is to be used. The quality information equipment subsystem provides the procedures for procuring this measuring and control equipment. Such activity has advanced development aspects, which include study of the long-range needs of the company's business with respect to measuring equipment based upon new products, new processes, and improvements in product quality, flow, and costs. Special studies are made to develop new basic measuring techniques and their adaptation and integration into mechanized and automated manufacturing equipments. Procedures for programming advanced information equipment development are included in the system.

Procedures for equipment design and application include development of design requirements; analysis of the quality system to determine most effective and economic measurements, required precision, and accuracy and to determine the best method for measuring each quality characteristic; development of specifications for quality information equipment and cost estimates covering design, development, construction, and initial application costs; execution of such work, keeping the quality information equipment updated to meet new needs arising as a result of design changes, process revision, and application experience in the field; provision for proper maintenance and calibration; origination and maintenance of schematics, blueprints, layouts, replacement parts lists, and operating and maintenance instructions, including safety precautions; and means for measuring overall effectiveness of the quality information equipment area.

As manufacturing operations become more mechanized and automated, the quality information equipment activity gains increasing importance. As a matter of fact, a proper degree of development in automated measurements is often a prerequisite to automated manufacture. This topic is discussed further in Chapter 12.

6.10 Quality Training, Orientation, and Work Force Development

The procedures under this component of the quality system provide the means for developing the "people capability" required to properly operate the quality system. It includes not only those persons in the company directly engaged in control-of-quality work but those in other functions and whose training affects product quality. Programs for training personnel not directly engaged in quality control are directed at the following: product know-how; quality-control-function indoctrination; shop-operations indoctrination in quality-control methods, procedures, and techniques; management quality-control-program orientation; specialized education in quality-control techniques for product-design engineers, manufacturing engineers, and buyers and other specific areas of activity; shop personnel proficiency evaluations; quality-mindedness programs, trainee education, vendors, and industrial customers.

Programs for those directly connected with control-of-quality work include the following: basic quality-control principles, rotational programs, trainee assignments, personnel-performance measurement, guidance, and counseling; company-sponsored course participation, professional society participation, university extension courses, work force inventory, and promotion programs; continuous quality training through letters, bulletins, periodicals, and personal association.

The effectiveness of quality training, orientation, and work force development is measured by personnel capability that has evolved as a result of this part of the quality system. Availability of capable persons to fill open positions is also a measure of its timeliness and its effectiveness.

6.11 Postproduction Quality Service

When the customer or consumer purchases a product, the purchase is, in effect, of the *function* the product is expected to perform. Furthermore, the purchaser expects that the product will continue to provide that function over some period of time. If, for some reason, the product fails to perform its intended function over its life expectancy, most companies feel obligated to see that the customer receives the product function which was expected as a result of purchase. Many companies have an organizational component known as *product service* which fulfills this function. Although such an organization has many of the primary responsibilies in this area, Quality Control has a number of contributing responsibilities. A close working relationship between the components is essential to success (see the relationship chart, Fig. 8.3, in Sec. 8.11).

The total activity in this area is covered by that component of the quality system known as *postproduction quality service.* Here procedures are established for answering complaints and making adjustments that will result in a satisfied customer. More specifically, this component of the quality system includes procedures covering the following activities: review of product guarantees and warranties to establish relationship with respect to product reliability, to place limitations on the company's liability, and to make adjustments or concessions beyond the warranty period; comparative tests and quality evaluations with competitive products; information to Marketing about quality costs, timing, and adverse effects of schedules on quality, anticipated difficulties, and corrective action being taken; quality-certification plans as advantage to the customer in buying the particular company's products; quality audits on warehouse stocks for deterioration and damage on purchased material shipped directly to the customer and on repair items; renewal parts, including technical data, quality control, and required availability period; review for adequacy and recommendation for improvements in instruction books covering installation, maintenance, and use; review of serviceability of the product, tools, and techniques for repairs; review of quality, cost, and timeliness of service work; field failure rates and costs and the reporting system for these, including the data processing and analyzing systems; correlation of field failures with the factory quality index; information from Marketing to Manufacturing and Engineering about unanticipated difficulties and adverse trends.

6.12 Management of the Quality Activity

This component of the quality system includes the procedures the manager uses in getting the job of managing done, namely, procedures for planning, organizing, integrating, and measuring. These procedures include the following: accumulation, compilation, and reporting of quality costs; establishment of quality-cost-reduction goals and programs; development of systems for measuring the true outgoing quality level of the product; establishment of product-quality improvement goals and programs by product line; establishment of objectives, goals, and programs for the quality-control organizational component and the publication of these for use by appropriate personnel; classification of quality-control work as to generic kinds of work; organization to get the work done and staffing of the organization; issuance of position guides or job descriptions; issuance of procedures for getting the work done; acceptance of the work assignments by individuals; integration of all individuals in the quality-control organizational component; development of measures of effectiveness to determine the contribution of the quality-control function to the profitability and progress of the company.

6.13 Special Quality Studies

This component of the quality system provides procedures and techniques for identifying specific quality problems and finding specific solutions for such problems. Included in these procedures and techniques are machine- and process-capability analysis; quality-measuring equipment capability and repeatability analyses; studies on economic partitioning of tolerances; formal analyses of specific areas of manufacturing variability contributing to high manufacturing losses, high cost of evaluating and controlling quality, and high complaint expenditures; evaluation of proposed new methods, new processes, and new materials and their effects on ease of manufacture, quality, and quality costs; optimum adjustment of processes based upon correlation of product-quality characteristics with process conditions; diagnosis of quality problems, taking corrective action, and following up to measure effectiveness of action.

6.14 Key Areas of Systems Measurement

The control and management of quality hinge upon the interrelationships of many different quality-related activities performed throughout the industrial cycle. Without adequate standards for management measurements and reporting, the fundamental feedback theory of control—which requires measurements against such standards as a basis for evaluation and control—cannot work effectively.

Built into the total quality system, then, are numerous checks and balances by which to assess its performance.[4] While there are many ways to "score" quality results, experience with successful total-quality-control programs has shown certain principal areas of measurement to be particularly useful indicators. These measurement areas can be summarized as follows.

Measurement of Costs

The periodic collection and analysis of quality costs monitors the cost effectiveness of the quality system. The objective is to track quality-cost trends both in total, as well as individual, quality-cost areas. This very important quality measurement, which is discussed at length in Chapter 7, is fundamental to the quality-systems goal of full customer quality satisfaction at the lowest possible quality costs.

Measurement of Quality

Timely measurement and reporting of quality level data are used in assessing quality performance, setting quality-level goals, and evaluating corrective-action efforts. Such information becomes the basis for establishing improvement goals, priority schedules, and so forth. The delineation of quality-level requirements, determination of quality-level measurements, and quality information feedback are considered in Part 4, "Engineering Technology of Quality." Statistical techniques used to track quality levels are discussed in Part 5.

Measurement of Customer Satisfaction

Intensive examination of small samples of finished product solely from the viewpoint of the user can be a useful predictor of customer satisfaction. Results of this type of customer-centered quality audit, together with other measurements after the product is in use, evaluate the effectiveness of the quality system from the viewpoint of the customer. Such measurements include data on field failures and service-call rates and analysis and reporting of customer-attitude trends regarding product quality, safety, service, and reliability. Such data not only alert management to the need for rapid product corrective action, they provide valuable input toward the development of new models and similar products. Feedback of quality information from the field is discussed further in Section 10.27.

Measurement of Systems Conformance

Auditing and assessment of the quality-system procedures identify deviations from system effectiveness before these deviations can develop into major quality problems. Such data determine whether adequate quality plans continue to be established and are current; whether quality responsibilities and procedures established by quality plans are being satisfactorily fulfilled; and pinpoint areas where improvements are necessary. The entire range of quality auditing is examined throughout the remainder of the book as it applies to the several technologies of quality control. In particular, Section 11.23 and beyond review specific auditing techniques.

6.15 Key Systems Activities for Quality Control—An Example

An examination of the steps taken by a large and rapidly growing manufacturing company to implement a total quality system may be useful to put these key quality-systems activities in perspective.

The soundly based and well-managed company found itself faced with spiraling and potentially very damaging quality and liability problems which it was unable adequately to control. This was in direct contrast to the strong management control of other business areas, such as production flow and the control of cost budgets.

To help solve its quality problems, management decided to initiate a strong, enduring total quality system. As work proceeded, quality requirements evolved and were documented throughout the total quality system in a Quality-Systems Manual to which all functions had input and to which all personnel could refer.

For example, in the area of incoming material, the quality-systems work for the firm took into account such diverse factors as:

- *Incoming-material-control procedures,* including applicable sampling plans, instructions, data recording, and reporting
- *Applicable vendor relationships,* including the delineation of quality requirements to vendors—as well as classification of quality characteristics and acceptable quality levels; the correlation of measurement methods; vendor quality capabilities; facilities surveys and evaluations; incoming-material rating; feedback of quality information to vendors; corrective action and follow-up; certification to ensure scheduled quality output; certification of incoming material
- *Quality information equipments to be used for incoming-material control,* including the necessary accuracy, capacity, service connections, and floor space and maintenance requirements, calibration, and periodic balancing with vendors' devices
- *Laboratory-acceptance testing,* including sample requirements and laboratory results reporting
- *Material disposition,* including identification, routing for scrap, return to vendor, and detailed inspection
- *Incoming-material audit*
- *Incoming-material-personnel requirements,* including qualifications and special training

Such thorough systems planning across all the main-line functions resulted in an operating quality framework for the firm and major improvements in product quality and quality costs. In effect, installation of a strong quality system provided a significant competitive advantage for the firm.

6.16 The Quality-Systems Manual

The "right" quality-systems design for a particular company will be based upon specific and varying requirements, as discussed earlier in Section 6.3. It thus follows that the tangible operational reference, or Quality-Systems Manual, for each company will also vary in format and content. Indeed, a whole range of such Quality-Systems Manuals exists in different forms and different degrees of detail to orient quality-systems work to specific industrial situations. What is important is not so much *what* the Quality-Systems Manual covers but that it covers *all* the relevant information, in sufficient detail to embrace the *overall* procedures necessary to define *essential* operating functions and responsibilities.

From this viewpoint, the Quality-Systems Manual for the company just described might be considered typical in thoroughness of documentation of a comprehensive system for total quality control (Fig. 6.2). Far from being merely a thick book of details, however, such thorough documentation (as discussed in Sec. 5.7) provides a quality "road map" marking the shortcuts and detours and alternative routes as well as the usually traveled expressways. It provides instant and graphic direction for every member of the firm when choosing his or her most expeditious route to genuine quality assurance.

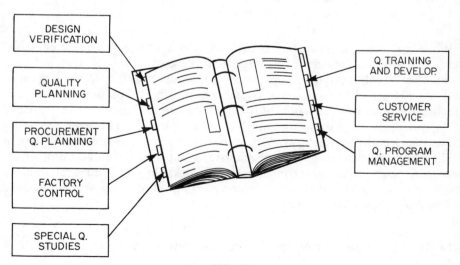

FIG. 6.2

6.17 Quality-Systems Management

Because of the power and scope of total quality control, it is necessary that the ongoing management and maintenance of the quality system be carried on as explicit operating responsibilities. For example, there must be provisions for such activities as the following:

- Provide overall management of *all* activities of the quality system.
- Create, coordinate, and distribute quality-motivation programs.
- Establish performance standards and evaluation of overall quality progress in the areas of key systems measurements.
- Review the effectiveness of corrective-action programs.
- Resolve any intersystem incompatibilities which cannot be concluded by personnel immediately involved.
- Ensure effectiveness of the system-audit program and quality information feedback.
- Provide the focus of management attention to the activities of the quality system, ensuring their effective application toward achieving a common objective.
- Provide or obtain priority decisions for quality-system activities when they compete with other programs for resources.
- Provide intracorporate liaison on the quality system.
- Assure that the quality system is revised as required.
- Assure the continuing effectiveness and business contribution of the quality-cost program.
- Provide leadership to ensure the effective use of the quality system as a specific factor in the company's business strategy.
- Assure, as appropriate, the effective visibility of the quality system to customers and other relevant groups.

While the ongoing control of the quality system to this degree of effectiveness is clearly the concern of management, responsibility for assuring such control will be delegated to appropriate functions throughout the organization. As discussed in Chapter 8, overall responsibility for the creation, implementation, and maintenance of the quality system is normally the province of the quality function organized for that specific purpose. However, the policy leadership for the systems program must come from top-level management itself, to ensure that an *overall* mechanism is put in place to accomplish the necessary managerial and technical systems work. Only such integrated, high-level control will assure that management is running its quality operations rather than being run by them.

6.18 Recognizing an Effective Quality System: A Summary

The strong quality system can be identified by its accomplishments in 12 fundamental areas. The system hallmarks are that:

1. *It controls quality on an integrated, organizationwide basis* which begins with the marketing conception and the product design and continues through procurement, production, and product service. This recognizes that quality and liability problems are not respecters of organization boundaries and a quality program, to be realistic, must be constructed accordingly.

2. *It provides for primary quality decision-making ties with upper management,* based upon fundamental general management quality policy which is periodically demonstrated by deeds rather than words throughout the organization. This recognizes that *quality-related operations have become so extended, so intricate, and so involved that the need for integrated, high-level control of these operations becomes of primary rather than secondary importance, as in the past.*

3. *It fosters a sufficient budgetary base and technical competence to permit preventive effort* to get quality and reliability engineering accomplished during the product-design planning and manufacturing-process design stage, where it can do the most good.

4. *It establishes quality control as a set of disciplines to be applied* by functions *throughout the business* systematically rather than as a single functional organization in one part of the business.

5. *It builds in quality control's coupling with customers on a positive feedforward basis* as well as a feedback basis, thereby providing, in this era of rapid product change, a great deal of data about customer-use requirements before production—not after problems have exploded.

6. It clearly *structures and reports quality costs* both of assuring quality and failures in this assurance as a formal part of the cost accounting program —not merely in the curiosity status of a periodic memorandum—and it employs these costs as a guide to quality resource allocation in as systematic a way as that through which production or engineering or sales resources are allocated in the company.

7. It *makes quality motivation a continuous process* of quality goals, quality measurements, and an attitude of quality-mindedness beginning with general management.

8. It *structures an unique technological contribution* to the plant and company through quality and reliability engineering work. This recognizes that the once secondary role of quality engineering confined, for example, to do only inspection or quality planning within the already preordained industrial engineering plan—but without contributing to the original concept of that plan—no longer meets today's production demands for a direct quality technical role to optimize quality results fully as much as cost and volume results. Quality and reliability engineering instead is needed to make primary technical contributions to the product, the production layout, and the service concepts of the business.

9. *It provides for continuously measuring and monitoring actual customer quality satisfaction* with the product in use, including adequate levels of inspection and testing, as the basis for generating the facts that lead to immediate corrective action.

10. *It provides good product service rapidly and economically,* generating demonstrable customer acceptance as opposed to creating additional customer dissatisfaction.
11. *It integrates product-safety and product-liability-control considerations* with all aspects of the quality program.
12. *It adds a major, companywide workscope to the quality function.* This makes quality control the technical and managerial extension of the general management of the company into the quality field. And it places a major new planning and control dimension—and a new stature—upon what is meant by the quality function of a company.

For companies which have given strong attention to modern quality control, a total quality system has given their customers the high quality they seek in three key features: the kind of *control* it brings—in dovetailed, organizationwide actions and procedures; the kind of *commitment* it is—based upon foresighted investment in quality, shared responsibility for quality, and quick remedial action toward quality when the need arises; and the kind of *confidence* it brings—in measurable quality progress—highly visible, highly auditable, and highly maintainable.

Notes

[1]The terms "total quality system" and "quality system" hereafter will be used interchangeably in this book.

[2]This discussion closely follows and is based upon the work of Donald S. Feigenbaum. See, as a basic discussion, "Systems Engineering—A Major New Technology," *Industrial Quality Control,* vol. XX, no. 3, September 1963. See also "The New Look in Quality Control," *Automotive Industries,* Oct. 15, 1972; "Effective Systems Improvement Control," *Journal of Systems Management,* November 1974; "Return to Control," *Quality Progress,* May 1976; "Systems Engineering and Management—Operating Framework of the Future," *Journal of Systems Management,* August 1971.

[3]Full consideration must be given to all relevant requirements already established, whether by industry or government. A number of these quality documents exist for products ranging from nuclear reactors to automobiles, toys, drugs, and prosthetic devices.

[4]The importance of systems measurements was discussed in Sec. 5.6.

Quality Costs—Foundation of Quality-Systems Economics

Satisfactory product and service quality goes hand-in-hand with satisfactory product and service cost.

One of the major obstacles to the establishment of stronger quality programs in earlier years was the mistaken notion that the achievement of better quality required much higher costs. Nothing could have been further from the facts of industrial experience.

Unsatisfactory quality means unsatisfactory resource utilization. This involves wastes of material, wastes of labor, and wastes of equipment time—and consequently involves higher costs. In contrast, satisfactory quality means satisfactory resource utilization and consequently lower costs.

A major factor in these mistaken past concepts of the relationship between quality and cost was the unavailability of meaningful data. Indeed, in earlier years, there was a widespread belief that quality could not be practically measured in cost terms. Part of the reason for this belief was that traditional cost accounting, following the lead of traditional economics, had not attempted to quantify quality. Correspondingly, quality cost did not easily fit into older accounting structures.

Part of the reason was that some quality-control proponents themselves were unwilling to encourage the measurement of quality costs. They were concerned that such identification might lead to unwisely drastic reductions in these costs and consequently to reductions in quality programs themselves.

Today, we not only recognize the measurability of quality costs but that these costs are central to the management and engineering of modern total quality control as well as to the business strategy planning of companies and plants. Quality costs provide the economic common denominator through which plant and company management and quality-control practitioners can communicate clearly and effectively in business terms. Quality costs is the basis through which investments in quality programs may be evaluated in terms of cost improvement, profit enhancement, and other benefits for plants and companies from these programs. In essence, quality costs are the foundation for quality-systems economics.

Chapter 7 reviews key aspects of quality costs as a major area of total quality control.

7.1 What Is the Scope of Quality Costs?

Since the concept of quality costs was first presented by the author,[1] the measurement and control of these costs have become essential elements in the accounting system of companies. Today, when the cost of quality can be comparable in importance to labor costs, engineering costs, and selling costs, quality costs are budgeted by departments, used in major capital investment decisions, and are part of significant business determinations by modern companies striving to maintain and improve their competitive position.

The preponderant use of quality-cost data has thus far been by producers, who have made very great strides in the quantitative measurement of factory- and plant-oriented *operating quality costs* (discussed in Secs. 7.2 through 7.11). In actual fact, however, quality costs are generated not only throughout the marketing-design-manufacturing-inspection-shipping cycle but continue to accrue throughout the total life cycle of the product in service and use.

Thus, the incidence of quality costs is very broad and falls not only upon producers but upon consumers and merchants and indeed, upon activities throughout the entire production and consumption process. As such, quality costs have become an increasingly important indicator in the economics of Gross National Product (GNP) measurements, with the economic significance of product and service quality becoming more and more widely recognized. There is no doubt that the measurement of product life cycle–oriented costs, including user quality costs and other wider-ranging quality costs, will continue to evolve and be approached with the same precision now devoted to the more traditional producer operating costs, defined next in Section 7.2.

7.2 What Are Operating Quality Costs?

Quality costs in plants and companies are accounted so as to include two principal areas: the costs of control and the costs of failure of control (Fig. 7.1.). These are producer *operating quality costs,* or

> Those costs associated with the definition, creation, and control of quality as well as the evaluation and feedback of conformance with quality, reliability, and safety requirements, and those costs associated with the consequences of failure to meet the requirements both within the factory and in the hands of customers.

QUALITY COSTS

COST OF CONTROL

COST OF FAILURE
OF CONTROL

FIG. 7.1

The principal quality-cost areas are broken down as in Figure 7.2.

The costs of control are measured in two segments: *Prevention costs* keep defects and nonconformities from occurring and include the quality expenditures to keep unsatisfactory products from coming about in the first place. Included here are such cost areas as quality engineering and employee quality training. *Appraisal costs* include the costs for maintaining company quality levels

QUALITY COSTS

SEGMENTS

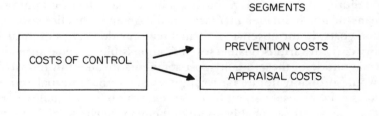

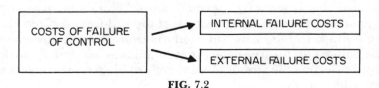

FIG. 7.2

by means of formal evaluations of product quality. This includes such cost areas as inspection, test, outside endorsements, quality audits, and similar expenses.

The costs of the failure of control, which are caused by materials and products that do not meet quality requirements, are also measured in two segments: *internal failure costs,* which include the costs of unsatisfactory quality within the company, such as scrap, spoilage, and reworked material, and *external failure costs,* which include the costs of unsatisfactory quality outside the company, such as product-performance failures and customer complaints.

Because operating quality costs include key costs associated with quality, as defined in Section 1.3, it is important to be aware that they embrace the achievement of such characteristics as reliability, safety, maintainability, and other relevant quality characteristics. Operating quality costs thus relate to the total-customer-oriented aspects of quality, as discussed in Section 1.4.

7.3 How Are Quality Costs Reduced by Total Quality Control?

Since the introduction of the concept of total quality control, experience has demonstrated the effectiveness of total quality systems in improving the quality of products and services while reducing quality costs. The reason for the satisfactory better-quality result is fairly clear from the very nature of the prevention-centered, step by step, technically thorough program. But the explanation may not be nearly so obvious for the accompanying by-product of lower overall quality cost. This needs to be spelled out, especially since it includes, in the long run, lower expenses for the quality-control activities themselves as compared with the costs of traditional inspection and testing.

The reason for the favorable cost result of total quality control is that it cuts the two major segments of a company's quality costs, internal failure and external failure costs—as well as having a beneficial effect on appraisal costs —by means of much smaller increases in the smallest quality-cost segment: prevention costs. In the absence of formal nationwide studies of these operating quality costs in various businesses, it is impossible to generalize about the relative magnitude of these quality-cost segments throughout industry. However, it would probably not be far wrong to assume that internal and external failure costs may represent about 65 to 70 cents out of every quality-cost dollar and that appraisal costs probably range in the neighborhood of 20 to 25 cents. In many businesses, however, prevention costs probably do not exceed 5 to 10 cents out of the total quality-cost dollar.

In a nutshell, this cost analysis suggests that we have been spending our quality dollars the wrong way: a fortune down the drain because of product failures; another large sum to support a sort-the-bad-from-the-good appraisal screen to try to keep too many bad products from going to customers; comparatively nothing for the true defect-prevention technology that can do something about reversing the vicious upward cycle of higher quality costs and less reliable product quality.

The fact is that historically under the more traditional type of quality-control function, failure and appraisal expenses have trended together, and it has been extremely difficult to pull them down once they have started to rise. The reason is clear.

An unprofitable cycle is at work that operates something like this: The more defects or nonconformities produced, the higher the failure costs. The traditional answer to higher failure costs has been more inspection. This, of course, means a higher appraisal cost.

Now this tighter inspection screen does not really have much effect in eliminating the defects. Some of the defective products are *going* to leave the plant and wind up in the hands of complaining customers. Appraisal costs thus stay up as long as failure costs remain high. And the higher these failure and appraisal costs go, the higher they are likely to go without successful preventive activity. So the total-quality-control approach is to turn this cost cycle downward by establishing the right amount of prevention, supporting the right, though modest, amount of quality engineering, process-control engineering, quality information equipment engineering, and other significant quality-system-oriented improvement expenditures.

This plainly means an increased expenditure for prevention to bring about reduced failure costs *and* reduced appraisal costs, with the balance of quality-cost dollars going to profit. The 5 to 10 cents out of every dollar that is now being spent for prevention may well need to be doubled and tripled, with much of the increase going toward improved efforts in the systems engineering activities of quality control. These increases in prevention are financed by a portion of the savings in failure and appraisal cost; they do not represent net, long-term additions to total company quality cost.

Let us examine what actually does happen, costwise, with total quality control and a total quality system:

First, when prevention costs are increased, to pay for the right kind of systems engineering work in quality control, a reduction in the number of product defects and nonconformities occur. This defect reduction means a substantial reduction in failure costs.

Second, the same chain of events takes place with appraisal costs. An increase in prevention costs results in defect reductions, which, in turn, have a positive effect on appraisal costs because defect reduction means a reduced need for routine inspection and test activities.

Finally, when there is an upgrading of quality-control equipment, personnel, and practices, an additional reduction in appraisal cost results. Better inspection and test equipment, a general modernization of quality-control practices, and the replacement of many routine operators by less numerous but more effective process-control inspectors and testers have a positive downward pull on the cost of the appraisal function.

The end result is a substantial reduction in the cost of quality and an increase in the *level* of quality. Improvements of one-third or more in quality costs are not unusual. The major element of this improvement goes into profit improvement for the company, making the quality system one of the most attractive return on investment opportunities available.

Moreover, lower quality costs bear a strong relationship to major improvements in the total productivity of plants and companies.[2]

7.4 Quality-Cost Establishment

The establishment of a quality-cost program for total quality control involves three stages: (1) the identification of quality-cost items; (2) the structuring of quality-cost reporting, including the related analysis and control; and (3) the ongoing maintenance of the program to ensure that business objectives of higher quality at lower cost are being met.

Such ongoing maintenance requires the dissemination and use of quality-cost information as an explicit operating responsibility. For example, there must be provision for such ongoing activities as the following:

- Provide overall management of the quality-cost program.
- Establish routines and mechanisms to accumulate quality-cost data.
- Supervise processing of quality-cost data either by computer data processing or manually, as has been determined to be the most cost-effective manner.
- Coordinate and distribute quality-cost data in its most useful form to top, middle, and line management via quality-cost reports on several different bases.
- Monitor, analyze, and report quality-cost trends in the various departmental cost accounts.
- Document those areas requiring modification to improve control.
- Review effectiveness of quality-cost audits and quality-cost feedback.
- Review effectiveness of corrective-action programs.

7.5 Identifying Quality-Cost Items

An essential element in operating a total-quality-control program is thus the identification, analysis, and control of quality costs for the business. Let us consider the general approach to typical items that make up these *operating quality costs.*

Listed below are representative items in each of the four segments of operating quality costs and the definitions of these items. Each company must determine the significant items it will include in its quality costs. Companies will find it desirable to include additional items in this list and to develop the quality-cost structure best suited to their particular needs. Figure 7.3 is an example of a brief summary report, consolidating key quality-cost items.

XYZ Company
Operating Quality Costs
Detailed Monthly Report

DATE July 19____   YEAR ____   MONTH June

Acc't	Title	002	003	005	008	010	015	Other	Total
1.1	Quality Management		10,311			28,734			39,045
1.2	Process Studies								
1.3	Quality Information EQ.				30,032				30,032
1.4	Training								
1.5	Misc.								
1.0	**Prevention**		**10,311**		**30,032**	**28,734**			**69,077**
2.1	Incoming Inspection					4568			4568
2.2	Calibration and Maintenance		2937						2937
2.3	Production Tests	1017	52,256			16,717			69,990
2.4	Special Tests and Audits								
2.0	**Appraisal**	**1017**	**55,193**			**21,285**			**77,495**
3.1	Scrap							85,752*	85,752
3.2	Rework—Production	7410	4869						12,279
3.3	Rework—Vendor	246							246
3.4	Corrective Action	3369	2630						5999
3.0	**Internal failure**	**11,025**	**7499**					**85,752**	**104,276**
4.1	Warranty Expenses	2706	12,108						14,814
4.2	Postwarranty Expenses								
4.3	Customer Services						52,765		52,765
4.0	**External failure**	**2706**	**12,108**				**52,765**		**67,579**
	Total	**14,748**	**85,111**	···	**30,032**	**50,019**	**52,765**	**85,752**	**318,427**

*Scrap costs include $72,243 for special unit scrap.

FIG. 7.3

115

Definitions of Operating Quality-Cost Items

1. Cost of prevention

   a. Quality planning

Quality planning represents costs associated with the time that all personnel —whether in the quality function or in other functions—spend planning the ongoing details of the quality system and translating product-design and customer quality requirements into specific manufacturing controls on quality of materials, processes, and products through formal methods, procedures, and instructions. It also represents costs associated with the time spent doing other quality-planning work, such as reliability studies, preproduction quality analysis, and writing instructions or operating procedures for test, inspection, and process control.

   b. Process control

Process control represents costs associated with the time that all personnel spend studying and analyzing manufacturing processes (including vendors') for the purposes of establishing a means of control and improving existing process capability, and providing technical support to shop personnel for the purposes of effectively applying or implementing quality plans and initiating and maintaining control over manufacturing operating processes.

Note: Quality planning and process control may be performed in some businesses by the same personnel. The first activity may be thought of as preproduction planning and the second as providing technical support during production. Process control is aimed at controlling process-quality problems. This should be distinguished from test and inspection, defined under 2, cost of appraisal.

   c. Design and development of quality information equipment

Design and development of quality information equipment represent costs associated with the time that personnel spend designing and developing product- and process-quality measurement, data, control, and related equipment and devices. This item does not include the cost of equipment or depreciation.

   d. Quality training and work force development

Quality training represents the cost of developing and operating formal quality training programs throughout the company operations, designed to train personnel in the understanding and use of programs and techniques for the control of quality, reliability, and safety. It does not include training costs of instructing operators to achieve normal quantity proficiency.

   e. Product-design verification

Product-design verification represents the cost of evaluating preproduction product for the purpose of verifying the quality, reliability, and safety aspects of the design.

   f. Systems development and management

Systems development and management represent the cost of overall quality systems engineering and management and support for quality-systems development.

   g. Other prevention costs

Other prevention costs represent administrative costs involving quality and reliability organizational costs not otherwise accounted for, such as managerial and clerical salaries and travel expenses.

2. Cost of appraisal

a. Test and inspection of purchased materials

Test and inspection of purchased materials represent the costs associated with the time that inspection and testing personnel spend evaluating the quality of purchased materials and any applicable costs of supervisory and clerical personnel. Also, this may include the cost of inspectors traveling to vendors' plants to evaluate purchased materials.

b. Laboratory-acceptance testing

Laboratory-acceptance testing represents the cost of all tests provided by a laboratory or testing unit to evaluate the quality of purchased materials.

c. Laboratory or other measurement services

Laboratory or other measurement services represent the cost of laboratory measurement services, instrument calibration and repair, and process monitoring.

d. Inspection

Inspection represents the costs associated with the time that inspection personnel spend evaluating the quality of the product in the plant and applicable costs of supervisory and clerical personnel. It does not include the cost of inspection of purchased materials included in 2a, inspection equipment, utilities, tools, or materials.

e. Testing

Testing represents the costs associated with the time that testing personnel spend evaluating the technical performance of the product in the plant and applicable costs of supervisory and clerical personnel. It does not include the cost of testing purchased materials included in 2a, test equipment, utilities, tools, or materials.

f. Checking labor

Checking labor represents the costs associated with the time that operators spend checking quality of own work as required by the quality plan, checking product or process for quality conformance at planned points in manufacturing, sorting lots which are rejected for not meeting quality requirements, and other in-process evaluations of product quality.

g. Setup for test or inspection

Setup for test or inspection represents the costs associated with the time that personnel spend setting up product and associated equipment to permit functional testing.

h. Test and inspection equipment and material and minor quality equipment

Test and inspection material represents the cost of power for testing major apparatus, such as steam or oil, and materials and supplies consumed in destructive tests, such as life test or tear-down inspections. Minor quality equipment includes costs of noncapitalized quality information equipment.[3]

    i. Quality audits

Quality audits represent the costs associated with the time that personnel spend performing audits.

    j. Outside endorsements

Outside endorsements represent external laboratory fees, insurance inspections costs, and so on.

    k. Maintenance and calibration of quality information test and inspection equipment

Maintenance and calibration of test and inspection equipment represent the costs associated with the time spent by maintenance personnel calibrating and maintaining quality information test and inspection equipment.

    l. Product-engineering review and shipping release

Product-engineering review and shipping release represent the costs associated with the time of product engineers who review test and inspection data prior to release of the product for shipment.

    m. Field testing

Field testing represents the costs incurred by the department while field testing the product at the customer's site prior to final release. These costs might include traveling costs and living expenses.

3. Cost of internal failure

    a. Scrap

For the purpose of obtaining operating quality costs, scrap represents the losses incurred in the course of obtaining the required level of quality. It should not include materials scrapped for other reasons, such as obsolescence, overruns, and product-design changes resulting from further evaluation of customer needs. Scrap might be further subdivided, e.g., between fault of own manufacture and fault of vendor.

    b. Rework

For the purpose of obtaining operating quality costs, rework represents the extra payments made to operators in the course of obtaining the required level of quality. It should not include extra payments to operators for any other reasons, such as rework caused by product-design changes resulting from further evaluation of customer needs. Rework might be further subdivided, e.g., between fault of own manufacture and fault of vendor.

    c. Material-procurement costs

Material-procurement costs represent those additional costs incurred by the material-procurement personnel in handling both rejects and complaints on purchased materials. Such costs may include getting disposition from vendors for rejected materials, making certain that vendors understand quality requirements for either rejects or complaints, and so on.

    d. Factory contact engineering

Factory contact engineering represents the costs associated with the time spent by product or production engineers who are engaged in production problems involving quality; e.g., if a product component or material does not conform to quality specifications, a product or production engineer may be requested to review the feasibility of product-specification changes. It does not include engineering development work which may be performed on the factory floor.

4. Cost of external failure

    a. Complaints in warranty[4]

Complaints in warranty represent all costs of specific field complaints within warranty for investigation, repair, or replacement.

    b. Complaints out of warranty

Complaints out of warranty represent all accepted costs for the adjustment of specific field complaints after expiration of the warranty.

    c. Product service

Product service represents all accepted product service costs directly attributable to correcting imperfections or special testing, or correction of defects not the result of field complaints. It does not include installation service or maintenance contracts.

    d. Product liability[5]

Product liability represents quality-related costs incurred as a result of liability judgments related to quality failures.

    e. Product recall[6]

Product recall represents quality-related costs incurred as a result of the recall of products or components of products.

7.6 Collecting and Reporting Quality-Cost Information

Much of the cost data necessary to provide an operating quality-cost report may be available from the existing plant and company accounting system. Quality-cost information may be obtained from time sheets, expense reports, purchase orders, rework reports, credit and debit memos, and many other similar sources. Often, data obtained from such sources can be pulled together to provide the different items of quality cost and to place these in the segments and categories previously discussed. When data are not available for a certain item, e.g., time spent by design engineers interpreting quality requirements, it is often possible to make accurate estimates to arrive at a value for the element. However, the accounting component should make such estimates on a sound financial basis.

With these data, it then becomes necessary to structure the forms of quality-cost reporting that best meet the plant and company requirements. At first, it may be necessary for the Manager–Quality Control to put together a few consolidated quality-cost reports to demonstrate what quality cost is and how it can be used (Fig. 7.4). When the value of the report has been demonstrated, the quality-cost reporting function should be taken over by the accounting function because it is the appropriate component to issue financial data. For example, in Figure 7.4, the relative magnitudes of each of the four segments

XYZ Company
Operating Quality Costs
Summary Report

DATE July 19   MONTH June

Net sales (X1000)   Month $3072   Year to Date $8318.4

Area of cost	Production			Qual. control			Engineering			Field serv.			Other			Prior Year Total		
	Mo $×10³	YTD % of sales	PR YR	Mo $×10³	YTD % of sales	PR YR	Mo $×10³	YTD % of sales	PR YR	Mo $×10³	YTD % of sales	PR YR	Mo $×10³	YTD % of sales	PR YR	Mo $×10³	YTD % of sales	PR YR
Prevention	10.3	0.48		28.7	0.99		30.0	0.80		. . .						69.0	2.3	
Appraisal	56.2	1.89		21.3	0.73		. . .			. . .						77.5	2.6	
Internal fail	18.5	0.76		. . .			. . .						85.8	2.66		104.3	3.4	
External fail	14.8	0.42		. . .			. . .			52.8	1.67					67.6	2.1	
Total	99.8			50.0			30.0			52.8			85.8			318.4		
% of sales	3.3%	3.5%		1.6%	1.7%		1.0%	0.8%		1.7%	1.7%		2.8%	2.7%		10.4%	10.4%	

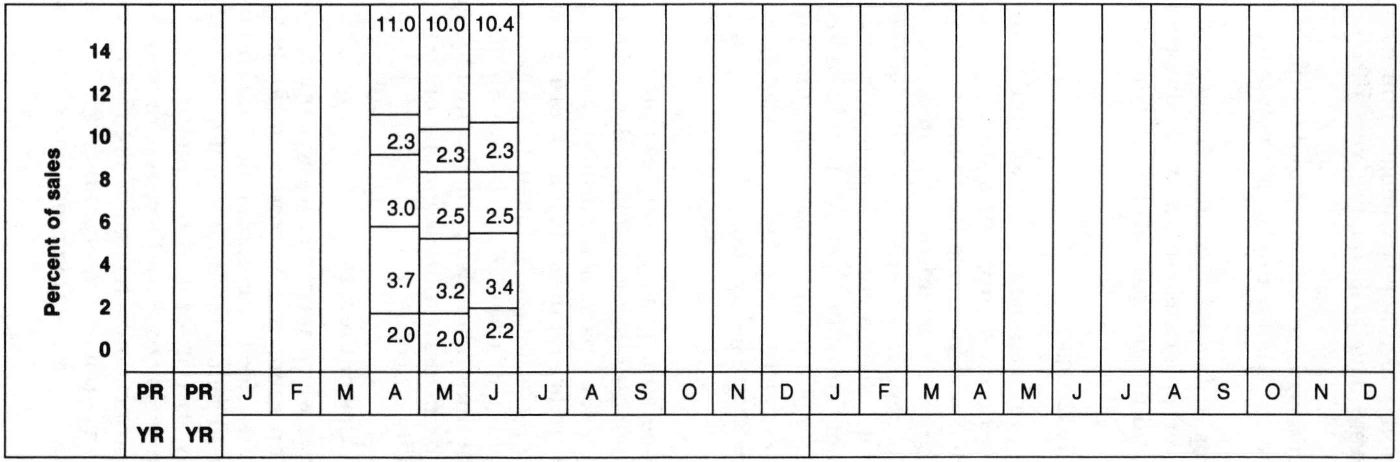

Percent of sales

14 12 10 8 6 4 2 0

	PR PR	J	F	M	A	M	J	J	A	S	O	N	D	J	F	M	A	M	J	J	A	S	O	N	D
	YR YR																11.0	10.0	10.4					
																		2.3	2.3					
																		3.0	2.5	2.5				
																		3.7	3.2	3.4				
																		2.0	2.0	2.2				

Note: Sales and percentages data for year to date (YTD) are for the period April through June only.

FIG. 7.4

121

—particularly prevention, which appears initially unusually high, suggesting inclusion of questionable data—will require very careful examination and structuring.

Computer data processing is an important tool for quality-cost reporting in many companies, either through a centralized computer operation or on a distributed-data basis.

Moreover, quality-cost data are increasingly being established as a part of management information programs (Sec. 3.6). Quality-cost information thus becomes an ongoing and integral part of the company data base.

7.7 Analysis of Quality Costs

After quality costs have been identified and structured, it is necessary to analyze them as a basis for any appropriate action. The analysis process consists of examining each cost item in relation to other cost items and the total. It also includes a time-to-time comparison, i.e., comparing one month's operations with the previous several months' operation, or one quarter with the previous several quarters. Such a comparison is more meaningful when the absolute dollars of quality costs for a period are related to the degree of total manufacturing activity for that period. For example, this quantity can be stated as a ratio of quality-cost dollars to the dollars of manufacturing output or to other suitable bases, as discussed below.

Comparison Bases

It is suggested that operating quality costs be related to at least three different volume bases. The bases selected will vary, depending upon the product and type of manufacture for a particular business. Examples of volume bases that should be considered are (1) direct labor, (2) productive direct labor, (3) shop-cost input, (4) shop-cost output, (5) manufacturing-cost output, (6) contributed value, (7) equivalent units of productive output, and (8) net sales billed. In addition, the interrelationship of the four quality-cost segments should be of interest, particularly the relationship of costs of external failure to total operating quality costs.

Breakdown by Product Line or Process

To pinpoint the areas which merit the highest priority of quality effort, a breakdown of overall operating quality costs by major product lines or areas of the process flow is often needed. For example, with cost information readily available, it is possible to report certain items of quality costs for a particular machining or assembly area or for a specific model.

Figure 7.5 shows the quality costs for three separate product lines: A, B, and C. Line A shows a disproportionately high failure rate with very little prevention and appraisal effort. Appraisal appears high for line B. Although a high percentage of prevention effort is going into line C, internal failure remains

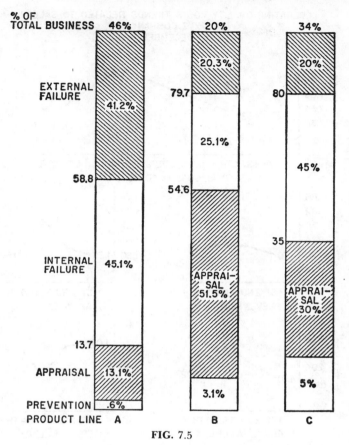

FIG. 7.5

high. This indicates that a greater proportion of existing preventive effort should be expended in reducing internal failure.

Reports

Regular operating quality-cost reports should be issued periodically, weekly, monthly, or quarterly as required. These reports include the expenditures for the items selected from Section 7.5 and the comparison bases. The reports include quality-cost data applicable to previous periods for the purpose of indicating trends. Figures 7.6 and 7.7 demonstrate two methods of showing cost trends.

The various items of operating quality cost are classified under the four segments of quality costs. Figure 7.8 is an example of a quality-cost report which shows a breakdown by the four major segments. In addition, a further breakdown is made with respect to significant items of quality cost.

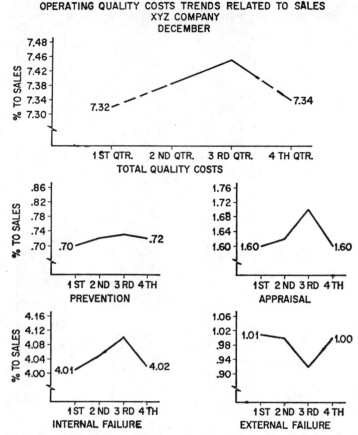

FIG. 7.6. When considering operating quality costs, keep in mind that they may be related to bases other than sales.

7.8 Selection of Measurement Bases for Operating Quality Costs

Measurement bases are an important part of the operating quality costs and should be selected carefully. Because of diversified businesses, bases selected for one may not satisfy the requirements of another; therefore, it is best to consider the advantages and disadvantages of several measurement bases before making selections.

Some Questions to Consider for the Selection of Measurement Bases

1. Are they sensitive to increases and decreases in production schedules?
2. Will they be affected by mechanization and the resulting lower direct-labor costs?

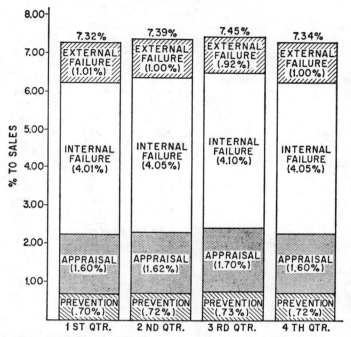

FIG. 7.7 **When considering operating quality costs, keep in mind that they may be related to bases other than sales.**

3. Are they affected by seasonal product sales?
4. Are they oversensitive to material price fluctuations?

If the business is affected by such influences as these, bases should be selected to reflect current relationships. Because of the possibility of these influences occurring at a future date and making past data obsolete, it is advisable to select more than one measurement base. Such selections should, in the majority of cases, include three from each of these four bases: labor, manufacturing cost, sales, and units of product.

Descriptions of the suggested bases will be broken down into two parts:

1. Advantages and disadvantages
2. Definitions and calculations

OPERATING QUALITY COSTS
XYZ Company
December

	1st qarter	2nd quarter	3rd quarter	4th quarter
Expenditures (in thousands of dollars):				
Prevention	$ 142	$ 146	$ 151	$ 143
Appraisal	321	335	372	332
Internal failure	841	862	922	831
External failure	204	214	214	201
Total	$1508	$1557	$1659	$1507
Percent to Sales:*				
Prevention	.70	.72	.73	.72
Appraisal	1.60	1.62	1.70	1.60
Internal failure	4.01	4.05	4.10	4.02
External failure	1.01	1.00	.92	1.00
Total	7.32	7.39	7.45	7.34
Percent to sales—Significant Categories:*				
Quality planning	.32	.35	.36	.37
Inspection	.70	.71	.83	.82
Scrap and rework	3.90	3.92	3.98	3.72
Complaints	.80	.82	.81	.81

* Other bases such as shop cost of output, total direct labor, or contributed value may be used.

FIG. 7.8

1. Advantages and disadvantages
    a. Labor bases
        (1). Total direct labor
        (2). Operation or standard labor
Operation or standard labor, when available, is always superior to total direct labor because it represents planned performance rather than planned plus variances.

Both labor bases are sensitive to the ups and downs of the business. They are not appreciably affected by material price changes, by many end products, by sales lagging production, or by long manufacturing schedules.

Both are affected by mechanization that results in a reduction of operators.
    b. Manufacturing cost bases
        (1). Shop cost of output (SCO)
        (2). Manufacturing cost of output (MCO)
        (3). Shop cost of input (SCI)
Manufacturing cost of output is superior to shop cost of output where the product has a high technical content, because MCO reflects the design engi-

neering cost. Conversely, if the design engineering cost is less of a factor, SCO is a better base.

If the manufacturing cycle is extremely long, both output bases would have little relationship with current quality costs. For these conditions SCI would be a better base.

    c. Sales bases

        (1). Net sales billed (NSB)

        (2). Contributed value (NSB minus direct material)

Both these bases are considered good if the manufacturing cycle is relatively short and the product is sold soon after completion.

Contributed value is used in preference to NSB whenever material is a large part of the sales dollar and where price fluctuations in material would distort a NSB base.

    d. Unit bases

        (1). Production related to contributed value

        (2). Production related to quality costs

        (3). Quality-cost dollars per equivalent unit of production output

These three bases are useful because they relate unit output or actual production to a dollar base. The first two bases are not recommended where there are several end products of different values. A change in the production mix would distort the base but would not be reflected in the total production. Of course, this is not an influential factor where quality costs are kept by product lines.

By selecting and using several of the bases recommended, it is possible to measure more accurately the trends in quality costs. If all bases do not show the same improvement, the cause of discrepancy in any base should be determined.

  2. Definitions and calculations

    a. Total direct labor (self-evident)

    b. Operational labor (planned direct labor)

    c. Direct labor ⎱ Shop
       Direct material ⎰ cost
       Indirect cost plus ⎰

    d. Production engineering costs ⎱ Manufacturing
       and expenses cost
       Provision for complaints
       Box, pack, and ship ⎰   ⎱ Cost of
                                 sales

    e. Contract-engineering costs and expenses
       Product-installation construction and
       miscellaneous direct charges
       Other accounts (plant, etc.)

    f. Net sales billed
       Minus cost of sales equals gross margin

Minus commercial and administrative expense equals income before taxes

Minus taxes equals income after taxes

g. Contributed value is equal to net sales billed minus direct materials

h. Production related to contributed value: Multiply the contributed value per unit times the production for the period

i. Production related to quality cost: Divide the total quality cost by the number of pieces produced and express as dollars per unit or per thousand units

j. Quality-cost dollars per equivalent unit of production output: When more than one end product is involved and the manufacturing cost of each is unequal, it is desirable to equate the production to equivalent units before relating to quality costs. To do this, follow these steps:

(1). Select the end product that makes up the largest dollar volume and call it product 1.

(2). Get the manufacturing cost or contributed value (whichever is more applicable) of product 1.

(3). Assign this cost the factor 1.

(4). Get the manufacturing cost or contributed value of product 2.

(5). Find related value factor for product 2 (divide step 4 by step 2).

(6). Multiply the production of product 1 times the factor 1.

(7). Multiply production of product 2 times the factor from step 5.

(8). Total of steps 6 and 7 is the equivalent units of production output.

(9). Total quality costs divided by equivalent units of production output in step 8 gives the quality-cost dollars per equivalent unit of production output.

Example:

Product	Unit mfg. cost of contributed value	Factor	×	Production output for period	Equiv. prod. output for period
A	$250	1	×	10,000	10,000
B	$400	1.6	×	3,000	4,800
C	$ 50	0.2	×	10,000	2,000

Total equivalent units of production output = 16,800

Assuming total quality-cost dollars for this period amounted to $59,976, the relation is

$$\frac{\$59,976}{16,800} = \$3.57 \quad \text{quality-cost dollars per equivalent unit of production output}$$

As the product mix in the output changes, the equivalent units produced will also change. This provides an extremely sensitive and easily understood comparison base which closely follows production.

Complaint Comparisons

In some businesses, the reporting of complaint expenditures lags actual production from 6 to 24 months. In these cases, the inclusion of complaint charges with current quality costs may give a somewhat distorted picture. Under these circumstances, it may be well to make two comparisons: (1) total quality costs to the applicable comparison bases and (2) total quality costs *less the complaint component of external failure costs* to the applicable comparison bases.

7.9 Establishment of Quality-Cost Goals

When an analysis of quality costs has been completed, it has to be interpreted for actions that will be taken. Certain goals must be set in bringing about the desired relationships. For example, a balance is sought between dollars invested in preventive effort versus dollars saved as a result of reducing failure costs. When a quality-cost program is first initiated, it may be found that a dollar spent in prevention will save many dollars in failure costs. As the program progresses, and the most costly cases of failure are brought under control, further prevention effort may not pay off at as high a ratio. The right level of total operating quality costs is that level at which the quality-cost segments are in optimum balance. Complete reporting and analysis of quality costs help determine this optimum point.

For example, if prevention dollars are spent in design review activities in the new-design control job for a product or process to eliminate defects, there will be less need for inspecting or testing the product and less cost for failures in the plant or complaints in the field. Because of this interrelationship, expenditures in any one of the four quality-cost segments must be evaluated in terms of the resultant savings in the others.

This does not mean, however, that a straight dollar-for-dollar relationship exists between the various items of quality costs. For example, the quality costs included in the segment of costs of external failure often should be given considerably greater significance than the items falling within costs of internal failure. A dollar of complaints is normally of much more market impact than a dollar of scrap.

The usual situation is covered by the foregoing discussion, but there are other situations that require special consideration with respect to operating quality costs. One must always bear in mind the objective of the business. For example, some companies may be doing research and development work, in which case the only manufacturing would involve a few prototypes. This should mean a heavy investment of preventive effort toward obtaining designs of product and process that result in high product reliability. Such expenditure would have to be analyzed and then agreed to to assure meeting the long-range objectives of the business even though external failure costs are, and would be, extremely low because of limited current production.

7.10 Applications of Quality Costs

Company and plant management, together with functional heads, and assisted by the Manager–Quality Control, are constantly making decisions which affect the costs in the various segments in order to obtain the minimum total operating quality cost at the desired outgoing quality level. Quality costs provide some basically sound "tools" for arriving at such decisions. They may be used as follows.

Quality Costs Serve As a Measurement Tool

Since quality costs are broken down into segments, it is possible to obtain a dollar measurement on each quality activity. For example, the dollars invested in quality planning can be measured as to the quality-engineering costs devoted to that activity. Justification for this investment can be measured by reduced failure costs as a result of quality planning and by reduced quality-appraisal costs as a result of more efficient inspection methods.

Quality costs provide comparative measurements for evaluating quality programs versus the value of the results achieved.

Quality Costs Serve As a Process-Quality Analysis Tool

To use only the measurement tool is not enough; it is also necessary to analyze particular quality costs. Quality costs, when properly broken down by product lines or segments of the process flow, will pinpoint major problem areas and serve effectively as an analysis tool.

Quality Costs Serve As a Programming Tool

An analysis provides a basis for specific courses of action. Planning for carrying out these courses of action involves establishing a program. One of the important functions filled by a program is the assignment of available labor, and other resources, for carrying out the action. Since resources are usually limited, quality costs are a means for identifying those actions which provide the highest potential payoff, hence those actions which should have priority with reference to time sequence.

Figure 7.9 is an example of such a program. Note that it specifically describes the action and states when it is to start, the individual responsible for the action, the time required in each period, and the results expected. This type of programming provides a means for obtaining maximum contribution from company personnel toward product-quality improvement and quality-cost reduction.

Quality Costs Serve As a Budgeting Tool

Quality costs are a guide to budgeting the necessary expenditures for accomplishing the desired quality-control programs. Such programs, of course, take into account the objectives and goals of the business. As shown by a previous example, the long-range objective may be to attain high product reliability. In such a case, one aspect of the program would be directed toward staffing a strong quality engineering effort to do preproduction evaluation and quality planning.

All programs may not be immediately feasible in view of available resources. Programs may have to be brought along successively, building toward goals that take 2 to 3 years to realize. Such a procedure helps assure realistic budgets and attainment of specific reliability goals.

Quality Costs Serve As a Predictive Tool

Quality-cost data provide the controls to evaluate and assure performance in relation to the goals and objectives of the company. They are effective in producing valid cost estimates in obtaining new business in service or products and in meeting competition in the marketplace. Quality-costs data also aid in the positive evaluation of product performance in relation to service and warranty, including repairs and replacements and product-recall or -liability expenses (including the cost of liability insurance).

An Example of Operating Quality Costs

Let us look at a medium-sized company as an example of what can be achieved when quality costs are used as a tool for programming and arriving at supporting budgets to reach specific goals. This company had many trying problems in the quality area and was fighting desperately to pull out of a loss position.

An analysis of quality cost showed the high rate of 9.3 percent to shop cost of output (SCO). Furthermore, little was being spent for preventive effort. The 9.3 percent was divided as follows: prevention, 0.2 percent; appraisal, 2.8 percent; and failure, 6.3 percent to SCO. The company decided to start a total-quality-control program throughout the company, including investing in a quality-systems engineering activity to take leadership for the necessary kinds of technical work. In a little less than 2 years and after this investment for preventive effort, total quality costs dropped from 9.3 to 6.8 percent. Prevention went from 0.2 to 0.6 percent, appraisal dropped from 2.8 to 2.2 percent, and failure from 6.3 to 4.0 percent to SCO. This improvement was brought about by reductions in a number of quality-cost items as follows:

- Appraisal costs were reduced $430,000.
- Scrap and rework were reduced $2,068,000.
- Complaints were reduced $536,000.

PROPOSED PROGRAM

Date: _____

XYZ COMPANY

MATERIAL QUALITY COST REDUCTION AND IMPROVEMENT

Quality-control Work	Area, Line, or Product	Basis of Input Measurement	Input Coverage Current	Goals 3/31	Goals 6/30	Goals 12/31	Proposed Start Date	Function Basically Responsible	Indiv. Responsible	Key Assoc. in Other Components	Man-hrs	$	Jan-Feb	Mar-Apr	May-Jun	Jul-Aug	Sep-Oct	Nov-Dec
Formally classify quality characteristics on purchased material as to relative importance, and establish acceptable quality levels and standards considering manufacturing process requirements as well as end-product requirements.	Product A	% of all parts, and materials fully covered	20	25	45	70	Feb. 4	Q.C. Engr. *	J. Dunn	George-Engr., Green-Purch., Arp-Mfg. Eng.	180	...	15	50	40	30	25	20
	Product B		15	20	40	65	Feb. 18	Q.C. Engr. *	C. Brill	Jones-Engr., Black-Purch., Smith-Mfg. Eng.	180	...	10	40	50	30	30	20
Develop specific methods, procedures, and operations for each acceptance test, inspect or check on each part or material, and reduce to formal written planning.	Product A	% of all parts, materials, and quality characteristics fully covered by written planning	30	40	60	85	Jan. 6	Q.C. Engr.	R. True	George-Engr., Dunn-Q.C.E., Silk-Insp. & Test, Equip. Design	240	1,300	35	60	60	20	40	25
	Product B		15	25	50	80	Feb. 4	Q.C. Engr.	R. True	Jones-Engr., Brill-Q.C.E., Silk-Insp. & Test, Equip. Design	280	600	30	80	70	25	50	25

Est. Total Input Req. (Man-hr by Indiv. Respons. and Dollars Other Than Compens.) — columns: Man-hrs, $.
Estimated Effort Application by Individual Responsible (in Man-Hr) — columns: Jan-Feb, Mar-Apr, May-Jun, Jul-Aug, Sep-Oct, Nov-Dec.

Improvement Results Expected in Quality-cost Flow

	Performance Measurement	(Current) Jun-Dec	Goals Jun-Dec	Goals	% Rel. Improv. Per Year
Productivity	1. Dollars of direct material processed per dollar of incoming-material acceptance costs	198	210	240	20
Effectiveness	2. % incoming-material acceptance costs divided by manufacturing losses attributable to vendors	44%	47%	60%	36
	3. % manufacturing losses (O.V.) recovered divided by total manufacturing losses attributable to vendors	15%	25%	40%	165
Timeliness	4. % of lots found not fully meeting all quality requirements as received	8%	12%	5%	38
	5. Average number of lots per week not processing through in less than a day	120	70	30	75

Reduction in acceptance costs and net losses Year 1 = $55,000

Reduction in annual rate of acceptance cost and net losses Year 2 = $109,000

Activity	Product	Measure					Date	Q.C. Engr.†		Responsibility							
Formally delineate quality requirements including relative (importance and acceptance levels on individual quality characteristics) to vendors through purchasing of direct materials and parts. Includes checks to be made by vendor and data to be supplied.	Product A	% of all parts, materials, and quality characteristics fully delineated to vendors, understood, and accepted	0	20	40	70	Jan. 6	through Purchasing	J. Dunn	Green–Purch. White–Prod. Contr.	220	150	50	40	40	30	40	20
	Product B		0	15	35	60	Jan. 20		C. Brill	Black–Purch. Rogers–Prod. Contr.	220	150	30	50	50	30	40	20
Perform vendor quality servicing to assure scheduled quality output.	Product A	Av. no. of vendors not consistently supplying material meeting all quality requirements.	27	24	18	3	Mar. 1	Qual. Control (Process Control Spec.)*	A. Mack	Brill, Dunn} QCE; White, Rogers} Prod. Cont.	190	650	...	60	45	30	35	20
	Product B		18	15	12	2	Mar. 1		A. Mack	Green, Black} Purch.; Blue–Insp.; Fore.	210	400	...	70	70	25	25	20
Establish systems of measuring the productivity, effectiveness, and timeliness of incoming-material control. Develop feedback to ensure that corrective action is taken as required.	Product A	% of functional performance measurements in place and reported monthly.	0	100	100	100	Jan. 6	Mgr. Qual. Control	D. Adams	King–Mgr. Mater.	20	...	15	5				
	Product B		0	100	100	100	Jan. 6		D. Adams	Borne–Acctg.	20	...	15	5				
Remaining elements of work in *incoming-material control*, major area of the total quality system.	Products A and B	...	...	...	...	...	Jan. 6	Qual. Control generally	C. Brill J. Dunn R. True A. Mack F. Blue D. Adams	As indicated or required	290	500	10	20	40	60	80	80
TOTAL.............	...	...	...	...	...	...	...	...	...	...	2,050	3,750	210	480	465	280	365	250

* Previously divided responsibility.
† Responsibility not previously specifically assigned.

FIG. 7.9

In total, this company made a net quality-cost improvement of more than $2,760,000 in a little less than 2 years; its product quality is now looked upon as one of the best in its field, with minimal external failure costs.

This kind of quality and cost improvement clearly helped this company progress successfully to a profit position within the first year's operation of the program. A solid profit position was attained in the second year. In small businesses or large businesses, this same approach can be taken, and experience has shown that comparable results can be achieved.

7.11 Return on Investment and Quality Costs

Quality costs are becoming an increasingly central factor in the determination of return on investment.[7]

Return on investment considerations deal with the establishment of the amount—in dollars—and timing—in months or years—of the return expected on the investments made in particular programs and projects by companies and plants. The "appropriation requests" which summarize the specific details of these programs usually include the related return on investment information, which becomes a key factor in the management decisions concerning whether to proceed with the project. The return on investment information serves also as an important measurement of the degree to which the project has, in fact, met its objectives, through comparison of the return on investment actually achieved in the project with that which had been established in the original appropriation request.

There are two principal ways quality costs enter into this. The first way has to do with the use of expected improvements in quality costs—together with improvements expected in other costs such as production and engineering—while establishing the return expected from investments in new capital equipment or in other improvement projects. This use of quality costs in the capital equipment return on investment equation has been relatively recent and parallels the establishment of quality costs as an important ongoing part of company accounting practice. Prior to that, investments in production equipment or engineering facilities were primarily related to the return expected from more traditional cost areas, such as direct labor or direct material.

The second way quality costs have become basic in return on investment determinations has to do with the economic evaluation of total quality programs themselves. The expenditures for the installation of the quality program and the ongoing prevention activities are related to the return in lower internal and external failure cost, in lower appraisal costs where appropriate, and frequently in improvements in other measurable costs of the business.

Such return on investment approaches to quality programs, based upon quality costs, have become increasingly characteristic for many plants and companies, and the return on investment results from quality programs have been excellent.[8]

7.12 Other Quality-Cost Categories in Quality-Systems Economics

Operating quality costs provide the foundations for the economic measurement and control to maintain an effective total quality system. However, there are other categories of quality costs of decision-making importance to quality-systems economics. When operationally justified, some or all of these cost areas may be established as key areas in the total quality-cost program of plants and companies.

Five of these quality-cost categories are discussed here as being significant: *indirect quality costs and vendor quality costs* (Sec. 7.13), *intangible quality costs and "liability exposure" costs* (Sec. 7.14), *equipment quality costs* (Sec. 7.15), and *life cycle quality costs,* particularly *user quality costs* (Secs. 7.16 to 7.18). Section 7.19 then considers other measures for decision making.

The explicit structuring of these five quality-cost categories must take place in accordance with the specific factors relating to different plants and companies. The following discussion covers key aspects of the scope and detail of quality costs that must be taken into account in such detailed structuring.

7.13 Indirect Quality Costs and Vendor Quality Costs

Indirect quality costs represent those quality costs which are hidden in other business costs. It is essential for overall cost improvement that the important segments of these costs are identified and reported so that specific attention will be given to reducing these items of cost.

An extremely important indirect cost is that of unnecessary extra manufacturing operations made standard for reasons of uncertain quality. Also important are the costs of unnecessary design features introduced because of weak control of quality.

Other indirect quality-cost reductions as savings unequivocally attributable to total-quality-control activities include design improvement requiring less labor, material, or equipment; process improvement requiring less labor, material, or equipment; reduction in inventory of materials held for inspection and test, rejected materials awaiting disposition, overstocking of purchased material as a hedge against rejections; reduction in down time; savings to customers through elimination of their incoming inspection afforded by the producer certifying product quality.

Vendor Quality Costs

A very significant indirect cost results from the fact that the purchase price of materials includes, in effect, the supplier's (operating) quality costs. These costs, which may be thought of as vendor quality costs, represent a key economic factor for both vendor and purchaser.

Some suppliers with strong total quality programs and good operating quality costs consider it a major competitive advantage to review these costs with the buying company's purchasing and quality-control functions to demonstrate very favorable quality results. Sometimes these costs are specifically disclosed by suppliers during purchasing negotiations because the buyer's emphasis on tight pricing makes detailed review of certain key costs a competitive necessity.

Where supplier quality-cost information is not available, and under circumstances where it is appropriate to do so, buying company quality control will estimate the possible ranges of these quality costs as a key factor in developing a vendor relationship. If, with the purchaser's quality-engineering help, the supplier can reduce such quality costs by a substantial amount, this reduction might be, in part, reflected in a lower sales price to the customer as well as additional sales volume and sales profit margin to the supplier.

7.14 Intangible Quality Costs and "Liability Exposure" Costs

Intangible quality costs are those costs associated with the loss of customer goodwill as the result of unsatisfactory quality as perceived by customers. Marketplace evidence has increasingly confirmed quantitatively what judgment has always suggested: namely, that lower levels of product sales result from higher levels of quality failure and of product service costs in today's markets.

However, whether such loss of sales is caused by specific experience with the product, or whether it is the result of unfavorable publicity generated by such events as product recalls or high-dollar liability penalties, the reduction of sales due to "tarnishing" of the company quality image can be of considerable magnitude.

Indeed, the very fact of what might be thought of as "liability exposure"—even in cases where the producer is not judged liable and "wins" the suit—can produce a significant loss of customer goodwill and incur a high penalty in intangible quality costs.

Moreover, the directly quantifiable costs associated with liability exposure—whether actual or only threatened—can be substantial. They include such cost items as time of personnel involved with investigating the problem and preparing a "case." When a case actually comes to trial, expenses include such costs as the time of company personnel who must testify, attorney fees, expert witness fees, and other court costs.

The general scoping of intangible quality costs, as well as potential liability costs for company and plant products—while necessarily estimates—nonetheless can play a very useful part in the determination of the prevention approach and the degree of prevention expenditures that are needed in quality programs.

7.15 Equipment Quality Costs

Equipment quality costs represent the capital investment in quality information equipment specifically obtained to measure product quality for purposes of acceptance and control, together with the related equipment amortization, the buildings (in the case of major testing, environmental and other installations), and the occupied floor space.

This cost is expended for some of the same reasons that operating quality costs are incurred, namely, for prevention of quality failures and for economies in appraisal. In the case of operating quality costs, these costs are expended mostly for personnel services; in the case of equipment quality costs, they represent investment expenditures for measuring equipment (inspection and test machines), for process quality-control devices, and increasingly for quality information data processing computer equipments.

When properly identified, amortized, and consolidated with operating quality costs, a more complete and realistic basis for measuring the effectiveness of the total-quality-control program is provided by equipment quality costs.

One of the major areas of the increasing importance of equipment quality costs concerns the growing utilization of automatic test equipment (ATE) in quality programs. For instance, the availability of computers and microprocessors has not only expanded the range and capabilities of ATE, it has exponentially increased their potential effect upon quality-cost improvement.

The selection of ATE serves, therefore, as a typical example of the factors taken into account relative to the equipment quality-cost-oriented decisions as to the type of equipment and its potential payback. Estimated product life, for one example, can strongly dictate the choice among several different types of automatic equipment: short product life expectancy may indicate that heavy investment in ATE is impractical, while a longer product life expectancy may well merit a substantial product testing and diagnostics investment and still yield excellent returns in savings.

Another consideration is the availability of adequate software planning and personnel and the costs to assure software quality. Trained people must be provided to get the programming results within expected time schedules. Still another consideration is the traffic the equipment may be called upon to bear. Very often, the enthusiasm which greets a new test machine results in overloading with work that in many cases could and should be accomplished by lower cost testing means. Adequate and realistic workload forecasting is required, always taking into consideration periodic production problems or unexpected hitches with incoming material.

Economic considerations are fundamental to buy or not-buy decisions concerning ATE. Not only the cost of the equipment, but the cost of programs and of fixtures and cost of discovering failures at a subsequent level of testing must all be factored in.[9]

In earlier years, when equipment utilization was a smaller element in quality-cost improvement, equipment quality cost was thought of as an incidental factor in the overall structuring of aggregate quality-cost areas. Today, it has become an important quality-cost area in itself as equipment quality costs are becoming a larger and larger proportion of overall plant and company equipment investment and as the importance of good quality results grows.

7.16 Life Cycle and Use-Oriented Quality Costs

The importance of product life cycle costs was discussed earlier.[10] A growing factor in such life cycle costs is what might be thought of as *use-oriented quality costs,* or:

> Those costs associated with maintaining product quality over a reasonable period of product use, including such costs as those for service, repairs, replacement parts, and similar expenditures.

The principal incidence of use-oriented quality costs is upon producing companies (or merchants), upon buyers and customers, and upon some combination of these.

It has become vital for companies to quantify these use-oriented quality costs for three principal reasons:

First: When use-oriented quality costs are unsatisfactorily high, they are likely to have a major negative effect upon product sales.

Second: One of the principal effects of today's increasing emphasis upon producer-quality responsibility has been to place upon the producing companies themselves a growing proportion of use-oriented costs—over and beyond the more traditional limited warranties and responses to customer complaints. When use-oriented quality costs are without effective measurement and control, the external failure-cost segment of a company's operating quality costs can thus be subject to progressively higher, longer-term, and often unpredicted cost increases.

Third: Data on use-oriented quality costs are an essential input to the corrective-action activities of the total quality program of plants and companies. Indeed, these costs can be generated throughout many areas of the industrial quality cycle: as examples, the product installation which has put a filter in backward in the cold water copper tubing for a new refrigerator icemaker, the assembly line which improperly solders electronic joints in 300 chassis before the fault is discovered and after the chassis have gone into industrial products, the mislabeling of the morning's shipment of garments which will ultimately result in complaints because of poor clothing fits, the high cost that can be associated with so-called dead on arrival consumer electronics product opened in the store, and the engineering quality oversights which later may result in a reactor shutdown. The causes of such unduly high use-oriented costs must be dealt with by suitable actions of the company quality program.

Together, these three reasons also make clear the two quite different respects in which the measurement of use-oriented quality costs is important to companies. One is that as a buyer of materials, and equipment—typically referred to as "original equipment manufacturer" (OEM) purchases—the company is itself a user. The other respect is that the company also sells its products to users.

When considered this way, it is clear that a knowledge of use-oriented quality costs can be of dual advantage to a company. As a buyer, such information can lead to cost savings on OEM purchases; as a seller it can enhance sales of marketed products.

7.17 Life Cycle and Use-Oriented Quality Costs—Structuring the Costs

To be effective, use-oriented quality costs must be structured by a company through a carefully established program. This program must recognize that the customers and users of the company's products and services are likely to be widespread geographically, are likely to buy in very different ways, and are likely to have widely varying practices concerning the maintenance of use-oriented data.

For just one example, an automobile bought in fleet-sized quantities may have very precise user data maintained by the firm making the large purchase; however, in the case of the identical automobile purchased by an individual consumer, there may be very little specific data maintenance by the user.

Experience has shown that, to be effective, the use-oriented quality-cost program of a company must be precisely structured in the following 11 areas:

1. The specification of the maintenance, service, repair, replacement parts, and other relevant cost accounts that will be measured
2. The selection of the measurement bases that are most effective and relevant for the analysis and comparison of costs
3. The establishment of the cost data input procedures—including statistical sampling as appropriate—that will govern the product quantities, mix, geographic distribution, and other relevant factors in the use-oriented quality-cost program
4. The organization of the cost data collection activities, including the necessary personnel training, that will govern the reporting of the costs
5. The establishment of the data handling procedures—both manual and computer—that will govern the processing of the cost data
6. The provision for the necessary electronic data processing equipment, as appropriate, that will be required
7. The establishment of the detailed time frame and schedules for the cost data collection, processing, and reporting
8. The determination of the report formats in which the use-oriented quality costs will be assembled by the company, especially including the management consideration of what will be required in these reports
9. The establishment of the procedures for the review of the trend and meaning of these costs—including suitable statistical analysis—as to the measurement bases that have been selected
10. The specification of the corrective action steps that will be taken by the plant and company to assure the effective control of use-oriented quality

costs to help assure the company of customer quality-satisfaction improvement and of company quality-cost reduction

11. The establishment of the audit activities to verify the accuracy and the effectiveness of the use-oriented quality-cost program.

7.18 Life Cycle and Use-Oriented Quality Costs—Cost Input and Measurement Bases

Among the bases for establishing inputs of use-oriented quality costs, the following four are among the most important:

High Value, Highly Engineered Products

In these products—such as aircraft, railroad propulsion units, military weapon systems, and similar equipments—the producing company can often establish the use-oriented quality-cost program in very close cooperation with the customer. Trained people in the customer organization can, in many cases, provide the data inputs as an integral portion of their regular duties.

Leased Products

In these products—such as office units, data processing and computer equipment, graphic reproduction units, and similar equipments—the ongoing maintenance may be provided by the leaser, which may be a component of the producing company itself. With suitable structuring and training, these service and maintenance people can, in many cases, provide the data inputs as an integral portion of their regular duties.

Mass-Distributed Products

In these products—such as household articles and many similar articles—which are very widely distributed to a very large number of individual users, the producing company must establish a program of ongoing use-oriented quality-cost data with carefully established and stratified samples of users. This requires precise determination of the cost inputs because users may often be rather casual in this, and very careful training of the producing-company people who will perform the data collection actions. Very often, it requires providing premiums or other motivators to the user for obtaining the necessary data.

Mass-Distributed Products with Some Large-Scale Users

In these products—such as home appliances that may be purchased in large quantities by apartment builders, fleet purchase of small pickup trucks, and similar equipments—a concentrated group of large users constitutes a very small but important user proportion of the total number of products in use. In many cases, cooperation with these large users can be arranged by the producing company as a central basis for providing use-oriented quality-cost data.

MEASUREMENT BASES FOR USE-ORIENTED QUALITY COSTS

The selection of the suitable measurement bases for the use-oriented quality costs of a plant or company is a significant factor in the effectiveness of the program. Such bases must be determined as to what is most relevant for the product. While there will be different determinations of this among different products and different companies—including the very important relationships of use-oriented quality costs to external failure costs—one of the most basic measurement bases in life cycle terms is that of original purchase price of the product.

Prior to installation of a total quality program in a plant or company, such use-oriented quality costs, as related to original purchase price, have often been the random end result of a variety of uncoordinated marketing, engineering, production, and service actions throughout the firm. These costs may vary from a relatively small proportion of the original purchase price in the case of some short life cycle products to use-oriented quality costs that may be very high, as compared to the purchase price, in long life cycle products.

The forward planning of use-oriented quality costs is thus of increasingly great importance in company operations. The identification and measurement of use-oriented quality costs, as a basis for their progressive management and control, is a very significant area in the modern total quality programs of plants and companies. It provides the foundation for the establishment of the objectives for reasonable levels of use-oriented quality costs and for the achievement of these objectives, in an organized and systematic program.

7.19 Other Measures for Decision Making in Quality Control[11]

A number of other numerical quality-cost measurements are needed in management of the total quality program and will have to be developed as required by the particular situation. The approach to developing such measurements may be illustrated by examples in relation to job 2 of total quality control: incoming-material control.

Productivity Measurement

The first example concerns a productivity measurement which reflects the relative quantity of work performed. The performance measurement is

$$\frac{\text{Direct material dollars}}{\text{incoming appraisal costs}}$$

Productivity is normally measured by *output* over *input*. In incoming-material control, direct material represents *output*. Incoming appraisal costs, which include all incoming testing, inspection, and laboratory-acceptance testing, are the quality-related input. This ratio provides a direct measure of productivity

—output over input—reflecting the relative *quantity* of work performed. As *more* work is appraised for quality at *less* cost, productivity rises.

Effectiveness Measurements

The next measurement is one of *effectiveness*, which reflects the relative quality of work performed. Here we need two measures.

The first measure is

$$\frac{\text{Incoming-material appraisal costs}}{\text{manufacturing losses attributable to outside vendors}}$$

Incoming-material appraisal costs reflect the effort applied. Manufacturing losses attributable to outside vendors reflect the effectiveness of the applied effort in keeping poor-quality incoming material from reaching the factory floor.

As the *quality* of the applied effort in appraising incoming material rises, associated manufacturing losses should *decrease* and effectiveness should *go up*.

This effectiveness index shows no bona fide improvement by merely increasing incoming appraisal costs. These increasing appraisal costs will also make the *productivity index* go down, thus indicating no legitimate overall improvement.

The second measure of effectiveness is

$$\frac{\text{Outside vendor losses recovered from vendors}}{\text{total losses attributable to vendors}}$$

The quality of work performed in incoming-material control applies *both* to effectiveness in screening out poor quality and to effectiveness in being able to recover increasingly higher percentages of vendor-associated losses. This recovery percentage is as low as 15 percent in some businesses and the total outside vendor-attributable losses as high as several hundred thousand dollars to several million dollars a year. This is another important measure of potential for increasing profits through improvement of the effectiveness of work performed. The better the job done by the total quality program in the defect-prevention and after-the-fact phases of incoming-material control, the greater is the probability that Purchasing will be able to recover higher percentages of vendor losses.

Timeliness Measurement

Timeliness of action provides another measurement reflecting the timeliness of work performed. Here again we need two measures to present potential contribution to profits fairly.

The first measure is:

Percent of lots failing to meet fully
all requirements as received

This is a measure of *timeliness of defect-prevention work* in the incoming-material control area. It is one thing to become increasingly effective in sorting good from bad. It is equally or more important to take preventive action which ensures the proper quality as received. Better defect-prevention work done not only with vendors but with Engineering and Purchasing should reduce the percent of lots failing to meet all requirements. A reduction in this percentage is reflected as an improvement in timeliness of action.

The second measure for timeliness of action reflects efficiency in processing incoming material:

Average number of lots per week *not* processing through from receipt
at receiving dock to release for stock or use in less than 1 day
(24 hours)

Timeliness of action here is reflected in material *not* processing through rapidly, of material awaiting disposition or corrective action before release for stock or use. A high number of lots reflects poor timeliness of action. Very positive contributions to profits are available from reduced purchasing lead times, lower inventories, fewer production holdups for needed material, and fewer "use-as-is" disposition of marginal-quality material to keep production lines running. As materials flow through faster and disposition procedures are improved, timeliness of action through incoming-material control improves.

Managerial Decision Making

How are these performance measurements used as managerial decision-making tools? The measures that have been discussed are ratios in the three basic performance areas of *productivity, effectiveness,* and *timeliness of action* in incoming-material control. To be of value, these ratios must be converted into decision-making tools. This is done by plotting *performance* versus *time* and noting the relative improvement achieved and progress made in meeting goals.

As an example, consider the first of these measurements as a graph, namely, productivity for incoming-material control in a business. The actual numbers on the graph are typical of some businesses. Figure 7.10 shows productivity reflecting the *quantity* of work performed.

For direct material dollars divided by incoming-material appraisal costs, productivity has become static at $200 of direct material for every dollar of incoming appraisal costs. This level is considerably below the $240 goal set in the total quality program for productivity improvement by year's end. If this goal is to be achieved, decisions must be made by the responsible individuals to *ensure* that action is taken. It may be a decision to make a work-sampling study to determine what percentage of total incoming appraisal time is *nonproductively* spent handling materials, obtaining blueprints and measuring devices,

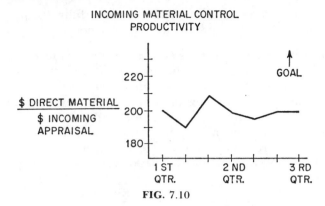

FIG. 7.10

and keeping records. It may be a decision to look into the substantial amount of dollars being expended in routine laboratory-acceptance testing. A substantial portion of this routine laboratory testing might well be *reduced* to skip-lot sampling with *no loss* in protection.[12]

These are just two of many possible avenues to explore to bring productivity up to the goal of more work performed at less cost. The important point is that company management *knows* productivity has become static and recognizes the need for a *decision* to motivate positive action. It has a direct measure of how sound this action was in achieving the desired results in the productivity area. Similarly, graphs can be constructed for the remaining four performance indices that have been discussed in the incoming-material control area.

Combined Measurements

The basic performance indices, just noted, each tell a separate story. Any one alone could provide an erroneous measure of the contribution being made. In combination, however, these performance indices are a powerful decision-making tool for increased profits through positive and effective incoming-material control.

They provide also a sound, numerical basis for *establishing* specific *programs, goals,* and *budgets* and for a close, cooperative relationship between the incoming-material and the quality function. Equally important, these performance indices make an excellent report for top management. The control of quality and its contributions to profits are translated in terms that are readily understood and, in graphical form, readily measured.

In this discussion, only one area, incoming-material control, has been considered. Performance indices covering productivity, effectiveness, and timeliness of action can likewise be developed for each of the major jobs of total quality control. Periodic reports on all indices provide a composite, continuing measure of performance for the quality system in a business.

If positive improvements can regularly be reported in a high percentage of these performance indices, the indications are good that the quality component and the quality system are operating satisfactorily in making contributions to the effectiveness of the business.

Managing through appropriate indices such as those discussed, and within the framework of operating quality-cost data, is one of the major keys to sound total quality control for a company.

7.20 Quality Costs and Economic Growth: A Summary

The close new relationship between economic growth and the cost of quality means that quality control and quality economics must become two of the principal elements of a company's strategic planning and its major managerial actions for achieving competitive economic strength in national and international markets. Quality control and quality costs must be directed in a way that provides the firm with major added business value. Thus, the measurement and control of quality costs will increasingly assume a position of central importance in company management plans and actions as the general rule—not as the special case, which has sometimes been the condition in earlier and less demanding times.

Notes

[1] See A. V. Feigenbaum, *Total Quality Control; Engineering and Management,* McGraw-Hill Book Company, New York, 1961, and "Total Quality Control," *Harvard Business Review,* vol. 34, no. 6, November–December 1956.

[2] Total productivity was reviewed in Secs. 3.2 and 3.3.

[3] Section 7.15 reviews major quality information equipment costs.

[4] Warranty was discussed in Sec. 2.7.

[5] Product liability was discussed in Sec. 2.6.

[6] Product recall was discussed in Sec. 2.8.

[7] See Sec. 1.14 for a discussion of the great importance of return on investment as an economic indicator.

[8] Figure 1.5 illustrated the high value of these results.

[9] For a discussion of automatic test equipment, see J. Richard Lucas, "General Purpose A.T.E.'s Are Not for Everyone," *32nd Annual Technical Conference Transactions,* American Society for Quality Control, Chicago, 1978.

[10] See especially Sec. 2.1 for a review of modern buyer life cycle "mentality" and Sec. 2.10 for the specific effects of life cycle costs upon product sales and acceptance in the marketplace.

[11] This section is according to a paper by F. J. Berkenkamp.

[12] Skip-lot sampling and other published sampling plans are discussed in Sec. 15.11.

PART THREE

Management Strategies for Quality

CHAPTER **8**

Organizing for Quality

Since total quality control guides and coordinates the actions of people, machines, and information across the whole range of key company activities, it is essential that quality be organized effectively and economically company-wide.

There are three considerations in the development and operation of this total quality organization. The first is the identification and confirmation of the specific quality work and teamwork—including the responsibility, authority, accountability, and relationships for quality—of each of the key individuals and groups in the company and the plant.

The second consideration is the identification and confirmation of these same areas for the quality-control function itself so that it may help the company achieve its quality objectives.

The third consideration is the leadership of company and plant management itself in the establishment and ongoing maintenance of quality organization.

The basic managerial and technological foundation for the work and interrelationships of this organization is provided by the total quality system of the company and plant. Without a strong quality system, there cannot be a strong quality organization.

This chapter reviews the approach, principles, and basic structure for achieving effective and solid total quality organization.

8.1 What Are Today's Requirements for Quality Organization?

Several modern marketplace, technological, and economic factors have established major new requirements upon organizing for quality. Four of these factors are particularly important, as follows:

1. Traditional quality programs were, in the past, thought of as a single function in the company. Today, instead, they must be recognized as a systematic group of quality disciplines, to be applied on a coordinated basis by all functions throughout the company and plant.
2. Traditional quality programs were, in the past, several organization layers removed from satisfactory direct, ongoing contact with the buyers and customers of the company's products and services. Today, instead, they must be continuously coupled with the buyer and customer on both a feedforward and feedback basis.
3. Quality problems transcend and do not respect individual functional organizational boundaries within companies. Today, the quality program must be organized accordingly, if it is to be realistic.
4. Quality-related operations in companies have become so extended, intricate, and involved today that the need for integrated, high-level control is of primary rather than secondary importance, as in the past. This is necessary to assure orientation to the real facts of the quality of new products under development, to receive "early warnings" of impending production-quality problems, and to permit management to run its quality operations rather than be run by them.

Together, these four factors represent the forces that are placing the establishment of strong total quality organization at the primary level of general management attention.

Organizing to meet these new quality requirements is not a matter of any one universal organization structure; this can vary for many reasons, but it is a matter of following clear principles and specific disciplines which firmly and clearly establish quality organization in that particular pattern which fits the company's marketplace and economic and social requirements.

For example, factors 1 and 2 are central determinants in establishing effective *companywide* quality organization, discussed in Sections 8.2 through 8.9.

Similarly, factors 3 and 4 are central determinants in establishing, within this companywide pattern, effective *quality-control* organization, discussed in particular in Section 8.10 and beyond.

8.2 Defining the Organizationwide Impact of Total Quality Control

As a definition:

> Total quality control's organizationwide impact involves the managerial and technical implementation of customer-oriented quality activities as a prime responsibility of general management and of the main-line operations of marketing, engineering, production, industrial relations, and service as well as of the quality-control function itself.

The need for such organizationwide impact is demonstrated in company after company throughout the world. Experience shows that as much as 80 percent and more of the fundamental quality problems requiring improvement today are outside the scope of traditional quality-control departments (Fig. 8.1). Or, in other words, as few as 20 percent or less of important quality problems have tended to be dealt with effectively under these more traditional quality approaches.

These important quality problems may exist in production because of the installation and continuance of manufacturing operations that do not meet quality requirements. They may exist in development and engineering because of product designs that have been established in purely technological terms and do not adequately consider quality over the product life cycle.

They may exist in marketing because of customer specifications that emphasize superficial product appearance and features but not the actual uses to which the product will be put by customers. They may exist in product service programs that provide a "quick fix" of quality problems but not satisfactory ongoing product operation. And, very importantly, they may exist in some management attitudes and practices which speak generally about quality but do not, in specific detailed actions, provide the necessary support, emphasis, and budget for quality improvement.

In recognition of this organizationwide impact of quality problems, modern quality programs are structured to deal with all these key quality problems (Fig. 8.2) as a primary managerial, economic, and technical responsibility of the key individuals throughout marketing, engineering, production, and service in the firm—as well as in quality control and general management itself.

QUALITY PROBLEMS REQUIRING IMPROVEMENT

80 %
OUTSIDE TRADITIONAL
QUALITY CONTROL

20 %
INSIDE

FIG. 8.1

QUALITY PROBLEMS REQUIRING IMPROVEMENT

ALL KEY QUALITY PROBLEMS
PRIMARY
MANAGERIAL
RESPONSIBILITIES

FIG. 8.2

Modern quality organization provides for the work necessary to enter thoroughly into the customer-use aspects of marketing specifications—for example, to help establish the roadability of a new automobile, the service rate of a new computer, or the efficacy of a new pharmaceutical—not occasionally or just in reaction to problems, but systematically and regularly.

It assures that the activity go deeply into planning the basic capability of all production processes—both those newly purchased and those already in operation. It fosters the work to assure the fundamental reliability and safety of all product designs. It provides for activity toward creating standards for all product service. It involves work continuously to measure customer satisfaction with the product in use. And, through continuing motivation and participation, it provides for explicit activity toward making positive quality-mindedness a way of life in the factory and in the office.

8.3 The Task of Quality Organization

The task of quality organization, therefore, is operation and integration, in the framework of the total quality system, of the activities of the persons and groups who work within the technological framework represented by the four quality-control jobs.

The spirit motivating this organization must be one which stimulates an aggressive quality-consciousness among all company employees. This spirit depends upon many intangibles, among which management's attitude toward quality is paramount.

It also depends upon some very tangible factors. The most important of these is that the structure of the quality organization permit a maximum of results and integration with a minimum of personal friction, overlap of authority, and dissension among functional groups.

Establishing an adequate quality organization for a company is a job of human relations. Guides to the structural patterns that are useful may be found in industry's experience during the past several years. This experience may be gaged against the backdrop of the organization planning methods which are widely and effectively used.

The patterns emerging as most successful may be readily summarized regarding their essentials:

Basic quality responsibility rests in the hands of company top management. Over the past several decades, top management, as part of the general industrial trend toward specialization, had delegated portions of its quality responsibility to such functional groups as Engineering, Manufacturing, Marketing, Product Service, and Quality Control. In addition, the all-important responsibility of each worker for producing quality products has, if anything, increased over this period of years with the increasing complexity both of products and production machinery.

In present-day industry, the four jobs of total quality control cannot be effectively pursued unless those functional quality responsibilities for their various elements are clearly defined and structured. Moreover, there must be an associated mechanism to assist in integrating and measuring these responsibilities. In the larger companies where top management cannot of and by itself act as such a mechanism, present-day management establishes an organizational component as a pivotal point of its total-quality-control organization to provide the required integration and control.

Creation of this quality-control component does not relieve other company personnel of their delegated quality responsibilities, for the discharge of which they are best qualified. The component does, however, make the quality-control whole for the company greater than the sum of its individual engineering, manufacturing, inspection, and marketing parts, through the functions of integration and control. It thus provides the core of the organizational pattern for making effective the total-quality-control technological framework, an effectiveness which has not been at all equaled by the more traditional quality-control organizations of the past.

8.4 What Has Been the Formal Organization for Quality in the Past?

The importance of such clear structuring is emphasized in the fact that even in some companies which have devoted significant concentration to quality activities, many have given only casual attention to quality organization. Most of their time and effort has been devoted to reacting to quality problems or to developing the technological aspects of quality control. Quality organization, however, has been neither well thought through nor properly clarified.

Too often, quality organization has been created as a short-term response to major quality pressures, such as a rapid growth of internal failure costs in the plant, or a group of newly recognized product-safety hazards, with the potential for major product-liability claims or a major product-recall program.

Under these circumstances, dealing explicitly with the organizationwide impact of quality has sometimes been overlooked. Various portions of quality work have been carried on, not as a part of the preconceived plantwide total-quality-control program, but as uncoordinated—often informal—portions of the regular responsibilities of several functional groups in the plant. New-design-control activities have usually been the province—sometimes formal, sometimes informal—of Design Engineering and, possibly, Manufacturing Engineering. Incoming-material control has generally been supervised by Inspection and Laboratory Engineering, sometimes with Purchasing.

Product control has often been exclusively directed by Production Supervision. Special process studies have frequently resolved into free-for-alls in which all groups would participate at one time or another.

Indeed, organizing for quality has often been approached primarily as organizational considerations bearing upon the work of the quality-control component itself. As a result, several company quality-control components have "just growed." They have become appendages to existing inspection departments, "new" functional groups developed with little preliminary analysis of what their function should really be or additional assignments for strong personalities in the plants. On some occasions, a "central quality-control office" has been established, reporting to top management, but with little clear authority or direct relationships with actual company quality actions.

The quality-control organizations that are formally recognized on company organization charts are often not adequate to serve in the quality-control jobs. Some plants do not recognize that all four jobs are within the province of their quality-control organization. Often a quality-control program is allied with a renamed but nonetheless still traditional inspection department. It concerns itself with job 2, incoming-material control, and with certain phases of job 3, product control.

Equally frequently encountered is the practice of creating a quality-control organization simply by adding such methods as statistical sampling to the activities of the plant's existing inspection department.

Again, there are often basic inadequacies in the program of those plants which concentrate upon the development of "new" functional quality-control organizations. Many of these groups have been built around a single quality-control technique or a single quality-control objective. Some of these groups are statistical bureaus; others carry on specialized versions of sampling work or study only "manufacturing losses"; still others are responsible for trouble-shooting field complaints or for writing factory inspection and testing instructions, and certain others are assigned primarily to evaluation and testing regarding new product introduction. A few groups are established for the primary purpose of maintaining customer quality relations.

These groups are limited in scope to job 1, new-design control; job 3, product control, or job 4, special process studies. Their members typically are extremely conscientious and often gain local successes in the individual projects they attack. In the final analysis, however, as is almost inevitable, the results of their work in relation to the overall plant quality objective may be analogous to the results obtained by attempting to restrain a balloon by squeezing one end.

Failure to meet the company quality objective is not the only difficulty that has been experienced from these types of quality-control organizations. They have often been characterized by lack of integration among the several activities and by sprawling, disjointed quality-control planning. The new quality-control techniques, most of which cut across all four quality-control jobs, are frequently overlooked or misapplied because there has been no single channel through which they might be introduced companywide.

Some companies have organized in such a way that product-reliability responsibilities are set up separate from basic product-quality responsibilities. Large and costly reliability organizations have been established which, in some cases, largely duplicate the product-quality responsibilities that already exist. Naturally, conflicts between the two groups develop, and the interests of neither overall product quality nor its product-reliability element are served.

The same diffusion of responsibility and coordination also exists in some companies with regard to other major quality-related areas, such as product safety. With regard to the all-important field of product liability, Section 3.9 thoroughly reviewed the significant difficulties created for companies which have allowed walls to exist between their quality programs and their liability loss prevention activities.

8.5 What Has Been the Status of Quality Responsibilities in These Organizations?

In the final analysis, many of these past quality organizations have been so informal or so restricted in scope that they have not been quality organizations at all in the total-quality-control sense of coordinated administration of an integrated program of the four quality-control jobs.

Knotty personality problems have sometimes arisen when management has been led to expect from these forms of quality organizations the overall improvements in quality and reductions in cost that have been reported in the literature. Friction among company groups and employees and high turnover of quality-control personnel themselves have sometimes characterized these programs. Employees throughout the company are often not clear as to the scope of the quality-control organization itself and sometimes level "empire-building" charges against its members.

On the one hand, management becomes dissatisfied with its quality-control program and suspicious of the national claims being made for the activity. On the other hand, members of the quality-control organization become frustrated and privately berate management for its lack of understanding and its refusal to grant the group more power.

Management has thus been paying a high price for quality organization in many plants and companies. The issue in quality organization today is therefore *not* "Shall we organize for administration of the quality-control jobs?" It is rather "What is the most effective type of quality organization that will provide customer satisfaction and low costs?"

8.6 What Issue Has Arisen from This Distribution of Responsibilities?

It may be granted that the hydra-headed responsibility and lack of genuine organization for the four quality-control jobs are major causes for the high costs of industrial quality and for the occasional low quality of these products. As everybody's job, quality control may often become nobody's job.

It may be granted that coordination among quality-control activities has occurred more according to whim than to any adequate organizational procedure. Budget factors and personality considerations have tended to Balkanize product-quality responsibilities and insulate functional groups from each other.

It may be granted that several of the quality-control activities have developed in contradictory directions. Product-quality responsibilities are so widely distributed that it is naive to expect that they will synchronize with each other "spontaneously."

It may be granted that modern quality problems are too complex technically to be adequately solved on this hit-or-miss basis. Industrial quality problems have simply outgrown the organization structure designed in a previous era to cope with them.

But what is to be done about this situation?

The basic issue at stake is that these individual quality responsibilities are integral parts of the day-to-day work of the line, staff, and functional groups which hold them. They cannot be effectively separated out from the other activities of these groups. The few efforts to organize quality control in this direction have proved abortive.

Thus, responsibility for specifying tolerances and other quality requirements and for making suitable tests to determine what this quality should be is intimately connected with the product engineering function. An important part of manufacturing engineering work is development of the assurance that the tools and processes selected will produce parts of the required quality standard.

It is right and appropriate in most companies that key responsibilities for product quality be distributed among various organizational components. How can quality control be organized so that integration and control are provided without relieving the rest of company personnel of their basic responsibility for quality?

8.7 What Is the Process of "Control"?

This problem of diffused responsibility is not so knotty as it may seem at first glance. It has been faced and solved by management on several previous issues.

It was faced in the development of organization for personnel administration. It was inconceivable that all personnel activities be stripped from the hands of the line organization and placed in the hands of a personnel group.

It was faced in the development of production-control organization. It was clearly seen at the outset of this program that responsibility for many phases of production must remain where it was: in the hands of the factory supervisor, the engineer, and other parties to the production process.

It was faced in the development of financial and cost accounting organization. It was obvious that responsibility for expenditures should be placed with the many individuals and groups who knew about the work being done; such responsibility could not be totally placed in the hands of a cost accounting group.

The organizational technique developed by management to meet these conditions can be simply described. It may consist initially in leaving untouched responsibilities and authority in the hands of the groups to which they have been delegated. This procedure is followed whether this delegation had previously been formally made by management or the responsibilities had informally gravitated to the groups in question.

A means is then created for assuring management that the results of these groups are satisfactory in relation to preset management standards. In the process of this results check, it may become necessary to coordinate the activities of the several delegates and redistribute some of their responsibilities.

Management often has no time to carry on the work that is required. It may therefore "extend its personality" by creating a functional individual or functional group to do this work for it.

As discussed in Section 1.5, this process is one of control. The term "control" is usually applied to the organization that is correspondingly created, as in budget "control," production "control," financial "control," and, of course, quality "control."

This process may be rephrased in relation to product quality. Analyzed from this organizational point of view, quality control becomes merely what the phrase implies: management's control over product quality. It is a device whereby management delegates authority and responsibility for product quality, thus relieving itself of unnecessary detail and permitting the benefits of specialization while retaining for itself the means for ensuring that quality results will be satisfactory for top management's standards and policies.

8.8 Organizing Principles

Fundamental to building the organization structure which puts this process to work, and thereby brings the four quality-control jobs to effective use, are two quality organizational principles that sum up the concepts discussed above. The first principle is that *quality is everybody's job* in a business. (Section 8.9 discusses the implementation of this principle.)

In defiance of this principle, many businesses over the years have attempted to centralize their company quality responsibility by organizing a function whose job has been handsomely described as "responsibility for all factors affecting product quality." These experiments have had a life span of as long as 6 to 9 months, that is, when the job incumbent had the advantage of a strong stomach, a rhinoceros hide, and a well-spent, sober childhood. Others not similarly endowed did not last the 6 months.

The simple fact is that the *marketing specialist* can best evaluate customer's quality preferences. The *design engineer* is the only person who can effectively establish specification quality levels. The shop *supervisor* is the individual who can best concentrate upon the building of quality.

Total-quality-control programs thus require, as an initial step, top management's reemphasis of the respective quality responsibilities and accountabilities of all company employees in new-design control, in incoming-material control, in product control, and in special process studies.

The second principle of total-quality-control organization is a corollary to this first one: *Because quality is everybody's job in a business, it may become nobody's job.* (Section 8.10 discusses the implementation of this principle.)

Thus, the second step required in total quality programs becomes clear. Top management must recognize that the many individual responsibilities for quality will be exercised most effectively when they are buttressed and serviced by a well-organized, genuinely modern management function whose only area of *specialization* is product quality, whose only area of *operation* is in the quality-control jobs, and whose only *responsibilities* are to be sure that the products shipped are right—and *at the right quality cost.*

8.9 The First Principle: Key Organizationwide Quality Responsibilities and Authorities

In the determination and confirmation of key quality responsibilities, organizationwide, a typical breakdown of some of the major functional groups which have key responsibilities and authorities for product and service quality is as follows:

1. *Product Planning, Marketing, and Sales,* for the product description that will best fulfill the customer's wants and needs in use, the presentation of

product-quality data to the customer, and the determination of quality standards with the customer

2. *Product Engineering,* for the original product design, the writing of specifications, the establishment of guarantees, and the selection of materials, tolerances, and operating characteristics

3. *Manufacturing Engineering,* for the selection of machining and processing equipments; the design of appropriate jigs and fixtures; analysis of certain types of manufacturing difficulties which may arise in producing quality of the desired standard; and the selection of methods, development of work places, and provision of satisfactory working conditions

4. *Purchasing,* for choosing vendors and the quality guarantees demanded from the vendors

5. *Laboratory,* for the quality standards set for materials and processes; the approval of the quality of critical materials, either purchased or processed; and recommendations on the use of special processing techniques

6. *Production Supervision,* for operator education; proper attention to, and care for, manufacturing facilities; proper interpretation of drawings and specifications; and for actual control over the manufactured parts as they are being produced

7. *Production Employees,* for skill, care, and quality of workmanship

8. *Inspection and Testing,* for judging the quality of incoming parts and materials and appraising the conformance of manufactured parts and assemblies to specifications

9. *Packaging and Shipping,* for the adequacy of the container into which the product is placed and for the shipment of the product

10. *Product Service,* for providing the customer with the means for fully realizing the intended function of the product during its expected life: for example, maintenance and repair instructions and replacement parts

Other groups like Production Control, wage rate, and Personnel share in these quality responsibilities. Some specialized activities—motivational research, for example—have product quality as one of the major reasons for their existence.

8.10 The Second Principle: Key Quality-Control Responsibilities and Authorities

To help general management and the heads of these several functions meet their own quality responsibilities so as to obtain the necessary business quality results, the two basic authorities of a modern quality-control function may be formally stated as *first,* to provide quality assurance for the business's products, and *second,* to assist in assuring optimum quality costs for those products.

To exercise these authorities, three principal responsibilities must be assigned to the quality-control function:

First, the modern quality-control component has a *business responsibility,* whereby quality control provides a primary and direct contribution to the business planning and business-implementation actions of the firm's market growth, its cost control, and its product planning in customer life cycle quality terms. This is in direct contrast to the quality component being asked to react to business quality problems only after they have occurred.[1]

Second, the quality-control component has a *systems responsibility,* whereby quality control provides the primary leadership in the company for the engineering and management of a strong total quality system that assures quality and quality cost from marketing and engineering through production and service.[2]

Third, the quality-control component has a *technical responsibility,* whereby quality control provides for the major operating control and assurance activities.[3]

These three quality responsibilities represent a far bigger job than in the quality-control function of a few years ago—whose work was usually limited to some form of technical responsibility. These three responsibilities represent the necessary work that modern quality control must accomplish to provide the positive quality contribution that is so essential to business health today.

8.11 Structuring Total Quality Organization—General Management Responsibility

To make clear and concrete the work, authorities, and responsibilities involved in implementing the two basic principles of modern quality organization, general management must clearly and specifically document—and communicate to all employees—the quality structure of the company and the plant in the necessary organizational detail. This quality organizational manual will include the publication of suitable position guides, where appropriate.

This structure, covering companywide quality responsibilities throughout all four jobs of total quality control, represents the organizational realization of the formal published quality policy of the company.[4]

Only through such documentation will it be possible for individuals and groups throughout the company to understand clearly their accountability for the specific customer-oriented quality results for which they are being measured and to which their personal commitment is essential. Chapter 9 discusses in some detail the achievement of this positive total quality commitment.

Because of the high degree of integration that is required in companywide and plantwide quality programs, this documentation must also identify the principal areas of teamwork and relationships among individuals and groups. Otherwise, the necessary high degree of cooperation and coordination will not be facilitated.

Figure 8.3 shows a typical set of relationships among quality responsibilities, including those of the quality-control function. This diagram, called a relationship chart, is a most useful means for analyzing, identifying, and establishing the primary quality responsibilities of the various organizational components of the company.

RELATIONSHIP CHART
(Applied to Product Quality)

Code: (R) = Responsible
C = Must contribute
M = May contribute
I = Is informed

Areas of Responsibility	General Manager	Finance	Marketing	Engineering	Manager-Manufacturing	Manufacturing Engineering	Quality Control	Materials	Shop Operations
Determine needs of customer			(R)						
Establish quality level for business	(R)		C	C	C				
Establish product design specs				(R)					
Establish manufacturing process design				C	M	(R)	M	M	C
Produce products to design specs			M	C	C	C	C	C	(R)
Determine process capabilities					I	C	(R)	M	C
Qualify suppliers on quality							C	(R)	
Plan the quality system	(R)		C	C	C	C	(R)	C	C
Plan inspection and test procedures						C	(R)	C	C
Design test and inspection equipment						C	(R)		M
Feed back quality information			C	C	I	M	(R)	C	C
Gather complaint data			(R)						
Analyze complaint data			M	M			(R)		
Obtain corrective action			M	C	C	C	(R)	C	C
Compile quality costs		(R)	C	C	C				
Analyze quality costs		M					(R)		
In-process quality measurements							(R)		C
In-process quality audit				C		C	(R)		
Final product inspection				C	C	M	C	(R)	

FIG. 8.3

8.12 The Three Quality-Control Subfunctions

These authorities, responsibilities, accountabilities, and relationships of the modern quality-control component itself are fulfilled through its three subfunctions, which are quality engineering, process-control engineering (including also inspection and testing), and quality information equipment engineering.

Quality engineering develops the detailed quality planning, which contributes to and implements the quality system for the company.

Process-control engineering (including also inspection and testing) monitors the application of quality control on the factory floor and thus gradually supplants the older policing inspection activity.

Quality information equipment engineering designs and develops the inspection and testing equipment for obtaining the necessary measurements, controls, and information flow for quality. Where justified, this equipment is combined with production to provide automatic feedback of results for control of the process. All pertinent results are then analyzed as a basis for adjustment and corrective action on the process.

The basic structure for such a quality-control function is shown in Figure 8.4. Figure 8.5 is a typical position guide for the manager of the function. Figure 8.6 reviews typical work activities of the quality-engineering, process-control-engineering (also including inspection and test) and quality-information-equipment-engineering subfunctions.

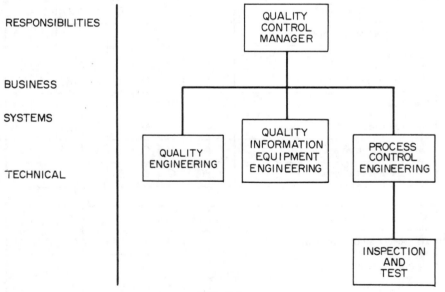

FIG. 8.4

8.13 Organizing the Quality-Control Function in a Company

Companies vary widely in products and history and markets and personalities. So too will it be appropriate for them to vary in their particular adaptations of the basic quality-control structure shown in Figure 8.4.

What is the right way for a particular company to go about organizing the three subfunctions of the quality-control component? Should some quality-control work be decentralized, or should the function be centralized? To whom should Quality Control report? Should a quality-"assurance" component be established separately from a quality-"control" component? The next sections of this chapter are directed toward answering these questions.

Let us turn first to the six steps for planning any sound quality-control organization structure.

First: Define the company quality purposes for whose realization the organization is being created.

Second: Establish the objectives that the organization must achieve if it is to implement these purposes.

Third: Determine the basic work activities that must be accomplished in meeting the organization objectives. Classify these work activities into an appropriate number of basic functions.

Fourth: Combine these basic functions into job packages which pass the screen of seven acid-test questions:

1. Does the position comprise a logical, separate field of responsibility?
2. Is the position clear-cut and definite as to scope, purpose, objectives, and results to be achieved?
3. Can a single individual be held responsible and know the measuring sticks by which he or she is being judged?
4. Are the functions of the position closely related and do they "belong together?"
5. Does the position have authority commensurate with its responsibility? In other words, is it tooled up for results?
6. Does the position have easy, workable relationships with other positions in the organization?
7. Can the number of people reporting to the holder of the position be genuinely supervised?

Fifth: Consolidate the job packages into an organization component or components best suited to specific company requirements, recognizing the particular character of the organization component that has been created.

Sixth: With this in mind, locate the component in that segment of the larger company organization where it can do its job and achieve its objectives with maximum effectiveness and economy and a minimum of friction. Establish the

FIG. 8.5

XYZ COMPANY

POSITION GUIDE
MANAGER–QUALITY CONTROL

I. Broad function

The Manager–Quality Control has three basic areas of responsibility to the company, as follows:

Business Responsibility: The Manager–Quality Control will provide customer quality assurance for the products and services of the company and assist in assuring the achievement of the optimum quality costs for the company. The Manager–Quality Control will participate in the strategic business planning of the company. The manager will help formulate and document basic company quality policy and quality organization. The manager will contribute his experience to help establish realistic quality goals and feasible supporting tactics in company business plans. The manager will participate in all major quality-related decisions in all phases of business activity. The manager will place emphasis upon such areas as potential liability of the company's products, the reliability and safety of all products, and the minimization of such hazards in achieving full customer quality satisfaction as product recalls. The manager will assist in bringing the full effect of the company quality program to the improvement of productivity in both the office and the factory.

Systems Responsibility: As delegated by general management, and in close cooperation with all key company and plant functions, the Manager–Quality Control will provide leadership in quality-system establishment and maintenance. The manager will also assure and contribute to the regular collection and analysis of quality costs to measure the business effectiveness of the systems economics of the quality program for achieving optimum balance among prevention, appraisal, and failure costs.

Technical Responsibility: The Manager–Quality Control will provide for suitable company and plant operation and application of the engineering and statistical technologies of quality control. This will be exercised through the three subfunctional areas of quality engineering, process-control engineering, and quality information equipment engineering. This includes maintenance of suitable activities to audit quality effectiveness, especially planning programs of audits; procedure audits, quality-systems audits, and product audits. (These audits are reviewed in Sections 11.23 through 11.27.)

II. Principal responsibilities

To implement the basic business, system, and technical responsibility, the Manager–Quality Control has managerial and functional responsibilities in the company for the operation of the quality-control component. The manager is responsible for assuring that customer quality requirements have been adequately defined to permit appropriate quality planning and implementation and that these quality requirements have been met. The manager's quality responsibilities will include the necessary activities bearing upon all major customer quality-related characteristics, such as product reliability, product safety, and similar characteristics.

Within the limits of approved policies, programs, budgets, and procedures, the Manager–Quality Control is responsible for and has the authority to fulfill the duties listed below. The manager may delegate portions of responsibility together with the necessary authority for their fulfillment, but the manager may not delegate or relinquish overall responsibility for results.

A. Managerial responsibilities

The Manager–Quality Control is responsible for providing leadership to all employees of the quality-control component by performing the work of a manager, in which the manager will, as to

1. Planning

    a. Personally keep informed and keep the supervisors informed of the objectives, policies, plans, and budgets of the business.

    b. Develop the company's quality program, including policies, objectives, plans, organizations, procedures, and appraisals, and assure the documentation of the program and its distribution to company personnel to promote the proper concept of the quality program.

2. Organizing

    a. Develop a sound organizational structure for the performance of all phases of the quality-control component activities.

    b. Establish appropriate subfunctional components within the quality-control component, staff them with qualified personnel, and delegate appropriate responsibilities and authority for conducting their particular phases of the quality-control program.

    c. Instruct, advise, counsel, and review the performance of the unit and subunit supervisors of the quality-control component.

3. Integrating

    a. Provide for the systematic utilization of all resources of the component to achieve effectively and economically the desired objectives.

    b. Acquaint everyone in the component with their responsibilities, authority, and accountability and promote individual development and the necessity for unity of effort.

4. Measuring

    a. Establish standards for measuring the performance of the Unit and Subunit heads and other personnel of the quality-control component and inform them of their progress.

    b. Analyze and appraise the progress of the component as measured against the objectives set up and take or suggest action necessary for improvement.

B. Functional responsibilities

The Manager–Quality Control, by contributing personal knowledge as well as working through those reporting directly to the manager, will

1. Formulate basic policies, plans, programs, standards, and techniques necessary to carry out the objectives of the Quality–Control component, and upon their approval will carry out such policies, plans, and programs.

2. Provide the adequate facilities and equipment necessary for inspecting, testing, and measuring the quality of the company products and the most economical maintenance of such equipment and facilities.

3. Provide and have distributed to all appropriate personnel the business programs designed to promote the spirit of quality thinking throughout the component and encourage participation of Quality-Control personnel in any educational courses that may be available to keep themselves informed of the newest developments that involve quality-control procedures.

4. Maintain relationships with Marketing units to understand thoroughly the functions of the product necessary to fulfill customer needs, as well as the ongoing product service requirements.
5. Maintain relationships with Engineering units to discuss quality considerations as early as possible in the product-design stage.
6. Maintain relationships with Manufacturing units to assure adequate process-capability and quality information feedback.
7. Maintain proper relationships with vendors to ensure that their products meet company quality standards.
8. Work with Finance units to determine quality costs so that these costs can be easily analyzed and controlled.

III. Authority and reservation of decision-making authority

The Manager–Quality Control has full authority to make decisions and take action necessary to carry out the responsibilities assigned so long as such action does not deviate from established business and company policies, practices, and position guides and is consistent with sound business judgment, except for the following specific limitations placed upon the manager's authority:

1. Certain additions to payroll and salary adjustments of certain employees
2. Changes in the organizational structure at the unit level or above
3. Major changes affecting the other components
4. Approval of certain expense accounts

IV. Accountability

The Manager–Quality Control is fully accountable for the fulfillment of responsibilities and their proper interpretation. The manager may not delegate or relinquish any portion of this accountability. Performance of the Manager–Quality Control will be measured by the extent or degree to which the manager and the quality-control component fulfill the following accountability measures:

1. The assurance of product quality for the customer
2. The economy of quality costs
3. The effectiveness of the quality system in operation
4. The cooperation and quality leadership relationship with the key functions of the company, including Marketing, Engineering, Production, Service, Industrial Relations, and others.
5. The quality of the manager's leadership in all areas of the quality-control component.
6. The quality and timeliness of the manager's decisions and actions as to all responsibilities of the position.
7. The quality of managerial leadership by personal actions and the action of others in the quality-control component reporting directly to the manager.
8. The attainment of the objectives and fulfillment of the responsibilities of the manager's position as indicated by the level and trend in such typical areas as

a. The control of the quality of incoming materials and completed parts as compared with engineering specifications
b. Action taken to correct cause of complaints because of poor material or quality of work
c. Adequacy of equipment and facilities with which to perform quality-control functions
d. Adequacy of process measurements to provide necessary information to Production Operations for process control
e. Adequacy and timeliness of quality information feedback to organizational units that can take corrective action
f. Accuracy in diagnosing quality difficulties and analyzing underlying causes
g. Accuracy of product-quality measurements indices and reflecting the true quality of the product reaching the customer.
h. Realization of cost-reduction and manufacturing-loss goals.
i. Safety of component personnel as indicated by the frequency and severity of accidents in the subsection
j. Morale of the component employees as indicated by the number of grievances and absenteeism, employee turnover, and productive work-hours lost because of work stoppage
k. The effectiveness of promotion of the suggestion plan and other employee benefit plans as measured by comparative employee participation in the benefit plans
m. The effective utilization of the work force, facilities, and equipment indicated by the work produced against predetermined standards.
n. The standards of quality mindedness and of quality motivation throughout employee actions.

---

relationships with other organization components that are necessary to the organization objectives.

The first four steps were discussed earlier in this and previous chapters. When steps 5 and 6 are considered, the detailed ways in which Quality Control can be organized begin to take shape.

Sections 8.14 to 8.17 discuss the considerations involved in step 5, namely, the factors involved in establishing specific organization structure for Quality Control.

Section 8.18 discusses the considerations involved in step 6, namely, the factors involved in placing this quality-control structure within the larger structure of the company organization.

8.14 Basic Questions for Organization Structuring

When establishing the specific organizational structure for quality control, a company must answer these basic questions:

FIG. 8.6

WORK ACTIVITIES OF THE
QUALITY-CONTROL COMPONENT

The major subfunctions in Quality Control are

· Quality Engineering
· Quality Information Equipment Engineering
· Process-Control Engineering, including Inspection and Testing

The work of these subfunctions involves suitable attention to all key characteristics of customer quality satisfaction, including reliability, product safety, and other related quality characteristics.

QUALITY ENGINEERING

General Description

This component of the quality-control function has responsibility for the action required to

1. Determine that quality objectives and goals have been defined sufficiently to permit adequate quality planning to satisfy customer expectations.
2. Review proposed products and processes to avoid or eliminate unnecessary quality difficulties.
3. Plan the quality measurements and controls on materials, processes, and product to provide adequate control of quality at minimum quality-related costs.
4. Determine that manufacturing processes have sufficient capability to meet quality requirements.
5. Analyze quality information and feedback analyses and recommendations for adjustment to product design, manufacturing process and equipment, and the quality system.
6. On behalf of the Manager–Quality Control, carry out key steps in establishing and maintaining the company and plant quality system.

Work Activities

1. *Quality objectives and goals.* Recommend to top management realistic company product-quality objectives and goals. Work with Marketing and Engineering in establishing specific quality requirements on individual products based upon customer need, the function of the product, and its reliability, salability, and value.
2. *Preproduction quality ability.* Review new and revised designs for quality ability, including assurance of product reliability and product safety. Recommend to Engineering improvements that increase product uniformity and reliability and improve quality characteristics to reduce field failures and complaints. Recommend improvements for simplifying control of manufacturing processes and evaluating quality, thereby reducing costs.
3. *Review of engineering prototype evaluation.* Review performance, environmental reliability, safety, life, shipping test results, and other information resulting

from Engineering development work. Analyze and evaluate prototype performance as a basis for reliability and safety studies and for planning the required controls on quality and associated information feedback.

4. *Quality standards.* Participate with Marketing and Engineering in establishing and defining those quality standards which cover such items as appearance, surface roughness, color, noise, and vibration.

5. *Shop-practice standards.* Participate with Manufacturing Engineering and Production Operations in establishing shop standards that will be followed in the absence of engineering specifications, e.g., radii on bends and squareness of sheared stock.

6. *Product- and process-quality planning.* Determine and establish the required quality procedures for controlling product and process quality, including reliability and safety. Planning should include the relative importance of quality characteristics and required quality levels; points in the flow for quality measurements to be made; methods and procedures for quality measurements by operators, quality checkers, inspectors, testers, auditors, and so forth; applicable statistical quality-control techniques; quality information feedback; required quality measurement and control equipment; defective-material disposition procedures; and other pertinent quality procedures. Assure incorporation of applicable quality measurements into the manufacturing process planning. Provide appropriate components with cost estimates and time schedules pertaining to the preceding quality controls. Periodically review quality planning to assure continued adequacy and effectiveness.

7. *Purchased-material quality control.* Determine the relative importance of purchased-material quality characteristics and the required quality levels, keeping in mind design, manufacturing process, and reliability and safety requirements. Assure adequate delineation of quality requirements to vendors through Purchasing. Designate quality characteristics to be measured and methods and procedures for performing quality evaluations, including sampling plans and required inspection and test equipment. Evaluate new vendor facilities and systems for controlling quality. Plan for vendor ratings and materials certification by vendors.

8. *Controls on production devices directly affecting quality.* Assist Manufacturing Engineering in specifying the required quality capability of new production devices directly affecting quality, i.e., equipment, tools, dies, fixtures, and so on. Establish methods and procedures for evaluating original adequacy to the required quality capability. Establish procedures for ensuring adequate preventive maintenance controls, qualitywise, on the above.

9. *Quality capability requirements.* Determine that manufacturing processes and equipment have sufficient capability to meet quality requirements by analyzing process-capability studies, control charts, and other statistical data. Determine which product- and process-quality characteristics require process-capability studies. Analyze results of studies and feedback recommendations for selection or improvement of machine or process to meet manufacturing quality requirements.

10. *Outgoing product-quality index.* Establish a current, timely, and continuous index of outgoing product quality by customer-oriented quality audits and ratings, including life, reliability, safety, and environmental evaluations.

11. *Quality information feedback.* Ascertain the specific quality information feed-

back needs of General Management and all key personnel in Manufacturing Engineering and Marketing; ensure timely delivery of action-centered data and reports which make for optimum quality-related decision making.

12. *Manufacturing quality problems.* Diagnose chronic manufacturing quality problems referred by Process-Control Engineering to determine basic cause of difficulties. Also provide technical assistance as required to other functions. Present analysis of facts to establish the nature of the problem for solution and action by the appropriate component. Follow and report progress to applicable management.

13. *Quality-cost analysis.* Analyze all elements of quality costs, and provide analyses as a basis for initiating positive action in the areas of prevention, appraisal, and failure for overall reduction in quality costs.

14. *Product-quality certification.* Develop quality-certification plans for products shipped to customers. Assist Marketing in publishing brochures outlining the quality system, showing the advantages to the customer of buying quality-controlled and certified products.

15. *Customer complaints and field failure analysis.* Analyze, identify basic causes, and feedback analyses and recommendations, participating with other functional components in instigating corrective action. Follow and report progress to appropriate management.

16. *Quality-control training.* Develop and implement quality-control orientation programs for all operational personnel in the company to ensure understanding of quality-control objectives, programs, plans, and techniques. Provide quality training programs for personnel in Shop Operations and other subfunctional components.

17. *Quality-control communication.* Develop and initiate efficient methods for regularly reporting to managers and other interested personnel the current status of product quality with respect to quality objectives and goals to stimulate quality improvement and continued quality efforts. Keep management regularly informed on status and progress made on quality-control programs and plans.

18. *Quality-system establishment and maintenance.* Play a key role in quality-system determination and ongoing operation.

General Comments on Quality Engineering

In a small business, it is possible that all the preceding work activities would be assigned to one position. In larger companies, these work activities might be divided among several positions. For example, Advanced Quality Engineering would be responsible for work activities 1 and 2 and 18. The quality engineer who does the planning of specific controls on quality would be responsible for work elements 3 to 10 and 14. Work activities 16 and 17 would normally be assigned to the appropriate engineer or engineers by the Manager–Quality Control. The remainder would be given to a quality engineer assigned to a product line. In some cases, a quality analyst would be assigned to the numerical analysis portion of the quality-engineering work elements.

*Work activities which normally are not delegated to other functional components.

QUALITY INFORMATION EQUIPMENT ENGINEERING

General Description

This component of the quality-control function has responsibility for the action required to develop, design, and provide the required quality-measurement equipment for evaluating, measuring, and controlling product and process quality, including reliability, safety, and other major customer requirements.

Work Activities

1. *Test and inspection equipment design.* Design, construct, and prove in required testing equipment, inspection tools, fixtures, and gages or procure this equipment or service. Plan for continued effectiveness of such equipment and tooling, including calibration schedules.
2. *In-process quality-measuring devices.* Ensure that in-process quality-measuring devices are provided to indicate, and in some cases record, the quality at the instant it is produced so the operator can provide rapid control of the process and have proof of in-process quality. Plan for continued effectiveness of such devices, including calibration schedules.
3. *Mechanization and automation.* Work with Manufacturing Engineering to incorporate, where possible, the quality-measurement and control devices with the manufacturing equipment to provide optimum mechanization and automation through integrated analysis and feedback of quality data.
4. *Advanced Quality-measuring techniques and equipment.* Devise, develop, and prove feasibility of advanced quality-measurement and control techniques and equipment required to achieve continually improving manufactured product quality, including reliability, at reduced costs. Emphasize continuing development of metrology, nondestructive evaluation, and related measurement areas.

PROCESS CONTROL ENGINEERING

General Description

This component of the quality-control function has the responsibility and takes the action required for

1. Providing technical assistance for understanding quality standards and solution of Manufacturing quality problems
2. Evaluating the quality capability of processes and providing quality maintenance throughout Manufacturing
3. Interpreting the quality plan and assuring its understanding and effective implementation throughout Manufacturing
4. Assuring the maintenance and calibration of quality information equipment and safe operating practices, including suitable metrology and nondestructive evaluation procedures
5. Assuring that the quality level of the finished product, purchased materials,

*Work activities which normally are not delegated to other functional components.

and components are commensurate with engineering specification and the quality plan.

6. Performing the actual physical operation required to help provide quality assurance, such as inspecting, testing, and quality auditing

7. Appraising the quality plan and contributing to its continuing effectiveness.

Technical Work Activities

1. *Appraise the quality plan.* Appraise the continuing effectiveness of the quality plan for quality levels, nature of manufacturing quality problems, customer complaints, and economical operation as the result of implementing and working with the plan.

2. *Interpretation of quality plan.* Furnish to Production Operations and other Manufacturing organization components all necessary interpretation of the quality plan: its use, operation, and intent.

3. *Review and maintain quality standards.* Inspect all quality standards, both written and physical, for clarity and furnish interpretation to assure understanding and proper use. Provide for the maintenance of all quality standards. Also provide for or maintain necessary companywide primary and secondary standards, such as electronic instruments and gage blocks.

4. *Determine conformance to quality planning.* Provide to Production Operations and others an evaluation of conformance to quality planning, to help make effective use of such planning.

5. *Temporary quality planning.* In urgent situations, when not prescribed in the quality plan, temporarily provide Production Operations with inspection, test, and process-control criteria, procedures, measurements, and so on.

6. *Quality troubleshooting.* Provide advice, counsel, and assistance in the understanding and solution of quality problems in manufacturing.

7. *Contribute to reducing quality cost, including manufacturing losses.* Seek out and demonstrate ways for reducing quality costs, including manufacturing losses. Work closely with Quality Engineering, Manufacturing, and Production Operations in effecting such improvements.

8. *Product special testing.* Conduct, or arrange for, special tests as an aid to Engineering and other organization components for product development, product specification development, and new processes and equipment development.

9. *Laboratory tests, measurements, and analyses.* Make, or arrange for, laboratory tests, measurements, and analyses of materials, processes, and products for process- and product-quality control. Provide special tests and measurements as required.

10. *Material and product disposition.* Investigate nonconforming materials, components, and products for causes. Work closely with Engineering, Manufacturing Engineering, Materials, and Production Operations for prompt and economic use or disposition and correction of the cause for nonconformance.

11. *Customer contacts.* Work closely with Marketing in maintaining contact with the customer's inspection or quality-control representative as to current quality problems. Interpret standards, specifications, quality requirement, and quality planning for in-plant customer inspection.

12. *Analyze rejected and returned product.* Analyze products returned because of

customer complaints to determine the cause of complaint. Advise and counsel appropriate organization components for corrective action.

13. *Service and repair shops contacts.* Consult with, and offer advice to, Service and Repair Shops on evaluating returned product quality. Also assist in evaluating the quality of the repaired product.

14. *Intercompany quality responsibility.* Investigate differences in interpretation of quality criteria between companies in a supplier-customer relationship. Promote quality understanding and acceptance practices that result in increased use of company-built components and products. Work closely with Purchasing, Ordering, or Production Control as required.

15. *Quality of manufacturing equipment.* Assure that all purchased equipment, tools, dies, and fixtures meet quality capability specifications by interpreting results of capability studies and requirements of the quality plan.

16. *Vendor contacts.* Work closely with Purchasing in maintaining contact with the vendor's quality-control representative as to the vendor's quality performance and interpreting the standards, specifications, requirements, and objectives of the quality plan. Serve as direct contact with in-plant vendor inspection. Refer chronic problems to Quality Engineering with recommendations for solution.

17. *Determine process and equipment quality capability.* Perform quality-capability studies of processes and manufacturing equipments, tools, and dies to assist in the solution of manufacturing quality problems and to provide quality information to be used in improving the quality plan.

18. *Record quality data.* Record quality measurements and maintain quality records as required by the quality plan.

19. *Foster quality awareness.* Aid in fostering quality-mindedness throughout Manufacturing and in suppliers of purchased materials.

20. *Maintenance of quality-control equipment.* Provide for standardization, calibration, and maintenance for process instrumentation, process-control and test equipment, laboratory equipment, inspection equipment, meters, and gages.

21. *Improve metrology, nondestructive evaluation, and measuring techniques.* Recommend to Quality Engineering and Quality Information Equipment Engineering improvements in measuring techniques.

22. *Operational safety.* Provide safety rules and practices for use in the design, operation, and maintenance of quality information test and inspection equipment. Inspect designs and resulting quality information equipment for safety. Establish and maintain safe working conditions, equipment, and procedures for all such equipment used in the component. Advise managers as to safety training needs and provide for the safety training of users of quality information equipment.

Inspection and Test Work Activities

1. *Operational planning and scheduling.* Plan inspecting and testing work load, in accordance with overall schedules and available facilities, to meet production requirements.

2. *Receiving inspection and test.* Perform specific inspection and test operations to

*Work activities which normally are not delegated to other functional components.

confirm that only materials meeting established specifications are accepted. Make use of vendor contacts, process analysis, other laboratory data, and application of incoming-material certification plans.

3. *In-process inspection and test.* Perform specific inspection and test operations to confirm that parts in process meet established specifications.
4. **Final inspection and test.* Perform specific inspection and test operations to confirm that only finished products meeting established specifications are shipped. Assure that all products furnished to customers conform to engineering specifications and the quality plan, making use of information from in-process controls, inspection, performance testing, quality auditing, and customer contacts.
5. **Quality auditing.* Perform quality audits as required.
6. **Quality-records maintenance.* Maintain accurate up-to-date inspection and test records as prescribed by the quality plan to indicate quality trends and need for corrective action.
7. **Training personnel.* Ensure that inspection and test personnel are trained in job requirements.

Comments on Process-Control Engineering

With today's manufacturing practices, an advantage is gained by having a technically competent engineer on the manufacturing floor to handle the day-to-day quality problems as they arise and to implement the quality plan. Process-Control Engineering fulfills this responsibility. Such an arrangement relieves the quality engineer of short-range quality problems so the engineer can accomplish the function of quality planning. It provides specialized technical assistance on matters of quality in the shop, thus permitting routine in-process inspection and test work to be assigned to Production Operations. Final inspection and testing and receiving inspection and testing are normally assigned to the process-control-engineering component.

General Comments on Work Activities

Elements denoted by asterisks are normally retained in the quality-control component. Under certain circumstances, the unmarked elements may be delegated to other components in the business.

*Work activities which normally are not delegated to other functional components.

---

1. Are all the work activities (as shown in Fig. 8.6) of the three subfunctions to be placed in a central quality-control component reporting to the Manager-Quality Control? Or should suitable work activities be decentralized and placed in other components in the company? As one example of such decentralization, should some routine inspection and test work be assigned to the superintendent in charge of production?

   These questions are discussed in Section 8.15.

2. When the decisions have been made as to how centralized the quality-control component is to be, another series of questions follows. How is the work assigned to the quality-control component to be structured in detail? For example, should there be one or more quality-engineering components reporting to the Manager–Quality Control? Should there be more than one process-control-engineering group? Is the quality-information-equipment-engineering activity of a sufficient magnitude to warrant a separate component, or should it be combined with quality engineering in a single component?

Perhaps the most typical question is whether inspection and testing should be broken out of process-control engineering to form a separate component reporting to the Manager–Quality Control. In turn, should there be more than one inspection component or more than one test component?

These questions are discussed in Section 8.16.

3. When determinations have been made concerning centralization or decentralization of quality work activities to the quality function—or to other components of the company—and after structuring has been considered for the work assigned to the quality function, a further area of consideration can be made. This is centralization or decentralization—within the quality function itself—into a quality-"assurance" component and a quality-"control" component. Section 8.17 discusses these questions.

8.15 Should the Quality-Control Function Be Centralized or Decentralized?

Figure 8.7 illustrates those work activities of quality control which, industrial experience indicates, can be considered "fixed" within the quality-control component and those activities which are "variable" and may be suitable for decentralization to other organizational functions in the company. Note from the chart that the work elements appropriate for decentralization are primarily found in the process-control-engineering component and include in-process inspection and testing activities.

Inspection and Test Reporting to Production Operations

In companies with a well-established quality-control organization of proved effectiveness, certain advantages may be obtained by assigning the routine in-process test and inspection elements of process-control engineering to production operations and components. Certain criteria must be observed to make this decentralization effective. Typical of these criteria are the following:

1. That a suitable written quality plan must be prepared by Quality Engineering and vigorously followed by Production Operations

FIXED AND VARIABLE WORK ELEMENTS

	Quality Engineering	Quality Information Equipment Engineering	Process Control Engineering
• FIXED (Always retained within subfunction)	• Quality objectives. • Pre-production quality definition, including reliability, safety, and related quality characteristics. • Prescribe quality-control plan: where when, who, how, and how much to inspect and test, for example. • Quality-cost analysis. • Quality-control training. • Quality information feedback. • Diagnosis of quality problems.	• Design and provide quality information equipment. • Mechanization and automation of quality-measuring equipment. • Measurement development.	• Interpret and implement quality-control plan. • Quality audit. • Process-capability studies. • Maintenance of quality-control equipment. • Receiving inspection and test. • Final inspection and test.
• VARIABLE (May decentralize to production Operations)			• In-process inspection and test. • Data recording. • Operational planning.

FIG. 8.7

2. That a process-control-engineering function must exist within the quality-control component to provide competent technical support to Production Operations for help in solving day-to-day quality problems

3. That Process-Control Engineering must conduct a continuous audit on product quality being shipped.

4. That Process-Control Engineering must conduct a continuous audit on the degree to which the planned quality procedures are being followed
5. That quality information equipment must be maintained on a planned schedule to assure accuracy and precision of measurements
6. That inspectors and testers must be trained to have the capability required to perform the work to which they are respectively assigned and that this training be kept up-to-date
7. That there must be a clear and continuous understanding of the primary responsibilities for accomplishing each portion of quality work on the part of each organizational component in the company and the continuous fostering of the quality-mindedness which encourages high-quality work

A relationships chart proves quite useful in establishing this primary responsibility for each organizational component. A segment of a typical chart is shown in Figure 8.8.

Figure 8.9 shows an organization where all the variable elements of routine inspection and testing have been decentralized from Quality Control and assigned to Production Operations.

RELATIONSHIP CHART
(Applied to Product Quality)

Code: (R) = Responsible
C = Must contribute
M = May contribute
I = Is informed

Areas of Responsibility	General Manager	Finance	Marketing	Engineering	Manager- Manufacturing Manufacturing Engineering	Quality Control	Materials	Production Operations
Analyze quality costs	M					(R)		
In-process quality measurements						C		(R)
In-process quality audit				C		C	(R)	
Final product inspection			C	C	M	C	(R)	

FIG. 8.8

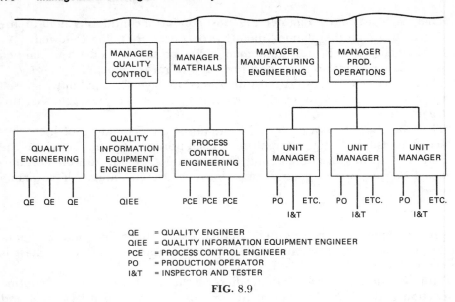

FIG. 8.9

The Closed Feedback Loop in Quality-Control Organization[5]

Note from Figure 8.7 that the major part of the work activities can tend to be in the fixed category because the quality-control function itself is primarily a planning and control, or "feedforward" and "feedback," function in which "too much division" changes the basic purpose of the function. The continuous feedback cycle of quality-control activities are as follows:

First, *quality planning* is done by Quality Engineering; this provides much of ongoing planning and control detail within the basic framework of the quality system for the company's products. Included also is planning for the quality-measurement equipment, which is performed by Quality Information Equipment Engineering.

Second, *quality appraising* is performed by Process-Control Engineering (also including inspection and testing). It evaluates, in accordance with the quality plan, the conformance and performance of the parts and products with engineering specifications.

Third, there is rapid feedback by Process-Control Engineering for *quality analysis*, which results in new planning, thus completing the cycle (Fig. 8.10). This analysis also fosters corrective action for product-quality deviations.

Within this structure, the fixed portions of quality-control work provide for clear-cut responsibility. Through the structure, the Manager–Quality Control is able to make a direct contribution to product quality in the company by having full accountability for two basic responsibilities of assuring the right quality at the right quality cost.

Of at least equal importance, as discussed earlier in the chapter, there is clear

THE FEEDBACK CYCLE IN QUALITY CONTROL

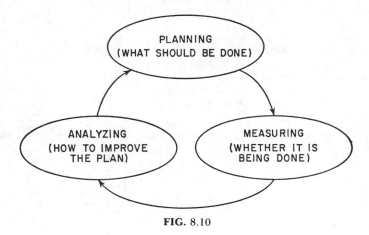

FIG. 8.10

and full accountability on the part of all other company functions for their basic quality responsibilities. The managers and superintendents in Production Operations, for example, have the clear responsibility for producing in accordance with the specifications and the quality system and for performing the "variable" work activities of their own in-process measurements.

But now let us see what happens to these direct responsibilities for the feedback cycle if some of the fixed work portions are removed from the quality-control function.

Figure 8.11 is as an example. Here all the fixed activities of quality-engineering work remain with the quality-control function. But a part of the fixed portions of process-control-engineering work is removed from the quality-control function and assigned to the superintendents of Production Operations. Also assigned to the superintendents is the in-process inspection and test function.

Single, clear-cut responsibility for the feedback cycle no longer resides with the quality-control function. Because of the elimination of the fixed elements of process-control-engineering work, the fundamental character of the quality-control component has been changed.

It instead becomes a loosely knit activity which carries on only certain portions of quality-control work; the feedback cycle itself can come together only at organizational levels above that of the quality-control function. In fact, however, it is unlikely that this feedback cycle will be brought back together at these upper management levels because of the many other responsibilities that exist there.

For such divisionalization of what here have been called fixed work activities in fact distorts the basic purpose of quality-control organization, as discussed in Section 8.10. Top management no longer has, in its quality-control func-

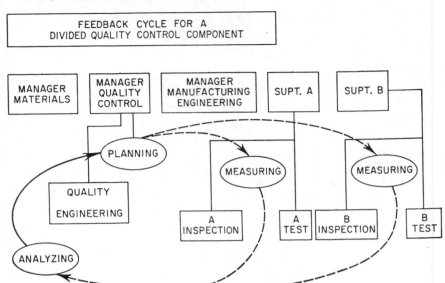

FIG. 8.11

tion, a device whereby it delegates authority and responsibility for product quality, thus relieving itself of unnecessary detail and permitting the benefits of specialization while retaining for itself the means for assuring that quality results will be satisfactory for top management's standards and policies. In substance, top management has no such device.

Lack of understanding of this basic feedback and planning-and-control nature of the quality-control function has perhaps been the primary reason for the large number of failures in quality-control organization that have taken place throughout industry. There may be full agreement about the work as summarized in Figures 8.5 and 8.6, but a company may nonetheless assume —wrongly—that the contribution of its quality-control function can be adequate so long as all these work elements are assigned "somewhere" rather than on an organized, fixed and variable structure discussed here.

This philosophy assumes that quality-control organization is merely the bits-and-pieces sum of its individual quality-engineering, process-control-engineering, and quality information equipment engineering activities. It assumes that, so long as strong individual responsibilities have been established for each of these activities and each is located somewhere in the larger organization, then a strong quality-control contribution will necessarily result, regardless of the assignment of responsibility.

One way to demonstrate the flaw in this reasoning is to compare the diagram of the quality-control feedback cycle of the organization structure in Figure 8.10 with one for the structure in Figure 8.11. Figure 8.12 reflects the properly

organized structure; Figure 8.11 reflects the improperly organized structure.

Note that Figure 8.12 shows short, direct tie-ins among the three feedback
phases. In contrast, Figure 8.11 shows dashed rather than direct tie-ins and
additional loops and lengths that must be traveled to complete the cycle.
Readers familiar with technical feedback circuits will no doubt suspect from
these diagrams that in Figure 8.11, as compared with Figure 8.12, there is a
tendency to slower response and back-and-forth "hunting"—or "buck passing"—in organizational language. They will suspect that it is inherently a more
difficult loop to organize and probably cannot be made to work entirely effectively. That suspicion is, in fact, confirmed both by organization theory and
organization practice.

Recent experience throughout industry shows that not only is slowness of
action a problem with such back-looping structures but that the resulting
hunting may lead to dissatisfaction with the quality-control organization pattern on the part of all company personnel and to the gradual disappearance
in actual practice of any dashed-line relationship at all. Quality Control, whose
very life blood is the fast, automatic response of the feedback loop to help
company personnel prevent poor quality, will be eliminated as a feedback
function, as a result of the improper structuring of fixed work activities from
the quality-control function. Only some individual bits of quality-engineering,
process-control-engineering, and information equipment work will remain in
the function. Certainly, total-quality-control programs cannot be pursued with
so piecemeal an organization.

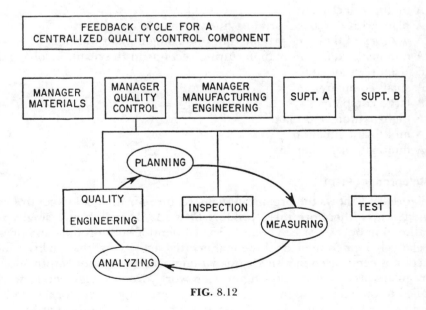

FIG. 8.12

8.16 How Should the Quality-Control Component Be Structured?

After deciding what quality-control work is to be decentralized to other organizational components, the next task is the internal structuring of the quality-control function itself. There are many alternatives for structuring the quality-control component, depending upon the particular situations faced by a company. A few of the alternate ways of structuring the quality-control function are discussed in this section. When such alternatives are being chosen, certain criteria need first to be considered. A few of the more important of these criteria are the following:

1. Keep "layers" of supervision to a minimum so lines of communication can be kept as short as possible.
2. Keep "spans" of supervision as broad as possible. (This follows if "layers" are to be kept to a minimum.) The "span" is the number of persons reporting directly to a supervisor or manager. The lower in the organization one goes, the greater the spans should become, because the work of the reporting positions usually becomes more uniform in nature.
3. Place similar portions of work into a single work package that can be handled by a person in the position considered.

With these criteria in mind, let us look at some examples of particular situations in which companies have structured their quality-control component best to suit certain situations. The following examples will be considered:

1. A multiproduct plant
2. A plant with one basic product line at a single location
3. A number of different product lines in a single plant location
4. A number of different manufacturing sections in the plant, involving specialized technologies
5. A small company
6. A large company
7. A highly automated plant
8. A multiplant situation
9. A multinational company

A Multiproduct Plant

Figure 8.13 shows the organizational structure for the quality-control component where there are three product lines (A, B, and C) at a single plant location of moderate size. The technical content of both product and process is relatively limited; hence all the engineering activity for the quality-control function is centralized in a single quality-engineering component. In addition to regularly assigned quality-engineering work, process-engineering work is applied to the respective product lines as required. Quality information engineering work is also done by this same component as the need arises.

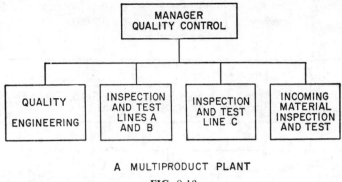

A MULTIPRODUCT PLANT

FIG. 8.13

Inspection and testing are decentralized, according to product line. One inspection and test component serves lines A and B, which are assembly operations of similar products. Another inspection and test component serves line C, a fabrication line. The incoming-material inspection and test component checks purchased materials and product components for all lines.

One Basic Product Line—Single Plant Location

Figure 8.14 shows a situation in which a single product is being manufactured at a single plant location. At first one might think this is even simpler than the previous example. In this particular case, however, the manufacturing operation consists of a number of closely integrated processes, each involving its specialized technologies. The size of the operation is such that it is difficult to justify assigning a single quality-engineer to each process section. Consequently there is one quality-engineering component which does the quality planning for all the processes. The total process-control-engineering demand is high; however, the load varies considerably from process to process depending upon where current quality problems arise. Hence, a single process-control-engineering component serves all processes as the needs arise. A quality-control information equipment component serves the entire plant.

Each process is assigned its separate inspection and test component since the type of inspection and/or test is highly specialized with respect to each of the processes.

A Number of Different Product Lines

The quality-control organization shown in Figure 8.15 is for a single plant location of moderately large size that has a number of different product lines. The technical content of each product line is comparatively high with respect to the process. As a result, process-control engineering is decentralized by product line. Inspection and test activities are included within the process-control-engineering components in this particular plant. In one case, lines B

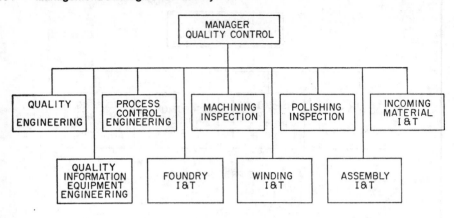

ONE BASIC PRODUCT LINE–SINGLE LOCATION
FIG. 8.14

and C are combined to occupy fully one person's time with respect to process-control work. Line responsibility has also been combined (A with D and B with C) to round out the various quality-engineering assignments. One quality information equipment component serves all product lines since the work is similar regardless of the type of product line being served. One or more engineers are employed in this component, depending upon the work load.

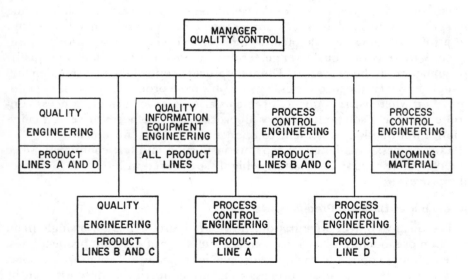

A NUMBER OF DIFFERENT PRODUCT LINES
FIG. 8.15

Manufacturing Involving Specialized Technologies

Figure 8.16 shows a quality-control organization for a large heavy-apparatus company. Although the plant is in a single location, each component is manufactured in its respective building. Some buildings are separated by as much as a mile. The process technologies differ considerably. For example, the insulator section requires a chemical engineer or ceramics engineer to fill the process-control-engineering position. Tanks involve steel plate fabrication, welding, and painting; cores involve coil winding, treating, and baking; and laminations involve metal stamping and enameling. As a consequence, a process-control engineer is located in each of the manufacturing buildings to provide the required specialized technical backup for shop operations. In contrast, Quality Engineering is organized along functional lines. Quality planning for the entire plant is centralized in one component. Statistical analysis is performed by another component. Incoming material and quality information equipment engineering are covered by a third component.

A Small Company

Another dominant influence upon quality-control organization is the physical size of the plant in number of products, number of processes, number of operators, and square feet of floor space. Figure 8.17 shows a small quality-control component where three functions, quality-control management, quality engineering, and quality information equipment engineering, are combined

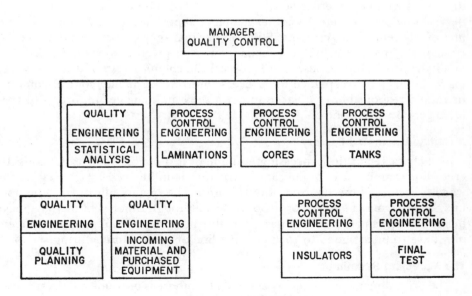

SPECIALIZED TECHNOLOGIES

FIG. 8.16

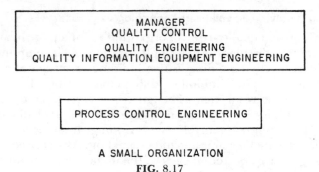

A SMALL ORGANIZATION
FIG. 8.17

into one position. Reporting to this position is a process-control engineer for providing hour-to-hour technical support to shop operations.

A Large Company

In contrast to the small company is the inherent complexity of the large company. The number of highly specialized operations increase, there are often a number of product lines, and the degree of automation may tend to increase. The very number of positions that must be filled to handle the quality-control function properly in a large company dictates an organization similar to that shown in Fig. 8.18. To keep the span of the Manager–Quality Control within reason, it is necessary to place managers or supervisors over the specialized engineering activities. All the quality-engineering work is supervised by one manager. Another manager supervises quality-control information equipment engineering. Still another manager supervises the process-control-engineering activity. A manager is also given responsibility for the quality-control laboratories, where physical and chemical tests and analyses are made for material acceptance and process control. The quality-control-component field responsibility is placed under a separate manager reporting to the Manager–Quality Control.

A Highly Automated Factory

The character of the processing equipment is a major factor to be considered. For example, the organization structure is influenced by the degree to which a factory is mechanized or automated. The quality information equipment activity may be of major proportions, although other subfunctions may be moderately small. In such a case, a quality information equipment engineer may have to be assigned to each product line or each manufacturing section.

The Multiplant Situation

The preceding pages implicitly assumed that there is only one administrative unit in the plant or company for which the quality-control component must be

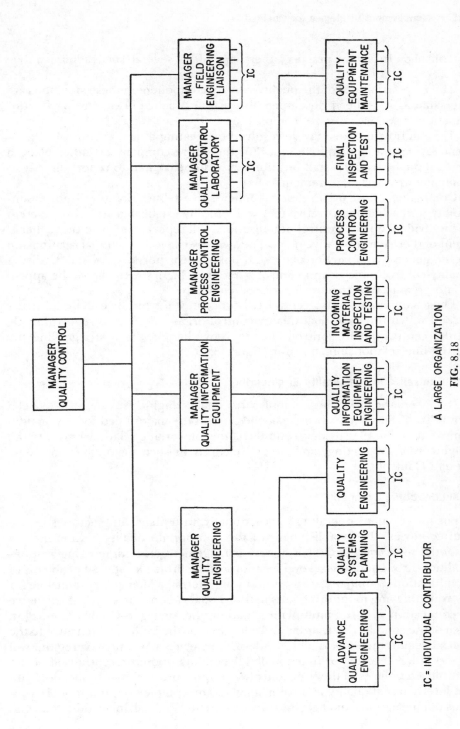

A LARGE ORGANIZATION

FIG. 8.18

IC = INDIVIDUAL CONTRIBUTOR

established. In actual practice, there are often several such administrative units.

The responsibilities of the quality-control component in these situations are the same as have been developed above. But practice in organizing for this situation is somewhat more complex.

The multiplant issue may be resolved by creating a quality-control component for each administrative unit. For the entire company or entire plant, a general quality-control staff position may also be created to report directly to company or plant management.

Companies whose organizational policy is to establish decentralized responsibility for each administrative unit will typically establish a structure wherein the individual quality-control organizations will report directly to the management of their administrative units. They will also have a functional relationship to the general company or plant staff position for purposes of standardizing quality-control policies and control personnel. Figure 8.19 shows the appropriate organization pattern for a large company.

Those companies with a centralized concept, will typically establish a structure in which the individual quality-control organizations will report directly to the central quality-control staff, thereby changing to a straight-line the dotted-line relationship shown in Figure 8.19.

The Centralization of Quality Engineering

Note from the preceding examples that quality engineering has usually been centralized. This occurs principally because of the major need for the quality-control function to provide a central channel of working relationships with the Engineering, Marketing, and other functions in such major areas as New-Design Control.

A Multinational Company

For the company operating internationally, with plants and factories in several countries, the establishment of the appropriate quality organization is essential to provide cohesive quality management and engineering responsibilities throughout the several locations of the firm. The special problems of a multinational company are assisted by appointing a Manager responsible for coordinating and monitoring international quality control. As discussed above in connection with the multiplant situation, the Manager–Quality Control in each of the company's locations and countries, as the individual sensitive to the special requirements of quality work of the particular country or region, will report either directly, or functionally, depending upon the centralized or decentralized policies of the firm, and always with a professional connection with the international quality-control manager. The complex organizational problems of international quality control are discussed in detail in Sections 8.23 and 8.24.

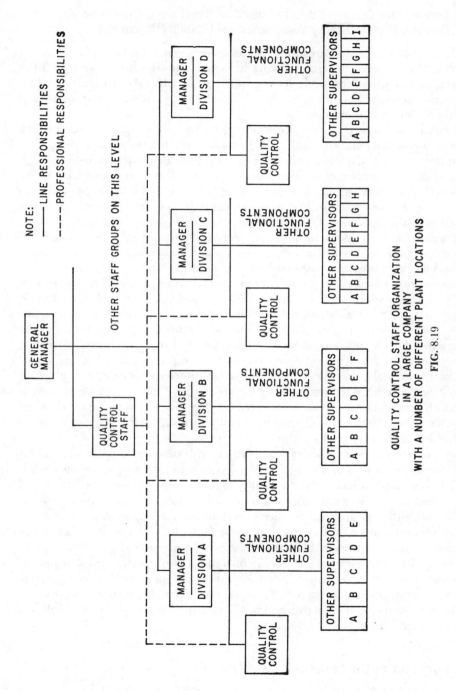

QUALITY CONTROL STAFF ORGANIZATION
IN A LARGE COMPANY
WITH A NUMBER OF DIFFERENT PLANT LOCATIONS

FIG. 8.19

8.17 Should the Quality-Control Function Itself Be Centralized or Decentralized–Quality Assurance and Quality Control?

A further fundamental question in determining centralization or decentralization is the possible division of work activities among more than one functional quality-control component. The question usually takes the form of division between what has come to be called a quality-"assurance" component and a quality-"control" component.[6]

In companies which have decentralized the quality-control function into these two components, the approach has generally been the following:

For the three basic quality-control responsibilities discussed in Section 8.10, as the quality-assurance component has evolved in these companies in recent years, its activities are more likely to be in the business and systems responsibility areas, with some technical responsibilities that include substantial concentration in audit activities. The quality-control component's activities in these companies are more likely to be in the technical responsibility areas—principally inspection and testing activities—with some limited systems responsibilities and a lesser business responsibility concentration.

This division of the quality-control function has thus provided these companies with the opportunity to concentrate the emphasis of and attention to particular areas of quality-control work quite precisely between these components. Because of the differing backgrounds and skills that may be required for these two components—together with the different degree of attraction they correspondingly have for qualified managers, engineers, and technicians—companies may also be able to staff these components more effectively.

However, as compared with an integrated quality-control component which covers all quality control on a unified basis,[7] this division must be established with careful development and must be equally carefully maintained. Two principal reasons for this are as follows:

The first reason is that, unless established with detailed organization planning, the division between two functional components can evolve significant overlap and duplication between quality-assurance-component activities and quality-control-component activities. This can lead to unclear responsibilities, conflict of authority and personalities, and additional expense.

The second reason is illustrated by the fact that the establishment of a separate quality-assurance component has been approached by a few companies as an alternative for directly facing into the achievement of total organizationwide quality involvement. While for quality-control work this may contribute to some upgrading of capabilities from traditional inspection and testing, it will only postpone the establishment of total quality programs and will not be a substitute for it.

8.18 Location of the Function

Where should the quality-control function be placed in the larger structure of company organization? Should it be a part of Marketing, of Engineering, of

Manufacturing? Should it invariably report directly to general management?

While there are no categorical answers to these questions, because of the growing recognition of the importance of high quality to overall business results, the trend increasingly has been for the quality-control function, just as the other main-line company functions, to report directly to general management (Fig. 8.20).

The direct-report approach of one firm may be of interest. In this successful company, business growth has been and continues to be significant. There is considerable emphasis upon the development of new products with high technical content. The business operates and sells worldwide.

The total quality system developed by this company assigns quality responsibility across all the main-line functions, as follows:

The marketing component is responsible for evaluating customer quality preferences and determining the prices these customers are willing to pay for various quality levels.

The engineering component is responsible for translating Marketing's requirements into exact drawings and specifications.

The manufacturing component is responsible for building products to these drawings and for knowing that it has done so.

The quality-control component is responsible for quality leadership in both business strategic planning and the technology of quality control. Because of its vital contributions to business planning and decisions, the quality-control function in this company reports directly to general management.

There is, however, no single organizational rule as to the optimum location of the quality function. Certainly, Quality Control in any company should report high enough so that it can implement its responsibilities for quality assurance at optimum costs. Certainly, also, it should be close enough to the firing line so that it will be able to fulfill its technological role. Because companies vary widely in their objectives, their character, their philosophies of organizational structure, and their technology, the answer to the question of where to locate Quality Control will necessarily vary also.

For an example of a somewhat different organizational form, which in earlier years was employed by some companies, quality control was positioned as integral to the Manufacturing component and the Manager–Quality Control

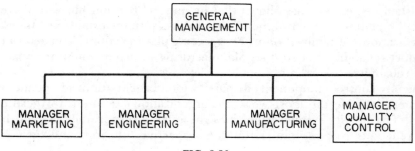

FIG. 8.20

reported directly to the Manager–Manufacturing—at the same organizational level as the Manager–Materials and the Manager–Manufacturing Engineering.

The basic concept in this approach was that each major organizational component should have direct measurements of its own work. Thus, Manufacturing not only must know that it has produced products of specified quality, but it also must be responsible for the costs incident to assuring a specified quality level. However, this concept assumes that quality is primarily a function of manufacturing activity, and today experience demonstrates that it is a function of businesswide activity for most companies.

The particular placement decision must be made by each company, based upon its individual circumstances. The decision for the most effective location of the quality-control function will be based upon (1) a determination of quality responsibilities as they exist in the larger structure of the total company organization and (2) establishing where the quality-control component will make the greatest contribution.

8.19 Organizing for Reliability and Other Product-Quality Parameters

As was noted in Chapter 1, certain product "qualities" are singled out and incorrectly used as the description of the *composite* total quality of the product. One of the more significant of these has been "reliability." Other terms that have more recently come over the horizon are "maintainability" and "serviceability." It is vitally important to recognize that these, while important, are nonetheless individual "qualities" of the product and must be considered together with all the other quality characteristics that make up product quality. To do otherwise creates the danger of excluding important characteristics. Frequently, under the stress of specific quality problems, the temptation arises to organize separately for these individual problems. This makes achieving overall product quality more difficult.

It has been argued that reliability is a very special product quality of overriding importance and, hence, deserves special consideration and emphasis. Some have sought to gain this emphasis by means of special reliability organizations. These organizations have sometimes tended to become large and costly "empires," often duplicating, or in conflict with, other product-quality organizations in the company. When a separate reliability organization is established, experience has shown that its integral relationship with the many other "qualities" of the product often conflicts with the established functional organization. Certainly, Product Engineering plays a major role in determining product reliability, but so does Manufacturing in maintaining, or enhancing, that reliability.

Quality-control components as part of total organizationwide quality management provide the most workable organizational solution to these problems. The quality system establishes the quality responsibilities, and hence the reliability responsibilities, for the respective functions and their corresponding organizational components. It also identifies the "interfaces" among these components and establishes procedures for smooth handling of all quality matters. Total quality control also provides a truly "open-ended" organizational solution, meeting other quality requirements that inevitably will receive emphasis in the future, such as maintainability, serviceability, system effectiveness, and the like. The point is to organize in a comprehensive structure for the purpose of quality on a full "strength-of-the-company" flexible basis.

8.20 What Are Some Problems in Organizing for Quality Control?

It is only to be expected that the critical problems in organizing for total quality control will be matters of human relations. The major difficulty usually faced is the natural resistance by members of the organization to change of any sort.

One example of this resistance is the automatically negative reaction with which some company employees may greet a program like quality control. Such grumbled statements may be made as "We're doing exactly what we did before, except that they call it a quality system now, and that person they have as head of the quality-control organization gets all the credit for our work."

A major cause for attitudes of this sort is that delegation of product-quality responsibilities preceded by many years the creation of the quality-control organizational component. Unless they are convinced otherwise, holders of these responsibilities may fear that the quality-control component will somehow usurp their prerogatives.

A different type of human problem is represented by the initial administrative difficulties that the new quality-control component may face. One functional group may try to pass responsibility to another group. The engineering and marketing groups may rail against lack of interest in quality by the manufacturing group and refuse to cooperate because "It won't do any good unless those manufacturing people become more quality-minded."

Manufacturing may, in its turn, criticize Engineering for lack of realistic quality standards and criticize Inspection for unnecessarily harsh product rejections. Manufacturing Supervision may see reasons for going slow with the introduction of statistical methods. Overzealous proponents of these methods may wish to place a control chart on every factory operation and be sharply critical if this is not done.

After an initial fanfare in introducing the quality program, top management may forget that the quality component is only an extension of itself and give it the lukewarm support which may be the kiss of death to the quality-control program. Marketing and Sales may be extremely polite to the advisory efforts of the component but feel that the quality-control program is really only an internal plant matter.

Some quality-control programs have been well-organized on paper but have failed to meet their objectives because they were improperly introduced to the company. The statement is sometimes made by quality-control personnel in this type of program that their company organization is "not quality-conscious" and that it "isn't going along with the quality-control program." This may be largely an admission by the quality-control leaders that, in introducing their program, they took into proper account only technical and not human factors.[8]

To foster the spirit of quality-mindedness and commitment to quality which is essential to the successful introduction of total-quality-control programs, some companies have considered what is called a Quality Promotion unit. This group, which sometimes reports to the quality-control function, and sometimes directly to management, is responsible for quality education and training, for "watchdogging" quality problems, and for acting as liaison on quality matters between the various company functions.[9]

8.21 What Is a Broad Behavioral Science View of Quality-Control Organization?

In the behavioral science terms of the psychologist and the sociologist, quality-control organization is both (1) *a channel of communication* for product-quality information among all concerned employees and groups; in effect, an information system; and (2) *a means of participation* in the overall company quality-control program by these employees and groups.

The problems of communication that have been generated by the high degree of specialization in the modern industrial organization are well known by management. Inspection may not know what product characteristics Engineering considers really important until production has started and articles are actually in the hands of customers.

Operators may not understand that the close tolerances to which they are working are critical for proper product performance. A complete meeting of minds may never take place between the supervisor and the inspector about what is important on certain machined parts.

Equally well known to management is the need by employees to feel "part of it." Some factory operators and functional specialists feel that "our quality responsibility is so small a portion of the whole that we're not a part of the company quality-control program or important to it."

With proper quality organization, the production supervisor will more readily get the chance to suggest to Engineering certain design changes that would make manufacture easier and more economical. These suggestions will be forthcoming before production has started instead of becoming criticisms afterward. Quality Control will have the opportunity to participate with Manufacturing Engineering in the development of key inspection stations while a manufacturing layout is still on the drafting board.

8.22 What Is the Size of the Quality-Control Component?

Under the total-quality-control approach, the Manager–Quality Control can focus attention upon meeting the company's quality objectives at the lowest quality cost, and the dollars for quality control can be budgeted upon the basis of producing such a result rather than upon the basis of a historical inspection and test ratio. The size of the quality-control component then is balanced by considering what can be accomplished at most economical levels. The collection, analysis, and use of quality costs, discussed in Chapter 7, are means for determining this economic balance.

As a matter of fact, it may be noted from industrial experience that sound total-quality-control organization requires no long-term increase in quality-control expense. Quite the contrary, quality-control expense, as a proportion of total company expense, will be reduced in the long run. Improvements of one-third or more in overall quality costs are not unusual. When the organization of the quality-control component includes, as has been shown in this chapter, technically competent individuals whose efforts can be devoted to preventive quality efforts, inevitably the number of persons in the quality-control organization will be fewer than in earlier, less technical forms of organization.

8.23 The Special Quality Requirements Imposed by Internationalism

For the company whose business interests are international in scope, a new dimension is imposed on quality organization. The growing trend toward internationalism, discussed in Chapter 3, in which products may be designed in one country, materials procured in other countries, and manufacturing operations and markets spread throughout the world, mandates the establishment of viable quality programs *inter-* as well as *intra*nationally.

The specific form of internationalization will itself vary widely among companies. This is because of such differences as company history and organizational philosophy, product mix, marketing strategies, production volumes, policies toward suppliers, and the geographic location of manufacturing facilities. However, there are many common denominators in the work to achieve effective internationalization, and this is coming to represent a significant dimension of quality professional knowledge, skills, and attitudes.

For example, an international quality-control program must take proper account of many vitally important factors throughout the countries that are involved. These include differences in culture; governmental policies and controls on imports and exports; standards; testing practices; levels of technical skill and its concentration in a few areas only, rather than throughout an entire country; the importance—or lack of it—placed upon quality achievement; managerial and leadership approach and philosophy; employee work patterns and motivation; and differences in many other areas of similar importance.

These differences can be very fundamental. For example, the very word "control" can have quite different connotations in different cultures and different languages. A simple translation of the term "quality control" in transferring the program of one country to another country and another language may not at all adequately convey the intended managerial and technical meaning.

An activity as basic as inspection can vary widely in expected work content and objectives. In some regions, inspection work is quite technical, with an illustrious industrial background. In others, inspection is synonomous with policing. And in still others, inspection may signify routine parts stamping. Hence, to be effective, the movement of "inspection planning" from one region to another can require far more than technical changes which account for differences in manufacturing equipment only.

Corrective-action programs, which are fundamental to routine quality operations, can also encounter wide responsibility and authority variations. In some regions, quality control can be expected to take the lead. In others, however, the "controller" is one who measures and records but is far removed from any more-positive action. So, a quality-improvement program that has been established for one country can require basic redevelopment if it is to be applied elsewhere.

Audit programs may range from activity which is well executed by trained people to a concept that is essentially unknown and somewhat suspect. A quality program depending upon audit can therefore encounter basically different reactions in different regions, no matter how precisely it is defined for execution.

One of the most important areas of difference can be in the quality and the quality levels of similar parts and products produced in different geographical regions. The differences can be particularly significant in the international sourcing of a part or product by a company for the purpose of achieving better availability or lower cost than has been possible from the traditional domestic sourcing. The quality and the quality levels of these internationally sourced products may be consistently and surprisingly better than those presently purchased domestically—with a very positive effect on customer satisfaction. Or, after the approval of the first samples, the quality may turn out to be disastrously poorer—eliminating any cost advantage and creating a major availability problem because of defectives rather than solving one. Vendor-source control, therefore, can have an even more significant dimension in quality operations than in domestic ones.

These basic examples, taken together with the many more complex ones that could be added, illustrate the demanding nature of international quality work. They illustrate the importance of an organized approach to the successful internationalizing of quality operations.

8.24 Organizing for International Quality Control

These 10 principles are among the keys to a systematic program for international quality work:

1. International quality operations must be based upon a clear, consistent, uniformly applicable structure of quality activities throughout all regional operations—specifically targeted to meet fully the customer satisfaction and the quality-cost requirements of the company's worldwide business.

    Experience shows that consistency and clarity of control is necessary to assure compatibility of quality, both throughout international customer markets and among regional factories which use parts produced elsewhere. It is also essential to the accomplishment of effective quality planning and to the achievement of useable and meaningful quality information feedback. And it is a fundamental requirement for international communications.

    These international quality systems, to be most effective, build in the basic proven principles of prevention, clear specifications and standards, reliability verification, vendor evaluation, positive employee motivation, process control, product testing, customer-attitude measurement, audit, and other essentials for quality achievement—even though they may not have been effective previously in all the regional quality operations.

2. The specific activities and procedures that implement this structure must be carefully and thoroughly adapted to the particular country and regional operation, consistent with maintenance of the basic quality objectives and standards.

    Without such adaptation, the necessary quality activities may never be fully understood nor accepted. To be effective, they must be absorbed into regular, day-to-day operations in the country or region. Without this, quality control will be something apart.

3. International quality operations should be based upon regional and country strengths.

    Some areas are, for example, outstanding in the quality of their assembly skills, others in employee quality motivation; and still others in technical strengths such as nondestructive evaluation and effective testing practices. The quality operations in these regions should correspondingly be built on these advantages.

4. Authority for quality should be placed directly at the local product source in the country or region, and this should be clearly understood and uniformly practiced.

    The specific responsibility for day-by-day quality achievement in design, purchasing, production, or service must be located wherever in the international operation that the product or part is engineered, manufactured, or serviced. Otherwise, the accountability and the motivation for quality achievement will be very difficult to maintain and measure.

5. Good communications must be recognized as an essential foundation for international quality operations, and they must be carefully established and continuously practiced, rather than be an occasional fireworks display in response to crisis.

   Formalized information-processing networks are a key requirement. However, there is also no substitute for the strong encouragement of periodic, personal, face-to-face intercommunications among key quality personnel throughout the several countries and regions.

6. Training and motivation in the knowledge, skills, and attitudes essential for quality achievement must be programmed and budgeted as ongoing activities throughout all regional and country quality operations.

7. Audit, both of quality results and maintenance of the quality-control structure, must be systematically performed throughout all countries and regions as a management measurement of the adequacy of quality performances.

8. Quality policy and organization structure for international quality operations must be clearly identified and established as an integral part of the complete international organization and management pattern of the company.

   While the particular forms will vary because of different conditions among companies, there are several common characteristics. One is the clear delineation of the international quality policy whose principles will provide quality guidance throughout all countries and regions. A second characteristic is establishment of central company international quality leadership—to lead in structuring the basic international quality system; in audit activities; in motivation and training; in technical and managerial quality innovation; in quality-cost and other measurement; and in similar activities. A third characteristic is establishment of quality management and engineering responsibilities throughout all regions and countries. A fourth characteristic is structuring the relationships that link the quality aspects of the design-purchasing-production-service cycle when each takes place on a geographically separated basis.

9. International quality structure should be developed with the widest possible participation throughout all countries and regions, and ongoing maintenance of the structure should be based upon the continuation of this involvement.

   This provides widespread inputs and constructive considerations throughout all international company operations. Also, of very great importance, it recognizes that each country is a sovereign entity and will have requirements that must be assured.

10. The effectiveness of international quality operations depends upon deep quality commitment in each regional and country operation.

The starting point is, of course, the visible and continuing commitment of management at all levels. The basic objective is the development and maintenance of deep quality commitment—and of the pride that accompanies such commitment—among all employees throughout all countries and regions. The test of such commitment is the degree to which it has become a way of day-to-day life.

Experience shows that application of principles such as these are essential in the establishment of international quality operations which meet what has been called the test of the 6 C's: namely, that these international quality programs be clear, consistent, communicable, cost-effective, encourage cooperation, and provide competitive advantage to the company in its international marketplace.

Notes

[1]Sections 1.10 through 1.14 explored the new role of quality as a major management strategy.

[2]The quality system, including quality economics, was discussed in Chaps. 5 through 7.

[3]The technical aspects of the quality function are considered in detail in Part 4.

[4]Establishment of the formal quality policy of the company is more fully discussed in Sec. 10.4.

[5]Part of Sec 8.15 according to an unpublished paper by J. S. Macdonald.

[6]Chapter 1 made clear that total quality control, as discussed in this book, includes the work involved in what has come to be called quality assurance as well as in the work of quality control.

[7]The organizational designation given this component varies widely, depending upon the circumstances and policies of different companies, and may be titled Quality Control, Quality Assurance, Reliability, Product Assurance, Product Integrity, and several other designations.

[8]The approach to introducing total-quality-control programs is discussed in more detail in Chap. 9.

[9]Ikuro Kusaba, "The Role of the QC Promoting Department," Nagoya Institute of Technology, June 1980.

CHAPTER 9

Achieving Total Commitment to Quality

The quality of products and services results from the quality contributions of many different individuals with many different technical, production, and managerial skills. Central to quality achievement, then, is the enthusiastic participation and support of all these individuals—that is, the *positive commitment to quality* which is fundamental to programs for total quality control.

There are many ways such quality commitment evolves and is achieved, depending upon company history, policies, personalities, resources, and so forth. It must be based upon a strong total quality system and an organizational structure which makes clear the company and management commitment to quality. As discussed in Chapter 8, organizing for quality identifies for *every* employee explicit responsibility for quality as expected job performance—not only for those employees in such visible functions as reliability engineering or quality control—but for *all* individuals in the organization as one of the measureable activities in the consideration of their compensation and promotion.

Achieving genuine and widespread commitment to quality is a process which has many dimensions, and one—it is important to realize—which can never be considered "finished." A perishable strength, subject to continually changing challenges, demands, and unexpected influences from many quarters, quality commitment can usefully be regarded as an ongoing program which is basic to total quality control and total quality systems.

Chapter 9 thus reviews total quality control from the quality-commitment viewpoint of sound human relations, both within the plant and company and as concerns outside suppliers and the public. The growth of the quality profession is also considered.

9.1 The Scope of Quality Commitment

Achieving widespread commitment to quality involves a very broad range of ongoing actions throughout the total quality program activities of the company. It is based upon sound quality policy, careful quality planning, and enlightened quality management. Clear specifications, adequate process equipment, good tooling, careful screening of vendors and suppliers, routine feedback, and evaluation of quality information—all these activities together with many others contribute to the achievement of true quality commitment.

Total quality control and total quality systems may thus involve a wide range of programs to emphasize the assurance of positive quality motivation and strong quality achievement on the part of company personnel in at least three fundamental areas:

The *first* area is their quality *attitudes*. Essential here is the genuine belief by company employees in the importance of good quality, excellent workmanship, well-conceived designs, and service-centered selling.

The *second* area is their quality *knowledge*. Vital in this connection is employee understanding of the kinds of quality problems that bear both upon their individual jobs and the plant in general; appreciation by the employees of the existence of up-to-date methods for solving their specific quality problems; positive acceptance by them of the principles, facts, and practices of modern means for building, maintaining, and controlling quality.

The *third* area is their quality *skills*. Important here are the abilities, both physical and mental, through which plant personnel actually perform the operations essential to quality as they are called for.

The range of such programs can include quality education and training activities of the broadest sort, from planned activities to maximize on-the-job exposure and experience—to formalized classroom situations—to organized employee participation in quality problem solving and troubleshooting.

Sections 9.2 through 9.5 discuss the objective for quality education and the quality-education process. Quality-mindedness as a fundamental to quality commitment is discussed in Section 9.6, and several participative approaches to quality are reviewed in Section 9.7.

9.2 The Role of Quality Education

Among the areas fundamental to the achievement of quality commitment is that of quality education. The basic management objective for company quality education may, therefore, be readily formulated. This objective may be stated as

> *The development for company personnel—in all functions and at all levels—of those attitudes, that knowledge, and those skills in quality which may contribute to company products at minimum cost consistent with full customer satisfaction.*

Such an objective is not a new one. Long before total-quality-control programs had attracted widespread attention, plant managements were attempting to emphasize quality in the training of new operators, in the courses designed for foremen and supervisors, and in the types of assignments used in the planned rotation of engineers and salespeople.

The objective is one whose achievement can be based only in part upon the use of formalized classroom types of training such as those just cited. Much of the quality learning process—especially in attitudes but to an appreciable extent also in knowledge and skills—takes place very informally and almost imperceptibly during the course of an employee's regular day. Part of it is forced upon the individual during the finger-burning of on-the-job experience; a great deal of it comes about as a result of the daily contacts between worker and boss; part of it results from exposure to fellow workers.

The management quality-education objective is one for which the means of achievement vary widely over periods of time. Quality problems have only one certainty: Their content will be subject to continual change. Hence the solutions to quality problems will be a book to which chapters are constantly being added but for which the final chapter is never written. Quality education never ends for the healthy, aggressive company whose products compete effectively in the fast-moving modern marketplace.

9.3 Quality Education As a Process

Education in the quality problem is a process that, with varying degrees of effectiveness, has been taking place in industry for many years, in many forms, and in many ways. The successful introduction of total quality control and total quality systems thus must begin with the recognition of an *existing* fund of quality attitudes, knowledge, and skills—good or bad, current or hopelessly antiquated—on the part of company personnel. It recognizes that they begin with a regularly functioning, informal learning process which is continually adding to this fund of education. And to the extent that such activities have been in operation, it must take into account the existing formal process of on-the-job, vestibule, orientation, and classroom training activities in job skills as related to quality.

It is interesting to observe that many of the modern quality-education efforts that have proved unsuccessful for companies are those which have paid little or no attention to this principle, that to determine where an individual or a program or a quality-education activity is going, it is first necessary to learn where the individual or program or educational activity has come from, and then to act accordingly. Although much attention was lavished on their content and teaching methodology, the unsuccessful company quality-education activities never really fitted deeply into the company for which they were presumably designed. Some were offered prematurely or were not sufficiently down to earth; others were couched in quality terminology that completely threw overboard the traditional plant designations for rejects, losses, and quality faults;

still others took no advantage at all of the quality-education process that had been going on in the plant for many years; collectively, they never really came to grips with the company and its quality problems as they really existed at the time the educational programs were begun.

Experience seems strongly to indicate, therefore, that the first step in appraising needs for modern total quality education is to analyze carefully the *existing* company quality-education process, determine its characteristics and its strengths and weaknesses, and then build educational planning from there.

9.4 Analysis of the Existing Quality-Education Process

There are three basic questions that must be asked about the existing quality-education process during this analysis:

Question 1: *What are the scope, magnitude, and effectiveness of the company's formalized training for plant personnel in the specific job knowledge and skills that are required for the designing, building, and maintenance of good quality?*

Even if a company has an officially designated training staff which carries on all formal training activity and which may have ready well-organized answers to this question, it is important to go much deeper than the analysis that would be provided through this type of evaluation by these training men and women whose horizon is almost necessarily highly specialized. It is necessary to go to the grass roots of this training effort to see and analyze the emphasis placed by the technical training school upon relative types of quality knowledge and skills; the amount of time actually spent in the vestibule room in teaching new operators job skills relating to quality; the reaction of supervisors to the caliber of the knowledge and skills gained by employees in such training; the reality, as compared with the company's current quality problems, of the inspection-training manual used in the plant; the degree to which development and design engineers come to be acquainted with the realities of modern requirements for product reliability and the analytical techniques for dealing with these requirements as well as with modern design techniques for quality.

If the company has no formal training staff, it may be necessary to dig deeply even to establish just what formal training efforts in quality are being carried on by various sections and supervisors. It is vital that such facts be established because a major purpose of the analysis of the current quality-education process is to gain a picture of the total hours—hence total dollars—being expended on formal training for quality, and their effectiveness.

Question 2: *What is the net effect on the quality thinking of company personnel because of the informal, on-the-job, day-by-day influences of experience, contacts, and exposure that are so basic to the process of quality education in a company?*

The single most useful criterion with which to answer this question is the degree of quality-mindedness that exists, section by section, throughout the company. Although not an exact science, quality-mindedness can be sharply and readily appraised quantitatively by those experienced in quality control.

Question 3: *What are the scope, magnitude, and effectiveness of the company's formalized efforts to train plant personnel in the modern concepts of quality and the programs and methods of total quality control?*

Typically, in the early days of installation of a total-quality-control program for a company, the answer to this question was "Almost nothing is being done." It remains, however, a very useful practical question to ask. It is surprising how often material that relates directly to modern quality and its control techniques may turn up in some dark corner of the company's educational process. Years ago someone may have inserted such material in a foreman's training course, in which it has effectively though obscurely since been used. Possibly some supervisors or workers to whom the terms $\overline{X}$, R, or p charts would be a new language have instinctively found how useful it seems to be to chart reject percentages or tally readings on parts from certain machine tools, and these supervisors or workers have educated or are trying to educate those around them in the value of these methods. Such home-grown material, as well as the people who have used and developed it, can be tremendous assets in any formalized quality-control training courses being planned. To use such material, however, requires awareness that it exists.

9.5 Use of Answers to the Questions

Recognizing that the totality of the company's quality-education process is one of the most important influences that must be utilized on behalf of the total quality program, answers to these three questions provide much of the basic material for planning the types and kinds of modernization that must take place to bring this education process up to date.

Action to be taken in the area of question 1—*formalized training in specific job knowledge and skills as related to quality production*—relates to the quality aspects of training all employees—both those with long service as well as new employees. It recognizes the importance of quality orientation in "how to" instruction as an integral part of employee development.

In the area of question 2—*the informal process of quality education*—what is involved in solution to the various problems of developing and maintaining quality-mindedness is another major field for quality-control attention. This subject is discussed in Section 9.6. Section 9.7 reviews several participative quality-mindedness approaches. An example of a quality-mindedness program is given in Section 9.8.

Question 3—*the formal training of personnel in modern quality problems and control techniques*—is an issue of prime interest in programs for total quality control. It is considered in Section 9.9.

9.6 Quality-Mindedness

One of the three objectives is in the matter of attitudes, as noted in Section 9.2, for company education in total quality control.

Quality attitudes of plant personnel historically have been shaped by a broad process of quality education which involves not only formal quality-control courses but, to a much larger extent, many informal quality influences. These influences are the actions and deeds that occur daily in connection with the job and which probably are the most significant factors in molding the attitudes of the individual.

The individual operator in the plant is the key to the production of products of satisfactory quality. In most instances, this individual wants to do a good job; it is important, however, that the correct "climate" is provided for this accomplishment. The operator looks to supervisors and managers to provide the necessary quality system, the tools with the required capability, suitable training for the development of necessary skills, and quality information equipment to measure his or her performance and guide the operation of the process for which he or she is responsible. In the final analysis, it is this person—the individual operator—around whom the quality-system program of the company is designed.

But this program is normally a technological one; it must be supplemented by a human climate which motivates the individual operators to *want* to use the program to produce good quality. This motivation is largely supplied by the actions and deeds of the supervisor. For example, unless *top* management shows continued interest in product quality by deed as well as word, not much will happen in the balance of the organization. Intermediate managers tend to concern themselves with those problems that appear important to top management.

Quality-mindedness for top management must be more than a matter of lip service. The most earth-shaking pronouncement in support of product quality fades into nothingness for shop operators when an order comes down to the factory to ship products of substandard quality to meet a delivery commitment.

Interest in quality has to be genuine and borne out by action, periodic meetings to discuss quality problems, adherence to the quality policy for the company, and balanced interest in behalf of product quality. Unless such interest is evident, lack of support is felt by those who daily seek to attain quality standards. If this support is withheld for long periods, morale begins to suffer and ineffectiveness inevitably results. Resistance to compromising product quality may be lacking when such resistance is most needed.

The functional managers of the business are expected to carry out the policies of top management and at the same time get functional work done according to plan. Unfortunately, things do not always work according to plan, and conflicts arise. For example, a new design may have hit a snag, creating a quality problem. There may be an introductory date that has to be met. Will half measures be used, and a temporary fix used—and not proved—to meet the introductory date? It is at times like these that quality-mindedness is really put to the test and the integrity of the individual put on trial. Certain loyalties develop, to both the organization and the product. At times like these, functional managers can do much to set the tone of quality-mindedness in the plant by their actions in behalf of sound product quality.

One of the key figures in any quality-mindedness campaign is the shop supervisor. This individual represents first-line management, in fact as well as name, to the people who report to the supervisor. If a good employee relations program is in place and working, the supervisor's position as part of management is well-established, as are the lines of communication. The employees look to the supervisor to keep them informed about the company's problems and successes. Thus in a quality-mindedness campaign, the shop supervisor is the spokesperson for the company. Furthermore, the supervisor's actions on behalf of product quality must be backed by intermediate and top managers all the way up the line. If this is done, the supervisor deals from strength and will champion the cause of product quality.

This is the positive situation workers like to see. They take pride in belonging to an organization where the day-to-day actions of supervisors are consistent with the aims of the enterprise. To them, this typifies a strong organization that knows where it is headed. They are challenged as individuals to put their best effort and skill into producing quality products when they know that the best of research work and the best of engineering, manufacturing, and marketing work have been used to provide the customer a product of satisfactory quality.

A number of media can be used in promoting quality-mindedness. These media should be used over a predetermined period—say, 2 to 3 months. Even a modest promotion can effectively use the following devices:

1. Short write-ups in plant paper.
2. Cartoons in plant paper.
3. Poster displays in work area. (These can be of a general nature of showing "Why do it better" or "How to do it better.")
4. Quality slogans.
5. Increased suggestion awards for quality-improvement suggestions.

As noted in Section 8.20, a separate Quality Promotion Unit is sometimes established to assist in promoting quality-mindedness throughout the organization. Whatever the organizational approach selected, it is important to obtain the participation of all personnel. This provides a group appeal. If individual employees have not fully appreciated the value of producing product quality as personally rewarding, they may consider its importance to the group. Thus individuals may feel that the welfare of the group is important to their own welfare. This builds an esprit de corps throughout the organization. Several of the many different approaches to group involvement in quality are reviewed next.

9.7 Participative Approaches to Quality Commitment

As earlier pointed out in Chapter 1, the most underutilized resource of many companies is the knowledge and skill of employees. That this is so has made improved use of the potential of this resource a key company objective—for the benefit of employees and the organization of which they are a part, and certainly for the benefit of the customers of the company's products and services.

Among the many examples of approaches to achieve this objective are factory and office jobs designed to use employees minds as well as hands, production operations established for team manufacturing to permit flexibility and significant employee involvement in selecting the most efficient production procedure to fit situations as they develop, and electronic data processing and other devices which maximize the utilization of employee skill through the automation of routine support tasks.

The underlying principle of such approaches is that work becomes more challenging and interesting for employees as their knowledge and skills are improved and when they are increasingly able to influence decisions affecting their jobs. Also basic to such programs is the recognition that what is good for individual employees is also good for the organization of which they are a part, and the major process and cost improvements documented from such approaches reflect this.

One of the most important of these approaches is specific programs to enhance greatly employee participation in actions for improvement of operations. Many plants and companies have long recognized and emphasized the importance and value of widespread and genuine employee involvement as a basic characteristic of their operating practice. In some companies, "employee roundtables"—many different terms and many different structures have been used by companies for these periodic group sessions among a relatively small number of employees—has for many years been an important factor in plant operations.

Behavioral Science Developments Which Support Employee Participation

The value and significance of such employee participation have been assisted by conceptual and theoretical developments of the social sciences, which have come to identify those patterns of human behavior likely to foster both productive job contributions and human job satisfaction. The eminent industrial sociologist Elton Mayo, working and publishing in the 1930s, was among the pioneers who recognized that if industrial productivity is to be enhanced, many disintegrative social factors involved in twentieth-century industrialization would require far more effective employee involvement in plant actions than had earlier been the case. One consequence of his work was the Hawthorne Experiments, conducted and published in the late 1930s by sociologist F. J. Roethlisberger and W. J. Dickson of the Western Electric

Company, which was one of the early landmarks of the consideration of group participation.

In the 1940s and thereafter, developments in participation and involvement by such pioneering psychologists as Kurt Lewin—in his evaluation of concept of group dynamics—and Douglas McGregor, A. H. Maslow, Rensis Likert, Frederick Herzberg, and many other leading social scientists, created the important area of what has come to be called behavioral science. This led to a number of industrial applications which, in some companies, also had influence on the practical form of "roundtables." A growing number of these applications of behavioral concepts were developed by individuals like Alfred J. Marrow.[1]

These behavioral science developments provide several contributions of successful foundations for fostering employee commitment to quality. For one major example, they make clear one of the very powerful motivational principles of psychology. This principle is that the group of which the individual is a part can be thought of as the "ground" on which she or he stands in an industrial organization, and the individual's actions in the firm are largely influenced by perceptions of what "his" or "her" group is and how the individual may contribute to the group's objectives.

The implications of this are, first, that improvement approaches which are directed to the individual worker—and not also to the group of which the worker is a part—are doomed to be only minimally effective no matter how inspired the techniques. Second, if the worker thinks of "her" or "his" group as being only a small factory work group rather than the full plant team— including the quality organization, engineering, production—then this individual will correspondingly be narrowly oriented to the equally narrow benefit criteria of the group and no amount of "motivational activity" in the traditional sense will change that very much to the mutual benefit, including the plant as a whole. Third, however, if the worker's perception is of being part of the entire plant group, then quality and productivity improvement possibilities become much more significant very quickly.

While most of more widely used forms of employee participation—such as quality circles, quality of working life, and others to be discussed— have been primarily the outgrowth of practical plant and company practice, it is important in total quality control to consider them also with regard to their behavioral science implications.

Principles of Participation

Indeed, a series of 10 principles have emerged from these developments, both in companies and out of behavioral science, which are very important guidelines for the establishment of employee-involvement programs that contribute to quality commitment in total quality control. These principles are:

1. Successful employee-involvement programs require genuine—not superficial—management involvement. Moreover, there must be full under-

standing throughout all levels of management concerning the multifaceted purposes served by the program.

2. Employee contributions and ideas must receive serious consideration—and be placed into operation whenever the recommendations are sound and relevant—for the program to have real value.

3. A principal requirement—and one of the real tests of effective programs—is that they have long-term continuity in contributing to plant and company operations. In contrast, a tendency of some employee-involvement programs—one to be avoided—is to be a short-term activity in which interest and value quickly fade after the initial spotlight is removed.

4. Involvement programs are fully as important for office employees as for factory employees.

5. Program organization must be kept clear and simple. One of the great weaknesses of some involvement programs has been their overorganization, with a superstructure which soon falls of its own weight.

6. As a corollary to 5, successful involvement programs require very careful initial preparation. While participants and leadership may be selected at the beginning of the program, the greatest possible emphasis should subsequently be placed upon voluntary participation with a minimum of program "forcing."

7. Involvement sessions, to be effective, must be purposeful from the point of view of the participants. Sessions that are thought to be a "waste of time" by participants may, in fact, have negative effects. Training in group participation and in analysis and synthesis of problems and their solution is particularly important.

8. The substance of the involvement sessions—as well as the overall program itself—must be kept fresh, relevant to current plant issues, and up to date. As one participant put it ". . . part of our task in these sessions is to be sure we move on to other activities when the present activities have been gotten into for a long enough time. . . ."

9. The leadership of the involvement sessions should be from and oriented to line operations in the plant and company—so as to assure direct operating participation—rather than only from staff.

10. Of the most vital importance, in the achievement of customer quality satisfaction, involvement programs are an important ingredient to, but not a substitute for, the companywide and plantwide total-quality-control program's demanding work in marketing, engineering, production, and service actions—some of which can provide inputs to involvement-program activities and benefit from some of their outputs.

Experience clearly demonstrates that involvement programs will be genuinely meaningful only when they are developed within the plant and company total-quality-control program and established at the time in which they can be effective in that program. Some plants have plunged into premature involvement programs which could not be successful because they simply were not structured to handle the necessary quality actions to be dealt with. As earlier discussed in Section 1.9, without the guidance and the strong decision-making framework of total quality control, individual quality activities, particularly including participation programs, will not realize their promise.

9.8 Participative Approaches to Quality Commitment—Quality Circles, Quality of Working Life (QWL), and Other Key Approaches

Among the key approaches to employee group involvement, three areas in particular will now be discussed:

· Quality circles
· Quality of working life (QWL)
· Other key approaches

Quality Circles

One of the most widespread forms of employee group participation is the *quality circle.* A quality circle is a group of employees—usually from one area of plant and company activity and usually small in number—which meets periodically—often 1 hour per week—for such practical purposes as:

· To pinpoint, examine, and analyze and to solve problems, often of quality but also of productivity, safety, work relations, cost, plant housekeeping, and others
· To enhance the communication between employees and management

One of the unique characteristics of the quality circle, among the several employee-involvement concepts, is the structural emphasis upon the organized solution of relevant plant and company issues and problems. One of the principal factors in quality-circle activity is the training of circle participants in such analysis and synthesis techniques.

The quality-circle group usually includes 8 to 12 employees, whose participation normally is voluntary, with a group leader who may typically be a volunteer or—as is often the case at the startup of the program—one assigned for the purpose. While organization varies widely among plants, each group will also have a coordinator whose role is administration of the quality circle. Each group may also have what has come to be called a "facilitator"—a term from behavioral science. The role of the facilitator includes helping a specific circle get started, training the circle leader as well as circle members in problem-solving techniques, sometimes acting as a technical consultant, and assisting the circle through some difficult periods. Depending upon the plant situation, the position of coordinator and facilitator may sometimes be combined.

Typically, the quality-circle program for a plant will be guided by a steering committee, whose membership—it can be from 5 to 15 people—provides overall cognization and direction of the plant quality-circle program. This steering committee may include plant management personnel, production supervision, employee relations personnel, engineering personnel, marketing personnel, as well as circle leaders and production and office employees. In all cases, the organization of the steering committee must stem from plant management.

This steering committee is the company or plant management mechanism for orientation of the quality-circle program and normally deals with such areas as identifying overall circle objectives, encouraging circle activity, providing plant resources to make circle activity possible, authorizing circle actions as well as establishing policies and guidelines, suggesting areas for suitable circle attention and indicating areas that are not suitable, providing recommendations for how circle leaders and members can most effectively be selecting, developing measures for determining circle effectiveness, and offering other areas of direction.

Within these criteria established and maintained by the steering committee, fullest emphasis is placed upon the quality circle selecting its own targets and for membership to be voluntary when the program enters ongoing operation. During the startup stage—which can be initiated in many parts of the company or plant and for many purposes—front-line supervisors are often identified as the first leaders and certain employees in the factory or office are invited to attend. Later, orientation sessions are held for employees, who are then asked if they wish to participate.

A principal characteristic of quality circles is that they are normally structured to direct their attention to plant and company problems in an organized way. The quality-circle leaders will be trained in techniques for identifying plant issues and problems requiring attention and in how this attention can be directed effectively. This training usually includes the concepts of group participation, creativity and brainstorming, issue identification and problem solving, the development of quality and productivity consciousness, straightforward statistical techniques such as those discussed in Chapter 13, and other areas.

The value of quality circles is far less dependent upon the mechanics of particular forms of organization structuring than upon the effectiveness through which these human motivational, behavioral, statistical, problem-oriented, and other practices are presented and implemented.[2]

The impetus to establish a quality-circle program often comes from the quality-control function of the plant and company because of the contribution that can be made both to quality commitment and quality improvement. The evolution of the program, however, is most effectively implemented through direct leadership by the production function and, depending upon the organization location of the quality circles, by the design engineering, the product service, and, in some cases, the marketing functions. Quality control is a very strong ongoing contributor and participant in the quality-circle program, particularly as to its orientation to the real plant quality and productivity programs and to its encouragement of the continuity of circle activity.

Experience has shown that the longer-term effectiveness of quality circles relates to how closely their ongoing operation continues to be related to the 10 guideline areas discussed in Section 9.7. While all areas are significant, among the areas of particular importance are principle 5—simplicity of organization—where great attention must be given to structuring the circle program in a way that its administration does not become an increasingly complex burden; and principle 9—line leadership—where direction of quality-circle activity only by staff groups are likely to limit their scope.

Principle 1 is another area of vital importance. In one plant, for example, an industrial engineering supervisor observed about the problem-solving value of quality circles that ". . . one of my industrial engineers could do more about that methods problem in one full day than the circle has done in four months. . . ." His observation, which reflected a limited understanding of the program, overlooked the several-sided role of quality circles as a communications area as well as one that prepares the way for "selling" the acceptance of the new method when it is implemented. Nonetheless, steering committees—and the circles themselves—must continually assure themselves that the activities of the circle are meaningful in problem-oriented terms and not primarily 1 hour a week of "going through the motions."

Perhaps the greatest vulnerability of quality circles has been in principle 10. Quality-circle programs have been approached in some plants as the activity which must carry the principal quality-improvement leadership in the plant quality program—and to proceed "on their own" in doing so. This is sometimes because participation programs are highly visible initially and—at least during the "honeymoon" of their beginnings—they can seem to be a way for a plant to be taking some steps in quality, but nonetheless avoid facing into deep quality changes that must be made in engineering designs, production facilities, service practices, sales claims, or, indeed, in management quality standards. Only when quality circles have been seriously integrated within the companywide total-quality-control framework can their effectiveness be suitably strong over the long term.

Quality of Working Life (QWL)

For many years, several different forms of programs have brought together employees with supervisors and managers so that all can consider improved ways and means to deal with improvements of the overall *quality of working life* (QWL). One of the earliest of these programs was initiated by Joseph Scanlon, a major trade union official and later a lecturer at the Massachusetts Institute of Technology, in what has come to be known as the Scanlon Plan.

One of the more recent and widely recognized forms of program has itself come to be described as the quality of working life and is based upon the principle that a commitment to quality results most naturally where workers are closely involved in the decisions which directly affect their work.[3]

QWL activities in different companies have taken many different forms: workers may be called upon to help design their own assembly lines or work stations; production teams may be responsible for selecting and training new team members without direct management supervision; they may assume other traditional management responsibilities, such as forecasting material and work force requirements, and may even evaluate their own performance.

Some companies with QWL programs routinely provide workers with the sort of information once considered the "business" of only management and stockholders, such as strategic goals and productivity indices. Still other companies encourage and fund advanced education for employees, both in-plant and in nearby colleges and universities; some companies have instituted policies for promoting largely from within their ranks. Whatever the specific activities, the QWL approach assumes the perspective of the individual worker as regards his or her skills, potential and feelings about the job, and promotes meaningful recognition for the worker as an individual.

Other Key Approaches

The achievement of quality-mindedness and quality commitment is dependent upon the genuine enthusiasm and widespread contribution of employees throughout the plant and company in the planned activities for total quality control. There has been a wide variety of different participative programs and approaches to achieve a spirit of quality-mindedness in plants and companies in addition to quality circles and QWL. Among the motivational programs which have received major attention are Employee Quality Councils, the Zero Defects approach, Employee Suggestion Programs, Management by Objectives, Quality Goal Setting, as well as a whole spectrum of job-enrichment efforts known by various titles: "work reform," "work restructuring," "sociotechnical systems," and others. These programs, together with many additional forms, have been effective in certain situations for certain companies.

Participative approaches to the fostering of quality commitment in many plants and companies have proved their value over the years. The key to effectiveness has been the selection of that participative approach and that program of employee involvement which most genuinely meets the needs and conditions of the specific company—there is otherwise no one "best" solution to achieving quality-mindedness.

Indeed, one of the basic tasks in the establishment of genuine plantwide total commitment to quality is the tailoring of the particular program for such employee involvement which fits the plant and company, carefully avoiding an activity lifted bodily from another plant and company just because it is quickly available and quickly packaged.

The plant and company employee relations function plays a major role today in this creation and maintenance of these activities in the plant total-quality-control program so that they be sound and effective—not superficial and transitory.

The establishment by a company of that particular quality-improvement program which evolves from its own requirements and history can be especially effective in many cases. One such example[4]—in this instance a program focused upon individual production teams—is termed a "Quality Visibility Program." This particular program is one which brought together the elements for quality commitment in this particular company.

In the Quality Visibility Program, a major aircraft manufacturer placed responsibility for quality on small groups working together as teams to produce a specific assembly from start to finish. This team approach extended even to the members of each manufacturing unit sharing the same vacation schedule.

Each team's performance (usually stated as number of defects per hour) was plotted graphically on a wall chart prominently displayed in a central Quality Visibility Center. Also plotted were improvement goals established by Manufacturing. (A replica of each chart was also displayed at individual stations on the plant floor.) The charts were coded to clearly delineate above-standard as well as substandard performance.

The Visibility Center provided an established meeting ground for a supervisor and crew to "hash out" production problems. Here, the individual group could call on Engineering, Incoming Material, Inspection, Tooling, or any other relevant company function for help in quality improvement. The Center was also used for weekly meetings of supervisors and management; when a problem had been noted, the responsible supervisor outlined the specific corrective action planned and named a date by which the improvements would become effective. The results, in turn, would show up on the team's performance chart.

At work for this company, then, were the psychological effects of progress made visible to each worker's peers, together with a spirit of competition between crews to show a good quality record.

9.9 Formalized Training in Quality Control

Members of the teaching profession who have studied the learning process of groups and individuals at all levels of the modern company have repeatedly told us of their unanimous conclusion: Adult men and women in industry will learn and retain only those things which they think they need to know, which they genuinely believe will help them in their work, which they think will most likely help them to solve the problems which daily plague them, and which, in effect, they really want to learn.

It follows from this, and experience in quality education certainly confirms it, that the most effective quality-control training courses are those which are quality-problem-centered rather than quality-theory-centered; those whose course content is built around specific assistance in helping men and women do their quality job better; those whose objective is the dissemination of principles and practices for solving basic, down-to-earth quality issues rather than the dissemination of broad, general theories for quality discussion only.

The *first* and most universal principle in building a quality-control training program, therefore, is the following:

Principle 1: Keep it down to earth and centered upon real company quality problems. Concentrate upon practical, meaningful quality material and case studies.

Several other principles have simmered out of recent industrial experience and may be readily cited:

Principle 2: In developing quality-control training programs, the quality engineer and training staff should work and consult with the line organization to the fullest extent possible, especially in regard to the scope and kinds of material to be used in the programs. After all, the line organization must do the bulk of quality problem solving for the company and, from a marketing point of view, represents with its employees the customer for quality-control training. Line people should, therefore, be encouraged to feel that course work is being carried on by Quality Engineering as an assistance to the line rather than as a substitute for it.

Principle 3: The quality-control training programs should be based upon recognition that the solutions to industrial problems—therefore, the solutions to quality problems—are always changing; consequently, education in quality-control methods and techniques can never be considered as completed, including education for the educators themselves. It follows that participants in the quality-control courses should be strongly encouraged to continue their education on a self-training basis after completion of the formal course, through whatever means are most appropriate for this purpose. It also follows that formal quality-control training courses should have definite, organized provisions for periodic, brief refresher courses for plant personnel who have completed the basic training courses.

Principle 4: The training programs should, in the long run, include and involve as participants all levels of personnel, from general management to the skilled machinists. Since interests and objectives differ widely among organization levels, individual courses in the quality-control training program should be tailored to fit these several needs; no attempt should be made to force a single quality-control training course to fit such widely different needs as those of the general manager, the quality-control trainee, and the inspection supervisor.

9.10 The Range Covered by Quality-Control Training Programs

In large companies, a long-range program of quality-control training may include any or all of such training activities as the following:

1. A brief and general course for first-line supervision in modern methods of planning and controlling quality, concentrating essentially upon the physical elements affecting product quality.
2. A general orientation discussion for middle- and upper-management levels, portraying total quality control as a management planning and control technique and concentrating upon the financial aspects of quality as well as upon the general outline of the technologies of quality control itself.

3. Orientation training in quality for new company employees. This work may be carried on as a part of regular new-employee plant-orientation activity.
4. A brief, simple, visual presentation of some of the machine and assembly aspects of quality control for skilled workers and assembly operators.[5]
5. A course in the practice of quality-control techniques for inspectors, testers, laboratory personnel, selected supervisors, and others whose daily work requires new and better quality training. Such a course emphasizes engineering, manufacturing, sales, testing, and inspection phases of quality control. It will cover a general and brief review of the technological and statistical methods that may be involved.
6. A course in the technologies and statistical methodology of total quality control for company technical employees—development or design engineers, manufacturing engineers, and so on—whose work in the total-quality-control system makes such training essential.
7. Detailed training courses for persons who are, or may become, full-time members of the quality-control organization or whose work and background make such training desirable. Such courses involve not only detailed discussion of quality engineering and of practical quality techniques and methods but provide a basic knowledge of the statistical methods that may be useful in a total-quality-control program. Concentration will also be in such areas as metrology, nondestructive testing, data handling, computers, advanced instrumentation, auditing, and so forth.

These detailed quality-control training courses will involve some aspects of all three technologies of total quality control: Quality engineering, process-control engineering, and quality information equipment engineering. Of fundamental importance to their effectiveness is that they be consistent among themselves within the company in the point of view they take toward total quality control, and that this point of view also be consistent with the actual operating company quality-control policies and practices. The course should not teach one thing while the company practices another.

The growing complexity of quality methodology has made it difficult for any one individual to be thoroughly competent in every facet of industrial quality-control technology. There is thus a growing need both for specialists and for engineers and managers whose generalized knowledge in many areas will allow them to coordinate and direct the specialists' work. Increasingly, quality-control professionals must devote explicit attention just to keeping abreast of new knowledge in their particular area.

9.11 Alternative Resources for Quality-Control Training Programs

Whether a company is large or small will not influence the content of the training courses to any appreciable extent. For the smaller company not wishing to develop special training material, a number of textbooks about quality control are available. If the number of persons to be trained is limited, some of the groups listed in Section 9.10 may be combined into a single course. For example, executives and engineers could make up one group, with executives attending only the initial indoctrination sessions and the engineers continuing to study the technical and statistical aspects of quality control in the later sessions. Another group could be made up of factory personnel, including operators and inspectors.

For the company that does not wish to undertake its own in-plant training in quality control, a number of universities and colleges offer suitable quality-control courses. Although these institutions may offer quality-control courses as part of the regular curriculum, they present special courses to cater to those regularly engaged in industry. These courses are of two types: The first is an intensive course of 1- to 2-weeks' duration; the second is an evening course given 1 or 2 nights a week over a period of 12 to 15 weeks. Although many of these courses have had a statistical quality-control orientation, others are broader in scope to include consideration of other aspects of total quality control.

A number of other outside sources in quality-control instruction are also available through a variety of professional associations.

9.12 Responsibility for Quality-Control Training

As noted in Section 6.10, quality education and training is a direct and ongoing activity of the company quality system. As such, it must be organized for, with specific responsibility assigned for its various activities.

While overall responsibility for education and training developmental programs is likely to rest with the employee relations and personnel component of the firm, with assistance from the quality function, it will usually involve within the organization a number of other functions whose level of training and education will affect product quality. Suitable leadership for the education activities will thus be drawn from across the full line of the organization as appropriate to the needs of the particular company.

COMMUNICATING QUALITY COMMITMENT

Two major areas requiring direct attention for the establishment of total quality control are (1) the technical complexities involved in establishing the quality program framework and (2) the human, organizational, and timing complexities involved in getting it off the ground. The range of technical approaches is considered in appropriate chapters throughout this book. Sections 9.13 through 9.19 review the psychology of introducing programs for total quality control.

Very important in this work is the related process of communications. The new quality program will have a significant effect on activities throughout the company. It will alter managerial guidelines, and it will call for much tighter integration among human actions and machine and information flow. The clear communication of the very real benefits in and from the new, strong quality program is therefore basic to obtaining the genuine quality commitment of individuals throughout the company.

This total quality communications process may be summarized by seven underlying requirements:

1. A crystal-clear statement that can be understood by all of what is required in and from the total quality program
2. A definite review of how the program will be created and introduced
3. An assurance of the professional competency of those who will do the work
4. An opportunity for all key members of the organization to become involved in the information-gathering portion of the project
5. An opportunity for the key organization people to participate directly in the work as it develops
6. The communication throughout the enterprise of the specifics of the resulting program activity
7. A very concrete statement of the economic and other benefits that are accruing to the organization from the evolution of total quality control

9.13 Motivation for the Development of Total Quality Control and Total Quality Systems

The motivation for proposing the introduction of total quality control may come from a number of different quarters within the organization. It may be initiated by top management, which may have been impressed with the necessity for improved quality-control activity in the company or may have seen success of such a program in other plants. It may be proposed by functional managers such as the head of Manufacturing or Engineering. Quite frequently, total quality development is suggested by relatively young members of the company organization who are technical specialists.

The proposal to initiate total quality control may be made as a sheer defense mechanism in the face of severe pressure on the company, in the form of many field complaints, extremely high manufacturing losses, or bitter internal feelings among plant personnel caused by unresolved quality problems. The initiatory proposal may be made as a suggestion to improve an already-operating series of activities devoted toward the control of quality.

Wherever the total-quality-control proposal is born and under whatever circumstances, it is safe to say that it will not be suitably effective without obtaining a genuine commitment to quality from all parties involved. Thus, the first major task for total quality proponents is a uniform one: A concrete, practical, and attractive approach must be developed for initiating the program and for communicating the ultimate objectives of a quality system for the plant.

At least four general considerations must be taken into account during development of this approach.

Individual Tailoring: An essential requirement is that the company's quality needs should first be carefully reviewed. The quality-control program being introduced should be one with procedures and terminology tailored to the individual plant requirements determined from this review. It should not be a "prepackaged" program lifted bodily from another company or from the literature in the field.

Economic Balance: The scope of the quality-control activities recommended by the program should be based upon sound economic analysis rather than developed without reference to the economics of company quality needs. The scope should be determined by striking a balance between the range of the quality problems in the company and the cost of the minimum amount of control required to face and solve them.[6]

The field of quality costs, as reviewed in Chapter 7, offers many of the tools needed for this analysis. Problems that quality-control components encounter when introducing their proposals in terms of their technical details alone disappear quickly when they show the potentialities in the business language of quality costs.

Participation: The quality-control program will undoubtedly recommend action and cooperation from many functional groups and persons in the plant. The support, involvement, and motivation of these persons and groups are far more likely to be secured if they have participated in formulation of the program.

Emphasis on Benefits: The program should emphasize the tangible benefits that may be derived from quality control and should indicate the measuring sticks that will be regularly used to evaluate the results produced.[7] To the extent that actual applications of individual quality-control projects that have been successfully carried on in the plant can be cited, the salability of the entire program will be much enhanced.

It must be noted, in connection with the development of such a program, that attention should be paid to the circumstances under which the total-quality-control proposal is being initiated. Appreciation of these circumstances should strongly influence the approach planned for introduction of the program.

The program sponsored by top management, for example, will have to point toward the encouragement of spontaneous and genuine approval and participation by the lower-echelon members of the company organization. The program promoted by functional heads will have to overcome the immediate reaction by members of other functions that total quality control represents simply an "empire-building" device on the part of the Quality-Control Manager or the Managing Engineer.

The program which is developed primarily because of high manufacturing losses must guard against restricting its coverage solely to the product-control aspects of total quality control. The program generated by numerous field complaints must exercise caution against concentrating primarily upon special process studies troubleshooting.

9.14 Sequence For Obtaining a Commitment to a Total-Quality-Control Program

Acceptance of the proposed quality-control program by top management, with whatever adaptations and improvements it wishes to make, is an essential without which no further genuinely effective selling can be done in the factory. Quality-control proponents in many plants may properly be called upon to render considerable tangible evidence of the value of the activity before this approval is obtained for their program. The approval may well be tentative, with complete acceptance contingent upon the results from initial quality-control applications.

When the program has been accepted by management, tentatively or otherwise, a sequence of several steps will be followed to bring its proposals into actual operation in the plant. This sequence will develop the program through the stage where widespread tangible evidence of the actual value of quality-control activities will be available to all members of the company organization. It will carry on the program to the ultimate point where an overall, company-wide program of quality is in operation of the sort discussed in this book.

This "sales sequence" includes at least four general steps which are quite fundamental in introducing total quality control under a wide variety of industrial circumstances. These steps are:

1. Introduction by top management to concerned key personnel of the quality-control program and the initial steps for placing it in operation. A report is made of selection of the head of the quality-control component if the assignment has not heretofore been made known.
2. A systematic beginning for the program in the company, with full management support. Analysis and presentation of the company's quality costs, and an evaluation of the opportunities for substantial improvement in them, can be extremely effective in encouraging top-level support for the program.
3. Regular appraisal of tangible results as the program evolves; growth and development of the program and its gradual evolution and integration toward the form of the planned companywide total-quality-control system.
4. Communication of quality objectives and of information on quality-control activities to all company personnel; encouragement of as wide a degree of participation as possible in the program from personnel; establishment of quality-control education and training work.

9.15 Steps in Achieving a Widespread Quality-Control Commitment

Introduction of Program by Top Management: Some degree of resistance among company personnel to a program like total quality control is inevitable unless it is properly presented. This resistance is generally caused by lack of information as to the procedures and objectives of the program.

Before any action is taken for establishing the activities proposed by the basic quality-control program, therefore, it is highly desirable that top management present the essentials of the program to all key people. A presentation of this sort accomplishes several purposes: It provides a means for communicating to key personnel the basis for total quality control; it tangibly demonstrates that the proposed program has genuine top-management support; it furnishes a channel wherein those individuals who have not yet had such an opportunity may participate in an overall review of the proposed activities.

This introduction by management may be carried on quietly and informally if a private meeting is deemed best for company conditions. Or management may wish to encourage widespread enthusiasm in the launching of total quality control by holding a "full-dress" promotional meeting.

The promotional meeting may begin with formal presentation of the program by top management, possibly followed by some device such as a slide film with commentary to review the details of the quality-control activity.

This introductory meeting furnishes an excellent opportunity for announcing the selection of the leadership of the program. Wherever possible and practical, it may be most beneficial that the individual thus selected be someone who is already a member of the company organization, familiar with its quality problems and personally familiar with many of the individuals in the plant.

A Step-By-Step Beginning: In turn, the actual initiation of the new company quality activities is more likely to develop smoothly when it is coordinated systematically. The step-by-step installation of the program may thus be carried on sequentially. In parallel with the ongoing development of the program, attention may also be concentrated, where appropriate, toward handling particularly troublesome quality problems.

Tangible Results: Since growth of the quality-control program will be directly dependent upon the results it produces, it is extremely important that adequate means for reporting these results be established. These reports are made by the Quality-Control Manager to top management and other key personnel periodically, perhaps monthly. The initial reports are made on the first individual steps of the program, and the coverage of the report is expanded as the quality-control activities expand. Great care is exercised in the reports to point out that the quality-control results are a result of the cooperative efforts of several functional groups and individuals rather than the personal successes of the quality-control people.

The measuring sticks used may be drawn from a wide variety of areas, depending upon the situation. Of great importance is the use of quality costs as a key measuring stick. Others are improvements in design and manufacturing process, customer acceptance, enhancement of personnel quality-mindedness, and reductions in overruns.

Many of the important results thus reported will be intangibles. But the most effective of all these results is that which can be measured against the very tangible measuring stick of dollars-and-cents savings. Quality-control reports used during this phase of development may tend, therefore, to give quality-cost savings the most prominent place among all the measuring sticks used.

Communication and Participation: The greatest quality resource of a plant is conscientious workmanship. Essential, therefore, to genuine quality commitment is the development of a real feeling of quality responsibility among all members of the company organization.

Growth of this attitude is fostered by communication of quality objectives to all personnel in the plant. Media that can be used are the plant newspaper; special quality-control publicity releases; meetings with employees to review the quality features of products of the plant; quality cartoons posted on bulletin boards; and presentations before employee-information meetings of skits, discussions, and sound or slide films on quality. Most effective of all means for communicating quality objectives and quality-control activities is the face-to-face relationship between supervisor and employees, whereby the required information is passed along. This chain of communication starts, of course, with top management.

Growth of quality-mindedness is also fostered by encouraging employee participation in actual quality activities: plantwide quality drives with definite objectives, shop quality committees which meet periodically to make and review recommendations for quality improvements—each may be extremely effective. Encouragement at employee-information meetings of two-way discussions between supervisor and employee about the identification and solution of quality problems is also of great importance.

Success of this phase of quality-control development is judged by the extent to which all employees in the company come to recognize the importance of their individual efforts to the design, manufacture, sale, and shipment of a product of acceptable quality.

9.16 The Attitude for Quality Proponents Themselves

Important to the success of the proponents of the quality-control program in carrying through the "development" process discussed above is the basic attitude they bring to the task of introducing total quality control into the plant. It is interesting to note, in this connection, that there is much in common between the attitude of effective quality-control proponents and that of successful sales engineers for industrial products.

When successful, well-trained sales engineers make a call to sell a product to a new and prospective customer, they proceed according to a carefully planned course of action. They may use selling materials such as samples and charts whose value has been carefully tested. They will recognize that they bear the burden of proof and that the prospects will be interested only if they can be shown that sufficient benefit will be gained from the product to justify its purchase.

Sales engineers are able to adapt their sales arguments to meet the interests of their prospects. With the design engineer, they must be able to discuss technical details; with top management, they must be able to talk of the dollars-and-cents benefits to be derived from their product; with manufacturing people, they must be able to talk about the effects upon plant personnel of the installation of the product.

As with industrial sales engineers, two basic sales precepts which quality-control proponents must follow are that

1. They must always concentrate in sales discussions upon the benefits of their product, which is quality control.
2. They must always be able to discuss these quality-control benefits from the individual viewpoint of the "prospect"; in their case, the design engineer, the shop supervisor, the purchasing agent, the inspector, or top management.

While quality-control proponents may themselves be personally impressed, for example, with the logic and clarity of the statistical aspects of the activity, they must not simply assume that everyone else in the plant is similarly impressed. If the organizational aspects of quality control are of interest, this phase must be emphasized in sales discussions and not statistics; if human relations aspects are of interest, this matter must be emphasized.

Again, as with sales engineers, successful quality-control proponents do not blame their failure upon the prospect when they do not make a sale. Instead, they try to analyze that part of their approach which failed to make a satisfactory impression. Perhaps the costs quoted for the program were unduly or unrealistically high; perhaps there was excessive emphasis upon the organizational and administrative aspects of quality control; perhaps there was too little emphasis upon the benefits to be gained from application of quality-control technology. If the fault was in the approach used, the quality-control proponents try to improve their approach; if the fault was in the form of the quality-control program proposed, they will rework the program, if deemed necessary, so that its undesirable features will be eliminated.

Throughout, quality-control proponents lean upon their deep conviction of the benefits to be gained by their company from quality-control applications. They recognize, however, that these benefits will probably never be realized unless they can so present them that they will be joined in their acceptance of and enthusiasm for quality control by the great majority of the plant organization and particularly by top management.

9.17 Introducing Quality Control in the Multiplant Company

Much of the discussion in this chapter has implicitly assumed that the organization to which total quality control is being introduced is a company with a single plant. Quality-control programs must, of course, also be presented under other conditions: in the company which operates many plants at differ-ent geographic locations and in the plant at a single geographic location which includes several semi-independent operating divisions.

The approach used in this multiplant or multidivision situation is, however, similar in principle to that reviewed with reference to the company with a single plant. A quality-control program must be prepared, approval must be obtained from top management, and a step-by-step beginning is highly desirable.

Introducing quality control in the large, multiplant company will naturally call for a great deal of flexibility in the basic quality-control program presented to company top management. This program must be adaptable to meet the different needs of the various plants of the company, and it must be in such a form that will be attractive to the managements of these plants.

As compared with the single plant, quality-control development in the multi-plant company may require a wider degree of initial participation in program development and much more extensive way-paving before applications may be initiated. Since there will be, however, a larger organization to support the associated expense, the multiplant situation may have the advantage that more attention can be devoted to preparation of extensive quality-control materials for use in the early phases of the introduction of the program.

As the quality-control program is being introduced step by step in the operating sections of the multiplant company, it is necessary to develop con-currently a hard core of personnel in each plant who have developed the proper quality attitudes, quality knowledge, and quality skills to support suc-cessfully the quality-control program.

9.18 Communicating Quality Commitment to Vendors

The high quality of suppliers is an important ingredient to the success of total quality control. Therefore, the quality commitment of suppliers is essen-tial. Communicating the total-quality-control program to vendors involves the same basic principles that are used to communicate the program internally; i.e., the vendor must be led to appreciate the benefits to be gained by using total quality control.

A number of companies have published attractive brochures encouraging their suppliers to join with them in specific quality-improvement and quality-control programs. One such company agrees to do certain things for the benefit of the vendor; the vendor, in turn, agrees to do certain things for the supplier. Chapter 19 discusses this in detail.

In general, the purchaser company may agree to do the following:

1. To let the vendor know all the facts in connection with an order, including all the quality requirements
2. To encourage exchange visits to promote understanding and solution of mutual problems
3. To place, whenever possible, facilities of research, development, and tech-

nical service at the disposal of suppliers in helping to solve quality problems and improve quality

4. To plan procurement schedule sufficiently in advance of requirement dates
5. To supply the vendor with a written understanding concerning the quality program to be followed by supplier and purchaser
6. To arrive at an understanding with respect to handling of unsatisfactory material
7. To maintain a consistent cost policy
8. When mistakes are made, to acknowledge them quickly and take corrective action quickly
9. To develop with the supplier the knowledge and conviction that the most important requirement is the quality of the end product.
10. To preserve the dignity of the relationship with the supplier

In turn, the supplier's responsibilities may include

1. To supply materials to specification on schedule
2. To maintain quality-control procedures which assure consistent meeting of specifications
3. To be willing to react quickly on the disposition of unacceptable product
4. To inform the purchaser as far in advance as possible of circumstances affecting cost
5. To maintain efficiency of operation that assures competitive costs
6. To maintain a progressive viewpoint aimed at constant quality improvement
7. To grow with the purchaser's business
8. To service the customer and thereby protect the best interests of the consuming public
9. To promptly bring the attention of the purchaser to any factors which may impair the relationship
10. To look upon the association as a long-term partnership

Along these same lines, a large consumer electronics manufacturer[8] has sought to promote product quality with its suppliers by a vendor-performance-recognition award program.

In summary, the program outlines 13 specific mutual benefits from good purchaser-vendor relationships:

1. Improved quality.
2. Improved reliability.
3. Faster approvals.
4. Fewer rejections.
5. Saving of environmental test time.
6. Better assurance of the vendor's quality.

7. Vendors better informed of what is expected of them and their products.
8. Through reporting of control dimensions, vendor will know where to concentrate inspection.
9. Shipping cost savings.
10. Rework and scrap cost savings.
11. By use of recognized quality-control techniques, vendors have reliable records of their quality.
12. Better vendor-company relations.
13. Better incoming-material quality resulting in better product quality and increased sales—also a vendor benefit.

A number of companies have conducted "vendor clinics," which are organized programs whereby vendors are brought into the host plant in groups to hear presentations by various managers and quality-control personnel with respect to quality policy, quality levels, quality-control procedures, handling of engineering changes, and similar subjects. Opportunity is taken to show the vendors where the part they furnish fits into the final product and why certain requirements are important. Brochures or programs are printed, including a résumé of subjects discussed.

The representative from the vendor establishment should be a person of responsibility. This individual should be in a position high enough in the vendor organization to bring about changes in policy and procedures. The host plant will organize the program in a way that provides full opportunity for discussion among participants.

The size of the groups attending a vendor's clinic may vary from 10 to several thousand persons. This will depend upon what is to be accomplished. If announcement of a new policy is being made, it can be done in a large group. However, if two-way communication is necessary, the smaller group will encourage more response from the vendor or the vendor's representatives.

9.19 Communicating Quality Commitment to Customers

It is an established fact that customers will buy where they receive the greatest value. Some of the values customers look for in products are durability, convenience, reliability, attractiveness, adequate performance—all these are *qualities* of the product. The manufacturer who can provide these desired qualities without exceeding the price for competitive offerings gains product leadership.

If a manufacturer has provided the customer good values and demonstrated a commitment to quality, the company has established a reputation with the customer and can expect the customer's continued patronage. Even beyond that, the customer may become an active booster for the company's products and recommend them to associates, thus demonstrating the customer's own commitment to quality. Any salesperson knows the advantages of being able to sell quality as compared with selling price.

When a manufacturer has established a reputation as a producer of quality products, there is a great deal of advantage in advertising the fact. This is a case where acts must back up words. If they do not, the words can prove to be very embarrassing and very damaging to the manufacturer. Examples can be identified where firms are no longer in business because they could not back their claims for quality products. On the other hand, those companies which have been able to advertise themselves truthfully as producers of quality products have established themselves in a very sound position.

The best product-quality assurance a manufacturer can provide to customers is the operation of a total-quality-control program.

The company with a well-established, effective total-quality-control program in place can emphasize it as an added value for the customer. Well-documented quality-control procedures build confidence and assure customers that great care is used in delivering a quality product to them.

Numbers of procurement agencies, for example, are placing increasing reliance on suppliers having a well-organized quality system in place. Experience has shown that less inspection and fewer rejections have to be made on the part of the procuring agency when the supplier has a sound quality system.

This viewpoint with respect to the quality system is of equal importance to industrial customers. Plant visits can be effectively used to demonstrate to customers just how the company's total quality system operates: how materials are controlled, reliability tests conducted, quality check points operated, and product quality certified.

For example, a midwestern electrical manufacturer had tried unsuccessfully to secure the account of a large appliance manufacturer for his motor requirements. Not until he arranged a thorough visit for the appliance company's purchasing agent and its quality-control manager was he able to establish the favorable climate needed for obtaining the order. A review of the plant convinced the potential customers that the motor concern had an added value to offer its customers in the form of its well-planned quality system.

In effect, the use of product quality as a sales mover is an example of "the art of being good, qualitywise, and getting credit for it."

9.20 Communicating Quality Control Precisely

An important factor in obtaining and maintaining a commitment to quality is the clarity of the communications process used for quality. Concern about the misuse or imprecise use of quality terminology has been expressed not only by quality professionals but by business managers and government and legal sectors. Whether internally in plants and companies or externally to customers and the public, communicating the principles of quality commitment and total quality control will be enhanced when expressed in mutually clear and understandable terms.

A great variation in quality-related terms is perhaps only natural because quality is a concept applied to many different types of products and services, one which embraces a variety of disciplines, ranging from statistical techniques through physical and social sciences. As one example, the terms "defect" and "defective" in the past were often used to describe what actually could be a variety of very different circumstances covering their basic intent to describe units that do not meet requirements. What was termed a defect might have been a relatively minor and almost unnoticeable flaw in a product or service and which had no effect upon performance. On the other hand, it might have been a blemish that rendered the product unacceptable as to appearance. Or the term defect could also describe a serious quality problem which rendered a product or service not suitable for customer use, or even make it hazardous.

It is therefore essential that there be clear categories for units that do not meet requirements. The following example illustrates the confusion that may arise without such clear categories.[9]

Consider the manufacture of 5-centimeter-wide gummed labels. Suppose the operation failed to completely cover the back of the label with gum, leaving a 0.6-centimeter-wide gap in the center area. This might never be noticed by the customer—the label would "work" adequately; it might be of interest to the manufacturer as an indication that something was interrupting the smooth flow of the gum and corrective action was required. Now suppose this same-sized gap were located along the edge of the label, leaving it loose at one end so that the envelope to which it was stuck might jam an automatic sorting unit. This would likely be evaluated more severely in terms of acceptability, both by the manufacturer and the user. If the manufacturing operation of the gummed labels should happen to be performed with a very wide roll of paper that is coated with gummed material and later slit into 5-centimeter rolls before being cut into individual labels, in those instances where the gap coincided with the slitter setting, a defective product would result.

There has been considerable progress in the development of improved terminology in quality control to meet these purposes of precision, including such terms as defect, nonconformity, and blemish. Sections 14.16 and 15.5 discuss this subject of quality-control terminology in more detail.

9.21 Commitment to Quality: Growth of the Quality-Control Profession

Today's quality movement increasingly encourages genuine management-oriented and multifunctional-wide quality understanding, commitment, and support. Traditionally, the early training and formative work experience of many plant managers and operations managers have been in the industrial engineering area. In sharp contrast, as the realization of the importance of the quality area has grown, in a company group that some years ago represented one of the early applications of total quality control, of 21 plants in the group, 19 are now managed by men and women whose early training, formative work assignments, and original professional experience were in quality control. There is little doubt that quality will continue to become an increasingly significant management enterprise.

With product quality a prime motivation for customer purchases, and with quality costs looming as one of the most significant elements of product cost that must be minimized to permit the setting of the right price to the customer, total quality control is one of the most potent new professional work areas in modern business today for improving sales, productivity, and profitability.

The culmination of these developments is that total quality control—the basis for quality-engineering professionalism—is fast assuming its place as the newest of the major technological and managerial areas that make fundamental contributions to those businesses which grow, prosper, and contribute to general economic well-being. Total quality control and total quality management are the future for quality-control professionals and their functions. It is a future that, with proper application of effort, will be a happy and productive one for these individuals and their careers, for the prosperity of their companies and their companies' customers, and for the optimum utilization of resources in the economy as a whole.

9.22 Commitment to Quality: Worldwide Growth Of the Quality Field

There has been a literal explosion in recent years throughout every continent and in many countries of the numbers of men and women practicing quality control in factories and offices in some area of quality—managerial or supervisory, quality engineering, test equipment, inspection planning, and so forth. Some are very highly professional in practice; many others are very rapidly becoming so. The population explosion of the worldwide quality-control community may be summed up in three central points that are vitally important to all men and women in the quality field:

The *first* point is that the practice of quality control is no longer concentrated in a very few countries and among a relatively small number of men and women.

Second, the innovative developments and progress in quality control are correspondingly widely and importantly based throughout many countries of the world.

Third, to practice quality control in a way consistent with the best and most up-to-date methodology, it is becoming increasingly important to keep abreast of quality-control progress and activities on a far more internationally oriented basis than before.

Modern quality professionals therefore owe it to the business development of their companies or plants—as well as to their own career growth—to become increasingly closely acquainted with the international aspects of modern quality control.

In the face of the rapid growth of internationalization, the prospects are that this will greatly deepen and further broaden the contribution that quality professionals can make to the growth and to the business health of companies as they face today's increasingly smaller and more competitive world.

Notes

[1]For a discussion of some of the classic behavioral science works, see for instance F. J. Roethlisberger and W. J. Dickson, *Management and the Worker,* Harvard University Press, Cambridge, Mass., 1939. Also, Douglas McGregor, *The Human Side of Enterprise,* McGraw-Hill Book Company, New York, 1960; A. H. Maslow, *Motivation and Personality,* Harper & Brothers, New York, 1954; Frederick Herzberg et al., *The Motivation to Work,* 2d ed., John Wiley & Sons, Inc., New York, 1959; Rensis Likert, *The Human Organization: Its Management and Value,* McGraw-Hill Book Company New York, 1967; Alfred J. Marrow et al., *Management by Participation,* Harper & Row, Publishers, Incorporated, New York, 1965.

[2]Quality circles have been developed and are in use in many parts of the world. For a summary of experience in the United States, see Frank M. Gryna, Jr., "Quality Circles, A Team Approach to Problem Solving," *AMA Research Study,* American Management Association, New York, 1981. For a discussion of the widespread experience with quality circles in Japan, see particularly Yoshio Kondo, "Human Motivation and Quality Control," *Proceedings of the Joint Conference of the European Organization for Quality Control—International Academy for Quality,* Venice, 1975; "Roles of Manager in QC Circle Movement," *Proceedings, 30th Conference American Society for Quality Control,* Toronto, 1976; "The Smallest Common Denominator or the Largest Common Divisor for Human Motivation," *Proceedings, International Academy for Quality,* Kyoto, Japan, 1978. See also Kaoru Ishikawa, "Quality Control in Japan," published in connection with the International Conference on Quality Control, Tokyo, 1969.

The role of the author of this book in the origination of the quality-circle concept is discussed by Peter F. Drucker, "Learning From Foreign Management," *The Wall Street Journal,* June 4, 1980.

[3]Robert H. Guest, "Quality of Work Life—Learning from Tarrytown," *Harvard Business Review,* July–August 1979. For a report on a research study of QWL, see Paul S. Goodman, "Quality of Work Life Projects in the 1980's," *Proceedings of the 1980 Spring Meeting,* Industrial Relations Research Association, University of Wisconsin, Madison, pp. 487–494.

[4]See Nat Wood, "Quality Visibility at Northrop," *Quality,* vol. X, no. 10, October 1977, pp. 20–22; and Jim Frankovich, "Quality Awareness Through Visibility," *Quality Progress,* vol. XI, no. 2, February 1978, pp. 22–24.

[5]For a discussion of visual training and work standards, see Jay W. Leek, "Benefits from Visual Standards," *Quality Progress,* vol. IX, no. 12, December 1976, pp. 16–18.

[6]Chapter 7 discussed this economic balance.

[7]Key quality measurements were discussed in Sec. 6.14.

[8]Paul J. Breibach, "Vendor Quality Assurance and Reliability," *32nd Annual Technical Conference Transactions,* American Society for Quality Control, Chicago, 1978, pp. 11–20.

[9]Richard A. Freund, "Saying What You Mean To Say," *Quality Progress,* vol. X, no. 2, February 1977, pp. 16–20.

PART FOUR

Engineering Technology of Quality

CHAPTER 10
Quality-Engineering Technology

Real assurance of quality today requires far more than good intentions, testing and inspection activities, and a traditional quality-control department. It takes the same business, managerial, and technical depth to assure the quality and quality cost of a product as it does to design, make, sell, and service the product itself—depth that starts well before production begins and ends only with a satisfied customer.

The total management and organization of quality for basic business, systems, and economic responsibilities, as well as for the important area of proper communications, were considered in previous chapters. Educating and training for total quality control also were discussed. It is important now to gain an understanding of the specialized technical aspects of the modern program for quality control.

The engineering technology of quality is a group of disciplines required at every stage of the industrial cycle. It embraces fundamental operating techniques and approaches which are fully as useful to the machinist and production-line assembler and computer software programmer and laboratory technician as they are to the design engineer, the manufacturing engineer, the shop foreman and the quality engineer. All key men and women in the organization who influence product and service quality must draw upon certain aspects of this body of technology to implement their individual responsibilities for quality.

For the quality function itself, this engineering technology of quality is inherent in its contributions toward making the companywide quality program a reality. It is through application of this technology that the quality function carries out its major responsibility of widespread and vitally important technical contributions to quality control.

Part 4 therefore reviews the engineering technology basic to the modern program for total quality control. This technology has three major disciplines: "Quality-Engineering Technology" (discussed in Chap. 10), "Process-Control-Engineering Technology" (Chap. 11), and "Quality Equipment Engineering Technology" (Chap. 12).

10.1 The Technological Triangle

Figure 10.1 shows the technological triangle, which is a useful structure for relating the engineering technology of quality control to the overall total quality program of companies and plants.

The apex of the triangle provides the caption for the *field:* total quality control. The first tier establishes the structure for total quality control through the quality system. The second tier indicates the technical work areas, or jobs of quality control: new-design control, incoming-material control, product and process control, and special process studies. These technical work areas are underlaid by commitment to quality throughout the plant and company and by quality education and training. The third tier of the triangle identifies the three major disciplines whose application is fundamental to carrying out the technical aspects of the jobs of quality control: Quality-Engineering Technology, Process-Control-Engineering Technology, and Quality Information Equipment Technology.[1]

On the next tier are some of the techniques which can be employed to accomplish these jobs. It is important to point out that any single technique or combination of techniques may be selected by any one of the three technologies for use in any one of the technical work areas. This area of techniques can be looked upon as a storehouse of tools from which all the technologies are free to draw for accomplishing work in the technical work areas. The bottom tier shows the applications for the various techniques in accomplishing certain parts of the work. For example, the technique of quality-cost optimization may be applied to cost reduction and product-design selection and many other listed applications.

This chapter and Chapters 11 and 12 discuss the three technology disciplines of total quality control and typical techniques they employ. A few examples of specific applications are given. In Part 6, detailed examples are given, showing how these techniques are used in the four jobs of quality control throughout industry.

10.2 Quality-Engineering Technology[2]

Quality-engineering technology may be defined as

> The body of technical knowledge for formulating policy and for analyzing and planning product quality in order to implement and support that quality system which will yield full customer satisfaction at minimum cost.

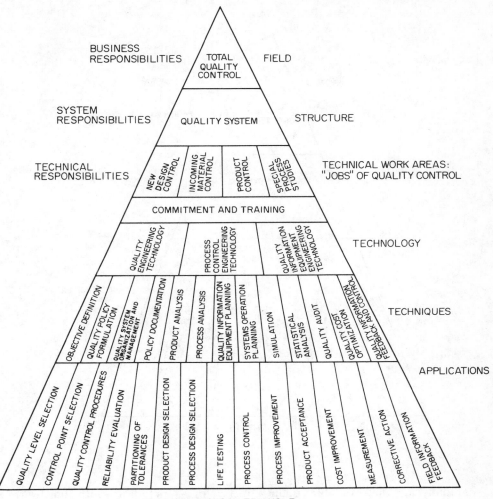

THE TECHNOLOGY TRIANGLE
FIG. 10.1

Figure 10.1 showed the technological triangle, relating the engineering technologies to the overall field of total quality control. Figure 10.2 now shows the counterpart triangle for quality engineering. Quality engineering becomes the field, or apex, of the triangle. The technical work area of the discipline—quality-systems implementation—is shown in the first tier.[3] The second tier then shows the principal techniques of quality-engineering technology.

Quality engineering relates the particular requirements of the plant and

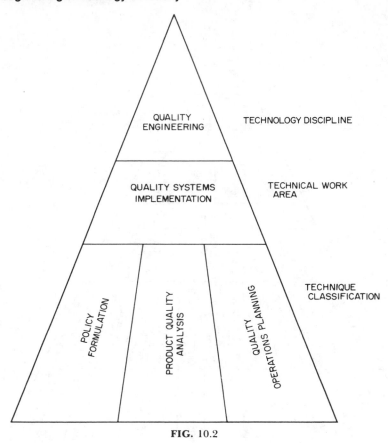

QUALITY
ENGINEERING

TECHNOLOGY DISCIPLINE

QUALITY SYSTEMS
IMPLEMENTATION

TECHNICAL WORK
AREA

TECHNIQUE
CLASSIFICATION

POLICY
FORMULATION

PRODUCT QUALITY
ANALYSIS

QUALITY
OPERATIONS PLANNING

FIG. 10.2

company to the available quality technology—including both hardware equipments and planning and control actions—[4] to put in place much of the ongoing operating detail of the quality-systems framework for the firm.

Quality-engineering technology thus provides the technical areas to deal with such questions as the following: What are the specific details of the control activities to take place during the development and production and service cycle? Will these quality activities best be accomplished through the use of quality information equipment or by the use of people guided by procedures? What information and material inputs will be needed? What type of information data is required? How should it be analyzed, and what sort of feedback should be used? Depending upon the differences in the product-quality levels encountered, what criteria are there for alternative courses of corrective action?

10.3 The Techniques of Quality Engineering

The entire range of techniques used in quality-engineering technology may be grouped under three major headings:

1. *Formulation of quality policy.* Included here are techniques for identifying quality objectives and quality policy of a particular company, as a foundation for quality-analysis and -systems implementation. Techniques for quality policy formulation are discussed in Section 10.4
2. *Product-quality analysis.* Techniques for analyzing include those for isolating and identifying the principal factors that relate to the quality of the product in its served market. These factors are then studied for their effects toward producing the desired quality result. (Techniques used for analyzing are discussed sequentially in Secs. 10.5 through 10.16.)
3. *Quality operations planning.* Techniques for implementing the quality system emphasize the development in advance of a proposed course of action and methods for accomplishing the desired quality result. These are the quality planning techniques underlying—and required by—the documentation of key activities of the quality system. (Quality planning techniques used for implementing the quality system are discussed sequentially in Secs. 10.17 through 10.38.)

TECHNIQUES FOR FORMULATION OF QUALITY POLICY

10.4 Quality Objectives and Quality Policy

A prerequisite to implementing a total quality program is the clear delineation of the quality objectives and the quality policy of a company. Until the company knows where it is going with respect to product-quality standards and product-quality levels, no foundation is provided upon which to build functional quality plans. Policy must be established to provide the limits within which quality-related decisions by the functions of the business will assure a proper course of action in meeting quality objectives. This policy is the broad strategic pattern to guide and govern all management decisions in the product-quality areas, including safety, reliability, and other necessary quality characteristics.

So that these quality objectives be clearly understood by every employee of the company, it is important that they be explicitly stated in a formal, written document. In its statement of quality policy, management has the opportunity to make its quality targets crystal clear. It can identify its objective of quality leadership in the markets served by the company's products and services. It can point to the key role the quality of the firm's products or services plays in their acceptance by its customers, and thereby in the business success of the company and its employees. It can stress that, for this reason, quality considerations are of a primary importance consistent with other major business factors in corporate strategy, planning, and priority. And it can emphasize the importance of each employee knowing and understanding individual and organizational responsibilities toward the company quality goal. Such policy provides the guidance originating at the top of the organization, which will then be shaped into procedures and instructions of increasing detail as responsibility for carrying them out is delegated down throughout all operations.

A quality policy statement thus puts in place the major road signs leading to total quality control. The route itself will be mapped out specifically by each function of the company in terms appropriate to its products, markets, and business situation. It will lead to what might be thought of as "off-line" quality control during research and development and production engineering, fully as much as the "on-line" control of quality during production itself.[5]

Quality-engineering techniques play a key role in this formulation of quality policy, which is in fact one of the major quality-engineering contributions to the business. These techniques relate to integrating the company's customers and their quality desires into the necessary policy framework. In particular, there must be identification of (1) the quality decisions that must be made and (2) the quality problems that must be solved, which then lead to (3) the specific documentation and achievement of the quality policy.

Decision Identification

First, the integrated product plan for the business is charted step by step from inception of a product idea through all the actions required to deliver the product to the customer and to service that product. All the quality-related decisions are identified at each step.

Then the limitations that have to be placed on each decision, to ensure meeting the quality objectives of the business, are identified. These limitations provide the guidelines within which managers are free to make alternative decisions and take courses of action toward reaching quality objectives.

For example, when a particular product concept has been completed for a company by one of its marketing product planners or design engineers, a decision must be made by the company whether to accept the concept as developed. Individual cases, taken of and by themselves, may cause internal frictions incident to such a decision. When it has been established by policy that design reviews always are necessary to assure desired product quality, then the issue instead becomes just how the design review will be conducted.

Guidelines, in the form of supporting procedures, will delineate the components or individuals from the various functional organizations who will participate in the review. These procedures also will identify the criteria to be used in accepting the design concept.

This area of decision identification is one of the approaches required in formulating the elements of company quality policy. Another is through identification of quality problems.

Problem Identification

All the quality problems that have been encountered with the product under any circumstance, during development, in customer service, and so on, are listed. The question is put in each case as to how the problem came to be a problem. Then the further question is posed: "What decision could have been made that would have prevented this from becoming a problem?" The required element of policy is then identified by putting the question "What policy is required to assure getting these 'right kinds' of decisions?"

For example, in a Western company, a consumer-product model was rushed to market to gain the advantage of an innovation in design. Insufficient time was scheduled to determine the reliability of the model. As a result, many quality complaints were received from the field. A policy element was subsequently established which required a specified reliability at a specified confidence level before future models in the product line could be released for market.

When the elements of policy have been established through use of the techniques in decision identification and problem identification, the third area of policy formulation—documentation—becomes active.

Policy Documentation

There are many different forms of presentation that can be used to document policy, depending upon the individual requirements of particular companies. Many of these forms in their fundamentals are equally effective in communicating written policy to the company managers. However, the majority include a basic format that covers the following points:

- Policy title
- Need for policy
- Policy statement (this defines the basic quality interests that must be preserved for the company)
- Courses of action (these are the guidelines for the procedures that are followed for implementing the policy)
- Responsibility and authority (this area defines the position assignments in the organization that have responsibility for enforcing the policy and interpreting it)
- Definition of terms (if needed)

To assure adherence to the quality policy and to provide for its proper implementation, the required step is a formal communication to the managers responsible for administering the functional work within the company.

These policies are thoroughly communicated to and discussed with all plant and company employees. The quality policy thereupon becomes one of the major factors in emphasizing quality as a "way of working life" throughout the complete organization.

Figure 10.3 shows a representative section of a quality policy formulated by an Atlantic seaboard electronics manufacturer.

XYZ Electronics Company
Product Quality Policy

Need for Policy

To enhance the Company reputation, competitive position, and profitability, it is necessary to produce products of good quality. Meeting this objective requires a properly directed approach by all functions to the elements which concern product quality.

Statement of Policy

It is the policy of the XYZ Electronics Company to market only products of a quality that will merit and earn customer satisfaction by performing expected functions reliably and effectively in accordance with customer expectations and which are discernibly better than competitive offerings. In support of this objective, the XYZ Electronics Company continuously strives to lead its product field in research and development, design, manufacture, marketing, and product service related to its area of business responsibility.

Courses of Action

1. *Selection of business opportunities.* This Company will not accept business which will compromise its product-quality reputation. In this regard the customer's specifications will be reviewed to determine that they serve the common interests of the customer and the Company and to ensure that appropriate quality standards can be met. When these conditions are not met, the Company will not submit a proposal. A comprehensive contract review will be carried out by all functional areas before a contract is signed in accordance with Company instructions.
2. *Product development and design.*
   a. Only approved components and processes shall be used. In cases where new components and processes are needed to meet product requirements, adequate qualification tests or process capability measurements will be carried out prior to their use. Department instructions shall specify procedures for obtaining component and process approval.

FIG. 10.3

TECHNIQUES FOR PRODUCT-QUALITY ANALYSIS

10.5 Approaches to Analysis

A key factor in implementation of the quality system and in meeting the objectives and quality policy of the business is thorough analysis of the quality aspects of the product itself and those of the served market.

Analysis of all the quality factors bearing on the product defines the areas in which policy-oriented courses of action must be followed to meet business objectives. After those needed have been identified, planning can then be undertaken to establish the methods and procedures for carrying out the courses of action.

A subsequent section, 10.17, considers some of the general approaches to planning. This section considers some of the general approaches to analyzing.

The act of analyzing involves breaking down a situation into all its segments and then synthesizing these segments back to the whole. In quality-control work there are many separate segments to any product-quality situation. Some examples are:

1. Customer-use needs and wants
2. Function to be performed by the product
3. Environments encountered by the product
4. Life and reliability requirements
5. Safety requirements
6. Requirements specified by regulatory agencies and government industry standards
7. Attractivity or appearance
8. Product design
9. Manufacturing process
10. Shipping conditions
11. Traceability of product
12. Liability loss control
13. Installation
14. Maintenance and services
15. Characteristics of served market
16. Competitive offerings

Each item can be further analyzed. For example, item 8, product design, can be described in terms of each individual quality characteristic of the product, and even further analysis can be made by considering various aspects of these quality characteristics. They can be analyzed according to their importance in supporting the principal functions of the product. They also can be analyzed by considering each quality characteristic with respect to its producibility, that is, its ability to be manufactured easily and economically.

Basically, the important quality abilities (Sec. 1.2) of the product must be carefully determined by the techniques necessary for the purpose. Sections 10.6 through 10.16 consider some representative examples of these specific analyzing techniques used in quality-engineering work. Section 10.6 presents in tabular form these representative techniques related to the purpose of the analysis.

10.6 Quality-Engineering Analytical Techniques

Purpose of analysis	Technique
To identify the needed quality	"Delineation of Quality Requirements" (Sec. 10.7)
To examine the proposed design	"Designed Experiments" (Sec. 10.8) "Economic Partitioning of Tolerances" (Sec. 10.8) "Analysis of Prototype Tests" (Sec. 10.8) "Analysis of Product Reliability and Life Cycle (Sec. 10.9) "Analysis of Environmental and End-Use Effects" (Sec. 10.10) "Analysis of Safety" (Sec. 10.11) "Review of Designs" (Sec. 10.12)
To examine the effect of process and methods	"Evaluation of Effects of New Methods, New Processes, and New Materials" (Sec. 10.13) "Adjustment of Product and Process for Compatibility" (Sec. 10.14)
To study vendors	"Vendor-Facilities Evaluation" (Sec. 10.15)
To evaluate the quality-cost balance	"Quality-Cost Optimization" (Sec. 10.16) "Simulation Techniques" (Sec. 10.16)

10.7 Delineation of Quality Requirements

A detailed delineation of quality requirements for each product and its components and subassemblies is a necessary technique in the attainment of the desired quality in the finished product. This means that each quality characteristic of any significance must be specified with allowable tolerance limits. Where appropriate, acceptable quality levels can then be established for each quality characteristic.

For this to be done intelligently requires a thorough knowledge of the product and how each quality characteristic affects its function. The setting of the product specification is usually accomplished by the product-design engineer, who should be most knowledgeable with respect to the product parameters. The functions the customer expects from the product, the environments and conditions under which the customer uses it, the expected life and product reliability, the product safeguards—all have a determining influence on the design parameters. They must be established based upon careful determination of customer-use patterns.

Quality requirements are applied in determining the precision and accuracy of manufacturing equipment employed for making the product. They are also used in determining required quality information equipment and quality-control procedures.

10.8 Designed Experiments

These provide the technique for selecting the best of several design approaches or the best of alternative manufacturing methods.[6] The effects of significant factors at different quality levels or values are studied. Such analysis permits selecting the most favorable combination of quality levels for the significant factors. This type of analysis is a sound basis for planning the design for the product and process. Designed experiments are discussed more fully in Section 16.10.

Economic Partitioning of Tolerances

Where two or more dimensions are involved in a fit, it may be possible to take more tolerance on one member, provided the tolerance is tightened up on the other member of members. Economies may be possible by applying the technique of economic partitioning.

If certain conditions can be met, tolerances of individual parts can be increased without exceeding the total tolerance of the buildup. The certain conditions that must be met are discussed in Section 16.8. This section also shows how the tolerance on certain dimensions may be increased without causing an excessive buildup in the total tolerance.

Analysis of Prototype Tests

The building and testing of prototypes are significant techniques for analyzing product quality. During prototype testing, it is necessary to log carefully the history of the prototype as to the characteristics of materials, along with any special operations or processes required to produce it. Such a log is used to analyze differences in performance between handmade prototypes and tool-made products, or products from the actual production process.

Prototype test results aid the subsequent quality planning. They indicate the characteristics that may offer difficulty from a quality-control standpoint. They also help establish cause-and-effect relationships between process and product. Materials and components that represent extremes of tolerance can be represented in prototypes so their effects on function can be studied.

10.9 Analysis of Product Reliability and Life Cycle

An essential area of product analysis is determination of the reliability of new product concepts, designs, and manufactured units, including the reliability of principal components that will be used in the product. Reliability techniques today make possible such analyses with a high degree of engineering and mathematical validity.

All too often in the past, reliability programs were carried out with inadequate planning, limited testing facilities, ambiguous reporting, and uncertain recommendations. A reliability testing program involving 50 test units for a new electronic product design might, for example, be reported as having "experienced one failure." In actual fact, there may have been several failures which the design engineer sincerely believes can be easily corrected, thereby presumably not requiring the designation of "failures." Such a "one failure" reliability report and program of the past had little value in an efficient program for quality control.

The proper definition of the reliability testing program for a new product; the assurance of the suitable performance of the program; its reporting, together with recommendations—these today constitute important areas relating to quality engineering. This work is also closely related to the establishment of product-quality life cycle patterns.

Chapter 17 discusses key approaches to product reliability.

10.10 Analysis of Environmental and End-Use Effects

A properly planned prototype testing program should include tests which thoroughly represent the actual environments and end-use conditions which the product will "see." The same can be said of tests conducted on the first tool-made samples resulting from the pilot run.

With industrial products, it is essential that such tests be conducted, as appropriate, with the use of equipment that is suitable for accomplishing the necessary technical results. This requires the use of altitude and temperature chambers, shock testing devices, spectroscopy techniques, pressure boxes, noise-measurement devices, and a very wide range of nondestructive evaluation (NDE) practices.

Particularly with consumer products, where customer-use patterns may be less predictable in technical terms than are industrial products, the employment of the consumer test panel technique can be useful. This can range from placing a group of new models of major household appliances in a selected group of homes to determine performance results through the bringing together of groups of consumers to determine usage patterns on new small tools, household devices, or clothing.

A prototype testing program is operated over an extended period of time to simulate usage the product would experience during the early stages of its life. It shows up "weak links in the chain"; that is, it establishes modes of failure. When the weaknesses of the product are identified, they are corrected by changing the design or the method of manufacture so the customer will not experience premature product failure or breakdown.

10.11 Analysis of Safety

As products have become more complex and as customer-use patterns have become more intricate, the analysis of product safety has become a major product-quality-analysis-related area. Where there is unsatisfactory product quality, there may also be unsatisfactory product safety.

Product-safety programs today must involve safety analysis of design, purchased components, manufacture, service. To be meaningful and dependable, design-safety analysis must determine not only potential safety hazards in anticipated product operation—the traditional concentration of design safety—but potential safety hazards inherent in a range of possible customer-use patterns. As one design safety analyst put it, "If it can happen, it will happen; and safety determination must evaluate the incidence and the significance of the abnormal as well as the normal product-use pattern."

Purchased-component safety analysis has assumed an increasing importance in today's safety programs as a number of companies have come to place great emphasis upon "buy" versus "make" policies in the procurement of parts and materials. One of the difficulties experienced in product-safety programs of the past has been the limited attention they have placed upon hazard evaluation of purchased components, and this has been a principal reason why the safety problems of some products have been caused by supplier parts. The problem has not necessarily been lack of care by the supplier but, instead, the misapplication of the part—for example, the purchased pressure blow-off valve that does not operate when critical pressure ranges are reached because the valve has been used in a product whose operating conditions place upon the valve stresses that were neither intended nor understood by the supplier.

The importance of careful safety attention to product manufacture and product service requires equally great emphasis in modern safety programs. The way a product is manufactured and the procedures in accordance to which a product is serviced can be essential determinants as to whether a basically safe product design is maintained or whether unsafe conditions may be created. Safety analysis is an essential contributor to the establishment of what will be acceptable manufacturing methods and service practices, and such thoroughgoing safety attention is a necessary condition in the establishment and operation of a modern product-quality analysis program.

Safety analysis and safety testing programs are important factors in the program of the company for product liability—including its all-important safety aspects. (Liability loss control is reviewed in Sec. 10.28.)

10.12 Review of Designs

Review of product designs is the technique of examining product concepts, drawings, specifications, production plans, and other technical documents related to product development, to ensure that the product design and its production will provide the intended customer quality satisfaction in use and that all necessary information and requirements are clearly specified for this purpose. Among the areas that may be considered are specific customer quality requirements, including product features, reliability and safety test data; requirements specified by regulatory agencies or appropriate government and industry standards; manufacturing feasibility, including facilities, equipment, and scheduling; inspection and test requirements consistent with "state of the art" capability; product-liability considerations; vendor part and material dependability; reasonable tolerances; clearly defined criteria for product acceptance; life cycle considerations; appropriate service and maintainability features; adequate packaging requirements; and many other factors.

Design review considers components and parts and subassemblies as well as the full assembly and final equipment itself—and enters into such other areas as software, as required. Design review will be procedurized to take place at key phases of product introduction. This may include, as appropriate, *preliminary* design review during product-concept development and first drawing and model stage; *intermediate* design review during the completion of design product testing and production and process planning; and *final* design review prior to final product approval, qualification, and release. Reviews of detail design and production design take place within the process.

To be effective, design review must be routinely required by company and plant policy and specifically structured with regard to participation, criteria, decision-making authority, and reporting. Product Engineering normally has a major role in the evaluation of its own designs, with intensive participation by Manufacturing Engineering, Production Operations, Product Service and Field Engineering, Marketing Product Planning—together with very intensive participation by Quality Control. Indeed, the quality process-control and quality information equipment engineers are in an especially favorable position to review the design and offer suggestions because of their quality experience with previous, similar designs.

The reviewers look for situations that can be recognized as having the potential for creating quality problems. Such an examination eliminates situations that carry quality risks. Correction of the situation prevents the problem from arising when production starts.

A careful analysis is made by relating each quality characteristic to all other pertinent characteristics and applicable process to see if experience would indicate creation of quality problems. Furthermore, pilot runs and tests of the product under end-use conditions may reveal problems where experience has been incomplete and which may be fed back for additional design review, when needed. Identified problems are assigned to the appropriate organizational component for permanent corrective action.

Several sections of Chapter 18 review key aspects of design review in operation, in particular Sections 18.10 to 18.14.

10.13 Evaluation of Effects of New Methods, New Processes, and New Materials

Planned experiments involve techniques to evaluate the effects of new factors entering a process. Effects on ease of manufacture, product quality, and quality costs can be evaluated if it is possible to place numerical values on the causal factors and their effects. Some of the special statistical techniques discussed in Chapter 16 (such as Latin squares, factorial designs, regression analysis, and analysis of variance) can be used for this application. Involved experimental designs can be programmed on computers for saving time and money.

This technique has its application in analyzing the effects of technical changes so that quality plans can be revised to accommodate such changes properly.

10.14 Adjustment of Product and Process for Compatibility

This technique is the basis upon which the design and the process can be brought into compatible relationship with each other without curtailing design function or requiring process capabilities beyond the limits of feasibility and cost.

When design engineers start the product design, there are certain functional objectives they are trying to meet with the product. They not only have to consider what is possible from a design standpoint within the limitations of delivery time and prices but what is possible from a manufacturing point of view. Consequently, they collaborate with manufacturing engineers early in the design cycle. In this manner, the design engineer hopes to design a product that will perform the functions the customer expects and, at the same time, design a product that can be built within the imposed time and cost limitations.

Unfortunately, unforeseen difficulties may arise whereby the related manufacturing processes do not meet expectations with respect to precision or accuracy. Problems may arise with the product design itself in that it does not come up to the required performance. In either case, adjustments have to be made to bring about a compatible relationship among (1) the product requirements, (2) the design, and (3) the manufacturing process.

In some cases, adjustments may have to be made in all three factors to obtain a feasible product. The technique of adjusting product and process to a compatible relationship has its application in what has come to be called "negotiating product feasibility."

10.15 Vendor-Facilities Evaluation

Before important orders are allocated to vendors, it is necessary to use the technique of vendor-capability evaluation. This will determine probability of the vendor being able to deliver the required quality on schedule at the quoted price.

Such an evaluation is based upon a thorough survey of the vendor's facilities and experience, usually through an on-site examination. It takes into account the vendor's quality system, whether the vendor's past experience has included products similar to those being ordered, and the research and engineering skills and manufacturing facilities available in the vendor's organization.

This technique has its application in the selection of vendors based upon their respective quality capabilities.

10.16 Quality-Cost Optimization

Evaluation of the various segments of quality costs discussed in Chapter 7 permits balancing of preventive and appraisal costs against failure costs. The technique of quality-cost optimization involves the selection of a course of action that will result in a minimum total quality cost.

Use of such an analyzing technique helps establish inspection points in the process that are strategic from an overall quality-cost standpoint. For example, a circuit test to check accuracy of wiring may prove economical, particularly if a subsequent operation makes the wiring inaccessible, requiring an expensive dismantling operation. Such analysis influences the quality planning for the product.

Simulation Techniques

The technique of simulating a system or an organism involves operation of a model or simulator which is a representation of the system or organism. The model is amenable to manipulations which would be impossible, too expensive, or impracticable to perform on the entity it portrays. The operation of the model can be studied, and from it properties of the behavior of the actual system or organism are inferred.

Today, such simulation is becoming important in quality control. For example, a mathematical model may be built to represent the inspection system for the product. Manipulation of the model, through use of a computer, with various percent nonconformities originating at different processes, and use of various inspection stations can predetermine the location of inspection stations that give the greatest overall economy.

For a further example, the entire area of physical model building of the product is significant, particularly for safety testing. Environmental tests are used to simulate the end-use conditions under which the product is required to operate.

TECHNIQUES USED IN PLANNING

10.17 Approaches to Planning

The act of planning is thinking out in advance the sequence of actions to accomplish a proposed course of action in doing work to accomplish certain objectives. So that the planner may communicate the plan to the person or persons expected to execute it, the plan is written out with necessary diagrams, formulas, tables, and so on.

Planning in the field of quality control must, of course, be geared fundamentally for delivering satisfactory product quality to the customer at minimum quality cost. These objectives are realized only by carefully planning the necessary quality procedures which establish the required operational detail.

To achieve product and service quality, many different pieces of work must be performed, by many people, and in a certain time-phased sequence. Different techniques are used in accomplishing the work. Therefore, the establishment of effective quality plans is based upon using the results of the techniques of analysis progressively to answer the following questions:

1. What specific quality work needs to be done?
2. When, during the product-development, production, and service cycle, does each work activity need to be done?
3. How is it to be done: by what method, procedure, or device?
4. Who does it: what position in what organizational component?
5. Where is it to be done: at what location in the plant, on the assembly line, in the laboratory, by the vendor, or in the field?
6. What tools or equipment are to be used?
7. What are the inputs to the work? What is needed in the way of information and material inputs to get the work accomplished?
8. What are the outputs? Do any decisions have to be made? What are they and what criteria should be used for making them? Does any material have to be identified and routed?
9. Is any record of the action to be made? If so, what is the form of the data? Is computer data processing required? What kind of analysis is required? To whom is it sent? What form of feedback is to be used?
10. Are there alternative courses of action to be taken, depending upon certain differences in the product quality encountered?
11. What are the criteria for these courses of action?
12. Is any time limit imposed on the work? If so, what is it?

Many more questions are developed as the planning assumes a finer degree of detail.

The final output of the planning process is the set of detailed instructions necessary to carry out the prescribed courses of action in meeting the quality objectives of the business and in carrying out the established quality policy. As earlier discussed in Chapter 9, to foster quality commitment, these detailed instructions must be clear and definitive enough to be clearly understood by all plant and company employees yet general enough to provide effective quality technology approaches to the work.

Fundamental areas of a portion of such a quality plan, which require documentation applying to the incoming-material control job of quality control, are

---

Materials

1. Incoming-material-control Procedures
   a. Sampling plans
   b. Instructions
   c. Data recording
   d. Reporting
2. Vendor Relationships
   a. Delineation of quality requirements to vendors, including classification of quality characteristics and acceptable quality levels
   b. Correlation of measurement methods
   c. Vendor quality capability, facilities, and quality systems surveys and evaluations
   d. Incoming-material rating
   e. Feedback of quality information to vendors
   f. Corrective action and follow-up
   g. Servicing to assure scheduled quality output
   h. Certification of incoming material
   i. Interpretations
3. Incoming-material-control Measuring Devices
   a. Specification (method, accuracy, precision, capacity, service connections, floor space, etc.)
   b. Maintenance
   c. Calibration
   d. Periodic correlation with vendor's devices
4. Laboratory Acceptance Testing
   a. Test specifications
   b. Samples for laboratory
   c. Request for tests
   d. Laboratory results reporting
5. Material Disposition
   a. Identification
   b. Requests for deviation
   c. Routing (scrap, rework, salvage, return to vendor, detail inspection, etc.)
6. Incoming-material Audit
7. Incoming-material Quality-control Personnel Requirements
   a. Number
   b. Qualifications
   c. Special training

FIG. 10.4 **Quality plan outline, incoming material.**

shown in Figure 10.4. Figure 10.5 shows a page of an instruction covering one of these activities within this particular quality plan, giving the detailed procedure for sampling and testing one type of purchased material, namely, fuel oil.

Sections 10.18 through 10.38 consider some representative examples of quality techniques.

Section 10.18 presents in tabular form the techniques of planning related to the purpose of the plan.

10.18 Quality-Engineering-Planning Techniques

Purpose of planning	Technique
To establish acceptance criteria	"Classification of Characteristics" (Sec. 10.19) "Acceptance Sampling" (Sec. 10.20)
To provide acceptance procedure and an acceptance facility	"Determination of Quality Measurements to Be Made" (Sec. 10.21) "Determination of Quality-Measuring Equipment Requirements" (Sec. 10.22)
To document the plan	"Documentation of Quality Planning" (Sec. 10.23) "Review of Technical Instructions, Procedures, and Manuals" (Sec. 10.23)
To communicate and work with vendors	"Making Quality Requirements Understood by Vendors" (Sec. 10.24) "Servicing of Vendors" (Sec. 10.25) "Material-Certification Plans" (Sec. 10.26)
To establish quality information	"Quality Information Feedback" (Sec. 10.27) "Liability Loss Control" (Sec. 10.28) "Data Processing and the Use of Computers" (Sec. 10.29) "Software Control" (Sec. 10.30) "Communication with Other Functions" (Sec. 10.31) "Feedback of Information from the Field" (Sec. 10.32)
To assure corrective action	"Corrective Action" (Sec. 10.33)
To establish audit	"Audit Planning—Product, Procedure, and System" (Sec. 10.34)
To assure continuing customer satisfaction	"Quality Control in the Field" (Sec. 10.35) "Renewal Parts Quality Control" (Sec. 10.35) "Customer Attitude" (Sec. 10.36)
To promote quality to the customer	"Promotion of Quality to the Customer" (Sec. 10.37)
To maintain product configuration	"Configuration Control, Design Changes, Traceability" (Sec. 10.38)

QUALITY INSTRUCTION
COMPANY R

Subject: Fuels, and Oils, including Process Chemicals

IV. SAMPLING JET FUELS AND LUBRICANTS

A. Fuels and lubricants are subject to 120-day sampling by ABC Laboratory.

B. Receiving Inspection will maintain a complete file of records and will be responsible for the schedule of sampling and the preparation and delivery of the samples to the Plant Laboratory.

C. Samples will be processed in accordance with requirements of military fuel specifications.

1. All samples will be analyzed by the Plant Laboratory and the composite report of both ABC and Plant Laboratory findings will be reported to the Receiving section submitting the samples.

V. SAMPLING ON 90-DAY BASIS

A. It is the option of the Quality Supervisor of each section in the Company to require 90-day sampling for the purpose of maintaining a control check on incoming quality of materials.

B. It is the responsibility of the Receiving section to set up the necessary record control for such sampling program.

C. The Plant Laboratory will perform the analysis and furnish a report to the Receiving section submitting materials under a 90-day quality control program.

VI. PROCESS CHEMICALS

A. Process chemicals shall be ordered and received in the same manner as fuels described in paragraph II.

B. It shall be the responsibility of each Operating Section to issue and to conform to detailed instructions providing the necessary control of these materials.

C. Sampling shall be performed at the option of the Quality Supervisor of each Operating Department, analysis to be performed by the Plant Laboratory on request.

APPROVED: *John Smith*

Manager – Quality Control
Company R

DATE: *March 10*

March 12

Date Issued	Superseded Issue	Dated	Page	No.

FIG. 10.5

10.19 Classification of Characteristics

This technique involves the classification of numerous quality characteristics of a product, such as dimensions, speed, hardness, and weight, according to their relative importance in contributing to the quality of the product. The technique also involves the classification of key process-quality characteristics in parts-making, subassembly, assembly, packaging and shipping, and installation and service. Such classification is a valuable tool for weighing the relative importance of these characteristics.

For example, a fourfold classification frequently used is that of critical, major, minor, and incidental. For *product-*quality characteristics, this may involve such classifications as the following:

- A *critical* characteristic is one which threatens loss of life or property or makes the product nonfunctional if it was outside prescribed limits.
- A *major* characteristic is one which makes the product fail to accomplish its intended function if outside prescribed limits.
- A *minor* characteristic is one which makes the product fall short of its intended function if outside prescribed limits.
- An *incidental* characteristic is one that will have no unsatisfactory effect on customer quality.

For *process-*quality characteristics, this may involve such classification as the following:

- A *critical* characteristic is one where any significant variation from the tolerance that may occasionally occur will cause a significant and unacceptable average long-term nonconformity or defect rate.
- A *major* characteristic is where any measurable to significant variation from the tolerance that may occasionally occur will cause an unacceptable average long-term nonconformity or defect rate.
- A *minor* characteristic is one where any variation from the tolerance that may occasionally occur may cause a small average long-term nonconformity or defect rate.
- An *incidental* characteristic is one where any variation from the tolerance that may occasionally occur will have no average long-term nonconformity or defect consequences.

The specific classification structure, and the definition of the classifications, must be established by companies for their particular product and process requirements. Within the classification structure established by the total quality program, the product-design engineers normally are in the best position to classify the individual product-quality characteristics, working closely with quality engineers. The manufacturing engineers normally are in the best position to classify the individual process-quality characteristics, working closely with quality engineers.

Such classification of characteristics enables the quality effort to be directed to the matters of greatest importance, thereby assuring required quality and continuous production at minimum quality cost. The effect is very important during the completion of product design, assisting the design engineer and the design review team to review the tolerancing and other dimensions of the product for that which is truly of critical and major importance in the product. The effect is very important during production, helping to guide the inspection and testing to the correct control emphasis, rather than allowing it to be determined by casual and uneconomic practices. And the effect is very important during vendor selection and incoming-material control, providing specific parameters to the vendor concerning what is and what is not critical and major and providing more efficient control and economy to both the company and the vendor.

Classification of characteristics also permits selection of sampling plans with producer and consumer risks limited according to the critical nature of the characteristic. For a quality characteristic classified as critical, for example, it is likely that any risk involving acceptance of nonconforming products is undesirable. In such a case, no sampling could be permitted; that is, 100 percent inspection would have to be used to assure that every item in a lot conformed to specification.

If, on the other hand, a certain quality characteristic were classified as minor, a sampling plan might be chosen that would permit acceptance of items in terms appropriate to the character of this kind of quality characteristic.

The technique of classifying characteristics has application in quality planning. The degree of inspection commensurate with the importance of the quality characteristic is applied.

10.20 Acceptance Sampling

If the vendor is producing to the required quality level, it should be unnecessary to inspect or test the purchased product 100 percent. Selection of a statistically determined sample from the lot is a valuable technique for accepting or rejecting the lot based upon a maximum permissible number of defects or nonconformities found in the sample.

Purchasers can thereby protect themselves against very poor lots with considerable economy of inspection. Unacceptable lots are generally returned to the vendor for sorting. Chapter 15 reviews the tables available to give various acceptable quality levels (AQLs) at given producer and consumer risks.

There is a wide selection of sampling plans to cover almost any situation that might arise in practice. Basic to the selection of a sampling plan is a decision with respect to the quality level that the inspected material must adhere to, for proper use, if it is to be accepted. Following this decision is the subsequent choice of single, double, or multiple sampling plans. Then the decision must be made as to the type of measurement taken, i.e., attribute (go and not-go) or variable (continuous scale). Sample size and acceptance number are given by the plan chosen.

This type of sampling finds application over a wide range: acceptance of materials or components or assemblies.

10.21 Determination of Quality Measurements to Be Made

The technique of reviewing product function, design, and manufacturing process leads to the determination of which quality characteristics should be measured.

- This technique includes considering and deciding upon the methods used for taking the measurement.
- It also includes determining the point in the process flow where the measurement should be taken.
- It further includes the decision about the extent of measurement, i.e., every article or a sample from the product flow.
- This technique also establishes the mechanism for taking the measurement.
- In some cases, the operator may be the only person who should make the measurement. In other cases, the product might pass through an inspection or test station, where inspectors or testers make further measurements. Or such measurements might be made by automatic quality-control equipment and the data automatically processed and used for adjustment of the process.

This planning technique establishes the economic balance between the cost of taking quality measurements and the value of quality control and product acceptance.

Process sheets or flowcharts, which show each step in the process, are used as basic working documents. The significant quality characteristics generated at each step are identified, and strategic inspection points are selected according to the process sequence. Often, computer operator planning provides an effective means for generating this planning.

Figure 10.6 shows a process sheet, with inspection points noted by circling at certain specific operations.

DRAWING No. *10IR233*	Pt or Gt. *9* / Oper *X* / Ser. *3*	Issued By *J. SISKA*	METHOD SPECIFICATIONS — REMARKS										
MAT'L DATA		Date *3/14/60*											
		Sheet *6*											
		of *9*											
		Work Station *ZA35*											

	SEQUENCE DESCRIPTION	Surf. #	MEASURING EQUIPMENT	TOOLS FIXTURES	# Cuts	NO. Pass	MAX. DEPTH	FEED	SPEED	LG. of CUT	Handling	Machining	% TOOL MAINT.
52	CHMF HOOKS	11	"	"	2	R	–	.008	6.7	1/16"			
53	CHMF HOOKS	12	"	"	2	R	–	.008	6.7	1/16"			
54	CHMF HOOKS	13	"	"	2	R	–	.008	6.7	1/16"			
55	CHMF HOOKS	14	"	"	2	R	–	.008	6.7	1/16"			
56	CHMF HOOKS	15	"	"	2	R	–	.008	6.7	1/16"			
57	FORM RAD. VIEM "M"	16	TEMP IOIR233-IIA	165-108-1	1	R	–	.010	9.6	3/8"			
58	TURN PC. OVER, JAWS, STRAPS, IND. TO ALIGN												
59	FIN.FC. ($^{29.719}/_{29.708}$ PLUS $^{.26}/_{24}$)	1	STRAIGHT EDGE INSIDE MIKE	H.S.S.	1	R	.060	.015	8.2	3/4"			
60	FIN. FC.–RECORD DIM. AT (3) PLACES	2	"	"	1	R	.060	.010	9.6	4 1/4"			
	120° APART (1)												
	(2)_____(3)_____												
	OPER._____												
61	FIN. BO. RECORD DIA._____	3	VERNIER CALIPER	"	2	R	–	.008	9.6	5/16"			
	F.I.R. RUNOUT_____OPER._												

FIG. 10.6 **Process sheet.**

10.22 Determination of Quality-Measuring Equipment Requirements

Specifications usually attempt to identify the product in terms of measurable characteristics of the end product. When the end-result specifications cannot be written, the technique of specifying measurable characteristics of the process is used as test-methods specifications. In order that the product function can be assured, certain tests must be run regularly to evaluate process characteristics. With the aid of these test specifications, together with an analysis of the product function, the product design, and the manufacturing process, detailed test procedures can be planned. They describe test methods, test equipment, test sequence, and test frequency.

After the methods used for taking the measurements are decided, the equipment to implement the measurement must be developed, designed, built, or procured. Its specification must take into consideration floor space and power requirements, capacity, accuracy, precision, and safety. Chapter 12 discusses application of this technique.

Quality Personnel Requirements

Upon completion of the inspection and test plan, including inspection- and test-equipment requirements, the number of persons required to implement the plan is determined. Not only must this total number be determined, but the number in each classification must be established, according to training and experience.

10.23 Documentation of Quality Planning

Detailed quality procedures and instructions must be documented so that all quality-assurance activities are clearly identified. This is essential to communicate the quality plan to the many positions in a plant that have responsibility for implementing various parts of the plan. The necessary types of communication include use of reports, the procedures for the calibration of measuring equipment, the routing and disposition of material, the form of quality audits, and the necessary inspections and tests, all of which will be routinely audited for conformity and specifically identified so that there can be no confusion with documents relating to established product lines.

As computer application in quality planning has grown in companies, it is increasingly practical to maintain this quality planning with the data processing and word processing systems of the plant. Each inspection and test instruction for particular inspection and test devices is indexed and coded, providing ready replacement when needed. When such computer capability is not available, manual procedures, such as use or quality planning binders, will be used.

An example of an instruction is shown in Figure 10.7.

Review of Technical Instructions, Procedures, and Manuals

In this area, manuals are reviewed and issued to cover installation, adjustment, testing, repair, maintenance, and user application of the product. Suggestions are also made on the basis of product and process knowledge that will assure customer satisfaction with minimum complaint and service cost.

10.24 Making Quality Requirements Understood by Vendors

At the time vendors are asked to prepare quotations for material or components, the technique of clearly delineating quality requirements to them should be exercised. They should be provided with a formal package which includes a classification of the quality characteristics so that they know what is of critical, major, minor, and incidental importance. The package should include the criteria by which the product will be accepted or rejected, i.e., the inspection plan that will be used and the maximum percentage of nonconformities, if any, that is permissible. Chapter 19 discusses this in detail.

Such communication to the vendors is essential in directing their resources so that critical quality characteristics will be given the needed attention. In this way, the highest degree of conformance can be obtained without adding excessive costs to materials and components.

MACHINE ROOM INSPECTION

PUNCHED PARTS – DIES

In addition to the usual procedure of inspection certain additional measurements and recording of dimensions will be made. This added procedure will require the assistance of the Machine Room foreman and operator. The procedure will be as follows:

1) The usual setup and in-process spot checking by the inspector will continue.

2) In addition, 4 times during the production run, or once each hour, whichever yields the most samples, the operator will select three parts, tag them, respectively, sample lot 1, 2, 3, etc.

3) These samples will be turned over to the Machine Room inspector, who will measure them immediately if possible, or at the earliest convenient time within the shift period. Measurements will be recorded on the appropriate card currently used. The job will run regardless of whether these samples can be measured immediately. If such measurements can be made with simple measuring tools, such as scale, calipers, or micrometers, it is expected that the operators will make them merely as a control to determine that parts are within tolerance, so that defective parts will not continue to be made.

4) If the inspector finds that dimensions are in error either before or after the job is completed, the tool will be tagged defective until such time as an investigation can be made to determine whether die, operator, or procedure error is the cause. The tool must not be returned to the tool crib until measurements of samples are completed and disposition is given by the inspector. If the die is rejected, it will be properly tagged and forwarded to the tool room. Appropriate remarks will be made on the inspection record card.

5) After each run is completed, assuming the die is still acceptable, an average of the dimensions measured ($\overline{X}$) will be plotted on the Quality Control Chart Data sheet. Control limits for the dimensions measured serve as the upper and lower control limits. This plot will serve two purposes:
    A) A record of inspection of $\overline{X}$ plots.
    B) An indication as to: (1) when die is approaching need for repair; (2) normal variation of die; (3) accuracy of setup; and (4) effectiveness of control by operator.

W. E. John
SUPERVISOR – QUALITY CONTROL

FIG. 10.7

10.25 Servicing of Vendors

The technique of providing technical service to vendors upon request safeguards the scheduled flow of purchased material.

Initially, vendors should be advised of any unsatisfactory trends in the products they ship the company, so that they will be able to adjust their processes before they get into trouble. If scheduled delivery of acceptable material is threatened because of quality problems in the vendor's plant, it may be advisable for the purchaser to send a representative to the vendor's plant to help the vendor promptly locate and eliminate the quality difficulty.

In many respects, the success of a company depends upon the success of its vendors. Where a vendor is providing a critical part, requiring special technologies and complex processes, the purchaser will do well to keep in close touch with the vendor on all matters pertaining to quality. For example, joint investigation may reveal a drifting of measuring devices which affects correlation of measurements between purchaser and vendor. Where the purchaser has specialists that can serve the vendor in emergencies, their assistance may enable the vendor to solve quality problems quickly and resume shipment of parts and components without disrupting schedules.

10.26 Material-Certification Plans

Material certification is a technique for establishing a set of procedures whereby the vendor furnishes the purchaser inspection data and test results as objective evidence that a particular lot of material or parts meets its quality requirements.

Today, certification plans are being used to stop the uneconomic procedure of double inspection, i.e., inspection by the vendor before shipment and inspection by the purchaser upon receipt of the purchased material. Often the purchaser waives inspection if the vendor provides objective data showing that quality requirements have been met.

Such data are included along with the shipping papers accompanying the material or are mailed in advance of shipping. Agreement is reached between purchaser and vendor about the quality characteristics to be measured and the amount of data required. Since much of the required data are already available from the vendor's quality-control system, usually no increase in price results from including certification as a service. In fact, better planning, brought about by certification, often reduces quality costs, thereby enabling negotiation of cost improvement with the vendor.

An audit of quality is made periodically on received lots to maintain correlation between vendor's and purchaser's measurements.

10.27 Quality Information Feedback

One of the important planning techniques of quality engineering is the establishment of *quality information feedback* for the plant and the company. Quality information may be thought of as the "intelligence" of the total-quality-control program. The effectiveness through which this intelligence is structured, transmitted, and used is one of the principal parameters of the effectiveness of the program.

In principle, this quality-engineering technique can be looked upon as the establishment of communications among positions generating information and positions receiving and using information.

The objective is to structure in the form of the necessary procedures the actual, physical information feedback loops which were discussed in concept in Section 8.15. Through these loops, the specific quality results are measured, analyzed, and then fed back for use in replanning. This quality information is the factual basis upon which the correct and timely quality decisions can be made and action taken.

The following are three primary aspects of emphasis (Fig. 10.8) in this activity, two of which concentrate in individual quality areas (1 and 2) and one of which is oriented to the overall plant and company (3):

**Primary Aspects of Quality
Information Feedback**

1. Identification of the explicit information
2. Establishment of information flow
3. Integration of quality information

FIG. 10.8

1. Identification of the explicit information, as appropriate, in all existing quality plans—whether in customer quality determination, design review, process-capability analysis, and similar areas. Too often in the past, the planning of quality operations dealt only casually or indirectly with the quality information aspects of the plan and procedure.
2. Establishment of essential quality information flow procedures, in such areas as inspection and test reporting, customer complaints, and vendor performance.
3. Determination of the overall plant and company quality information flow requirements, evaluation of the effectiveness of the existing flow pattern, establishment of the overall plan for evolving the existing information flow to that which is needed, creation or adaptation of the necessary quality information procedures, and integration of overall quality information flow pattern.

In each of these areas, the most thorough possible use must be made of modern information-processing approaches and technology—including data flow analysis and planning—which have been developed with great success throughout industry. Today, this represents an essential discipline in the development of quality information requirements.

However, experience over the years has made very clear that the quality information requirements must first be developed for the *needs of the user*—whether in management, production, marketing, engineering, or quality control itself—and second, in terms of the data processing patterns and equipment that are the *most efficient.* The quality-control function has a primary information-handling leadership role in this first area; it must work closely with the data processing function of the company, wherein the expertise will most likely reside concerning the second area.

There are several important areas in establishing the needs of the user. One is the explicit establishment of these needs for all key positions in the plant and company. A second area is standardization of reporting throughout the plant and company so that there are common understanding and clear communications, ranging from defect definition in quality levels and scrap listing in quality costing to reliability assessment in vendor performance reporting on electronic components. A third is establishing the reporting formats, routines, and time frequency as well as the functions to receive the reports and the types of quality-engineering analysis that will be performed.

There are also several important areas in establishing the most efficient handling of quality information. One is to standardize and correlate the measurements of parts and components when the same measurements are made by different methods or equipment at different points in the design and production cycle. A second is to provide that there will consistently be, in quality plans, analysis of measurement data to seek out relationships between like process operations or like parts. For instance, it may be discovered upon examination that while cost or quality data from a given line or process area show no tendency to indicate an out-of-control condition, the same data when rearranged and looked at in respect to a single part, such as 1-inch diameters turned at a particular station, may show a definite trend toward an out-of-control condition. A third is to distinguish between short loop information flowing within a single work station or process line—which will require almost immediate or "real time" feedback—and longer loop information flowing throughout the plant or business, which may be handled in batch or "off-line" fashion.

In structuring the information for quality plans and procedures, quality control, data processing, and other key functions of the plant or company must determine the answers to such questions as the following:

- What kinds of information are essential?
- How much information is needed?
- What are the sources of the information?

- How should the information be transmitted—manually, by computer, by some combination of the two?
- To what positions should information be sent?
- How frequently should the information be sent?
- How fast must it be received to be effective?
- In what form should it be presented to be immediately usable as a basis for decision and action?
- How can the existing plant and company data base be used as a quality data input and for quality data output?

The effectiveness of the quality information system that is planned for the answers to these questions should, in turn, be measured periodically to ensure that it remains efficient. Such measurements must determine that

- Hard copy paperwork is kept to a minimum.
- Only usable data are being transmitted.
- Data are going to positions whose responsibilities call for its use.
- Data are adequate and being properly applied.
- The information flow is being adequately maintained.
- The information is producing effective and timely decisions for corrective action.
- Quality information processing takes place in the most cost-effective operation-equipment-work force-data utilization.

For ongoing operation of quality information feedback, the two major methods for collection and transmission of quality data are manually and by computer. In any increasing number of total quality programs, quality information is an integration of manual and computer methodology to furnish timely and accurate information.

The extent of computerization is fundamentally an economic determination and generally depends on the type, size, and needs of the plant and company. However, to assure most efficient computer use for the actual user applications, the original planning of information feedback will typically be manual, to prove adequacy of information, to assure the clarification of user needs, and to confirm the quality requirements of the business. The important area of data processing equipment and computers is discussed in Section 10.29.

10.28 Liability Loss Control

The integration with quality-control activities of the company liability loss prevention program—including its insurance carrier aspects—is a significant planning technique to assure improved company protection from liability risk and unfavorable liability litigation.

Liability exposure exists at every phase of product development (Fig. 10.9): from marketing product conception to the first preliminary design, through all

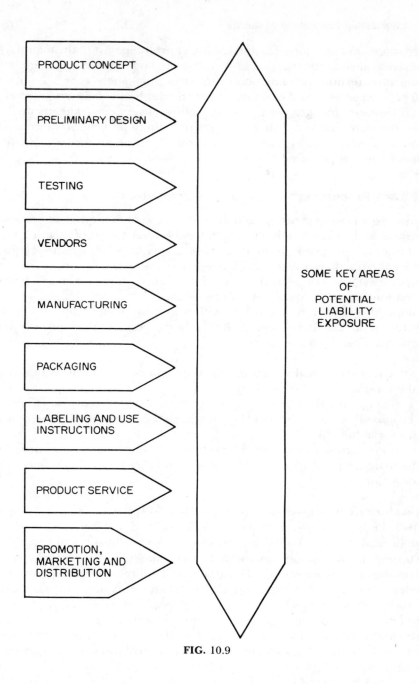

PRODUCT CONCEPT

PRELIMINARY DESIGN

TESTING

VENDORS

MANUFACTURING

PACKAGING

LABELING AND USE
INSTRUCTIONS

PRODUCT SERVICE

PROMOTION,
MARKETING AND
DISTRIBUTION

SOME KEY AREAS
OF
POTENTIAL
LIABILITY
EXPOSURE

FIG. 10.9

design stages and development and testing of prototypes; into the manufacturing phases—including negotiation of contracts and vendors; through actual manufacture, testing, and assembly; into packaging, labeling, and use instructions; product service; and ultimately to the methods of promotion, marketing, and distribution, including warranty periods and service arrangements.

It is therefore essential that all aspects of liability prevention be related to individual quality-control plans and that quality information be consistently monitored for all potential liability loss indicators.

10.29 Data Processing and the Use of Computers

A major quality-engineering technique is the use of modern data processing equipment and computers, integrated into all relevant areas of quality control. This not only can speed up the timeliness of quality information—frequency today can be fractions of a second, if needed, to minutes or hours as compared to days or even weeks as in the past—but in some cases can make possible information flow that could not otherwise exist.

Computer application, integrated within careful quality-engineering planning, can be a very useful tool in dealing with the basic demands of quality information flow, which are that:

- Effectiveness of quality information is dependent upon the promptness of the report.
- Time lags that discourage prompt corrective action must be eliminated.
- Trouble spots must be quickly brought to the attention of those who can do something about it.
- Good reporting formats must be established which indicate responsibility for action, type of action, and follow-up with a measure of the effectiveness of action.

Computer hardware—that is, equipment—and software—that is, programs to drive the hardware—are today available for, and are used in, a very wide range of quality-control applications, from customer quality data and prototype testing through incoming-material and production-quality-level results to field testing and service reports. Hardware availability for quality control today includes mainframe computers, on which certain forms of quality data can be run; minicomputers which can be directly dedicated to such quality-control operations as product testing; and microprocessors, which can be integrated with inspection devices to provide control-limit evaluation as part of the metrological work. Software availability for quality control today includes a variety of programming languages, from machine languages through high-level languages—including FORTRAN, COBOL, BASIC, PASCAL, and others—which have application to particular quality-control usages.

Close cooperation between the quality-control function and the data processing function is essential in computer application to quality control. However, it is important that the quality-control function itself develops and organizes the necessary capability for understanding and application of computers to quality control. This is, in part, because—as discussed in Section 3.6—the importance of computer application to quality control has only recently been recognized in some companies and so much user-oriented know-how must be supplied by the quality-control function. It is, in part, because the structuring of quality information feedback—the quality-control procedures for data collection, tabulation, analysis, and distribution—is an essential precondition to make the computer application operational.

And it is, in part, because the unduly high degree of data processing centralization and the correspondingly heavy load and delays on central mainframes in some plants and companies increasingly requires what has been called distributed data processing. Here, operation of data processing in quality control is decentralized to quality-control microprocessors and minicomputers that are suitably linked to the control data base of the plant and, as appropriate, to the company mainframe computers. However, processors, printers, cathode ray tubes, memory devices and other equipment as well as a wide variety of peripheral devices are directly located at the quality operations whose information handling needs they serve.

Some of the areas of computer application that are particularly important in total-quality-control programs today are the following:

- Complaint reporting by field engineers can be provided, either by telecommunications or through tapes and disks, to make customer quality performance as well as other pertinent data quickly available. Similar reporting can also be used to maintain spare parts inventories, where the input data is the trigger for replacement planning. Also, this reporting can maintain, as required, customer traceability information in the event of design modifications or, if needed, product recall.
- Incoming-material quality reporting upon discrepant lots, providing all necessary information to measure quality, rate vendors, analyze costs, and measure the work load and flow of material through incoming inspection.
- In-process control, inspection, and test data reporting for recording quality information such as type of nonconformity or defect, area of occurrence, responsibility for nonconformities or defects, number inspected, number nonconforming or defective, and disposition.
- Reliability and maintainability data for key components.
- Quality planning and instructions through word processor techniques.

Until recently, the great majority of computer applications in quality control have been batch-processed—that is, on an essentially off-line basis, with an issue frequency ranging from hours to days and, in some instances, weeks. This batch operation is generally satisfactory for many of the hierarchy of management and operations reports that are basic in the four jobs of total quality control, some examples of which are shown in Figure 10.10.

New-Design Control

- Prototype test results
- Component reliability assessment trends
- Design review corrective action tracking

Incoming-Material Control

- Receiving inspection reports
- Vendor survey status
- Vendor corrective action reports
- Material review status

Product Control

- Production-line defect rate reports
- Functional test percent-nonconforming summary
- Audit status
- Field quality reports

Special Process Studies

- Corrective action status
- Statistical trend surveys

FIG. 10.10 **Computer reports in the quality-control jobs.**

Real-time measurements, controls, and reporting are rapidly becoming increasingly important in the process-control and product-control areas of total quality control. Small computers, directly integrated with production operations, operate in a direct feedback and control mode in both parts-making—ranging from integrated circuit and printed board manufacturing—to assembly—where robots with direct computer quality controls built in check their own work and make necessary adjustments.

10.30 Software Control

Software control is a significant quality-engineering planning technique because of the importance that the quality of software has come to have in three principal areas.

The first area is the need for high quality in the software that will be used in conjunction with the computers which the plant purchases or leases in connection with its data processing programs. The second area is the assurance of the software used in conjunction with the OEM mini- and microcomputers that are purchased by the plant for incorporation in the product which will be sold to customers—microcomputers for aircraft-engine controls or minicomputers for large-scale power turbine installations. The third area is the quality control of the software created by the company itself that will be an important component of the complete product sold to customers, such as telecommunication and avionic equipment.

In all three areas, quality-engineering planning must apply the same product-quality qualification demands that are required for any other sophisticated incoming material, complex component, and final product.

One of the unique factors in software control is that software failures are generally caused by errors in design. These errors show up not only in original program execution but particularly when the program is being exercised under a range of user operating conditions. Thorough reliability evaluation is therefore an essential activity within the overall software-control program, with emphasis upon software-reliability measurement, estimation, and prediction. Some approaches to software reliability modeling are reviewed in Chapter 17.

Software control requires close integration with the company software function and the quality-control function to establish the unique requirements for *testing, verification,* and *validation* that have been developed for software quality control. Figure 10.11 shows these three primary considerations in software control. Software control has therefore become an essential part of company total-quality-control programs. Effective software control requires attention to such unique quality activities as the following:

- Design of the software program, including *design analysis* and *requirements analysis*
- Evaluation of the software under the wide variety of conditions that may be demanded, including *module testing* and *system testing*
- Matching of the software and computer hardware, including *integration testing* and *acceptance testing*
- *Installation testing*
- Ongoing maintenance of the software program, including *service testing*

Section 20.23 discusses a further example of software control as an essential factor in product control (Chap. 20).

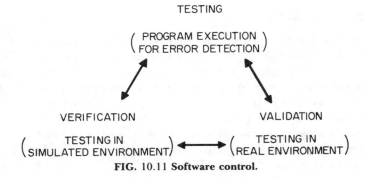

FIG. 10.11 **Software control.**

10.31 Communication with Other Functions

Establishing a systematic exchange of information among Quality Control, Marketing, and Product Engineering is an effective technique for establishing up-to-the-minute, customer-oriented quality goals.

Specifically, the flow of information includes data about the effect of marketing schedules on product quality and quality cost. It includes news about any special tools and techniques that prove valuable in service work.

Early warning of *potential* field problems that may result from preproduction or factory quality problems, as well as progress reports about corrective action being taken to eliminate quality problems, can also help salespeople hold customer confidence. Such data also will be invaluable in the event of product difficulties, including the extreme cases of product recall.

Finally, short training programs on the key benefits of the company's total quality control are helpful to sales personnel and distributors, especially in a very competitive product line.

10.32 Feedback of Information from the Field[7]

The field organization has an important responsibility in feeding back information to the factory. Such flow provides a further information technique for obtaining action in improving product quality and is a most useful measurement of quality progress.

Any design features that cause difficulty in servicing need to be made known. Actual product performance data are necessary, along with supplementary data concerning conditions under which the performance data were taken.

Field failure data and customer complaints should be sufficiently detailed to provide a means for analyzing the causes, so that proper corrective action can be applied. Report formats can be designed to make it easy for repair personnel to note the cause of the malfunction of a product.

Correspondingly, field engineering should be alerted to possible anticipated problems when evidence is encountered at the plant. A typical flow pattern for providing such information is shown in Figure 10.12.

10.33 Corrective Action

Corrective action means, in total-quality-control programs, the permanent correction of a quality problem—of parts deviation, production defects, process errors, customer-product malfunction, and a host of the other quality deficiencies that may occur. While one of the oldest of the quality-engineering techniques, corrective action has also in the past been one of the weakest in application in some companies.

This weakness has taken many forms. It has existed because of the long delay in reporting basic quality problems; the careless "hip shooting" that might have gone into diagnosis of the problem; the "quick fix" that may have repre-

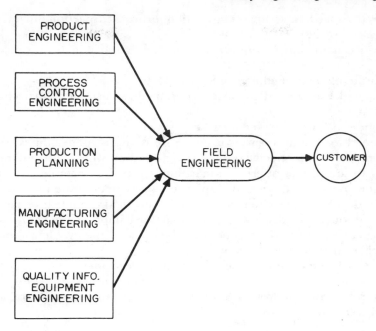

FIELD ENGINEERING INFORMATION
FIG. 10.12

sented the efforts toward solving the problem, which turned out to be no solution at all; the extensive time span that may have occurred in dealing with the problem in a conclusive fashion—which may have been a matter of months and even years; and the tendency for some important problems not to have come to top-level attention prior to having reached customer crisis proportions.

The effectiveness of a company's corrective action is, therefore, one of the key indicators of the strength, realism, and practicality of the company's quality program. Corrective action is a primary quality-planning area of total quality control.

This quality planning must recognize that the quality problems requiring action will be obvious to the entire plant organization only in such cases as a major production defect or a surge of customer complaints. In many other cases, the quality problem—for example, a design defect which shows up with very low frequency but which may ultimately lead to a major product recall—may not be obvious at all and will require careful analysis and fact gathering.

The inputs for an existing or potential problem may come from many sources in total quality control including design review, prototype tests, vendor source inspection, receiving inspection, process inspection, final test, and customer complaints.

Corrective action must therefore be structured so that quality problems are:

· Thoroughly identified and quickly reported
· Validated with regard to their importance to customer satisfaction and quality cost
· Diagnosed for the problem causes
· Planned for the necessary corrective steps and responsibilities
· Corrected for the specific sequence of deviations which initiated the problem: In the case of discrepant machined parts, for example, first, rework of the parts which were the specific causes that created the problem; second, retooling of the machine tool which had too much variation and thus produced the discrepant parts; and third, improvement of the specific practices or policy which generated the cause of the problem—improved machine maintenance, for example
· Reviewed to ensure that the correction is permanent

Chapter 21, "Special Process Studies," more fully discusses several areas of problem solution.

10.34 Audit Planning—Product, Procedure, and System

The planning of audit, to measure the degree of effectiveness of quality operations, is a quality-engineering technique that is structured to meet several purposes of the company quality program, as follows:

Product audits to determine, in user terms, the degree to which customer satisfaction is likely to be achieved.

Procedure audits to establish and report the degree of compliance. Quality operations in the office, factory, laboratory, and field are evaluated as to whether and how each step of the quality procedure is being followed in the prescribed manner.

System audits to assess the effectiveness of the quality system and to determine the degree to which system objectives are being achieved.

The implementation of these audit plans through process-engineering technology is discussed in Sections 11.23 through 11.27.

10.35 Quality Control in the Field

The technique of establishing quality standards in the field and controlling service work to these standards results in maintenance of satisfactory service in the field. The product service component of the company can establish controls on the quality it generates in the field as a result of servicing the product. Such quality is as important as that of the original product because the customer expects equivalent quality when it is necessary to call for service.

To make this result possible, quality standards are established for service work. Means for auditing the work are provided to ensure that the standards are being met. Training programs are established for service personnel to provide the skills necessary in meeting these quality standards. Quality manuals and bulletins issued to the field, while important, may not be enough in themselves to assure this thorough understanding and appreciation of the controls on quality which stand behind the product. Additional education may be necessary in the form of plant tours and visits, demonstrations, and formal presentations detailing the company's quality objectives.

In the case of purchased components shipped directly to the customer, the field control objectives remain essentially the same: to assure that the quality of the purchased materials is compatible with the product supplied and representative of a quality level at least equal to that of the supplied product. Among the alternatives open to the quality engineer are source inspection by a field inspector prior to shipment, vendor certification with each shipment to a customer, site inspection or audit of material shipped directly by the vendor, or "sample shipments" which will be carefully appraised.

A further technique of quality control in the field is the periodic audit of finished-goods inventory in the warehouse. Stock is reviewed for improper identification and damage, deterioration, and obsolescence.

Also very important for this purpose is the quality planning of field product installation. As an example, for a consumer product such as a major household appliance, many factors having to do with installation procedures will bear directly both upon quality costs and customer satisfaction. Should the product front panel, which is available in a choice of finishes and colors, be shipped separately from the product itself to minimize dealer inventory and to reduce the chance of damaged or scratched panels because they will be put in place after the appliance has been installed? Will the extra handling and packaging costs justify this? In the matters of required electrical connections, the size and type of cables, and so forth, requirements and associated costs are usually defined by local electrical codes; however, the recommended height and location of the installed unit, the venting and insulation material and methods, and other such decisions can directly affect the performance of the unit and thus influence the customer's satisfaction with it. The relationships of these end-use requirements must be factored into the total-quality control-program to assure trouble-free customer installations.

Renewal Parts Quality Control

Renewal parts should have a quality level at least as high as, or higher than, that found in the original equipment. The customer may forgive the manufacturer once if the original part fails but is slow to forgive a second failure. The planning of quality-control work related to renewal parts is, therefore, an important technique.

A major need for this technique is when material is shipped directly from the vendor to the customer, because difficulty of control is greatly increased;

however, procedures must be established that assure compatibility with the original product supplied and the quality of the part. These may include procedures for purging part stocks to eliminate undesirable or obsolete items.

Application of this technique provides a continuing product function to the customer.

10.36 Customer Attitude

Customer-attitude determination is intended to obtain and measure the opinions, impressions, reactions, and degree of satisfaction of individual customers regarding the overall efforts of the company toward providing quality for its products and/or services. The results of such a program are a basis for determining which factors customers regard as most important in a product, for establishing corrective action on reported problems, and for achieving improvement in customer attitudes.

Among the important attitudes which can be measured are the following:

1. Quality of shipment
2. Quality of product installation
3. Quality of product operation
4. Quality of product functional design
5. Maintainability (ease of being restored to service if product fails)
6. Serviceability (easily followed instructions, easily obtainable tooling, and so on)
7. Quality of service

There are many methods to collect this information. One of the most generally used is the questionnaire sent directly to the customer. Other approaches include telephone interviewing (sometimes used when the customer fails to respond to a questionnaire) or personal visits by a company representative (usually reserved for on-site audits). Useful information can also be gained by examination of buying trends, comparisons with competitive products, model-to-model comparisons, geographic area differences, and so forth.

Although the favorable attitude and goodwill of each single customer is important to a company, it is apparent that some accounts are more critical than others regarding volume, size, revenue, cash, profit, potential business, prestige, image, and so forth. For this reason a "customer rating plan" is sometimes adopted as a means of weighting customer response between "critical" customers and "major" customers (Fig. 10.13).

10.37 Promotion of Quality to the Customer

The technique of communicating product-quality values to customers is important in sales work. The system by which a business maintains quality has special significance and may be of great interest to customers. It assures them

Comparison of Response
Classification and Demerit Rating

Classification of response	Critical customer demerit weight	Major customer demerit weight
Very Serious	100	50
Serious	50	25
Not serious	10	5
Complete satisfaction	0	0

Quality Rating by Questionnaire

Demerits by questionnaire	Quality rating by questionnaire
0–24	Excellent
25–49	Good
50–99	Poor
100–up	Unacceptable

FIG. 10.13 **Customer-attitude response.**

that every precaution has been taken to provide a product which measures up in every way to its advertised features. Even more to the point for industrial products, quality and reliability levels can be certified. This enables customers to relax incoming inspection systems with confidence.

This type of information is an effective sales mover. It may appear in many forms, such as institutional advertising, brochures, packages, and instructions.

10.38 Configuration Control, Design Changes, Traceability

Configuration control is the planning technique to assure continuing customer quality satisfaction by maintaining the integrity of the product in the face of design changes, application differences, vendor alterations, product cost reductions, production-process changes, and several other impacts of the passage of time in relation to a particular product.

This technique relates to establishing that the product at all times contains the intended parts and subassemblies, is produced in accordance with approved processes, provides the intended functions, and is maintained and serviced in the intended modes. Accomplishing this requires, from the beginning of the product design, clear specifications, bills of materials, parts listing, vendor listings, and other complete product documentation.

All subsequent changes require explicit approvals before being included in the product configuration. Such approvals take place in accordance with engineering, marketing, production, and service procedures; through decision by responsible management; and, where appropriate, with awareness of suitable regulatory and standards authorities.

An important corollary is the technique of design-change approvals by systematic reviews of what are often termed Engineering Change Notes (ECNs). All ECNs that are approved for introduction in the product configuration will be scheduled with regard to the corresponding changes in materials and processes that may be required, the vendor alterations that may be needed, the field parts inventory substitutions that may take place, and the service training that may be needed. The organized scheduling of such changes will be monitored to assure continuing product-quality effectiveness. Similar change control can be maintained, where appropriate, for processes and field service practices.

For some highly engineered products—aircraft, nuclear reactors, military weapon systems, and others—configuration control is a basic requirement to assure product safety and reliability. For many other products—consumer appliances, electronic controls, machine tools—economic forms of configuration control are a valuable quality-engineering tool which contributes to parts and product traceability as well as spare parts and updating product traceability, which is itself discussed in more detail in Section 20.22.

Notes

[1]The business, systems, and technical responsibilities of the quality organization (as indicated on the technological triangle) were discussed in Sec. 8.10.

[2]The quality-engineering techniques described here have been developed by a number of professional quality engineers. Although too numerous to mention individually, it is these men and women who have created the substance of modern quality-engineering technology.

[3]Quality-systems approach and the establishment of the quality system were discussed in Chaps. 5 and 6, Part 2.

[4]The principles of quality-systems engineering are outlined in Sec. 6.2.

[5]This concept has been explored by Professor Genichi Taguchi. See "Introduction to Quality Evaluation and Quality Control," *International Conference on Quality Control*, Tokyo, 1978.

[6]For an example of the role of designed experiments and other qualitative tools in assessing complicated processes, see John L. Bemesderfer, "Approving a Process for Production," *Journal of Quality Technology*, vol. II, no. 1, January 1979, pp. 1–12; for a discussion of the role of designed experiments in product design, see Genichi Taguchi, "Design and Design of Experiments," *Annual Meeting of American Association for the Advancement of Science*, Washington, D.C., January, 1982.

[7]Field quality information is basic to the measurement of quality, as discussed in Sec. 6.14.

CHAPTER 11

Process-Control-Engineering Technology

We are rightfully impressed by the flood of worthwhile new devices that modern product technology has provided us. The ingenuity of their design and the intricacy of their function are striking.

An equally striking story, however, is represented in the technological developments behind the manufacturing processes which make these products possible. There has been an almost phenomenal growth in new methods for compounding, molding, cutting, and shaping mechanical, electronic, chemical, and other parts. Many new alloys and materials that were not known a relatively few years ago are being handled in the manufacturing plants of today. These processes not only operate at faster rates of speed, but the greater demands placed on them have tended to make them more complex.

These developments have not been directed to new processes alone. Much greater precision has been developed in the more traditional production equipments. Thus, high-speed, complex, precision processes in drilling, milling, and boring have required closer control; in many cases, automatic control. Older methods, which employed an operator making manual adjustments, are no longer fast enough or precise enough to be applied to modern processing. Nor have these developments been confined to parts and components-making: Assembly processes, once the most manual area of production, are today becoming mechanized at a very rapid rate, aided by robotized and other new production equipments.

Much greater precision is required in the parts entering some of these processes—high-reliability microcomputer assembly, for example, where processes must in some cases measure components in terms of number of non-conforming parts per million (which we now designate as *PPM*) in place of more traditional programs which earlier measured in terms of parts-per-thousand and even per-hundred.

The *control* of processes today assumes significantly new importance not only because it helps these modern processes work more efficiently but because many of them are simply not economically practical without satisfactory process control. If a high-speed, complex process goes out of control, major losses in terms of worthless product can mount up with terrifying speed. Even if the product has deviated only slightly from its specification, its later use in complex end assemblies may represent a high risk because of ultimate expensive teardown operations to replace it.

After the quality program is established through use of quality-engineering techniques, therefore, implementation within the framework of the program requires an intensive schedule of process measurement and analysis applied directly to incoming material, on the manufacturing floor, and in the field. Furthermore, rapid feedback of the resulting analysis is required to maintain control of quality throughout all the production processes. The technology of process-control engineering provides the quality-control tools for accomplishing this work.

While these tools are heavily used by the Process-Control-Engineering component—including Inspection and Test—of the quality-control functions, they also represent techniques that are also widely used by other key functions, such as product engineering, development laboratory, manufacturing engineering, materials specialists, production supervision, service engineers, and others. The relationship of the Process-Control-Engineering component with other company functions in the use of these techniques is discussed in Section 11.28. Section 11.29 then summarizes some of the key principles and checkpoints for process control.

11.1 Process-Control-Engineering Technology[1]

Process-control-engineering technology may be defined as

> The body of technical knowledge for analysis and control of process quality, including direct control of the quality of materials, parts, components, and assemblies as they are processed throughout the entire industrial cycle.

The many techniques employed by this technology may be grouped under four major headings:

1. *Process-quality analysis.* Included here are techniques for analyzing the measurements that have been planned by quality-engineering technique. These measurements describe the behavior of the process while it is operating, so that there will be sensitive and rapid means for predicting process trends.

(Techniques used in process analysis are discussed in Secs. 11.2 through 11.11.)

2. *In-process control.* Included here are techniques for actually applying results of the process analysis to adjust process parameters and environments to keep the process in a state of control. (Techniques used for in-process control are discussed in Secs. 11.12 through 11.16.)

3. *Implementation of the quality-program plan.* Involved here are techniques for adjusting and revising parts of the quality plan to take into account the dynamic changes of the day-by-day production situation. (Techniques for implementing the quality program are discussed in Secs. 11.17 through 11.22.)

4. *Quality-effectiveness audit.* Included here are techniques for performing the constant monitoring that has been planned by quality-engineering techniques. The monitoring covers product and process—as well as the attendant costs to ensure that the planned quality results are achieved—together with procedures and the full quality system itself. (Techniques for quality-effectiveness audit are discussed in Secs. 11.23 through 11.27.)

In the final analysis, these process-control-engineering techniques are directed toward providing immediate quality information to the operator. This individual is thus able to make parts right the first time and *know* that they have been made correctly. To do this, however, requires that the operator be provided with the necessary quality information equipment. As this is done and as this method of operation becomes effective in the plant, the inspectors can then back away from routine sorting in favor of more positive activity. Instead of simply policing manufacturing processes, Inspection and Test can become true parts of the process-control subfunction of Quality Control, as discussed in Chapter 8. These types of process-control men and women can provide positive assistance in the *production* of the right quality as follows:

- By becoming auditors of the good quality practices that have been pre-planned
- By providing as much as possible on-the-spot, shop-floor analysis of non-conformities
- By feeding back facts about these nonconformities for corrective action
- By beginning to truly understand process behavior as the basis for process analysis and control

TECHNIQUES USED IN PROCESS ANALYSIS

11.2 Process-Control-Engineering Analytical Techniques

Among the significant techniques associated with process analysis, 14 will be reviewed as representative. They are covered as follows:

Purpose of analysis	Technique
To determine capability	"Machine- and Process-Capability Analysis" (Sec. 11.3)
	"Process-Reliability Maturity Analysis" (Sec. 11.3)
	"Quality-Measuring Equipment Capability and Repeatability Analysis" (Sec. 11.4)
To determine degree of conformity to planned values	"Analysis of Pilot-Run Results" (Sec. 11.5)
	"Incoming-Material Testing, Inspection, and Laboratory Analysis" (Sec. 11.6)
	"Quality-Assurance Inspection" (Sec. 11.7)
	"Nondestructive Testing and Evaluation" (Sec. 11.7)
	"Production Testing" (Sec. 11.8)
	"Sorting Inspection" (Sec. 11.8)
To determine source of variation	"Process-Variation Analysis" (Sec. 11.9)
	"Analysis of Variable Quality-Cost Performance" (Sec. 11.9)
To identify causes of nonconformance	"Test-Data Analysis" (Sec. 11.10)
	"Scrap and Rework Analysis" (Sec. 11.10)
	"Field Complaint Analysis" (Sec. 11.11)

11.3 Machine- and Process-Capability Analysis

Use of this technique permits the prediction of the limits of variation within which a machine or process will operate. Hence it provides a means for measuring the machine and process capability and comparing this against the tolerance required by the specification.

Every machine and every process has inherent variability. For example, if a lathe is set up to turn shafts to an outer diameter of 1.000 inch, it is known that all the shafts produced will not be exactly 1.000 inch. The majority will be near this value, but there may be a few percent that are as low as 0.998 or as high as 1.002 inches (Fig. 11.1). As is discussed in more detail in Chapter 13, each machine has a natural pattern of variability; machine- and process-capability analyses establish this pattern on the basis of actual measurements taken under controlled conditions.

On the basis of this "behavior pattern," it is possible to predict what the machine or the process is capable of producing. If the spread of the pattern is less than that of the tolerance, the machine is capable of producing parts to tolerance. If it is broader than the tolerance, the machine will have to be replaced with one of greater precision or the process will have to be changed.

A detailed procedure for conducting process-capability studies is presented in Section 20.16, along with examples of process capabilities.

An application of a process-capability study is a study conducted by a Philadelphia manufacturer. The study was conducted to determine the capabilities of a numerically controlled six-spindle, automatic, turret-drill press. Accuracy

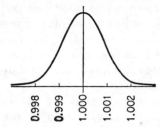

FIG. 11.1 **Machine variability as shown by a frequency-distribution graph.**

of hole location was determined under each operating condition ordinarily encountered in practice. Two different methods were employed: one using the master plate to indicate positioning without actually cutting metal, and the other putting a random series of holes in a number of sample pieces.

The sample pieces were measured and analyzed, using the methods discussed in Section 20.16. The study proved very comprehensive and provided the following information:

1. Accuracy of each of the six spindles when *(a)* drilling, *(b)* reaming, and *(c)* boring
2. Accuracy of hole locations without center drilling
3. Repeatability of the machine in coming back to "zero position" after performing a series of operations
4. Accuracy of the machine in different areas of the worktable
5. Comparison of accuracy with dial- versus numerically controlled operation

This information was used for programming the machine so it would meet drawing tolerances. This permitted acceptance of the work from the machine with a minimum amount of inspection and a maximum assurance that the pieces were accurate.

PROCESS-RELIABILITY MATURITY ANALYSIS

This technique is an integral part of a company reliability program to qualify a new product and the production processes which will produce it. A design maturity test, which will have qualified the basic reliability of the product design, will be followed prior to the start of production by a process maturity test to ensure that the production operations provide satisfactory reliability to maintain this qualified design. Process maturity analysis applications are considered in more detail in Chapters 17 and 18.

11.4 Quality-Measuring Equipment Capability and Repeatability Analysis

Just as a piece of manufacturing equipment has a pattern of variability, so does a piece of measuring equipment have its own pattern of variability. For example, if a gage block measures to 1.0000 inch and then repeated measurements are taken on it with an ordinary pair of micrometers, it will be found that most of the readings fall around 1.0000 inch, but a few percent of the readings may be at 0.9998 and 1.0002 inches. The techniques of quality-measurement equipment capability and repeatability analysis relates to identifying and controlling this pattern of variability.

For example, one of the most traditional of all measurement devices—micrometers without a vernier scale—would be unsuitable for measuring a dimension that had a total tolerance of 0.005 inch, because the variability of the measuring instrument, including human variability, is almost as great as that of the process. A rule of thumb is that the precision of the measuring equipment should be such that its total variability does not exceed one-tenth of the tolerance being measured.

For example, if a shaft has a tolerance of ± 0.001 inch—total tolerance, 0.002 inch—the variability of the measuring equipment desirably should not exceed 0.0002 inch. This equipment should be capable of being read to 0.0002-inch calibration marks, dividing the total tolerance into 10 increments. If such a rule is followed, the observed measurement should be within 1 percent of the actual measurement.

11.5 Analysis of Pilot-Run Results

This analytical technique compares actual versus planned quality performance by means of a pilot run. Any departures from planned performance with respect to either the product or the process calls for investigation and possible adjustment of both.

A pilot run is a trial production run using regular production tooling and production compounds—electronic, mechanical, chemical, and other. The first manufactured units are subjected to end-use tests and field test to see if the product meets performance requirements.

Besides analysis of data resulting from tests of the pilot-run product, a careful analysis of the pilot run itself should be made to determine which, if any, manufacturing processes depart from planned results and are contributing to the deterioration of product quality.

It is important to point up quality trouble spots so correction to the process or product design can be made prior to the start of production. An evaluation of the effectiveness of the corrective action should also be made.

The pilot run may also show up inadequacies or "overdesign" in the quality-control plan, i.e., points in the process flow where more quality information should be obtained or, conversely, where less quality information would suffice.

As the result of a thorough pilot-run analysis, for example, it was discovered that a special wrench for installing valve orifices in a device was slipping and cutting slivers of metal from the valve body. These slivers would later lodge in the orifice and cause the device to fail. As a result, a new locking wrench that prevented slippage and the attendant quality problem was designed.

11.6 Incoming-Material Testing, Inspection, and Laboratory Analysis

Analytical techniques applied to the physical and chemical properties of materials permit measuring the degree to which the materials conform to the quality-program plan.

The services of a laboratory are often necessary for making these chemical and physical analyses. This can serve for both incoming-material control and process control.

The technique of incoming-material testing and inspection and laboratory analysis is applied to the acceptance of materials, parts, components, and subassemblies that qualify as meeting quality standards. By having the laboratory equipment located in the receiving inspection area, much "trotting" of samples to the laboratory and mailing back of laboratory reports can be eliminated, thereby speeding up the whole acceptance procedure.

Examples of such equipment include tensile test machines, testers for checking strength of packing materials, hardness testers, radiation testers, moisture testers, ultrasonic testers, signature analysis, laser machines, spectrophotometers, and other state-of-the-art nondestructive evaluation techniques. The rapid evaluation of such equipments used in nondestructive testing and evaluation technology is discussed in more detail in Chapter 12.

11.7 Quality-Assurance Inspection

The technique of quality-assurance inspection is the measuring of the various quality characteristics generated in a production process or inherent in the material. This type of inspection can be a check made on each piece produced (100 percent inspection) or a check made on a statistical sample of the lot. The inspection may be a mechanical or electronic measurement or a visual inspection, the results of which are compared with standards.

The inspection can be performed by the operator or worker making the part or component, by a second person who is responsible for measuring only, or performed entirely by computer-controlled measurement.

This inspection assures that the products being produced meet the standards of quality and quality levels which have been previously established.

NONDESTRUCTIVE TESTING AND EVALUATION

Nondestructive testing and evaluation, used in process-control engineering, is the technique for thoroughly examining key quality characteristics of parts materials and products without imposing change or other deformation in the component or product. From an operating and production point of view, nondestructive testing is highly dependent upon skill in recognizing opportunities and initiative and ingenuity in recommending ways of making the necessary tests—fully as much as it is of providing the necessary equipment. Often the equipment is technically available well ahead of the suitable number of opportunities, and so the Process-Control Engineer, technical specialist, tester, or inspector should be continuously on the lookout for opportunities for such tests.

When a need is found, the Process-Control Engineer can often recommend a practical test method. Then, by consultation with other quality engineers, nondestructive tests can be planned and the necessary equipment procured or developed. This work of the Process-Control Engineer is very important and contributes to the establishment of more and better process controls as a result of increased ability to measure hard-to-measure quality characteristics.

11.8 Production Testing

Production testing is the technique of operating the product under actual or simulated load conditions to determine that the unit will function properly. The actual operating conditions are usually varied to simulate the field conditions, including tests for overload. Tests may be made on each unit of product or on a representative sample. The test method used may involve automatic equipment or conventional manual methods and equipment.

Tests of this type not only assure that the product will function but help reduce customer annoyance due to the product's not being properly adjusted. Factory adjustment, where feasible, is less expensive and more accurate than field adjustment. Tests also assist in-process control by making the information available for feedback to contributing processes.

Sorting Inspection

This inspection technique sorts those parts which conform to the applicable drawings and specifications from those which do not conform. It is used where the process that produces the part does not have the capability to produce parts to the quality levels required or where a process goes out of control and the lot quality is below the acceptable level. Where the capability of the process is below that required to meet the design requirements of assembly, selective assembly may be used. Under these conditions, the sorting inspection consists of separating the parts into categories or classes according to the dimensions actually generated.

11.9 Process-Variation Analysis

Through the techniques used for studying process variations, it is possible either to eliminate or reduce the cause, thereby decreasing the variation and bringing it under control.

In some cases, it may not be possible to identify assignable causes for variation; i.e., the variation may be constant and under control. This situation shows that a fundamental change in the manufacturing process is required to bring about the desired results.

If such basic changes in process are not possible within knowledge, time, and cost limitations, the product design must come under consideration. It may be possible for the product-design engineer to "design around" the difficulty and accomplish the same product function by a different arrangement, for example, using an electronic approach rather than a mechanical one. To assist the design engineer here, it is necessary to analyze the design by studying the effects of significant design parameters at varying levels by means of designed experiments.

Analysis of Variable Quality-Cost Performance

Where a high degree of manufacturing variability is contributing to losses and production delays, and especially to high quality costs, a formal analysis of the trend is made. The various factors that cause the variability of the process can be studied, and those factors which contribute most to variability can be sorted out and identified by various statistical techniques, as discussed in Part 5. Application of these techniques permits elimination or closer control of the factors causing variability; hence it is possible to reduce process variability.

11.10 Test-Data Analysis

Fundamental to the maximum usefulness of the technique of test-data analysis is good data on which to base the analysis, such as measurement of the significant parameters at the correct levels and in the proper sequence. These data provide means for detecting symptoms that tell much about the quality of the device being tested.

Proper analysis of data is directed at getting as much quality information as possible from the available measurements. Normal variation in operating parameters such as output voltages and currents, horsepower, noise level, and vibration can be distinguished from abnormal behavior by use of statistical techniques.

The resulting analysis often serves to diagnose the basic cause for abnormal operation so that corrective action can be taken on the particular unit under test. It is also a means for going back into the design or process to make changes that will get away from borderline quality. The analysis of component failure, assembly errors, and finish defects can be used to point out areas where corrective action should be taken or where further study should be made.

Scrap and Rework Analysis

Basic to this technique is the analysis of causes for scrapped parts and necessary rework operations. The collection of data in sufficient detail permits pinpointing of trouble sources. Such data are often available as a by-product of a good quality cost accounting system. In such a system, the organizational component responsible for causing the scrap or rework is charged for the loss or repair.

11.11 Field Complaint Analysis

Basic to this technique is the analysis of causes of customer dissatisfaction with company products, structured so that necessary areas of corrective action can be pinpointed to the production operations requiring quality improvement. The prompt collection of data which include all pertinent information not only aids in identifying the possible problems within the manufacturing process but helps pinpoint which company function should be responsible for corrective process-oriented action—for example, Engineering, Manufacturing, Materials Control, Quality Engineering, or others. The computerization of this quality information is increasingly making such data more timely and more valuable.

Likely sources for such data are service-shop tickets, service-call reports, service-engineers' reports, installation reports, returned apparatus reports, and data on other complaints. When the systematic collection of such data is included in the quality cost accounting system of the company, the organizational component found responsible for causing the customer complaint can be charged for the repair or replacement costs.

The accumulated data of field complaint analysis is useful in many process-oriented ways. By structuring the information into various identifying categories, such as part number, application, and geographical location of the customer, patterns will develop which can be further analyzed as a basis for ongoing improvement of process variation. Not only can service-call rates and complaint-service expenses be reduced, but improved outgoing product-quality levels can be targeted to improve productivity of production operations.

TECHNIQUES USED FOR IN-PROCESS CONTROL

11.12 Process-Control-Engineering Techniques Used for In-Process Control

Representative techniques for applying results of the process analysis for control purposes are presented by four typical cases as follows:

Purpose of control	Technique
To control quality during processing	"Vendor Rating and Vendor Performance Rating" (Sec. 11.13) " 'Structure Table' Control" (Sec. 11.14) "Control Charts" (Sec. 11.15) "Work Sampling" (Sec. 11.16)

11.13 Vendor Rating and Vendor Performance Rating

Evaluation of vendors is an important activity to assure the dependable high quality of incoming material in the plant and company. Two principal techniques are basic to this activity:

Vendor Rating

This technique provides vendor-to-vendor assessment, whereby each vendor is measured against another specific vendor, or group of vendors, for price, quality, delivery, and other important performance measures. Vendor Rating, typically reported quarterly, results in decisions concerning future business activities with the vendor. This technique is discussed in detail in Chapter 19.

When vendors are compared against their competitors, they may insist that the only fair basis is comparison on a given component, not on an overall average performance, because some vendors may have more difficult requirements to meet for a particular kind of part not being made by their competitors.

Vendor Performance Rating

This technique involves objective appraisal of one vendor's specific products. Product performance is assessed in depth, and the results fed back to the vendor. In the case of a poor quality situation, this information can be used by the vendor to affect corrective action and improve standing and reputation with the company. The Vendor Performance Rating report is generally published monthly in the case of high-usage products.

Together, Vendor Rating and Vendor Performance Rating comprise an effective incoming-material control mechanism in the total quality program.

11.14 "Structure Table" Control

A "structure table" is a technique for tabulating knowledge in a logical sequence. In quality-control work, such a table is established for a part or a process. The knowledge required for control of the quality attributes is contained in the structure table. Planning for similar parts or operation can be quickly extracted from such tables with a minimum of effort.

Quality information in the body of the table includes process-capability values and percentage yields. Analysis of this information provides a basis for machine routing and expected yield.

For example, if production of a given part involves several different turning operations, the process-capability data will show which lathes should be used to generate a given dimension to a required tolerance. By progressing a step further, the tables will show the expected quality levels which will be produced by following the recommended routing.

Figure 11.2 is an example of a structure table.

MACHINE #273
(LATHE−O.D.)

TABLE 0331

A. Q. L. − %	←————————— .1 —————————→				
CAPABILITY − (%) OF TOLERANCE)	≤10	≤25	≤50	≤75	≤75
CHECK−(# PIECES)	1	1	6	10	REJECT
ACCEPTANCE BAND− (% AROUND NOMINAL)	85	64	40	13	REJECT
NEXT TABLE	0332 —————————→				NONE

←———— 1.0 ————→						←———— 2.5 ————→					
≤10	≤25	≤50	≤75	≤90	<90	≤10	≤25	≤50	≤75	≤90	≤90
1	1	4	10	10	REJECT	1	1	1	6	10	REJECT
88	70	51	32	18	REJECT	90	73	46	38	29	REJECT
←———— 0332 ————→					NONE	←———— 0332 ————→					NONE

←———— 5.0 ————→						←———— 10 ————→					
≤10	≤25	≤50	≤75	≤90	<90	≤10	≤25	≤50	≤75	≤90	<90
1	1	1	4	6	REJECT	1	1	1	2	4	REJECT
90	76	51	43	35	REJECT	92	79	57	45	42	REJECT
←———— 0332 ————→					NONE	←———— 0332 ————→					NONE

FIG. 11.2 **Structure table.**

11.15 Control Charts

The control chart technique is used for in-process control to give an hour-by-hour or day-by-day picture of the process to the shop personnel and the process-control engineer. By use of these charts, the control limits of the process are established, and control of the process is maintained by periodic sampling and plotting the results. By observing the charts, any out-of-control condition of either the central tendency or the spread of the distribution can be detected. Through study of the data plotted on a control chart, advance indications can often detect a process that is tending toward an out-of-control condition. Further investigation and analysis have to be made to determine the cause. Then corrective action has to be taken, preferably before a nonconforming product is made.

Control charts can be used to control such processes as machining, finishing, assembly, chemical processing, and any other process where the quality characteristics are measurable. The theory and practice of control charts is the subject of Chapter 14.

11.16 Work Sampling

Work sampling is a statistical technique for making a large number of instantaneous or flash observations of a job or worker randomly and for recording the quality activity or state observed. The ratio of each quality activity or state observed to the total observation measures the proportion of time spent on various activities. This ratio further determines such information as delay time, the amount of time spent on clerical work, the magnitude of interruptions, and the time spent on different products of a product mix.

It is an analysis tool to obtain facts for programming improvements and to assist in measuring the productivity of an activity. It is an excellent technique to determine where further study is necessary to improve productivity. Studies made before and after improvements are done can be used as a measure of an improvement.

Work sampling is an especially useful technique in quality-control work. The variety of different operations that make up most quality-control jobs may be effectively analyzed by this method. Excessive time being spent on makeready work can be identified, such as making electronic connections for testing, collecting samples, or getting report blanks. More efficient, productive quality-control work patterns are often possible as a result of studies using this technique.

TECHNIQUES USED FOR IMPLEMENTING THE QUALITY PLAN

11.17 Process Engineering Techniques for Implementing the Quality Plan

Typical of the techniques for implementing and adapting the quality plan to the production situation are the five presented here:

Purpose	Technique
To implement the quality plan	"Use of Manuals and Standing Instructions" (Sec. 11.18) "Interpretation of Drawings, Specifications, and Quality Planning" (Sec. 11.19) "Temporary Quality Planning" (Sec. 11.20) "First-Piece Inspection" (Sec. 11.21) "Disposition of Discrepant or Nonconforming Material" (Sec. 11.22)

11.18 Use of Manuals and Standing Instructions

Preparation of process-quality manuals and standing instructions within the framework of the quality program represents an important process-control technique. These manuals codify and communicate various procedural details, such as operative procedures and standards of workmanship, which ordinarily are not spelled out on drawings. Specific process references and tolerances should appear on a drawing or in a specification, but generally it is cumbersome to include the detail required for operative procedures and standards of workmanship. Too often, these instructions are not written anywhere; they are transmitted verbally, and like all verbal communications, the information will change each time it is communicated.

Typical manuals are

- *Process-quality procedures manuals,* which include such instructions as material-disposition procedures, instructions for completion of forms, maintenance of files, gage-inspection procedures, and procedures for making process-capability studies.
- *Standard shop-practice manuals,* which include such information as the definition of flatness, finish, squareness, undercut for threading, spotweld depressions, and the like. Instructions of this type are difficult to write, so pictures, sketches, and visual or physical samples may be required to convey fully the meaning of the instructions. Manuals of this type become the reference material for judging quality of workmanship and are useful for training new personnel and for reviews by experienced personnel.

11.19 Interpretation of Drawings, Specifications, and Quality Planning

Interpretation of drawings, specifications, and quality planning is often a necessary technique for their proper implementation in production. Even though these instructions are written as clearly as possible, there is always the chance that they may be misunderstood by production personnel. These personnel do not always have the same background information that is available to the product engineer who develops the design or the quality engineer who develops the plan. This activity helps give an image of a good part and emphasizes its important characteristics. Information given in this manner is more acceptable than criticism of mistakes and errors by an operator or assembler that result from lack of understanding.

The need for interpretation should never be used as a crutch for poor drawings, instructions, or quality plans. When additional information is required, the instruction, drawing, or plan should be changed to include it.

Drawings, specifications, and quality planning can be interpreted to the operator, using different methods of communication. This can be accomplished in orientation sessions with either groups or individuals. Another method is to communicate the information to supervisors or lead personnel so they can instruct their operators. Samples, pictures, and drawings may be used as visual aids. Proper instruction of operators is essential to the "make-it-right-the-first-time" principle.

11.20 Temporary Quality Planning

Temporary quality planning is the technique for instituting a temporary set of quality-control instructions where the established quality-program plan does not apply. These instructions are generally necessary when the normal or planned production method or planned quality information equipment cannot be used. These situations arise when machines break down and equipment or tooling is removed for maintenance. In other instances, material substitutions are made because of slow delivery or unacceptable purchased material. It is necessary that temporary planning be instituted immediately and on the spot where the problem exists so that the overall product quality will be maintained and remain under control, even under adverse conditions.

Temporary planning is generally instituted on the production floor, using such equipment and gaging as is readily available. In those instances where a permanent change is made in the production process, temporary planning should be used only until quality-engineering techniques are used to modify the regular quality-program plan. It is important that a follow-up be made on all temporary quality plans so that inspections, operator checks, laboratory analyses, or reliability tests which were used to control a temporary condition do not continue beyond their need.

11.21 First-Piece Inspection

First-piece-from-a-new-tool checking technique is a detailed inspection of a part made using a new tool, fixture, or die under actual operating conditions. This inspection measures accurately every specified characteristic generated by the new tool and compares it with the part drawing. Each measurement is recorded, and any deviations of the generated characteristic from the drawing are noted. Particular attention is given to such characteristics as squareness, wrinkling, radii, and tool marks. Any deviations recorded must be resolved by either reworking the tool or changing the part drawing to agree with the product.

First-piece inspection is the first step in proving in the production tooling and obtaining correlation between manufactured parts and the part drawing. This technique helps resolve major discrepancies between tooling and the product specification. Part-to-part variation can then be determined by a process-capability study.

11.22 Disposition of Discrepant or Nonconforming Material

Disposition of discrepant or nonconforming material is the technique used for removing nonconforming material from the operating quality system. Occasionally, material or parts are produced which do not meet specifications because of vendor problems, material substitution, design or production errors, equipment failures, or material variation. Whatever the reason, a decision must be made to use the material or part as is, to rework the part to drawing, to rework it to a planned deviation from drawing, or, finally, to scrap the material or part.

Disposition procedures are orderly ways for the discrepancy to be analyzed for its effect on product. A recommendation is then made for disposition on the basis of the analysis and the necessary approvals requested. A secondary purpose is served by the follow-up for corrective action. The general procedure consists of these steps:

1. The discrepancy is reported on a form with all pertinent inspection and test data.
2. The discrepancy is analyzed for the effect the defect will have on outgoing product quality.
3. Disposition is recommended.
4. Where design is affected, the design engineer who developed the product specification should approve the disposition.
5. The signed report becomes the authority for disposition and copies are distributed.
6. Copies are directed to production for corrective action.

TECHNIQUES USED FOR AUDITING QUALITY EFFECTIVENESS

11.23 Process Engineering Techniques—Quality Audit

One of the major developments of modern quality control is the growth, both in concept and techniques, of the quality-audit function of total quality control. Implementing and carrying out such audits is today one of the most significant areas of process-control engineering technology.

As a definition,

Quality audit is evaluation to verify the effectiveness of control.

Quality audit is not a different form of parts inspection or a more intensive type of product testing or a more elaborate procedure for vendor rating. Those plants which, in the past, have tried to upgrade such in-line product control practices by labeling them "audits" have overlooked the basic function of objective overview through which modern quality audit contributes to modern quality control. They have pyramided the cost of inspection and testing without gaining the benefits of quality auditing.

Quality audit will be, in some of its forms, the inspection of parts inspection, the testing of product testing, and the procedure for evaluating the procedures for vendor rating. The purpose is not duplication of product or process controls but assurance that there *is* control.

Among the several different considerations in the establishment of quality audits to meet different quality-program objectives are the following:

- *Quality purpose*—including audits that may be directed to product; process; a variety of specific areas such as measurements; procedures; and the quality system itself
- *Quality-audit performance*—including audits that may be performed by a single process-control engineer, a group from the quality function, a multifunctional plant team, a companywide team drawn from other plants, an outside organization
- *Audit frequency*—including audits that may be performed on predetermined frequencies such as daily, weekly, monthly, quarterly, or other and those performed without advance notice
- *Quality-audit reporting and documentation*—including audits that are quantitatively measured in index numbers or reported in a summary document—with both quantitative and qualitative data—measured in terms of comparative trends showing improvement or deterioration, or evaluated in terms of performance standards
- *Audit corrective action*—including corrective actions explicitly identified by product, area, process, organizational component, time schedule, and follow-up responsibility

Among the techniques for auditing quality effectiveness, the following will be reviewed as representative:

Purpose of audit	Technique
To measure effectiveness of product control	"Product Audits" (Sec. 11.24)
To measure effectiveness of quality planning and execution	"Procedures Audits" (Sec. 11.25)
To measure effectiveness of quality system and execution	"Quality-System Audits" (Sec. 11.26)
To measure effectiveness of specific quality areas	"Other Areas of Quality Audit" (Sec. 11.27)

11.24 Product Audits

A major process-control-engineering technique is the implementation of the product audits whose quality-engineering planning was discussed in Section 10.34. In process-control-engineering activities, this product audit is a technique for—from the point of view of the customer—evaluation of a relatively small sample of product upon which all operations, tests, and inspections have been performed and which awaits shipment. This evaluation is performed in accordance with a carefully established quality-engineering plan.

All quality characteristics that have previously been examined are evaluated. Certain additional life, environmental, and reliability tests that cannot be performed under production conditions may also be performed. Examination of the product under customer-centered use conditions is the orientation for the audit steps.

Where necessary, the work is done in facilities whose primary purpose is performing audits. However, product-audit work may under some circumstances be performed directly at the end of the production line, or, in the case of products where certain components and subassemblies become effectively encapsulated in the completed product, it may also take place in certain in-process areas. The location depends upon where quality characteristics can best be evaluated with the required technical effectiveness and necessary objectivity.

Audit frequency must be geared to the production volume and the production cycle time conditions. In the case of high production products with short production cycles, audit frequency will be daily, in recognition of the rapid quality changes that can take place under high-volume conditions. Weekly audits will be scheduled for products of medium production volume. Monthly audits may be required for long production cycle products. However, except for job-shop products, such as large turbines produced over a very long time, audit cycles longer than 1 month will allow too long a time for objective evaluation of possible deterioration in control practices.

In many products, such as minicomputers, diesel engines, and television chassis, product audits are performed by process-control engineering together with other technical personnel of the plant. In products such as certain foods, where qualitative characteristics are of particular importance, a panel of experienced plant personnel will be required for objective, effective audit. In products such as automobiles, the audit will include road performance use tests by experienced personnel.

In the quality-engineering structuring of the product-audit planning, each quality characteristic is classified in accordance with its importance (Sec. 10.19) and a series of demerits is established, weighted in accordance with the importance of the quality characteristic. Depending upon the plant circumstances and approach, this demerit system may, for example, establish a base of 100 as "without product-quality discrepancy"—which is then reduced by demerits assigned during auditing. The actual details of the demerit structuring will depend upon particular plant, product, customer, and marketplace conditions and must be established by each plant for these specific conditions.

During product-quality audit, each quality characteristic is evaluated for demerits assessed for each quality discrepancy identified. An index is computed by totaling the demerits and relating them to a comparison base, for example, demerits per unit of product. The index is plotted graphically with time to determine trends of product quality and the effectiveness of product control. Figure 11.3 illustrates such a quality-audit index trend for a tightly controlled electronic product produced by a major industrial control manufacturer.

The audit data are carefully analyzed to identify specific areas which call for investigation of design, processing, control methods, or procedures. In Figure

PRODUCT QUALITY AUDIT RATING
ELECTRONIC ASSEMBLY <u>GF15</u>

PERIOD: <u>Week 11 through 27</u>

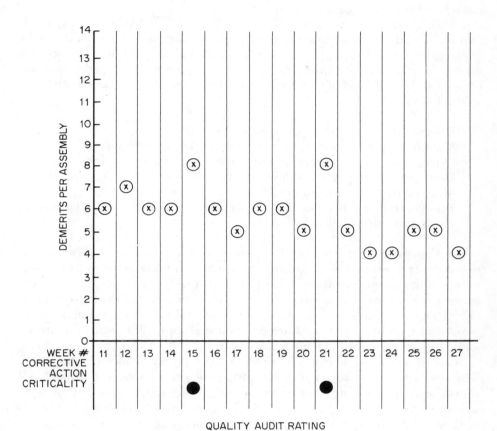

QUALITY AUDIT RATING
FIG. 11.3 **Quality audit rating.**

11.3, weeks 15 and 21 require critical corrective action. These corrective actions become a central area of the plant and of the company corrective-action program.

11.25 Procedures Audits

An additional major process-control-engineering audit technique is the implementation of the procedures audits whose quality-engineering planning was earlier reviewed. In process-control-engineering activities, this procedures audit operates as a technique for a formal examination and verification in accordance with the specific audit plan that detailed procedures in the quality plan are being followed. The primary purpose of the audit is assurance of the effective execution of all aspects of the quality procedure. However, if indicated, identification will be made that the procedure design is inadequate and must be reviewed for improvement.

The audit plan will be designed to be directed to key procedural areas, which may include, depending upon the plant requirements, differences in the audit frequency required for certain procedures. The audit plan may be directed both to certain key individual procedures—such as employee quality instruction—and those groups of procedures that, for example, bear upon such areas as the following:

· In-process quality documentation and records
· Manufacturing-process equipment and tooling maintenance
· Quality information equipment measurement and calibration
· Conformance to process requirements
· Material handling and storage practices
· Product testing conformance to applicable specifications and quality standards and other similar key areas

Frequency of audits is established based upon the rate of possible operational changes—such as in variation in production volume, employee turnover, new production introductions, and others—that will impact the plant: In fast-moving operations, certain procedures—such as employee training—and certain groups of procedures—such as equipment calibration and maintenance—may require monthly audits. Other procedure groups will require a quarterly audit and, in some cases, semiannual audits.

Some procedures audits will be performed by process-control engineering. The performance of audits of some groups of procedures with major multifunctional impact—such as product testing conformance to applicable specifications and quality standards—will take place by an audit team composed of functional representatives together with process-control engineering.

In addition to regularly scheduled procedures audits on a frequency established on a published basis, unscheduled procedures audits—periodically performed by process-control engineering—can represent an important area of the audit program under some plant circumstances. The objective is not that of policing but that the audit not become too routine a matter.

In the quality-engineering structuring of the procedures-audit planning, a measurement rating program for the audits will be established. This may involve identification of such categories as excellent, satisfactory, poor, and unacceptable, with clear definitions for each that may be applied to each procedure as a result of audit findings. Direct quantitative ratings are also established, when appropriate for the procedure, for example, aggregating to a scoring rating of 100 in the case when no deviations are found.

During the audit evaluation, each procedure is evaluated for this measurement structure, with identification made for each deviation from procedure practice. Careful records are maintained for each rating, including applicable documentation.

As a matter of audit practice, a preliminary report of the audit results will be provided to the managers and supervisors of the area under audit, directly at the conclusion of the audit. This permits all audit activities to be as visible as possible, permits review and discussion, and permits any necessary corrective action.

The formal and documented procedures-audit report will then be provided to all key individuals. It will also identify corrective action, including recommended responsibilities for such corrective action.

Where appropriate, the results of the procedures audit will be quantified as summary scores of the audit. These scores can be plotted to indicate trends of managerial control of the quality procedures. Figure 11.4 shows the procedures-audit index for the calibration and maintenance area of a large mechanical parts manufacturing plant.

The implementation of the indicated corrective actions will be a key area of attention for subsequent audits. Where major corrective actions are indicated, a follow-up audit may take place in advance of the normal schedule.

11.26 Quality-System Audits

The quality-system audit assesses the effectiveness of implementation of the quality system and determines the degree to which system objectives are being achieved. The audit is system- rather than product-oriented. It is not explicitly hardware-oriented, except where that hardware may contribute to the assessment of the overall system.

System auditing is a major area of total quality management and technology and will take place in accordance with a thoroughly structured program which will include evaluation of all key activities of the system.

The auditing will usually be performed by a multifunctional team. Some audits may have the participation, when appropriate, of one or more members of top plant or company management.

Audit frequency will depend upon plant circumstances and will always be scheduled so that full system measurement takes place within a time frame so that any potential deterioriation of systems practices will not be able to continue. Procedures audits of particularly critical system areas will thus be scheduled to take place at a much greater frequency than the full system audit itself.

The audit report will be formally documented and reported to all key individuals and groups and to plant and company top management. Areas of systems-implementation weakness will be thoroughly identified, necessary corrective action steps will be established, and improvement responsibilities will be proposed. Areas where the quality system itself has deficiencies will be identified so that necessary systems-design improvement can take place.

The corrective-action steps become an integral part of the top priority man-

QUALITY PROCEDURES AUDIT
PERFORMANCE TRENDS

MFG. UNIT/AREA: Calibration & Maintenance   AUDIT TEAM: P.C.E. & Team

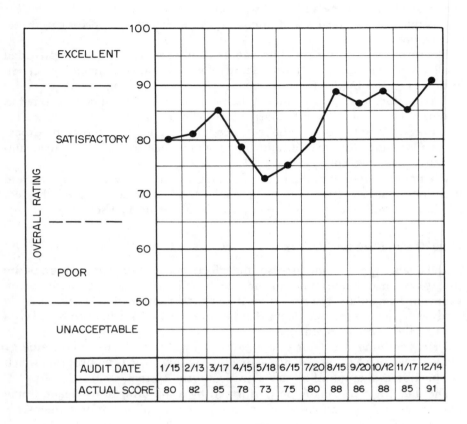

AUDIT DATE	1/15	2/13	3/17	4/15	5/18	6/15	7/20	8/15	9/20	10/12	11/17	12/14
ACTUAL SCORE	80	82	85	78	73	75	80	88	86	88	85	91

FIG. 11.4 **Quality procedures rating.**

agement- and engineering-scheduled projects of the plant and company. Follow-up audit in these necessary areas will be an integral part of the system audit program to ensure that the necessary improvements have, in fact, taken place.

11.27 Other Areas of Quality Audit

Plant and company circumstances may call for the basic principle of quality audit to be applied in particular areas, either periodically or on a one-time basis. Included among these areas are:

· Product Service Quality Audit—oriented to field product evaluation of a small sample of product following product service
· Quality Measurement Audit—oriented to measurement practices evaluation of particular forms of metrology
· Process Audit—oriented to audit of process-control practices in critical processing areas
· Vendor Quality Practice Audit—oriented to audit of key vendor quality procedures relating to critical purchased parts and subassemblies
· Laboratory Reliability Testing Audit—oriented to audit of the reliability of key areas of reliability testing

11.28 Use of the Technology by the Process-Control-Engineering Component

The Process-Control-Engineering component—including Inspection and Test—of the Quality-Control function heavily employs process-control-engineering technology in its work. The relationship between this component and other functions of the plant and company in the use of these techniques is a significant factor in the effectiveness of the technology.

The basic responsibility and decision-making authority of the Process-Control-Engineering component lies in two principal areas: the interpretation of quality standards and the final acceptance of product for customer use. Thus, the relationship of Process-Control Engineering with the other two engineering activities in total quality control, Quality Engineering and Quality Information Equipment Engineering, is a straightforward one. Quality Engineering establishes the quality plan, including the process-control plan, and specifies the what, when, where, and how to get the desired control. Process-Control Engineering provides information about process capabilities on which the process-control plan is based and then follows through and puts the plan itself into action. A closed-loop information flow exists between these two technical groups. A similar relationship exists between Process-Control Engineering and Quality Information Equipment Engineering with regard to relevant hardware for measurement and control.

Process-Control Engineering's relationship begins during the product-development stage with Manufacturing Engineering and Materials so as to coordinate the process-control plan for the new product with the planning for the production machines and production personnel, and the materials of acceptable quality. In their own turn, these functions will expect from Process-Control Engineering both capability information and operating quality data on which to base their decisions regarding process and material sources.

Production also depends upon the Process-Control-Engineering component for key activities. To ensure that planned quality controls are carried out on the production floor, Process-Control Engineering must see that personnel have the correct understanding of the control plan and that they operate the quality information equipment correctly. It must also see that personnel receive timely quality information feedback designating required process adjustments, efficient disposition decisions for off-specification items, feedback from product-quality measurements, and technical help in resolving quality problems and improving process capability. Production will also expect technical help in avoiding production delays and resolving quality problems, such as efficient disposition decisions for off-specification process conditions and materials quality.

To carry out many of its responsibilities, the Process-Control-Engineering component will have to obtain decisions from still other company functions. As examples, decisions to deviate from drawings must be determined by Design Engineering, and decisions to return vendors' material must be worked out with Purchasing.

11.29 Key Checkpoints for Process Control

Twelve checkpoints for process-control effectiveness can be summarized as follows:

1. Are understandable product- and process-quality requirements available and throughly documented in production operations?
2. Are process capabilities and relationship of inputs to outputs clearly delineated?
3. Are causes of process variation explicitly identified and is there an organized procedure for their elimination if needed?
4. Have practical methods been established to control quality of process inputs?
5. Do all production personnel have readily available information about physical, chemical, and other standards; quality routines; and decision rules for taking quality corrective action?
6. Have all quality plans and quality information equipment been thoroughly tried out in the production environment and proved effective and practical?
7. Have all control practices and equipment been tested on pilot runs prior to their routine operation?
8. Has study begun of process behavior and function in the design and development stage of new product introduction?
9. Have product and process designs and quality plans been balanced with production capabilities?
10. Has provision been made for analysis and immediate corrective follow-through of field complaints in the relevant production operations?
11. Are the data analyzed in such a way as to expedite product traceability and recall?
12. Have sufficient monitoring, auditing, and feedback provisions been made to maintain and support control?

Note

[1]The process-control-engineering techniques discussed here have been developed by a number of professional quality engineers. Although too numerous to mention individually, it is these men and women who have created the substance of modern process-control-engineering technology.

CHAPTER 12

Quality Information Equipment Engineering Technology

Modern process control and final product testing demands equipment which can make quality measurements of precision. The thousandths-of-an-inch pocket micrometer, which once epitomized exactness, is being made obsolete by electronic gages that measure millionths of an inch. The dimensional gaging, formerly characterized by manually operated mechanical height gages and surface plates, is now increasingly being accomplished by dimensional measuring machines which are computer-controlled.

Dimensional characteristics are but one of a long list of quality characteristics needed for the evaluations of today's products. A whole array of electronic parameters must be measured: voltage, current, power, resistance, capacitance, and frequency, in a wide range of values. Chemical measurements are increasingly common, even in the mechanical goods and electrical industries. Physical strength, thrust, flow, pressures, temperatures, surface and subsurface flaws, and times (in microseconds) are more and more widely used measurements, as are an array of radiation, optical, and energy-sensitive measurements.

Add to this the additional requirements that these measurements must be made rapidly and accurately during the manufacturing cycle, must be compatible with it, and often must be made automatically. Furthermore, consider that these measurements may be used to adjust the process itself automatically. This may involve feeding the measurements into a computer, comparing the results with standards, and then feeding back the needed information for correction of the process, all automatically, while the resulting data are stored for future recall. Many of the measurements may have to be performed for nondestructive test and inspection evaluation, and some must take place on a noncontact basis.

Final inspection and test itself must include more and more reliability and other functional checking to provide the necessary complete product evaluation required by today's marketplace. This thorough evaluation requires, for accuracy and economy, equipment that is as automatic as possible and increasingly mini- or microprocessor computer-based.

Equipment in the field of quality control is thus assuming a new and much more significant role than was played by the traditional inspection and testing devices. Historically, inspection equipment was essentially a small incident in the work of the factory methods planner, and the primitive equipment and low productivity of such equipment certainly demonstrated this. Even test equipment, although somewhat more extensively covered, was still largely a matter of selecting manually programmed hand-wired test circuits that could be mounted in a suitable metal box.

These older equipments had the principal job of accepting or rejecting parts and products. Their being made automatic usually meant only that they would electrically, electronically, or mechanically sort the bad product from the good, which made no other contribution to the plant's quality objective than that bad parts and products might be identified more quickly than had ever before been possible. These devices were often set up with almost no preplanned relationship to other segments of the plant quality-control work.

12.1 The Job of Modern Equipment

In contrast, today it is clear that the basic job of modern quality-control equipment is not merely to inspect or test; it is also to provide usable information about product and process quality. This information may still be used, in part, as the basis for acceptance or rejection. But its other major use is for rapid manual, mechanized, or fully automatic feedback for process control and for true *control* of product quality—often for the first time in some operations.

In fact, these modern quality *information* equipment devices are the representation, in physical equipment, of portions of the quality system of the plant. As such, they are an essential segment of this system and must be fully compatible with its other segments.

The rapid growth of modern manufacturing technology—regarding processes, production mix and volume, and parts and assembly tolerances—has been a major factor in causing the need for this improvement in the effectiveness and the operation of quality equipment. These quality equipments have become recognized as essential elements in planning and installing modern manufacturing and total quality operations in today's production plants.

The testing and inspection equipments that are designed according to the quality *information* concept are often much lower in *total* cost to the plant and less complex in design and operation than are devices developed according to the older testing and inspection concepts. This is because it has been all too frequent to mechanize and electronicize unproductive quality equipment which turns out to be much more complex and costlier than the planned quality requirements demand.

An example is the midwestern motor plant that purchased a motor tester for final, 100 percent, go and not-go checking of 17 quality characteristics. This $190,000 piece of checking equipment did nothing to improve the basic quality level of the motors; its principal asset was that it provided much more rapid separation of the bad motors from the good.

Study, employing the techniques of quality engineering, established for the plant a quality plan which specified two pieces of in-process equipment to measure and process quality information. These two equipments, whose total cost was $24,000, helped control the motor process. They soon made the costly, elaborate, final motor tester unnecessary.

Lessons learned from application of the first several generations of modern quality equipments have had what might be thought of as a forcing action on the necessity for effective quality-engineering work in the specification and use of such equipments regarding what the *quality system calls for*. This is in contrast to trying to fit the system to some technically optimized but not quality optimized piece of testing or inspection hardware which simply cannot provide the prevention-oriented results required in total quality programs.

The principle is this: What is significant is not better quality devices as such but those information equipments which integrate with low-cost, high-efficiency quality systems.

The increasing importance of such equipment is demonstrated by the trends in its use. Only a few years ago, this type of equipment commanded just a few cents out of every dollar spent by plants on their equipment investment. Today, 25 percent and more of the industrial plant investment dollar can be budgeted for quality-control equipments related to sound, necessary, and quality- and cost-improving projects.

The technology of quality information equipment engineering provides the quality-control tools that must be considered here. As a major area of total quality control, the work of quality information equipment engineering complements and coordinates with the other primary quality technologies: quality engineering and process-control engineering.

12.2 Quality Information Equipment Engineering[1]

Quality information equipment engineering may be defined as:

> The body of technical knowledge relating to techniques and equipment which measure quality characteristics and which process the resulting information for use in analysis and control.

There are many techniques used in this technology, any one of which may have several applications. One example is the design of computer-controlled measuring equipment to provide, by electronic probe, accurate and thorough inspection of many dimensions of complex machined parts. A coordinate measuring machine, used to measure major aircraft parts, produced by numerically controlled machines, typifies such equipment (Fig. 12.1).

While substantial use of these techniques takes place in the quality information equipment engineering component of the quality-control function, they are also widely employed in the product engineering, manufacturing engineering, laboratory science, and service engineering areas of a plant and company.

The full complement of techniques of quality information equipment technology may be grouped under four major headings:

1. *Advanced equipment development.* Included here are techniques for creating measurement practices and instrumentation and control procedures for application to those quality information requirements that are established by quality-engineering and process-control-engineering techniques. (Techniques used for advanced equipment development are discussed in Secs. 12.6 to 12.18.)
2. *Equipment-specification planning.* Included here are techniques for establishing the actual specification of the quality information equipment, which is required within the framework of the quality plan. (Techniques for equipment-specification planning are discussed in Sec. 12.19.)
3. *Design, procurement, and construction.* Included here are the techniques for the design and procurement of the individual components for the specified

FIG. 12.1 **Computer-controlled coordinate measuring machine used to measure parts produced by numerically controlled machines. (Courtesy General Dynamics Company, Fort Worth, Texas.)**

equipment. Also included are techniques for constructing the equipment. Further included are techniques for procuring the equipment in total, when this is the indicated step for a company. (Techniques for design, procurement, and construction are discussed in Sec. 12.20.)

4. *Installation, checkout, and follow-up.* Included here are techniques for the installation and application of the quality information equipment following its construction. (Techniques for this phase are discussed in Sec. 12.21.)

Some companies, which are large enough, will organize their technical efforts so that the entire range of techniques is covered from development through installation. As a practical matter, this means that these companies will design and make their own quality information equipment, except for various major new quality information concepts.

Other companies will organize to concentrate most heavily upon the techniques relating to specification and procurement. This means that they will buy their quality information equipment from one or more of the vendor firms which themselves cover some of the techniques of development, design, construction, and installation.

But the same fundamental need for applying the technology of quality information equipment exists for both types of company; both must specify the type of equipment required by their quality-program plan and must have considered the other information equipment techniques sufficiently to assure the feasibility and proper operation of this equipment. The determination of how this equipment will be obtained then becomes a matter of economics: a practical make-or-buy decision.

12.3 The Relationship among Quality Information Equipment Engineering, Quality Engineering, and Process-Control Engineering

The creation and installation of effective prevention-oriented quality equipment depend upon clear and well-structured working relationships among the three engineering areas within the quality function, together with effective working relationships between the quality function and Product Engineering, Manufacturing Engineering, and other technical functions of the company.

The quality-engineering planning of the plant must input, to the quality information equipment engineering component, the key parameters that define the requirements which must be served by the equipment. This will include such areas as the following:

1. The quality characteristics of process and product that must be measured
2. The location in the production process flow—in cooperation with manufacturing engineering—at which the measurements are to take place and the necessary inspection and testing cycle times

3. The degree of inspection and test that is to take place—100 percent or sampling
4. The data requirements—variable or attribute—and the data recording and other quality information needs
5. The intended quality measurement accuracy and limits
6. The intended users of the data
7. The feedback desired for process and product correction and improvement
8. The corrective-action procedures and the control practices

Many considerations must be taken into account in the development of this planning, such as customer requirements, relevant industry and regulatory standards and codes, product-reliability requirements, and production and process complexity—all in relation to the product engineering specifications.

Moreover, process-control engineering—which will have a major role in implementing the actions indicated by the measurements—must also make many significant inputs to the quality information equipment engineering component concerning elements that will be involved in actual ongoing quality-oriented operation of the equipment. This is particularly with regard to the practical considerations dealing with use of the equipment in the production environment. An important portion of these inputs has to do with human factors—that is, who is likely to operate the equipment and under what conditions—as well as many factors of calibration and maintenance.

The time available before the quality information equipment is needed can also be a big factor in what course of action is taken. Therefore, the quality engineer should bring the quality information equipment engineer into the quality program as early as possible, to establish preliminary quality plans which can be refined as more knowledge becomes available. Both engineers must jointly discuss the relevant quality planning and work closely to assure the right equipment for the job at hand.

Under those special circumstances when there is insufficient time to design and install the right equipment, it may be advisable to consider using temporary quality information equipment for a short time, rather than settling for inadequate equipments. Otherwise, such overly limited equipments may remain in use for a very long time, but without the ability to justify eliminating them and getting the right equipment for the job.

In preproduction quality evaluation, the quality engineer must be alert to factors which will influence the quality information equipment and get the quality information equipment engineer into the situation to resolve difficulties. Especially to be considered are design configurations to allow access for measurement and designation of specifications so they are measureable. In many instances it is possible to make a design configuration which is conducive to easy measurement. This is especially worthwhile in high-volume manufacture, so tests can be conducted automatically, or in processing, where measurements can be taken during processing.

12.4 The Relationship among Quality Information Equipment Engineering, Quality Engineering, and Process-Control Engineering—Some Examples

Such basic quality areas as soldering control of electronic part joints and numerically controlled machining of parts and their computer-controlled inspection are examples of the essential character of these equipment-oriented relationships within the quality function and among it and the other technical functions.

Soldering Control of Electronic Part Joints

The assurance of acceptable soldered joints, which is one of the fundamental quality-measurement objectives in many electronic manufacturing processes, illustrates the importance of close cooperation between quality engineering and quality information equipment engineering. This is because there are several alternatives for equipment location and determination.

One option is postprocess measurement of, for example, noise generated by the joint; infrared measurement of heat-rise characteristics; or by mechanical or even visual-aided means. Another option is preprocess measurement of the solderability of the parts to be joined and the characteristics of the solder and its related catalysts. And in-process measurements can also take place through control of the parameters of the soldering process. Section 12.10 discusses the area of point-of-process-identification in more detail.

The selection of the correct, most practical, and most cost-effective basis for the quality information equipment specification is thus not purely a unilateral decision based solely upon quality-engineering or quality information equipment considerations. It requires a cooperative determination, based upon the particular plant, process, and other operating factors.

Numerically Controlled Machine Parts

Whether to inspect parts from numerically controlled (NC) machines is an area which illustrates the significance of process-control engineering and quality information equipment cooperation.

In some plants there has been, from time to time, the view that quality equipment for inspection of parts from NC machines is unnecessary in the expectation that all parts produced from a proven NC program will necessarily be satisfactory. However, this may be incorrect because of the realities of the process experience. There may be a fixture problem, a tool setter may set a tool too deep or insert a ⅝-inch drill when a ½-inch drill is called for, or the override switch that some NC machines incorporate to compensate for a tool that is not quite the correct size may be adjusted and then forgotten or overlooked by an operator when a tool change takes place.

Process-control engineering inputs, based upon this realistic production experience, provide an important guide to the specification of the necessary quality equipment for these NC applications in specific plant operations.

12.5 Some Forms of Quality Information Equipment

The modern inspection and testing devices which result from use of quality information equipment technology take many forms, from the very simple, very low cost to the very complex.

For example, in electronic components manufacturing, quality information equipment engineering has made automatic testing equipment (ATE) as essential in the design and production of integrated circuits (IC) as the manufacturing processes themselves. To the fullest extent possible, the ATE is programmed for the complete range of produced ICs and the measurement of their key quality characteristics, instructed and controlled by minicomputer or microcomputer devices. Plant quality engineering establishes quality data summaries—structured by IC failures—and, to the extent possible, their root causes. These are provided in quick computer readouts, both printed in hard copy and provided in cathode ray tube soft copy as required for corrective action use by process-control engineering and other concerned individuals and functions.

For a quite different example, a midwestern plant producing thin metallic rod at fast processing speeds and in a hot and chemical atmosphere accurately measures the often-whipping material with optically based noncontact gages which feed back continuous signals to the upstream processing equipments. These equipments are automatically adjusted for the correct quality characteristics, and the process variability is tracked on a control chart basis and audited by process-control engineering. Other forms of nondirect-contact measurements are used in the plant to measure bearing races on a high production basis by induced-current magnetization technique.

An example of a job-shop kind of operation is in the plant of the manufacturer of complex airborne electronic radar gear. Here, computer programs automatically drive test routines which exercise the gear under a wide variety of conditions. Hard copy data readout compare performance under test with the quality requirements. The thoroughness of the testing for quality-assurance purposes is enhanced by test runs that require only minutes but which formerly required several hours.

In mechanical and automotive manufacturing, automatic subassembly functional testing has become an increasingly essential factor in production quality maintenance. The quality information equipment programs subassembly operation under various conditions and performs dozens of quality tests, including pressure, leakage, noise, vibration, and others. Digital data evaluation provides ongoing quality information concerning production trends and potential service conditions. Applications are now moving to complete assembly operations.

In addition to these equipments that incorporate already well-developed technical principles, there are those that continue to emerge from development work on new technical applications, such as laser-based quality information scan techniques for examining metals, computer-image enhancement to improve the effectiveness of radiography in areas such as the detection of small defects in ceramic-type units, computerized ultrasonics for surface and subsur- face flaw detection, and many others. Figure 12.2 is an example of laser diag- nostic method for measuring torsional vibration in rotating equipment.

Although these examples are representative of outstanding progress in the field of quality information equipment, they also illustrate the opportunities for further progress that are immediately ahead. As a case in point, with the exception of the fast-moving metal example, none of the previous examples has the fully integrated closed-loop feedback for control of the manufacturing process that is increasingly essential for truly effective process control.

ADVANCED EQUIPMENT DEVELOPMENT

12.6 Advanced Development Areas

Advanced equipment development relates to establishing the fundamental principles of measurement, instrumentation, data processing, and control that will provide the foundation for the later work of the detailed design of quality information equipment. This section reviews some general concepts underpin- ning advanced development, after which Section 12.7 discusses the equipment system viewpoint that threads through the work. Sections 12.8 through 12.16 consider some of the more specific techniques for actual points-of-process application of quality information equipment. Section 12.17 discusses infor-

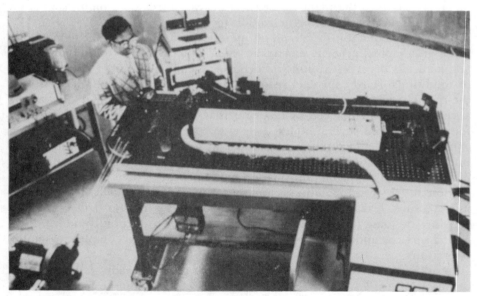

FIG. 12.2 **Laser doppler velocimeter. (Courtesy General Electric Company, Schenec- tady, N.Y.)**

mation recording, analysis, and feedback. Section 12.18 then presents evaluation techniques relating not to new equipment but toward planning to improve existing equipment.[2]

Advanced equipment development basically falls into two general areas:

1. *Generalized* development
2. *Specific* advanced developments

General Development

General advanced development consists of continuous research and investigation of quality information equipment in toto. Programs in this area of advanced development are not normally directed at any particular product but at a group of them. These programs consist of a systematic approach to the process-control and final product-quality requirements inherent in the quality-program plans.

The basis for these programs lies both in the long-range quality plans of the business and in current or new products of the company which have the greatest growth potential.

It is also related to maintaining close familiarity with technical developments that are relevant to quality information equipment. There is today perhaps no comparable field in which there is an increasingly rapid explosion. For example, the instruction-and-control potentials of mini- and microcomputers for testing and inspection equipment has only begun to be realized. For measuring techniques—both contact and noncontact—a growing array of effective and increasingly economic developments are coming into operation. These cover integrated radiographic inspection[3] (material handling, TV monitoring, video tape recording, x-radiation unit, and other elements); laser technique; advanced signature analysis; energy differential testing; photogrammetry; electron scanning; thermography; and many other areas. Moreover, the integration of data and information-processing equipments is providing quality information flow with new speed and accuracy capabilities of major proportions.

By studying the literature of electronics, computer processors, and industrial instrumentation practices; by attending equipment exhibits and shows; by exchanging visits with engineers of companies providing such equipment elements; by continually studying the latest trends in control systems design, information processing, and feedback systems, the quality information equipment engineering component can keep itself relevant to the new developments through which it must serve its plant and company.

Specific Developments

The second type of advanced development is that pertaining to the *specific* current or new products to which the business is committed and to those future products currently undergoing development. The application of quality measurement and control, integrated to the fullest extent with the manufacturing processes, must start at this stage to assure practical success. At this time also the guide rules for development of the quality information equipment are originated. These rules include the following:

1. The preliminary specifications of that quality information equipment which the quality-program plan indicates should be applied to process or product performance measurements. Figure 12.3 illustrates such a specification for incoming-material testing of transformers.
2. The preliminary quality information equipment cost estimates with breakdowns and cost follow-up procedures. Figure 12.4 is a checklist of cost considerations for quality information equipment.
3. The estimated schedules for design, procurement, construction, checkout, and release of each quality-control equipment component. Figure 12.5 is such a schedule, showing percentage of time and cost represented by each step together with the position responsible.

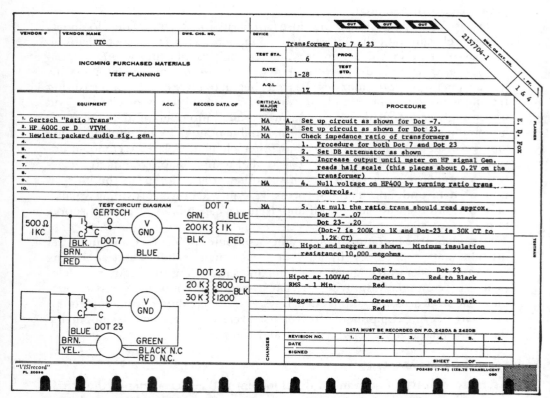

FIG. 12.3 Preliminary specification for quality information equipment, incoming-material test for transformers.

CHECK LIST OF FACTORS TO CONSIDER IN ESTABLISHING EQUIPMENT COST

I. Equipment Cost
    Initial cost
        Development
        Design
        Construction
        Basic equipment
            Individual components
            Purchased complete
        Fixturing or tooling
        Masters for calibration
        Equipment for work handling
        Accessory equipment
            Recorders, etc.
        Safety features
        Installation
            Footings
            Enclosures
            Services
            Rearrangement of existing facilities
        Debugging
        Operator training
        Replacement parts and spares

II. Equipment Operating Cost
    Facilities and services
        Power
        Storage
        Water
        Air
    Maintenance
    Calibration
    Operator labor
    Setup
    Floor space
    Amortization period

III. Operating Costs Affected by Equipment Design
    Cost of bringing work to equipment
    Cost of bringing equipment to work
    Information value toward prevention of defects
    Increased production capacity
    Increased machine utilization
    Improved process capability
    Improved product assurance
    Improved safety
    Equipment utilization

FIG. 12.4

QUALITY INFORMATION EQUIPMENT
DEVELOPMENT SCHEDULE

% Time	Step	Description	Responsibility	Cost %
10	1	Development of program concept and problem requirements; analysis of approaches	Qual. Info. Equip. Eng. & Qual. Eng.	5 / 10
20	2	Development of tentative (conceptual) design approach, review against requirements, evaluation of economics of program, establishment of schedule	Qual. Info. Equip.	25
40	3	Development experimentation, breadboarding special mechanisms and circuitry, obtaining of test data and analysis, establishing of materials and components decisions	Qual. Info. Equip.	40
	4	Design of circuitry, subassemblies and components, including layout	Qual. Info. Equip.	
55 / 60	5	Preliminary drafting, parts list and purchasing of prototype materials, review of schedule and economics	Qual. Info. Equip.	
	6	Prototype construction, debugging modifications and improvements	Qual. Info. Equip. Eng.	65
	7	Pilot run-capabilities evaluation	Qual. Info. Equip. Eng. & P. C. Eng.	
80 / 85 / 90	8	Final drafting, calibration and maintenance plans, theory of operation write-up, operating instruction, time studies, program report	Qual. Info. Equip. Eng. & P. C. Eng.	85 / 90
100	9	Program application, final economics analysis and program evaluation (3 months to 1 year) after program completion or installations	Qual. Info. Equip. Eng. & Qual. Eng.	95 / 100

FIG. 12.5

4. The productivity and operational cost figures to be associated with each equipment.
5. The organization and personnel required for the quality information equipment design program. Figure 12.6 shows the work of the quality engineer, quality information equipment engineer, and process-control engineer with relation to the development steps.
6. The organization and personnel required for operation and performance maintenance of the equipment, along with the associated times and labor costs to be attained.

Equipment-development efforts in this stage are of a conceptual nature.

Whether applicable to existing or to new products, the advanced development programs depend on, and to a large extent are guided by, the advanced planning being carried on in the quality-engineering area. When new product designs are involved, however, the quality information equipment design cycle must also integrate with the work of the product planning group which is materializing new product specifications; it must also continue into the detailed design of the product by engineering.

Throughout this advanced quality information equipment-development activity, recommendations will develop for product-engineering design changes to permit more effective product and process measurement and control. Similarly, recommendations will be developed for Manufacturing Engineering rela-

QUALITY INFORMATION EQUIPMENT — RESPONSIBILITY VS. TIME						
Product Development Steps		*Quality Engineering*		*Quality Information Equipment Engineering*		*Process Control Engineering*
1 Product planning		New design evaluation Review product specifications Product tolerance; analysis based on capability studies Provision for automatic inspection and test Provide broad equipment requirements	1	1 Develop program concept, problem requirements; analyze approaches	1	Preprocurement assistance counsel on operating problems and limitations of processes and personnel
				2 Develop tentative design approaches Review and evaluate Establish schedule		
2 Engineering study and design				3 Broadboarding mechanisms and circuitry; obtain data for analysis Decisions on materials and components	2	Equipment design evaluation: Counsel on operation, operator controls, data displays Calibration and maintenance problems
3 Procurement		Quality planning: Classify quality characteristics Determine locations for measurements Develop measurement planning	2	4 Design and layout of circuitry, components, and subassemblies		
4 Preproduction runs				5 Drafting, parts lists, purchase materials, review schedule		
5 Product manufacturing				6 Construct prototype debug, modify, and improve.		Operational acceptance: Cooperate on checking out by measuring product under operating conditions Review operating instructions Obtain capability study
		Measurement and Feedback: Plan audit and other techniques to measure and feedback for control	3	7 Pilot-run-capabilities evaluation	3	
				8 Final drafting, plans, and instructions		
				9 Equipment application, cost analysis, and program evaluation		

FIG. 12.6

tive to the application of measurement equipment to tie in with the processing equipment itself, for corrective process control or adjustment of the product.

12.7 Quality Information Equipment Functional Concept

To recognize both the scope and similarity of quality-measurement problems, it is well to consider the quality information equipment from a functional, *systems-design* viewpoint before considering individual components of such a system. Among the several approaches, one of the most useful is to conceive quality information as consisting of the following seven basic functions:

1. *Programming.*[4] This function consists of instructing the actual performance of measurements, which includes defining the sequence in which measurements are to be performed, the equipment to be used for measuring the individual quality characteristics, the procedure through which the measurements are accomplished, the sampling plan where indicated, and the results that are required.

   What is coming to be called computer-aided quality (CAQ) is an increasingly important approach to this function in some plants with regard to computer-controlled quality information equipment, as further discussed in Section 12.9.
2. *Selecting.* Here the function is that of selecting the material, part, or product that is to be tested or inspected, the connections to it, the input signals to be applied, the output terminations required, and the measuring devices applicable. This may also include disposition of the material, part, or product at the conclusion of its evaluation.
3. *Measuring.* Involved is determining the range of measurements to be used and then performing the measurement of product- or process-quality characteristics.
4. *Data recording and processing.* This function consists of recording pertinent measurements of product or process quality and then tabulating this information in usable form for analysis.
5. *Information analysis and decision.* Here the function is to perform computations on the measurement information, compare these computations with the required results, and determine their acceptability individually and by trend. This function also includes establishing the corrective or controlling action desired.
6. *Feedback.* Involved is communication of the corrective or controlling action required to the proper controlling areas and thereupon providing an indication that proper corrective action has been performed.
7. *Controlling.* Here the function is performance of the required corrective or

controlling action on the product design, the manufacturing process, or the individual material, part, or product itself.

The basic block diagram for a quality-measurement system, involving these seven functions, is illustrated in Figure 12.7, with the functions indicated by number for easy reference. All seven functions may be performed by equipment, or only part of them. All must, however, be considered and accounted for while doing the preliminary planning for the equipment that will fit into the quality plan. The equipment finally chosen may be nothing more than a simple, inexpensive gage to perform function 3, with the other six functions performed manually or through paperwork; or the choice may be for a fully automatic equipment which performs all seven functions without human intervention.

The selection of the balance of the quality information system among the functions performed by people, procedures, and equipment is a practical matter. It depends upon the particular company situation: economics, the labor-to-equipment ratios, and the nature of the manufacturing processes. As noted in Section 12.1, the decisions for this selection are based upon the principle that what is significant is not better quality devices of and by themselves but the choice of those equipments which permit the greatest *overall* efficiency and operation for the total quality system.

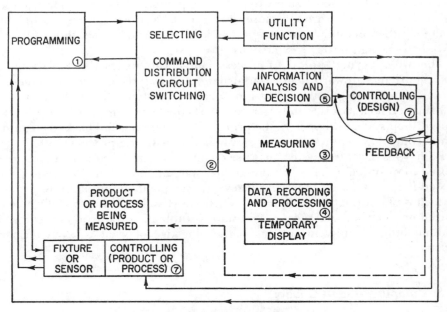

QUALITY INFORMATION SYSTEM BLOCK DIAGRAM
FIG. 12.7

12.8 Degree of Mechanization for the Control of Processes

The degree to which this selection leans toward equipment for the control of processes, rather than toward people and procedures, may be determined by several considerations. These considerations guide what will be the degree of "mechanization" or "electronicization" of the quality information system.

The first consideration, and one of the more important, is that of economics: to establish the balance between the cost of accomplishing specific functions automatically as compared with performing them manually. Studied in this establishment of economic balance are processing costs under the two alternatives. Further studied is the value of improved product quality as such.

Although the economic consideration is important, other criteria must go beyond that point. For example, product-quality requirements may be very exacting with relation to the capability of available manufacturing processes. When such a situation exists, the process must either have a high degree of inherent stability or be rapidly adjusted when disturbances occur as a result of changing conditions.

In many such high-speed processes, the human being cannot observe, decide, and adjust rapidly and accurately enough to prevent the manufacture of large amounts of nonconforming product. When this is the case, operator adjustment must be replaced by fully automatic equipment control.

Another consideration on which a decision for fully automatic equipment control should be based is safety to operating personnel. Greater safety might be assured not only through closer control of hazardous processes but by removing the operator from hazardous locations, for example, those subject to radiation, high heat, or explosions.

The two opposing "poles" of process control can be described as *open-loop control,* oriented toward manual adjustment, and *closed-loop control,* oriented toward automatic adjustment. In the open-loop system (Fig. 12.8), process-information feedback is to the operator who is the "controller," whereas in the closed-loop system (Fig. 12.9), the process information is fed back to an automatic control system which is physically tied in with the process.

Both types of control system may use quality information equipment, but the closed-loop system uses by far the greater amount. In its strictest sense, the closed-loop system ties together all seven basic quality information functions by means of information equipment. When this is accomplished by fully mechanized or electronicized means, continuous automatic production is achieved without human intervention; this is the objective of what is often termed *automation.*

12.9 Computer-Aided Quality

For those products and parts where there has been engineering computer-aided design (CAD) and computer-aided manufacturing (CAM), the same en-

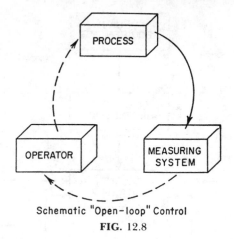

Schematic "Open-loop" Control
FIG. 12.8

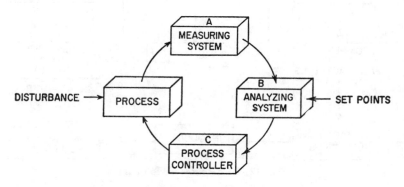

SCHEMATIC PROCESS CONTROL LOOP
FIG. 12.9

gineering data base may be utilized by quality information equipment engineering to provide one of the major approaches to computer-aided quality (CAQ). This integrates the engineering data base that designed the part and the product and guided its manufacture with the inspection and test of the part and product. Further economy and effectiveness can be obtained from the quality program module by establishing computerized sampling plans for key quality characteristics.

While this quality work involves its own modules, together with those for engineering and manufacturing, the key to CAQ, coordinated with CAD and CAM, is a centralized data base. This is defined by the technical functions of the plant, working in cooperation. Figure 12.10 shows this approach.[5]

Each module is operated and controlled by the various functional users,

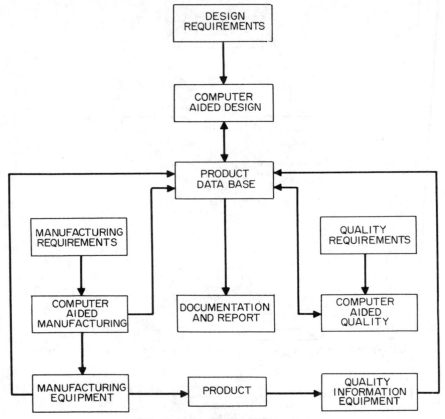

FIG. 12.10 **Computer-aided quality.**

providing direct cost and efficiency control. Functions can interact in an auto-mated mode by providing timely and accurate feedback. With this system it is possible to program audit points, information checks, and production "stop" points into various modules and store them in the central data base. Moreover, it greatly improves the approach to software quality assurance.

The integration of CAQ, in general, is adaptable to any type of product design. Among the most significant operating benefits are the following:

- To provide a common data base for the storage and extraction of technical data
- To provide an effective control of data and minimize redundancy
- To provide consistency of interpretation of data and consistency of output
- To minimize recurring manufacturing and quality programming and pro-vide backup operating programs
- To assure manufacture and quality measurements to design and standards
- To provide configuration control, revision control, and historical records as well as timely quality information reporting

- To provide error checking, improved cost assignment and visibility, and defect visibility and responsibility assignment
- To minimize print development and control problems

NC Parts Computer-Controlled Inspection

One of the most significant applications of this approach to CAQ is the computer-controlled dimensional gaging of major NC machines by coordinate measuring machines (CMM). Every part characteristic that can physically be evaluated by the electronic measuring probe is examined; characteristics that cannot be handled this way are inspected by manually aided gaging.

Increasingly, the programs for this kind of computer-controlled inspection-controlling movements and measurements of the CMM are prepared by the quality-engineering component itself within the framework of the quality information equipment and from the integrated data base for the product and part.[6]

The quality-engineering component will also establish the necessary sampling plan and accomplish the programming for its application as a part of the quality program for the CMM. Since the actual—that is, variables—quality data for each part dimension measured are available through the computer data entry and recording process, a variables sampling plan of the MIL-STD-414 Lot Sampling Plan type can be used.[7] The tables for size of the sample and the acceptance and rejection of this MIL-STD-414 can therefore be programmed into the computer. When the operator of the CMM identifies the NC part number and the lot size to be inspected into the computer, the CMM computer then automatically governs the inspection procedure: required sample size and comparison of results to the known variance data base so that an acceptance/rejection decision may be made for the part. In the case of a reject decision, the computer points out the characteristics that constituted the reject decision.

12.10 The Points of Process for Application of Quality Information Equipment

In Section 12.7, the various functions performed in the equipment system were discussed. In Section 12.8, a set of criteria was presented on which decisions could be based concerning the degree to which the quality plan should be automated. These criteria included economics, human safety, required speed of adjustment, and accuracy of adjustment.

This section discusses still another factor to be considered when designing the equipment system: the *point of application* in the manufacturing process flow.

Mechanization and electronicization of measurements, process control, and final product evaluation may be accomplished in one or a combination of several different stages of the manufacturing process, depending on the quality requirements placed on the product and the processes by the quality plan. Five of the most important are:

- Preprocess measurement and control
- In-process measurement and control
- Postprocess measurement and control
- Combinations of process measurement and control
- Integrated process control

12.11 Preprocess Measurement and Control

Preprocess measurement and control may be required to monitor or control the materials or parts entering the process or to control the product or the process based on input measurements. The measurement may range from the physical characteristics of copper strip moving into a drawing process, the performance patterns of an IC device entering into a printed circuit board assembly machine, or the mechanical integrity of a component part conveyorized into a control rod subassembly process; to the rough dimensions of an engine block casting entering automatic finishing, the electrical characteristics of a small capacitor placed in the parts tray for television assembly, and the bar stock being evaluated for the detection of surface discontinuities by laser-scan technology prior to entrance into processing (Fig. 12.11).

One fundamental schematic diagram of preprocess control is shown in Figure 12.12.

The measurement control of material entering the process is quite necessary

FIG. 12.11 Fully automated laser scan unit detects surface discontinuities of bar stock. (Courtesy of Magnaflux Corporation, Chicago, Ill.)

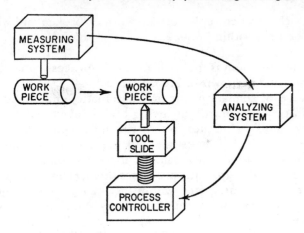

SCHEMATIC DIAGRAM OF PREPROCESS CONTROL
FIG. 12.12

in those process industries which require close control of the mix of the constituents of the product by weight or volume. It is also a safeguard against expensive, nonpredictable down time in mechanical, electronic, and electrical products industries which use long, continuous lines of automatic equipment.

A simple example of such equipment is a gage that automatically checks cast-iron castings for heatiron soleplates prior to a completely automatic milling and machining line. If a casting is undersize so the ogive will not clean up, or if it is oversize so it will not fit down in the pockets of the milling machine turntable, the casting is eliminated. In the latter case, cutter breakage with attendant delays is prevented.

12.12 In-Process Measurement and Control

Control applied from in-process measurement is based on a measure of the controlled quality characteristic as the product is generated. This in-process measurement and control can initiate signals to regulate or stop the process to prevent substandard production. For instance, in the case of machining processes, signals from the in-process control system may be used to

1. *Regulate the speed or degree of generation.* This may be a signal which changes the tooling from a roughing to a finishing cut as final size is approached for control of accuracy, finish, and eccentricity.
2. *Stop the generation when the predetermined value of the controlled variable is reached.* This is the signal that causes the tool to retract when finish size is reached, or the one that shuts off the furnace when the unit is at the required temperature.
3. *Stop the generation or the process when it is out of control.* This is the signal that

stops the machine when tools become worn or broken and when parts can no longer be held within limits.

In-process measurement is the basis for the in-process control of a process. One basic schematic is shown in Figure 12.13.

A broad range of semiautomatic and automatic equipments is becoming available for in-process control, including both contact and noncontact measuring and signaling techniques, often with microcomputer command-and-control devices into which process sampling plans are programmed in the case of high-volume operations. Increasingly, these equipments are included as elements of the basic design of the processes themselves. The quality information equipment is thus integrated within the manufacturing equipment and, with modern processes, may amount to a very significant proportion of the total equipment cost.

Quality information equipment engineering works closely with manufacturing engineering with regard to the necessary equipment. This can provide both greater economy and efficiency as compared to the earlier approaches of physically "hanging" in-process control devices onto processes, which too often never matched each other in operational characteristics.

A basic example of the principle can be illustrated in outside-diameter grinding of precision bearing parts. The process controller is programmed so that it directs the grinding wheel to traverse in at a fast feed until it gets within 0.001 to 0.003 inch of finish size, as signaled by the measuring gage, and then traverse at slow feed to about 0.0001 inch from nominal size, where the in-feed stops and allows the wheel to start to "spark out." When the process-control analysis has determined from the information transmitted from the gage that

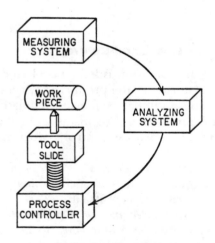

SCHEMATIC DIAGRAM OF
IN−PROCESS CONTROL
FIG. 12.13

the piece is ground to nominal size, it tells the controller to retract the grinding wheel. The result is a high-quality part, a fast production cycle time, and low production and quality costs.

12.13 Postprocess Control Techniques

Control applied from postprocess, or output measurement, is based on measurement of the quality characteristics of the completed product. In electronics assembly, this may mean, for example, that quality information equipment engineering establishes automatic end-of-assembly testing of the range of quality characteristics of printed circuit boards (PCBs) to provide final assurance of board quality. In metallurgical manufacturing it may mean the final inspection of a large motor casting, as a whole, by overall magnetization; or it may mean the quantitative and qualitative alloy evaluation of welds in the casting by microprocessor-based x-ray fluorescence analysis.

In the case of machining operations, postprocess measurement and control may be desirable or necessary for a variety of reasons:

- It may not be possible to design in-process measurement devices within the manufacturing equipment.
- Process environment—chips, coolant, temperature, and so on—may be of a nature which makes in-process measurement undesirable.
- It may be desirable to gage the part when it is not under the influence of the processing chuck or fixture.
- The accuracy specified may be beyond the capability of the process, and so the parts may have to be measured and classified for selective assembly.

One schematic of postprocess control is shown in Figure 12.14.

In parts-making processes, the workpiece may be moved out of the chuck or fixtures and into a gaging station, or the gage may be brought to the part before it is moved. In some cases, the gaging station is adjacent to the processing operation; in others, it may be some distance away and the parts from several machines directed to it in sequence.

Signals from the postprocess controller may be used to

1. *Stop the process when it is out of control.* As in in-process control, this is the signal that stops the machine or process when the tools become worn or damaged.
2. *Adjust the process when the product is approaching specified limits.*
3. *Actuate a classifying or segregating mechanism* to identify parts as good, oversize, or undersize, or by size groups for selective assembly or processing.

Postprocess measurements may also be used automatically to control the process by the technique of zone control. As shown in Figure 12.15, a precontrol zone, which is something less than product tolerance, is established, and

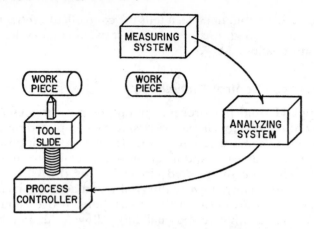

SCHEMATIC DIAGRAM OF POST−PROCESS CONTROL
FIG. 12.14

no process correction is made when products are produced within these control limits. This concept is fully discussed in Section 14.22 under "Control Gaging."

This precontrol zone is one answer to the back-and-forth, or hunting[8], effect of controls which attempt to correct for the normal, inherent dispersion of the process. The precontrol system recognizes the difference between "scatter" and "drift" and corrects only for the drift. The recommended process capability for this type of control is approximately one-half the product tolerance.

The operation of such a precontrol system is as follows: Each part is measured after it is produced, and if the dimension in question falls within the precontrol limits, no correction is made and the process receives a go-ahead signal for the next piece. If two successive parts (or, in some cases, three or four parts) fall outside the precontrol limits but are within the product toler-

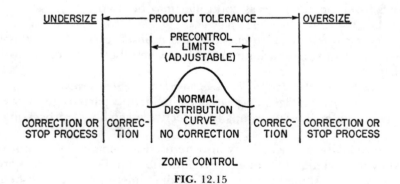

ZONE CONTROL
FIG. 12.15

ance, a tool correction is made with a signal to the process-controlling element. When a measurement indicates that the dimension in question is outside product tolerance, either undersize or oversize, a correction is made (may be indexing a new cutting edge); if the next piece is also outside product tolerance, the machine is automatically shut down.

12.14 Postprocess Control—Major Quality Information Equipment Requirements

Some of the most extensive quality information equipment demands are found in modern postprocess control. Two major areas are the following:

- Reliability test equipment for laboratory evaluation
- Complete testing of major products

Reliability Test Equipment for Laboratory Evaluation—Electronic Switches

Some of the most exacting quality information equipment engineering is required in the postprocess measurement and control stage for product-reliability evaluation. An example is life cycle-oriented tests of completed electronic switch assemblies, wherein the quality information equipment is designed to be fully mechanized and electronicized over all seven quality information functions. Considerable ingenuity is required in engineering all seven areas, particularly in accurately simulating end-use conditions.

The equipment must be sufficiently flexible so as to provide for the complete range of customer-use circumstances. To provide accurate reliability evaluation, all the conditions that the product may see in use must be duplicated in the combination sequences and time durations that the product will encounter. This means that a number of environments may be in combination, such as temperature, pressure, vibration, and shock. The levels for these environments are dynamically varying with time. Simultaneously, the loading on the product may be varying.

This calls for some very elaborate programming of test conditions, with a variety of inputs to the product under test and readout of product performance at different stages of the test. Duration of tests for individual switch conditions may be a few minutes up to many days, or even months, depending upon the type of product being tested. Reliability testing procedure, to which such equipment must respond, is discussed in detail in Chapter 17.

Complete Testing of Major Products—Large Engines

One of the principal quality information equipment engineering demands for postprocess control is the testing of completed large-scale products. Such tests must be comprehensive, accurate, meet quality engineering requirements for information, and performed within a cost-effective time frame. An example is the final testing of large engines produced in high-volume quantities.

The quality information equipment engineering approach is to establish the testing procedure in engine test cells which are designed in mini-computer-controlled test (CCT) terms, which both improves testing effectiveness and greatly shortens testing time as compared to traditional manually controlled test cells. Each test cell is designed to monitor instantaneous values for more than 85 parameters of the completed tested engine. CRT terminals can display 25 test parameters at a time, and printers provide certified test results to customers who require them and furnish a permanent record for problem correction and product improvement. Test engineers are able to complete the minicomputer engine test in about 25 percent of the time formerly required by manual testing. Furthermore, the computer-based quality information equipment provides more information faster and more accurately than was possible with manual testing.

12.15 Combined Process Measurement and Control Techniques

Combined gaging is a type of process control which utilizes both in-process and postprocess measurement, as shown schematically in Figure 12.16.

Under this arrangement, the postprocess system monitors the performance of its companion system on the machine and, when corrective action is necessary because of machine drift, causes the system on the machine to reset or zero itself, either in increments or by an amount equal to the variation.

This way the in-process system, whose characteristic function is to control random deviation, also compensates for machine drift at the command of the postprocess system. This combined action can permit close control over quality level of machine or process output for extended periods of time.

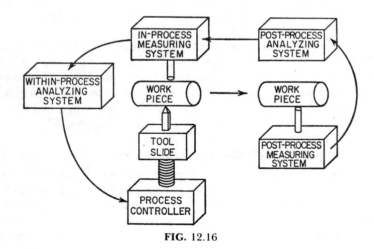

FIG. 12.16

12.16 Integrated Process Control

Pre-, in-process, and postprocess measurement control techniques, as they were discussed in the previous sections, are increasingly being integrated in modern manufacturing and processing facilities. On-line control programs for essentially continuous processes represent one of the significant application areas.

An example is in a major Japanese steel manufacturing plant, which produces to a wide diversity of customer specifications.[9] Because the plant uses hot ingots which are transferred directly from the melting shop to soaking pits for "blooming," accuracy of quality information on each preceding process is extremely important.

Five subsystems make up the overall computerized system, four on-line subservice systems and the other a batch-type subsystem. The former process main production-line activities, such as production order entry, issuance of instruction, and collection of data. For example, one subsystem covers operations from the melting process to the blooming production process. Other subsystems cover such areas as billet allotment and yard control. All five subsystems are related and combined so that quality data are fed to a central data base.

When a customer order is accepted, the system automatically decides every specification using information stored in a standard production file. Necessary instructions, including modification instructions for melting and blooming, are shown on color displays in every operations room. Data are collected automatically and can be used at any point in the process to perform a simulation of the process and to indicate necessary changes in production. The computer also contributes to optimum yield by suggesting the ideal amount of scrap and other raw materials and by calculating optimum length of the billet. A daily checklist indicates inspection items to be completed, all with the objective of fully integrated process control.

12.17 Information Recording, Analysis, and Feedback

Sections 12.10 through 12.16 discussed several of the areas for application of quality information equipment. All seven functions, as discussed in Section 12.7, must be taken into account by the quality information equipment engineer to provide the economic and effective evaluation of the materials, parts, subassemblies and products of each point of process as specified by the quality plan.

When establishing the necessary structure to meet the requiremer ts of functions 4 to 6 (data recording and processing, information analysis and decision, and feedback, respectively), it is essential to assure the efficient performance of what might be thought of as *quality data processing*—not only for each discrete unit under inspection and test but for the retention and handling of integrated quality data across similar units, similar defect codes, similar reliability parameters, and other similar areas that are important to the plant and company quality data base. Thus essential quality information is not "wasted." Proper planning of such data structuring is one of the most demanding areas of the working relationships between quality engineering and quality information equipment engineering because clear experience retention and careful quality analysis represent one of the fundamental strengths of a plant's total quality program in such areas as the following:

- Vendor parts performance—both for quality purposes and for production planning purposes in the plant's material requirements planning (MRP)
- Component defect rates—for all volume parts used in quantity
- Parts reliability
- Subassembly and final product-quality level and other similar areas

As an example, a large West Coast electronics manufacturer has established quality data processing to concentrate upon quality experience for two primary classifications:

- All high-usage components—not only passive units such as resistors and capacitors but IC chips—that pass through process-control test
- All high-usage PCBs that pass through post process test

Distributed data processing patterns provide essentially real-time test data for each component and PCB at each minicomputer- or microcomputer-based test station throughout the plant. These are also coupled with the plant main-frame computer installation, which provides consolidated quality data trends and analysis. Quality data can be presented in many modes, from reliability data, broken down by various component codes and various forms of statistical analysis, to the routine performance of specialized analyses of linearity and various complex data manipulations.

This quality data bank is an essential tool in many areas of the plant quality program, including use by both design engineers and quality engineers who participate in the company new-design control activity (Chapter 18).

12.18 Evaluating and Analyzing the Measurement Operation

The foregoing discussion outlined some basic principles used in planning equipment systems. Use of these principles is essential, not only for providing efficient, effective measurement facilities for new installations but for the equally important task of improving quality information equipment that is in service and has been operating for some period of time.

This section discusses a method for evaluating the current status of such equipment with respect to the functions it performs and the degree of mechanization and electronicization that is indicated. The discussion uses, as its example, the evaluation of a testing position by an analytical procedure called *TAG (test automation growth) charting.*[10] The same analytical procedure is equally applicable to inspection positions, quality-audit position, and so forth.

Its current mechanization level can be plotted for each element of a test operation on the TAG chart (Fig. 12.17), and after analysis and study of each of these elements, a second, or theoretically desirable, level of mechanization, electronicization, or automation can be established. With the test costs, savings, and other benefits listed for each element and for the test operation as a whole, the chart can be readily used as an aid by the quality information equipment engineer in planning and scheduling for increased mechanization of measurement operations. To measure and gage the mechanization level of a series of operations effectively, it is necessary to

TEST AUTOMATION PLANNING SHEET

TEST _____ DATE _____

INSTRUCTIONS

1. Classify all test operations into basic elements, such as shown on tag chart.
2. Analyze each element; mark automation level on the tag chart. Connect points.
3. Obtain element time (either manual or total) and write in as per cent of total.
4. Obtain test cost for each element (or group) and record (use labor or total test cost).
5. For each element, analyze possible mechanization methods. Consider all improvement potentials and savings. Estimate equipment costs.
6. Determine the highest justified automation level for each test operation element. Mark levels on chart; connect points.
7. Use the work planning section to plan sequence and work schedule for mechanization or automation of test elements.
8. Indicate operation element, initiation date, work detail schedules with completion dates, and show equipment cost (design material, labor etc.), and actual net savings expected. (Use appropriate base-yearly or per unit.)
9. Indicate at bottom completion date and total costs and savings.

TAG - - - TEST AUTOMATION GROWTH - - - TAG

Tag Chart Benefits
Aids in:

1. Picturing present and proposed test operations.
2. Making a systematic analysis of a test operation.
3. Planning improved test methods.
4. Integrating test operations with manufacturing operations for continuous flow.
5. Analyzing test cost and savings.
6. Spotlighting pay-off areas.
7. Developing realistic improvement schedules.
8. Preparing estimates for equipment appropriations.
9. Selling equipment improvement programs.
10. Maintaining good Employee Relations through adequate and timely information.

FIG. 12.17 Test automation planning sheet.

1. Classify the operations into discrete and definable elements.
2. Establish a method of evaluating the various levels of mechanization and electronicization that presently exist and those that may be developed.
3. Conceive and study methods of mechanizing and electronicizing tests.
4. Evaluate proposed changes from an economic and improved quality point of view.

A discussion of each of these four steps follows.

Classifying the Elements of the Test Position

1. Classify all operations for this test into basic elements, such as those shown on the chart (Fig. 12.17, reverse side).
2. Analyze each element and mark its standing in the proper "automation level." Connect the points thus plotted.

DATES			Element	Brief Description of Change		Equipment	Cost	Net Savings
Initiate	Target	Complete						
Completion Date						TOTALS		
Special Benefits								

TAG -- TEST AUTOMATION GROWTH SCHEDULE - TAG

TEST OPERATION ELEMENTS
1. Set up - Prepare test equipment for test.
2. Position - Prepare for test; move into place.
3. Connect - Connect product with motivating sources, measurement devices, etc.
4. Select test - Select for each test: voltages, currents, measuring equip., gages, etc.
5. Operate - Apply power; actuate; bring up to operating condition; etc.
6. Measurement - Perform function of measuring or comparing, including necessary setting of instruments; balance; adjust, etc.
7. Adjust - Adjustments, corrections, settings, etc. on unit to obtain specified operation of unit under test.
8. Record - Record measurement data or results, identification, etc.
9. Data Analysis - Classification of data; computations; preparation for feedback.
10. Information Feedback - Transmit test results or analyses to shop operations. Q.C. Engineering, or Design Engineering.
11. Disconnect - Disconnect motivating sources, etc.
12. Reject - Removal of defective unit.
13. Remove - Remove from test position or location.
14. Test Tear Down - Dismantle set up of test facilities and equipment.

TEST AUTOMATION LEVELS
1. Hand - Use of human faculties alone.
2. Hand + Mechanical Aid - Use of hand operated switches, screw drivers, etc.
3. Hand + Powered Aid - Use of powered clamps, hoists, screw drivers, etc.
4. Operator Cycled - A powered piece of equipment controlled by an operator.
5. Operator Initiated - Completely automatic with the exception of starting.
6. Automatic Program - An operation directed by a fixed cycle programming device.
7. Simple Decision - An operation controlled by a decision from a sensing device.
8. Self Checking - Test equipment compared to standard to insure desired performance.
9. Fault Indicating - Indicates source of faults in test equipment, product or process.
10. Decision and Correction - Sensing device initiates feedback for automatic correction.
11. Anticipation, Decision and Correction - Corrective action before fault occurs.

FIG. 12.17 **Test automation planning sheet (reverse side).**

Evaluating the Levels of Mechanization and Electronicization

1. Add the numerical values assigned to each individual element and divide by the total number of elements to determine the average "automation level." (This numerical rating is an arbitrarily assigned value from 0 to 100 for general rating purposes.)
2. Determine the manual or elapsed time (whichever is under study) for each test operation element and show the percentage of the total time in the space provided.
3. Obtain the test cost for each element (or group of elements) and record in the space provided. All costs relating to the test should be analyzed for inclusion here because for some operations, power or fuel consumed may be more significant than labor costs, or vice versa.

Figure 12.18 is an example of how the test position for an electrical relay comes out diagrammatically when plotted. Note that, although some of the elements are in the automatic area, several are in the hand stages. Note also the division of the testing time. For instance, in this example, almost half the time of the test is consumed in selecting power sources, meters, and so on.

Studying for Improvement

1. For each test element, analyze the possible mechanization and electronicization methods.

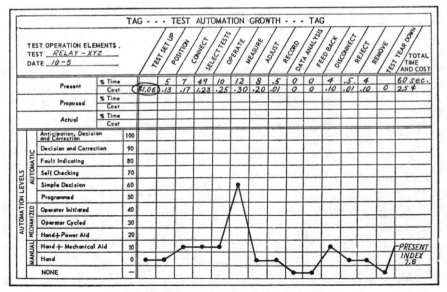

FIG. 12.18 TAG chart for electric relay.

2. Consider all the improvement potentials and savings which would be realized. Estimate the equipment costs for upgrading the various elements.

Evaluating the Necessary Changes

1. Determine the highest automation level which is justified for each test operation element, in light of the costs and savings involved.
2. Mark these new levels for each element in the appropriate box on the same chart. Connect the new points, using dashed lines or a different colored pencil.
3. This new growth line shows where the advance planning work of the quality information engineer should be directed. The completed TAG chart for the relay test example is shown in Figure 12.19.

EQUIPMENT SPECIFICATION PLANNING

12.19 Specifying the Equipment

When a new product design is approximately halfway through its time cycle, the transition of the quality-control equipment-design job begins from advanced conceptual development, as discussed above, to detailed design planning. The design planning phase consists of finalizing the measurement and control methods, techniques, and equipment in a form that can be used as a specification either for detailed design within the company or for deciding

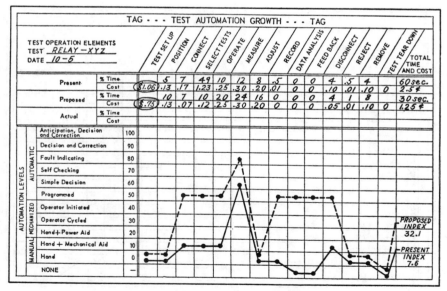

FIG. 12.19 Completed TAG chart for electric relay.

upon procurement of the equipment from an outside vendor. Detailed cost estimates for the design and development of equipment are prepared. The specifications for the overall quality information system are firmly determined, and the detailed specifications for each individual equipment are established, including accuracy, capacity, size, operational requirements, safety, productivity, and operational costs including provision for calibration and maintenance.

As discussed in earlier sections of this chapter, there are many equipment alternatives open to the quality information equipment engineer in making decisions as to how the seven functions are to be performed. The continuing rapid development in those equipment areas make discussion of their functional details beyond the purpose of this chapter. However, Figure 12.20 shows key aspects of a checklist for specifying or designing quality information equipment. The schedule of equipment design, procurement, construction, checkout, and release for operation is timetabled and coordinated with the other segments of the quality-program plan.

At this time the details of prototype, sample, and preproduction testing are established and coordinated among quality information equipment engineering, quality engineering, and process-control engineering to provide for a team operation of product- or process-performance analysis and/or determination of rapid corrective action to assure smooth continuity of manufacturing operations.

DESIGN, PROCUREMENT, AND CONSTRUCTION

12.20 Getting the Equipment Built

The transition from the design planning stage into the design-procurement and construction phase of the equipment job is essentially one from the planning and organization portion of the program to that of performance and measurement of results. In this phase of the equipment job the detailed design and development of the individual pieces of equipment are either performed within the company or externally subcontracted. Sketches, layouts, circuit diagrams, software requirements, itemized material lists, and detailed equipment specification sheets are originated. The associated test and inspection operation instructions, which have been developed by quality-engineering technology, are finalized, and the required equipment-operating instructions and calibration and maintenance procedures are drafted. Material is ordered and received and the necessary construction of equipment and facilities performed.

Normally during this phase of the quality information equipment job, when new product designs are involved, the prototype new design is completed and subjected to detailed design evaluation tests to confirm its performance to product requirements and specifications. It is often essential that these tests be followed closely and in detail by the quality information equipment engineers because performance failures and accompanying design corrections may directly affect the quality-program plan and its associated equipment.

FIG. 12.20 **Quality information specification checklist.**

Quality Information Equipment Specification
Checklist for Specifying or Designing Equipment

1. Applicable standards, codes, and drawings

ANSI	Sketches
IEEE	Preliminary designs
	Drawings
ASME	Engineering specifications
EIA	Data processing and software planning
Other Applicable	
Safety Codes	Operational planning

2. General information and alternative plans

Function of equipment

Environmental conditions

General

Specific

Shock	Lubricants
Temperature	Dirt
Moisture	Chips

Delivery requirements

Alternative systems of equipment that may fulfill requirements

3. Design and operational requirements

Characteristics to be checked

Voltage	Dimension
Current	Chemical property
Frequency	Physical property
Power	

Where will characteristics be checked?

Preprocess

Process

Assembly

Final

Input and output requirements

Power	Connections
Frequency	Shielding
Voltage	Pressure

Speed of operation

Number of measurements per unit time

Time available per measurement

Dwell time of paced components

Delay time for information feedback

Time for memory storage of data

Time required for computations

Time required for work classification

Safety requirements

Grounding

Interlocks

Barriers
Safety control circuits
Type of equipment this unit must operate with
Special maintenance features
  Plug-in components
  Rack-mounted units
  Adjustment elements in accessible locations
  Test points available
  Failure-indicating system
Provision for expansion or additions
  Physical size
  Speed of operation
  Quantity of work handled

4. Accuracy and calibration
State accuracy required
  System
  Components
    Digital readouts
    Meters
    CRT's
    Transducers
  Reliability
  Calibration
    Frequency of calibration
    Time required
    Self-calibrating
  Service availability
  Error risk inherent in equipment design
  Usage amount
  Consequences of errors—product, plant, customer
  Separate calibration
    At location where used
    At location other than where used
  Master piece required
  Standard required

5. Information input and data processing requirements
Software programs
Data codes and base
Memory demands
Distributed or mainframe data handling
Mode of input
Telecommunications

6. Information output requirements
Classification of work checked
Visual readout
Records required
  Statistical chart
  Digital data

Analog data
Work identification
If used for feedback control
 What is to be controlled?
 Control input requirements
 Connections

7. Materials and construction
 Material in

Cabinet	Cabling
Chassis	Control handles
Knobs	Transducers
Meters	Sensors
Panels	Readouts and CRT's

 Construction features
  Limitations of
   Size
   Space
   Weight
  Conformance to
   Other equipment—give requisition number if available
   Materials-handling equipment
  Physical appearance
   Sloping front
   Layout of components
   Layout of controls
   Paint requirements
   Type of lettering
   Nameplate data
  Method of mounting
   Fixed
   Soft tires
   Portable
   Locking wheels
  Special precautions
   Exclude dust and dirt
   Radiation
   Explosion proof
  Safety precautions
   Ground straps
   Polarized connectors

8. Provision for instructions
 Operating instructions
 Calibrating instructions
 Maintenance instructions
 Software instructions
 Installation instructions
 Parts list
 Spare-parts list
 Schematic drawings

      Wiring diagrams
      Assistance of manufacturer to set up
      Where to get operation assistance

9. Acceptance Checks
      Availability of equipment at manufacturer's plant to ascertain quality of
      materials and workmanship
      Surveillance of tests to ascertain compliance
      Provision for specified evaluation period after installation
      Process-capability parameters
      Workpieces required for evaluation
         Quantity
         Rate needed

Planning for Calibration and Maintenance

A key factor in quality equipment design is to minimize the need for—and the costs of—calibration and maintenance. Moreover, since most quality information equipment will require periodic calibration to ensure suitable accuracy throughout its operational use, these calibration requirements must be specifically spelled out during equipment design. Key factors in specifying these calibration and maintenance requirements are identified in area 4, Figure 12.20.

An organized calibration and maintenance program incorporating planning of facilities, equipment, and training, determination of appropriate cycles, and detailed schedules and procedures is an essential plan to be established as part of the design, procurement, and construction activity.[11] Particularly with very complex information equipment, it is very important that attention be payed in this plan to control of the possible accumulation of errors in a sequenced buildup of calibration.[12] Where the equipment can be established as an economic part of a larger calibration operation, computer application may be used either through batch processing to provide an "automatic file" for maintenance timing or, where practical, through on-line computer control of calibration.

INSTALLATION, CHECKOUT, AND FOLLOW-UP

12.21 Getting the Equipment into Operation

The fourth and last set of techniques of quality information equipment engineering involves equipment installation, checkout, and follow-up. This phase usually commences just prior to the preproduction run and continues through the buildup to full-rated manufacturing operation. It consists of "debugging" the various equipment components of the quality program, verifying equipment applications and operating, calibration, and maintenance instructions, and instructing and training the operating personnel in equipment usage.

In addition, a capability study is made on the quality information equipment as well as a detailed analysis of the performance of the quality information equipment against its individual specifications.

The concern at this point is in two areas: with the capabilities of the equipment to perform satisfactorily to the specifications and with the capability of the equipment as it works in conjunction with all the process variables as required by the quality program plan. The process-control engineer is responsible for checking the equipment for speed, accuracy, repeatability, and safety under operating conditions. There may be, for example, a large margin of safety on accuracy but poor performance on repeatability in the assigned application.

The quality information equipment engineer may institute a record system, which may serve as notification to the process-control engineer that equipment is being built or is on order from a vendor. The process-control engineer may then be alerted to ensure that proper incoming checks are made on the equipment. If the equipment has been designed and constructed internally, the equipment engineer will evaluate it against the design specifications; if it is purchased equipment, satisfactory evaluation may have been performed on a representative unit prior to purchasing the equipment.

When the process-control engineer has evaluated the equipment for use under operating conditions, it may be desirable to retain the notification record from the equipment designer. If the equipment does not perform satisfactorily when installed, or if modification would improve its usefulness, the process-control engineer then sends the record to the equipment designer with a request for the needed changes. For example, it may be found that a locating pin on a checking fixture is to drawing but insertion of the product into the fixture scratches one face of the product, or shop-supply voltages fluctuate radically, thus requiring voltage regulation to be added to a piece of testing equipment.

The quality information equipment is jointly released for production use when the quality information equipment engineer and the process-control engineer have ensured that the equipment itself functions properly and that it can be used properly in this application. Subsequently, quality information equipment capability will be periodically reviewed to ensure that it is being used and updated for best performance and cost savings and that quality information equipment capability satisfies the needs of the product and process.

To relate these four phases of the quality information equipment design cycle to the steps in the normal cycle of product development, the chart in Figure 12.21 is shown.

12.22 Summary of Quality Information Equipment—Basic Factor in Productivity, Mechanization, and Electronicization

The essential role of total quality programs in the achievement of productivity, as emphasized in Chapter 3, is particularly significant in these modern

PRODUCT DEVELOPMENT CYCLE

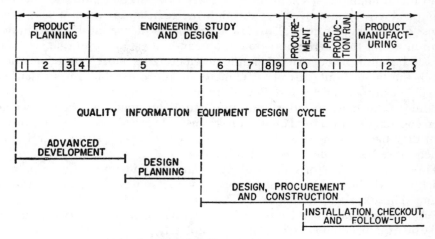

1. Request for product development.
2. Review by product planning.
3. Tentative management approval.
4. Development authorization approval.
5. Preliminary design.
6. Prototype manufacture.
7. Review and final recommendations by Product Planning.
8. Management approval.
9. Final drawings.
10. Conditional manufacturing release.
11. Preproduction manufacture.
12. Full manufacturing release.

FIG. 12.21

quality information equipment programs. Principal means for productivity achievement are mechanization and electronicization. A key lesson to be derived from industrial experience is that the areas of mechanization, electronicization, and productivity are very highly interrelated with quality programs.

Mechanization and electronicization may, in this sense, be thought of as

The progressive use of work-saving and -improvement equipments and devices, the most advanced form of which is automation.

Productivity may, in this sense, be thought of as

The effectiveness with which the resource inputs—of personnel, materials, machinery, information—in a plant are translated into customer-satisfaction-oriented production outputs and which today involve all the relevant marketing, engineering, production, and service activities of the plant and company rather than solely the activities of the factory workers, where traditional attention has been concentrated.

Experience demonstrates that improvements in productivity today depend to an increasingly great extent upon quality's role in mechanization actions. This productivity improvement through mechanization will not take place unless quality is given central attention, together with the mechanization program in a very thoroughly integrated, human-motivated, and organized way. This is because productivity depends not merely on more output per hour within the factory but, in today's climate, on more useable output that will provide customer satisfaction. See Sections 3.1 to 3.3.

While some mechanization and automation installations which have not been coordinated with total quality programs have greatly speeded up production, they have not increased productivity. They have, instead, merely produced more bad product faster than before.

Three factors make for successful mechanization and automation programs, which provide both substantial productivity and substantial quality improvements. These three factors are:

First: Mechanization and automation programs, from their very beginnings, must be organized and carried out as completely planned business programs with full attention to their effects upon the human, motivational, material, informational, and economic resources of the plant; they cannot be approached as purely mechanical or electronic equipment design and installation projects, with all other matters dealt with on an incidental, secondary basis.

Second: The modern total quality program must be integrated with all phases of the conception, installation, and ongoing control of the mechanization program. Quality information equipment must be taken into account in all aspects of mechanization and electronicization.

Third: Similarly, mechanization of quality control itself through quality information equipment must be accomplished as an integral part of the quality program of the plant; it cannot successfully proceed on an individual-piece-of-hardware-by-individual-piece-of-hardware basis.

An illustration of the importance of these three factors is found in the quality technology application to meet the quality requirements placed upon the magnetic bearing support assembly previously discussed in Section 3.5.

This support, which is a precision instrument component, is a relatively simple device consisting of four parts: Two washers, between which is assembled the third part, a permanent magnet with a hole in its center, through which the fourth part, a fastener, passes to hold together the washers and the magnet.

The original production operation consisted of a manual production line along which the washers, magnets, and fasteners were progressively assembled by workers using simple hand tools. Quality standards were high. Incoming inspection of the washers was to a 1 percent AQL for the production line.

The mechanization objective was to eliminate this manual assembly line in favor of a rather fast mechanical process in which the washers, magnets, and fasteners flowed in through hopper feeds, were joined, assembled, and packed at the rate of 720 assemblies per hour—one every 5 seconds. The mechanical design of this new process was quite demanding technically. The quality-technology activity to assure the economic health and the productive operation of this new process was equally demanding as the mechanical design and installation which, in earlier years of the plant, would probably have been all that was seriously considered in planning the program.

Two instances illustrate the quality-technology activities: The *first* instance was the impact of the mechanization program upon necessary changes by quality engineering in the relevant quality planning. This was made necessary because the 1 percent AQL for washers, which was so highly satisfactory a quality level for the manual operation, was a totally unacceptable quality level for mechanization. With the 1440 washers that were required for 720 assemblies an hour, the 1 percent AQL would have meant 14 potential machine stoppages per hour, 1 every 4 minutes, a completely impossible situation. What was needed for mechanization was a washer quality level that would be far better than for the manual operation and would provide a potential machine stoppage risk that would be acceptable for economical production flow.

Such quality levels could not be achieved by better postprocess washer inspection before the mechanized operation. They instead required the establishment of a much stronger in-process-oriented, process-control engineering program—including better control and more frequent punching-tool sharpening—in the punching press operations which actually produced the washers in another building of the factory and where such tighter process control had never before been necessary.

The *second* instance was the need for quality information equipment that had not before been necessary. The permanent magnets had required no dimensional inspection devices in the manual production line because the experienced workers themselves had inspected with their fingers to determine chips, rounded edges, or burrs which meant magnets that should not be used. With mechanization, the workers disappeared, and so did the inspection by their fingers. This established the need for the development of electronic gage-based optical quality information equipment to accomplish the same purpose. This equipment was installed in the incoming hopper for magnets, to assure their 100 percent inspection, because these permanent magnets are so inherently brittle that process control during and after their actual production could assure satisfactory production magnets, but chipping could and would occur during transportation and so had to be controlled prior to the new process.

This quality-technology-program installation, together with the mechanization program, contributed to a very successful modern assembly operation with both high productivity and high quality.

This example illustrates two contributions of a modern quality program that are needed to support the increased quality requirements inherent in today's mechanization and automation programs:

> To identify and bring about the quality-engineering and process-control-engineering changes that will be needed in certain parts of the quality plan

to assure the quality requirements which will make the mechanization program successful

Through quality information equipment engineering, to identify and make available the quality equipment that will be needed within the mechanization project itself

These steps, when properly executed, are an activity to be integrated with mechanization and automation programs and which is essential to ensure that more productive useable output per hour will result rather than merely more output both useable and unuseable.

Notes

[1]The equipment concepts and developments considered here have been created by many quality-engineering and equipment engineering professionals, whose work has established the basis for modern quality information equipment.

[2]Section 12.6 and material related to it in this chapter are, in part, according to unpublished material developed by Donald D. Ward and Walter P. Sime.

[3]For a detailed discussion, see Murray E. Liebman, "Real-Time Radiographic Inspection Systems," *14th Annual Technical Conference Transactions*, International Academy for Quality, 1979.

[4]The term "programming" is used here in the general technical sense of planning and, where appropriate, may include, but is not confined to, computer programming, which is oriented to those quality information equipments that are computer-based.

[5]For a discussion of computer-aided quality, see William Riemenschneider, "CAQ Starts with CAD," *32nd Annual Technical Conference Transactions*, American Society for Quality Control, 1978, pp. 105–109.

[6]For a discussion of a full-scale CMM application, see Maurice Puma, "Quality Technology in a Changing Manufacturing Environment," *Quality Progress*, vol. XIII, no. 8, August 1980.

[7]Section 15.21 discusses MIL-STD-414 plans in more detail. The newer variables plan, ANSI/ASQC Z1.9, is also suitable for this purpose. Section 15.23 discusses this plan.

[8]The hunting effect is an oscillation of the controller caused by overcorrecting the process, with subsequent swings correcting the overcorrections.

[9]This is discussed by Yoshihiko Hasegawa, Kiyomi Tanaka, and Teruo Yanagi, "On-Line Quality Control System at Daido Steel, Chita Plant," *International Conference on Quality Control*, Tokyo, 1978.

[10]The TAG chart was developed by E. S. Acton, E. T. Angell, and D. D. Ward after principles originally published by James R. Bright, General Electric Company.

[11]For a description of a quality and productivity measurement program in a metrology environment, see Roland Vavken, "Productivity of Quality Measurement in Metrology," *31st Annual Technical Conference Transactions*, American Society for Quality Control, 1977.

[12]See, for example, Jimmy E. Hilliard and J. R. Miller III, "The Effect of Calibration on End Item Performance in Echelon Systems," *Journal of Quality Technology*, vol. 12, no. 2, April 1980, pp. 61–70.

PART FIVE

Statistical Technology of Quality

CHAPTER **13**

Frequency Distributions

The greatly increased precision demanded of manufactured parts and products has been accompanied by the need for better methods to measure, specify, and record it. That statistics, the so-called science of measurements, is one of the most valuable techniques used in the four quality-control jobs has long been evident.

Over the years, statistical techniques and statistical methodology have become more and more widely used and generally accepted throughout industry. With the availability of today's computers and advanced data processing equipments, their practical application continues to multiply and deepen. Statistics play a major role in modern programs for total quality control.

However, the current popularity of the statistical approach was not easily achieved. Much early opposition was encountered in plants and companies, partly because of the natural resistance met during the introduction of any new and unfamiliar method—and more specifically because of factory supervisors' distrust of mathematical symbols which seemed to cloak industrial statistics with an air of mystery.

In part, this opposition was due to the overabundance of technical statistics and the underabundance of practical administrative applications that characterized the literature which reached industrial management. In part, it was because of the simple fact that the formal education of many graduate engineers overlooked concentration on this subject. Today there is a growing wealth of material about the practical aspects and theoretical details of industrial statistics. The statistical terminology and mathematics have been reduced to simple arithmetic and algebra for general use. A surprisingly large number of industrial employees has been trained in these methods.

The victory of statistical methods in industry really represented a compromise between "pure" statistics and the practical realities of industrial situations. Statistical methods, as actually practiced in total quality control, do not represent an exact science. Their character is strongly influenced by human relations factors, technological conditions, and cost considerations.

A plant quality-control program may, for example, be faced with the problem of choosing between two sampling tables. One table may be quite precise statistically but difficult for production people to comprehend. The other table may not be so precise statistically but much easier to administer. It would be quite typical for the plant to select the latter table.

Probably more important than these methods themselves has been the impact upon industrial thinking of the philosophy they represent. The "statistical point of view" resolves essentially into this: *Variation* in product quality must be constantly studied

- Within batches of product
- On processing equipments
- Between different lots of the same article
- On critical quality characteristics and standards
- In regard to pilot runs of a newly designed article

This variation can best be studied by the analysis of samples selected from the lots of products or from units produced by the processing equipments.

This point of view, which emphasizes the study of variation, has had a significant effect upon quality-control activities wherein the actual statistical methods themselves are not used, and the study of variation that is recommended has become useful in other administrative areas like time study, safety engineering, personnel administration, and service functions.

Five statistical tools have come to be widely used in the quality-control jobs:

1. Frequency distributions
2. Control charts
3. Sampling tables
4. Special methods
5. Reliability

Some understanding of these tools is necessary for full technological comprehension of total quality control. For this reason, Part 5 discusses them in some detail in its five chapters.

Moreover, this is also essential to the effective use of computers, whose importance in total quality control was discussed in Chapter 12 and in other sections of this book. An ever-widening software library of computer programs is now available to greatly expedite the speed and accuracy of statistical calculations. This computer application takes place most effectively in a company when quality practitioners themselves—whether in engineering, production, marketing, service, or general management or quality control itself—have the basic necessary statistical understanding.

The discussion follows a pattern whereby the general approach to each of the five tools is first presented in the appropriate chapter. Later sections of the chapter present some of the qualifications and limitations that may be required by particular industrial applications of the tool. Industrial experience with presenting the point of view of statistics, as used in quality control, indicates the desirability of this pattern of presentation.

THE CONCEPT OF THE FREQUENCY DISTRIBUTION

13.1 The Universal Nature of Manufacturing Variations

One characteristic of modern manufacturing is that no two pieces are ever made exactly alike. The variations may be small—as in the case of gage blocks, which have been guaranteed to two-millionths of an inch. Whether large or small, variations exist in parts manufactured in all production processes, whether they be NC machine tools, blanking presses, fluidized bed processes, annealing furnaces, painting machines, or potting and encapsulation of delicate electronic components.

Some variations are so great that they are immediately indicated by modern measuring equipments. Other variations are so minute that successive readings on measuring equipment will reflect primarily the variation of the measuring equipments themselves rather than that of the parts.

Among the types of parts variation, three classifications useful for analytical purposes are

1. *Variations within the part itself,* as illustrated by a small shaft which is out of round at one end and within tolerance at the other end
2. *Variations among parts produced during the same period of time,* as illustrated by the variation in the length of studs produced by a screw machine during a 5-minute period
3. *Variations among parts produced at different periods of time,* as illustrated by the variation in length between studs produced at the beginning of the first shift as compared with those produced at the end of the shift

There are many factors that contribute to any or all of these variations, including tool wear, bearings that loosen, machine vibrations, faulty jigs and fixtures, poor raw materials, careless or untrained operators, and weather changes. Industry has long recognized the inevitability of these variations. It includes, on drawings and specifications, tolerances which designate the permissible deviation from the standard shape, thickness, color, size, and other parameters.

DAILY REPORT AUTOMATIC SECTION		
PART	NO. INSPECTED	NO. REJECTED
STUD DWG. 53415	863	67
BRACKET DWG. 6753	1892	103
STUD DWG 52318	657	112

FIG. 13.1

13.2 Recording Parts Variations

As closer and closer tolerance limits have been specified, it has been increasingly necessary for production and engineering personnel to keep a close check on dimensions. *Go* and *not-go* inspection has been the most widely used procedure for this purpose. Out-of-limits parts are sorted from those which are within limits. Figure 13.1 is a record of such an inspection.

These data may tell a production foreman that corrective action must be taken to reduce rejects. But they will provide few guides to what that action should be. Were the rejects caused by improper machine setups? By tool wobble? By operator carelessness? By poor materials?

Another type of record was developed by the inspection supervisor of an eastern plant to tabulate the outer-diameter dimensions of shafts. The nominal value for this shaft diameter is 0.730 inch, with a tolerance of ± 0.002 inch.

The form used is called a *tally card*. Shaft dimensions from 0.725 to 0.735 inch are listed across the bottom of the card. While examining completed shafts, inspectors record the outer-diameter measurements by placing an *x* in the appropriate spot on the tally card. Figure 13.2 shows such a card.

As compared with Figure 13.1, this type of record gives a much more effective guide for corrective action. It furnishes at a glance a *picture* of just what and where parts variations are rather than indicating whether the shafts are simply "good" or "bad."

The *where* of parts variations may be learned in many cases because there are certain pictures which are characteristic of causes of variation. If the picture

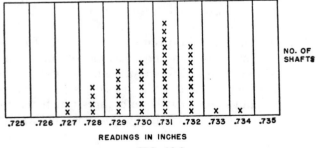

READINGS IN INCHES

FIG. 13.2

shows a widely spread distribution, it may, as in the case cited above, indicate tool wobble. A picture which shows parts bunched below the nominal 0.730-inch dimension may indicate that the machine-tool setup requires a change.

Figure 13.2 is a form of *frequency distribution*. The common sense of the inspection foreman led him to the use of the graphic tally, which is the heart of the frequency distribution.

13.3 Defining the Frequency Distribution

The frequency distribution may be defined as a

Tabulation, or tally, of the number of times a given quality-characteristic measurement occurs within the sample of product being checked.

The tabulation may be plotted with frequency of occurrence on the vertical axis and some quality characteristic (inches, volts, magnetic strength, radioactivity, pounds, hardness) plotted on the horizontal scale. It then is properly called a *frequency curve*.

Industrial usage, however, has come to term this type of tabulation a *frequency-distribution curve* or, most popularly, simply a frequency distribution. The latter term is used here.

13.4 A Frequency-Distribution Example

The length characteristic of a certain type of brass stud is an interesting example of the frequency distribution. These studs are produced on a screw machine. Their length is determined by a cutoff operation. The drawing specification for this length calls for 0.500 ± 0.005 inch.

Fifty pieces may be arbitrarily chosen as the size of the sample to be checked. The studs are selected as they are successively completed by the machine. The resulting measurement readings may be recorded as shown in Figure 13.3.

This mass of numbers may be scanned for some time without gaining any

LENGTH OF STUD – .500 $\pm$ .005

1.	.498	11.	.500	21.	.505	31.	.503	41.	.502
2.	.501	12.	.499	22.	.502	32.	.501	42.	.501
3.	.504	13.	.501	23.	.504	33.	.504	43.	.504
4.	.502	14.	.502	24.	.504	34.	.501	44.	.502
5.	.503	15.	.504	25.	.501	35.	.500	45.	.500
6.	.504	16.	.499	26.	.503	36.	.502	46.	.502
7.	.502	17.	.503	27.	.502	37.	.499	47.	.504
8.	.505	18.	.502	28.	.500	38.	.502	48.	.501
9.	.503	19.	.503	29.	.501	39.	.503	49.	.503
10.	.500	20.	.502	30.	.501	40.	.503	50.	.503

FIG. 13.3

FREQUENCY DISTRIBUTION ON LENGTH OF STUD – .500 $\pm$ .005

LENGTH	FREQ.	FREQ. IN %
.495		
.496		
.497		
.498	I	2%
.499	3	6%
.500	5	10%
.501	9	18%
.502	12	24%
.503	10	20%
.504	8	16%
.505	2	4%
TOTAL	50	100%

FREQUENCY DIAGRAM
FIG. 13.4

useful concept of the overall conformance of the sample of 50 studs to the drawing specification. To clarify this picture, the data can be grouped by like dimension; that is, all 0.500-inch readings will be grouped together, all 0.501-inch readings will be so grouped, and so forth. A card can be prepared which lists the suitable divisions. As in Figure 13.4, the number of times a reading occurs can be recorded opposite the appropriate division. This represents its *frequency* of occurrence. These divisions are usually termed *cells*.

Figure 13.4 can be converted into a graph by substituting individual *x*s for the numbers listed in the frequency column. Figure 13.5 is the result.

LENGTH	FREQUENCY
.495	
.496	
.497	
.498	X
.499	XXX
.500	XXXXX
.501	XXXXXXXXX
.502	XXXXXXXXXXXX
.503	XXXXXXXXXX
.504	XXXXXXXX
.505	XX

FREQUENCY DISTRIBUTION
FIG. 13.5

It is possible to go still further and to join the tops of the columns of xs. This results in the frequency-distribution curve of Figure 13.6.

The steps illustrated by Figures 13.3 and 13.4 are often eliminated in practical factory use. Measurements are directly recorded as in Figure 13.5.

Figures 13.5 and 13.6 present a picture of the length characteristic of the sample of brass studs. Such features about the group quality of stud lengths are shown as

1. *The approximate central value.* This will usually reflect the dimension at which the screw machine was set up.
2. *The spread of the values.* This will reflect the variability of raw materials or possibly that of the screw-machine cutoff operation itself.
3. *The relation of the values to the drawing tolerance.* This will be important as a guide to any necessary corrective action.

13.5 The Analytical Use of This Frequency-Distribution Picture

Suppose that the 50 studs shown in Figure 13.6 are being checked for the purpose of approving the setup of the screw machine preliminary to a long production run. Is the setup satisfactory?

Since all the studs are within the drawing tolerance, approval on a go and not-go basis would undoubtedly result in an O.K. for the setup.

The frequency-distribution picture of Figure 13.6 furnishes a far more useful basis for approval than this go and not-go approach. It provides a wealth of information that would be unavailable from a go and not-go check. The inspector, operator, or supervisor who glances at Figure 13.6 may see the following:

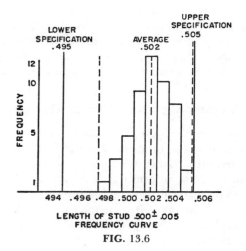

LENGTH OF STUD .500 ± .005
FREQUENCY CURVE

FIG. 13.6

1. From the way that parts are bunched around 0.504 and 0.505 inch, common sense dictates that some parts may be produced during a long production run that will measure 0.506 or 0.507 inch and so be unacceptable. This condition is all the more critical because, in this particular operation, tool wear tends to produce longer studs. There may be a tendency for parts to measure well over 0.506 or 0.507 inch during the latter part of the run.
2. The total variation of the parts checked is 0.007 inch. This compares favorably with the 0.010-inch total tolerance allowed by the drawing.
3. The machine is set up about 0.002 inch above the nominal dimension; 0.502 inch seems to be the central value on Figure 13.6.

This information might suggest the appropriate corrective action to production personnel: A longer, more economical production run may be obtained by taking advantage of the acceptable 0.007-inch spread. The screw machine may be reset so that 0.500, rather than 0.502 inch, will be approached as the nominal reading; or considering the tool wear, 0.499 inch may be used as nominal.

In the actual situation represented by this example, the screw machine was reset this way; a successful production run was obtained from this action.

This type of application, treating the frequency distribution as a simple picture with no algebraic analysis, is one of its most popular industrial uses. There are many adaptations of this application: different sample sizes are used; different forms are made up for plotting the distribution.

Production people sometimes like to plot in dotted limit lines at the upper and lower ends of the distribution, as shown in Figure 13.6. These dotted lines are often called *process limits.*

Production people usually also plot in somewhat heavier lines, which represent the actual drawing specification. Compared with these heavier lines, the process limits furnish a simple prediction of the quality that may be expected from a particular setup on a given machine or process.

Broadly speaking, process limits can be distinguished from specification limits as follows: A process limit is set by the operation itself; a specification limit is usually established by a human being—often the design engineer—who takes into account factors external to the operation.

13.6 The Frequency Distribution As a Way of Thought

Fully as valuable as its application as an analytical method is the use of the frequency distribution as a way of viewing modern product manufacture.

The frequency-distribution concept emphasizes that variation is inevitable in manufactured parts. This variation generally takes a definite frequency pattern, which cannot be learned by examination of only two or three pieces.

Men and women in industry are often prone to think of manufactured parts as individual items, each uniquely representative of the process by which and the design to which they were produced. To learn about these processes and designs, production people may feel that only a few pieces need be examined. This point of view is probably a carry-over from the days when manufacturing was on an individual job-lot basis.

The frequency distribution states that these individual pieces tell relatively little when they are studied by themselves. The lot of which those pieces are a part yields the significant information. Individual pieces are best thought of as units of a larger lot. To truly represent the quality characteristics of these pieces requires the study of a sample of adequate size drawn from the lot to which the pieces belong.

Costly errors occur when this concept is not appreciated. An engineer may spend a great deal of time in the design and development of a new product, being certain that the article can be produced satisfactorily on the factory floor.

When active production begins, however, manufacturing difficulties may be reported by the production organization. A large number of articles may be rejected by Inspection. Days may occur when the various parts will not fit together into the assembly of the article.

The engineer may bitterly feel that the plant has not organized itself adequately to produce the article. In its turn, production personnel may feel that the engineer has turned out an incomplete design.

What may actually have happened is that the engineer did devote a great deal of attention to tests on two or three sample assemblies and checks on five or six parts. But the engineer did not test a sufficient number of articles to give a representative picture of the total variation to be expected when all possible variables have come into play.

Figure 13.7 represents this situation. The two xs represent the units actually tested by the engineer. The dotted frequency curve represents the total distribution of which these two units are a part. It is the effect of this distribution curve which may be mirrored in the difficulties the plant is having with this article.

A similar error may occur when a machine-tool setup is being approved preliminary to a long production run. Only two or three pieces may be checked. In some instances, such as when the variability of the machine is known, this sample size might be satisfactory. In many cases, however, it will

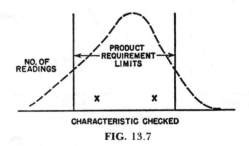

FIG. 13.7

not be at all representative of the total variation that may be expected during the production run.

The frequency distribution, therefore, makes such important contributions to the concept of product manufacture as the following:

1. It helps to establish the *principle* that some amount of variation must always be expected among manufactured parts.
2. It helps to establish the *general nature* (see Sec. 13.7) of the graphical shape that this variation will take.
3. It helps to establish an *important approach* to the study and control of this variation.

Thus, it will help answer such questions as

1. Is the variation in a process such that parts can be produced within specification limits as far as a particular quality characteristic is concerned?

    In the left-hand chart of Fig. 13.8, the answer to this question is "Yes"; in the right-hand chart, "No." The shaded area represents out-of-tolerance parts.
2. How does the average value for the quality characteristic compare with specification limits?

    Figure 13.9 illustrates graphical answers to questions of this sort.

13.7 The General Shape of Industrial Frequency Distributions

Industrial frequency-distribution studies have been made on a wide variety of manufactured products. Intensity of cathode ray tubes, thickness of ceramic substrates, consistency of varnish, and the strength of permanent magnets have all been plotted.

It has come to be recognized that some similarity exists among the shapes

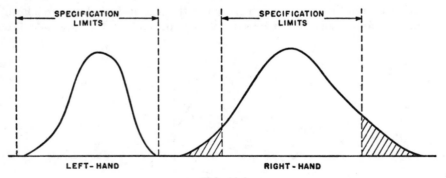

FIG. 13.8

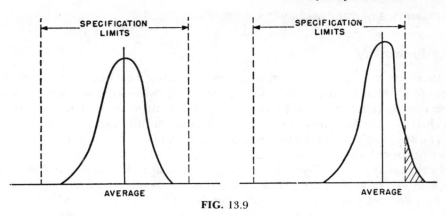

FIG. 13.9

of these industrial frequency distributions. Figure 13.10 represents an example of this general curve shape; it shows the distribution of the thickness of about 150 slabs of sheet steel.

Pictorial analysis of the sort that has been discussed above has been very useful in many of these studies. But in other applications there has been need for a more precise sort of analysis. The demand is for consolidation into a set of numbers of the essential information shown by the graphs of Figures 13.6 and 13.10.

The algebra necessary for this job is found in the so-called probability mathematics.

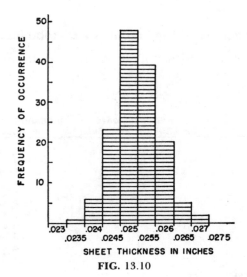

FIG. 13.10

MATHEMATICS OF THE FREQUENCY DISTRIBUTION

13.8 Probability

Everyone who is familiar with games of chance has heard or asked the question "What are the odds?" This question represents the popular recognition that there are *probabilities*, rather than certainties, associated with games of chance—whether tossing coins or waiting for a full house in poker.

The throwing of dice furnishes a useful example of the application of the laws of probability to games of chance.

In throwing one six-sided die, each of the six sides has an equal chance of coming up. In several throws, a 4 should occur as often as a 3.

Two dice may be thrown at once, and their top numbers added. This sum might range from 2 to 12. When two dice are thrown, however, fewer sides are available to turn up totals like 2 or 12 than to turn up a 7. A definite probability, or "set of odds," is associated with this situation and is shown in Figure 13.11. In the long run, actual throws of two dice would conform closely to this pattern.

A frequency-distribution curve of the data in Figure 13.11 can be plotted as shown in Fig. 13.12. The similarity of this curve shape to the industrial distributions already discussed is readily apparent. Presumably, the many variables in an industrial production process have roughly the same effect upon parts variations as the so-called chance factors have upon a game such as dice throwing.

The significance of this similarity is that the algebraic measures developed in the field of probability can be used to analyze industrial frequency distributions.

13.9 Algebraic Measures of the Frequency Distribution

Consider the two characteristics of the frequency distribution that have been mentioned:

SUM OF FACES OF DICE	NUMBER OF WAYS OF GETTING THE SUM	"PROBABILITY" OR CHANCE OF OCCURRING
2	1	1/36
3	2	2/36
4	3	3/36
5	4	4/36
6	5	5/36
7	6	6/36
8	5	5/36
9	4	4/36
10	3	3/36
11	2	2/36
12	1	1/36
TOTALS	36	36/36

FIG. 13.11

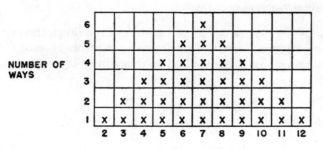

SUM OF FACES OF DICE

FIG. 13.12

1. Its *central tendency,* that is, what is the most representative value
2. Its *spread,* or *dispersion,* that is, how much variation is there

For industrial use, the two most valuable measures of central tendency are the *average* and the *median.*

The two most useful measures of spread are the *standard deviation* and the *range.*

13.10 Measures of Central Tendency

Average

The *average* is the most useful measure of central tendency. It is obtained by dividing the sum of the values in a series of readings by the number of readings, or symbolically:

$$\overline{X} = \frac{X_1 + X_2 + X_3 + \cdots + X_n}{n} \tag{1A}$$

where
$\overline{X}$ = average value (called "X bar") of the series
$X_1, X_2, \cdots, X_n$ = value of successive readings
n = number of readings

To avoid the awkward numerator in Formula (1A), it has become customary to speak of the "sum of the Xs" and to use the Greek capital letter sigma (Σ) to denote this sum as (ΣX). Thus, Formula (1A) becomes

$$\overline{X} = \frac{\Sigma X}{n} \tag{1B}$$

If there is a set of five readings—11, 12, 13, 15, 16—the average is obtained as shown:

$$\overline{X} = \frac{11 + 12 + 13 + 15 + 16}{5} = 13.4$$

In a series where there is a large number of readings, the calculation of the average is greatly simplified by first grouping together readings in suitable cells and then summing up these cells. For this condition, Formula (1B) may become

$$\bar{X} = \frac{\Sigma fX}{n} \tag{2}$$

where f = frequency of readings within a given valued cell (X)
   ΣfX = sum of the product of successive cell values and the number of readings associated with each of these respective cell values

When the values of the average for each series of readings in a number of series are calculated, it may be desirable to compute the average of these several averages. This measure is termed the *grand average*.

Symbolically, it is shown as $\bar{\bar{X}}$ (X double bar) and is calculated as in the following formulas:

$$\bar{\bar{X}} = \frac{\bar{X}_1 + \bar{X}_2 + \cdots \bar{X}_r}{r} \tag{3A}$$

for r samples of equal size.

And, for r samples of size $n_1, n_2, \cdots, n_r$, the formula is:

$$\bar{\bar{X}} = \frac{n_1\bar{X}_1 + n_2\bar{X}_2 + \cdots n_r\bar{X}_r}{N} \tag{3B}$$

where $N = n_1 + n_2 + \cdots n_r$

The grand average has its chief value in control chart work.

The samples upon which these calculations of the average and grand average are based are drawn from a larger "population" which may consist of a single lot or, more generally, a production flow represented by a series of lots. This *population average* is designated as μ (Greek lowercase letter mu). In most practical quality-control situations, it is seldom known. $\bar{X}$ and $\bar{\bar{X}}$ which are, in effect, estimates of the population average, are fully satisfactory for most industrial applications and are the central tendency measures in predominant industrial use.

Median

The *median* is sometimes used for industrial work. It is that value which divides a series of readings arranged in order of the magnitude of their values so that an equal number of values is on either side of the center or "median" value.

Thus, in a set of readings—11, 12, 14, 16, 17—the value of the median is 14. In another set of readings—8, 9, 9, 10, 11, 11, 12, 12, 13, 13, 13, 15—the value of the median is 11.5.

The median is likely to be somewhat erratic as compared with the average but is often much easier to obtain.[1] For that reason it is preferred in several types of work, particularly with control charts in machine shops.

13.11 The Standard Deviation

The *standard deviation* is used as the measure of spread for almost all industrial frequency distributions. It is usually computed for samples drawn from larger lots, and in these cases it is called the *sample standard deviation* (denoted by small letter s). The sample standard deviation is the positive square root of the sum of the squared deviations of readings from their average divided by one less than the number of readings, or symbolically:[2]

$$s = \sqrt{\frac{(X_1 - \overline{X})^2 + (X_2 - \overline{X})^2 + (X_3 - \overline{X})^2 + \cdots + (X_n - \overline{X})^2}{n - 1}} \tag{4A}$$

where
$$\begin{aligned} s &= \text{sample standard deviation} \\ X_1, X_2, \cdots X_n &= \text{value of each reading} \\ \overline{X} &= \text{average value of the series} \\ n &= \text{number of readings} \end{aligned}$$

Thus, in the series 4, 5, 6, 7, 8, where the average is 6, the sample standard deviation can be calculated as follows:

$$\begin{aligned} s &= \sqrt{\frac{(4 - 6)^2 + (5 - 6)^2 + (6 - 6)^2 + (7 - 6)^2 + (8 - 6)^2}{5 - 1}} \\ &= \sqrt{\frac{4 + 1 + 0 + 1 + 4}{4}} = \sqrt{\frac{10}{4}} \\ &= 1.581 \end{aligned}$$

Where there is a large number of readings in a series, it is usually convenient to group together readings of the same value into individual cells before undertaking the calculation of the standard deviation. When the readings have been so grouped, a useful formula is

$$s = \sqrt{\frac{\Sigma f X^2 - n\overline{X}^2}{n - 1}} \tag{4B}$$

where $\Sigma f X^2 = $ sum of the product of readings in the successive cells times the square of the value for cells

The *average* sample standard deviation, $\bar{s}$ (small letter s bar) is widely used in plant control chart applications. The average sample standard deviation is the average value of the sample standard deviations when each sample has the same number of readings, or symbolically:

$$\bar{s} = \frac{s_1 + s_2 + \cdots + s_r}{r} \tag{5}$$

for r sample deviations.

As similarly discussed in Section 13.10 in connection with the average, the samples upon which these calculations of the sample standard deviation are based are drawn from a larger "population" which may consist of a single lot or, more generally, a production flow represented by a series of lots. This *population standard deviation* is designated as σ (Greek lowercase letter sigma).

For certain statistical reasons, a sample standard deviation s slightly underestimates the σ of the population from which the sample was drawn. A factor designated as c_4 (small c subscript $_4$) must therefore be used to estimate the value of the population standard deviation when the value of the sample standard deviation has been determined. This calculation is as follows:

$$\sigma = \frac{s}{c_4}$$

Values for c_4 are given in Figure 13.13.

While the sample standard deviation is generally the most widely applied standard deviation measure in many plant applications, the population standard deviation measure is also very important in such applications as the evaluation of the ongoing quality of a continuous process and the long-term quality of vendor shipments over time.[3]

As noted from the c_4 factors in the table in Fig. 13.13 and as more fully discussed in Section 13.18, the accuracy of s as an estimator of the population standard deviation increases substantially as sample size also increases. In many plant quality-control applications where frequency distribution sample size is relatively large and where high precision of the estimate of σ is not needed, then s is considered as a useful practical indicator of σ. However, where sample size is small and where precision is required—as in various electronic, medical, safety-oriented, and other applications—σ must be calculated from s as shown above to establish the necessary values. For plant control chart applications (discussed in Chap. 14) and where sample size is relatively small, this distinction between the values of s and σ is particularly important.

CALCULATING THE SAMPLE STANDARD DEVIATION

In the practical calculation of the sample standard deviation, and when there is a large number of readings, several techniques may be found useful for simplifying the calculation. Four of these techniques are:

"Coding" the Readings in a Series

Some series have readings whose values are extremely cumbersome. A case in point is a series whose values are 839.38, 839.42, 839.63. In instances like

n	c_4	c_5	n	c_4	c_5
2	0.7979	0.6028	32	0.9920	0.1265
3	0.8862	0.4633	34	0.9925	0.1226
4	0.9213	0.3888	36	0.9929	0.1191
5	0.9400	0.3412	38	0.9933	0.1158
6	0.9515	0.3075	40	0.9936	0.1129
7	0.9594	0.2822	42	0.9939	0.1101
8	0.9650	0.2621	44	0.9942	0.1075
9	0.9693	0.2458	46	0.9945	0.1051
10	0.9727	0.2322	48	0.9947	0.1029
11	0.9754	0.2207	50	0.9949	0.1008
12	0.9776	0.2107	52	0.9951	0.0988
13	0.9794	0.2019	54	0.9953	0.0969
14	0.9810	0.1942	56	0.9955	0.0951
15	0.9823	0.1872	58	0.9956	0.0935
16	0.9835	0.1810	60	0.9958	0.0919
17	0.9845	0.1753	62	0.9959	0.0903
18	0.9854	0.1702	64	0.9960	0.0889
19	0.9862	0.1655	66	0.9962	0.0875
20	0.9869	0.1611	68	0.9963	0.0862
21	0.9876	0.1571	70	0.9964	0.0850
22	0.9882	0.1534	72	0.9965	0.0838
23	0.9887	0.1499	74	0.9966	0.0826
24	0.9892	0.1466	76	0.9967	0.0815
25	0.9896	0.1436	78	0.9968	0.0805
26	0.9901	0.1407	80	0.9968	0.0794
27	0.9904	0.1380	84	0.9970	0.0775
28	0.9908	0.1354	88	0.9971	0.0757
29	0.9911	0.1330	92	0.9973	0.0740
30	0.9914	0.1307	96	0.9974	0.0725
31	0.9917	0.1286	100	0.9975	0.0710

FIG. 13.13 **Adapted with permission from I. W. Burr, "Applied Statistical Methods," Academic Press, New York, 1974, p. 437.**

this it is often useful to "code" the readings by subtracting a constant value from each one.

In the case cited, 839.00 might be subtracted from each reading. This would leave values such as 0.38, 0.42, and 0.63, which are much easier to handle.

A general rule is: Any constant value can be added or subtracted from the values in a series without changing the value of the standard deviation. Note, however, that if the values in a series are multiplied or divided by the same factor, the value for the standard deviation will be multiplied or divided by that factor. To convert back to the original readings, it is necessary to divide or multiply the value for the standard deviation for the coded values by the same constant with which the readings were coded.

"Grouping" the Readings in a Series

One form of grouping the readings in a series has already been mentioned, namely, to gather together readings of the same value into several individual cells. This practice causes difficulties when it creates too many of these cells.

Thus, there may be 200 readings in series, ranging from a low of 52.01 through 53.73 to 59.33 on to a high reading of 62.00. All are recorded to the nearest hundredth.

Grouping together all readings which are 52.01, 53.73, and so on may result in 50 to 75 cells. This would probably be a cumbersome total with which to work.

It is possible to group these data in a relatively small number of cells by selecting cells arbitrarily. Thus group 1 may include readings from 52.01 to 53.00 inclusive, group 2 may include readings from 53.01 to 54.00 inclusive, and group 10 may include readings from 61.01 to 62.00. Two hundred widely varied readings can thus be reduced to 10 cells, a far more manageable number than 50 to 75 cells. From 8 to 20 cells are found in industrial frequency distributions, about 12 cells being the most popular number.

The resulting value for the standard deviation for the example cited will be given in terms of the cell interval taken as a unit. This figure can be converted back to the original values for the readings simply by multiplying by the cell interval selected, which in the case cited is 1.00.

"Zeroing"

When the readings have been coded or grouped, there are two major alternatives for carrying through the standard deviation calculation:

1. Carry through the calculation with the data as they stand in coded or grouped form. This type of calculation is illustrated in Section 13.16.
2. Carry the grouping a step further by selecting one cell arbitrarily as zero, considering the cells in the lower part of the table below the zero cell as positive and those in the upper part of the table as negative. With such grouping, the numbers with which it is necessary to work are often smaller. This is advantageous in certain types of calculations. This procedure is briefly used in Section 13.17.

Electronic Calculators and Computers

In recent years, there have been great improvements in electronic means for calculating the standard deviation along with other statistics. Large-scale digital electronic computers have been used successfully for solving complex problems using programmed statistical techniques similar to those outlined in Chapter 16. Smaller and more specialized electronic calculators and computers are commercially available for the calculation of specific statistics.

Also available are other special-purpose calculators, such as the process-capability slide rule, discussed in Section 20.16, for computing the standard deviation.

There can be little question but that technical devices have eliminated much of the time formerly required for the standard deviation and other statistical calculations.

13.12 The Range

The *range* is the difference between the lowest and the highest readings in a series, or symbolically:

$$R = X_{\text{high}} - X_{\text{low}} \tag{6A}$$

where R = range value
X_{high} = highest reading in series
X_{low} = lowest reading in series

In the series 11, 12, 13, 15, 16, X_{high} is 16 and X_{low} is 11. The range is therefore

$$R = 16 - 11$$
$$= 5$$

When the values of the range for each series of readings in a number of series are calculated, it may be desirable to compute the average of these ranges. This measure is termed the *average range*. Symbolically it is shown by $\overline{R}$ (R bar) and is calculated as follows:

$$\overline{R} = \frac{R_1 + R_2 + \cdots R_r}{r} \tag{6B}$$

for r sample ranges, each range with the same number of readings.

13.13 Comparing the Standard Deviation and the Range

Although the standard deviation usually provides more reliable information about the spread of a sample than does the range, the range is far simpler to calculate. In a series with 10 readings, the range can be obtained at a glance; the standard deviation would involve a computation.

Because of its relative simplicity, the range has enjoyed wide industrial usage, particularly in control chart work. Statistically, however, its accuracy decreases as the number of readings increases.

Common sense immediately gives two reasons for this decrease in accuracy of the range as sample size increases. In large samples there is more chance of including a "wide-of-the-mark" reading. These "maverick" readings are inevitably reflected to a high degree by the range, which simply measures the spread from the lowest to the highest reading. Also, the range considers only the two extreme readings and disregards the other observations, so all the available information is not used in calculating the spread.

The standard deviation does not have these failings to so great a degree. It is a much more effective reflection of *all* the readings in a series, and any maverick will have far less effect upon its value.

A simple generalization, therefore, is that the standard deviation can be used with samples of almost any number of readings. The range should be used only with samples of small size. A sample of no more than 10 readings is preferred, and 15 readings is a practical, rule-of-thumb maximum.

13.14 The Normal Curve

Historically, much of the analytical use of the algebraic measures described above revolved around a type of frequency distribution termed a *normal curve.* This normal curve is the frequency-distribution curve approached in many situations where chance is given full play, as in the case of a large number of throws of dice.

Figure 13.14 illustrates this curve. It has a unique bell shape, which has been likened to a London bobby's hat.

An extremely important relationship exists between the population standard deviation and the normal curve. When the standard deviation is computed for a normal frequency distribution, 68.27 percent of all the readings in the distribution will occur between plus and minus one standard deviation of the average ($\overline{X} \pm 1\sigma$), 95.45 percent of all readings in the distribution will occur between plus and minus two standard deviations of the average ($\overline{X} \pm 2\sigma$),

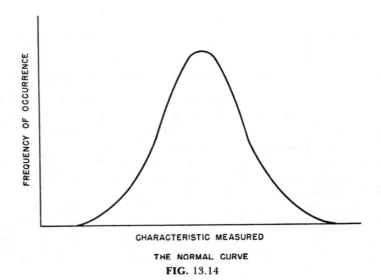

CHARACTERISTIC MEASURED

THE NORMAL CURVE

FIG. 13.14

99.73 percent of all the readings in the distribution will occur between plus and minus three standard deviations of the average ($\overline{X} + 3\sigma$).[4]

Figure 13.14a shows this relationship between the standard deviation and the normal frequency distribution.

The importance of this relationship may be readily appreciated. With the average and the standard deviation calculated for a normal distribution, it is possible to compute two additional features of that distribution:

1. The percentage of values that will fall between any two readings of different values. In actual practice, this will be any two dimensions.
2. The total amount of variation that may for all practical purposes be expected from that distribution ($\overline{X} \pm 3\sigma$). This so-called 3-sigma value is the algebraic parallel for the process limits that were obtained in Sec. 13.5 by simply drawing dashed lines at the extremes of the distribution.

The task of determining the percentage of readings which fall between any two given dimensions is considerably simplified by the use of the table shown in Figure 13.15. This table relates the decimal fractions of normal curve area to varying distances from the average, $\overline{X}$. The x/σ shown in the table equals $(X - \overline{X})/\sigma$, where X is the individual reading. Since the normal curve is symmetrical, most tables calculate areas for only one side of the curve.

The importance of the use of this relationship is also equally powerful when s, the sample standard deviation, is the generally applied measure of dispersion in plant quality-control activities. When precision and accuracy are required, the analysis of values between any two readings or of total variation will be made up by converting s into σ as earlier discussed in Sec. 13.11. An example of this in plant quality-control application is given in Sec. 13.30. In plant situations where large sample sizes are used and where the demand exists for quick corrective action with no high demand upon the absolute precision of readings, the value of s itself is sometimes determined to be a satisfactory estimate of σ in these calculations. An example of this is given in Sec. 13.16.

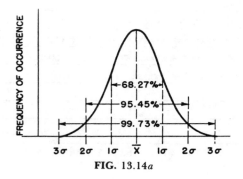

FIG. 13.14a

DISTANCE FROM AVERAGE DIVIDED BY STANDARD DEVIATION x/σ	AREA	DISTANCE FROM AVERAGE DIVIDED BY STANDARD DEVIATION x/σ	AREA
0.0	0.00000	2.0	0.47725
0.1	0.03983	2.1	0.48214
0.2	0.07926	2.2	0.48610
0.3	0.11791	2.3	0.48928
0.4	0.15542	2.4	0.49180
0.5	0.19146	2.5	0.49379
0.6	0.22575	2.5758	0.49500
0.7	0.25804	2.6	0.49534
0.8	0.28814	2.7	0.49653
0.9	0.31594	2.8	0.49744
1.0	0.34134	2.9	0.49813
1.1	0.36433	3.0	0.49865
1.2	0.38493	3.1	0.49903
1.3	0.40320	3.2	0.49931
1.4	0.41924	3.3	0.49952
1.5	0.43319	3.4	0.49966
1.6	0.44520	3.5	0.49977
1.7	0.45543	3.6	0.49984
1.8	0.46407	3.7	0.49989
1.9	0.47128	3.8	0.49993
1.96	0.47500	3.9	0.49995
		4.0	0.49997

FIG. 13.15

13.15 An Example of the Algebraic Analysis of the Frequency Distribution

The philosophy of algebraic analysis of the frequency distribution is similar to that for pictorial analysis, as discussed in Section 13.5. The chief difference is the mechanical one of calculating the average and the standard deviation.

DIMENSION	TALLY	TOTALS
.023		
.0235	X	1
.024	XXXXX	6
.0245	XXXXXXXXXXXXXXXXXXXXXXX	23
.025	XXXXXXXXXXXXXXXXXXXXXXXXXXXXXXXXXXXXXXXXXXXXXXXXXX	48
.0255	XXXXXXXXXXXXXXXXXXXXXXXXXXXXXXXXXXXXXXXXX	39
.026	XXXXXXXXXXXXXXXXXXXX	20
.0265	XXXXX	5
.027	XX	2
	TOTAL VALUES	144

TALLY SHEET FOR STEEL SHEET THICKNESS MEASUREMENTS
FIG. 13.16

An example of such an analysis is a study made by a New York State punch-press factory. This shop wished to examine the amount of variation existing in the sheet steel it was purchasing for its stamping presses.

One hundred forty-four thickness measurements were made on a sample of steel sheets. An indicator gage, reading to an accuracy of 0.0005 inch was used. Figure 13.16 pictures the tally card which resulted from this series of measurements.

With 144 readings, many of which were the same value, grouping into cells was a simple matter. The first two columns of Figure 13.17 show this grouping. With data grouped in this fashion, the appropriate formula for the average in Section 13.10 is Formula (3). Formula (4B) is most appropriate for the standard deviation, as presented in Section 13.11.

The last two columns in Figure 13.17 show how grouped data can be further tabulated in a form most useful for substitution into these formulas.

Thickness (in mils) (X)	Frequency f	Frequency times thickness fx	Frequency times thickness^2 fx^2
23.5	1	23.5	552.25
24.0	6	144.0	3456.00
24.5	23	563.5	13805.75
25.0	48	1200.0	30000.00
25.5	39	994.5	25359.75
26.0	20	520.0	13520.00
26.5	5	132.5	3611.25
27.0	2	54.0	1458.00
Totals( )	144	3632.0	91663.00

Average:
$$\overline{X} = \frac{\Sigma fx}{n} = \frac{3632}{144} = 25.222 \text{ mils} = 0.025222 \text{ inches}$$

Standard deviation:
$$s = \sqrt{\frac{\Sigma fx^2 - n\overline{X}^2}{n-1}}$$

$$= \sqrt{\frac{91663 - 144(25.222)^2}{143}}$$

$$= \sqrt{\frac{91663 - 91605.496}{143}}$$

$$= \sqrt{\frac{57.504}{143}}$$

$$= \sqrt{0.4021258}$$

$$= 0.6341 = 0.6 \text{ mils} = 0.0006 \text{ inches}$$

FIG. 13.17

The calculations for the average and the standard deviation are shown at the foot of Figure 13.17. The importance of carrying enough decimal places in the standard deviation calculation should be noted.

Some of the information that this analysis made available to management of the punch-press factory was the following:

1. The nominal, or average, thickness for the steel sheets being received was 25.222 mils (thousandths of an inch). ($\overline{X} = 25.222$ mils.)
2. The total variation in the sheet steel was ± 1.8 mils ($\pm 3s = \pm 1.8$ mils), or a total variation of 3.6 mils.[5]

The standard deviation figures are rounded off. Three-decimal-place accuracy is meaningless in a situation where the accuracy of the measuring instrument is only 0.5 mil.

An interesting practical circumstance is illustrated by these data. A glance at the tally of Figure 13.16 would have provided almost the same information as was obtained through these calculations. This glance would have indicated that the spread of the values was from about 23.5 to 27.0 mils.

This condition often arises in actual application of the frequency distribution. For this reason much of the use of this distribution is as a simple picture. As more fully discussed below, however, there is an important need for calculating the standard deviation in certain types of industrial analyses.

13.16 Algebraic Frequency-Distribution Analysis

Management of the punch-press plant may now wish to study another question. How much of this sheet steel would be out of limits were a specification to be established of 25 ± 1 mil, or from 24 to 26 mils?

With a sample size as high as 144 obtained under well-planned circumstances and with the degree of data precision required, the plant determined that the value calculated for s was a satisfactory estimate of σ and the answer to this question could be simply obtained by use of the table of areas in Figure 13.15. Before this table can be used, two values must be calculated:

1. The deviation from the average of the two dimensions in question (24 and 26 mils)
2. The value of this deviation from the average, divided by the standard deviation (x/σ)

Calculation of these numbers is shown in Figure 13.18.

From Figure 13.15 it may be seen that an x/σ of 2 corresponds to an area of 0.47725, or 47.725 percent of the normal-curve area. It may also be seen that an x/σ of 1.3 corresponds to an area of 0.40320, or 40.320 percent of the normal-curve area. Therefore, the spread between an x/σ of 2 (representative of a reading of 24.0 mils) and an x/σ of 1.3 (representative of a reading of 26.0

Computation	Lowest value (24 mils)	Highest value (26 mils)
x	$x_L = X_1 - \bar{X}$ $x_L = 24.0 - 25.2$ $x_L = -1.2$	$x_H = X_2 - \bar{X}$ $x_H = 26.0 - 25.2$ $x_H = +0.8$
$\dfrac{x}{\sigma}$	$\dfrac{x_L}{\sigma} = \dfrac{-1.2}{0.6}$ $\dfrac{x_L}{\sigma} = -2$ The algebraic minus sign simply means that this deviation represents a value below the average of the series	$\dfrac{x_H}{\sigma} = \dfrac{+0.8}{0.6}$ $\dfrac{x_H}{\sigma} = +1.3$ The algebraic plus sign simply means that this deviation represents a value above the average of the series

where x_L = deviation from the average of the lowest value
$\quad\quad x_H$ = deviation from average of the highest value
$\quad\quad X_1$ = lowest value (24 mils)
$\quad\quad X_2$ = highest value (26 mils)
$\quad\quad \sigma$ = standard deviation (0.6 mils)

FIG. 13.18

mils) equals the sum of these two percentages:

$$47.7 \text{ percent} + 40.3 \text{ percent} = 88.0 \text{ percent}$$

Consequently 88.0 percent of the area of the distribution falls between 24.0 and 26.0 mils. As a corollary, 12.0 percent of the area falls outside 24.0 to 26.0 mils. Were this distribution representative of the thickness of steel sheets henceforth to be received by the punch-press plant, it would indicate that about 12 percent of the sheets would be unsatisfactory and would be rejected.

13.17 Another Method for Calculating the Sheet-Steel Distribution

Another method for preparing the data of Figure 13.17 would have been to arbitrarily select the cell with the highest frequency (referred to as the *mode* of the distribution), 25.0, as the middle, or "zero," cell. The next cell with a value higher than 25.0, namely 25.5, would have been considered as +1; 26.0 would have been considered +2; and so on. Similarly, the next cell with a value lower than 25.0, namely 24.5, would have been considered as −1; 24.0 would have been considered −2; and so forth.

This procedure would result in much smaller numbers in the calculations. In those cases where such a circumstance is desirable, this zeroing technique is very useful for calculating the average and standard deviation.

After the data have been coded and zeroed according to the procedure discussed in Section 13.11, the calculations for the average and the standard deviation are exactly the same as shown in Figure 13.17. When these calculations have been made, however, they must be converted back into original values for the readings. Formulas for this conversion are now shown.

Conversion for average:

$$\text{Average in original value} = \text{value of "zero" frequency} + (\overline{X} \text{ times cell interval}) \tag{7}$$

Conversion for standard deviation:

$$\text{Standard deviation in original value} = \text{value of } s \text{ times cell interval} \tag{8}$$

Figure 13.19 shows the use of this procedure with the steel-sheet data of Section 13.15. It may be compared with the similar calculation in Figure 13.17.

13.18 Sample Size and the Frequency Distribution

The following question was asked of several groups of production supervisors in quality-control training classes: "Suppose that a lot of several thousand electronic relays, produced at the same source and under the same manufacturing conditions, is placed on a final test bench preparatory to shipment. The tester at this bench wishes to get a picture of the group quality of the voltage characteristic of these relays. He decides to select a sample of five relays for this purpose.

"Suppose, now, that the tester selects these five relays at random, checks the voltage characteristic of each relay, and plots his results in the form that would be used for a frequency-distribution plot. He calculates the average and the standard deviation for the plot. . . . Do you feel that this five-reading plot will give the tester a good picture of the central tendency and spread of the voltage characteristic of the lot of several thousand relays?"

The answer of the class members was almost unanimously that they did not feel that the plot would give a satisfactory picture.

A second question was then asked of the groups: "Suppose that the tester returns the five relays to the lot and selects five more relays at random. He checks their voltage characteristics and analyzes the resulting plot. . . . Do you feel that the values for the average and standard deviation for the second set of relays will represent about the same picture as that for the first set?"

Again the answer was "No."

The class members were then queried as to why they had answered as they had. Their almost unanimous retort was that the sample size of five was "too small to be representative."

These class members had intuitively placed their fingers on the core of the problem of the sample sizes that should be used to represent the plot or frequency distribution. The class members had pointed out that a sample which is too small may not accurately portray the average and standard devia-

(X)	(f)	(fx)	fx²
−3	1	− 3	9
−2	6	−12	24
−1	23	−23	23
0	48	0	0
+1	39	+39	39
+2	20	+40	80
+3	5	+15	45
+4	2	+ 8	32
Totals	144	+64	252

Average: $$\overline{X} = \frac{\Sigma fx}{n} = \frac{64}{144} = 0.4444$$

Standard deviation: $$s = \sqrt{\frac{\Sigma fx^2 - n\overline{X}^2}{n - 1}}$$

$$= \sqrt{\frac{252 - 144\,(.4444)^2}{143}}$$

$$= \sqrt{\frac{252 - 28.4387}{143}}$$

$$= \sqrt{\frac{223.56126}{143}}$$

$$= \sqrt{1.5634}$$

$$= 1.25$$

Conversion:

Average in original value = value of "zero frequency" + ($\overline{X}$ times cell interval)

$$= 25.0 + (0.4444)(0.5)$$
$$= 25.0 + 0.2220 = 25.222 \text{ mils}$$

Standard deviation in original value = value of s times cell interval

$$= (1.25)(0.5)$$
$$= 0.6 \text{ mils or } 0.0006 \text{ inches}$$

FIG. 13.19

tion of the lot from which it is drawn. They had noted that two or more samples which are too small may vary quite widely in their respective averages and standard deviations even though they have been drawn from the same lot.

The general principles that hold in these cases can be simply stated: The larger the sample size, the less the spread among averages and standard deviations for samples drawn from the same lot, and hence the more closely will these measures correspond to the comparable measures that would result if the entire lot were analyzed.

The smaller the sample size, the greater the spread among averages and standard deviations for samples drawn from the same lot, and hence the less closely will averages and standard deviations correspond to the value for the average and standard deviation that would result if sampling were discarded in favor of analyses of the entire lot.

It follows from the above statements of principle that, for samples drawn from the same lot, values of averages and standard deviations have standard deviations of their own. This standard deviation for the average is symbolized by $\sigma_{\bar{X}}$ (sigma subscript X bar). The standard deviation for the sample standard deviation is symbolized by σ_s (sigma subscript s).

These particular measures of spread are represented in the following formulas:

$$\sigma_{\bar{X}} = \frac{\sigma}{\sqrt{n}} \qquad (9)$$

where $\sigma_{\bar{X}}$ = standard deviation of the sample average
σ = population standard deviation of the lot from which the sample was drawn
n = sample size

and

$$\sigma_s = \sigma\sqrt{1 - (c_4)^2}$$

where σ_s = standard deviation of the sample standard deviation
σ = population standard deviation of the lot from which the sample was drawn
c_4 = factor for calculation of population standard deviation from sample standard deviation (as earlier discussed in Sec. 13.11 and Fig. 13.13)

The rather cumbersome expression $\sqrt{1 - (c_4)^2}$ has been converted into a factor designated as c_5 (c subscript 5). Values for c_5 are given in Figure 13.13. The formula for the calculation of the standard deviation of the sample standard deviation is therefore as follows:

$$\sigma_s = c_5\sigma \qquad (10)$$

Note in the definition of the terms used in Formulas (9) and (10) that σ is said to represent the population standard deviation of the "lot" from which the sample was drawn. In the electronic relay example noted in this section, the "lot" is a physically segregated, already produced group of units.

This sort of lot is only one of many types covered by the term. Broadly, the term may refer to an entire stream of units either already produced or to be produced in the future by the same source and under the same manufacturing conditions. Thus, a "lot" of studs from an automatic screw machine might be the entire output of the machine over a long period under the same setup and operating conditions fully as much as the "lot" might be a single hour's or day's production. Under practical industrial conditions, the decision as to what is or is not a "lot" is often a fairly arbitrary one.

When the frequency distribution for individual readings is normally distributed, then the frequency distribution for the spread of averages, as in Formula (9), follows the normal distribution pattern. That for the spread of standard deviations, as in Formula (10), is not a perfectly normal curve, but it approaches normality as the sample size increases.

The determination of that sample size of electronic relays wherein the total spread of averages from samples drawn from the same lot will be no greater than 0.90 volt may serve to illustrate the use of one of these formulas. For the sake of simplicity, it may be assumed that, from other data, the population standard deviation of the lot is known to be 1 volt. Also, each calculation will assume a sample average of 14 volts. The relays in question are the same lot that has been discussed in this section.

Using first a sample size of five relays, substituting in Formula (9) shows

$$\sigma_{\bar{X}} = \frac{\sigma}{\sqrt{n}} = \frac{1}{\sqrt{5}} = \frac{1}{2.25}$$
$$= 0.44 \text{ volt}$$

Since the distribution of averages is normal, the total spread of averages of samples of five relays will be

$$\bar{X} \pm 3\sigma_{\bar{X}} = 14 \pm 3(0.44)$$
$$= 14 \pm 1.32 \text{ volts}$$

The value for averages computed from a sample of five relays may be expected to range from 12.68 to 15.32 volts when the average value is 14 volts. This represents a spread of 2.64 volts and is greatly in excess of the target of a spread of 0.90 volt.

Additional trial of other sample sizes would show that a sample size of 50 relays would be most appropriate. Substituting in Formula (9) shows

$$\sigma_{\bar{X}} = \frac{\sigma}{\sqrt{n}} = \frac{1}{\sqrt{50}} = \frac{1}{7} = 0.14 \text{ volt}$$

and

$$\bar{X} \pm 3\sigma_{\bar{X}} = 14 \pm 3(0.14)$$
$$= 14 \pm 0.42 \text{ volt}$$

In this case, the value for averages in a sample of 50 relays may range from 13.58 to 14.42 volts. This represents a spread of 0.84 volt and, as such, meets the target that the spread be no greater than 0.90 volt.

13.19 What Sample Size Should Be Used in Connection with Frequency-Distribution Calculations?

Use of Formulas (9) and (10) for deciding upon the size of a particular sample in many practical industrial applications often requires knowing in advance the value of the population standard deviation of the lot from which the sample is to be drawn. In actual industrial practice, this value is often unknown in advance. As a result, Formulas (9) and (10) are useful chiefly as conceptual guides rather than as mathematical determinants of industrial sample sizes.

The practical industrial decision as to the appropriate size for a particular sample usually takes into account two factors:

1. *The economics of the situation;* that is, how much does it cost to take each reading?
2. *The statistical accuracy required;* that is, how much error is permissible in the values obtained for spread and central tendency?

These two factors usually operate in different directions. The economics of the situation calls for the smallest sample size that can possibly be allowed. The statistics call for a generally larger sample size to yield a maximum of protection.

As a result, the sample size that is appropriate for a given frequency-distribution analysis is often not decided in industry on a fixed statistical formulation. It is developed from a balance between the statistics and the economics of the situation. Past experience with the process in question and judgment of the individuals concerned play a very large part in this decision.

Since the cost of readings and the required statistical accuracy will naturally vary from industry to industry, any generalization about sample size will of course be subject to individual adjustment. For practical purposes, however, a sample size of 50 readings is usually sufficiently reliable for most industrial frequency-distribution analyses for production application. This sample size of 50 is widely used in this book.[6]

When the cost of taking individual measurements is low, or when accurate analyses are required, sample sizes of 100 readings or more may be used. In situations where the distribution analysis is relatively new, the individual without formal statistical training may be well-advised to use a sample size below 50 readings only in the special cases of competent statistical advice, extensive past experience with the process variation, or where only extremely rough approximations are desired.

Note that no mention has been made of the size of the lot from which the samples have been drawn. No effort has been made to relate sample size to lot size because, in general, the reliability of a sample depends largely upon the size of that sample rather than the ratio of the size of the sample to the size of the lot from which it was drawn.

This principle is of great importance in the development and use of sampling tables and is discussed more fully in Chapter 15.

PRACTICAL ASPECTS OF THE FREQUENCY DISTRIBUTION

13.20 Shapes of Industrial Frequency Distributions

Many industrial frequency distributions do not follow the bell shape of the normal curve. Sometimes these nonbell shapes represent the standard, accepted condition for the process in question. They may be a reflection of the engineering and manufacturing fundamentals of this process.

Sometimes these shapes represent a purely temporary process condition. They may serve as a guide to detecting the presence of some unusual factor like defective materials or tool chatter.

There is no magic about the normal curve in the sense that those distributions which closely approximate its shape represent "good-quality" processes and those which are not so smooth represent "bad-quality" processes. How "good" the shape of an industrial frequency distribution is is almost entirely a matter of economics.

The jagged, spread-out distribution, which is well within specification limits, may be a good distribution for that particular purpose. The smooth, normal-curve-shaped distribution, which is outside specification limits, may be a bad distribution. Simply because a distribution is "flat-topped," "jagged," or "skewed" is no infallible indication that the process it represents is inferior to that represented by a smooth, normal-curve-shaped distribution.

Five of the typical shapes taken by these distributions are

1. Skewed curves
2. J-shaped curves
3. Bimodal curves
4. Curves of articles that have been 100 percent inspected
5. Curves of articles that have been 100 percent inspected but are subject to variation after the inspection has been completed

13.21 Skewness

Figure 13.20 represents the distribution shape that is typical for a powdered-metal process in an eastern factory. This type of distribution is termed a *skewed* curve. The number of readings decreases to zero more rapidly on one side of the "hump" of the curve than on the other side.

A distribution may be skewed to the right, as in Figure 13.20. It may also be skewed to the left, as in Figure 13.21, which represents a quality characteristic of a screw-machine part.

Skewness is often the result of the operation of some strong factor or factors. These factors are felt to be fundamental to the powdered-metal process and

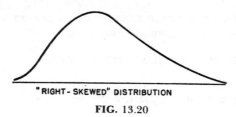

"RIGHT- SKEWED" DISTRIBUTION

FIG. 13.20

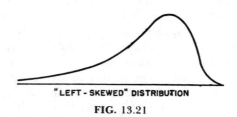

"LEFT - SKEWED" DISTRIBUTION

FIG. 13.21

would be very difficult to identify. For this reason and because the distribution is well within specification limits, its shape is accepted by the factory as standard for this process.

A skewed curve is not, however, accepted as standard for the screw-machine part of Figure 13.21. Skewness here is often characteristic of tool chatter. If such action is required to meet the part specifications, the screw-machine process can be investigated for tool chatter and the chatter eliminated.

13.22 J Shapes and Bimodality

When readings are taken of "run-out" or the "out-of-round" of shafts, a distribution shape similar to that of Figure 13.22 results.

This J-shaped curve is an extremely nonsymmetrical distribution, where one limit is zero and the number of readings approaching the other limit is high.

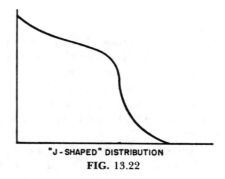

"J - SHAPED" DISTRIBUTION

FIG. 13.22

Batches of similar product from two different sources—different machines, different vendors—may sometimes be mixed together. A distribution shape such as that of Figure 13.23 may result in these cases.

This *bimodal* curve is a distribution with two peaks, where data of two or more different origins are included.

Bimodality may also result from a shift in conditions when data are being taken on a single machine or process. The machine tool in question may be located on a gallery, and its tool setting may be jarred whenever the crane rumbles by.

13.23 100 Percent Inspection Curves

When products whose variation may be wider than that of their engineering specification are subjected to 100 percent inspection, a distribution shape similar to that of Figure 13.24 may result. It is sometimes possible for a customer to determine from just such a frequency-distribution analysis the amount of inspection the vendor is placing on a product.

A product of the sort shown in Figure 13.24 may be subject to slight changes in its quality characteristics during transportation from vendor to customer. Or there may be some degree of variation between the vendor's measurements equipment and that of the customer. In these cases a distribution shape similar to that of Figure 13.25 may result.

This distribution is typical of those which obtain on some products, the

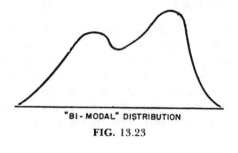

"BI - MODAL" DISTRIBUTION

FIG. 13.23

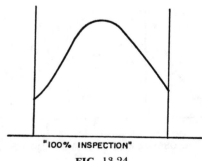

"100% INSPECTION"

FIG. 13.24

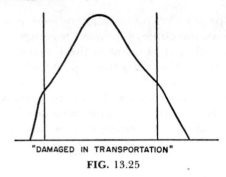

"DAMAGED IN TRANSPORTATION"

FIG. 13.25

caliber of whose inspection is in question. The vendor may insist that the lot has been subject to rigorous inspection before shipment has gone. The customer may insist that the product as received contains many defectives—which is also the case.

Some products, such as resistors, are 100 percent sorted by the vendor and segregated into groupings dependent upon the degree of variation from nominal. For example, Figure 13.26 shows the distribution of parts shipped to a customer whose tolerance requirements are very broad; the factory has already removed the ± 5 percent tolerance parts for shipment to tight tolerance customers.

13.24 "Normality" and the Frequency Distribution

If curves of the sort discussed above depart so widely from the shape of the normal curve, how meaningful has been the discussion in Sections 13.8 to 13.19 of the mathematics of the frequency distribution? The discussion there was predicated upon the fact that the industrial distributions would quite closely approximate the shape of the normal curve.

This issue is not so serious as it might seem at first glance. It may be shown that most of the concern with this particular issue is quite academic.

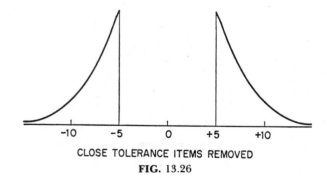

CLOSE TOLERANCE ITEMS REMOVED

FIG. 13.26

Some reasons for the propriety of using normal-curve analysis and algebra as a guide to the study of industrial frequency distributions are the following:

1. Algebraic measures like averages and standard deviations apply to all frequency-distribution shapes. It is only in their interpretation that the degree of similarity of a given industrial distribution to the normal curve may be of importance.
2. Much of the industrial use of the frequency distribution involves no algebraic analysis. The distribution is used as a simple picture.
3. When algebraic analysis is required, experience has shown that a very large number of industrial frequency distributions *do* sufficiently closely approximate the shape of the normal curve.
4. When a distribution is badly skewed or otherwise distorted, the distribution is often used simply as a guide to corrective action. Algebraic analysis may not be made until after this corrective action has been taken. If it is made both before and after, values for the average and the standard deviation furnish excellent indices to the effect of the corrective action.
5. Distribution analyses of many industrial conditions do not require a great deal of precision. In these cases the normality of a distribution may not be of major significance.
6. Normal-curve analysis need not be used where it is inappropriate. There is no magic about these instances. An experienced individual may determine them by a simple glance at curve shape and then apply the corrections that are discussed in Section 13.25. There are also several analytical and graphical methods for determining normality, one of which is the *probability paper*, discussed in Sections 16.3 to 16.6.

Industrial users of these statistical methods know that they are not working with an exact science. No matter how precise their algebraic methods, it is the data used in these formulas that are important. These data are highly perishable in their value. The conditions that the data represent may change overnight.

As a result, algebraic analysis of the frequency distribution is used more as a cautious industrial guide than as a precise and final calculation. If an analysis is improperly made, the rapid industrial production conditions will make that fact soon known.

As these methods come to be used in individual applications, over a period of time, they will probably become flavored with the circumstances of that application. Formulas used will become adaptations to the particular distribution shapes that are involved if these shapes are not normal. In these cases, normal-curve analysis simply furnishes the initial guide for the development of the algebra of the application.

In the final analysis, the measurements-taking philosophy of the frequency distribution is its greatest practical contribution. Once this philosophy has been established, the methods to support the measurements taking will gradually adapt themselves to the particular industrial application.

Frequency-distribution analysis is of course subject to the same misuse that characterizes any analytic method. But its users remain safe when they understand its philosophy and limitations, appreciate that it is an inexact science, and use common sense in its application. Once this background has been developed, abstract discussions of "normality and the frequency distribution" become matters of no great practical concern.

13.25 Frequency-Distribution Analysis of Nonnormal Distributions

Section 13.14 described the relationship between the normal curve and the standard deviation, whereby 99.73 percent of all readings fall within $+3\sigma$ of the normal-curve average. Section 13.16 showed how this relationship could usefully be applied in resolving such questions as expected reject percentages.

This particular relationship between the frequency distribution and the standard deviation does not of course hold true when a frequency distribution is appreciably nonnormal in its shape. Yet other useful relationships do still exist between nonnormal frequency distributions and the standard deviation. These relationships can be used to analyze a distribution with just the same approach as described in Section 13.16, except that the formulas presented below now obtain.

For a distribution that is skewed, either to right or left as in Figures 13.20 and 13.21, but has only one hump and whose average value approximately coincides with the most frequent value, the percentage of values between $\pm$ (t) σ is shown as[7]

$$\text{Percentage of readings} \geq 1 - \frac{1}{2.25t^2} \tag{11}$$

For a very badly skewed or jagged distribution, Figure 13.23, for example, the relationship is shown as[8]

$$\text{Percentage of readings} \geq 1 - \frac{1}{t^2} \tag{12}$$

Thus, Formula (11) shows that about 95 percent or more of all values are between $+3\sigma$ of a perceptibly skewed frequency distribution, while about 89 percent or more of values are, in Formula (12), between $+3\sigma$ of the most badly distorted curve shapes that will be found.

Figure 13.27 shows a comparison among areas under frequency distributions which conform both to the conditions of Formulas (11) and (12) and that of the normal curve.

There are also ways to "normalize" some of these nonnormal distributions by such techniques as transformations and computing independently the variation for each half of the distribution.[9]

PER CENT OF AREA UNDER DIFFERENT FREQUENCY DISTRIBUTION SHAPES			
WITHIN ⟶	$\bar{x} \pm 1\sigma$	$\bar{x} \pm 2\sigma$	$\bar{x} \pm 3\sigma$
"NORMAL CURVE" DISTRIBUTION	68.27 %	95.45 %	99.73 %
"SKEWED" DISTRIBUTION	≥55 %	≥89 %	≥95 %
BADLY DISTORTED DISTRIBUTION	—	≥75 %	≥89 %

FIG. 13.27

13.26 The Predictive Value of the Frequency Distribution

It has been implied above that two uses for the algebraic analysis of the frequency distribution are

1. To predict the characteristics of an entire lot of completed units from the characteristics of a frequency-distribution sample drawn from that lot
2. To predict the characteristics to be expected in the *future* on a process or product design from the characteristics of a frequency-distribution sample drawn from that process or units of that product design

Certain limitations must be recognized in connection with both these important applications of the frequency distribution.

Lot Characteristics

The prediction of the average and standard deviation of a lot can be performed accurately and reliably if the following conditions are observed:

1. The sample size must be sufficiently large to permit accuracy.
2. The sample must be properly selected.
3. Practical matters must be dealt with, such as adequate measuring equipment and proper recording of readings.

These sampling details are discussed in some detail in Chapter 15.

Future Performance

The accuracy of a machine tool in performing a given operation may be sought. Appraisal of the performance of a new semiconductor may be checked by a pilot run whose characteristics must be analyzed. Approval of the setup of a processing equipment, preliminary to a long production run, may be required.

It is not sufficient in these applications merely to be certain that the sample is of adequate size and has been properly selected and measured. A problem of equal importance is "How representative of future conditions is this sample?"

This question can never be answered with complete certainty. But a sample can be made more representative of these conditions in several ways. Past experience with the process in question can be used to gage the seeming reasonableness of sample results. Samples can be examined at separate intervals of time and the uniformity of their results compared. Analysis can be made of the major variables that may be expected to have an effect at *some* time in the future, and these variables can be introduced into the articles in the sample.

In judging the process capability of a new machine tool, experience has taught personnel in one factory that they must make three or four distribution sample checks at intervals of several days. They then compare the results of these checks, consolidate them if it seems appropriate, or make more checks if such a step seems indicated. Chapter 20 details a method for making a study of this type.

This factory uses only one distribution sample to approve the setup on processing equipments that are already installed. They have had previous experience with this equipment, and sometimes there are available the results of process-capability study on it, such as has been discussed above.

There is no substitute for technical judgment in predictions of this sort. If proper conditions and variables have not been taken into account, mere statistical accuracy in dealing with the data at hand means very little. If the resulting prediction does not conform to common sense, then it is likely to be wrong and should be carefully rechecked. Until they have gained some experience, the new users of industrial statistics in particular should make haste slowly in this predictive use of the frequency distribution.

13.27 Some Guides to the Use of the Frequency Distribution

The frequency distribution sometimes enjoys a better initial reception in the production organization when it is simply called a *tally*. Its record forms may be termed *tally cards*. A wide variety of forms are used for these tallies; Figure 13.28 shows one of them.

Nothing is more disheartening than to analyze a set of readings only to find that they are worthless. The data recorded on these tally cards must be accurate. This requires proper record keeping on the part of the individual assigned that task. The importance of adequate gaging equipment to make the required measurements cannot be overemphasized.

Carelessness or ineffectiveness on the part of the recorder may be a critical problem. Occasionally the readings that are so carefully analyzed in the front office have generated in the head of this record taker. This person may have wished to save the effort of making the checks or may have forgotten to make them.

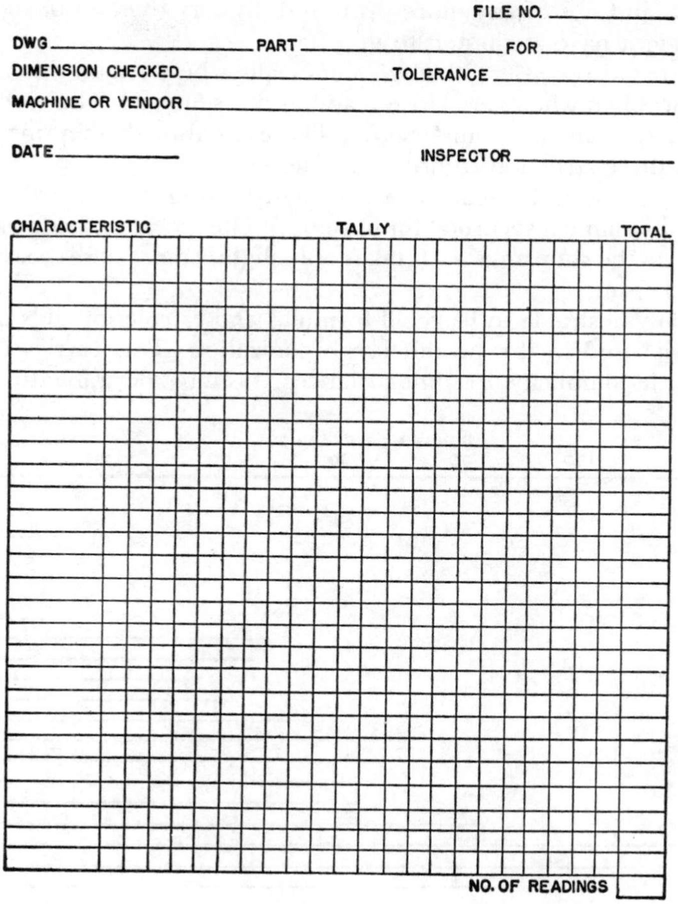

FILE NO. _____

DWG _____ PART _____ FOR _____

DIMENSION CHECKED _____ TOLERANCE _____

MACHINE OR VENDOR _____

DATE _____   INSPECTOR _____

CHARACTERISTIC   TALLY   TOTAL

NO. OF READINGS

FIG. 13.28

The record taker may be untrained in the proper use of gages and instruments or may make a series of reading errors that are not discovered for some time.

When the frequency distribution shown on the tally card seems to take a unique or puzzling form, very careful attention should be paid to its readings. Figure 13.29 illustrates an interesting example of this sort.

The characteristic measured is voltage. The frequency distribution of these voltage readings shows peaks and valleys far more numerous than would be expected because of sampling variation. But note that the peaks occur at some multiple of 5 and the valleys occur in between.

In this set of readings, the recorder simply "liked" to read numbers that were some multiple of 5 because the instrument was calibrated with markings at 5, 10, 15, 20, and so on. The unusual curve of Figure 13.29 is the result of this simple fact, and not of any more profound mystery than an unsophisticated observer might have attributed to it.

This matter of recorders "liking" some values better than others becomes a serious problem when very close readings are required. The recorders may unconsciously read the numbers they like even though they may have the desire and the instruction to do otherwise.

An extremely desirable feature of the tally-type frequency distribution is that sometimes it is almost secured "for nothing." The readings that make it up are often taken in the shop anyway. It takes only slightly more effort to record them on the tally form.

It is usually desirable to leave all formulas and calculation aids off the tally form that is used in the production organization. This carries further the evidence of its simplicity. In some instances, it is most desirable to analyze the

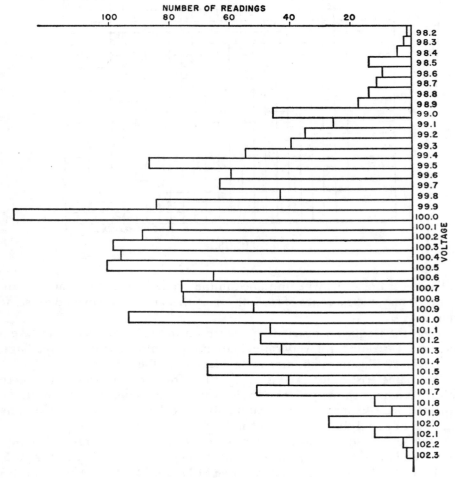

FIG. 13.29

readings away from the production line in the relatively more quiet, less hurried atmosphere of the office. In many cases, however, the tally can be set up for use directly at the factory workplace by the operator, as part of his or her direct quality program involvement.

THE FREQUENCY DISTRIBUTION IN ACTION—SOME EXAMPLES

13.28 The Frequency-Distribution and the Quality-Control Jobs

There are usually four steps in the analysis of a manufacturing process or an engineering design. They are

1. Taking readings
2. Analyzing the readings
3. Determining if the readings represent an economical operating condition
4. Taking corrective action where necessary

The frequency distribution is useful in each of these four steps: It furnishes a useful form for taking readings and a practical method for analyzing them, gives an indication of the economy of the process by comparing the resulting process limits with the specification limits, and furnishes a graphical and analytical guide for corrective action.

The frequency distribution is, therefore, useful in all four of the quality-control jobs.

1. *In new-design control,* it has a major application in predicting the performance of a new product (see example in Sec. 13.31).
2. *In incoming-material control,* its algebraic analysis may be very useful (see example in Sec. 13.30).
3. *In product control,* it is a technique for determining the amount of variation that may be expected from a given process or setup (see example in Sec. 13.32).
4. *In special process studies,* its uses as a picture may be very valuable (see example in Sec. 13.29).

Other uses of the frequency distribution in the quality-control jobs are

1. To determine the process capabilities of machine tools and other processing equipments
2. To compare inspection results between two factories or between two sections of the same plant
3. To examine the difference between the dimensional characteristics of similar parts produced in different molds
4. To indicate the variations among similar parts produced by each of two so-called duplicate sets of tools
5. To examine the accuracy of fit between mating parts
6. To analyze the effect of tool wear during a long production run on a machine tool

13.29 A Study of Regulating Equipments That Failed at the Customer's Plant[10]

Plant A produced regulating equipments in quantity for shipment to its customer, plant B. The two plants were about 150 miles apart. Plant B tested each of these equipments carefully after they were received, even though plant A had also tested them.

For the first 6 months of production, plant B found all the equipments it received to be satisfactory. Without warning, however, a large percentage of the regulators received by plant B in the seventh month were found defective in test.

Lot after lot shipped from plant A were found similarly defective. Plant B demanded that plant A take immediate corrective action.

Staff employees in plant A began to analyze the entire production process for the regulating equipments. They were primarily interested in the factors which affected the "voltage held" characteristic because this was most critical.

The frequency distribution was one of the analytical tools used. Figure 13.30

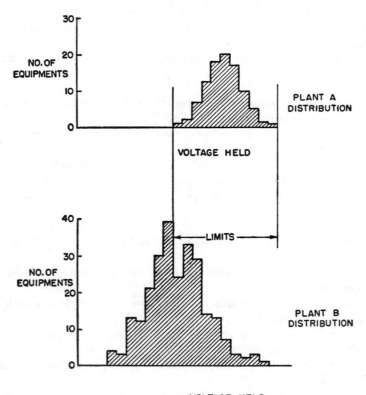

FIG. 13.30

shows the frequency distributions plotted for the voltage held characteristic. These distributions compare a sample of equipments tested in plant A after their manufacture with the same sample after its receipt and test in plant B.

These curves led the engineering staff of plant A to conclude that there were two major differences between the distribution as plotted in plant A and that plotted in plant B:

1. The plant B distribution had shifted lower on the voltage held scale. The engineers reasoned that this might have been due to difference in testing methods in the two plants.
2. The plant B distribution had a much wider spread than did the plant A distribution. The engineers reasoned that this might have been caused by some mechanical shift in the regulating equipments while in transportation between the two points.

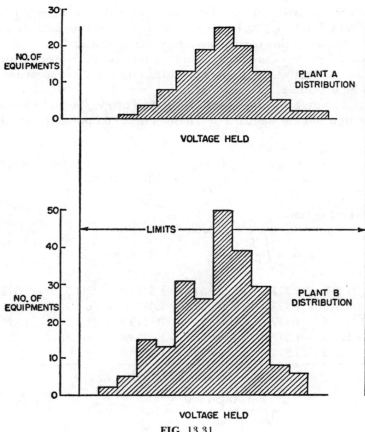

FIG. 13.31

These two speculations were pursued. After a great deal of investigation, they were borne out in test results. Production testing methods in plants A and B were geared together. A mechanical redesign was put into effect on those regulator parts that were shifting.

Another set of frequency distributions was plotted on samples manufactured and tested under these new conditions. This is shown in Figure 13.31, from which the end of the rejections could be predicted.

Subsequent production experience bore out the accuracy of this prediction.

13.30 Predicting the Quality of an Incoming Lot of Bronze Journal Bearings[11]

A shipment containing a large quantity of bronze journal bearings was received by an eastern factory. These bearings had been purchased for use in the production of an important device. Not completely certain of the work of the vendor from whom the bearings were secured, the factory wanted assurance of the quality of the lot.

The critical characteristic of these bearings was their inside diameter, whose specification was 1.376 ± 0.010 inch. It was decided to make a frequency-distribution analysis of this particular quality characteristic.

One hundred bearings were drawn from the lot, and their inside diameters were measured carefully. The frequency distribution of these measurements is shown in Figure 13.32.

An algebraic analysis was then performed. The two values to be calculated were the average and the standard deviation. These computations are shown:

Average:

$$\overline{X} = \frac{\Sigma X}{n} = \frac{137.730}{100} = 1.3773 \text{ inches}$$

Sample standard deviation:

$$s = \sqrt{\frac{\Sigma(X - \overline{X})^2}{n - 1}}$$

$$= \frac{\begin{aligned} &(1.370 - 1.3773)^2 + \quad (1.371 - 1.3773)^2 + \quad 2(1.372 - 1.3773)^2 + \\ &4(1.373 - 1.3773)^2 + \quad 3(1.374 - 1.3773)^2 + \quad 6(1.375 - 1.3773)^2 + \\ &16(1.376 - 1.3773)^2 + 14(1.377 - 1.3773)^2 + 24(1.378 - 1.3773)^2 + \\ &14(1.379 - 1.3773)^2 + \quad 9(1.380 - 1.3773)^2 + \quad 4(1.381 - 1.3773)^2 + \\ &(1.382 - 1.3773)^2 + \quad (1.383 - 1.3773)^2 \end{aligned}}{99}$$

$$= \sqrt{\frac{0.00054300}{99}} = 0.0023 \text{ inch}$$

and

INSIDE DIAMETERS	TALLY	TOTAL
1.370	x	1
1.371	x	1
1.372	xx	2
1.373	xxxx	4
1.374	xxx	3
1.375	xxxxxx	6
1.376	xxxxxxxxxxxxxxxx	16
1.377	xxxxxxxxxxxxxx	14
1.378	xxxxxxxxxxxxxxxxxxxxxxxx	24
1.379	xxxxxxxxxxxxxx	14
1.380	xxxxxxxxx	9
1.381	xxxx	4
1.382	x	1
1.383	x	1
	TOTAL READINGS	100

FIG. 13.32

$$\sigma = \frac{s}{c_4} = \frac{0.0023}{0.9975} = 0.0023 \text{ inch}$$

For a normal curve, 99.73 percent of the readings lie between $\overline{X} \pm 3\sigma$. Substituting the above values in this expression:

$$\overline{X} \pm 3\sigma = 1.3773 \pm 3(0.0023 \text{ inch})$$
$$= 1.3704 \text{ to } 1.3842 \text{ inches}$$

On this basis, the bearing quality is shown to be satisfactorily within the drawing range of 1.366 to 1.386 inches. This distribution is somewhat distorted and skewed to the left, however, so that the 3-sigma limits are not strictly accurate. But the distribution is well within drawing limits, and the amount of skew is not excessive, so the factory decided that it could accept the lot of bearings on this analysis.

This conclusion was found to be satisfactory when the bearings were actually used on the production lines.

13.31 Performance of a New Product

The engineering designers of a new product agreed that its most critical characteristic was "pickup volts." They decided that it would be extremely valuable to learn what might be expected from this characteristic when active production of the article was begun.

A number of samples of the device were made up on a pilot-run basis. The pickup volts of each article were tested, and a frequency distribution was made of the data. The resulting curve is shown in Figure 13.33.

A brief glance at this distribution showed the design engineers that unsatisfactory performance might be expected. An algebraic analysis of this distribution was made, using a table of areas similar to that of Figure 13.15. It indicated that about 20 percent of the devices could be expected to fall outside the specification limit of 15.5 volts that had been established for maximum pick-up.

The designers set about to analyze the various factors affecting pickup voltage. They discovered that a spring constant they had specified led to excessive variation. This spring supplied the mechanical force against which the electric force of the product's coil operated.

The problem resolved itself into making some simple change to compensate for the spring constant. It was found most economical to accomplish this by a minor mechanical design change on another part.

This change was made, and it was found to have eliminated the trouble that had been caused by the spring. The design engineers were pleased to have eliminated a potential source of manufacturing trouble before actual production had started.

When this article went into active manufacture, a frequency-distribution analysis was made of the pickup volts characteristic of the first production

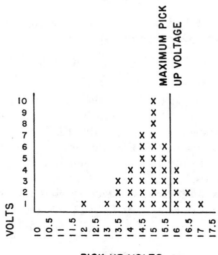

PICK UP VOLTS
WITH ORIGINAL SPRING SUPPORTS
FIG. 13.33

models. This distribution, given in Figure 13.34, showed that no trouble was being experienced.

13.32 Establishing the Shop Tolerance for a Drilling Operation

The drawing specification for a small, flat cover plate allowed a tolerance of ± 0.001 inch between the centers of two drilled holes. Considerable production difficulty was being experienced in meeting this tolerance, in addition to which a large number of cover plates were being rejected at final inspection.

The production foreman claimed that a ± 0.001-inch tolerance could not be met with existing drilling equipment. The experienced draftsman who had placed that tolerance on the drawing was equally certain that it could be met.

To resolve the question factually, a frequency-distribution analysis was made on a typical production lot. Both foreman and draftsman assured themselves that the drill press was properly set up, that its drills were well ground, and that the drill jigs were in good condition.

The resulting frequency distribution of Figure 13.35 showed a variation of ± 0.0025 inch in the center distances of the cover plates in the sample under examination. Since all had agreed that the sample was fully representative, it was decided that the ± 0.001-inch tolerance could not be met with existing equipment.

Three alternatives were open:

1. To continue to produce cover plates to this tolerance with existing equipment and make the resulting rejects a part of job cost

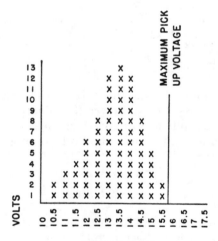

PICK UP VOLTS
WITH NEW DESIGN SPRING SUPPORTS
FIG. 13.34

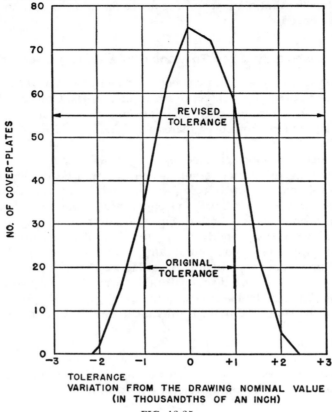

FIG. 13.35

2. To secure new equipment
3. To widen the tolerance

As is often the case in instances of this sort, investigation of the device on which the cover plate was assembled showed that a between-centers tolerance of ± 0.003 inch would be fully as satisfactory as one of ± 0.001 inch.

This change was made on the drawing, and no subsequent trouble was experienced on the part.

Notes

[1]The statistically minded reader will note that the median, as compared with the average, will tend to be erratic. With large samples, the median is likely to have about 25 percent more error than the sample average in representing the value for the "true" average (see Sec. 13.18).

[2]In the earlier years of statistical applications in quality control, this calculation was usually carried out on the basis of the sample root mean square deviation, as follows:

$$s_{(rms)} = \sqrt{\frac{(X_1 - \overline{X})^2 + (X_2 - \overline{X})^2 + (X_3 - \overline{X})^2 + \cdots + (X_n - \overline{X})^2}{n}}$$

In more recent years, and for certain statistical reasons, it has become more customary to use Formula (4A) to calculate the sample standard deviation in place of this root mean square approach.

[3]The term σ' (sigma prime) is also used in some statistical applications to represent the population standard deviation. In fact, while σ (or its equivalent designation σ') are entirely satisfactory values for dispersion in most practical quality-control situations, the "true" population standard deviation is seldom ever known for a variety of statistical and other causes. For this reason the population standard deviation is also sometimes designated as $\hat{\sigma}$—the symbol ^ denoting "estimate of" —particularly in circumstances where it is desired for precise statistical analysis purposes that when s represents the variability within a subgroup, σ as calculated from s will quite precisely represent the population within-subgroup variability and not necessarily the total variability within and between subgroups.

[4]$\overline{X}$ is an estimate of μ, the population central tendency measurement which, in technical statistical terms, is related in the normal curve to σ, the population standard deviation. As reviewed in Sec. 13.10, $\overline{X}$ is used in the above discussion and in Figures 13.14A and 13.27 because of its long-term employment and recognition throughout industrial applications and because of the usefulness of this estimate in most practical quality-control circumstances.

[5]The statistically minded reader will notice the unstated assumption of "normality" of the sheet-steel distribution made throughout this analysis. It is not until Sec. 13.20 and following that nonnormal distributions are formally introduced.

[6]The reader interested in further detail on this subject will find in the statistical literature methods for deciding upon a particular sample size with a great deal of statistical precision. See, for example, Irving W. Burr, *Statistical Quality Control Methods*, Marcel Dekker, Inc., New York, 1976.

[7]This formula is an adaptation, for practical use, of the formula known in the statistical literature as the *Camp-Meidel inequality*, which shows that

$$P_{t\sigma} \geq 1 - \frac{1}{2.25t^2}$$

where $P_{t\sigma}$ is the probability within the interval $\pm (t)\sigma$. The designation $\geq$ in the formula signifies "equal to or greater than."

[8]This formula is an adaptation, for practical use, of the formula known in the statistical literature as the *Tchebycheff inequality*, which shows that

$$P_{t\sigma} \geq 1 - \frac{1}{t^2}$$

where $P_{t\sigma}$ is the probability within the interval $\pm (t)\sigma$.

[9]For these and other such procedures, the reader will find much in the statistical literature. See, for example, Irving W. Burr, *Applied Statistical Methods*, Academic Press, Inc., New York, 1974. Another basic reference on the subject is Dudley J. Cowden, *Statistical Methods in Quality Control*, Prentice-Hall, Inc., Englewood Cliffs, N.J., 1957.

[10]Investigation made by R.B. Thomasgard and associates, Schenectady, N.Y.

[11]From a study discussed by Dr. C. F. Green, R. W. Hallock, and associates, Schenectady, N.Y.

CHAPTER 14

Control Charts

Controlling the quality of materials, batches, parts, and assemblies during the course of their actual manufacture is probably the most popularly recognized quality-control activity. Much of the literature on statistical methods in quality control has been devoted to this subject. The statistical tool most generally recommended for this work is the control chart, or some modification of it.

The control chart has been used in industry for many years. Its most prominent pioneer was the late Dr. Walter A. Shewhart, whose control chart approach remains the most widely used. Other forms of control charts have also come into use in recent years.

Only a few fundamentals are required for practical understanding of this tool. Although there are many adaptations of the basic control chart types, these are largely matters of changes in detail to meet particular situations.

CONCEPT OF THE CONTROL CHART

14.1 The Control Chart Approach

There are several alternative techniques for establishing drawing tolerances and specification limits. Sometimes these limits are carefully determined by test; sometimes they are arbitrarily "picked out of the air." Often they are based upon past experience with materials and manufacturing processes.

This experience has frequently been consolidated in writing in the form of "shop-practice" tolerance sheets. In other instances it exists as know-how in the heads of veteran production people.

It is common for a designing engineer to translate this know-how into engineering data. The engineer may ask the machine-shop foreman if a tolerance of ± 0.003 inch between drilled hole centers on bearing brackets can be maintained. The foreman's experience may lead to the answer, "Sure, we can do that." This answer may be the engineer's basis for placing a ± 0.003-inch tolerance on the bearing-bracket drawing.

The shop-practice experience may also be very important on the factory floor after drawings have been released to it by the design engineer. The machine shop may, for example, produce a lot of these bearing brackets whose between-centers variation is ± 0.005 inch instead of the ± 0.003 inch indicated. The shop foreman's immediate reaction will be that something "unusual" has occurred: perhaps the drill is running off center, perhaps it is improperly ground, perhaps the drill jig is worn. The foreman goes to the drill press with possible corrective steps well-formulated.

Experienced factory people thus intuitively separate manufactured parts variations into two types:

1. *Usual* variation, which is the amount of deviation that they have learned to expect. In the case of the bearing brackets, this is ± 0.003 inch.[1]
2. *Unusual* variation, which is the amount of deviation greater than they have learned to expect. In the case of the bearing brackets, this is the variation beyond ± 0.003 inch.[2]

Production people therefore conceive of "limits" of usual variation with respect to those parts and processes with which they are familiar. When these limits have been exceeded by the manufactured parts, they recognize that something unusual has occurred which requires correction.

Figure 14.1 illustrates this concept. The circled points are those requiring corrective action.

It is analysis of just this sort that is the basis for the most widely used forms of control charts. The philosophy of usual variation limits is carried into the control chart in the form of control limits. Because of the nature of control chart technique, however, the actual numerical value for control lim-

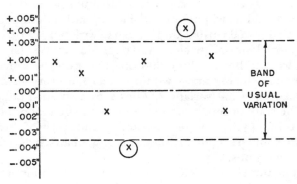

FIG. 14.1

its will ordinarily differ from the value for the corresponding usual variation limits.

14.2 Defining the Control Chart

The control chart may be defined as

> A graphical method for evaluating whether a process is or is not in a "state of statistical control".

In its most usual forms, the control chart is a chronological (hour-by-hour, day-by-day) graphical comparison of actual product-, part-, or other unit-quality characteristics with limits reflecting the ability to produce as shown by experience on the unit-quality characteristics.

The control chart method is a device for carrying out, factually, the production people's separation of variation into "usual" and "unusual" components. It compares actual production variation of manufactured parts with the control limits that have been set up for those parts.

When these limits have been computed and then judged acceptable for use in production, the control chart takes up its major role—aiding in the control of the quality of materials, batches, parts, and assemblies during their actual manufacture.

14.3 How Much Variation Is Acceptable?

The decision as to whether a set of control limits is acceptable is almost purely a question of economics. Is the usual variation they represent less than that required by the specification limits? If so, the control limits will generally be satisfactory.

Is the usual variation represented by the control limits greater than that required by specification limits? Will it cost too much to try to obtain closer conformance? If so, the control limits may be satisfactory. Will it be cheaper to improve the process than to accept the scrap and rework that seem inevitable? In this case, the limits will not be satisfactory and should not be accepted.

The distinction between usual and unusual variation is of course purely relative. What is usual for one machine and operation may be far different from usual variation for another machine and operation on the same material.

Plants and manufacturing areas within plants may vary in all the factors which go to make up usual variation. They may vary in the nature of their equipment, in the state of repair of machines, in the quality of materials used, in their skill in tooling jobs, and in the training and spirit of their employees. Thus, efforts to compare control limits among plants may often result in contradictory conclusions.

With skilled personnel to handle a certain job and with money to spend on it, the variation represented by control limits may almost certainly be reduced. In the example of drilling between centers cited in Section 14.1 the usual variation of ± 0.003 inch might well have been reduced to ± 0.0015 inch by new equipment and better materials.

Once accepted, however, the control limits can be used as an economic guide to corrective action on the job in question. It will cost too much to obtain greater uniformity. But if production results indicate more variation than is permissible by the limits, then it may be economical to spend money to trace down and eliminate the causes of this excessive variation.

14.4 Uses of the Control Chart

Depending for information about variation in product-quality characteristics upon what production people carry around in their heads is sometimes a risky business. Benefits in accuracy and record keeping result when this type of know-how is supplemented by the use of control charts.

The time period for learning about the usual variation represented by the control chart limits may also be greatly reduced. A period of hours or days may suffice in place of the much longer period necessary for the development of certain types of process know-how. This feature is of particular importance where there is a large proportion of green employees and newly appointed supervisors.

With control limits established for materials and parts manufacturing, a number of control chart applications are readily suggested, some of which are the following:

Determine Degree of Control of a Process

Readings on the quality characteristics of parts or products being produced can be analyzed to determine whether that process is in a controlled situation. If these readings show substantial variation both within and without the control limits that are calculated, then the process is visibly demonstrated to be an essentially uncontrolled one; various applicable forms of improvement action can be considered if they are needed and economic. If these readings show substantial "bunching" within the control limits that are calculated, then the process is visibly demonstrated to be an essentially controlled one; subsequent quality actions can be based upon this recognition of control.

This is a primary example of the first of the two most basic conditions for control charts—that for "analysis of past data" or, in technical statistical terminology, a control chart "no standard given"—further discussed in Section 14.5.

Predict Rejects Before Nonconforming Parts Are Produced

Quality troubles often gradually "drift" into a process. An improperly ground tool may cause a trend toward unusual variation which will finally result in the production of nonconforming parts. A chart which compares these actual production variations with control limits may "red-flag" the entrance into the process of this sort of quality trouble before scrap or rework is actually caused.

This application is illustrated by a popular comparison of control chart limits with highway boundaries. As the quality characteristics of manufactured parts approach the control-limit "shoulders," process correction may be called for to prevent the process running in a "ditch" by producing nonconforming parts.

This is a primary example of the second of the two most basic conditions for control charts—that for "adopted control limit values" or, in technical statistical terminology, a control chart "standard given"—discussed further in Section 14.5.

Judge Job Performance

The perennial question "Are we doing as good a quality job as we can expect with existing equipment?" may be answered factually by comparing actual manufacturing variations with the usual variation represented by control limits.

Establish Tolerances

Specification limits bear a relationship to usual variation only by coincidence. This is true because specification limits relate to the product requirements, whereas the expected variation relates to the process and its capability. However, it is advantageous for design engineers to be familiar with the capabilities of the existing processes so that they can "optimize" the utilization of these processes in their design selection.

Guide Management

The control chart furnishes management with a brief summary of the success or failure of plant efforts to control product quality.

Forecast Costs

Usual variation may be representative of a plant's methods of manufacture. To reduce this variation may be extremely expensive and may require new machinery, new methods, and better machine maintenance. Unusual variation, on the other hand, may represent temporary difficulties that can be eliminated without excessive expense.

Usual variation may for many processes be associated with the most economical way of manufacturing. Its determination is consequently useful for cost purposes.

In the special case wherein usual variation is wider than specification limits but, for some reason, the factory cannot improve the process, then it must be recognized that some scrap will be produced. The amount of this scrap can be forecast, minimized,[3] and made a part of job cost.

Develop a Factor for Nonconforming Material

Cost accountants have always had a problem dealing with the content of "manufacturing-loss" reports and adding to standard cost systems a realistic factor to account for rejected parts and assemblies. They have long recognized that 0 percent rejects may be both an impractical and uneconomic target.

A percentage factor is therefore often arbitrarily chosen at some figure which seems the most economical. This figure is frequently far too high or low—as the accountants themselves would be first to admit—simply because there may be no adequate data upon which to base an accurate estimate. Setting up control chart limits on various types of operations may furnish a more realistic basis for establishing these factors.

14.5 Types of Control Charts

Corresponding to the two types of inspection data that are taken in industry, two fundamental types of control charts are

1. *Measurements or "variables" charts* (of which the most popular are the so-called $\overline{X}$, R, s charts) for use when actual readings are taken
2. Charts for use with go and not-go or "attributes" data, of which *fraction or percent charts* (sometimes called p charts) are most popular

Much of the data taken in industry are of the go and not-go variety. As the complexity of products and processes increases, however, actual measurements are becoming more and more essential as their advantages in the prevention of nonconforming work become recognized.

Go and not-go data merely indicate that parts are "good" or "bad." But an important question for corrective action is "How good or bad?" In measurements data this question is more adequately answered. Hence, while there is an important place in total-quality-control applications for charts based upon each of these kinds of data, the greater control power of measurements data makes this type of chart the preferred control alternative wherever practical and economical.

There are two different conditions under which these control charts are used:

1. Charts used to investigate the state of control of a process, perhaps one that has not previously been examined, or one on which extensive process changes have been made, or one being examined for the state of ongoing control after a preliminary frequency-distribution analysis has demonstrated initial control. Readings on quality characteristics of parts or products are taken and analyzed for this investigatory purpose. Control limits and central tendency values are calculated as part of this analysis, and hence this condition is termed one of "no standard given." Often these control

limits and central tendency values are used in charts to maintain ongoing control.

2. Charts where central tendency and spread values are initially established, and hence this condition is termed one of "standard given." In all cases, the assumption is that these standard values are such that the process can operate at these levels and that available prior data—sometimes a no standard given procedure—has been used to determine that a state of control exists. In some plant and company situations, these standards are established in a relatively arbitrary way based upon particular economical or other practical circumstances based upon production or service needs or a desired or target value designated by a requirement or specification.

While the details for computing the control limits for the two types of charts —measurements and fraction or percent—differ, the basic approach is the same in both cases. It is based upon the laws of probability discussed in Chapter 13.

The steps followed in this approach are as follows:

No Standard Given

1. Select the appropriate quality characteristic to be studied.
2. Record data on a required number of samples, each sample composed of an adequate number of units.
3. Determine the control limits from these sample data.
4. Analyze the state of control in the process. Too much variation? Precipitous departures from a state of control and a sudden return to control? Well-controlled process? Appropriate action is taken, as needed and economical, based upon this analysis.

   In many instances, when control limits are first being computed for parts or assemblies, the processes are found to be "out of control"; characteristics of several samples exceed the control limits. On these processes, causes for the excessive sample variations can be traced down and eliminated. Steps 2 and 3 are repeated until the process becomes controlled.

   When a process yields samples whose characteristics remain consistently within the control limits, it may be termed a "controlled process."
5. In those instances where the control chart and its limits are then used to maintain ongoing process control, the procedure of steps 6 and beyond of the *standard given* condition (below) are followed.

Standard Given

1. Select the appropriate quality characteristic to be studied.
2. Establish the appropriate value for central tendency and spread that will be used. All available prior data must be used to determine that a state of control exists.

3. Determine the control limits from these "adopted" values.
4. Establish that these control limits are economically and practically satisfactory for the job.
5. Establish the values of the control limits and plot the limits on suitable graph paper.
6. Start to record the results of production samples of proper size, which are selected at periodic intervals.
7. Take corrective action if the characteristics of the production samples exceed the control limits.

Measurement control charts of the type reviewed above are discussed in Sections 14.6 to 14.11. Sections 14.12 to 14.15 then discuss the adaptation of these measurement control charts to control for specifications limits themselves, covering such applications as:

· Tool wear, trend control, and other modified control limits (Sec. 14.12)
· Using the process capability ("natural tolerance") as the base for the limits (Sec. 14.13)
· Acceptance control charts (Sec. 14.13)

Other forms of variables control charts, different from those discussed in Sections 14.6 to 14.13, have also been developed out of industrial statistical practice to meet particular plant control requirements, two of which are:[4]

1. Individual readings charts (Sec. 14.14)
2. Cusum charts (Sec. 14.14)

Sections 14.16 to 14.25 then treat charts for use with go and not-go data.

MEASUREMENTS CONTROL CHARTS

14.6 Form of the Chart

It was shown above that the computation of control limits really simmers down to a numerical calculation of what production people come to consider as usual variation limits. But how can this numerical calculation be made?

Chapter 13 discussed in some detail the universal nature of variation among manufactured parts. It described the frequency distribution as one medium for presenting and analyzing this variation. Sections 13.5 and 13.14 discussed frequency-distribution process limits, between which will fall practically all individual readings on production parts for the quality characteristic in question.

There is great similarity between these process limits and the usual variation limits that were described above in connection with the control chart. Indeed, usual variation limits may be thought of as the "natural tolerance" and "natural process limits" of the process in question. This concept of natural tolerances is very important throughout the practical application of statistical technology of quality.

Usual variation limits are, for most practical purposes, the process limits for the frequency distribution that would be "typical" for the product-quality characteristic in question. Figure 14.2 illustrates this concept.

Because of this similarity, one approach to the form for a measurements control chart might be simply an application of the type of frequency distribution discussed. Steps that might be followed are

1. Make several frequency-distribution analyses to arrive at the "typical" values for process limits.
2. Periodically obtain the readings on production parts required for a frequency-distribution sample.
3. Compare the picture of each frequency distribution with the process limits.
4. Take any indicated action.

Figure 14.3 shows the resulting picture of such an analysis.

Many practical problems are involved in this procedure. With a probable sample size of at least 50 readings required, it is possible that cost considerations would permit the measurement of only a few samples during each production period. Yet experience shows that the measurement of many samples selected at more frequent intervals during the production period is the more effective procedure for the control of product quality.

It would, in addition, be clumsy to compare the resulting frequency-distribution pictures with the process limits. It would also be relatively expensive to secure enough samples to calculate any acceptable "typical" values for these process limits.

One way to meet the objection of clumsiness would be to turn the frequency

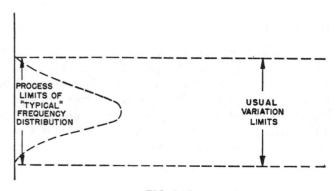

PROCESS LIMITS OF "TYPICAL" FREQUENCY DISTRIBUTION

USUAL VARIATION LIMITS

FIG. 14.2

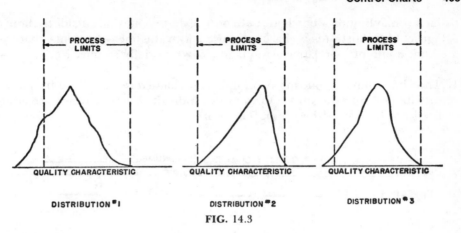

FIG. 14.3

distributions on their side. As shown in Figure 14.4, this would improve matters very little. And even if it improved them a great deal, the procedure of Fig. 14.4 would still force the measurement of few rather than many samples during the production period for the same reasons.

Because of difficulties of this sort, the modern measurements-control chart approach has been developed. Instead of the selection of the few samples comprising a relatively large number of units, this method permits the selection of many samples of relatively small size.

Rather than plotting the values for each individual reading in these small samples, measures of central tendency and spread are computed for each sample. These measures are then plotted on separate charts—one chart for central tendency and the other for spread. Control limits are established for each of these two charts, and the values of central tendency and spread for each individual sample of production parts are compared against the limits.[5] Correc-

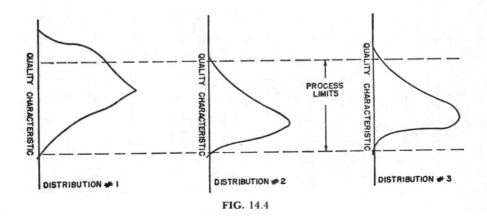

FIG. 14.4

tive action may be indicated when one or both of these values fall outside the limits.
    Figure 14.5 illustrates a chart form used with this measurements charting method. Some of its relative advantages may be briefly summarized:

1. The chart simmers out the two important characteristics of the frequency distribution into the simple form of two individual graphs which are easily used on the production floor. These are

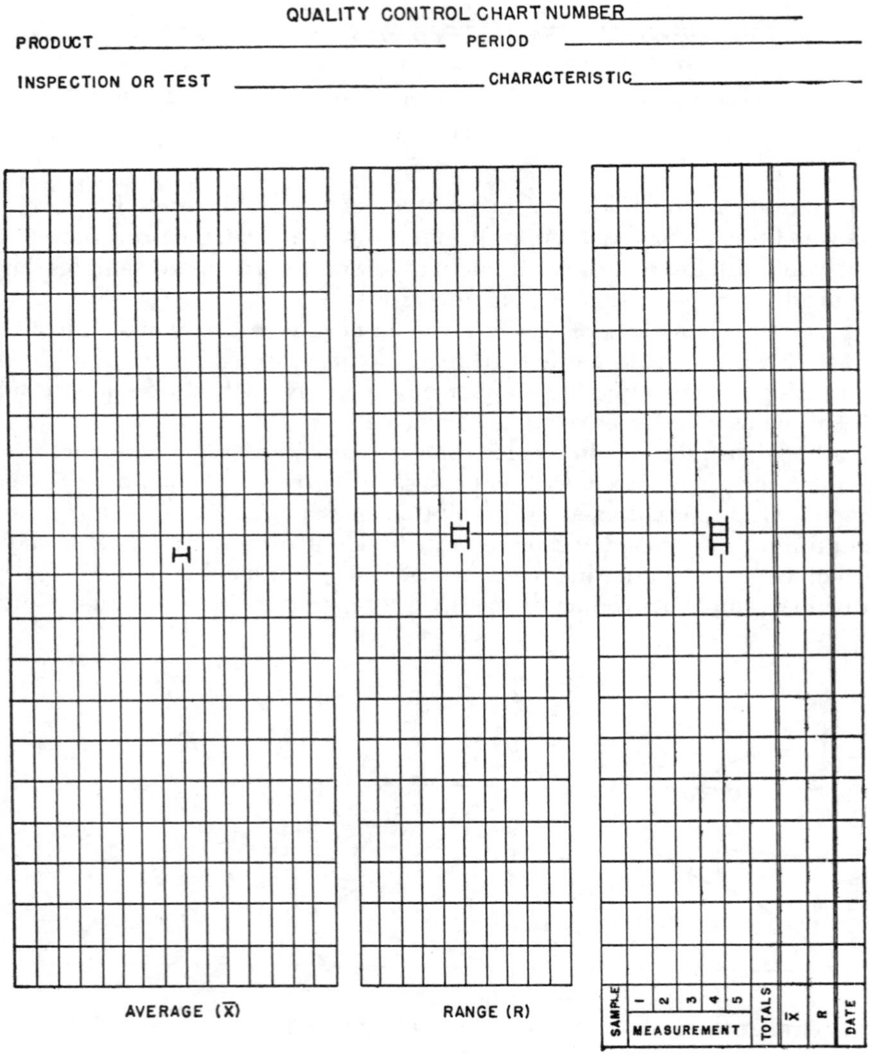

QUALITY CONTROL CHART NUMBER_____

PRODUCT _____ PERIOD   _____

INSPECTION OR TEST   _____ CHARACTERISTIC_____

AVERAGE (X̄)   RANGE (R)

| SAMPLE | MEASUREMENT 1 2 3 4 5 | TOTALS | X̄ | R | DATE |

FIG. 14.5

  a. A graph for measures of *central tendency.* The average $\overline{X}$ has been found the most useful measure here (see I in Fig. 14.5). However, any measure of central tendency will suffice.

  b. A graph for measures of *spread.* The range R has been found the most useful measure here (see II in Fig. 14.5). However, s—the sample standard deviation—is also widely used.

  Measurements-control chart limits are relatively easily computed for each of these two graphs and can be simply plotted on the appropriate portions of the graph.

2. The chart makes economical the selection of several samples, each with a few readings, in place of a few samples with as many as 50 readings (see III in Fig. 14.5).

14.7 Measurements-Control Chart Limits

  The basic principle for computing measurements-control chart limits is similar to that for computing the frequency-distribution process, or 3-sigma limits, discussed earlier. The difference between the two is that the measurements control limits are being established for *measures of central tendency and spread* from samples of relatively smaller size.

  Recall from Section 13.18 that values of central tendency and spread for samples drawn from the same lot have 3-sigma limits of their own. Limits for the two graphs in measurements control charts—the graph for central tendency and that for spread—are merely these same 3-sigma limits of Section 13.18. For the variation being compared in measurements control charts is that reflected in a series of samples drawn from what is presumed to be the same production stream or "lot"; values for central tendency and spread of these samples are simply gaged against their own 3-sigma limits, a technique that is in conformance with the principles of Section 13.18. As earlier discussed in this chapter, this comparison may take place either based upon analysis of past data with no standard given for the values for central tendency and spread or analysis of trends in terms of standard given for the values for central tendency and spread.

  3 sigma has been chosen in place of 2 or 4 sigma, for example, because experience has proved the 3-sigma value to be most useful and economical for control chart applications since so many frequency distributions encountered in industry tend toward "normality."[6]

  Computation of these measures of central tendency and spread for the various control chart conditions are greatly assisted by the use of constants that have been developed for these calculations. These constants are listed in Figure 14.6.[7]

  The formulas for computing these Shewhart measurements-control chart limits can be readily listed:

Factors for Computing Central Lines and 3-sigma Control Limits for $\bar{X}$, s, and R Charts

Observations in sample, n	Chart for averages — Factors for control limits			Chart for standard deviations — Factors for central line		Chart for standard deviations — Factors for control limits				Chart for ranges — Factors for central line			Chart for ranges — Factors for control limits			
	A	A_2	A_3	c_4	$1/c_4$	B_3	B_4	B_5	B_6	d_2	$1/d_2$	d_3	D_1	D_2	D_3	D_4
2	2.121	1.880	2.659	0.7979	1.2533	0	3.267	0	2.606	1.128	0.8865	0.853	0	3.686	0	3.267
3	1.732	1.023	1.954	0.8862	1.1284	0	2.568	0	2.276	1.693	0.5907	0.888	0	4.358	0	2.574
4	1.500	0.729	1.628	0.9213	1.0854	0	2.266	0	2.088	2.059	0.4857	0.880	0	4.698	0	2.282
5	1.342	0.577	1.427	0.9400	1.0638	0	2.089	0	1.964	2.326	0.4299	0.864	0	4.918	0	2.114
6	1.225	0.483	1.287	0.9515	1.0510	0.030	1.970	0.029	1.874	2.534	0.3946	0.848	0	5.078	0	2.004
7	1.134	0.419	1.182	0.9594	1.0423	0.118	1.882	0.113	1.806	2.704	0.3698	0.833	0.204	5.204	0.076	1.924
8	1.061	0.373	1.099	0.9650	1.0363	0.185	1.815	0.179	1.751	2.847	0.3512	0.820	0.388	5.306	0.136	1.864
9	1.000	0.337	1.032	0.9693	1.0317	0.239	1.761	0.232	1.707	2.970	0.3367	0.808	0.547	5.393	0.184	1.816
10	0.949	0.308	0.975	0.9727	1.0281	0.284	1.716	0.276	1.669	3.078	0.3249	0.797	0.687	5.469	0.223	1.777
11	0.905	0.285	0.927	0.9754	1.0252	0.321	1.679	0.313	1.637	3.173	0.3152	0.787	0.811	5.535	0.256	1.744
12	0.866	0.266	0.886	0.9776	1.0229	0.354	1.646	0.346	1.610	3.258	0.3069	0.778	0.922	5.594	0.283	1.717
13	0.832	0.249	0.850	0.9794	1.0210	0.382	1.618	0.374	1.585	3.336	0.2998	0.770	1.025	5.647	0.307	1.693
14	0.802	0.235	0.817	0.9810	1.0194	0.406	1.594	0.399	1.563	3.407	0.2935	0.763	1.118	5.696	0.328	1.672
15	0.775	0.223	0.789	0.9823	1.0180	0.428	1.572	0.421	1.544	3.472	0.2880	0.756	1.203	5.741	0.347	1.653
16	0.750	0.212	0.763	0.9835	1.0168	0.448	1.552	0.440	1.526	3.532	0.2831	0.750	1.282	5.782	0.363	1.637
17	0.728	0.203	0.739	0.9845	1.0157	0.466	1.534	0.458	1.511	3.588	0.2787	0.744	1.356	5.820	0.378	1.622
18	0.707	0.194	0.718	0.9854	1.0148	0.482	1.518	0.475	1.496	3.640	0.2747	0.739	1.424	5.856	0.391	1.608
19	0.688	0.187	0.698	0.9862	1.0140	0.497	1.503	0.490	1.483	3.689	0.2711	0.734	1.487	5.891	0.403	1.597
20	0.671	0.180	0.680	0.9869	1.0133	0.510	1.490	0.504	1.470	3.735	0.2677	0.729	1.549	5.921	0.415	1.585
21	0.655	0.173	0.663	0.9876	1.0126	0.523	1.477	0.516	1.459	3.778	0.2647	0.724	1.605	5.951	0.425	1.575
22	0.640	0.167	0.647	0.9882	1.0119	0.534	1.466	0.528	1.448	3.819	0.2618	0.720	1.659	5.979	0.434	1.566
23	0.626	0.162	0.633	0.9887	1.0114	0.545	1.455	0.539	1.438	3.858	0.2592	0.716	1.710	6.006	0.443	1.557
24	0.612	0.157	0.619	0.9892	1.0109	0.555	1.445	0.549	1.429	3.895	0.2567	0.712	1.759	6.031	0.451	1.548
25	0.600	0.135	0.606	0.9896	1.0105	0.565	1.435	0.559	1.420	3.931	0.2544	0.708	1.806	6.056	0.459	1.541

FIG. 14.6 Reproduced from ASTM-STP 15D by kind permission of the American Society for Testing and Materials.

No Standard Given

When Range Is Used As Measure of Spread

Average:	Lower limit	$= \bar{\bar{X}} - A_2\bar{R}$	(13A)
	Center line	$= \bar{\bar{X}}$	
	Upper limit	$= \bar{\bar{X}} + A_2\bar{R}$	(13B)
Range:	Lower limit	$= D_3\bar{R}$	(14A)
	Center line	$= \bar{R}$	
	Upper limit	$= D_4\bar{R}$	(14B)

When Standard Deviation Is Used As a Measure of Spread

Average:	Lower limit	$= \bar{\bar{X}} - A_3\bar{s}$	(15A)
	Center line	$= \bar{\bar{X}}$	
	Upper limit	$= \bar{\bar{X}} + A_3\bar{s}$	(15B)
Standard deviation:	Lower limit	$= B_3\bar{s}$	(16A)
	Center line	$= \bar{s}$	
	Upper control limit	$= B_4\bar{s}$	(16B)

where $\bar{\bar{X}}$ = grand average (see Sec. 13.10)
$\bar{R}$ = average range (see Sec. 13.12)
$\bar{s}$ = average sample standard deviation (see Sec. 13.11)

Standard Given

When Range Is Used As Measure of Spread

Average:	Lower limit	$= \bar{X}_0 - A\sigma_0$	(17A)
	Center line	$= \bar{X}_0$	
	Upper limit	$= \bar{X}_0 + A\sigma_0$	(17B)
Range:	Lower limit	$= D_1\sigma_0$	(18A)
	Center line	$= R_0$ (or $d_2\sigma_0$)	
	Upper limit	$= D_2\sigma_0$	(18B)

When Standard Deviation Is Used As a Measure of Spread

Average:	Lower limit	$= \bar{X}_0 - A\sigma_0$	(17A)
	Center line	$= \bar{X}_0$	
	Upper limit	$= \bar{X}_0 + A\sigma_0$	(17B)
Standard deviation:	Lower limit	$= B_5\sigma_0$	(19A)
	Center line	$= s_0$ (or $c_4\sigma_0$)	
	Upper control limit	$= B_6\sigma_0$	(19B)

where $\bar{X}_0$ = value of the average adopted for computing the center line and control chart limits
R_0 = value of the range adopted for computing the center line and control chart limits

s_0 = value of the sample standard deviation adopted for computing the center line and the control chart limits

σ_0 = value of the lot or population standard deviation adopted for computing the center line and control chart limits

Formulas (13A) and (13B) through (19A) and (19B) are used to compute measurements-control chart limits. The basic concept of these control limits is the same as that for process and normal variation limits. However, the physical location of the limits is different because these control charts consider the distribution of averages rather than the distribution of individual observations.

Drawing and specification limits establish the acceptable amount of variation for the individual pieces that are produced. As such, they can be compared with frequency-distribution process limits. These process limits can be directly measured against drawing and specification limits to determine whether an economically satisfactory state of control of product quality exists. Section 13.16 illustrated one way in which these limits could be so used.

Measurements-control chart limits, being based upon a distribution of averages, usually cannot be directly compared with drawing or specification limits. When a decision must be made as to whether these control limits indicate an economically satisfactory process condition, it is necessary to compare the drawing or specification limits in question with the frequency-distribution process limits. (The exception to this is the special case of charts for individual readings, which is reviewed in Sec. 14.14.)

Figure 14.7 illustrates a typical relationship among these limits.

Figure 14.8 illustrates some practical problems that may arise when this type of limits analysis is used to make a decision about the economics of a process condition. The process conditions are unsatisfactory in both charts of Figure 14.8, even though the reasons for their being unsatisfactory are almost completely opposed.

In the left-hand chart, the process has too much variation for the specifica-

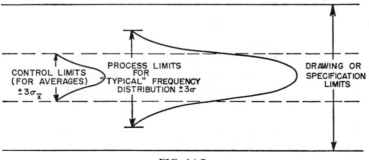

FIG. 14.7

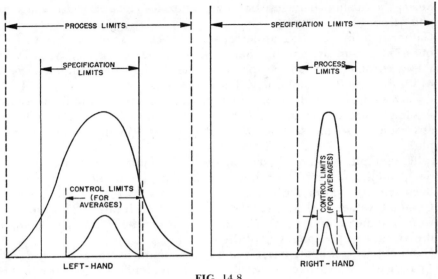

FIG. 14.8

tion limits. If the control limits were accepted as computed, nonconforming work would be produced. There are three possible alternatives here:

1. The process conditions can be improved.
2. The specification limits can be widened.
3. It can be recognized as part of job cost that, if no change is made, some scrap will be inevitable.

On the right-hand chart, the process condition is "too good." To reset a tool or change a process condition every time sample results showed out of control here would certainly be uneconomical. In this case, there are two alternatives: (1) the specification limits can be narrowed if this will tend to produce a better product, or (2) the control limits can be widened by some factor beyond the process limits which has proved satisfactory by experience with the chart in question. This matter is reviewed more broadly in Section 14.13.[8]

14.8 Computing Control Limits

The specific calculation of control chart limits is a very straightforward matter. The condition of "no standard given" carried through to ongoing process control is used in this section and 14.9 to illustrate this calculation. The range will be used as the measure of spread, and Formulas (13A) and (13B) and (14A) and (14B) will be applied.

There are eight steps to be followed in establishing a measurements control chart on this no standard given basis:

1. Select the quality characteristic to be controlled: length, width, hardness, and so on.
2. Gather data by selecting an adequate number of samples of the part in question and measuring the chosen quality characteristic. Adequacy will vary according to the specific process under examination, but for purposes of illustration, 25 samples have been selected.

   Each sample should contain an appropriate number of individual units. A sample size of five units has been found effective for many industrial applications, so the sample size of five is used in the following example.

   The samples should be taken at successive intervals (every hour, every day), and the data from each one must be recorded in the order that it has been selected and measured.
3. Compute values of the average and range for each of the 25 samples.
4. Compute the grand average $\overline{X}$ of the averages of the 25 samples. Compute the average of the ranges $\overline{R}$ of the 25 samples.
5. Compute control limits based upon these sample averages and ranges.
6. Analyze the average and range values for each sample with relation to these control limits. Determine if any factors requiring corrective action are present before the control limits are reviewed for approval.
7. Determine if the control limits are economically satisfactory for the process.
8. Use the control chart during active production as a basis for control of the quality characteristic in question so as to be assured that the process average and spread have not changed significantly.

14.9 The Calculation of Control Limits

A screw-machine setup had just been completed for the production of studs whose cutoff-length drawing tolerance was 0.500 inch $\pm$ 0.008 inch. A frequency-distribution analysis had been preliminarily carried on while the setup was being made. This analysis showed the setup to be satisfactory for the start of a long production run.

To establish a measurements control chart to analyze and then control the quality of these studs during the subsequent production run, the eight steps outlined above are followed in some detail:

Step 1: Select the Quality Characteristic

The cutoff length of the stud is most critical, and this is the characteristic for the control of which the chart is to be established.

Step 2: Gather Data for a Reasonable Time

About 150 studs are produced each hour. With a sample size of five units —one reading per stud on five studs—it can be arbitrarily assumed that one sample every hour may be selected for the purpose of setting the control limits. This decision is a practical matter of balancing such factors as cost, probable machine drift, availability of inspectors, and accessibility of gaging equipment.

Measurements of the required 25 samples will be taken by an inspector and recorded on a form similar to that shown in Figure 14.5. Figure 14.9 shows the actual form used in this case. The data taken are recorded on Figure 14.9 as they are gathered.

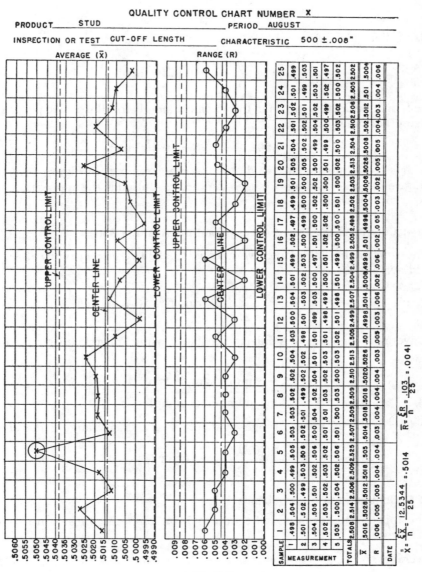

FIG. 14.9

Step 3: Compute the Average and Ranges for Samples

Referring to sample 1 of Figure 14.9, the five readings are

$$
\begin{array}{c}
0.498 \\
0.501 \\
0.504 \\
0.502 \\
\underline{0.503} \\
2.508
\end{array}
$$

Using Formula (1A):

$$\overline{X} = \frac{2.508}{5} = 0.5016 \text{ inch}$$

(The fourth decimal is shown in this example simply for illustrative purposes.)
Using Formula (6A):

$$R = 0.504 - 0.498 = 0.006 \text{ inch}$$

Similar calculations may be made for the other samples in Figure 14.9. The average and range readings for each sample are plotted in the appropriate spot on the control chart.

Step 4: Determine the Grand Average and the Average Range

The sum of the 25 sample averages is 12.5344. Using Formula (3A), the grand average is

$$\overline{\overline{X}} = \frac{12.5344}{25} = 0.5014 \text{ inch}$$

The average range may be similarly calculated, using Formula (6B) in the form that

$$\overline{R} = \frac{\text{sum of sample ranges}}{\text{number of samples}}$$

The sum of the 25 sample ranges is 0.103. The average range is therefore

$$\overline{R} = \frac{0.103}{25} = 0.0041 \text{ inch}$$

Step 5: Compute the Control Limits

The appropriate formulas in Section 14.7 for computing these control chart limits are

Averages: Lower limit $= \overline{\overline{X}} - A_2\overline{R}$ (13A)
               Center line $= \overline{\overline{X}}$
               Upper limit $= \overline{\overline{X}} + A_2\overline{R}$ (13B)

Ranges: $$\text{Lower limit} = D_3\overline{R} \qquad\qquad (14\text{A})$$
$$\text{Center line} = \overline{R}$$
$$\text{Upper limit} = D_4\overline{R} \qquad\qquad (14\text{B})$$

Referring to Figure 14.6 for the constants that are applicable for a sample size of 5, it is shown that

$$A_2 = 0.577$$
$$D_3 = 0$$
$$D_4 = 2.114$$

Substituting A_2 in Formulas (13A) and (13B), it is shown that

Formula (13A):

$$\text{Lower limit} = \overline{\overline{X}} - A_2\overline{R} = 0.5014 - (0.577)(0.0041) = 0.4990$$

Formula (13B):

$$\text{Upper limit} = \overline{\overline{X}} + A_2\overline{R} = 0.5014 + (0.577)(0.0041) = 0.5038$$

Substituting D_3 and D_4 in Formulas (14A) and (14B), it is shown that

Formula (14A):

$$\text{Lower limit} = D_3\overline{R} = (0)(0.0041) = 0$$

Formula (14B):

$$\text{Upper limit} = D_4\overline{R} = 2.114(0.0041) = 0.0087$$

These control limits may be plotted on the appropriate portions of Figure 14.9 by dashed lines. The center lines are also plotted on this figure, although some forms of control chart eliminate them.

Step 6: Use Limits to Analyze Sample Results

The control chart for the cutoff length of the screw-machined studs is fully constructed at the conclusion of step 5. Note from examination of Figure 14.9 that all sample ranges are within limits but that the average value for sample 5 is out of control.

It is possible that because only one sample reading is out of control, the reason may be pure chance. Recall that all these calculations are based upon the laws of probability. There is the chance (about 3 out of 1000) that an occasional good sample will show as out of control.

In this case, however, other reasons caused further analysis of sample 5. Investigation showed that the regular inspector had not taken the readings but had asked another employee to take them. The employee who was requested to take these readings was not qualified to handle precision measuring equipment. Other factors led to the suspicion either that sample 5 had not been measured at all or that the readings had been "faked."

For strict accuracy, therefore, the sampling procedure in steps 2 through 5 should have been repeated by gathering more samples. With somewhat less strict accuracy, the computation of steps 3 through 5 could have been re-worked, eliminating sample 5.

In this case, however, the control limits were allowed to stand as they had been originally calculated. It was felt, after examination of the stud data, that a recalculation would not yield sufficiently different results to justify the additional time that would be consumed by it.[9]

The circumstance illustrated by the results with sample 5 is typical of occur-rences while control limits are being initially established for a process or an operation. The sample results upon which the first computations have been made are usually examined with a judicious eye.

Often, several sample averages or ranges are found out of control during these initial computations. In these cases, efforts are made to trace down, identify, and eliminate the causes. The procedure of steps 2 through 5 is repeated until the process or operation is found to be "in control." This procedure is called *screening* control chart data.

As a result of this step, it can be determined that the process is in a state of control relative to the long-term production operation.

Step 7: Determine If the Control Limits Are Economically Satisfactory

The decision regarding the economics of control limits for the ongoing control of the process can effectively be made by the preliminary frequency-distribution analysis made before the control chart analysis took place, and in particular by coupling this analysis with an examination of the limits them-selves after they have been computed.

Chapter 13 pointed out that a process condition was considered economi-cally satisfactory if its frequency distribution was within tolerance limits and was well-centered. Section 14.9 noted that such a frequency-distribution analy-sis had been carried on while the screw machine was being set up for the production of studs. This analysis indicated that the 3-sigma or process limits for the cutoff length compared satisfactorily with the 0.492- to 0.508-inch tolerance limits.

The purpose of glancing at the control limits in addition to the process-limits analysis is to substantiate the frequency-distribution conclusions for the longer term conditions of the production run. Thus it is possible that the distribution sample might not have been representative (see Sec. 13.26) or that the process might be subject to factors causing variation which could not be taken into account by the preliminary frequency-distribution analysis.

With the studs, however, examination of the control limits plotted on Figure 14.9 merely tends to corroborate the frequency-distribution conclusions.

The center line of the $\overline{X}$ chart is on the "high side" of the tolerance rather than at the nominal side, but this is a situation often encountered in the shop. It resulted here, as is typical, from the desire of the machine operator to be "on the safe side of the tolerance."

What the operator had apparently done was to reset the tool so as to pro-duce studs whose average value was somewhat above the nominal length of

0.500 inch because studs that were on this "high side" could have excess material removed if a part happened to fall outside drawing limits, whereas studs on the "low side" would have to be scrapped if they fell outside drawing limits.

Yet the control limits are still satisfactory in spite of the high-side center line, although from a purist's point of view they might be improved by centering the process at the nominal value.

Step 8: Use Control Limits for Controlling Quality During Actual Production

With control limits computed and approved, a measurements control chart can be placed right at the screw machine producing the studs. This chart will have control limits plotted on it, and the values for average and range of the periodically selected samples will be marked in the appropriate chart spaces. This will be done by some designated individual, usually the machine operator on a "self-control" basis, with the periodic audit overview of the floor inspector or process-control engineer.

In theory, the frequency of making the sample checks may be calculated mathematically. In practice, this decision is an economic judgment based upon such factors as the quality history of the job, the quantity of hourly production, and how much it might cost to allow an out-of-control condition to exist undetected.

During the above procedure for computing control limits for the studs, samples were chosen every hour. This same policy is continued when the chart comes to be used for controlling quality of the cutoff length during actual production. For the studs, this hourly period is sufficient normally to highlight such factors as "drift," tool wear, or gradual loosening of setup bolts in sufficient time so that production of defective parts can be prevented.

Since the process conditions upon which the original computations are based may be subject to change, it is desirable that the control limits be reevaluated and possibly completely recalculated periodically. The need for such a computation depends, of course, upon the tendency of process and operation conditions to change. The frequency with which the calculation must be made may be 6 hours, 6 days, or 6 months, depending upon individual circumstances.

For the stud job, a 3-month period is adequate for recalculating limits. Should any methods change be made in the process during that period, however, recalculation of the limits would be required at once.

14.10 Measurements Control Charts: Differences in Detail

Control chart installations of various plants contain many differences in detail from the types of charts that were calculated in Sections 14.8 and 14.9. These differences are the result of efforts to meet individual plant conditions and relate to such matters as

1. Use of "standard given" approach
2. Use of sample standard deviation as measure of spread
3. Number of units in each sample
4. Measures of central tendency
5. Chart form
6. Methods of computing control limits
7. Warning levels and limits

1. Use of "Standard Given" Approach

When appropriate values of the average and the range can be adopted in advance of the construction of the control chart—recognizing, as discussed in Section 14.5, the importance of using prior data to confirm the existence of a state of control—the time for the establishment of the control chart limits can be reduced. Since the $\overline{X}$ and $\overline{R}$ calculations are no longer necessary to establish the values for the measures of central tendency and spread for the calculation of limits, steps 1 through 4 of Sections 14.8 and 14.9 are eliminated.

The adopted values of the average $\overline{X}_0$ (X bar subscript 0) and the range R_0 (R subscript 0) are used for the direct calculation of the control limits. Formulas (17A) and (17B) and (18A) and (18B) are used for this purpose, with the required control chart constants obtained from Figure 14.6.

The general control chart approach is the same as for the "no standard given" approach, except that the standard given approach begins in step 5 of Sections 14.8 and 14.9.

2. Standard Deviation As the Measure of Spread

Some plants prefer the standard deviation as the measure of spread in the control charts they use, particularly where sample size is more than 10 units. This type of measurements control chart is usually termed an $(\overline{X}, s)$ chart.

The procedure for calculating control limits is the same as when ranges are used. The chart forms used and the general approach are similar to those shown in Sections 14.8 and 14.9 and Figures 14.5 and 14.9, except, of course, that a sample standard deviation chart is used in place of the range chart.

The appropriate formulas from Section 14.7 for use in these computations are

No Standard Given

Average:	Lower limit	$= \overline{\overline{X}} - A_3\overline{s}$	(15A)
	Center line	$= \overline{\overline{X}}$	
	Upper limit	$= \overline{\overline{X}} + A_3\overline{s}$	(15B)
Standard deviation:	Lower limit	$= B_3\overline{s}$	(16A)
	Center line	$= \overline{s}$	
	Upper control limit	$= B_4\overline{s}$	(16B)

Standard Given

Average: Lower limit $= \bar{X}_0 - A\sigma_0$ (17A)

                 Center line $= \bar{X}_0$

                 Upper limit $= \bar{X}_0 + A\sigma_0$ (17B)

Standard deviation: Lower limit $= B_5\sigma_0$ (19A)

                 Center line $= s_0$ (or $c_4\sigma_0$)

                 Upper control limit $= B_6\sigma_0$ (19B)

3. Number of Units in Each Sample

The measurements-control chart sample sizes used in industry range from 2 to 20 units. Because of low accuracy, 2 and 3 units are infrequently used. Samples of 4 to 6 units are only slightly less popular than the 5-unit sample. Sample sizes of as many as 20 units are used in occasional cases. Multispindle machines are an example here; it may be desired to take one or more readings on units from each of several spindles, a procedure requiring a relatively large sample size.

The decision as to which of these sample sizes is appropriate in a given situation is one which must be made by striking a balance among such factors as the number of times samples may be selected in a particular period, the number of units that may economically be included in each of these samples, and the statistical accuracy that may be required for telegraphing unimportant "outs of control."

4. Measures of Central Tendency

The median is sometimes used as the measure of central tendency in place of the average $\bar{X}$. Under production conditions, the median is simpler to compute than the average because it can usually be determined simply by circling the reading of middle value in the sample.

The sample median is generally subject to greater statistical variation than the sample average (about 25 percent, generally for normal distributions), but for practical purposes it is sometimes more useful because of this ease of computation. The use of the median is influenced therefore by such factors as the availability of mathematically competent personnel, the degree of need for statistical accuracy, and the form of the distribution being observed.

5. Chart Form

Wide variation exists in the form taken by measurements charts developed for individual installations. On some jobs, it is not necessary to keep both an average and a range chart. For example, tool wear and other forms of process change have varying effects on different operations. There are instances where either the range or average remains almost constant or is unimportant, while there are wide changes in the other measure. Thus, a chart for either averages *or* ranges may be all that is required in these instances for control purposes.

Some control charts, as finally developed, lose their graphical form entirely.

Figure 14.10 illustrates such a chart that has been successfully used in a chemical factory for several years. This chart is not a graph, uses the median instead of the average, uses no range readings, and calls for action when the sample medians exceed a certain specified value. Out-of-limits readings are shown by a circle surrounded by bristles.

On some measurements control charts no numbers at all are recorded.

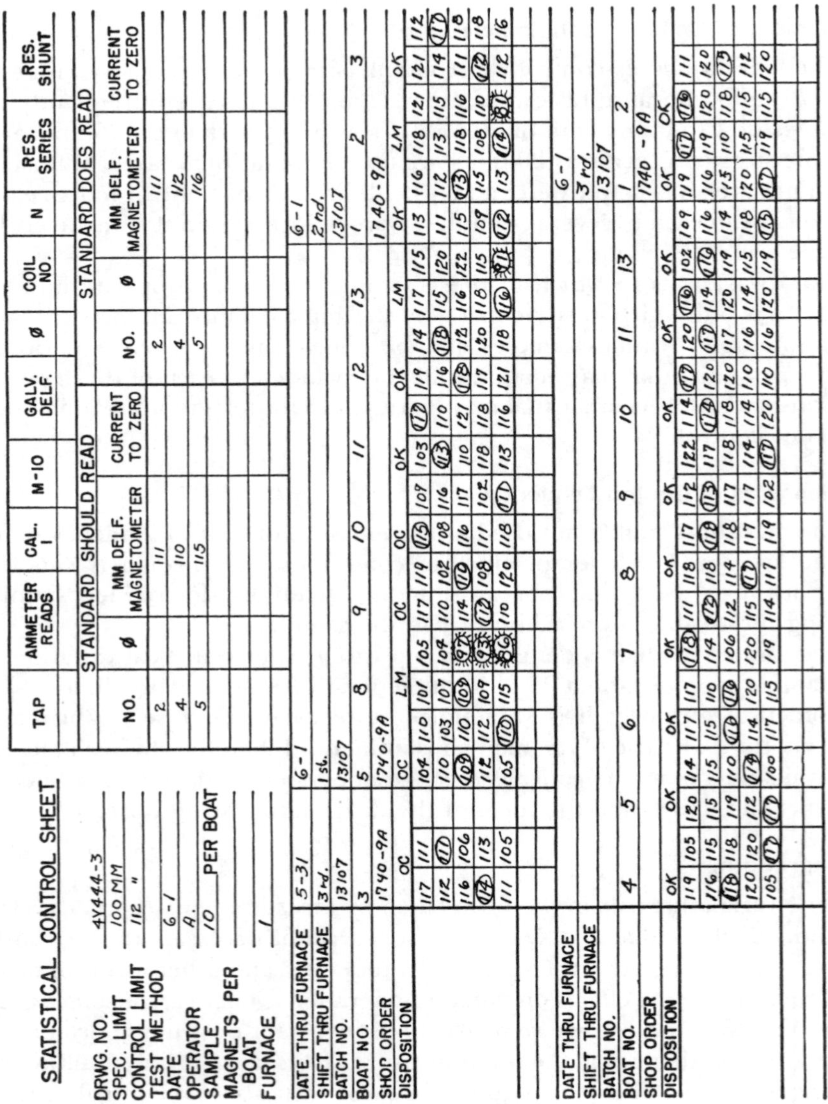

STATISTICAL CONTROL SHEET

DRWG. NO. 4Y444-3
SPEC. LIMIT 100 MM
CONTROL LIMIT 112 "
TEST METHOD
DATE 6-1
OPERATOR A.
SAMPLE 10 PER BOAT
MAGNETS PER BOAT
FURNACE 1

STANDARD SHOULD READ — STANDARD DOES READ

Column headings: TAP — AMMETER READS — CAL. I — M-10 — GALV. DEFL. — Ø — COIL NO. — N — RES. SERIES — RES. SHUNT

NO. Ø MM DEFL. MAGNETOMETER CURRENT TO ZERO   NO.   Ø   MM DEFL. MAGNETOMETER   CURRENT TO ZERO

DATE THRU FURNACE 5-31 / 6-1
SHIFT THRU FURNACE 3rd. / 1 sh.
BATCH NO. 13107 / 13107
BOAT NO. 3 / 5
SHOP ORDER 1740-9A / 1740-9A
DISPOSITION OK / OC

DATE THRU FURNACE 6-1
SHIFT THRU FURNACE 3rd.
BATCH NO. 13107
BOAT NO. 1
SHOP ORDER 1740-9A
DISPOSITION OK

FIG. 14.10

Individual Xs for every piece in each sample are plotted on an appropriate card form. If no more than a certain proportion of Xs in a sample fall outside the control limits, then the sample is considered representative of a satisfactory process condition. Figure 14.11 shows a typical form used here.

6. Computing Control Limits

There are many systems in use for computing measurements control limits. Graphs have been made of the constants of Figure 14.6. Some plants have issued data sheets upon which limits are computed for a wide variety of conditions. Some operations do the figuring "by hand," or with small electronic calculators. Other operations use digital computers or automatic line calculators. In some firms, $\overline{X}$ and R charts have been fully computerized, dramatically shortening computational time and ensuring accuracy. Increasingly, automated processes and automatic machine tools integrate certain $\overline{X}$, R concepts in their electronic control mechanisms.

There is no best form of measurements control chart; there are many varieties available, and the type of chart to suit particular needs can best be developed by the quality-control group of a given plant.

7. Warning Levels and Limits

There are some important process situations in chemical, electronic, and some mechanical operations where the production conditions require application of measurements control charts but where the basic process limits, while well-centered, are just within the specification limits. In the case of such products or components with especially strict or absolute specifications, some plants provide predetermined warning levels when the process output is closely approaching control limits. One widely used approach for such warning levels is to set the control chart warning limits at $+2\sigma$. A variety of other warning level approaches are used in plants to meet particular operating conditions.[10]

14.11 Economically Satisfactory Control Limits: Relation of Range and Standard Deviation

Particularly with long production runs of electronic or mechanical parts, it can be important to determine the long-term process limits. This is both to assure that control chart limits are likely to be economically satisfactory over the production run; and, also, for machine- and process-evaluation purpose, to assure that the longer-term process capability is satisfactory. An industrially useful procedure for this is based upon the fundamental statistical relationship between the average range and the population standard deviation.

When the average range $\overline{R}$ has been computed for a series of samples, showing controlled variation, as in Section 14.9, the value of the standard deviation for the "production stream" (Sec. 13.18) from which these samples

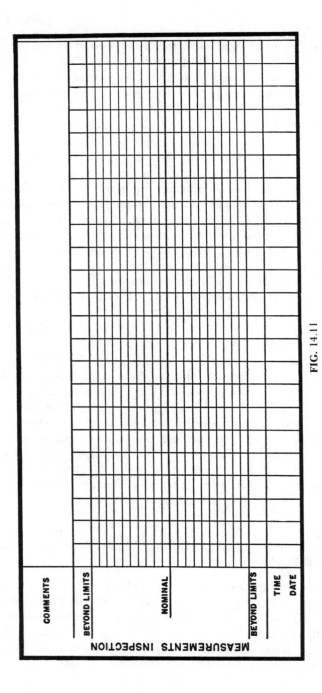

FIG. 14.11

were drawn bears a direct relationship to $\bar{R}$, if the distribution considered approximates the normal curve. This relationship is shown as

$$\sigma = \frac{\bar{R}}{d_2} \tag{20}$$

Figure 14.6 includes a tabulation of the d_2 conversion factor.

A very useful application of Formula (20) is found in those cases where it is desired to determine the spread for the individual units in the production stream and where control chart limits have been computed without also making an ongoing frequency-distribution analysis for process-capability evaluation purposes. As noted in Section 14.7, the control limits themselves cannot be directly compared with tolerance limits; 3-sigma, or process, limits for individual pieces must be calculated.

These 3-sigma limits for individual pieces can be computed easily by using the value of $\bar{R}$ that has already been calculated for use in the control limits. The 3-sigma limit can be developed as follows:

$$\sigma = \frac{\bar{R}}{d_2}$$

and

$$3\sigma = \frac{3\bar{R}}{d_2}$$

and

$$3\sigma = \frac{3}{d_2}\bar{R}$$

Now, in the case of no standard given, the 3-sigma limits for readings on individual pieces equal

$$\bar{\bar{X}} \pm 3\sigma$$

Substituting Formula (20), this formula becomes

$$\bar{\bar{X}} \pm \left(\frac{3}{d_2}\right)\bar{R}$$

The factor $3/d_2$ varies with different sample sizes and has been termed E_2 (E subscript 2). Figure 14.12 lists a tabulation of E_2 for different sample sizes.

Process, or 3-sigma, limits can be computed with this factor by use of the following formulas:

$$\text{Lower limit} = \bar{\bar{X}} - E_2\bar{R} \tag{21A}$$
$$\text{Center line} = \bar{\bar{X}}$$
$$\text{Upper limit} = \bar{\bar{X}} + E_2\bar{R} \tag{21B}$$

FACTORS FOR E_2

SAMPLE SIZE (N)	E_2
2	2.659
3	1.772
4	1.457
5	1.290
6	1.184
7	1.109
8	1.054
9	1.010
10	.975
11	.946
12	.921
13	.899
14	.881
15	.864

FIG. 14.12

Use of these formulas can be illustrated by reference to the control chart data of Section 14.9. With these data, the process-limit calculation can be made as follows.

Recall that, for the studs,

$$\overline{\overline{X}} = 0.5014 \text{ inch}$$

and

$$\overline{R} = 0.0041 \text{ inch}$$

From Figure 14.12, the value of E_2 for a sample size of five units is 1.290. Substituting these values in Formulas (21A) and (21B):

Formula (21A):

Lower limit $= \overline{\overline{X}} - E_2\overline{R} = 0.5014 - (1.290)(0.0041) = 0.4962$ inch

Formula (21B):

Upper limit $= \overline{\overline{X}} + E_2\overline{R} = 0.5014 + (1.290)(0.0041) = 0.5066$ inch

These limits compare satisfactorily with the tolerance limits of 0.492 to 0.508 inch, although they are again on the high side for reasons that were discussed in the previous section.

The computation carried out through Formulas (21A) and (21B) is sometimes not completely accurate when data used in the control chart computation are skewed. In the case of the studs, for example, close examination of the data would show that there is an appreciable skew to the left. Yet process limits are sufficiently within the drawing limits so that the above calculation is acceptable as a guide to the conclusion both that the control limits in question are economically satisfactory and that the longer term process capability is adequate.

This type of calculation, as a matter of fact, is encountered chiefly in the early stages of factory control chart installations. When experience has been gained with the control chart, the conclusion as to whether limits are economically satisfactory often becomes a rule-of-thumb decision which is made by simply glancing at the control chart data.

14.12 Modified Control Limits in Relation to Specification Limits—Tool Wear and Trend Control

Although the preceding methods for setting limits have been the most popular in industry, a somewhat different approach has much to recommend it in those cases where the process limits are narrower than the specification limits. In this method, control limits are established in relation to drawing or specification limits rather than to process averages.

The primary advantage to this modified limits approach is that it may result in more economical production runs. When control limits are established in relation to process averages, the average or nominal value often becomes the machine operator's target. Every effort may be made to set up and keep the job-quality characteristic at this average value.

On some jobs with long production runs, where tool wear is an important factor, this procedure may prove uneconomical. About one-half the variation allowed by the drawing or specification is simply discarded before the production run begins. The left-hand chart of Figure 14.13 illustrates this condition.

In the many cases where specification limits are wider than process limits, establishing control limits in relation to specifications may permit a more economical operating condition. These control limits will provide a guide to setting up the job, not at the nominal value but at that end of the control limits which is opposite the direction of tool wear. Thus in a job wherein the tool wear is in the direction of the upper specification limit, the lower control limit will be the target for the initial setup—when the basic long-term process capability and natural tolerance are sufficiently small. The right-hand chart of Figure 14.13 illustrates this situation. It may indicate a better long-term operating condition than does the left-hand chart of the figure because it may permit a much lengthier run without the need for tooling changes.

Another approach is the so-called slanting control lines for averages. In this application, the trend of the average values, as shown in Figure 14.13, is established, and control limits are established with relation to this trend.

However, these procedures may prove inappropriate, as in the case of machining certain mating parts whose overall tolerance when assembled has been

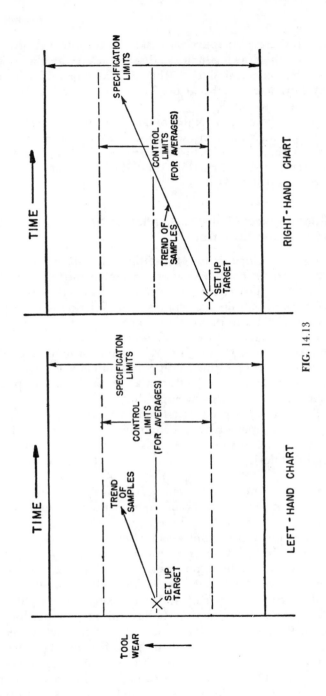

FIG. 14.13

424

established by the designing engineer on the assumption that the parts-quality target would be the drawing nominal value (see Sec. 16.8).

But for the run-of-the-mill parts that make up the bulk of production in many shops, control limits that relate to specification limits may prove highly satisfactory and extremely economical.

14.13 Computing Control Limits Based on Specification Limits— Process-Capability Charts, Acceptance Control Charts

There are also other types of plant operations where, as long as the spread of process sample values remains within control at levels acceptable for specification or tolerance levels, it is not necessary that the process remain in control about a single standard process level. This is typically true in the case of processes where changes or the "hunting" of the process is generally sufficiently small—and sometimes inherent—such that it is simply uneconomical to use a more tightly controlled measurement-control chart approach.

In these plant operations, the usual variation limits are narrower—often substantially narrower—than the tolerance and specification limits. This condition is sometimes encountered in certain electronic component and subassembly processes and in some mechanical, chemical, and nuclear-oriented operations.

The objective of computing control limits based upon the specification limit themselves is to allow definable shifts in process levels that are acceptable with regard to tolerance and specification levels but to control against large process shifts which are unacceptable in terms of these levels. A state of statistical control is important for the spread within the samples used for the procedure.

Two approaches used for this purpose in industry are (1) using process-capability values and (2) acceptance control charts.

Process-Capability Charts

One widely used approach to the establishment of these control limits involves the determination of the process conditions that generally apply to manufacturing of the parts in question and the development of a nomograph which is based upon this analysis.

An effective technique for accomplishing this objective is based upon computing, for each process, its *process capability*. Values for this process capability are equivalent to the process limits for the "typical" frequency distribution for the process in question, that is, the amount of variation that may ordinarily be expected from the process. Sections 20.15 to 20.18 discuss one means for determining these so-called process-capability values.

A procedure for computing control limits in relation to specification limits that is based upon process-capability values is as follows:

1. Determine the process-capability values for the process for which control limits are to be established. One procedure for computing this value is the

technique presented in Section 20.17, although some shops use know-how values based upon past experience with the process in question.

2. Determine the control limits from these process-capability values by the use of the nomograph (Fig. 20.19) discussed in Section 20.17, which has been established in relation to process-capability values. This nomograph may be used no matter what part is to be produced on the machine or process in question. The following formulas are used with the nomograph computation:

$$\text{Lower control limit} = \text{lower specification limit} + Q \qquad (22A)$$
$$\text{Upper control limit} = \text{upper specification limit} - Q \qquad (22B)$$

where Q = percent of the process capability as computed by the nomograph.

3. After they have been judged economically acceptable, plot these control limits on suitable graph paper.

4. Use the chart for controlling production quality of the parts. Select periodic samples, compute their average value, and compare this average value with the control limits to determine if corrective action is required.[11]

An example illustrating the use of this technique for setting control limits is in Section 20.17.

Acceptance Control Charts

An approach generally similar to the process-capability activity has been termed the "acceptance control chart," whose objectives are to examine a process both with respect to its ability to meet specification tolerances for a quality characteristic and whether it is in a state of control. In its strict form, the acceptance control chart differs from some other modified control limit charts in that it also takes into account (1) the probabilities of failing to detect process shifts of given size, (2) the probabilities of incorrectly identifying a change from the standard of what are termed "acceptable process zone levels," and (3) the identification of sample sizes to maintain these probabilities at desired levels of risk. In this sense, the acceptance control chart procedure follows practices more usual to acceptance sampling table procedure, which is reviewed in detail in Chapter 15.

The basic levels used in the acceptance control chart are those termed:

Zone of acceptable processes, which relates to a zone around a central or standard level which encompasses the levels for processes desired to have accepted. This is defined by an upper acceptable process level (UAPL) and a lower acceptable process level (LAPL).

Zone of rejectable processes, which relates to zones which encompass the levels for processes desired to have rejected. This is defined by an upper rejectable process level (URPL) and a lower rejectable process level (LRPL).

Zone of indifference, which relates to zones which encompass the levels for processes in which there is "indifference" as to whether it is desired to have acceptance or rejection. As further discussed in Chapter 15, every sampling situation has an indifference zone, but its relevance to the acceptance control chart is that it is usually undesirable and uneconomic for a process to be located in the indifference zone as contrasted to the acceptable process zone.

The procedure in establishing the acceptance control chart is to calculate acceptable control limits (ACL) to be the action criteria, as well as to calculate acceptable process levels (APL) and rejectable process levels (RPL). This takes place by establishing the following:

- The cutoff point termed z (for the Greek letter zeta), which identifies the distance of the ACL from the APL and the RPL in units of standard deviation of the process frequency distribution. This is established with two levels of risk termed z_α (z subscript alpha) and z_β (z subscript beta). Alpha and beta risks in sampling are defined and discussed in Section 15.5.
- The cutoff point termed z_{p1} (z subscript p subscript 1) and z_{p2} (z subscript p subscript 2), which identify, in the process frequency distribution, the distance of the APL and the RPL from the tolerance limits in units of standard deviation.

The specific calculation then proceeds according to the following formulas:[12]

Acceptable process levels:
$$\text{UAPL} = \text{UTL} - z_{p_1}\sigma \tag{23A}$$
$$\text{LAPL} = \text{LTL} + z_{p_1}\sigma \tag{23B}$$

Rejectable process levels:
$$\text{URPL} = \text{UTL} - z_{p_2}\sigma \tag{24A}$$
$$\text{LRPL} = \text{LTL} + z_{p_2}\sigma \tag{24B}$$

Acceptance control limits:
$$\text{UACL} = \text{UAPL} + \frac{z_\alpha\sigma}{\sqrt{n}} \tag{25A}$$

$$\text{LACL} = \text{LAPL} - \frac{z_\alpha\sigma}{\sqrt{n}} \tag{25B}$$

or

$$\text{UACL} = \text{URPL} - \frac{z_\beta\sigma}{\sqrt{n}} \tag{26A}$$

$$\text{LACL} = \text{LRPL} + \frac{z_\beta\sigma}{\sqrt{n}} \tag{26B}$$

Sample size in these calculations may be defined as:

$$n = \left[\frac{(z_\alpha + z_\beta)\sigma}{(\text{RPL} - \text{APL})} \right]^2$$

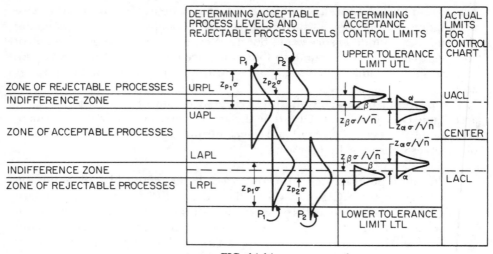

FIG. 14.14

Figure 14.14 illustrates this acceptance control chart approach.[13]

4.14 Other Forms of Variables Control: Individual Readings Charts; Cusum Charts

Section 14.5 mentioned two other forms of control charts, differing somewhat from those discussed above, which have been developed to meet particular requirements. These will now be reviewed.

1. Individual Readings Charts

There are some plant operations where, for a variety of operating reasons, there is no possibility of basing statistical control upon samples of units—which has been the approach of the charts discussed above—to provide values of central tendency and spread. This is the case, for example, in very long time cycle production operations where a single unit reading may represent a full operating shift—or an operating day, week, or even longer time interval. Another example is the case of production research situations where the unit reading is extremely expensive—or very lengthy as to the time such a reading takes.

These situations require charts related to individual readings, even though there are technical statistical questions as to whether they represent what might, strictly speaking, be termed control charts. Moreover, such individual readings charts do not provide any comparable control effectiveness as for sample-oriented control. The approach is, instead, based upon doing the best possible with the limited data available.

To obtain the values for central tendency and spread in the no standard given condition—which is often the case for individual reading control—estimates are obtained by means of *moving ranges*. This takes place by using $R_1 = |X_1 - X_2|$, $R_2 = |X_2 - X_3|$, and so on. The absolute value sign around $X_1 - X_2$ means that the positive value of this result is used. This procedure continues with $\overline{X}$ established as the average of the several individual readings and $\overline{R}$ for the average of the Rs.

The calculation of the control chart for individual readings is based upon use of Formula 20, Section 14.11, which relates the average range $\overline{R}$ to the population standard deviation σ. Adapting this formula to the use of the standard deviation for the individual readings, $X_1 \cdots X_n$, the formula becomes

$$\sigma_x = \frac{\overline{R}}{d_2}$$

with d_2 based upon sample size $n = 2$.

The control chart limits formula becomes

$$\overline{X} \pm 3 \frac{\overline{R}}{d_2}$$

and

$$X \pm \left(\frac{3}{d_2}\right) = \overline{R}$$

Adapting Formulas 21A and 21B to this case, the formula becomes (with the use of the constant E_2 for the expression $3/d_2$),

Lower control limit $= \overline{X} - E_2\overline{R}$ (27A)
Center line $\quad\quad\quad\ = \overline{X}$
Upper control limit $= \overline{X} + E_2\overline{R}$ (27B)

Because of a variety of conditions resulting from the minimum of readings associated with this approach and the long intervals that can occur between readings, some plant applications are based upon accepting an increased risk of searching for an assignable cause when none is present. These applications, therefore, compute the formula according to ± 2 sigma rather than ± 3 sigma.[14] The formula then becomes

$$\overline{X} \pm 2 \frac{\overline{R}}{d_2}$$

Constants for E_2 are in Figure 14.12; constants for $1/d_2$, when this latter approach is taken, are in Figure 14.6.

2. Cusum Charts

There are some processes in electronic, mechanical, chemical, pharmaceutical, nuclear-related, and other operations where effective control requires major sensitivity to process changes—particularly when the process is continuous or consisting of a flow of units. This is because a sudden, although continuing, process change can abruptly take place. It is important to detect this change, and a form of control chart termed the "cusum" (for cumulative sum) is sometimes used for this purpose.

Cusum charts are generally based upon the assumption that the spread of the process is in control. In the charts' plant application, the sensitivity of the approach can be such that care must be taken so that an undue number of process adjustments is not called for because this may limit the acceptability and economy of the approach in some production situations.

The basic approach in this form of chart is to track an average of a sample of readings, $\overline{X}$, with relation to a standard value, $\overline{X}_0$, by cumulating the deviations from $\overline{X}_0$. Then if $\overline{X}_0$ is actually close to $\overline{X}$, the cusum will tend to remain close to zero. But if it is different, the cusum will rapidly rise from zero—or go below if that is the arrangement between $\overline{X}$ and $\overline{X}_0$.

While upper and lower limits can be placed on this drift from zero, what is also of primary interest in this type of application is the steepness of the change. Thus, the cusum technique uses what has come to be called the V mask for cusum scaling. The key dimensions of the V mask are θ and d and are based upon α and β risks (see the discussion in Sec. 15.5) and the quality statistic. A factor termed K is used to relate the vertical scale unit to the horizontal scale unit.

The operating procedure is to place the movable V mask around the most recently plotted point; a shift is identified when any previous points are found outside the V. The concept of the cusum and V mask are shown as Figure 14.15.[15]

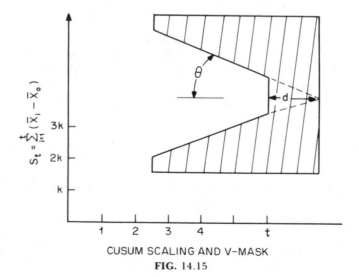

CUSUM SCALING AND V–MASK
FIG. 14.15

14.15 Measurements Control Charts: Summary

There are several additional applications of measurements control charts in factory operations over and above their use during actual production. Two typical applications are

1. Informing designing engineers of the manufacturability of the various possible alternative designs
2. Measuring tool wear as a guide to future tool and gage design

Detailed applications of this sort are discussed in Part 6, "Applying Total Quality Control in the Company." As far as use of these charts for quality control during production is concerned, formulas for use in computing the control limits are now summarized.

MEASUREMENTS CONTROL CHARTS

No Standard Given

When Range Is Used As Measure of Spread

Average:	Lower limit	$= \overline{\overline{X}} - A_2 \overline{R}$	(13A)
	Center line	$= \overline{\overline{X}}$	
	Upper limit	$= \overline{\overline{X}} + A_2 \overline{R}$	(13B)
Range:	Lower limit	$= D_3 \overline{R}$	(14A)
	Center line	$= \overline{R}$	
	Upper limit	$= D_4 \overline{R}$	(14B)
Process limits:	Lower limit	$= \overline{\overline{X}} - E_2 \overline{R}$	(21A)
	Center line	$= \overline{\overline{X}}$	
	Upper limit	$= \overline{\overline{X}} + E_2 \overline{R}$	(21B)

When Standard Deviation Is Used As a Measure of Spread

Average:	Lower limit	$= \overline{\overline{X}} - A_3 \overline{s}$	(15A)
	Center line	$= \overline{\overline{X}}$	
	Upper limit	$= \overline{\overline{X}} + A_3 \overline{s}$	(15B)
Standard deviation:	Lower limit	$= B_3 \overline{s}$	(16A)
	Center line	$= \overline{s}$	
	Upper control limit	$= B_4 \overline{s}$	(16B)

Standard Given

When Range Is Used As Measure of Spread

Average:	Lower limit	$= \overline{X}_0 - A\sigma_0$	(17A)
	Center line	$= \overline{X}_0$	
	Upper limit	$= \overline{X}_0 + A\sigma_0$	(17B)
Range:	Lower limit	$= D_1 \sigma_0$	(18A)

$$\text{Center line} \quad = R_0 \text{ (or } d_2\sigma_0)$$
$$\text{Upper limit} \quad = D_2\sigma_0 \tag{18B}$$

When Standard Deviation Is Used As a Measure of Spread

Average:
$$\text{Lower limit} \quad = \overline{X}_0 - A\sigma_0 \tag{17A}$$
$$\text{Center line} \quad = \overline{X}_0$$
$$\text{Upper limit} \quad = \overline{X}_0 + A\sigma_0 \tag{17B}$$

Standard deviation:
$$\text{Lower limit} \quad = B_5\sigma_0 \tag{19A}$$
$$\text{Center line} \quad = s_0 \text{ (or } c_4\sigma_0)$$
$$\text{Upper control limit} = B_6\sigma_0 \tag{19B}$$

LIMITS IN RELATION TO SPECIFICATIONS

Process Capabilities

$$\text{Lower control limit } = \text{ lower specification limit } + Q \tag{22A}$$
$$\text{Upper control limit } = \text{ upper specification limit } - Q \tag{22B}$$

Acceptance Control

Acceptable process levels:
$$\text{UAPL} = \text{UTL} - z_{p_1}\sigma \tag{23A}$$
$$\text{LAPL} = \text{LTL} + z_{p_1}\sigma \tag{23B}$$

Rejectable process levels:
$$\text{URPL} = \text{UTL} - z_{p_2}\sigma \tag{24A}$$
$$\text{LRPL} = \text{LTL} + z_{p_2}\sigma \tag{24B}$$

Acceptance control limits:
$$\text{UACL} = \text{UAPL} + \frac{z_\alpha\sigma}{\sqrt{n}} \tag{25A}$$

$$\text{LACL} = \text{LAPL} - \frac{z_\alpha\sigma}{\sqrt{n}} \tag{25B}$$

or

$$\text{UACL} = \text{URPL} - \frac{z_\beta\sigma}{\sqrt{n}} \tag{26A}$$

$$\text{LACL} = \text{LRPL} + \frac{z_\beta\sigma}{\sqrt{n}} \tag{26B}$$

INDIVIDUAL READINGS

$$\text{Lower control limit } = \overline{X} - E_2\overline{R} \tag{27A}$$
$$\text{Center line} \quad = \overline{X}$$
$$\text{Upper control limit } = \overline{X} + E_2\overline{R} \tag{27B}$$

CONTROL CHARTS FOR GO AND NOT-GO DATA

14.16 Percent and Fraction Control Limits

In go and not-go (or attributes) inspection, a unit is classified as simply meeting the specification limits or not meeting them. Frequently, go and not-go data are represented by the value of the fraction or percent of units that do not meet requirements. The fraction (often presented as a decimal) is the value obtained by dividing the total number of units inspected into the number of units that do not meet requirements. The percent is merely the percentage representation of the corresponding decimal value.

Thus, if 3 units are found that do not meet requirements out of a lot of 100 units, the fraction for that lot is 3/100, or 0.03. The percent for the lot is of course 3.

The universal variation among manufactured parts is to be found fully as much in these go and not-go data and their percent and fraction values as it is in actual measurements readings. Percent and fraction data can be described by values for their central tendency and spread fully as much as measurements readings. This is true because it can be shown that the binomial distribution (describing attribute data) for large samples approximates the normal distribution (describing variable data).

Terminology

As earlier discussed in Section 9.20, there has been considerable emphasis in recent years in making quality terminology more precise. The area of control charts has benefited from this emphasis.[16]

What has been termed above as "units that do not meet requirements"—designated as "variant units" in technical statistical terms—are generally expressed in one of two terms—nonconforming unit or defective unit—in specific percent and fraction control charts:

Nonconforming unit may be defined as

> A unit or service containing at least one departure of a quality characteristic from its intended level or state that occurs with a severity sufficient to cause an associated product or service to not meet a specification requirement.

Defective unit may be defined as

> A unit of product or service containing either at least one departure of a quality characteristic from its intended level or state that occurs with a severity sufficient to cause an associated product or service to not satisfy intended normal, or reasonably foreseeable, usage requirements; or having several imperfections that in combination cause the unit to fail to satisfy intended normal, or reasonably foreseeable, usage requirements.

The basic difference is that *defective unit*—and the corresponding term *defect* —is a term oriented to evaluation of units with regard to customer usage, and *nonconforming unit*—and the corresponding terms *nonconformity* and *nonconformance*—is a term oriented to evaluation of units with regard to conformance to specifications.

In some attributes control charts—such as where specification requirements are equivalent with customer-usage requirements—the two terms coincide.

Also, some customer contractual requirements may specify that any units deviating from the specification requirements are to be considered defective.

In other attributes control chart situations, the specification requirement may be internally established within the plant or company and be deliberately set tighter than the customer requirements—thus making nonconforming unit the more appropriate control chart term.

Many of the widely used attributes charts were originally developed with use of *defective* and *percent defective* as the basic terminology. Certain other attributes charts now have used *nonconformance* and *nonconforming* as the basic terminology, in accordance with this modern improvement of terminology; moreover this is also now being widely introduced into modern sampling tables, as discussed in Chapter 15.

Each plant and company will make its own determination as to which of these terms most precisely describes the "units that do meet requirements"—or "variant units"—with regard to its use of control charts. For clarity, for each chart and example discussed, this chapter uses the terminology employed by the company and plant referenced in the example. Since many plants continue to use the terms defect and defective for control, partly because they wish to emphasize customer effects, these terms will be widely used in the text below.

Control Chart Formulas

With percent data, the average is generally used as the measure of central tendency expressed as a percentage. The standard deviation is the measure of spread in successive sample percentages.

The average for percent data (expressed in integer notation, as in 3 percent) is symbolized by $\bar{p}$ (p bar). The symbol p, quantified as a fraction or a percentage, represents the *proportion* of defective or nonconforming units found in a single sample of n units. It is plotted as a point on a chart called a p chart. If the sample size n is kept constant for a successive set of k such samples, the average value of p is given by $\bar{p} = (\Sigma p)/k$. This average $\bar{p}$ is usually plotted as a solid line across the p chart and represents the *expected* proportion of unacceptable units to be found in a random sample of n units from the cause system under study.

With sample sizes which vary within the series of samples for which the average value is to be calculated, $\bar{p}$ can be computed by dividing the total number of units in the series into the total number of defects or nonconformities in the series as follows:

$$\bar{p} = \frac{\Sigma c}{\Sigma n} \times 100 \qquad (28)$$

where c = variable number of defectives or nonconforming units per sample.

The standard deviation of p is symbolized by σ_p (sigma subscript p). With constant sample size, it can be computed as follows:

$$\sigma_p = \sqrt{\frac{\bar{p}(100 - \bar{p})}{n}} \qquad (29)$$

where n = sample size

$\bar{p}$ = average value for percent defective or nonconformance

As in the case of measurements data, control chart limits are merely the 3-sigma values for p; in this case, p values for percent defective or nonconformance. These control limits may be represented as follows:

No Standard Given

$$\text{Control limits} = \bar{p} \pm 3\sqrt{\frac{\bar{p}(100 - \bar{p})}{n}} \qquad (30)$$

Standard Given

$$\text{Control limits} = p_0 \pm 3\sqrt{\frac{p_0(100 - p_0)}{n}} \qquad (30A)$$

where p_0 (p subscript 0) is the adopted standard level for average percent defective or nonconformance.

Fraction-defective or nonconformance control limits may be computed by a slight adaptation of the formula as follows:

No Standard Given

$$\text{Control limits} = \bar{p} \pm 3\sqrt{\frac{\bar{p}(1 - \bar{p})}{n}} \qquad (31)$$

In Formula (31), $\bar{p}$ is taken as the decimal value for average fraction defective.

Standard Given

$$\text{Control limits} = p_0 \pm 3\sqrt{\frac{p_0(1 - p_0)}{n}} \qquad (31A)$$

where p_0 is the adopted standard decimal value level for average fraction defective or nonconformance.

The lower control limits are zero when the calculated value is negative for the control-limit formulas listed above.

Interpretation of these control limits is similar to the interpretation for the measurements control limits that were described earlier in this chapter. When percent values for production samples fall outside the percent limits, a process change may be indicated, which may call for corrective action.

14.17 Two Types of Percent Control Charts

Control charts based upon percent data have proved quite effective in controlling quality during production. Two major variations in the charts used are

Type 1: Constant Sample Size

These are charts which are based upon comparing with control limits the percent or fraction values computed from samples of constant size. These samples are selected from the production process periodically—every hour, every 15 minutes, every morning.

Type 2: Varying Sample Size

These are charts established for parts and assemblies which have been 100 percent inspected as a part of regular factory routine. The sample size for these charts is the total production for the period in question and so may vary from period to period.

Establishing control chart limits for type 1 charts is a straightforward matter. The approach for setting the limits is the same as described in Sections 14.8 to 14.10, except that control limits are computed throughout with the use of Formula (30) or (30A) and only one chart for percent is maintained rather than individual charts for average and spread. Sample size with these charts is relatively larger than for measurements charts because of the lesser effectiveness of go and not-go data.

A sample size of 25 units is very popular for percent charts, although various rules have been suggested for determining the minimum sample size. The sample size must be small enough so that production and testing conditions can be presumed to be fairly uniform. Conversely, the sample size must be large enough to average at least 0.5 defective for $n\bar{p}$. Thus, if $\bar{p}$ is very small, this will require a large n.

A major application of type 1 charts is in those cases where measurements data may not exist—as in surface finish or possibly color—or where these measurements are difficult to obtain. Sometimes, also, constant sample size is made necessary by factors not directly connected with the control of quality, such as those cases where, for wage-payment reasons, the number of units in lots presented for 100 percent inspection is pegged at a certain number of units, like 500, 2500, or 4000.

Type 2 charts are probably the more important form of percent control chart. Blemishes or *imperfections* are a particularly important form of such attribute control chart application. In addition, because the procedure for computing their control limits is not quite so straightforward as that for type 1 charts, type 2 charts will be discussed below in some detail.

14.18 Form of the Percent Chart for 100 Percent Inspection

Most parts inspection in industry is of the go and not-go variety. Go and not-go examination of units is often 100 percent inspection, where the checking of each part is assumed to result in sorting all nonconforming units from the good units.

Records of the results of this go and not-go inspection have been maintained in many factories for a number of years. In too many instances, this record keeping has been a relatively fruitless task because the mass of numbers thus maintained may not furnish a very convenient guide for preventing the future production of nonconforming or defective units.

The effectiveness of this type of inspection in preventing the recurrence of defective or nonconforming work is, however, considerably increased by presenting go and not-go data in the form of a percent control chart. Figure 14.16 shows a typical chart form that has been developed in industry for this purpose, using values for defective units, because customer usage is the primary concern for variant units.

There are four major parts to this chart:

1. A graph for plotting the percent-defective (see I in Fig. 14.16)
2. A chart for recording the inspection information from which the percent-defective values can be computed (see II in Fig. 14.16)
3. A chart for periodically summarizing the percent-defective data (see III in Fig. 14.16)
4. A graph for plotting these summaries (see IV in Fig. 14.16)

The number of units inspected in each period—the sample size—will vary under normal shop conditions. Formula (30) cannot, therefore, be applied to compute a single set of control limits because the formula is predicated upon the assumption of constant sample size.

In theory, therefore, Formula (30) can be used to compute control limits only for the percent-defective data for each individual inspection period, taking the percent-defective value for that period as $\bar{p}$. This would, however, result in the unsatisfactory situation wherein there would be different control limits for each inspection period, making the interpretation of these limits quite difficult for practical shop purposes. Control limits for inspection periods where production was relatively low might be wider than control limits for inspection periods where production was somewhat higher.

In practice, if sample size does not vary more than a maximum of 20 percent, which is a practical criterion for most factory inspection periods, accuracy which is satisfactory for most industrial purposes may be gained by the computation and use of the *average* sample size over the inspection periods in question. This average sample size and other average values can then be substituted in Formula (30) as a form of standard given approach. The computation can be even further simplified by using charts of constants.

The following eight steps can be followed to establish a percent-defective chart of this sort:

1. Determine the quality characteristic to be controlled. This may be a single characteristic like length or weight; frequently it will be the total of all defective units found in those being examined.

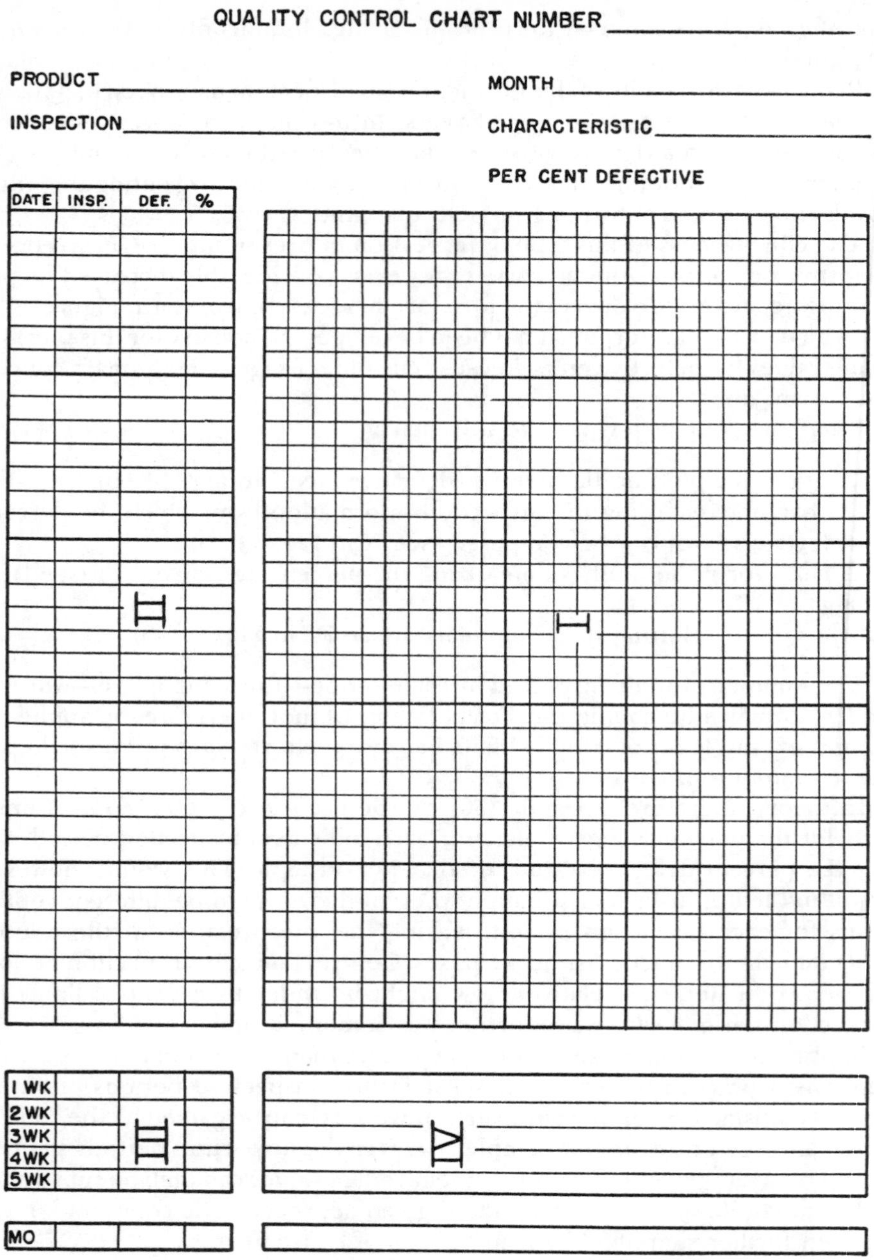
QUALITY CONTROL CHART NUMBER
PRODUCT
MONTH
INSPECTION
CHARACTERISTIC
PER CENT DEFECTIVE
DATE
INSP.
DEF.
%
I
II
III
IV
1 WK
2 WK
3 WK
4 WK
5 WK
MO

FIG. 14.16

2. Select an adequate number of samples. Each sample should contain an appropriate number of individual units. As in computing the control limits for variable data shown in Sections 14.8 and 14.9, the appropriate number will vary depending upon the process involved. For purposes of illustration, 25 samples are used. The "number of units" in each sample is, in this case, the total number of units examined during a standard inspection period like an hour or a day. The 25 samples must be taken at successive intervals (every hour, every day). The data from each one must be recorded in the order that the sample has been selected.
3. Compute the average sample size. In this case, where the total number of parts inspected in an hour or day is the sample size, sample size equals average hourly or daily production.
4. Compute the average number of defectives hourly or daily.
5. Compute control limits based upon the calculations of steps 3 and 4. Charts are available to simplify the computation that would be required if Formula (30) were used directly.
6. Analyze the percent-defective values for each sample with relation to these control limits. Determine if any factor requires corrective action before the limits are reviewed for approval.
7. Determine if the control limits are economically satisfactory for the process.
8. Use the control chart during active production as a guide toward control of the quality characteristics in question.

14.19 Establishing a 100 Percent Inspection Control Chart

In the manufacture of complicated motor end shields, there are a number of attributes which might cause an end shield not to meet requirements. Although later controls will eliminate such units, the plant uses the term "defective" to emphasize customer- and cost-oriented importance of any nonconformity. Some of these attributes are casting fractures, incorrect inner-bore diameters, and poor machined finishes. A typical application of the percent-defective control chart may be found in the 100 percent final inspection of these end shields, where any of these several attributes might cause rejection.

Production of end shields varies between 950 and 1050 units per day. The daily total of shields inspected will be considered sample size. The eight steps to be followed in making up a control chart of this sort are now followed in some detail.

Step 1: Determine the Quality Characteristic to Be Studied

In this case, any attribute which causes rejection of an end shield will be included.

Step 2: Take an Adequate Number of Samples

Data will be recorded on the inspection results for 25 successive days. These data are recorded in the appropriate section of Figure 14.17.

PRODUCT MOTOR END SHIELD_____ MONTH AUGUST_____

INSPECTION FINAL_____ CHARACTERISTIC ____ All DEFECTS____

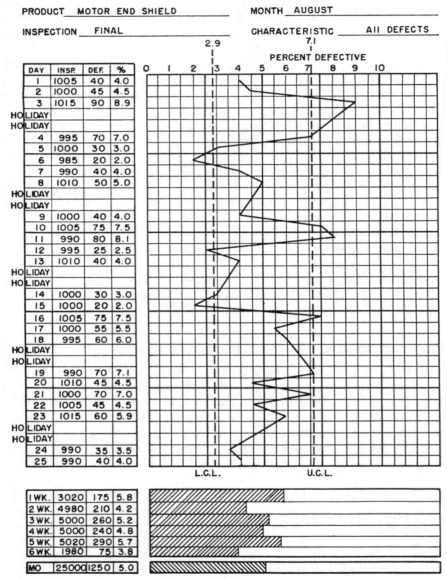

DAY	INSP.	DEF.	%
1	1005	40	4.0
2	1000	45	4.5
3	1015	90	8.9
HOLIDAY			
HOLIDAY			
4	995	70	7.0
5	1000	30	3.0
6	985	20	2.0
7	990	40	4.0
8	1010	50	5.0
HOLIDAY			
HOLIDAY			
9	1000	40	4.0
10	1005	75	7.5
11	990	80	8.1
12	995	25	2.5
13	1010	40	4.0
HOLIDAY			
HOLIDAY			
14	1000	30	3.0
15	1000	20	2.0
16	1005	75	7.5
17	1000	55	5.5
18	995	60	6.0
HOLIDAY			
HOLIDAY			
19	990	70	7.1
20	1010	45	4.5
21	1000	70	7.0
22	1005	45	4.5
23	1015	60	5.9
HOLIDAY			
HOLIDAY			
24	990	35	3.5
25	990	40	4.0

2.9 7.1

PERCENT DEFECTIVE

0 1 2 3 4 5 6 7 8 9 10

L.C.L. U.C.L.

1 WK.	3020	175	5.8
2 WK.	4980	210	4.2
3 WK.	5000	260	5.2
4 WK.	5000	240	4.8
5 WK.	5020	290	5.7
6 WK.	1980	75	3.8
MO	25000	1250	5.0

FIG. 14.17

Step 3: Compute the Average Sample Size

The total production for 25 days is 25,000 units. The average daily production is therefore 25,000/25, or 1000 units.

Step 4: Compute the Average Number of Defectives

The total number of defectives is 1250 units. The average value for daily defectives is therefore 1250/25, or 50 units.

Step 5: Compute Control Limits

Computation of control limits can be considerably simplified by the use of charts. Figures 14.18 and 14.19 show the charts that are useful for this work. Figure 14.19 differs from Figure 14.18 in that it has an expanded horizontal scale.

Use of these charts is as follows: The average number of defectives, 50, is located on the horizontal scale of Figure 14.18. Figure 14.19 is inappropriate because its horizontal scale does not extend beyond 17 average defectives. The two dashed curves marked Minimum No. of Defectives and Maximum No. of Defectives, respectively, cross the 50 line at 29 and 71 on the vertical scale of Figure 14.18. These values, 29 and 71, represent the minimum and maximum numbers of defectives that should be experienced in any day of production.

The upper and lower percent-defective control limits can now be calculated as shown in the following formulas:

$$\text{Upper control limit} = \frac{\text{maximum no. of defectives}}{\text{average sample size}} \times 100 \qquad (32)$$

$$\text{Center line} = \frac{\text{average no. of defectives}}{\text{average sample size}} \times 100$$

$$\text{Lower control limit} = \frac{\text{minimum no. of defectives}}{\text{average sample size}} \times 100 \qquad (33)$$

Recall from step 3 above that average sample size is equivalent to the average daily production of 1000 units.

Formula (32):

$$\text{Upper control limit} = \frac{\text{maximum no. of defectives}}{\text{average sample size}} \times 100$$

$$= \frac{71}{1{,}000} \times 100 = 7.1 \text{ percent}$$

$$\text{Center line} = \frac{\text{average no. of defectives}}{\text{average sample size}} \times 100$$

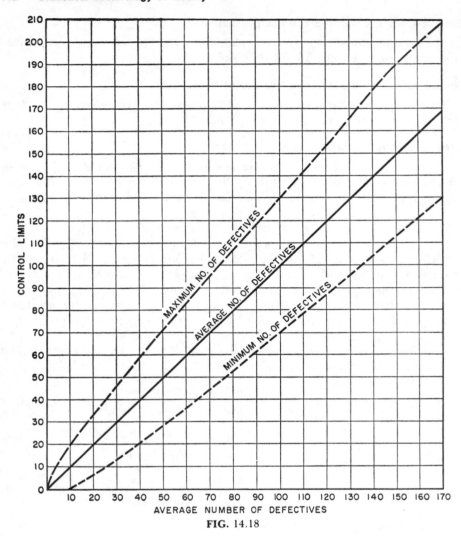

FIG. 14.18

$$= \frac{50}{1000} \times 100 = 5.0 \text{ percent}$$

Formula (33):

$$\text{Lower control limit} = \frac{\text{minimum no. of defectives}}{\text{average sample size}} \times 100$$

$$= \frac{29}{1000} \times 100 = 2.9 \text{ percent}$$

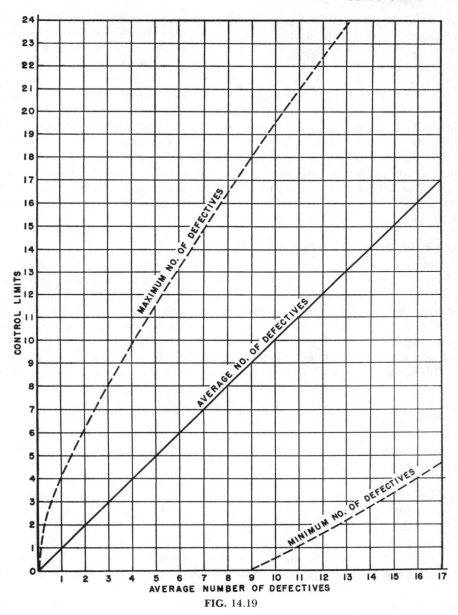

FIG. 14.19

These limits are plotted in the appropriate section of Figure 14.17.

Step 6: Analyze Results for Each Sample

Examination of Figure 14.17 shows that sample results on the third, sixth, tenth, eleventh, twelfth, fifteenth, and sixteenth days are outside the control limits. Investigation will be made of the causes of this variation. In the case of the points above the upper limits, the causes will be eliminated if possible. The causes for the points below the lower limits will be similarly identified if possible so that the reasons why quality improved on these days can be learned.

With 7 samples out of limits, it is likely that another set of 25 samples will be gathered after the appropriate process improvements have been made. New control limits will be computed, and sample results will be compared with these limits. The process of taking samples and computing limits will be repeated until the sample results show that the process is in control.

The new control limits that will be calculated should reflect the improvements that have been made in process conditions as a result of the investigation of out-of-limit samples. This sequence of computing percent-defective control limits thus serves as an effective guide to improving the process in question.

Step 7: Determine If Limits Are Satisfactory

The decision whether percent-defective control limits are economically satisfactory for use in the control of quality is based upon management judgment.

In theory, this decision should be based entirely upon economic factors because, with the careful 100 percent inspection as well as subsequent controls used in this factory, defective end shields will be screened from passing into customer use.

If the overall cost of accepting end-shield rejects, which average 5 percent and range from 2.9 to 7.1 percent, is lower than the overall cost of process improvements that would be required to reduce these rejects, then the control limits might be acceptable. If overall costs of process improvement are lower than the costs of rejects from 2.9 to 7.1 percent, then the limits might be unacceptable.

In practice, at least two factors make it difficult to make this decision based upon purely economic factors alone:

1. Particularly in shops which manufacture several products, it is sometimes very difficult to determine accurately the cost of accepting a certain percent defective for a given process or part.
2. Operator skill and interest may be much more important factors in process improvement than the much more easily evaluated costs of such factors as better machine tools or jigs and fixtures. A considerable reduction in rejections can be obtained in certain cases simply by posting the current control chart for all operators to see. In some cases, steps to improve morale may have much greater effect in reducing rejections than will investment in new equipment.

As a result, the decision whether control limits are satisfactory is based upon a combination of both the economic facts available and the past experience with the process.

In the case of the end shields, the 2.9 to 7.1 percent control limits represented a process condition unacceptable to management, and far lower limits were established as the necessary objectives. The thorough investigation of the end-shield manufacturing process that was initiated in step 6 was intensified, and some new equipment was ordered.

Although no "official" control limits were established for the process until this improvement program was completed, the 2.9 to 7.1 percent limits were used as informal gages to judge just how satisfactory the results of these improvements were. New limits were later calculated periodically as improvements were put into effect, the results of which demonstrated that this recalculation was necessary.

Step 8: Use the Limits for Control

When satisfactory control limits have finally been established for the end shields, these limits will be plotted on a form similar to that shown in Figures 14.16 and 14.17. These forms will be posted in plain view out in the shop as close as possible to the processing stations. (The percent-defective results of each day's production lots will be recorded on these charts.) Lots that show out of limits will be the signal for immediate investigation.

These control limits can also be used by the factory accountants as a basis for estimating the amount that should be applied to represent defective work in the standard costs for the end shields. The control limits may also be useful as a factual basis for setting bogeys for manufacturing-loss reports on the end shields.

As with measurements control charts, percent-defective control limits should be recalculated periodically in line with possible changes in process conditions.

14.20 Control Charts for Number of Units Defective or Nonconforming

These are some instances in go and not-go inspection where the number of defective or nonconforming units is preferred for control purposes over charts for percent or fraction. Control limits for these number-defective or number-nonconforming (np) charts can be computed for constant sample sizes as follows:

No Standard Given

$$\text{Control limits} = n\bar{p} \pm 3\sqrt{n\bar{p}\,(1 - \bar{p})} \tag{34}$$

where $\bar{p}$ = average value for fraction defective or nonconformance
$n\bar{p}$ = average value for fraction defective or nonconformance times sample size; average number defective or nonconforming

Standard Given

$$\text{Control limits} = np_0 \pm 3\sqrt{np_0(1 - p_0)} \tag{34A}$$

where p_0 = adopted standard value for fraction defective or nonconformance

Interpretation, procedures, and forms for computing these control limits are similar to those described above in connection with percent- and fraction-defective charts. p charts may easily be converted into the (np) form by changing scales and multiplying the central line and control limits by the sample size n.

14.21 Control Charts for Count Number of Defects or Nonconformities

With certain types of job-shop production, wherein go and not-go inspection is carried on, there are at least two reasons why percent or fraction control charts may prove of little value:

1. Production quantities may be too low. There may be only a few units produced every day, every week, or every month.
2. With physically large or complex products like wide-body aircraft, integrated engine systems, or turbines, some defects or nonconformities are almost always to be found at final assembly, such as bolts that must be pulled tighter, plates to be painted, or electronic systems to be coordinated. Under the conventional percent system, charts would almost always show 100 percent rejects, which would make them of little use for control of quality.

For situations of this sort, go and not-go inspection results are most effectively presented in the form of control charts for count. Thus, a complex engine might be found to have 30 nonconformities during its inspection, or an aircraft assembly might have 250 defects or nonconformities. Control limits would be expressed, therefore, by number of defects or nonconformities.

There are two types of count charts, depending upon the application:

1. The count of defects or nonconformities of a given classification observed on a single unit of product of constant size or character in successive inspections. This count is labeled c, and values of c are plotted on a chart called a c chart.
2. The *average* count or *average* number of defects or nonconformities of a given classification observed in a sample of n units of product of constant size or character in successive inspections. This average count is labeled u, where $u = c/n$, and values of u are plotted on a chart called a u chart.

c CHART

No Standard Given

$$\text{Control limits} = \bar{c} \pm 3\sqrt{\bar{c}} \qquad (35)$$

where $\bar{c}$ = average number of defects or nonconformities for n units of product

Standard Given

$$\text{Control limits} = c_0 \pm 3\sqrt{c_0} \qquad (35A)$$

where c_0 = adopted standard value for number of defects or nonconformities occurring in a unit of product

u **CHART**

No Standard Given

$$\text{Control limits} = \bar{u} \pm 3\sqrt{\frac{\bar{u}}{n}} \qquad (36)$$

where $\bar{u}$ = $(\Sigma u)/k$ for k values of u
$\quad\quad n$ = constant number of units used for each value of u

Standard Given

$$\text{Control limits} = u_0 \pm 3\sqrt{\frac{u_0}{n}} \qquad (36A)$$

where u_0 = adopted standard value

If u values are based upon unequal values of n, then

$$\bar{u} = (\Sigma c)/(\Sigma n) \quad\quad \text{and} \quad\quad \sigma_u = \sqrt{\frac{\bar{u}}{\bar{n}}} \text{ with } \bar{n} = (\Sigma n)/k$$

Likewise, $\bar{n}$ would be used in the standards given formula for control limits unless separate limits are to be computed and plotted for each unique sample size n.

14.22 Variations on Control Charts for Go and Not-Go Data

There are many variations from the types of control charts that were presented above. Typical of these variations are (1) difference in forms; (2) limits based upon specifications, including "control gaging"; and (3) precontrol. Each variation is now discussed.

1. Forms

The forms used to present go and not-go data in control chart form vary quite widely in industry from the charts shown in Figures 14.16 and 14.17. Sometimes the forms lose their graphical nature entirely, as in the case of an interesting tabulation developed by E. M. Schrock for control purposes.

This tabulation consists of listings of values for average percent and shows the minimum and maximum number of defective or nonconforming units to be expected with either varying or average lot sizes. Figure 14.20 shows one page of these tables.

It is in this area that distinctions between the control charts, as a method for controlling quality, and the sampling table, as a technique for controlling quality, begin to disappear. This matter is treated in more detail in Chapter 15.

RANGE OF REJECTS IN LOTS FROM A PROCESS HAVING A LEVEL OF 5 PERCENT DEFECTIVE

NUMBER INSPECTED	REJECTS SHOULD NOT EXCEED	FEWEST REJECTS EXPECTED
100	11	--
200	19	1
300	26	4
400	33	7
500	39	11
600	46	14
700	52	18
800	58	22
900	64	26
1000	70	30
1100	76	34
1200	82	38
1300	88	42
1400	94	46
1500	100	50
1600	106	54
1700	111	59
1800	117	63
1900	123	67
2000	129	71
2100	134	76
2200	140	80
2300	146	84
2400	152	88
2500	157	93
2600	163	97
2700	168	102
2800	174	106
2900	180	110
3000	185	115
3100	191	119
3200	196	124
3300	202	128
3400	208	132
3500	213	137
3600	219	141
3700	224	146
3800	230	150
3900	235	155
4000	241	159
4200	252	168
4400	263	177
4600	274	186
4800	285	195
5000	296	204

FIG. 14.20 From "Quality Control Tables for Attribute Inspection," E. M. Schrock. Reprinted by permission from "Quality Control and Statistical Methods," by E. M. Schrock, published by Reinhold Publishing Corporation.

2. Control limits based upon specifications, including "control gaging"

The desirability of basing control limits upon specification limits in certain cases was discussed in Sections 14.12 and 14.13. Various similar approaches have been adopted with control charts for attributes.

One example is what has been termed "control gaging." This relates to what, for many years, has been a controversial factory issue concerning the desirability of having two or more sets of specification limits for parts: one for use in factory processing and a wider set of limits for use in final inspection. This basic philosophy has been adopted as part of certain control chart installations, which have become compromises between measurements and percent control charts.

Very often, in establishing inspection stations in factory processing areas, so-called snap gages are employed. These gages have fixed limits which are set at the upper and lower specification limits for the part in question. With control gaging, these snap gages are made to a set of limits which is somewhat narrower than the actual specification limits. These control limits are established by the use of generalized formulas, which are usually a compromise between shop experience and statistical methods.

The gages must often be manufactured before the parts for which they are intended are started into actual production. As a result, the use of tools like the frequency distribution for deciding upon appropriate limits is necessarily eliminated in favor of standard tables from which the control-gage limits can be readily obtained. The basic approach is as discussed earlier in Section 14.14 with regard to charts for individual readings and the use of concepts as in Formulas (27A) and (27B).

Thus, the practice followed in control-gaging applications for sampling lots during the course of their processing is to use as the basis for control the *number* of readings in the sample which fall outside the gage limits. Thus two readings out of a sample of five might be allowed to fall out of limits. This type of procedure is extremely convenient under certain mass-production conditions.

As discussed in Section 14.14, instead of computing and plotting the average or median values for the sample, the individual readings for each unit in the sample are plotted on the control chart for averages. Suppose that these units are drawn from a sample whose average value is perilously close to the control limit. Obviously, about as many of these individual readings will ordinarily be outside the control limits as will be within these limits.

Since, with control gaging, it is these individual pieces which are being examined, it is quite possible and practical to establish gage limits at the control limits for average values and to allow the number of pieces which do not meet these gage limits to stand as an indication of the state of control of the process.

3. Precontrol

The activity of precontrol can lend itself to the use of snap gages or other methods for measuring go and not-go data. With control gaging and using the precontrol concept, the gages are made to a set of limits that is established based upon actual specification limits in accordance with procedures discussed in Sections 14.12 and 14.13. Then these gages are used to measure pieces to determine the correctness of the setup and the running portion of the operation in the following manner.

A specified number of first pieces are checked on the gage. If each piece falls within the precontrol limits, the setup is approved. Periodic checks are made on a one-piece sample during the manufacture of the parts. If the piece is within the precontrol limits, the operation is continued. However, if the one piece falls outside the precontrol limit, the next piece is checked. If the second piece falls within the precontrol limit, the operation continues. If the second piece also falls outside the limit, the operation is stopped and readjusted.

14.23 Critical, Major, Minor, and Incidental Classifications; Demerits Per Unit; Quality Score

In its most popular form, as noted in Section 14.19, some types of percent and fraction charts record totals of all types of defects or nonconformities which may be the cause for rejected units. The criticism sometimes leveled against this chart is that it considers all causes for rejection as equally bad, whether they be the simple matter of an easily replaced burred screw or basic flaws which will cause the scrapping of the entire assembly.

The effect of bulking together all types of rejects may have results in two separate areas:

1. On factory procedure for the internal control of product quality
2. On factory procedure for appraising product quality in regard to field performance

Each of these two matters is now discussed.

1. Internal-Control Procedures

When all types of rejects are bulked together in a percent or fraction chart, an out-of-control point caused merely by a quickly quelled minor epidemic of extremely inexpensive rejections may lead to unnecessary concern at the management level. On the other hand, management may be lulled into false security when it views an in-control point which includes three or four extremely expensive defects or nonconformities.

In spite of this, in many cases it remains sound practice to consider all defects as of equal weight. For one thing, handling time is one of the major product costs. It may be necessary to put fully as much rehandling time on a product with an inexpensive nonconformity as is required for a product with an expensive defect. Again, the repair cost of these expensive and inexpensive defects or nonconformities tends to balance off in the long run, permitting the consideration that all defects or nonconformities comprising the percent or fraction results may be treated as of equal weight.

In those cases where the relative seriousness of different types of defects or nonconformities does vary very widely, however, it may become desirable to weight them. Section 10.19 discussed this classification of quality characteristics of both product and process, to which these defects or nonconformities will be related.

For *product*-quality characteristics:

- A *critical* characteristic is one which threatens loss of life or property or makes the product nonfunctional if outside prescribed limits.
- A *major* characteristic is one which makes the product fail to accomplish its intended function if outside prescribed limits.
- A *minor* characteristic is one which makes the product fall short of its intended function if outside prescribed limits.
- An *incidental* characteristic is one that will have no unsatisfactory effect on customer quality.

For *process* quality characteristics:

- A *critical* characteristic is one where any significant variation from the tolerance, which may occasionally occur, will cause a significant and unacceptable average long-term nonconformity or defect rate.
- A *major* characteristic is where any measureable to significant variation from the tolerance, which may occasionally occur, will cause an unacceptable average long-term nonconformity or defect rate.
- A *minor* characteristic is one where any variation from the tolerance, which may occasionally occur, may cause a small average long-term nonconformity or defect rate.
- An *incidental* characteristic is one where any variation from the tolerance, which may occasionally occur, will have no average long-term nonconformity or defect consequences.

The comparative numerical weighting of critical, major, minor, and incidental will, of course, vary according to the individual product conditions. For example, a major defect may have twice the weight of a minor defect, or it may have 20 times its weight, depending upon relative circumstances. These weights may be used in control chart computations and will enable the chart to more accurately reflect the true economics of the process in question.

In the case of nonconformities which will be screened prior to customer receipt, these weights can be heavily determined in operations cost terms. If the true repair replacement or other relevant quality costs are known for the individual quality characteristics, the monetary operating quality costs can be used as the nonconformity weights.

2. Field Performance

With relatively complex products, different types of defects may have widely varying effects upon the performance of the product after it has reached the customer's hands. Bulking together all types of rejects in a percent-defective chart may tend to give management a false picture of the relative effect on performance of the defects shown.

As discussed in Section 10.19, defect classifications in these cases must be established according to the seriousness of the effect of various defects upon product safety and performance in use. In the case of process-quality characteristics, classifications may be established on the basis of their effect on unacceptable average long-term defect or nonconformity rates.

Comparative numerical weightings of these defects will, again, vary according to product conditions. And again, these weights can be used in control chart computations and will enable the chart to more accurately reflect an appraisal of the quality produced in the process in question.

In some instances, weighting of critical, major, minor, and incidental defects will include both internal economic and field performance appraisal factors.

Sometimes this classification procedure is carried still further by assigning demerits-per-unit weights to critical, major, minor, and incidentals. Thus, demerit weights of 100, 30, 10, and 1 might be assigned to critical, major, minor, and incidentals, respectively.

Control charts can be established based upon demerits per unit with a procedure and forms similar to those discussed above in connection with percent charts.[17]

With some products, management may require a single index of its product quality. Such a quality index or score may be obtained from use of demerit-per-unit data, as follows:

$$\text{Quality score or index} = \frac{\text{observed demerits per unit}}{\text{expected demerits per unit}}$$

This type of score may be extremely valuable in those factories where management wants a quality index in a form somewhat comparable to indices it receives on such matters as budget realization, weekly output, and wage costs. When quality costs associated with each type of nonconformity or defect are determined, then the quality index can be expressed in terms of quality-cost dollars and used as a gage against which to measure alternative courses of control and appraisal action.

14.24 Some Practical Aspects of Control Charts

A question that may have arisen in the minds of many readers during the foregoing discussions is: "In view of the effort and expense required to establish and maintain a single control chart for a single quality characteristic, how far can widespread application of control charts proceed in a factory with many parts and many processes?"

This question can be answered simply: "Control charts should be set up only in so far as it is economically desirable and physically practical to do so." Charts should be established only on important quality characteristics. They should be established only in those instances where customer quality satisfaction and costs justify close attention to the process. Control charts are simply one of many quality-control tools; any attempt which uses them indiscriminately as proof of a "well-functioning" quality-control program must be condemned.

Again, note that the foregoing discussions of methods for calculating control limits were a mixture of statistical computation and some fairly arbitrary decisions to adapt the control chart to the needs of particular situations. In factory practice, this adaptation to meet particular needs is widespread and takes many forms. For one instance, it is a policy in some shops never to plot lower control limits on those percent or fraction charts which are posted on the factory floor.

It has been found difficult to explain to the always-changing factory employees that these lower limits do *not* place a premium on a certain percentage of nonconforming or defective work. As a result, lower control limits are recorded only in the office, where they can be reviewed by interested management and the quality-control staff.

Again, as a preliminary to making decisions as to whether percent control limits are economically satisfactory, management aided by the quality-control staff may select arbitrary standard given control-limit targets for the process in question. In the experience of both management and the quality-control staff, these limits can eventually be achieved, and unless strong contrary evidence is presented, only these limits will be approved.

This practice, tempered with good judgment, is often very successful. This success is particularly notable on those many jobs where human relations factors are far more important than technological factors and where the mere selection of control-limit targets may have the psychological result of fostering quality improvements.

Moves such as these are perfectly reasonable parts of developing control chart installations for a factory. Experience seems to show that, in the long run, proponents of the control chart approach in a factory will be most successful if they concentrate upon promoting the fundamental concepts and points of view fostered by the control chart rather than upon endeavoring to push forward any particular control chart technique or form.

14.25 Summary of Formulas for Computing Go and Not-Go Control Limits

The formulas for computing control limits for charts using go and not-go data are summarized below:

No Standard Given

Percent control limits $\qquad = \bar{p} \pm 3\sqrt{\dfrac{\bar{p}(100 - \bar{p})}{n}}$ (30)

Fraction control limits $\qquad = \bar{p} \pm 3\sqrt{\dfrac{\bar{p}(1 - \bar{p})}{n}}$ (31)

Number of units control units $= n\bar{p} \pm 3\sqrt{n\bar{p}(1 - \bar{p})}$ (34)

(c) count control limits $\qquad = \bar{c} \pm 3\sqrt{\bar{c}}$ (35)

(u) count control limits $\qquad = \bar{u} \pm 3\sqrt{\bar{u}/n}$ (36)

Standard Given

Percent control limits $\qquad = p_0 \pm 3\sqrt{\dfrac{p_0(100 - p_0)}{n}}$ (30A)

Fraction control limits $\qquad = p_0 \pm 3\sqrt{\dfrac{p_0(1 - p_0)}{n}}$ (31A)

Number of units control limits $= np_0 \pm 3\sqrt{np_0(1 - p_0)}$ (34A)

(c) count control limits $\qquad = c_0 \pm 3\sqrt{c_0}$ (35A)

(u) count control limits $\qquad = u_0 \pm 3\sqrt{u_0/n}$ (36A)

Other useful formulas for particular applications of go and not-go data are

Average, $\bar{p}$: $\qquad \bar{p} = \dfrac{\Sigma c}{\Sigma n} \times 100$ (28)

Standard deviation of p: $\quad \sigma_p = \sqrt{\dfrac{\bar{p}(100 - \bar{p})}{n}}$ (29)

THE CONTROL CHART IN ACTION

14.26 Practical Applications of Control Charts

Uses of control charts were discussed in general terms in Section 14.4. It may now be of interest to depart somewhat from the general cases. Listed below are the brief discussions of five fairly specialized control chart applications to meet specific practical situations:

1. Percent nonconforming chart for control of final assemblies (see Sec. 14.27).
2. Measurements control chart for control of parts production (see Sec. 14.28).

3. Measurements control chart for control of incoming material (see Sec. 14.29).
4. Nongraphical control chart for control of screw-machine parts (see Sec. 14.30).
5. Measurements control chart to study tool wear (see Sec. 14.31).

14.27 Percent Nonconforming Chart for Electronic Measuring Equipments

Very high rejections were being experienced on preliminary subassembly of complex electronic measuring-equipment assemblies being manufactured by an eastern factory. The points at which most nonconformities were found were the intermediate inspection stations, at which more than 20 percent of all equipments submitted for inspection were being rejected. There were several attributes which led to nonconforming preliminary subassemblies, and any one of them could cause rejection at the inspection station.

To reduce the rejections, factory management undertook to develop a series of percent control charts established to show quality variations on the equipments at the intermediate inspection station. Later production and quality operations eliminated these nonconformities, but both productivity and cost depended upon improvement at intermediate inspection.

After an intensive period of effort in improving production conditions, altering engineering process parameters, changing machine tolerances, and educating operators, the figure of 20 percent average nonconformities was reduced to 7 percent. Management was presented with the control limits computed for the job at this 7 percent value for average percent—a lower limit of about 2 percent and an upper limit of about 12 percent. Past experience with similar production conditions led management to suggest experimentation with limits which would reflect only one-half of these standard 3-sigma limits.

These new limits ($\bar{p} \pm 1.5\sigma_p$) would mean that an indication of a process shift would occur more frequently when no actual process shift had taken place, but it also would result in a smaller process shift being detected sooner. This management decision was based upon such factors as the relative costs and production delays incurred when a process shift actually took place balanced against the machine adjustments when no process shift had occurred. The values used in the specialized application were 4.5 and 9.5 percent.

Figure 14.21 shows the chart for the month following management's approval of these limits for control purposes. This chart was posted right on the preliminary subassembly lines. A duplicate chart was posted in the management office. Control limits were used as a pictorial basis for judging the day-by-day job being done on the preliminary subassembly measuring-equipment production line.

Figure 14.21 was substantially duplicated from that month until the satisfactory completion of the job contract about 8 months later. The chart was a guide for several similar control charts developed for other equipment.

PRODUCT _MEASURING EQUIPMENT_____   MONTH __NOVEMBER_____

INSPECTION._FINAL_____   CHARACTERISTIC _ASSEMBLY_____

PERCENT NONCONFORMING

DATE	INSP.	NONCONF.	%
OCT.30	228	13	5.9
31	145	13	8.9
NOV. 1	186	13	7.0
2	196	13	6.6
3	144	9	6.3
4	144	12	8.3
WK.	1043	73	7.0
NOV. 6	157	14	8.9
7	-	-	-
9	172	11	6.4
10	137	8	5.8
11	132	12	9.1
WK.	598	45	7.5
NOV.13	146	13	8.9
14	141	14	9.9
15	211	19	9.0
16	167	18	10.8
17	199	18	9.0
18	148	15	10.1
WK.	1012	97	9.5
NOV20	152	13	8.6
21	141	11	7.8
22	206	15	7.3
23	193	9	4.7
24	180	10	5.6
25	198	10	5.0
WK.	1070	68	6.4
NOV.27	190	13	6.8
28	240	19	7.9
29	150	12	8.0
30	179	14	8.0
DEC. 1	180	7	4.0
2	189	12	6.5
WK.	1128	77	6.8

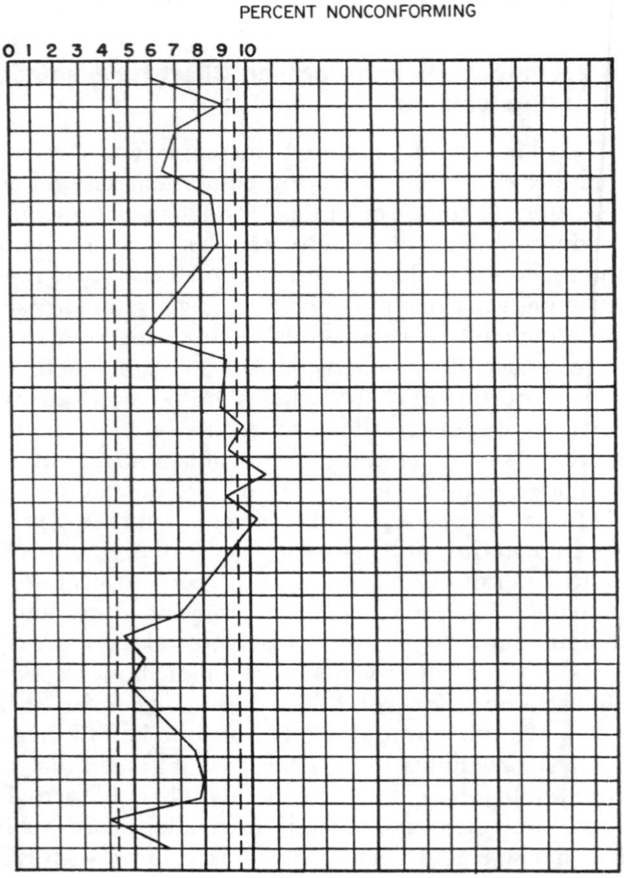

1 WK.	1043	73	7.0
2 WK.	598	45	7.5
3 WK.	1012	97	9.5
4 WK.	1070	68	6.4
5 WK.	1128	77	6.8

MO.	4851	360	7.4

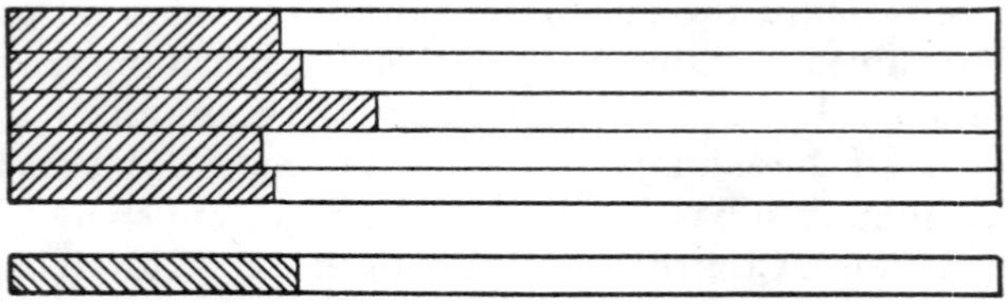

FIG. 14.21

14.28 Measurements Chart to Control Jewel-Screw Quality[18]

A measurements control chart was established to aid in controlling the quality of a jewel screw, in which the depth of drilling was critical with respect to a turned outside shoulder (see Fig. 14.22). The control limits for this chart were set up in relation to specification limits, using the procedure outlined in Section 14.13.

The first step in establishing these control limits was to make a frequency-distribution analysis on the five-spindle, automatic screw machine on which the jewel screw was produced. Each spindle was first studied separately, and then its data were combined with those of the other spindles to form the frequency distribution shown in Figure 14.22.

The process capability was found to be 1.2 mils, which compared favorably with the specification limits of 2.0 mils. This process capability was then used to determine the Q factor required for the control limit computation.

Using the nomograph (Fig. 20.25) with $p_1 = 0.3$ percent, $p_2 = 5$ percent, $n = 5$ shows the Q factor to be about 0.004 inch for a process capability of 1.2 mils. Control limits were then directly computed with this value for Q using Formulas (22A) and (22B).

Figure 14.23 shows the resulting measurements control chart, with these limits plotted. The procedure for using this chart for control purposes was established as follows: A sample size of five jewel screws per hour (one per

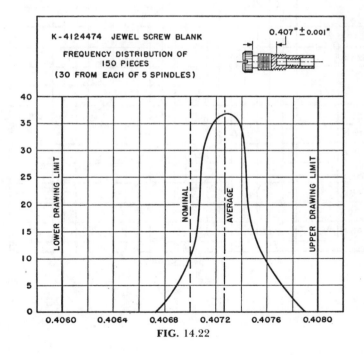

FIG. 14.22

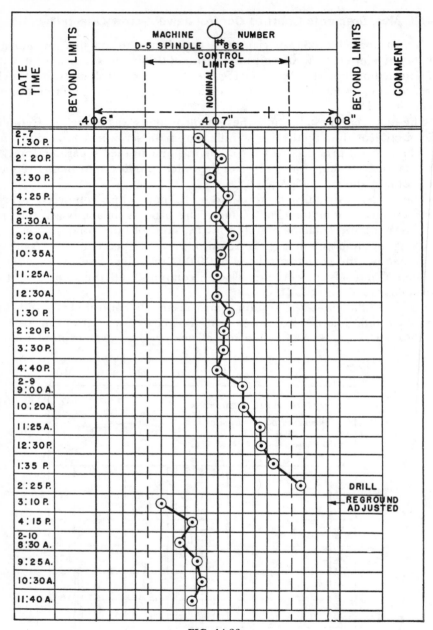

FIG. 14.23

spindle) was selected, with the average reading for each sample recorded on the chart (Fig. 14.23).

14.29 Measurements Chart for Control of Incoming Material[19]

An effective procedure for control of incoming sheet steel by measurements control charts was carried on by the punch-press section of a large factory.

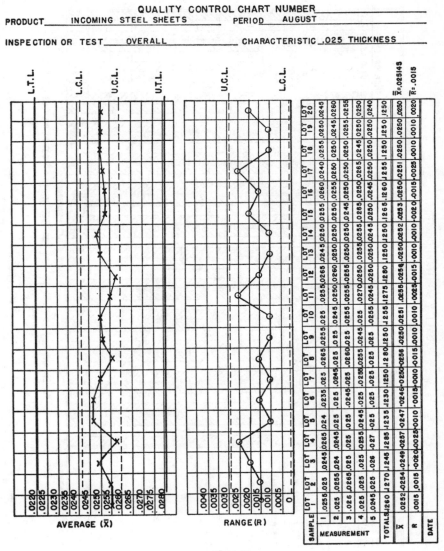

FIG. 14.24

Control limits were calculated for the average and the range of the sheet steel. Each lot of steel was sampled when it was received from the vendor, and the sample results were compared with the resulting control limits.

Previous difficulties that had been experienced because of the periodic acceptance of unsatisfactory lots of steel were eliminated by the use of this chart. Figure 14.24 shows one of the typical control charts used in this installation.

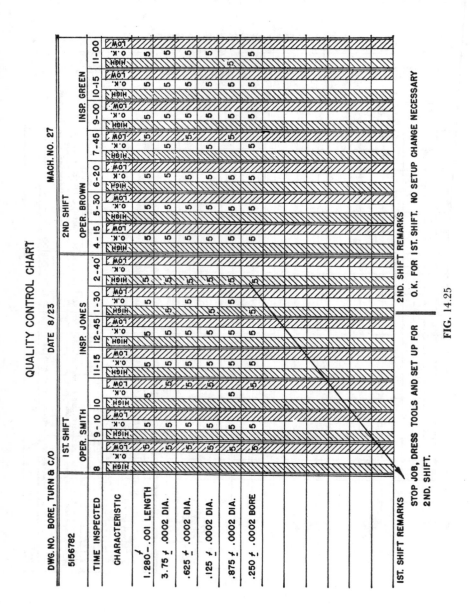

FIG. 14.25

14.30 A Nongraphical Control Chart for Screw-Machine Parts[20]

Figure 14.25 shows a nongraphical type of control chart that was used effectively in a screw-machine factory. This chart was used in connection with patrol inspection. The results of each machine check by the operator and patrol inspector were recorded on the chart, which was posted right at the machine.

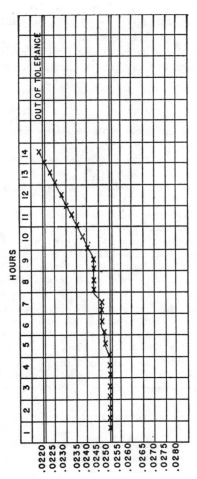

QUALITY CONTROL CHART NUMBER _____

PRODUCT PRO. & BLANK _____ PERIOD 8/28/ _____

INSPECTION OR TEST_____ CHARACTERISTIC .025 ± .003 HOLE

FIG. 14.26

During the period of its application, the chart resulted in a considerable reduction in parts rejects. Its extreme simplicity was very useful on the shop floor because only High, O.K., or Low classifications had to be checked by the inspector and machine operator.

The sensitivity of such a chart is limited in detecting small changes in the average. It is primarily effective in detecting operations with the process shifts capable of producing large percent nonconformances.

14.31 Measurements Control Chart to Study Tool Wear[21]

Figure 14.26 illustrates how a measurements control chart may effectively picture tool wear. The chart was used in a machine shop with valuable results.

This control chart for averages was established to study tool wear on a pierce and blank punch-press operation. It showed data that not only were useful for patrol inspection purposes but were of great value to tool and gage personnel for their future designs of pierce blank and punch equipment.

More detail about practical application of the control chart as a quality-control tool is in Part 6, "Applying Total Quality Control in the Company."

Notes

[1] The statistical control chart literature might refer to the causes of this type of variation as *unassignable* or *chance* causes.

[2] The statistical control chart literature might refer to the causes of this type of variation as *assignable*.

[3] See Sec. 20.18 for a discussion of how the scrap can be minimized when such a condition is present.

[4] Control charts continue to be developed for new applications as well as for particular conditions, such as cyclic data control and multivariate or multicharacteristic control. For a discussion, see R. A. Freund, "A Reconsideration of the Variable Control Chart," *Industrial Quality Control,* vol XVI, no. 11, 1960; Eric E. Johnson and Richard W. Counts, "Cyclic Data Control Charts," *Journal of Quality Technology,* vol. 11, no. 1, January 1979, pp. 1–12; and Isaac N. Gibra, "Recent Developments in Control Chart Techniques," *Journal of Quality Technology,* vol. 7, no. 4, October 1975, pp. 183–192.

[5] It is assumed that the general shape of the frequency distribution does not vary significantly. Moreover, experimentation shows that typically encountered differences in these shapes do not very much affect calculated values for sample sizes up to $n = 10$. For example, see Irving M. Burr, *Statistical Quality Control Methods,* Marcel Dekker, Inc., New York, 1976, p. 105.

[6] The use of the 3-sigma value was basically established in the original work of Dr. Shewhart. His justification was primarily empirical and pragmatic. However, there are also valid statistical foundations for this. See, for the classic work, W. A. Shewhart, *Economic Control of Quality of Manufactured Product,* D. Van Nostrand Company, Inc., New York, 1931.

[7] The reader interested in the development of these control chart constants may wish to review Burr, op. cit., pp. 97–101.

[8] In certain types of production situations where normality of data may not be present, errors can result from data analysis. In these instances see R. A. Johnson and M. Bagshaw, "The Effect of Serial Correlation on the Performance of Cusum Tests," *Technometrics,* vol. 16, no. 1, February 1974 and vol. 17, no. 1, February 1975; A. P. Stamboulis, "First Order Autoregressive Model

Applied to Quality Control," New York University memorandum, 1971; van Dobben de Bruyn, *Cumulative Sum Tests: Theory and Practice,* Hafner, New York, 1968; and Athanasios V. Vasilopoulos and A. P. Stamboulis, "Modification of Control Chart Limits in the Presence of Data Correlation," *Journal of Quality Technology,* vol. 10, no. 1, January 1978.

[9]Decisions of this sort must of course be based upon the circumstances peculiar to individual cases. Is the greater accuracy that would be gained by repeating the sampling procedure and "screening out" unrepresentative samples worth the additional time and effort that would be required? For further discussion of some economic factors, see A. J. Duncan, "The Economic Design of $\overline{X}$-Charts When There Is a Multiplicity of Assignable Causes," *Journal of the American Statistical Association,* vol. 66, no. 333, March 1971, pp. 107–121; Douglas C. Montgomery, "The Economic Design of Control Charts: A Review and Literature," *Journal of Quality Technology,* vol. 12, no. 2, April 1980, pp. 75–87; and W. K. Chiu and G. B. Wetherill, "A Simplified Scheme for the Economic Design of $\overline{X}$-Charts," *Journal of Quality Technology,* vol. 6, no. 2, April 1974, pp. 63–69.

[10]For a discussion, see Elaine M. Rainey, "Warning Limits for Shewhart Control Charts," *Quality Progress,* vol. XIII, no. 6, June 1980, pp. 34–36.

[11]Section 20.18 discusses the use of process capability studies.

[12]For a further discussion, see Raymond F. Woods, "Effective Economic Quality Through the Use of Acceptance Control Charts," *Journal of Quality Technology,* vol. 8, no. 2, April 1976, pp. 81–85.

[13]Figures 14.14 and 14.15 are after Figs. 1 and 2 of "Definitions, Symbols, Formulas and Tables for Control Charts," *ANSI/ASQC A1-1978,* p. 19, American Society for Quality Control, Milwaukee, Wisconsin.

[14]For a further discussion of this form of control chart, see Burr, op. cit., pp. 157–160.

[15]For a further discussion, see N. L. Johnson and F. C. Leone, *Statistics and Experimental Design in Engineering and the Physical Sciences,* vol. I, John Wiley & Sons, Inc., New York, 1964; A. J. Duncan, *Quality Control and Industrial Statistics,* 3d ed., Richard D. Irwin, Inc., Homewood, Ill., 1965; also A. F. Bissel, "Cusum Techniques for Quality Control," *Journal of the Royal Statistical Society,* ser. C, vol. 18, no. 1, 1969, pp. 1–30.

[16]An important contribution to this improvement in the precision of terminology is "Definitions, Symbols, Formulas and Tables for Control Charts," *ANSI/ASQC A1-1978,* American Society for Quality Control, Milwaukee, Wisconsin. This document was prepared by the following Writing Committee: Richard A. Freund, Chairman; Thomas W. Calvin, John W. Foster, John D. Hromi, J. Stuart Hunter, Norman L. Johnson, Jack V. Lavery, William M. Mead, Harrison M. Wadsworth, Jr. Several definitions in this chapter and book are in accordance with this document.

[17]For the classic discussion of such a control chart, see H. F. Dodge, "A Method of Rating Manufactured Product," *Bell System Technical Journal,* vol. 7, April 1928, pp. 350–358.

[18]From an unpublished paper by M. D. Benedict, Boston, Mass.

[19]From an analysis made by A. L. Fuller, Schenectady, N.Y.

[20]From a chart developed by N. G. Wickstrom, F. Helms, and J. Boyd, Schenectady, N.Y.

[21]From a study by A. L. Fuller, Schenectady, N.Y.

CHAPTER 15
Sampling Tables

Every industrial plant purchases some of its raw materials and component parts from outside sources. The vendors may be other companies or other plants of the same company. In the case of some large plants, one division of a plant may consider the output of another division of the plant an outside source.

Ensuring that these outside materials are of satisfactory quality has always been a major factory problem. Some of the approaches used to obtain this assurance have been 100 percent inspection, sampling of lots on a fairly arbitrary basis popularly termed *"spot checking,"* accepting from vendors certificates of test and inspection in lieu of an examination of the lot, and sometimes no inspection at all until production difficulties with the material call for it.

A more effective approach to this problem involves the use of statistical acceptance sampling tables. These tables have replaced in most instances all other approaches as the core of control of the acceptance of incoming materials and parts.

The tables also enjoy wide usage in the final inspections or tests made to assure that shipments to customers are of desired quality. Those government services which maintain inspection forces in industrial plants also use these tables as their basis for accepting lots of parts and assemblies that have been produced for them.

A somewhat different and equally important need for effective sampling tables relates to the control of parts and assemblies while they are being processed within the factory. Periodic examination of these parts by the so-called patrol, or roving, floor inspectors has too often been guided by hit-or-miss sampling procedures.

Statistical process-control sampling tables have been developed to meet this need. These tables have, indeed, been found very useful in many instances where application of the control chart cannot be made effectively.

This chapter surveys both acceptance sampling and process-control sampling tables.

THE CONCEPT OF ACCEPTANCE SAMPLING TABLES

15.1 Acceptance Sampling

Webster defines a sample as "a part . . . shown as evidence of the quality of the whole." From the discussion in Chapters 13 and 14, it is clear that samples and sampling methods are keystones of statistics as used in quality control. As a definition:

> Acceptance sampling is sampling inspection in which decisions are made to accept or not accept product or service; also the methodology that deals with procedures by which decisions to accept or not accept are based upon the results of the inspection of samples.

A statistical sampling table is another adaptation of the probability principles that were discussed in Chapters 13 and 14. It is possible to use "a part as evidence of the quality of the whole" for a simple reason. The variation that is inevitable for manufactured units usually conforms to a certain basic pattern for units that have come from the same manufacturing source. To determine this pattern, it may not be necessary to examine all units that have come from that source; the pattern may be sufficiently well-established after examination of only a *certain number* of units—in other words, by sampling. Statistical sampling tables consist of a series of these sampling schedules, each to serve somewhat different inspection objectives.

Sampling may be conducted on a go and not-go (or attributes) basis, that is, determining whether the units in the sample conform to specification requirements. Examination of the samples may also be conducted on a measurements (or variables) basis, that is, taking actual readings on the units in the sample.

An acceptance sampling plan may be defined as

> A specific plan that states the sample size or sizes to be used and the associated acceptance and nonacceptance criteria.

The first portion of the following discussion below is devoted to go and not-go acceptance. Since the majority of acceptance inspection is carried out on this basis, the usual type of acceptance sampling table is designed for go and not-go data. The second portion—Sections 15.20 to 15.22—is a treatment of measurements or variables sampling.

15.2 Why Sample for Acceptance?

When acceptance of incoming materials and parts is based upon inspection at the purchaser's factory, either 100 percent or sampling inspection can be used. Of these two methods, 100 percent inspection always has this clear-cut advantage over sampling: Only through thorough examination of each part in a lot—not through sampling—can complete assurance be obtained that all defective or nonconforming parts or materials have been removed from that lot.

Yet there are several features of 100 percent inspection which are undesirable as compared with effective sampling carried out on a modern statistical basis. Six of these undesirable aspects of 100 percent inspection are:

1. *It is costly.* Every part must be checked individually.
2. *It may lead to false assurance about the completeness of the inspection job.* The simple statement "100 percent inspection required" is often considered sufficient information to call for a complete and rigorous inspection job. 100 percent inspection is seldom, if ever, complete inspection of *all* the characteristics of a part; it is examination of only certain characteristics. The statement "100 percent inspection required" may leave the selection of the characteristics to be examined in the hands of individuals not at all familiar with those characteristics which are critical and important.
3. *It actually involves sorting.* In essence, 100 percent inspection means sorting bad parts from good. This is a postmortem procedure, which may be foreign to the preventive approach of total quality control. Under many types of manufacturing conditions, 100 percent sorting should be a last resort for use when some control procedure has broken down rather than a standard element of factory routine.
4. *It may result in accepting some nonconforming or defective material.* A number of independent checks on the reliability of 100 percent inspection in sorting out all bad parts from the good have cast considerable doubt upon its complete effectiveness in every instance. Where the percent nonconforming or defective in lots submitted is low, the monotony of repetitive inspection operations may result in the automatic acceptance of a number of defective parts. Where the percent nonconforming or defective is high, carelessness or lack of skill in the use of measuring equipments may result in the acceptance of large numbers of nonconforming or defective parts.
5. *It may result in not accepting some satisfactory material.* Some 100 percent inspection operators feel that they are not doing an acceptable job in the eyes of their supervisors unless they do not accept some parts. This sometimes results in the hypercritical interpretation of specifications and in the nonacceptance of satisfactory material.
6. *It may be impractical.* In cases where destructive testing is required, 100 percent checking is of course impossible.

In contrast to these liabilities of 100 percent inspection, reliable sampling procedures may be relatively inexpensive. If conditions permit sampling to be done, cost considerations may make it expedient to allow a certain predetermined percentage of nonconforming parts to remain in a lot until that assembly point is reached where they may be removed by production operators who find that the parts do not fit properly in the assembly.

Sampling may result in a considerable reduction in inspection monotony. The question of whether a lot will be accepted, based upon samples drawn from it, may become a matter of considerable interest for inspection operators.

Under many circumstances, sampling may have an effectiveness comparable to or greater than that of well-operating 100 percent inspection. Also, the instruction "sampling required" does not carry with it the impression of automatic accuracy which sometimes accompanies the instruction "100 percent inspection required." As a result, sampling usually forces the specification of those characteristics which *are* critical and those dimensional tolerances which *must* be maintained.

Obviously, in the case of destructive testing, only sampling is possible. Sampling procedures that have been developed for this destructive testing have achieved great effectiveness and success.

Sampling often lends itself to more efficient administration of the inspection force than does 100 percent inspection. The reduction in work load that may be permitted by substitution of sampling inspection for 100 percent examination may allow additional time for wider inspection coverage and for more accurate record keeping. Since sampling inspection may become somewhat of a game to inspection operators, this record keeping may develop into "keeping score" rather than being regarded as monotonous drudgery.

15.3 Early Forms of Acceptance Sampling

Many of these advantages of sampling over 100 percent inspection have been long recognized. As a result, sampling was carried on in industry long before its features were publicized by the current attention to the statistical sampling tables.

Many of these sampling procedures have been relatively crude and makeshift and have not resulted in the advantages over 100 percent inspection that were described in Section 15.2. "Spot checking" is the phrase usually applied to these hit-or-miss procedures.

In some plants, spot checking has meant a well-regulated and well-defined procedure for examining a certain percentage of the pieces in all incoming lots. In other plants, it has meant the occasional examination of a few pieces from those incoming shipment boxes which were easiest to reach or pry open. In still other plants, spot checking has resolved, in the final analysis, into a rough examination to determine if the amount of material in the lot corresponds to the amount billed by the vendor.

When, owing to these latter practices, bad material causes quality troubles on the production lines, the amount of inspection may be temporarily increased. This increase in inspection merely constitutes a postmortem step and does not help prevent the production of defective work.

The number of parts or the amount of material to be inspected and the size of the lot to be sampled are generally determined in arbitrary fashion under spot-check procedures. Occasionally, too many parts are checked—which is costly. Sometimes, too few parts are examined—which may permit defective materials to get into the production line.

Generally, little attention is paid to the risk of sampling variation (see Sec. 13.18) associated with the particular spot-check procedure in use. Nor is there any real understanding as to the quality "target" that is being aimed at.

Another feature of the usual spot check is its lack of agreed-upon acceptance or nonacceptance procedure. If a number of defective or nonconforming pieces are found, there is often no definitely specified system as to how to dispose of the lot.

One week, the spot check of a lot of incoming material may show five nonconforming or defective pieces, and the lot may not be accepted. A few weeks later, another spot check on similar material may show six nonconforming or defective pieces, and the lot may be passed on to the manufacturing floor. Such inconsistencies in procedure have as their inevitable result friction between vendor and customer, spotty quality of parts and materials released to the manufacturing floor, and strained feelings between the incoming-material inspectors and the manufacturing supervisors.

15.4 A Typical Spot-Check Procedure

Spot checking is often carried out with the procedure that a certain percentage of the pieces in a lot are examined. It is interesting to glance at the effectiveness of such a typical spot-check program. As described in a factory inspection instruction, the plan is presented, as follows: "Ten percent of the parts in all lots submitted for inspection will be examined on a go and not-go basis. Only those lots represented by samples containing no defectives or nonconformances will be accepted."

At first glance, the acceptance standard of this plan seems to be one which will afford a high degree of protection. Let us see, therefore, just how effective the plan actually is.[1]

Instead of using in our analysis manufactured parts or raw materials as the contents of the lots submitted for inspection, let us use a 52-card poker deck from which two deuces are removed. Lot size is therefore 50 cards.

Let us assume that the two one-eyed jacks in the deck are nonconformances or defectives. There will therefore be $2/50$, or 4 percent, nonconformances or defectives in the lot.

A 10 percent sample from this lot is five cards. The sample from the lot is therefore the equivalent of a five-card poker hand.

To determine the effectiveness of this spot-check plan, suppose that the following procedure is followed: A five-card poker hand is dealt from the deck of cards. The hand is examined to see if it contains a one-eyed jack. The five cards are then returned to the deck, which is shuffled. This procedure is repeated 19 times to represent a 10 percent spot check on 20 successive lots of 50 cards.

Students in quality-control training classes made this sort of check many times. Sometimes they found a one-eyed jack appearing in 3 hands out of 20, sometimes in 5 hands out of 20, sometimes in 4 hands out of 20. They found that under this plan, from 75 to 85 percent of the lots submitted for inspection will be accepted containing 4 percent nonconformances or defectives.

The probability calculation for the 10 percent spot check under these conditions shows that the most likely situation is that the plan accepts 80 percent of the lots submitted which are 4 percent nonconforming or defective. In the most usual case, 16 poker hands out of 20 will contain no one-eyed jacks—a solution that has not surprised poker players in the quality-control training classes.

Figure 15.1 shows a curve plotted from one of the probability calculations analyzing this sampling plan. Sample size (number of cards in the hand dealt) is plotted on the horizontal axis; the probability of accepting a lot with 4 percent defectives or nonconformances is plotted on the vertical axis.

It may be seen from Figure 15.1 that a sample size or "hand" of 34 cards would be required if it were desired, for example, to risk passing decks of cards with 4 percent nonconformances or defectives 10 percent of the time. This

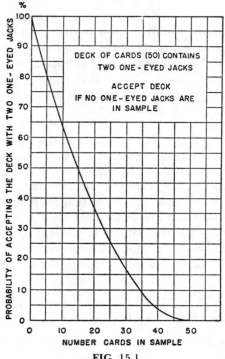

FIG. 15.1

sample size of 34 is in startling contrast to the 5-card sample size called for by the 10 percent spot check.

There are several other features of this spot-check plan which are undesirable. There is no agreed-upon quality target at which the plan aims. Is it satisfactory to pass lots which are 4 percent defective or nonconforming? If so, what risk can be taken that an occasional lot with more than 4 percent defectives or nonconformances will be passed? If not, what quality target should be established? The sampling plan has no answer for these questions.

The plan establishes no organized procedure for the disposition of decks of cards, samples of which contain defectives or nonconformances. It merely specifies that lots of which samples contain *no* defectives or nonconformances will be accepted. It states nothing about the plan of action when one or more defectives or nonconformances are found in a sample. Should the lot from which the samples are drawn not be accepted? Should another sample be drawn from the lot? Should the lot be 100 percent inspected? Again, the plan has no answers for important questions.

There is an additional element in this 10 percent spot check which makes it even more unsatisfactory in actual practice than the limitations described above would indicate. This element is that the protection afforded by the spot check varies with the size of the lots submitted. As a result, the plan may treacherously imply a quality assurance that it cannot fulfill.

Let us assume that the same sampling plan as described above is still in use but that now the lots submitted for inspection contain 1000 rather than 50 units. Analysis of the protection offered by the sampling plan under these conditions results in a far different picture from that shown by the analysis with a 50-unit sample size. Instead of the plan resulting in the acceptance of 80 percent of the lots submitted which contain 4 percent nonconformances or defectives, the 10 percent spot check now will result in acceptance of only 3 to 4 percent of the lots submitted.

Under typical factory conditions, it is inevitable that identical parts and materials will be received in lots of varying size. The span of the size of these lots will cover at least the range from 50 to 1000 units.

The quality target required by the manufacturing floor for this material, however, will obviously be independent of the size of the lots in which material is shipped by the vendor. Yet the protection afforded by the 10 percent spot check is very dependent upon lot size: The larger the lot size, the greater the protection. The reason for this situation was discussed in Section 13.19, namely, that the effectiveness of a sample depends chiefly upon its size rather than upon the ratio of the size of the sample to the size of the lot from which it was drawn.

15.5 Features of Statistical Sampling Tables

It is quite clear that the potential benefits of sampling as compared with 100 percent inspection are not to be realized from crude spot-check procedures of the sort described above. Industry's need for more effective sampling methods than these has been met by the development of modern statistical acceptance sampling tables.

In contrast to the unreliability and ambiguity of spot checking, modern statistical sampling procedures are reliable and quite specific. They are based upon well-defined probability principles, which have been translated into charts and formulas that are available for use in the construction of individual sampling plans to meet the needs of particular factory conditions.

One of the most important steps in the growth of statistical sampling has been the consolidation of certain of these individual plans into the form of acceptance sampling tables. Figure 15.2 shows such a table.[2]

In contrast to the crude spot-check plans, these tables represent disciplined structures for the performance of sampling in respect to the reliability of the procedures, the handling of the lots, and the costs that are involved. This discipline of acceptance sampling is represented in five definite features of the tables:

1. Specification of sampling data
2. Protection afforded
3. Terminology
4. Disposal procedure
5. Cost required

Each is now discussed.

Specification of Sampling Data

This is the size of samples to be selected from a given range of lot sizes, the conditions under which the samples are to be selected, and the conditions under which a lot will be accepted or not accepted.

Sample size, as shown in the tables, often is a compromise. The sample must be large enough so that it represents the quality of the lot from which it is drawn. This is a statistical question. The sample size, in some tables, may also take minimum inspection cost into account. This is an economic question, and sample size as well as other data in acceptance tables usually grow out of a balance between economics and "pure" statistics.

With some product units on which sampling can be accomplished, only a very small percent of nonconforming units may be allowed to pass on to the production line, for removal there. With other articles—nuts and bolts perhaps—higher percentages of nonconforming articles may be passed for removal on the production line. Thus, a series of sampling schedules with different percent-defective or percent-nonconforming values to meet varying conditions are provided in these tables.

Also established as part of the data is the quality index that is the common factor among the various sampling schedules of a particular sampling table. These indices are usually expressed as values for percent defective or percent

ACCEPTABLE QUALITY LEVELS (NORMAL INSPECTION)

LOT SIZE	SAMPLE SIZE	0.010		0.015		0.025		0.040		0.065		0.10		0.15		0.25		0.40		0.65		1.0		1.5		2.5		4.0		6.5		10	
		Ac	Re	Ac	Re	Ac	Re	Ac	Re	Ac	Re	Ac	Re	Ac	Re	Ac	Re	Ac	Re	Ac	Re	Ac	Re	Ac	Re	Ac	Re	Ac	Re	Ac	Re	Ac	Re
2-8	2	↓		↓		↓		↓		↓		↓		↓		↓		↓		↓		↓		↓		↓		↓		0	1	1	2
9-15	3	↓		↓		↓		↓		↓		↓		↓		↓		↓		↓		↓		↓		↓		0	1	1	2	2	3
16-25	5	↓		↓		↓		↓		↓		↓		↓		↓		↓		↓		↓		↓		0	1	1	2	2	3	3	4
26-50	8	↓		↓		↓		↓		↓		↓		↓		↓		↓		↓		↓		0	1	1	2	2	3	3	4	5	6
51-90	13	↓		↓		↓		↓		↓		↓		↓		↓		↓		↓		0	1	1	2	2	3	3	4	5	6	7	8
91-150	20	↓		↓		↓		↓		↓		↓		↓		↓		↓		0	1	1	2	2	3	3	4	5	6	7	8	10	11
151-280	32	↓		↓		↓		↓		↓		↓		↓		↓		0	1	1	2	2	3	3	4	5	6	7	8	10	11	14	15
281-500	50	↓		↓		↓		↓		↓		↓		↓		0	1	1	2	2	3	3	4	5	6	7	8	10	11	14	15	21	22
501-1200	80	↓		↓		↓		↓		↓		↓		0	1	1	2	2	3	3	4	5	6	7	8	10	11	14	15	21	22	↑	
1201-3200	125	↓		↓		↓		↓		↓		0	1	1	2	2	3	3	4	5	6	7	8	10	11	14	15	21	22	↑		↑	
3201-10000	200	↓		↓		↓		↓		0	1	1	2	2	3	3	4	5	6	7	8	10	11	14	15	21	22	↑		↑		↑	
10001-35000	315	↓		↓		↓		0	1	1	2	2	3	3	4	5	6	7	8	10	11	14	15	21	22	↑		↑		↑		↑	
35001-150000	500	↓		↓		0	1	1	2	2	3	3	4	5	6	7	8	10	11	14	15	21	22	↑		↑		↑		↑		↑	
150001-500000	800	↓		0	1	1	2	2	3	3	4	5	6	7	8	10	11	14	15	21	22	↑		↑		↑		↑		↑		↑	
500000 & over	1250	0	1	1	2	2	3	3	4	5	6	7	8	10	11	14	15	21	22	↑		↑		↑		↑		↑		↑		↑	

NOTES:

↓ = Use first sampling plan below arrow. If sample size equals or exceeds lot or batch size, do 100 percent inspection.

↑ = Use first sampling plan above arrow.

Ac = Acceptance number.

Re = Rejection number.

FIG. 15.2 Table is a modification of Table II-A of MIL-STD-105D in that inspection level II is used and corresponding lot sizes are incorporated directly into the body of the table.

nonconforming. Different sampling plans express these quality indices in different forms, among them being acceptable quality level (AQL), average outgoing quality limit (AOQL), and limiting quality level (LQL). Each quality index is designed to serve a somewhat different purpose, as is discussed in Section 15.7.

Protection Afforded

This is the element of risk that the sampling schedules in a given table will reject good lots or accept bad ones.

The very fact that sampling is done brings in such typical risks as (1) accepting an unsatisfactory lot as satisfactory and (2) not accepting a satisfactory lot as unsatisfactory.

Condition 1 will be of concern in a case such as that of a factory accepting lots based upon a given acceptance sampling table, because unacceptable material may thereby be released to its manufacturing floor. The term "consumer's risk" describes this characteristic of a sampling table.

The usual technical definition for consumer's risk is similar to the following: Consumer's risk is the probability, for a given sampling plan, that a lot will be accepted which has a designated numerical value which it is seldom desired to accept. This designated value is generally the limiting quality level (LQL) for the plan. Consumer's risk is expressed on a percentage basis: Thus a given sampling table may have a 10 percent consumer's risk.

Consumer's risk in technical sampling terms is designated as the β risk (beta risk) of the sampling plan.

Condition 2 will be of concern to the factory shipping the articles because the purchaser factory may return as unacceptable satisfactory material which has been rejected under the terms of the sampling table. The term "producer's risk" describes this characteristic of a sampling table.

The usual technical definition for producer's risk is similar to the following: Producer's risk is the probability, for a given sampling plan, that a lot will not be accepted, the quality of which has a designated numerical value representing a level which it is generally desired to accept. This designated value is generally the AQL for the plan. Producer's risk is expressed on a percentage basis: Thus a given sampling table may have a 5 percent producer's risk.

Producer's risk in technical sampling terms is designated as the α risk (alpha risk) of the sampling plan.

Terminology

As discussed in Section 9.20, there has been considerable emphasis in recent years on making quality terminology more precise. The area of sampling has particularly benefited from this emphasis.[3]

As also discussed in an identical way in Section 14.16 in connection with control charts, what has been termed "units that do not meet requirements" in the above definitions in this section—designated as "variant units" in technical sampling terms—are generally expressed in one or another of two terms in specific sampling plans:

Nonconforming unit, which may be defined as

> A unit or service containing at least one departure of a quality characteristic from its intended level or state that occurs with a severity sufficient to cause an associated product or service to not meet a specification requirement.

Defective unit, which may be defined as

> A unit of product or service containing either at least one departure of a quality characteristic from its intended level or state that occurs with a severity sufficient to cause an associated product or service to not satisfy intended normal, or reasonably foreseeable, usage requirements; or having several imperfections that in combination cause the unit to fail to satisfy intended normal, or reasonably foreseeable, usage requirements.

The basic difference is that *defective unit*—and the corresponding term *defect* —is a term related to sampling plans oriented to evaluation of units with regard to customer usage and that *nonconforming unit*—and the corresponding terms *nonconformity* and *nonconformance*—is a term related to sampling plans oriented to evaluation of units with regard to conformance to specifications.

In some sampling situations—such as where specification requirements are equivalent with customer-usage requirements—the two terms coincide. Also, some customer contractual requirements may specify that any units deviating from the specification requirements are to be considered defective.

In many other sampling situations, the specification requirement may be internally established within the plant or company and deliberately set tighter than the customer requirements—thus making nonconforming unit the more appropriate sampling term. It has been stated that the most commonly used type of variant for acceptance sampling purposes where the question of acceptability hinges on conformance to tolerance limits is likely to be a nonconforming unit.[4]

Many of the widely used sampling tables were developed with use of *defective* and *percent defective* as the basic terminology. Certain recently developed sampling tables have used *nonconformance* and percent *nonconforming* as the basic terminology (Sec. 15.23).

Each plant and company will make its own determination as to which of these terms most precisely describes the "units that do meet requirements"—or "variant units"—with regard to its use of sampling tables. For clarity, this chapter uses, for each sampling table and example discussed, the terminology prescribed by the table itself and by the plant and company referenced in the example.

Disposal Procedure

This is a set of rules that states what is to be done with the lots after sampling has been completed. Thus, a sampling table may contain the following information: "If the number of nonconforming units does not exceed the number specified in the table, accept the lot. Otherwise, reject or 100 percent inspect the balance of the lot."

Cost Required

This is average inspection cost required to accept or reject a lot. Some sampling tables, Dodge-Romig a particular case in point, are established to permit the use of the minimum amount of inspection necessary to hit a given quality target with a certain consumer's risk or producer's risk. Other sampling tables are established merely to afford a given degree of protection without necessarily providing the minimum inspection cost.

A sampling table will not of course specify its inspection cost in dollars and cents. When it is based upon providing minimum inspection, it will merely specify the minimum number of units that must be inspected or tested for a given set of conditions. The translation of the sampling schedules into cost figures is, however, an important feature of the use of sampling tables and is discussed later in the chapter.

15.6 Defining the Statistical Sampling Table

Statistical sampling tables therefore have the purpose of representing the probable quality relationships (usually expressed in percentage terms) of the lot or lots to the samples properly selected from that lot or lots.

As a definition, an *acceptance sampling table* or *scheme* may be defined as

> A specific set of procedures which usually consists of acceptance sampling plans in which lot sizes, sample sizes, and acceptance criteria, or the amount of 100 percent inspection and sampling, are related.

These typically also may contain rules for switching from one plan to another.

The effective sampling table not only must accurately represent the quality of the lot being sampled but also must specify the amount of risk that this representation may be either too high or too low. The number of calculations required to prepare these tables and the necessity for understanding the limitations of these calculations has made the development of sampling tables largely the province of the trained statistician. Yet the fundamentals upon which these calculations are based are quite simple and can be readily understood by all interested in this phase of statistical methods.

Modern sampling tables can be constructed for an almost unlimited variety of situations. The plans may be designed for any degree of accuracy, but they generally represent a balance between this accuracy and inspection cost.

In the final development of a particular table, practical production circumstances may be of much more importance than theoretical statistical factors. The attitudes of factory personnel and the pressure of everyday factory conditions may make for circumstances not anticipated during the mathematical preparation of the tables. As a result, the trained industrial statistician knows that the objective in preparing a sampling table is not that of constructing a plan which is a mathematician's joy. It is providing a useful tool to enable a factory to effectively judge its materials and parts—which inevitably involves a table in an easy-to-administer form.

A particular factory may have consolidated in a single card a sampling table that meets all its varying conditions of differing lot size and varying desired quality standards. In developing such a table, certain features of accuracy may have been sacrificed and certain "average values" used—procedures which could be readily criticized on a purely statistical basis. Yet such a table may be far more satisfactory for the use of the factory than would be a number of individual sampling plans which are statistically somewhat more accurate than the table but far more difficult for production personnel to use and be willing to understand.

15.7 Types of Statistical Sampling Tables

A typical procedure in the construction of a statistical sampling table can be simply expressed: First, it is to determine the probability of accepting lots containing various percents nonconforming when acceptance is based upon lot size (N) from which samples (n) are drawn containing (c) or less nonconformities. (c) is designated as the acceptance number (AN) of the plan. Second, it is necessary to consolidate into a table those sampling conditions which meet the particular requirements for which the plan is being established.

The relationship between the percent nonconforming in the lots being submitted for inspection and the probability of acceptance is termed the "operating characteristic," or OC of a particular sampling condition.[5] Every combination of lot size, sample size, and allowable number of nonconformities has a different operating characteristic, whose values are usually plotted in the form of a curve. The quality assurance offered by a given table may be judged by the OC curves associated with the table. Figure 15.3 shows such an OC curve for the following conditions:

$$N = 2000$$
$$n = 300$$
$$c = 11$$

Certain attributes of OC curves are of particular interest. One is that, generally, the larger the sample size, the steeper the slope of the OC curve. The steepness of the OC curve is an indicator of the power of a sampling plan to discriminate between acceptable and unacceptable quality. Another attribute

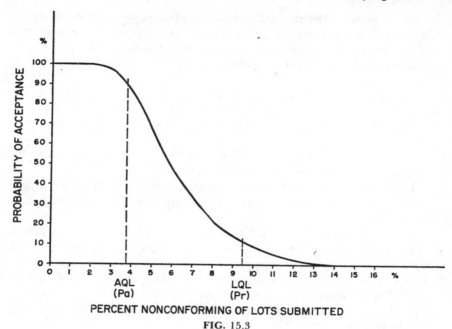

FIG. 15.3

of OC curves is that any increase in the acceptance number *(c)* is to shift the location of the entire OC curve to the right.

While the basic procedures in the construction of several statistical sampling tables may be similar, there are differences both in the details of the construction and the final form taken by these sampling tables. In line with two of the major types of quality protection desired for material being inspected and tested, two of the major approaches for which statistical sampling tables have been constructed are the following:

1. Those tables which are oriented to protection of the quality of the lots submitted for inspection and test. Two somewhat different quality indices are associated with this sort of table:

   Acceptable quality level (AQL), which may be defined as

   > The maximum percentage of units that do not meet requirements in a lot which, for the purposes of acceptance sampling, can be considered satisfactory as a process average.

   Tables which use AQL as the index are oriented to sampling a continuous series of lots and to providing high assurance of the acceptance of a lot when process quality is equal to or better than the specified AQL.

Recall from earlier discussion that the process average, as referred to in the definition of AQL, is the average value of process quality in terms of the percentage of units that do not meet requirements.

Limiting quality level (LQL), which may be defined as

> The percentage of units that do not meet requirements in a lot for which, for purposes of acceptance sampling, the consumer wishes the probability of acceptance to be restricted to a specified low value.

Tables which use LQL as the index are oriented to sampling with high emphasis upon the quality of individual lots.

Typical types of LQL tables are those for lot tolerance percent defective (LTPD), rejectable quality level (RQL), and unacceptable quality level (UQL).

The OC curve in Figure 15.3 can be indexed for AQL with a probability of acceptance designated as P_a (P subscript a) and for LQL with a probability of nonacceptance or rejection designated as P_r (P subscript r).

2. Those tables which are oriented to protection of the "in-the-bin" average quality of the material from a large number of lots after inspection. The type of quality index usually associated with this sort of plan is the average outgoing quality limit index.

Average outgoing quality limit (AOQL) may be defined as

> The maximum expected quality of outgoing quality over all possible levels of incoming quality, following the use of an acceptance sampling plan for a given value of incoming product quality.

Tables which use AOQL as the index are oriented to provide assurance that the long-run average of accepted quality will be no worse than the AOQL value —assuming screening and replacement of nonconforming units in lots that have not been accepted. This is the basic index for continuous sampling plans.

Average outgoing quality (AOQ) is itself defined as

> The expected quality of outgoing product following the use of an acceptance sampling plan for a given value of incoming product quality.

A sampling plan affording one of these two forms of protection will also afford some degree of protection of the other form. In addition, each of these two forms of sampling table has benefits for particular applications. One type of table cannot be termed "better" than the other.[6]

Where infrequent individual lots of material are received by a plant, lot-quality protection tables may be most appropriate. Where large numbers of lots are being inspected and the average quality of material being released to the factory floor is the important factor, then average outgoing quality protection may be desirable.

Each of these two types of sampling table is now discussed.

15.8 Lot-Quality Protection

When lot-quality protection tables are required, two of the most popular tables available are

1. Limiting quality level (LQL) tables
2. Acceptable quality level (AQL) tables

LQL Tables

Figure 15.4 shows the OC curves of four acceptance conditions. These four curves are similar in only one respect: They all pass through the point where the probability of acceptance on the vertical axis is 10 percent and the LQL on the horizontal axis is 4 percent. The meaning of this particular sampling table construction can be simply expressed: Under these acceptance conditions, the consumer is sure that 90 percent of the time lots which contain 4 percent nonconformances will not be accepted. For this particular schedule, the limiting quality level is thus 4 percent at a consumer's risk of 10 percent.[7]

AQL Tables

The OC curves for four other acceptance conditions are shown in Figure 15.5. These curves are similar in only one respect: They all pass through the point where the probability of acceptance on the vertical axis is 90 percent and the limiting acceptable quality level on the horizontal axis is 4 percent.

The meaning of this particular sampling table construction is as follows: Under these acceptance conditions, lots containing 4 percent nonconformances are assured of being accepted 90 percent of the time. There is a 10 percent producer's risk that lots conforming to this quality level will not be accepted. For this particular schedule, the acceptable quality level is thus 4 percent with a 10 percent producer's risk.

For these OC curves, when both the AQL and the producer's risk (α) and also the LQL and the consumer's risk (β) are specified, the sampling plan is completely determined when single samples (n) are taken. The need for n to be an integer requires the decision whether to index the plan to maintain the specified α risk of the plan or the specified β risk. For double or for multiple samples $(n_1, n_2, \ldots)$, the relationship among the samples must be identified.

15.9 Average Outgoing Quality Protection

When average outgoing quality (AOQ) protection is desired, average outgoing quality limit (AOQL) tables are most popular. These tables assure manu-

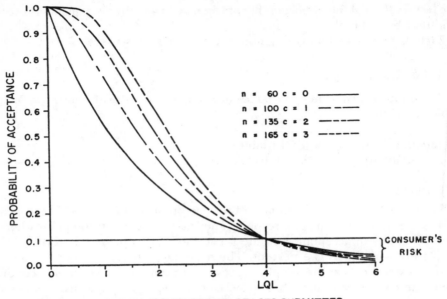

FIG. 15.4

PERCENT NONCONFORMING OF LOTS SUBMITTED

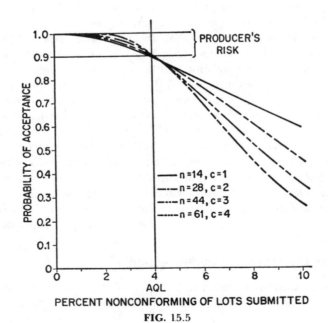

FIG. 15.5

PERCENT NONCONFORMING OF LOTS SUBMITTED

facturers that the percent nonconformance of their average outgoing quality will be equal to or less than a given level but require that the lots which are not accepted under the plan be 100 percent inspected and that the nonconforming units in these lots be replaced or repaired. The 4 percent lot tolerance percent nonconforming condition, with $n = 60$ and $c = 0$ as shown in Figure 15.4, is used to illustrate the AOQL form of sampling plan.

As shown in Figure 15.4, if lots with a percent nonconforming of 1 percent were submitted for inspection, these lots would be accepted 56 percent of the time. Therefore, 44 percent of the lots would be 100 percent inspected, and the nonconforming units in these lots would be replaced or repaired. The average quality after inspection, or AOQ, of these lots would be 44 percent × 0 percent + 56 percent × 1 percent = 0.56 percent.

If lots with a percent nonconformance of 1.5 were submitted for inspection, Figure 15.4 shows that 43 percent of the lots would be accepted and 57 percent of the lots would not be accepted and 100 percent inspected. Assuming again that this 100 percent inspection removes all nonconformances, the AOQ will be 43 percent of 1.5 percent, or 0.645 percent.

For lots submitted with a percent nonconformance of 2.0 percent, the AOQ will be 0.64 percent. This AOQ value grows progressively smaller for lots with 2.5 percent nonconformance, 3.0 percent nonconformance, and so on.

These several AOQ values are plotted in Figure 15.6, which shows that the maximum value for average outgoing quality under this plan is to be found with lots submitted for inspection which are 1.7 percent nonconforming. With lots which are 1.7 percent nonconforming, the AOQ value on the vertical axis, AOQL is 0.68 percent nonconforming.

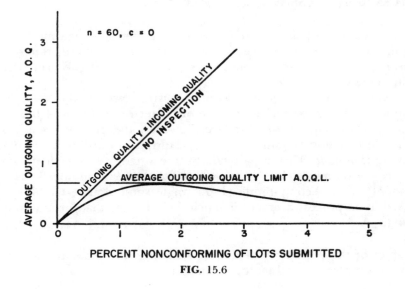

PERCENT NONCONFORMING OF LOTS SUBMITTED

FIG. 15.6

15.10 Single, Double, and Multiple Sampling

With each of these major types of statistical sampling plans there may be

1. *Single sampling,* that is, basing acceptance or rejection[8] of a lot upon the units in one sample drawn from that lot
2. *Double sampling,* that is, selecting one sample of units from a lot and, under certain conditions, selecting a second sample before accepting or rejecting the lot
3. *Multiple sampling,* that is, basing acceptance or rejection of a lot upon the results of several samples of units drawn from that lot

Of these three methods, double sampling has probably been the most popular, for reasons such as the following:

Double Sampling As Compared with Single Sampling

1. Psychologically, the idea of giving a lot of material a "second chance" before rejecting it has popular appeal. Double sampling is therefore sometimes easier to "sell" in the factory.
2. Double-sampling plans permit a smaller first sample than is called for by the sample size of the corresponding single-sampling plan. When the percent nonconformance is either low or high in material submitted for inspection, it is frequently possible to accept or reject lots based upon the results of the first sample. In these instances, therefore, double sampling permits lower sampling costs.

Double Sampling As Compared with Multiple Sampling

1. Double-sampling plans are often easier to administer than multiple-sampling plans. The need for selecting successive samples in the proper fashion may require greater administrative control and more highly skilled inspection operators.
2. In theory, multiple sampling may often permit lower total inspection than double sampling for a given degree of protection because of the smaller sample sizes required. In practice, however, the greater complexity of multiple sampling may, in some cases, return the overall cost advantage to double sampling. This is particularly true when the percent nonconformance in submitted lots is low—say, 0.1 percent—in these cases, the amount of inspection required by single- and double-sampling plans based upon process averages is much the same for that for multiple sampling.

In spite of the popularity of double sampling, there are certain benefits unique to both single and multiple sampling.

Single Sampling

1. Single sampling may be the only practical type of sampling plan under conveyorized production conditions when it is physically possible to select only one sample.
2. With lots of material whose percents nonconformance are close to the AQL, single sampling may offer more economical inspection protection than double sampling.

Multiple Sampling

1. When administrative costs can be kept low, multiple sampling may permit lower inspection costs for given degrees of protection than either single or double sampling.
2. Newer methods to simplify multiple sampling, among them computer-based sampling, may result in greater improved efficiency in administering these sampling plans.
3. Multiple sampling corresponds to the fashion in which an inspector normally selects samples.

The type of product and the way the product is presented for sampling—on a conveyor, in boxes piled on top of each other, and so forth—are the factors that must be taken into account.

Again, the choice of single, double, or multiple sampling depends upon the particular conditions for which the sampling plan is to be used. None of the three methods may be termed "best"; they may be merely "best for certain sampling conditions."

15.11 Published Sampling Tables and Plans

Of the many statistical sampling tables and plans that have been developed, many have been published in a form which makes them available for general use. Some of the most popular of these published plans are:

1. Dodge-Romig tables[9]
2. Military Standard 105D; ANSI/ASQC Z1.4; ISO 2859—all essentially similar[10]
3. Sequential plans[11]
4. Continuous sampling plans[12]
5. Chain sampling and skip-lot plans[13]
6. Columbia sampling tables[14]

Rather than designing their own sampling table, many industrial users of statistical quality-control methods have successfully used one or another of

Single Sampling Table for Average Outgoing Quality Limit (AOQL) = 2.0%

Lot size	0 to 0.04%			0.05 to 0.40%			0.41 to 0.80%			0.81 to 1.20%			1.21 to 1.60%			1.61 to 2.00%		
	n	c	$p_t\%$	n	c	$p_t\%$	n	c	$p_t\%$	n	c	$p_t\%$	n	c	$p_t\%$	n	c	$p_t\%$
1–15	All	0	...	All	0	...	All	0	...	All	0	...	All	0	...	All	0	...
16–50	14	0	13.6	14	0	13.6	14	0	13.6	14	0	13.6	14	0	13.6	14	0	13.6
51–100	16	0	12.4	16	0	12.4	16	0	12.4	16	0	12.4	16	0	12.4	16	0	12.4
101–200	17	0	12.2	17	0	12.2	17	0	12.2	17	0	12.2	35	1	10.5	35	1	10.5
201–300	17	0	12.3	17	0	12.3	17	0	12.3	37	1	10.2	37	1	10.2	37	1	10.2
301–400	18	0	11.8	18	0	11.8	38	1	10.0	38	1	10.0	38	1	10.0	60	2	8.5
401–500	18	0	11.9	18	0	11.9	39	1	9.8	39	1	9.8	60	2	8.6	60	2	8.6
501–600	18	0	11.9	18	0	11.9	39	1	9.8	39	1	9.8	60	2	8.6	60	2	8.6
601–800	18	0	11.9	40	1	9.6	40	1	9.6	65	2	8.0	65	2	8.0	85	3	7.5
801–1,000	18	0	12.0	40	1	9.6	40	1	9.6	65	2	8.1	65	2	8.1	90	3	7.4
1,001–2,000	18	0	12.0	41	1	9.4	65	2	8.2	65	2	8.2	95	3	7.0	120	4	6.5
2,001–3,000	18	0	12.0	41	1	9.4	65	2	8.2	95	3	7.0	120	4	6.5	180	6	5.8
3,001–4,000	18	0	12.0	42	1	9.3	65	2	8.2	95	3	7.0	155	5	6.0	210	7	5.5
4,001–5,000	18	0	12.0	42	1	9.3	70	2	7.5	125	4	6.4	155	5	6.0	245	8	5.3
5,001–7,000	18	0	12.0	42	1	9.3	95	3	7.0	125	4	6.4	185	6	5.6	280	9	5.1
7,001–10,000	42	1	9.3	70	2	7.5	95	3	7.0	155	5	6.0	220	7	5.4	350	11	4.8
10,001–20,000	42	1	9.3	70	2	7.6	95	3	7.0	190	6	5.6	290	9	4.9	460	14	4.4
20,001–50,000	42	1	9.3	70	2	7.6	125	4	6.4	220	7	5.4	395	12	4.5	720	21	3.9
50,001–100,000	42	1	9.3	95	3	7.0	160	5	5.9	290	9	4.9	505	15	4.2	955	27	3.7

Lot size	Process average 0 to 0.05%			Process average 0.06 to 0.50%			Process average 0.51 to 1.00%			Process average 1.01 to 1.50%			Process average 1.51 to 2.00%			Process average 2.01 to 2.50%		
	n	c	$p_t\,\%$	n	c	$p_t\,\%$	n	c	$p_t\,\%$	n	c	$p_t\,\%$	n	c	$p_t\,\%$	n	c	$p_t\,\%$
1–10	All	0	...	All	0	...	All	0	...	All	0	...	All	0	...	All	0	...
11–50	11	0	17.6	11	0	17.6	11	0	17.6	11	0	17.6	11	0	17.6	11	0	17.6
51–100	13	0	15.3	13	0	15.3	13	0	15.3	13	0	15.3	13	0	15.3	13	0	15.3
101–200	14	0	14.7	14	0	14.7	14	0	14.7	29	1	12.9	29	1	12.9	29	1	12.9
201–300	14	0	14.9	14	0	14.9	30	1	12.7	30	1	12.7	30	1	12.7	30	1	12.7
301–400	14	0	15.0	14	0	15.0	31	1	12.3	31	1	12.3	31	1	12.3	48	2	10.7
401–500	14	0	15.0	14	0	15.0	32	1	12.0	32	1	12.0	49	2	10.6	49	2	10.6
501–600	14	0	15.1	32	1	12.0	32	1	12.0	50	2	10.4	50	2	10.4	70	3	9.3
601–800	14	0	15.1	32	1	12.0	32	1	12.0	50	2	10.5	50	2	10.5	70	3	9.4
801–1,000	15	0	14.2	33	1	11.7	33	1	11.7	50	2	10.6	70	3	9.4	90	4	8.5
1,001–2,000	15	0	14.2	33	1	11.7	55	2	9.3	75	3	8.8	95	4	8.0	120	5	7.6
2,001–3,000	15	0	14.2	33	1	11.8	55	2	9.4	75	3	8.8	120	5	7.6	145	6	7.2
3,001–4,000	15	0	14.3	33	1	11.8	55	2	9.5	100	4	7.9	125	5	7.4	195	8	6.6
4,001–5,000	15	0	14.3	33	1	11.8	75	3	8.9	100	4	7.9	150	6	7.0	225	9	6.3
5,001–7,000	33	1	11.8	55	2	9.7	75	3	8.9	125	5	7.4	175	7	6.7	250	10	6.1
7,001–10,000	34	1	11.4	55	2	9.7	75	3	8.9	125	5	7.4	200	8	6.4	310	12	5.8
10,001–20,000	34	1	11.4	55	2	9.7	100	4	8.0	150	6	7.0	260	10	6.0	425	16	5.3
20,001–50,000	34	1	11.4	55	2	9.7	100	4	8.0	180	7	6.7	345	13	5.5	640	23	4.8
50,001–100,000	34	1	11.4	80	3	8.4	125	5	7.4	235	9	6.1	435	16	5.2	800	28	4.5

n = sample size; c = acceptance number.

"All" indicates that each piece in the lot is to be inspected.

p_t = lot tolerance per cent defective with a consumer's risk (P_C) of 0.10.

FIG. 15.7 Reprinted with permission from Harold F. Dodge and Harry G. Romig, "Sampling Inspection Tables," 2d ed., John Wiley & Sons, Inc., New York, 1959. Two tables: Single Sampling 2.0 percent AOQL and Single Sampling 2.5 percent AOQL, in app. 6, p. 201.

these published tables. They are, in general, sufficiently flexible to permit their being used in this fashion.

1. Dodge-Romig tables

These tables include both single- and double-sampling plans. They permit both AOQ limit protection and lot tolerance percent-defective (LTPD) protection. LTPD provides the limiting quality level (LQL) index approach for the tables.

To use AOQL tables, for example, it is necessary to know (a) the size of the lot submitted for inspection, (b) the AOQL protection desired for the material in question, and (c) the average quality or "process average" of the material presented for inspection.

The AOQL table used will indicate the sample size required and the allowable number of defectives in the sample inspected. If the sample contains no more defectives than are allowable, the lot is passed. If the sample contains more than the allowable number of defectives, the lot must be 100 percent inspected and the defective units repaired or replaced.

The tables specify the consumer's risk involved in each case, as well as other pertinent sampling data. They permit the minimum amount of inspection required for the degree of protection desired for material of a given process average.

Figure 15.7 illustrates a typical page from Dodge-Romig sampling tables. The figure shows single-sampling tables for AOQL of 2.0 percent and 2.5 percent. These are LTPD tables with a 10 percent consumer's risk.

2. MIL-STD-105D

These tables include the three types of sampling: single, double, and multiple. The AOQL for single sampling is mentioned in supplementary tables. Limiting quality (LQ) values are also provided in supplementary tables for consumer's risks of 10 and 5 percent.

To use these tables, it is necessary to know (a) the size of the lot submitted for inspection and (b) the AQL protection desired for the material in question.

The table in question will indicate the sample size required and the allowable number of defectives in the sample size. If the sample contains no more defectives than are allowed, the lot is passed. If the sample contains more than the allowable number of defectives, then the lot may be either rejected or 100 percent inspected. However, 100 percent inspection of rejected lots is not required for the maintenance of a given AQL.

There are also contained tables indicating when reduced, normal, or tightened inspection should be used. The criterion for the decision—called "switching rules" in technical sampling terms—is related to the magnitude of the estimated process average.

MIL-STD-105D provides sampling plans for both the case of fraction-defective inspection and defects per 100 units inspection.

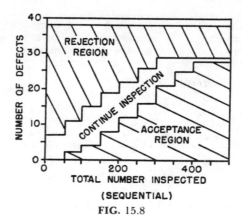

FIG. 15.8

3. Sequential plans

These plans have to do with sampling inspection in which, after each unit is inspected, the decision is made to accept the lot, not to accept it, or to inspect another unit. These plans involve individual units and thus differ from multiple sampling in AQL-type plans which involve sampling of groups of units.

The tables also differ in at least two ways from the types of single- and double-sampling plans discussed above:

a. Since sample sizes are smaller, sample results are analyzed much more frequently than with single-or double-sampling plans for their indication as to whether a lot should be rejected.

b. The plans are "double acting." Under standard tables, for example, it is necessary to specify only one quality index: A lot which is X_1 percent nonconforming will be acceptable, and it is satisfactory to run a Y_1 percent producer's risk.

With sequential plans, the double-acting feature enters in that it is also necessary to establish a second index: It is desirable to reject the lot if it contains more than X_2 percent nonconformities, and it is satisfactory to run a Y_2 percent risk of accepting a lot as bad as this.

As a result, sequential plans establish a "band of indecision" between an acceptance and a rejection region, as shown in Figure 15.8. Sampling is continued until the results from the samples indicate either acceptance or rejection of the lot because the sample results have crossed into either the acceptance or rejection region. This band of indecision may be illustrated in a 2 percent sequential sampling plan calling for a possible five samples and designed for lots ranging from 800 to 1299 units (see table, page 488).

With this sequential plan, if an inspector finds a single nonconforming unit in a sample size of 40, the inspector can neither accept nor reject the lot but must select another sample. The inspector is operating in the band of indecision. Examination of 20 more units will bring the sample size to 60, and if one more nonconforming unit is found, for a cumulative total of 2, a third sample must be selected.

Cumulative sample size	Cumulative acceptance number	Cumulative rejection number
40	0	4
60	1	5
80	2	6
100	2	6
120	3	7
160	7	8

This procedure can be carried on until the maximum sample size—160—is reached. At this point, the band of indecision disappears and acceptance or rejection of the material can be finally decided.

The average amount of inspection required with sequential sampling may be appreciably less than that required for comparable single- or double-sampling plans. Figure 15.9 shows the amount of inspection that would be required with a 4 percent AQL double-sampling MIL-STD-105D-type table to gain the same results as from the sequential plan shown in Figure 15.8. The much greater inspection area in Figure 15.9 is noteworthy: It illustrates one of the reasons for sequential sampling under appropriate circumstances.

Figure 15.10 illustrates one form of a sequential sampling table.[15]

4. Continuous sampling

These plans are designed for application to a continuous flow of individual units of product that (a) involves acceptance or nonacceptance on a unit-by-unit basis and (b) uses alternate periods of 100 percent inspection and sam-

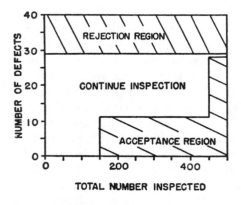

4% AQL MIL – STD – 105 D

FIG. 15.9

pling, depending upon the quality of the observed product. The variety of generally available continuous samplings are designated as CSP-1, CSP-2, CSP-3, CSP-A, CSP-M, CSP-T, CSP-F, CSP-V, and CSP-R.

The original continuous sampling plan, CSP-1, was developed by Harold F. Dodge and indexed for AOQL. The procedure is, at the beginning of production, inspect 100 percent of the produced units consecutively and continue until a certain number of units—designated i in technical sampling terms of CSP-1—are found to meet requirements. Then discontinue 100 percent inspection and inspect only a fraction—designated f in technical sampling terms —of the units, selecting the sample units one at a time to ensure an unbiased sample. Whenever a nonconforming unit is found, revert immediately to 100 percent inspection of succeeding units and continue until i units in succession are found clear of nonconforming units when sampling inspection is resumed. CSP-1 calls for replacement of all nonconforming units found with conforming units.

The protection provided by this plan is determined by the i and f constants chosen. The larger i is, the more difficult it is to begin sampling inspection or to return to it, and thus this provides more quality protection. The larger the proportion of f, the more quickly a possible nonconforming unit will be found, returning then to 100 percent inspection.

CSP-2 and CSP-3 were later developed by Dodge, assisted by Mary N. Torrey, to reduce the frequency of alternation between 100 percent sorting and sampling in continuous production situations. In CSP-2, the qualification for sampling is the same as in CSP-1—that is, i conforming units must be passed by 100 percent prior to going to sampling. However, when a nonconforming unit is found, 100 percent inspection is not immediately reinstituted; instead, careful records are maintained on the ensuing sampled units still at the f rate. If any of the next i sampled units is nonconforming, 100 percent inspection is reinstituted, but if no defective occurs within the next i units, the same procedure of "tracking but not 100 percent inspection" is followed. For example, the differences between CSP-1 and CSP-2 are shown in the table below.

AOQL	0.5%			1.0%			2.0%		
f	5%	10%	20%	5%	10%	20%	5%	10%	20%
i CSP-1	305	220	142	151	108	71	76	54	36
i CSP-2	390	293	200	194	147	100	96	72	50

In CSP-3, the objective is to provide additional protection against "spottiness" of production quality—that is, a sudden brief run of nonconforming units. CSP-3 starts with the same qualification for i as in CSP-2 and goes onto sampling at the specified rate f. When the first nonconforming unit is found, the next four units are inspected and any nonconformance in these four units leads to 100 percent inspection. If all four units are in conformance, then they

ACCEPTABLE QUALITY LEVEL (Percent Defective)

LOT SIZE	SAMPLE SIZE	0.1 A	0.1 R	0.25 A	0.25 R	0.50 A	0.50 R	0.75 A	0.75 R	1 A	1 R	1.5 A	1.5 R	2 A	2 R	3 A	3 R	4 A	4 R	5 A	5 R	6 A	6 R	7 A	7 R	8 A	8 R	9 A	9 R	10 A	10 R	12 A	12 R
499 OR less	40	→		→		→		→		0	3	0	3	1	4	1	5	1	6	2	6	2	7	3	7	3	8	4	9	4	9	5	10
	50	→		→		→		0	2	1	3	1	4	1	5	2	5	2	6	3	6	3	8	4	9	5	9	5	10	5	11	6	12
	60	→		→		→		1	3	1	4	1	4	2	5	2	6	3	7	4	7	4	9	5	9	5	11	7	10	7	13	9	14
	70	→		→		→		2	3	1	4	2	4	2	5	3	6	4	8	6	9	6	9	6	10	7	11	8	13	8	13	10	16
	80	→		→		→		3	4	3	5	3	4	4	5	5	6	7	8	8	8	8	9	9	10	10	11	12	13	12	13	15	16
500 to 799	40	→		→		•	2	0	2	0	3	0	3	0	4	1	5	1	5	1	6	1	7	2	8	2	8	2	9	4	10	4	11
	60	→		→		0	2	0	3	1	3	1	4	1	5	2	5	2	7	3	7	3	9	4	10	5	11	4	11	6	12	7	14
	80	→		→		0	3	1	3	2	4	2	5	2	6	3	6	3	8	5	8	5	11	6	12	7	13	8	13	9	15	10	17
	100	→		→		0	3	1	4	3	4	3	6	3	6	4	7	5	9	6	9	7	13	9	14	11	15	12	17	13	18	13	21
	120	→		→		1	3	3	4	3	5	5	6	5	7	7	8	8	9	10	10	12	14	16	16	18	18	19	20	21	19	20	21
800 to 1299	40	→		→		•	2	•	2	•	3	0	3	0	4	0	5	0	6	1	6	1	7	1	8	1	8	2	9	2	10	3	11
	60	→		→		0	2	0	3	0	3	1	4	1	5	1	6	2	7	2	8	3	9	3	10	4	11	4	12	5	12	6	14
	80	→		→		0	3	1	3	1	4	1	4	2	6	3	7	3	8	4	10	5	11	6	12	6	13	6	14	9	15	9	17
	100	→		→		0	3	1	3	2	4	2	5	3	7	4	8	5	10	7	11	7	13	9	14	9	15	11	17	12	18	12	21
	120	→		→		1	3	2	4	2	5	3	6	3	7	5	9	6	11	9	15	10	17	11	16	13	18	12	19	13	21	15	24
	160	→		→		3	4	4	5	4	5	6	6	7	8	9	10	10	11	13	14	15	18	16	17	18	19	19	20	22	22	25	26
1300 to 3199	50	→		•	2	•	2	•	3	•	3	0	3	0	4	0	5	0	7	0	7	1	8	2	9	1	9	3	10	3	11	3	13
	75	→		0	2	0	3	0	3	0	3	1	4	1	5	2	7	2	10	4	10	4	10	4	12	5	13	6	14	6	15	7	13
	100	→		0	2	0	3	1	3	1	4	2	5	3	6	5	8	8	11	8	12	8	15	9	16	8	15	9	17	10	18	11	17
	125	→		1	3	1	3	1	4	2	5	3	6	4	7	7	10	11	11	12	15	13	17	11	19	11	18	12	19	13	21	15	21
	150	→		1	3	2	3	2	5	3	6	6	8	6	8	10	15	17	18	17	18	17	18	20	21	22	23	25	25	27	28	19	25
	200	→		2	3	3	4	5	6	6	8	•	•	7	8	10	15	13	14	17	18	25	26	29	30	32	33	36	37	39	40	31	32
3200 to 7999	50	•	2	•	2	•	2	•	3	•	3	•	4	•	4	0	5	0	7	0	7	1	8	1	9	1	10	2	11	2	12	3	14
	100	•	2	0	2	0	3	0	3	1	4	1	4	1	5	2	5	5	10	4	11	9	13	5	15	6	16	8	17	9	19	10	17
	150	0	2	0	2	0	3	1	3	2	4	2	5	2	5	5	9	8	11	8	12	13	17	15	19	14	21	13	23	15	25	17	25
	200	0	2	1	3	1	3	2	4	3	5	4	6	4	7	9	15	11	17	15	18	17	21	19	24	22	26	25	29	28	31	32	36
	250	1	3	1	3	2	4	2	5	3	6	5	7	6	8	13	15	17	18	22	23	25	26	29	30	32	33	35	37	38	40	44	46
	300	2	3	3	3	4	4	5	6	7	7	8	8	10	11	15	15	17	18	22	23	25	26	29	30	32	33	36	37	39	40	45	46

		A	R	A	R	A	R	A	R	A	R	A	R	A	R	A	R	A	R	A	R	A	R	A	R	A	R	A	R	A	R		
	100	•	2	•	3	•	3	•	4	0	5	0	6	0	7	1	9	1	11	3	12	3	14	4	16	5	17	7	18			↑	↑
8000	150	•	2	•	3	0	4	0	5	1	6	2	7	2	9	3	11	4	14	6	16	7	17	9	20	10	22	12	24			↑	↑
to	200	0	2	0	3	0	5	1	6	2	7	3	8	3	10	6	13	7	17	10	19	11	22	13	24	16	27	18	30			↑	↑
21999	250	0	2	0	4	1	5	2	6	2	8	4	9	5	12	8	16	10	19	13	22	15	25	18	29	19	32	24	35			↑	↑
	300	0	3	1	4	2	6	2	7	3	8	5	11	6	13	10	18	12	22	16	26	19	29	22	33	24	37	29	41			↑	↑
	400	1	3	1	4	3	7	4	8	5	10	8	14	10	16	14	22	18	27	23	33	27	37	31	42	34	47	40	52			↑	↑
	500	2	3	3	4	6	7	7	8	9	10	13	14	16	17	22	23	28	29	34	35	40	41	45	46	50	51	58	59			↑	↑
	100	•	2	•	3	•	4	•	5	•	6	•	8	0	8	0	11	1	13	2	16	3	16									↑	↑
22000	200	•	3	•	4	0	5	0	6	1	7	1	10	3	11	3	15	6	18	8	20	10	24									↑	↑
to	300	0	3	0	4	1	6	1	8	2	9	3	12	5	14	7	19	11	23	14	26	17	31									↑	↑
99999	400	0	3	1	5	2	7	3	9	4	11	5	14	8	17	11	23	16	28	21	33	25	39									↑	↑
	600	1	4	2	6	3	9	5	11	7	14	10	18	14	23	19	31	27	38	34	46	39	53									↑	↑
	800	1	4	3	7	5	11	8	14	11	17	14	23	20	28	27	38	37	49	46	58	54	68									↑	↑
	1000	3	4	6	7	10	11	13	14	17	18	22	23	30	31	40	41	53	54	65	66	76	77									↑	↑
	200	•	3	•	5	•	7	•	8	0	9	0	13	2	13	2	18	4	20													↑	↑
100,000	400	•	4	0	6	0	8	0	10	3	12	3	17	7	18	9	25	14	30													↑	↑
and	600	0	4	1	7	2	10	2	12	5	15	7	20	12	22	17	33	24	40													↑	↑
up	800	1	5	2	8	4	11	5	14	8	18	11	24	18	29	24	40	34	50													↑	↑
	1000	1	5	3	9	5	13	7	17	11	21	15	28	23	35	32	47	44	60													↑	↑
	1200	2	5	3	9	7	15	9	19	14	24	19	32	28	40	39	55	54	70													↑	↑
	1600	4	5	8	9	14	15	19	20	24	25	33	34	45	46	61	62	86	87													↑	↑

A – Acceptance number

R – Rejection number

• Acceptance cannot be made at this sample size

↓ Use first sampling table below arrows
(Form larger lots, if necessary)

↑ Use first sampling table above arrows

FIG. 15.10

count as the first four of the i conforming units required to remain on sampling inspection.[16]

Another variation of continuous sampling plans is to use more than one sampling frequency. This plan is called "multilevel continuous sampling," growing out of the work of Lieberman and Solomon.[17] One of these multilevel plans, CSP-M, proceeds as follows: After i conforming units are accepted by 100 percent inspection, sampling is instituted at a rate f. If the next i units inspected under sampling are all in conformance, then the sampling rate goes to f^2. If the next i units sampled are all in conformance, then the rate goes to f^3, and so on. If conditions occur under which CSP-1, CSP-2, and CSP-3 would call for a return to 100 percent inspection, and sampling is taking place at a rate f^k, then the multilevel plan calls for a rate of f^{k-1}. If the sampling is at f, then 100 percent inspection is reinstituted.

These several approaches to continuous sampling have become characteristic of the wide variety of plans available for use in inspection under these conditions.[18]

5. Chain sampling and skip-lot plans

a. Chain sampling has to do with sampling inspection in which the criteria for acceptance and nonacceptance of the lot partly depend upon the results of the inspection of immediately preceding lots. These plans, designated ChSP-1, ChSP-C_1,C_2, and others, are oriented to the situation where the sampling acceptance number (c) is 0. In the more usual lot-by-lot sampling, where small samples are involved, there can be rather undiscriminating OC curves which can make it difficult to pass even high-quality lots.

Chain sampling was developed by Harold Dodge to provide greater probability of acceptance of lots of relatively high quality.[19]

b. Skip-lot sampling has to do with a plan in which some lots in a series are accepted without inspection (other than possible spot checks) when the sampling results for a stated number of immediately preceding lots meet stated criteria. This represents an application of CSP-1 to lots rather than to individual units.[20] It is an approach for eliminating inspection altogether on some fraction of the lots in a series when quality in the past has been sufficiently consistent.

6. Columbia sampling tables

These extremely flexible tables permit single, double, and multiple sampling as well as AQL and AOQL protection. Their use is similar to that of tables described above.

15.12 Normal, Reduced, and Tightened Inspection

The standard form of many sampling tables is generally called "normal" tables. Many well-conceived acceptance sampling procedures, such as MIL-

STD-105D, also provide for *reduced*-sampling and, in some cases, *tightened*-sampling plans for use to supplant normal sampling under certain circumstances. This is provided for in what is called the "switching rule of the plan" in technical sampling terms. While these reduced-sampling plans do not conform to the OC curves for the normal-sampling table in question, their use can be justified on the grounds that they take advantage of the additional information about the quality of lots submitted which has been obtained from the use of normal-sampling schedules.

When, for example, the quality of lots submitted for inspection is consistently better than the specified quality index value, which may be demonstrated by the fact that no lots are being rejected, then a reduced-sampling schedule may be used in place of normal sampling under certain acceptance plans. These reduced schedules are usually similar in form to the normal schedules, except that the first sample sizes, which correspond to a given lot size, are smaller. Such tables may have, for example, a first reduced sample one-fifth the size of the first normal sample.

Reduced sampling permits a decrease in inspection cost. This type of sampling can be continued until the quality of the material were to become poorer and call for a return to normal sampling.

When the quality of lots submitted for inspection is consistently poorer than the quality target aimed for, a tightened sampling schedule is called for. This tightened schedule is usually similar to the normal schedule, except that the allowable number of defectives for a given sample size is reduced.

Dodge-Romig tables approach this objective of flexibility and minimum amount of inspection by adjusting sample size to the process average. Instead of normal, reduced, and tightened categories, Dodge-Romig tables have degrees of inspection intensity; selection from among them is based upon the quality history of the part in question.

A variation of reduced sampling has evolved, called "discovery sampling."[21] The three major factors forming the basis of discovery sampling are as follows:

1. The entire sampling risk is contained in only the partially defective lots because any plan will accept the 100 percent good lots and reject the 100 percent-defective lots.
2. A small fraction defective occurs more frequently than does a large fraction defective.
3. The percentage of partially defective lots delivered to stock is a satisfactory process average measure.

To determine the sample size required for discovery sampling,[22] there are three factors to be considered: (1) the AOQL desired, (2) the ratio of lots containing some defectives to the total lots received (less the 100 percent-defective lots), and (3) the shape of the distribution of partially defective lots.

USING ACCEPTANCE SAMPLING TABLES

15.13 A Typical Acceptance Plan: Attribute

Figure 15.11 shows a MIL-STD-105D-type acceptance sampling table adapted for use by a multiplant organization to meet the widely varying incoming-material, in-process, and final inspection situations in its various factories. The table contains 16 different AQL schedules. Terminology has been adapted so that the table measures percent nonconformance.

Company personnel using this table are instructed to select their samples

1. *At random.* It is common sense that a sample may be most representative of a lot of material of unknown quality when the units in that sample have been chosen from all over the lot. As a result, each unit in the sample should be selected in such a way that each unit in the lot has a chance of being chosen.
2. *From a homogeneous lot.* As nearly as possible, the lot from which the sample is selected should consist of articles made under the same manufacturing conditions and drawn from the same manufacturing source.

This is important for practical rather than statistical purposes. For one example, a sample selected from lots shipped into a plant by two vendors may represent as satisfactory the quality of the combined lots. This situation may result only because the quality of one vendor's parts is far better than that required and the quality of the other vendor's parts far poorer than that required. The combined sample may mask this important difference in vendor shipments.

The table itself consists of five major sections, as shown in Figure 15.11.

I Lot size
II First sample
III Second sample
IV AQL (normal inspection)
V Procedure

Each section is now discussed.

I Lot Size

This column contains the various ranges of lot size covered by the table. When there is a choice as to what the lot size should be, the decision should be based upon including, within the lot, material from the same source.

If there are two lots each containing 5000 pieces, the question may arise as to whether lot size should be one lot of 10,000 pieces or two lots of 5000 pieces. If the two lots are from the same source—perhaps the same vendor—they may be treated as a single lot; if they are from two different sources—perhaps from two vendors—they should be treated as individual lots.

MIL-STD-105D — Double Sampling Plans for Normal Inspection (modified, Inspection Level II)

Legend for cells: `↓` = use first sampling plan below arrow; `↑` = use first sampling plan above arrow; `*` = use corresponding single sampling plan; numeric entries are "Ac Re".

LOT SIZE (I)	SAMPLE	SAMPLE SIZE	CUMULATIVE SAMPLE SIZE	0.010	0.015	0.025	0.040	0.065	0.10	0.15	0.25	0.40	0.65	1.0	1.5	2.5	4.0	6.5	10
2–8				NO DOUBLE SAMPLING PLANS FOR THESE SAMPLE SIZES; USE SINGLE SAMPLING															
9–15	First	2	2	↓	↓	↓	↓	↓	↓	↓	↓	↓	↓	↓	↓	↓	↓	*	0 2
	Second	2	4																1 2
16–25	First II	3	3	↓	↓	↓	↓	↓	↓	↓	↓	↓	↓	↓	↓	↓	*	0 2	0 3
	Second III	3	6															1 2	3 4
26–50	First	5	5	↓	↓	↓	↓	↓	↓	↓	↓	↓	↓	↓	↓	*	0 2	0 3	1 4
	Second	5	10														1 2	3 4	4 5
51–90	First	8	8	↓	↓	↓	↓	↓	↓	↓	↓	↓	↓	↓	*	0 2	0 3	1 4	2 5
	Second	8	16													1 2	3 4	4 5	6 7
91–150	First	13	13	↓	↓	↓	↓	↓	↓	↓	↓	↓	↓	*	0 2	0 3	1 4	2 5	3 7
	Second	13	26												1 2	3 4	4 5	6 7	8 9
151–280	First	20	20	↓	↓	↓	↓	↓	↓	↓	↓	↓	*	0 2	0 3	1 4	2 5	3 7	5 9
	Second	20	40											1 2	3 4	4 5	6 7	8 9	12 13
281–500	First	32	32	↓	↓	↓	↓	↓	↓	↓	↓	*	0 2	0 3	1 4	2 5	3 7	5 9	7 11
	Second	32	64										1 2	3 4	4 5	6 7	8 9	12 13	18 19
501–1200	First	50	50	↓	↓	↓	↓	↓	↓	↓	*	0 2	0 3	1 4	2 5	3 7	5 9	7 11	11 16
	Second	50	100									1 2	3 4	4 5	6 7	8 9	12 13	18 19	26 27
1201–3200	First	80	80	↓	↓	↓	↓	↓	↓	*	0 2	0 3	1 4	2 5	3 7	5 9	7 11	11 16	↑
	Second	80	160								1 2	3 4	4 5	6 7	8 9	12 13	18 19	26 27	
3201–10000	First	125	125	↓	↓	↓	↓	↓	*	0 2	0 3	1 4	2 5	3 7	5 9	7 11	11 16	↑	↑
	Second	125	250							1 2	3 4	4 5	6 7	8 9	12 13	18 19	26 27		
10001–35000	First	200	200	↓	↓	↓	↓	*	0 2	0 3	1 4	2 5	3 7	5 9	7 11	11 16	↑	↑	↑
	Second	200	400						1 2	3 4	4 5	6 7	8 9	12 13	18 19	26 27			
35001–150000	First	315	315	↓	↓	↓	*	0 2	0 3	1 4	2 5	3 7	5 9	7 11	11 16	↑	↑	↑	↑
	Second	315	630					1 2	3 4	4 5	6 7	8 9	12 13	18 19	26 27				
150001–500000	First	500	500	↓	↓	*	0 2	0 3	1 4	2 5	3 7	5 9	7 11	11 16	↑	↑	↑	↑	↑
	Second	500	1000				1 2	3 4	4 5	6 7	8 9	12 13	18 19	26 27					
500001 & over	First	800	800	↓	*	0 2	0 3	1 4	2 5	3 7	5 9	7 11	11 16	↑	↑	↑	↑	↑	↑
	Second	800	1600			1 2	3 4	4 5	6 7	8 9	12 13	18 19	26 27						

NOTES:

⇩ = Use first sampling plan below arrow. If sample size equals or exceeds lot or batch size, do 100 percent inspection.

⇧ = Use first sampling plan above arrow.

Ac = Acceptance number.

Re = Rejection number.

* = Use corresponding single sampling plan (or alternatively, use double sampling plan below, when available).

FIG. 15.11 Table is a modification of Table III-A of MIL-STD-105D in that inspection level II is used and corresponding lot sizes are incorporated directly into the body of the table.

From examination of the table, note that generally the larger the lot size, the smaller the percentage of articles that must be checked. Therefore, although it is most economical to use relatively large lot sizes, this policy should not be followed where it becomes necessary to mix materials from different sources. Exceptions to this rule occur where there is lack of information as to the origin of a lot or where practical experience shows that it is satisfactory to mix lots.

II, III First Sample, Second Sample

When the particular lot size in question has been chosen, the required sample sizes for that lot size can be read to the right horizontally. The row labeled First Sample indicates the number of units to be drawn from the lot and examined. If the acceptance conditions of the table indicate that a second sample must be drawn, its size is shown in the row labeled Second Sample.

IV Acceptable Quality Level (Normal Inspection)

There are 16 AQLs listed in the table, ranging from 0.010 to 10 percent. Each AQL has associated with it the allowable number of nonconforming units in the first sample (described as Ac) and the rejectable number of nonconforming units in the first and second samples (described as Re).

V Procedure

a. Choose the desired AQL.
b. Inspect the number of units equal to the first sample size given by the plan for the lot size involved.
    (1). If the number of nonconforming units containing nonconformities found in the first sample is equal to or less than the first acceptance number *(Ac)*, accept the lot.
    (2). If the number of nonconforming units found in the first sample is equal to or greater than the first rejection number *(Re)*, reject the lot.
    (3). If the number of nonconforming units in the first sample is between the first *Ac* and *Re,* inspect a second sample of the size indicated in the table.
    (4). Determine in the second sample the number of nonconforming units.
c. Add the number of nonconforming units found in the first and second samples.
    (1). If the cumulative number of nonconforming units is equal to or less than the second *Ac,* accept the lot.
    (2). If the cumulative number of nonconforming units is equal to or greater than the second *Re,* reject or 100 percent inspect the lot.

As an example of the use of the aforementioned table, consider the case of felt washers. The inner diameter of these washers is the critical quality characteristic, and these inner diameters are inspected when the material is received from the vendor's plant. An AQL of 2.5 percent has been established for this quality characteristic.

When a lot of 1000 washers is received in incoming inspection, the steps that will be followed in the use of the table are as follows:

1. *Select the appropriate lot size.* In Figure 15.11, the 1000-unit lot falls in the 501 to 1200 lot size.
2. *Select the first sample.* First sample for this lot size is 50 units.
3. *Measure the first sample.* With the 2.5 percent AQL, note that the allowable number of nonconformances for this lot size is two. If two or fewer nonconforming units are found, the lot can be accepted on the basis of the first sample. If the total number of nonconforming units is between two and five, then a second sample must be selected. If the total number of nonconforming units is five or more, the lot should be rejected or 100 percent inspected.
4. *Select and inspect the second sample.* If a second sample has been required, it is shown to be 50 units.
5. *Add the number of nonconforming units found in the first and second samples.* If the cumulative number of nonconformances is six or less, the lot can be accepted. If the cumulative number of nonconformances is seven or more, the lot must be rejected or 100 percent inspected.

15.14 Tightened Inspection Sampling

When the quality of lots has been demonstrated by normal inspection to require much tighter control, a tightened inspection sampling plan may be instituted for a period of time. This type of sampling is particularly used under circumstances where total rejection of the lot is not feasible—such as in the case of high-volume production of electronic components where the availability of a certain number of acceptable units may be critical. The tightened inspection sampling schedule (Fig. 15.12) permits production to continue while corrective action is being taken to eliminate the problem.

Typically, tightened inspection sampling is implemented and continued under the following conditions:

Condition A: The preceding five lots have been under normal inspection and two have been rejected. (This does not include lots or batches which have been resubmitted.)

Condition B: Tightened inspection shall be continued until five consecutive lots or batches have been considered acceptable on original inspection.

Condition C: In the event that 10 consecutive lots or batches remain on tightened inspection (or any other number of lots or batches designated by the quality program plan), acceptance under any circumstance should be discontinued until corrective action has improved the quality of submitted material.[23]

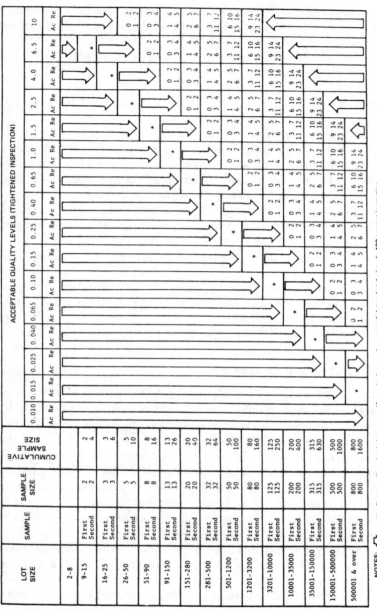

FIG. 15.12 Table is a modification of Table III-B of MIL-STD-105D in that inspection level II is used and corresponding lot sizes are incorporated directly into the body of the table.

498

15.15 A Reduced-Sampling Plan

As with many acceptance sampling tables, MIL-STD-105D has associated with it a series of reduced-sampling schedules. A section of the reduced-sampling table for double-sampling plans is shown in Figure 15.13. This table is designed for use if the following three criteria are met:

Condition A: The preceding 10 lots have been under normal inspection and none has been rejected. (Additional numbers of lots must be accepted under certain conditions specified in Fig. 15.14.)

Condition B: The total number of nonconforming units in the samples from the preceding 10 lots or batches is equal to or less than the applicable lower limit shown in Figure 15.14. If double or multiple sampling is used, all samples inspected should be included, not "first" samples only.

Condition C: Production is at a steady rate.

Use of the reduced-sampling table is similar to the procedure described in Section 15.14. Note that the economy of reduced sampling over normal sampling is that the size of the sample is far smaller than that for normal sampling.

Reduced sampling is particularly effective with such material as certain types of cast parts, where a lot is generally either uniformly satisfactory or uniformly defective. The small sample size may permit considerable reductions in inspection cost under these conditions.[24]

A major limitation of reduced-sampling tables is, however, this very element of small sample size. In many factories it usually carries with it the danger that the reduced tables may be used indiscriminately in place of normal tables in situations where reduced sampling is not applicable. As a result, the effective introduction of reduced-sampling tables in a factory is usually accompanied by means for careful control over the use of these tables.

15.16 A Lot-Sensitive Sampling Plan

Another quite different and useful approach has been designated as a lot-sensitive sampling plan. This single sampling plan is based upon the concept of acceptance with zero defects in the sample.[25] As an alternative to 100 percent inspection, it is more economical in that only a fraction of the lot is inspected. However, it is suitable only for those products where the state of the art permits near perfect quality levels to be economically produced. It is particularly useful in compliance and safety-related testing.

A lot-sensitive sampling plan (LSP) (Fig. 15.15) may be derived as follows:

1. Specify lot size N.
2. Specify the limiting quality level p_L that is to be protected by the plan.
3. Compute the product $D = Np_L$.
4. Enter the body of Table 1 at the nearest value of D and read the corresponding value of f as the sum of the associated row and column headings.
5. The sampling plan is sample size $= n = fN$.

ACCEPTABLE QUALITY LEVELS (REDUCED INSPECTION)†

Upper-left region of the body (small lot sizes / low AQL) is marked: **REDUCED INSPECTION NOT AVAILABLE** (shown blank in the table below).

LOT SIZE	SAMPLE	SAMPLE SIZE	CUMULATIVE SAMPLE SIZE	0.010		0.015		0.025		0.040		0.065		0.10		0.15		0.25		0.40		0.65		1.0		1.5		2.5		4.0		6.5		10	
				Ac	Re	Ac	Re	Ac	Re	Ac	Re	Ac	Re	Ac	Re	Ac	Re	Ac	Re	Ac	Re	Ac	Re	Ac	Re	Ac	Re	Ac	Re	Ac	Re	Ac	Re	Ac	Re
2-8																																			
9-15																																			
16-25																																			
26-50	First	2	2																							*		↓		↓		0	2	0	3
	Second	2	4																													0	2	0	4
51-90	First	3	3																					*		↓		↓		0	2	0	3	0	4
	Second	3	6																											0	2	0	4	1	5
91-150	First	5	5																			*		↓		↓		0	2	0	3	0	4	0	4
	Second	5	10																									0	2	0	4	1	5	3	6
151-280	First	8	8																	*		↓		↓		0	2	0	3	0	4	0	4	1	5
	Second	8	16																							0	2	0	4	1	5	3	6	4	7
281-500	First	13	13															*		↓		↓		0	2	0	3	0	4	0	4	1	5	2	7
	Second	13	26																					0	2	0	4	1	5	3	6	4	7	6	9
501-1200	First	20	20													*		↓		↓		0	2	0	3	0	4	0	4	1	5	2	7	3	8
	Second	20	40																			0	2	0	4	1	5	3	6	4	7	6	9	8	12
1201-3200	First	32	32											*		↓		↓		0	2	0	3	0	4	0	4	1	5	2	7	3	8	5	10
	Second	32	64																	0	2	0	4	1	5	3	6	4	7	6	9	8	12	12	16
3201-10000	First	50	50									*		↓		↓		0	2	0	3	0	4	0	4	1	5	2	7	3	8	5	10	↑	
	Second	50	100															0	2	0	4	1	5	3	6	4	7	6	9	8	12	12	16		
10001-35000	First	80	80							*		↓		↓		0	2	0	3	0	4	0	4	1	5	2	7	3	8	5	10	↑		↑	
	Second	80	160													0	2	0	4	1	5	3	6	4	7	6	9	8	12	12	16				
35001-150000	First	125	125					*		↓		↓		0	2	0	3	0	4	0	4	1	5	2	7	3	8	5	10	↑		↑		↑	
	Second	125	250											0	2	0	4	1	5	3	6	4	7	6	9	8	12	12	16						
150001-500000	First	200	200			*		↓		↓		0	2	0	3	0	4	0	4	1	5	2	7	3	8	5	10	↑		↑		↑		↑	
	Second	200	400									0	2	0	4	1	5	3	6	4	7	6	9	8	12	12	16								
500001 & over	First	315	315	*		↓		↓		0	2	0	3	0	4	0	4	1	5	2	7	3	8	5	10	↑		↑		↑		↑		↑	
	Second	315	630							0	2	0	4	1	5	3	6	4	7	6	9	8	12	12	16										

NOTES:

↓ = Use first sampling plan below arrow. If sample size equals or exceeds lot or batch size, do 100 percent inspection.

↑ = Use first sampling plan above arrow.

Ac = Acceptance number.

Re = Rejection number.

* = Use corresponding single sampling plan (or alternatively, use double sampling plan below, when available).

† = If, after the second sample, the acceptance number has been exceeded, but the rejection number has not been reached, accept the lot, but reinstate normal inspection.

FIG. 15.13 Table is a modification of Table III-C of MIL-STD-105D in that inspection level II is used and corresponding lot sizes are incorporated directly into the body of the table.

Table VIII. Limit Numbers for Reduced Inspection

Number of sample units from last 10 lots or batches	Acceptable quality level															
	0.010	0.015	0.025	0.040	0.065	0.10	0.15	0.25	0.40	0.65	1.0	1.5	2.5	4.0	6.5	10
20–29	*	*	*	*	*	*	*	*	*	*	*	*	*	*	*	0
30–49	*	*	*	*	*	*	*	*	*	*	*	*	*	*	0	0
50–79	*	*	*	*	*	*	*	*	*	*	*	*	*	0	0	2
80–129	*	*	*	*	*	*	*	*	*	*	*	*	0	0	2	4
130–199	*	*	*	*	*	*	*	*	*	*	*	0	0	2	4	7
200–319	*	*	*	*	*	*	*	*	*	*	0	0	2	4	8	14
320–499	*	*	*	*	*	*	*	*	*	0	0	1	4	8	14	24
500–799	*	*	*	*	*	*	*	*	0	0	2	3	7	14	25	40
800–1249	*	*	*	*	*	*	*	0	0	2	4	7	14	24	42	68
1250–1999	*	*	*	*	*	*	0	0	2	4	7	13	24	40	69	110
2000–3149	*	*	*	*	*	0	0	2	4	8	14	22	40	68	115	181
3150–4999	*	*	*	*	0	0	1	4	8	14	24	38	67	111	186	
5000–7999	*	*	*	0	0	2	3	7	14	25	40	63	110	181		
8000–12499	*	*	0	0	2	4	7	14	24	42	68	105	181			
12500–19999	*	0	0	2	4	7	13	24	40	69	110	169				
20000–31499	0	0	2	4	8	14	22	40	68	115	181					
31500–49999	0	1	4	8	14	24	38	67	111	186						
50000 & Over	2	3	7	14	25	40	63	110	181	301						

* Denotes that the number of sample units from the last 10 lots or batches is not sufficient for reduced inspection for this AQL. In this instance more than 10 lots or batches may be used for the calculation, provided that the lots or batches used are the most recent ones in sequence, that they have all been on normal inspection, and that none has been rejected while on original inspection.

FIG. 15.14 TABLE VIII-Limit Numbers for Reduced Inspection of MIL-STD-105D.

Table 1. Values of $D = Np_L$ Corresponding to f

f	0.00	0.01	0.02	0.03	0.04	0.05	0.06	0.07	0.08	0.09
0.9	1.0000	0.9562	0.9117	0.8659	0.8184	0.7686	0.7153	0.6567	0.5886	0.5000
0.8	1.4307	1.3865	1.3428	1.2995	1.2565	1.2137	1.1711	1.1286	1.0860	1.0432
0.7	1.9125	1.8601	1.8088	1.7586	1.7093	1.6610	1.6135	1.5667	1.5207	1.4754
0.6	2.5129	2.4454	2.3797	2.3159	2.2538	2.1933	2.1344	2.0769	2.0208	1.9660
0.5	3.3219	3.2278	3.1372	3.0497	2.9652	2.8836	2.8047	2.7283	2.6543	2.5825
0.4	4.5076	4.3640	4.2270	4.0963	3.9712	3.8515	3.7368	3.6268	3.5212	3.4196
0.3	6.4557	6.2054	5.9705	5.7496	5.5415	5.3451	5.1594	4.9836	4.8168	4.6583
0.2	10.3189	9.7682	9.2674	8.8099	8.3902	8.0039	7.6471	7.3165	7.0093	6.7231
0.1	21.8543	19.7589	18.0124	16.5342	15.2668	14.1681	13.2064	12.3576	11.6028	10.9272
0.0	*	229.1053	113.9741	75.5957	56.4055	44.8906	37.2133	31.7289	27.6150	24.4149

*For values of $f < 0.01$ use $f = \dfrac{2.303}{D}$; for infinite lot size use sample size $n = \dfrac{2.303}{p_L}$

FIG. 15.15 Table I of Lot Sensitive Sampling Plan, developed by Edward G. Schilling.

Always round up in computing sample size.

The plan is applied as follows:

1. Randomly sample n items from a lot of N items (i.e., sample a fraction f of the lot).
2. Reject if any defective units are found in the sample.

The use of the LSP plan provides LTPD protection to the consumer at the limiting fraction defective, p_L, specified. That is, the probability of accepting is 10 percent for a lot having fraction defective equal to p_L. If the fraction defective in the lot exceeds p_L, the probability that the lot would be accepted is naturally less than 10 percent. Specification of LTPD protection is equivalent to a reliability confidence coefficient of 90 percent; or, one can be 90 percent confident that a lot that has passed the plan has a fraction defective *less* than the value of p_L specified (or, equivalently, that it has a reliability of $1 - p_L$). In repeated applications of the plan, lots that are composed of exactly p_L fraction defective would be rejected 90 percent of the time.

Since a perfect lot has 100 percent probability of acceptance, for such lots the producer's risk of rejection is zero. For lots containing only a single defective unit (i.e., lots of fraction-defective $1/N$), the probability of acceptance is just $P_a = 1 - f$. The corresponding producer's risk of such a lot being rejected is $1 - P_a = f$. Thus, with a fraction of the lot inspected of $f = 0.21$ and a lot size of 100, there is a probability of acceptance of $P_a = 1 - 0.21 = 0.79$. For lots containing a fraction-defective $p = \frac{1}{100} = 0.01$, there is a corresponding producer's risk at that level of fraction defective of $1 - P_a = 0.21$. Thus the producer's risk for this type of sampling plan may be unacceptable unless most of the lots are perfect.[26]

15.17 When May Sampling Be Done?

Much consideration has been given to the economics of statistical sampling plans. A major problem in some industrial applications has been unwise use of these plans in situations for which they have no application. The widespread use of sampling plans is no end in itself; there are situations where either 100 percent inspection or no inspection is to be preferred over any type of sampling plan.

With the exception of those vital instances where destructive testing makes sampling imperative, the possibility of property damage or personal injury makes 100 percent inspection necessary, or where 100 percent inspection of safety parts may also be necessary, the decision as to whether sampling should be done may become almost entirely a question of practicality—that is, assurance that nonconforming units will be removed later in the production flow —and economics.[27]

The question resolves itself into the following two parts:

1. In the case of a given part, is it most economical to 100 percent inspect, to sample, or to carry on no inspection at all?
2. If sampling has been chosen, what sampling plan should be used and what quality indices should be chosen? In the instance of the MIL-STD-105D table discussed above, this question becomes "What AQL should be used?"

Industry decisions on these questions have most frequently been made in a fashion dictated by practical experience with the individual parts and individual suppliers. The development of sampling plans has now, however, made it possible to implement this practical experience by actual calculations of what the most economical inspection situation is.

In recent years, a number of very effective calculation approaches have been developed for this purpose. One of the simplest of these approaches, to obtain ready understanding under practical factory conditions to determine this most economical inspection situation for the MIL-STD-105D table discussed above, involves calculation of the "break-even point" (BEP). The BEP for a given part or quality characteristic may be defined as

> The percentage ratio between the cost of eliminating nonconforming units by inspection and the cost for repair when nonconforming units have been allowed to move onto the manufacturing floor.

The calculation of the BEP value can be made for a single part or quality characteristic as follows:

1. Determine the cost of removing nonconforming parts by inspection.
2. Determine the average repair cost for units—assemblies, for example—which are made using these nonconforming parts.
3. Calculate the resulting BEP by using the formula

$$\frac{\text{Cost of inspection (per part)}}{\text{Cost of repair (per nonconforming assembly)}} = \text{BEP} \qquad (37)$$

4. Determine the actual average percent nonconformance or process average nonconformity for the part or material in question. This value should be determined from the inspection results of several thousand parts.

    These parts should represent as many incoming lots as is practical, so that variations in the supplier's process can be evaluated. If the average incoming percent nonconformance is to be determined from the results of sampling inspection, only the results of the first samples should be used.
5. By comparing the BEP (from step 3) with the average incoming percent nonconformance (step 4), it can be determined whether 100 percent inspection, no inspection, or sample inspection is indicated.

    Four typical situations may be indicated:

a. If the percent nonconformance of incoming material is fairly close to the BEP, then sampling inspection may be the economical answer.

b. If the percent nonconformance of incoming material is somewhat higher than the BEP, 100 percent inspection will more than pay for itself.

c. If the percent nonconformance of incoming material is considerably lower than the BEP but erratic, sampling inspection may be indicated purely for purposes of protection.[28]

d. If the percent nonconformance of incoming material is considerably lower than the BEP and stable, then a case might be made for no inspection at all.

If it has been determined that sampling inspection is the most economical procedure in a given case, then some sampling plan and some quality index must be selected. Generalized procedures for relating various BEPs to quality indices are often used in this connection.

For the MIL-STD-105D table in Figure 15.11, this quality index is, of course, the AQL. Two alternative approaches may be used to select an AQL in Figure 15.11 which is appropriate to a given BEP. These approaches are simple and practical and are appropriate when an essentially "simplistic" approach to sampling can be taken; however, they must be closely reviewed in those cases where technical statistical considerations are important. These approaches are:

1. Select the AQL which is closest to or equal to the BEP. This procedure is quite popular because it has the virtue of great simplicity. It is relatively inaccurate, however, and in certain cases it sacrifices some of the economy possible with sampling.

    Figure 15.16 shows a typical calculation sheet developed by one factory for determining AQL in this fashion. In the example shown, inspection cost per unit has been determined as $0.01. Repair cost has been determined as $1 per unit.

    This results in a BEP of 1 percent which, in the procedure used in Figure 15.16, also becomes the AQL. If the actual incoming percent nonconformance of these parts is within the range of a 1 percent AQL, then the 1 percent value may become the quality target.

2. Relate the BEP to an AQL by using the table in Figure 15.17.

This procedure enables somewhat more economical use of sampling tables than permitted in alternative 1. Its use is similar to that of alternative 1 up to the point of calculation of the BEP; the difference is that the BEP value is then used to determine the appropriate AQL value. If the inspection cost per unit is $0.05 and the associated repair cost is $1, for example, then the 5 percent BEP will call for, as shown in Figure 15.17, an AQL of 4 percent.

Whether 1 or 2 will be used in a given factory—or whether this kind of calculation is appropriate at all—depends almost entirely upon the circumstances in that particular factory: the demand for sampling economy, the

---

SAMPLING PLAN

PART OR ASSEMBLY ___STUD___

DRAWING NO.   ___6947328___

A.   COST PER UNIT FOR COMPLETE INSPECTION OR TEST $0.01

B.   REPAIR COST IF NONCONFORMING UNIT IS FOUND IN
     ASSEMBLY   1.00

C.   ACCEPTABLE QUALITY LEVEL (AQL)=$\frac{A}{B}$ 1% *

---

*   THIS IS THE PROPORTION OF NONCONFORMING UNITS THAT CAN GET
    INTO ASSEMBLIES WITHOUT HAVING REPAIR COSTS EXCEED
    100 PER CENT INSPECTION COSTS.

a. F. Jones
_____
INSPECTOR

3/1
_____
DATE

FIG. 15.16

amount of paperwork entailed, the requirement for technical statistical accuracy, and so on.

15.18 Uneconomical Use of Sampling Plans

It is well to appreciate the results of indiscriminate use of a sampling plan in those cases where it is uneconomical. One instance occurs when the incoming percent nonconformance consistently exceeds the BEP. If a particular part or quality characteristic were 11 percent nonconforming in actual practice and the BEP were 7 percent, then use of Figure 15.17 would indicate a 6.5 percent AQL sampling plan.

Should such a sampling plan be used, the majority of incoming lots would be either rejected or subject to 100 percent inspection. This makes the plan meaningless at the outset and possibly an added cost burden. In addition, the

RECOMMENDED A.Q.L. VALUES
MIL−STD−I05D SAMPLING TABLE SHOWN IN FIG.15-11
FOR USE WITH VARIOUS BREAK-EVEN POINTS

BREAK-EVEN POINT	A.Q.L.	BREAK-EVEN POINT	A.Q.L.
$\frac{1}{2}$ % TO I %	$\frac{1}{4}$ %	6 % TO I0$\frac{1}{2}$ %	6.5 %
I % TOI$\frac{3}{4}$%	0.65%	I0$\frac{1}{2}$% TO I7 %	I0%
I$\frac{3}{4}$% TO 3%	I %		
3 % TO 4%	2.5%		
4 % TO 6%	4%		

FIG. 15.17

factor of sampling risk, as discussed in connection with producer's and consumer's risk, would indicate that a certain number of incoming lots would be accepted containing 11 percent nonconformances.

In the instance cited, therefore, 100 percent inspection should be carried on, not sampling, which is both uneconomical and impractical.

In actual practice, accurate details for the BEP calculation may not be readily available in a given factory owing to the type of accounting routines used. In addition, AQL selection is often dictated by past experience on a given part or quality characteristic before any detailed cost balance can or has been made.

As a result, the BEP, in common with other technical methods for answering the question of when sampling may be done, has as its main value the presentation of a point of view rather than the dictation of any hard-and-fast rule for a particular type of formal calculation. Sampling may be desirable under some conditions and undesirable under other conditions; it is imperative that the industrial user of sampling plans know what these conditions are. It is not so imperative, however, as to the form in which the user obtains and uses this information—whether to apply it in such an informal fashion as to make the selection of an AQL seem quite arbitrary or to use it as part of a formalized procedure for calculating cost balances.

When Dodge-Romig tables are used, some of this procedure to minimize the cost of sampling consistent with a given degree of protection is "built into" the sampling plan. These tables require that the value for average percent defective of the material in question be determined before a sampling schedule can be chosen. They automatically afford sampling schedules which minimize inspection in relation to a given quality target.

15.19 Sampling of Multiple Characteristics

The importance of selecting a suitable quality index value for a part has been emphasized in the previous discussion. But the problem of just what characteristics are covered by the "quality index value for a part" has not been fully analyzed. Does a 2.5 percent AQL for lots of incoming washers apply to all the characteristics of the washer? Does it refer only to the thickness and the outer-diameter characteristics? Does it simply apply to the inner-diameter characteristics?

For many parts, to be sure, only one characteristic is critical, so that it is readily obvious what is covered by the quality index value for that part. In the case of many industrial applications of springs, it is the "pull" of the spring that will be the only characteristic sampled.

Yet there are many other cases—certain semiconductor components, for example—where several characteristics are critical. In the case of cast parts, for instance, is may be necessary to sample thickness, weight, and length.

As a result, it is essential that the particular characteristics of a part for which the quality index value has been established be specified. When it is necessary to specify more than one such characteristic for parts being sampled, there are two major alternatives for accomplishing this objective:

1. *Establish a quality index value for each individual quality characteristic.* For round-head machine screws, an AQL of 2.5 percent may be established for the length characteristic, which is fairly critical, while an AQL of 10 percent may be established for the width of the screwhead, which may be of little importance. The lot may be rejected if either of these quality index values is not met.
2. *Establish an overall quality index value which applies to several of the part characteristics.* With washers, for example, the thickness, outer diameter, and inner diameter may be combined in a 2.5 percent AQL. If the sampling plan calls for rejection of the lot if more than five nonconformities are found, and if two thickness, two outer-diameter, and two inner-diameter nonconformities have been found—a total of six—then the lot may be rejected.

A similar approach to setting these quality index values involves the use of nonconformity classifications. These nonconformity classifications are derived from the classification of the characteristics concept reviewed in Chapter 10, "Quality-Engineering Technology," Section 10.19. Two alternative means for using this approach—for example, critical-major-minor defects or nonconformities—are the following:

1. Special sampling tables can be devised which allow for a single sample size to be used for several characteristics of a part but which provide separate columns for the allowable number of critical defects or nonconformities, the allowable number of major defects or nonconformities, and the allowable number of minor defects or nonconformities. The allowable number of minor defects or nonconformities is of course always larger than that for major defects or nonconformities, which in turn is larger than that for critical defects or nonconformities.

2. Standard sampling tables can be used, but the total number of defects or nonconformities in the lot under inspection is determined by weighting critical, major, and minor defects or nonconformities. Thus, with machine screws, minor defects or nonconformities may be weighed as one-fourth the importance of major defects or nonconformities. If the length of the screw is a major characteristic and the width of the screwhead a minor characteristic, and if the allowable number of defects or nonconformities is 5, the lot may be passed if 2 length nonconformities and 10 width nonconformities —total 4.5—are found.

Many other reasons can be cited for the importance of clearly specifying those characteristics to which a quality index applies. For one instance, lots of material are often rejected and shipped back to vendors as being "unsatisfactory" without any indication on the reject tag or in the inspection records as to just what is unsatisfactory—whether a single characteristic or a combination of characteristics.

Again, the vague statement that a certain part has a 2.5 percent AQL may leave the interpretation of the characteristics to which the 2.5 percent should be applied in the hands of an unskilled inspection operator unfamiliar with the relative importance of the various characteristics. Quite likely the operator will develop his own sampling specification for the part, which either may be too severe on unimportant characteristics or may place too little weight on important ones.

15.20 Sampling by Variables

There has been a great preponderance in industry of go and not-go inspection over sampling by actual measurements, or variables sampling. There have been many reasons for this condition, among which have been the lack of recognition of the effectiveness of variables sampling in many cases, the unavailability of the necessary measuring equipments in many factories, and, perhaps of greatest importance, the lack of the need in the past for the type of precision that may be furnished by actual measurements.

This situation is rapidly changing. The great growth in the precision demanded of products was extensively discussed earlier in this book, and there is now both quantity and quality of excellent measuring equipments available to much of industry.

The impact upon sampling procedure of taking actual readings is readily apparent. Much greater accuracy results from these measurements than from a simple statement that a part is "good" or "bad." The several advantages of knowing just where in the tolerance band a part falls as opposed to the mere statement that "it is O.K." may be recalled from previous discussions on frequency distributions and control charts.

Of equal importance but perhaps not so obvious is the fact that variables sampling may be less expensive than go and not-go sampling because information of equal value may be obtained from a smaller measurements sample than from a go and not-go sample.

Variables sampling takes many forms. One of the most typical is an application of the frequency distribution. A standard frequency-distribution sample size is often established—perhaps 50, perhaps 150 units—and a sample of this size is selected from each incoming lot of the material in question. The measured parts may be plotted on a tally card. Sometimes the sample size is kept flexible, sampling being stopped when an adequate distribution picture for the lot has appeared on the tally card rather than establishing a specific sample size.

Sometimes the resulting frequency-distribution picture is merely visually compared with the tolerance limits as the basis of acceptance or rejection of the lot. Sometimes the 3-sigma limits for the distribution are calculated and compared with the tolerance limits as the basis for acceptance or rejection of the lot. Figure 15.18 shows a lot of electronic capacitors that were accepted by visual examination of the frequency-distribution picture.

Measurements control charts are often used in variables sampling. The procedure involves the establishment of control limits for the part characteristic in question and selection of a sample size. Often this sample size is arrived at arbitrarily after some experience has been obtained with the parts in question.

In place of the methods described above, it is often both necessary and cost-effective to establish far more precise calculation of the sample size required for a given degree of protection. The individual features of such variables sampling plans are much more closely geared to the needs of particular conditions, and more economical sample sizes and procedures may result.

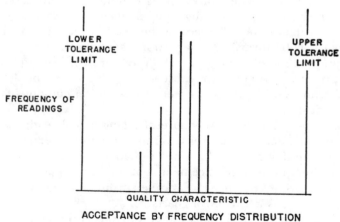

ACCEPTANCE BY FREQUENCY DISTRIBUTION

FIG. 15.18

15.21 An Acceptance Plan: Variables

Figure 15.19 shows the MIL-STD-414 variables acceptance sampling table for a single specification limit when the variability is known.[29] The table established 14 different AQL schedules, each of which is coupled with a specific operating characteristic curve describing the risks involved. Each operating characteristic curve is presented in MIL-STD-414.

The instructions for the selection of the samples are similar to those outlined for MIL-STD-105D in Section 15.13, for normal inspection, and in Section 15.14 for tightened inspection.

The table itself consists of five major sections, as shown in Figure 15.20:

I Lot size.
II Sample size (n).
III AQL (normal inspection).
IV AQL (tightened inspection).
V Acceptability constant (k).

Table D-1. Master Table for Normal and Tightened Inspection for Plans Based Upon Variability Known (*Single Specification Limit—Form 1*)

Lot size	Acceptable quality levels (normal inspection)													
	0.04		0.065		0.10		0.15		0.25		0.40		0.65	
	n	k	n	k	n	k	n	k	n	k	n	k	n	k
3–40														
41–65														
66–110													2	1.58
111–180									2	1.94	2	1.81	3	1.69
181–300							3	2.19	3	2.07	3	1.91	4	1.80
301–500	3	2.58	3	2.49	4	2.39	4	2.30	4	2.14	5	2.05	5	1.88
501–800	4	2.65	4	2.55	5	2.46	5	2.34	6	2.23	6	2.08	7	1.95
801–1300	5	2.69	6	2.59	6	2.49	6	2.37	7	2.25	8	2.13	8	1.96
1301–3200	6	2.72	6	2.58	7	2.50	7	2.38	8	2.26	9	2.13	10	1.99
3201–8000	8	2.77	8	2.64	9	2.54	10	2.45	11	2.31	12	2.18	13	2.03
8001–22,000	10	2.83	11	2.72	11	2.59	12	2.49	13	2.35	14	2.21	16	2.07
22,001–110,000	14	2.88	15	2.77	16	2.65	17	2.54	19	2.41	21	2.27	23	2.12
110,001–550,000	19	2.92	20	2.80	22	2.69	23	2.57	25	2.43	27	2.29	30	2.14
550,001–and over	27	2.96	30	2.84	31	2.72	34	2.62	37	2.47	40	2.33	44	2.17
	0.065		0.10		0.15		0.25		0.40		0.65		1.00	
	Acceptable quality levels (tightened inspection)													

All AQL values are in percent defective.

↓ Use first sampling plan below arrow, that is, sample size as well as k value. When sample size equals or exceeds lot size, every item in the lot must be inspected.

FIG. 15.19 Above table is a modification of Table D-1 of MIL-STD-414 in that inspection level III is used, corresponding lot sizes are incorporated directly into the body of the table, and lot sizes of 1301–3200, 3201–8000, and 550,001–and over are used.

Table D-1. Master Table for Normal and Tightened Inspection for Plans Based Upon Variability Known (*Single Specification Limit—Form 1*) *(Cont'd.)*

Lot size	Acceptable quality levels (normal inspection)													
	1.00		**1.50**		**2.50**		**4.00**		**6.50**		**10.00**		**15.00**	
	n	*k*	*n*	*k*	*n*	*k*	*n*	*k*	*n*	*k*	*n*	*k*	*n*	*k*
3–40	↓		↓		↓		↓		↓		↓		↓	
41–65	2	1.36	2	1.25	2	1.09	2	0.936	3	0.755	3	0.573	4	0.344
66–110	2	1.42	2	1.33	3	1.17	3	1.01	3	0.825	4	0.641	4	0.429
111–180	3	1.56	3	1.44	4	1.28	4	1.11	5	0.919	5	0.728	6	0.515
181–300	4	1.69	4	1.53	5	1.39	5	1.20	6	0.991	7	0.797	8	0.584
301–500	6	1.78	6	1.62	7	1.45	8	1.28	9	1.07	11	0.877	12	0.649
501–800	7	1.80	8	1.68	9	1.49	10	1.31	12	1.11	14	0.906	16	0.685
801–1300	9	1.83	10	1.70	11	1.51	13	1.34	15	1.13	17	0.924	20	0.706
1301–3200	11	1.86	12	1.72	13	1.53	15	1.35	18	1.15	21	0.942	24	0.719
3201–8000	14	1.89	15	1.75	18	1.57	20	1.38	23	1.17	27	0.965	31	0.741
8001–22,000	17	1.93	19	1.79	22	1.61	25	1.42	29	1.21	33	0.995	38	0.770
22,001–110,000	25	1.97	28	1.84	32	1.65	36	1.46	42	1.24	49	1.08	56	0.803
110,001–550,000	33	2.00	36	1.86	42	1.67	48	1.48	55	1.26	64	1.05	75	0.819
550,001–and over	49	2.03	54	1.89	61	1.69	70	1.51	82	1.29	95	1.07	111	0.841
	1.50		**2.50**		**4.00**		**6.50**		**10.00**		**15.00**			
	Acceptable quality levels (tightened inspection)													

All AQL values are in percent defective.
↓ Use first sampling plan below arrow, that is, sample size as well as *k* value. When sample size equals or exceeds lot size, every item in the lot must be inspected.

(**FIG.** 15.19 **continued**)

With the exception of IV and V, these sections are similar to those discussed in detail in Sections 15.13 and 15.14. Tightened inspection is included in the body of this table. The acceptability constant *k* is the value to which the sample average, the specification limit, and the variability are compared for disposition decision of the lot. How this is accomplished is detailed in the following example.

Consider the case of the felt washers used in Section 15.13. The inner diameter of these washers is the critical quality characteristic, and these inner diameters are inspected when the material is received from the vendor's plant. These washers are used to alleviate shock, so only a lower specification limit is specified. This lower limit (L) is 0.500 inch, and an AQL of 2.5 percent has been established for it. The process capability for this quality characteristic is known from past experience to be consistently 0.006 inch, or $\sigma = 0.001$ inch.

When a lot of 1000 washers is received in incoming inspection, the steps that will be followed in the use of the table are as follows:

1. Select the appropriate lot size. In Figure 15.20 it may be seen that the 1000-unit lot falls in the 801 to 1300 lot size.

2. Select the proper sample size (n). The proper sample size of 11 pieces is found at the intersection of the appropriate lot size (801 to 1300) and an AQL of 2.5 percent.

3. Compute the sample mean ($\overline{X}$). The inner diameters of the 11 pieces drawn at random were found to be as follows:

0.502 inch	0.503 inch
0.501 inch	0.502 inch
0.502 inch	0.503 inch
0.504 inch	0.501 inch
0.500 inch	0.502 inch
0.502 inch	

The sample mean $\overline{X}$ that equals $\Sigma X / n$ was found to be 5.522 inch/11 = 0.502 inch.

Table D-1. Master Table for Normal and Tightened Inspection for Plans Based Upon Variability Known (*Single Specification Limit—Form 1*)

	Acceptable quality levels (normal inspection)												
	0.04		0.065 III		0.10		0.15		0.25		0.40		0.65
I Lot size	**II** n	**V** k	n	k	n	k	n	k	n	k	n	k	n	k
3–40														
41–65														
66–110													2	1.58
111–180									2	1.94	2	1.81	3	1.69
181–300							3	2.19	3	2.07	3	1.91	4	1.80
301–500	3	2.58	3	2.49	4	2.39	4	2.30	4	2.14	5	2.05	5	1.88
501–800	4	2.65	4	2.55	5	2.46	5	2.34	6	2.23	6	2.08	7	1.95
801–1300	5	2.69	6	2.59	6	2.49	6	2.37	7	2.25	8	2.13	8	1.96
1301–3200	6	2.72	6	2.58	7	2.50	7	2.38	8	2.26	9	2.13	10	1.99
3201–8000	8	2.77	8	2.64	9	2.54	10	2.45	11	2.31	12	2.18	13	2.03
8001–22,000	10	2.83	11	2.72	11	2.59	12	2.49	13	2.35	14	2.21	16	2.07
22,001–110,000	14	2.88	15	2.77	16	2.65	17	2.54	19	2.41	21	2.27	23	2.12
110,001–550,000	19	2.92	20	2.80	22	2.69	23	2.57	25	2.43	27	2.29	30	2.14
550,001–and over	27	2.96	30	2.84	31	2.72	34	2.62	37	2.47	40	2.33	44	2.17
	0.065		0.10		0.15		0.25		0.40		0.65		1.00	

IV Acceptable quality levels (tightened inspection)

All AQL values are in percent defective.

↓ Use first sampling plan below arrow, that is, sample size as well as k value. When sample size equals or exceeds lot size, every item in the lot must be inspected.

FIG. 15.20 **Table is a modification of Table D-1 of MIL-STD-414 in that inspection level III is used, corresponding lot sizes are incorporated directly into the body of the table, and lot sizes of 1301–3200, 3201–8000, and 550,001–and over are used.**

Table D-1. Master Table for Normal and Tightened
Inspection for Plans Based Upon Variability Known
(*Single Specification Limit—Form 1*) *(Cont'd.)*

	Acceptable quality levels (normal inspection)												
	1.00		1.50 III		2.50		4.00		6.50		10.00		15.00	
I	**II**	**V**												
Lot size	**n**	**k**	**n**	**k**	**n**	**k**	**n**	**k**	**n**	**k**	**n**	**k**	**n**	**k**
3–40	↓		↓		↓		↓		↓		↓		↓	
41–65	2	1.36	2	1.25	2	1.09	2	0.936	3	0.755	3	0.573	4	0.344
66–110	2	1.42	2	1.33	3	1.17	3	1.01	3	0.825	4	0.641	4	0.429
111–180	3	1.56	3	1.44	4	1.28	4	1.11	5	0.919	5	0.728	6	0.515
181–300	4	1.69	4	1.53	5	1.39	5	1.20	6	0.991	7	0.797	8	0.584
301–500	6	1.78	6	1.62	7	1.45	8	1.28	9	1.07	11	0.877	12	0.649
501–800	7	1.80	8	1.68	9	1.49	10	1.31	12	1.11	14	0.906	16	0.685
801–1300	9	1.83	10	1.70	11	1.51	13	1.34	15	1.13	17	0.924	20	0.706
1301–3200	11	1.86	12	1.72	13	1.53	15	1.35	18	1.15	21	0.942	24	0.719
3201–8000	14	1.89	15	1.75	18	1.57	20	1.38	23	1.17	27	0.965	31	0.741
8001–22,000	17	1.93	19	1.79	22	1.61	25	1.42	29	1.21	33	0.995	38	0.770
22,001–110,000	25	1.97	28	1.84	32	1.65	36	1.46	42	1.24	49	1.03	56	0.803
110,001–550,000	33	2.00	36	1.86	42	1.67	48	1.48	55	1.26	64	1.05	75	0.819
550,001–and over	49	2.03	54	1.89	61	1.69	70	1.51	82	1.29	95	1.07	111	0.841
	1.50		2.50		4.00		6.50		10.00		15.00			
	IV Acceptable quality levels (tightened inspection)													

All AQL values are in percent defective.
↓ Use first sampling plan below arrow, that is, sample size as well as *k* value. When sample size
equals or exceeds lot size, every item in the lot must be inspected.

(FIG. 15.20 **continued)**

4. Compute the difference between the sample mean ($\overline{X}$) and the lower specification limit (L) in standard deviation units $(\overline{X} - L)/\sigma$. The sample mean ($\overline{X}$) is 0.502 inch, the lower specification limit L is 0.500 inch, and the standard deviation for this quality characteristic σ is 0.001 inch. Substituting in the formula, the result is found to be $(\overline{X} - L)/\sigma = (0.502 - 0.500)/0.001 = 2$.
5. Select the acceptability constant k. Using Figure 15.20, the proper acceptability constant $k = 1.51$ is found at the intersection of the appropriate lot size (801 to 1300) and an AQL of 2.5 percent.
6. Compare the difference found, $(\overline{X} - L)/\sigma$, with the acceptability constant k. If the value $(\overline{X} - L)/\sigma$ is less than k, the lot is rejected. If $(\overline{X} - L)/\sigma$ is greater than k, the lot is accepted. In this example, $(\overline{X} - L)/\sigma = 2$ inches is greater than $k = 1.51$, so the lot is accepted.

Note that in this example the accept decision was made using only 11 pieces, whereas in the case of the double-sampling attribute plan in Section 15.13, a first sample of 50 pieces was required.[30]

MIL-STD-414 considers other conditions with procedures similar to those in the above example, and, as in MIL-STD-105D, there are tightened sampling plans included in MIL-STD-414.

15.22 Computer-Based Sampling Plans

In many cases, computer programs for sampling tables have greatly contributed to their efficient use. A number of such programs have been developed for the most commonly used sampling tables.

One example of the approach is a program developed for Military Standard 414. It is capable of handling nine specific situations, all at inspection level IV as contained in Military Standard 414.[31] It covers situations where the process variance is both known and unknown. When the process variance is unknown, the user can specify either the sample standard deviation or the sample range. Given the above three situations, the following three cases can be handled: (1) One limit is specified (form 2), (2) two limits are specified with a single AQL value, and (3) two limits are specified with separate AQL values.

The program prints out a summary of the information required by the sampling plan selected. It also prints the required sample size, the estimated percent defective (EST PER DEF), the maximum allowable percent defective (MAX PER DEF), and states whether to accept or reject the lot. The user must correctly specify the number of items sampled before running the program.

The correct sample size is printed as a precautionary measure and should

---

Program Operation of a Computer Program for Military Standard 414

Card	Columns	Information
1	1–80	Format for data
2	1–6	The number of lots
3	1–5	Type of inspection (TYPEN, TYPET, TYPER)
4	1–6	Is the process variance known or not known (KNOWN, NKNOWN)
5	1–6	If the variance is unknown, the method desired (STDDEV, RANGE)
6	1–13	If the variance is known enter sigma using an E13.7 format
7	1–2	Coded lot size from Table 1
8	1	The number of limits specified
9	1–5	If only one limit is required, specify which one (UPPER or LOWER)
10	1–10	If LOWER is specified, enter the lower limit using E10.0 format
11	1–10	If UPPER is specified, enter the upper limit using E10.0 format
12	1–4	If two limits are specified, enter the number of AQL's as AQL1 or AQL2
13	1–2	If AQL1, enter the coded AQL from Table 2
14	1–2	If AQL2, enter the coded lower AQL from Table 2
15	1–2	If AQL2, enter the coded upper AQL from Table 2
16–on		Data from all lots according to the format specified on card 1

FIG. 15.21 **Program operation for computer program for MIL-STD-414, developed by Peter R. Nelson.**

Program Listing

```
      COMMON Y                                                                    001
      DOUBLE PRECISION UPPER, LOWER,AQL1,AQL2,KNOWN,NKNOWN,RANGE,                  002
     1TYPER,TYPET,TYPEN,TYPE,S,S1,S2,S4                                            003
      DIMENSION D(200),F(14,16,4),AQL(14),NR(16),FMT(80),                          004
     1N2 (16) ,N3(16) ,YNU(16) ,CC(16) ,NN(14,15,2) ,NNN1 (210) ,NNN2 (210),      005
     1FF1 (112) ,FF2(112) ,FF3(112) ,FF4(112) ,FF5(112) ,FF6(112) ,FF7(112),      006
     1FF8(112)                                                                     007
      EQUIVALENCE (FF1(1) ,F(1,1,1)) , (FF2(1) ,F(1,9,1)) , (FF3(1) ,F(1,1,2))     008
     1, (FF4(1) ,F(1,9,2)) , (FF5(1) ,F(1,1,3)) , (FF6(1) ,F(1,9,3)),             009
     1 (FF7(1) ,F(1,1,4)) ,(FF8(1) ,F(1,9,4)),                                     010
     1 (NNN1 (1) ,NN(1,1,1)) , (NNN2(1) ,NN(1,1,2))                                011
      DATA UPPER/ 'UPPER'/ ,LOWER/'LOWER'/ ,AQL1/'AQL1'/,AQL2/'AQL2'/,             012
     1KNOWN/'KNOWN'/,NKNOWN/'NKNOWN'/ ,RANGE/'RANGE'/,TYPER/'TYPER'/,              013
     2TYPET/'TYPET'/,TYPEN/'TYPEN'/                                                014
      DATA NR/1,1,1,1,2,3,4,5,5,6,7,7,8,9,12,13/                                   015
      DATA N2/3,4,5,7,10,15,20,25,30,35,40,50,75,                                  016
     1100,150,200/                                                                 017
      DATA N3/3,4,5,7,10,15,25,30,35,40,50,60,85,                                  018
     1115,175,230/                                                                 019
      DATA AQL/.04,.065,.1,.15,.25,.4,.65,1.,                                      020
     11.5,2.5,4.,6.5,10.,15./                                                      021
      DATA YNU/2.934,3.995,4.828,6.499,8.474,12.106,                              022
     119.355,22.986,26.611,30.236,37.486,44.735,                                   023
     262.856,84.601,128.091,167.958/                                              024
      DATA CC/1.91,2.234,2.474,2.83,2.405,2.379,                                  025
     12.358,2.353,2.349,2.346,2.342,2.339,2.335,                                  026
     22.333,2.331,2.33/                                                           027
      DATA FF1   /0.000,0.000,0.000,0.000,0.000,0.000,0.000,                      028
     1           0.000,0.000,7.590,18.86,26.94,33.69,40.47,                       029
     1           0.000,0.000,0.000,0.000,0.000,0.000,0.000,                       030
     1           1.530,5.500,10.92,16.45,22.86,29.45,36.90,                       031
     1           0.000,0.000,0.000,0.000,0.000,0.000,1.330,                       032
     1           3.320,5.830,9.800,14.39,20.19,26.56,33.99,                       033
     1           0.000,0.000,0.000,0.000,.4220,1.060,2.140,                       034
     1           3.550,5.350,8.400,12.20,17.35,23.29,30.50,                       035
     1           0.000,0.000,0.000,.3490,.7160,1.300,2.170,                       036
     1           3.260,4.770,7.290,10.54,15.17,20.74,27.57,                       037
     1           .0990,.1860,.3120,.5030,.8180,1.310,2.110,                       038
     1           3.050,4.310,6.560,9.460,13.71,18.94,25.61,                       039
     1           .1350,.2280,.3650,.5440,.8460,1.290,2.050,                       040
     1           2.950,4.090,6.170,8.920,12.99,18.03,24.53,                       041
     1           .1550,.2500,.3800,.5510,.8870,1.290,2.000,                       042
     1           2.860,3.970,5.970,8.630,12.57,17.51,23.97/                       043
      DATA FF2   /.1790,.2800,.4130,.5810,.8790,1.290,1.980,                      044
     1           2.830,3.910,5.860,8.470,12.36,17.24,23.58,                       045
     1           .1700,.2640,.3880,.5350,.8470,1.230,1.870,                       046
     1           2.680,3.700,5.570,8.100,11.87,16.65,22.91,                       047
     I           1790,.2750,.4010,.5660,.8730,1.260,1.880,                        048
```

516

1	2.710,3.720,5.580,8.090,11.85,16.61,22.86,	049
1	.1630,.2500,.3630,.5030,.7890,1.170,1.710,	050
1	2.490,3.450,5.200,7.610,11.23,15.87,22.00,	051
1	.1470,.2280,.3300,.4670,.7200,1.070,1.600,	052
1	2.290,3.200,4.870,7.150,10.63,15.13,21.11,	053
1	.1450,.2200,.3170,.4470,.6890,1.020,1.530,	054
1	2.200,3.070,4.690,6.910,10.32,14.75,20.66,	055
1	.1340,.2030,.2930,.4130,.6380,.9490,1.430,	056
1	2.050,2.890,4.430,6.570,9.880,14.20,20.02,	057
1	.1350,.2040,.2940,.4140,.6370,.9450,1.420,	058
1	2.040,2.870,4.400,6.530,9.810,14.12,19.92/	059

FIG. 15.22 Section from computer program for MIL-STD-414, developed by Peter R. Nelson.

agree with the number of sample data entries supplied by the user. For small lot sizes and very small AQL values, no sampling plans are available. If such a plan is requested, the program will print UNACCEPTABLE AQL. If the estimated percent defective is greater than 50 and the variance is unknown, the program so prints, and no further calculations are made.

Figure 15.21 summarizes the program operation. An example of the program listing is then given in Figure 15.22.

15.23 An Acceptance Plan: ANSI/ASQC Z1.9 Variables Sampling Symmetrical to MIL-STD-105D

Another variable acceptance plan, ANSI/ASQC Z1.9 (1980), is a revision of MIL-STD-414 and of its essentially equivalent civilian version designated ANSI Z1.9 (1972).[32] It is designed to be closely keyed to the widely applied attributes sampling plan using the MIL-STD-105D approach which has earlier been reviewed in this chapter.

While the basic sampling plans of ANSI/ASQC Z1.9 (1980) are similar to those of 414, the standard itself differs considerably from these previous standards, the previous civilian version of which was designated ANSI Z1.9 (1972).[33] It is closely aligned to the 105D tables. The "switching rules"—that is among normal, reduced, and tightened sampling—are essentially similar between Z1.9 (1980) and 105D, as shown in Figure 15.23.

Also, in ANSI/ASQC Z1.9 (1980), lot size ranges are adjusted from MIL-STD-414 to correspond to those in MIL-STD-105D. AQL's 0.04, 0.065, and 15.00 are eliminated to achieve a match of operating characteristics; inspection levels are relabeled to correspond to usage in MIL-STD-105D; and switching rules are essentially replaced by those of MIL-STD-105D.

Figure 15.24 shows a representative table from this standard, with some adaptation for particular use. In terminological areas, this sampling plan uses the designations of "nonconformity" for "defect," "nonconformance" for "defective," and "percent nonconforming" for "percent defective."

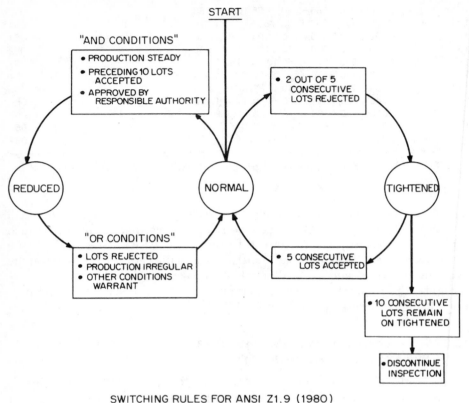

"AND CONDITIONS"
- PRODUCTION STEADY
- PRECEDING 10 LOTS ACCEPTED
- APPROVED BY RESPONSIBLE AUTHORITY

START

- 2 OUT OF 5 CONSECUTIVE LOTS REJECTED

REDUCED   NORMAL   TIGHTENED

"OR CONDITIONS"
- LOTS REJECTED
- PRODUCTION IRREGULAR
- OTHER CONDITIONS WARRANT

- 5 CONSECUTIVE LOTS ACCEPTED

- 10 CONSECUTIVE LOTS REMAIN ON TIGHTENED

- DISCONTINUE INSPECTION

SWITCHING RULES FOR ANSI Z1.9 (1980)

FIG. 15.23

PROCESS-CONTROL SAMPLING TABLES

15.24 The Approach to Sampling for Process Control

Many parts and materials are subject to several successive machining, robotized, or processing operations before they become finished units. Very often, also, products are assembled on conveyors where subassemblies are successively added and various operations are successively performed.

If lots of these finished units are examined for conformance to specification only after they have been completed, large quantities of defectives or nonconforming units may very well be found. The preventive approach of total quality control has made it inevitable that "process controls" would be established over the material during the course of actual production, irrespective of any acceptance procedures for examining them after completion.

That process-control sampling is essential has been recognized in industry for some time. The existence in many factories of the so-called patrol or roving

TABLE D-1
Master Table for Normal and Tightened Inspection for Plans Based on Variability Known
(Single Specification Limit -- Form 1)

LOT SIZE	Acceptable Quality Levels (normal inspection)											
	T		.10		.15		.25		.40		.65	
	n	k	n	k	n	k	n	k	n	k	n	k
2 – 15	↓		↓		↓		↓		↓		↓	
16 – 25												
26 – 50											2	1.58
51 – 90							2	1.94	2	1.81	3	1.69
91 – 150					3	2.19	3	2.07	3	1.91	4	1.80
151 – 280	3	2.49	4	2.39	4	2.30	4	2.14	5	2.05	5	1.88
281 – 400	4	2.55	5	2.46	5	2.34	6	2.23	6	2.08	7	1.95
401 – 500	6	2.59	6	2.49	6	2.37	7	2.25	8	2.13	8	1.96
501 – 1,200	7	2.63	8	2.54	9	2.45	9	2.29	10	2.16	11	2.01
1,201 – 3,200	11	2.72	11	2.59	12	2.49	13	2.35	14	2.21	16	2.07
3,201 – 10,000	15	2.77	16	2.65	17	2.54	19	2.41	21	2.27	23	2.12
10,001 – 35,000	20	2.80	22	2.69	23	2.57	25	2.43	27	2.29	30	2.14
35,001 – 150,000	30	2.84	31	2.72	34	2.62	37	2.47	40	2.33	44	2.17
150,000 and over	40	2.85	42	2.73	45	2.62	49	2.48	54	2.34	59	2.18
	.10		.15		.25		.40		.65		1.00	
	Acceptable Quality Levels (tightened inspection)											

All AQL values are in percent nonconformance. T denotes plan used exclusively on tightened inspection and provides symbol for identification of appropriate OC curve.

↓ Use first sampling plan below arrow; that is, both sample size as well as k value. When sample size equals or exceeds lot size, every item in the lot must be inspected.

FIG. 15.24 Table is a modification of Table D-1 of ANSI Z-1.9 (1980) in that inspection level II is used and corresponding lot sizes are incorporated directly into the body of the table.

floor inspectors is proof that some action has been taken in this direction. In essence, modern process-control sampling techniques represent a better controlled and better planned form of the patrol inspection that has been carried on for many years.

The approach to these modern process-control techniques has taken several forms. When actual readings are made, the measurements control chart has been found to be by far the most effective process-control technique. When go and not-go inspection has been carried on, percent-defective or percent-nonconforming control charts have had application and sampling tables for process control have been found particularly useful. The following discussion is devoted to a description of these process-control sampling tables.

15.25 Types of Process-Control Sampling Tables

Chapter 14 developed the thesis that parts can be most effectively controlled during production by examining small samples of these parts at frequent,

TABLE D-1 — Continued

Master Table for Normal and Tightened Inspection for Plans Based on Variability Known
(Single Specification Limit — Form 1)

LOT SIZE	Acceptable Quality Levels (normal inspection)											
	1.00		1.50		2.50		4.00		6.50		10.00	
	n	k	n	k	n	k	n	k	n	k	n	k
2 – 15	▼		▼		▼		▼		▼		▼	
16 – 25	2	1.36	2	1.25	2	1.09	2	.936	3	.755	3	.573
26 – 50	2	1.42	2	1.33	3	1.17	3	1.01	3	.825	4	.641
51 – 90	3	1.56	3	1.44	4	1.28	4	1.11	5	.919	5	.728
91 – 150	4	1.69	4	1.53	5	1.39	5	1.20	6	.991	7	.797
151 – 280	6	1.78	6	1.62	7	1.45	8	1.28	9	1.07	11	.877
281 – 400	7	1.80	8	1.68	9	1.49	10	1.31	12	1.11	14	.906
401 – 500	9	1.83	10	1.70	11	1.51	13	1.34	15	1.13	17	.924
501 – 1,200	12	1.88	14	1.75	15	1.56	18	1.38	20	1.17	24	.964
1,201 – 3,200	17	1.93	19	1.79	22	1.61	25	1.42	29	1.21	33	.995
3,201 – 10,000	25	1.97	28	1.84	32	1.65	36	1.46	42	1.24	49	1.03
10,001 – 35,000	33	2.00	36	1.86	42	1.67	48	1.48	55	1.26	64	1.05
35,001 – 150,000	49	2.03	54	1.89	61	1.69	70	1.51	82	1.29	95	1.07
150,000 and over	65	2.04	71	1.89	81	1.70	93	1.51	109	1.29	127	1.07
	1.50		2.50		4.00		6.50		10.00			
	Acceptable Quality Levels (tightened Inspection)											

All AQL values are in percent nonconformance.

Use first sampling plan below arrow; that is, both sample size as well as k value. When sample size equals or exceeds lot size, every item in the lot must be inspected.

(FIG. 15.24 continued)

regularly scheduled intervals. The objective of this sort of process check is to provide a continuous picture of the quality of parts being produced.

Plans that attain this objective represent a balance between inspection cost and the statistical accuracy required in indicating part quality. This balance must result in a plan wherein samples chosen are sufficiently representative and the intervals between each check are sufficiently close so that defective parts may be flagged to a stop as soon as they begin to appear in the manufacturing process.

It is this same fundamental approach around which effective process-control sampling tables have been designed. The tables specify

1. A series of sampling schedules, where possible, with quality indices providing a given degree of risk
2. The frequency with which these samples must be selected
3. The procedures to be used in implementing the sampling table: steps in accepting or rejecting lots, for example

Even more than acceptance sampling tables, these process-control tables represent a compromise between practical factory circumstances and "pure" statistics. This situation results from the greater need to recognize in process-control plans such intangibles as the conscientious application of operators and inspectors in the factory and such tangibles as the stability of the process in question.

As a result, some process-control sampling tables represent primarily a conscientious effort to place floor inspection on a scheduled basis; others are much closer to ideal statistical sampling procedures.

Perhaps the most important difference among process-control sampling tables relates to the type of production conditions for which the tables are designed. Three major types of process tables to be found are those that apply to

1. Production under those conditions when the output of a given period—a quarter hour, a half day—can be physically segregated in individual lots for process-inspection purposes. Brackets being slotted on a milling machine may, for example, be disposed between process-inspection checks in a tote box by the side of the machine.
2. Production under those conditions when continuous manufacturing flow makes it impractical physically to segregate the output of a given period. Integrated circuits being manufactured in an ongoing process are an example.
3. Production under those conditions when the lot for process-inspection purposes is automatically segregated during the manufacturing operation. Batch production of chemicals is an example of this type of situation.

The following sections discuss some of the process-control sampling techniques that have been developed for these production conditions.

15.26 Process-Control Table for Use When Output May Be Segregated

A process-control plan originally developed in industry has proved itself highly effective under those circumstances where it is convenient to separate the output of one period from the output of another period. Its primary objective is to discipline control practices under certain demanding production conditions, sometimes without fully precise statistical determination. Machining operations such as drilling and tapping have provided a particularly important field for use of this plan. This factory uses the designations defect and defective to identify units that do not meet requirements.

The plan consolidates the required process-sampling data into two tables, which are shown in Figure 15.25.

Schedule A provides information on the frequency with which sampling should be carried on.

Schedule B provides information on sample sizes appropriate to the desired acceptable quality level for the process or operation in question.

Frequency of sampling in schedule A is determined by two factors:

PROCESS CONTROL SAMPLING
PLAN

SCHEDULE A: HOW OFTEN TO SAMPLE - NO. HOURS BETWEEN CHECKS

HOURLY PRODUCTION	PROCESS CONDITION		
	ERRATIC	STABLE	CONTROLLED
UNDER 10	8 HOURS	8 HOURS	8 HOURS
10-19	4 HOURS	8 HOURS	8 HOURS
20-49	2 HOURS	4 HOURS	8 HOURS
50-99	1 HOUR	2 HOURS	4 HOURS
100 AND OVER	$\frac{1}{2}$ HOUR	1 HOUR	2 HOURS

"ERRATIC" - A PROCESS THAT IS INTERMITTENTLY GOOD AND BAD, OR THAT CHANGES FROM GOOD TO BAD WITH LITTLE ADVANCE NOTICE.

"STABLE" - A PROCESS THAT GIVES FAIRLY UNIFORM PERFORMANCE, BUT HAS GRADUAL CHANGE OR DRIFT IN ONE DIRECTION DUE TO TOOL WEAR OR OTHER FACTORS.

"CONTROLLED" - A PROCESS SHOWING PAST AND PRESENT EVIDENCE OF BEING UNDER CONTROL.

SCHEDULE B: SAMPLE SIZES FOR GO - NOT GO INSPECTION

DETERMINE ACCEPTABLE QUALITY LEVEL (A.Q. L.) AS A PERCENT DEFECTIVE; SAMPLE REGULARLY ACCORDING TO SCHEDULE A; USE SAMPLE SIZES BELOW.

ACCEPTABLE QUALITY LEVEL (AQL)	SAMPLE SIZE
UNDER 1.0%	20
1.0 - 1.9%	10
2.0 - 4.9%	5
5.0 OR MORE	2

JOB IS IN CONTROL WHEN NO DEFECTS ARE FOUND IN SAMPLE; WHEN OUT OF CONTROL, CORRECT PROCESS OR START 100% INSPECTION.

FIG. 15.25

1. *The production rate.* This rate is determined by simply computing the average number of parts produced each hour.
2. *The condition of the process.* This condition is determined on the basis of past experience. While such descriptions as "erratic," "stable," and "controlled" are necessarily general, the placing of a particular process in one of the three classifications is usually readily accomplished with a sufficient degree of accuracy for the purpose of the plan.

The size of the sample in schedule B is determined by the AQL for the process. This AQL may be either established as described earlier in this chapter or based upon past performance with the process. Selection of AQL based upon past performance is usually the practical alternative; either cost data may not be available or computation of individual BEPs for hundreds of operations may constitute an uneconomic task.

The use of this process-control sampling table usually proceeds with the following steps:

1. An AQL is established for the process or operation in question. Frequently a single AQL is set up to apply to all processes and operations within a manufacturing area. This procedure sacrifices accuracy in individual cases,

but it has the benefit of being simple and extremely economical, which in many situations tends to balance out its relative lack of accuracy.

2. Sample size for this AQL is determined from schedule B.
3. The average hourly rate of production is determined for the process or operation.
4. The frequency with which the sample check should be made is obtained from schedule A.
5. The plan is applied to actual production. Output between each process check is segregated. The required sample size is selected from the process at the required intervals. If one or more defects are found, process correction is immediately called for.
6. After the correction has been made, the same sampling procedure may be restored, or it may be made somewhat more rigorous for a period of time if conditions seem to call for such action.

Selection of the units in the sample from the production process may be made in three ways:

1. The sample may be selected at random from the segregated lot of parts.
2. The sample may be selected from the parts being produced at the time of the process inspection.
3. There may be a combination of 1 and 2.

Which of these three alternatives should be used depends upon the conditions of the individual process or operation. Repetitive punch-press operations, where the process is relatively stable for short periods of time but may have "trends" due to tool wear over longer periods, are often best controlled by the use of alternative 2. Drill-press operations carried on by relatively unskilled operators on rather crude fixtures, where the process has little "trend" during the production run but where carelessness over short periods of time may be an issue, are often best controlled by use of alternative 1. Alternative 3 is a compromise plan used in many cases.

15.27 Process-Control Table for Use When Output May Be Segregated: Example

The drilling operation on a critical hole in a shoulder plate may illustrate the use of the process-control sampling table of Figure 15.25.

Past experience has shown that this process varies intermittently from good to bad with little warning and that an AQL of 2.5 percent should be maintained on the operation. The required sample size may thereupon be determined from schedule B in Figure 15.25. The appropriate bracket for a 2.5 percent AQL is found by reading vertically down the AQL column to the 2.0 to 4.9 percent bracket. Reading horizontally across the table to the sample size column, note that a five-unit sample size is specified.

Average hourly production of these shoulder plates is 85 units. From schedule A of Figure 15.25, the hourly production column may be followed vertically downward until the suitable bracket is found. Eighty-five units will fall into the 50- to 99-unit bracket. Since the process varies intermittently from good to bad, a process condition of *erratic* applies here. Reading horizontally across the table to the process-condition column for erratic processes, a frequency between checks of 1 hour is specified.

Thus, with the drilling of a critical hole in the shoulder plates, the sampling condition prescribed is the selection of a sample of five units every hour.

15.28 Steps to Take in Application of This Process-Control Table

A series of steps are listed below that may appropriately be taken with the practical application of this process-control sampling table when the plan is being used on an overall basis in a processing area which includes several machine tools and processing equipments:

Step 1: Determine the average number of parts processed per hour by the machines and processing equipments over which control is desired. Determine the total number of machines and equipments that may be operating at the same time in the area.[34]

Step 2: Determine the overall process condition for the area. Using this and the average production figures from step 1, the frequency of sampling checks can be determined from schedule A in Figure 15.25.

Step 3: Determine the AQL for the area.

Step 4: Using the AQL decided upon, determine the sample size from schedule B in Figure 15.25.

Step 5: Determine the average number of parts that the present inspection force can inspect per hour at the machines in this area.

Step 6: Using the information from steps 1 through 5, determine if the present inspection force can apply process control in the area in question. If not, determine how to solve the problem by securing more inspectors, by more effective utilization of the present force, through better gages and equipments, by improving the process-control plan, and so on.

Step 7: Establish some means for recording the results of this process sampling. Usually a card filled in by the inspection department is placed on each machine. The information filled out on the card may be

1. Operator's check number or the machine number.
2. Operation number.
3. Date.
4. Process inspector's identification.

This card is usually divided into time periods so that the inspector can record in each space the condition of the process at that time.

Figure 15.26 illustrates a typical card used for this purpose. The face of this card carries space for such information as part drawing number, date, and machine number. For each time interval—7:00, 7:30—there are spaces for recording process condition in three categories:

1. "O.K.," that is, whether the parts checked are within tolerance.
2. "High," that is, whether the parts checked are above tolerance.
3. "Low," that is, whether the parts checked are below tolerance.

A column for "Reason" is provided wherein the number code for types of rejects, which is listed on the back of the card, can be used when a process is

---

SPECIAL MFG. DIVISION
INSPECTION

DWG. NO. _____ DATE _____

MACHINE _____ OPERATION# _____

STATION# _____ INSPECTOR _____

OPERATOR CHECK NO. _____

WITHIN TOLERANCE			TIME	REA-SON	STOP	S/L	IDLE
HIGH	O.K.	LOW					
			7:00				
			7:30				
			8:00				
			8:30				
			9:00				
			9:30				
			10:00				
			10:30				
			11:00				
			11:30				
			12:00				
			12:30				
			1:00				
			1:30				
			2:00				
			2:30				
			3:00				
			3:30				
			4:00				
			4:30				
			5:00				
			5:30				
			6:00				
			6:30				
			7:00				
			7:30				
			8:00				
			8:30				
			9:00				
			9:30				
			10:00				
			10:30				
			11:00				
			11:30				
			12:00				
			12:30				

FRONT

MACHINE ROOM

1- OVERSIZE	9 - DEF. MATERIAL
2- UNDERSIZE	10- BROKEN TAP
3- DEF. FIXTURE	11- BROKEN DRILL
4- ANGLE WRONG	12- BROKEN TOOL
5- DEF. GLS.	13- DEF. CUTTER
6- DEPTH OF HOLE	14-
7- DEF. BURRING	15-
8- DEF. FINISH	16-

PUNCH PRESS

17- ANGLE WRONG	22- UNDERSIZE
18- HOLES OFF. LOC.	23- DEF. MATERIAL
19- BURRS	24- DEF. FIXTURES
20- OVERSIZE	25-
21- UNDERSIZE	26-

SPOT WELD AND BRAZE

27- FLASH	32- DEF. FIXTURE
28- BURNING	33- WELD STRENGTH
29- ALIGNMENT	34-
30- SURFACE COND.	35-
31- DEF. WELD	36-

SHEET METAL

37- OUT OF SQUARE	51- WELD STRENGTH
38- OVERSIZE	52- UNDER CUT
39- UNDERSIZE	53- EXTRA WELDS
40- OMISSIONS	54- POOR GRIND
41- BURRS	55- ROUGH GRIND
42- WARPED	56- DEEP GRIND
43- DEF. MATERIAL	57- DEF. CORNERS
44- DEF. FINISH	58- SHARP EDGES
45- LOCATION	59- DEF. KNOCK OUTS
46- BROKEN WELD	60-
47- DEEP SPOTS	61-
48- FLASH	62-
49- BURNING	63-
50- DEF. FIXTURE	64-

COILS

65- O. DIAMETER	75- TERMINALS
66- I. DIAMETER	76- HARDWARE
67- LENGTH	77- NAMEPLATE
68- INSIDE LENGTH	78- EXPOSED WINDING
69- OUTSIDE LENGTH	79- POOR APPEARANCES
70- INSIDE WIDTH	80- LOOSE COVERING
71- OUTSIDE WIDTH	81-
72- OVER-ALL LENGTH	82-
73- STAMPING	83-
74- LEADS	84-

BACK

A TYPICAL PROCESS CONTROL CARD

FIG. 15.26

stopped. The "Stop" column is provided so that it can be punched when the operation is stopped for any cause.

The "S/U" column is included on the card so that it can be punched when inspection approval has been given to the initial setup parts at the start of the production run. The "Idle" column is printed on the card so that it can be punched if the machine is not operating when the inspector reaches it.

Step 8: Start the process-control sampling plan by filling out appropriate cards similar to the one shown in Figure 15.26 for each operation or machine for which the plan is being established. Place these tags on an appropriate location on the machines in question.

Step 9: Check the first production units as the operation is being set up. The process inspector should either approve the operation setup or refuse to let it start until the process is corrected to produce satisfactory parts. In the case of the card in Figure 15.26, the inspector will punch the "S/U" column to show approval of the operation.

Step 10: After approval the operator runs the job, checking the work as he or she feels necessary or, if the job is on an incentive plan, checking the work, as it may be paid in the time-studied price. As parts are completed, the operator disposes of them in a tote box provided beside the machine for that purpose. If the operator finds defective parts, the process should obviously be corrected.

Step 11: At the end of the proper interval of time, the inspector checks the required sample size for the job. These parts may be selected either as the pieces that have just been produced by the machine or at random from the tote box. The choice of which of these two means of sample selection should be used depends on the nature of the job and process (see Section 15.26).

If no rejects are found, the inspector disposes the parts that have accumulated since the last check into a "completed-work" tote box. With use of the card in Figure 15.26, the inspector will punch the card "O.K."

Step 12: If a reject is found, the inspector notifies the proper authority—usually the operator and the foreman—to get the process corrected immediately. The inspector may place a "defective tag" on the parts that have accumulated since the last check. It may be the responsibility of the operator to sort these parts or, under some systems, for the factory foreman to have them sorted. In the card in Figure 15.26, the inspector will record the appropriate reject number in the Reason space and will also punch either the High or the Low space or possibly both.

Step 13: Whenever the process is stopped to adjust or change the tooling, the procedure of step 9 is followed, as in the case of a new setup.

Step 14: The data on the tags may periodically be analyzed in any of several fashions. There may be daily or weekly breakdowns of reject causes, adjustment of the sampling schedules, examinations of the amount of idle time with the machines and equipments in question. Discussion of analyses of this sort is deferred for the product-control material of Chapter 20.

It is worth emphasizing that the process·control sampling table discussed in Sections 15.26 to 15.28 is a plan that has been developed to meet the needs of the particular factories for which it was designed. There is, for example, no magic in its specification that certain types of processes be checked only every 8 hours; this figure was based upon the fact that the factory worked 8-hour shifts. That the schedules of Figure 15.25 concentrate chiefly upon production quantities of less than 100 units per hour results from the situation that the factories operate at relatively low average hourly production quantities.

The form of process-control sampling tables depends upon the conditions of individual companies rather than chiefly upon any abstract statistical sampling conditions. It is important that this fact be recognized by those factories which are developing their own applications of such tables.

Also very important in the development of such plans is the relative work responsibilities of involved operators and inspectors. The application of the table reviewed above was one in which inspectors as well as operators have been heavily involved in the control actions. Other applications of the disciplines of this plan in factories, whose total-quality-control programs have strongly developed, have established a very high proportion of these process checks to be made by the operators themselves. The process engineering component of the quality-control function has provided audit and overview of the process-control actions.

15.29 Process Control When Output Is Not Easily Segregated

In those production situations where it may not be practical physically to segregate lots, the process sampling must be established accordingly. The same basic principles as earlier discussed in this chapter for continuous sampling plans—CSP-1, CSP-2, CSP-3, and others—are also particularly effective when applied to process-control objectives in the continuous production of parts or subassemblies. Examples include proceeding in an electronic component line or flowing forward on a mechanical assembly conveyor line.

Ross[35] made an interesting adaptation of this type of process-control plan. His plan is designed around the following characteristics:

1. An AQL of 2 percent at a producer's risk of 5 percent
2. A lot tolerance percent defective of 15 percent at a consumer's risk of 10 percent

Figure 15.27 shows the operating characteristic for this particular plan and the curve for average outgoing quality that is associated with it.

The sampling schedule developed under this plan requires the inspection of a continuous flow, or "sequence," of 32 parts without a reject. Then 1 part in every 18 is checked until a defect is found.

When a defect is found, a new sequence of 32 pieces without a reject must be found. Because this plan is based upon individual lot protection of the AQL type (see Sec. 15.8) rather than protection of overall output, as in the Dodge AOQL plan, it is not necessary to replace the defective units found to maintain the statistical accuracy of the plan.

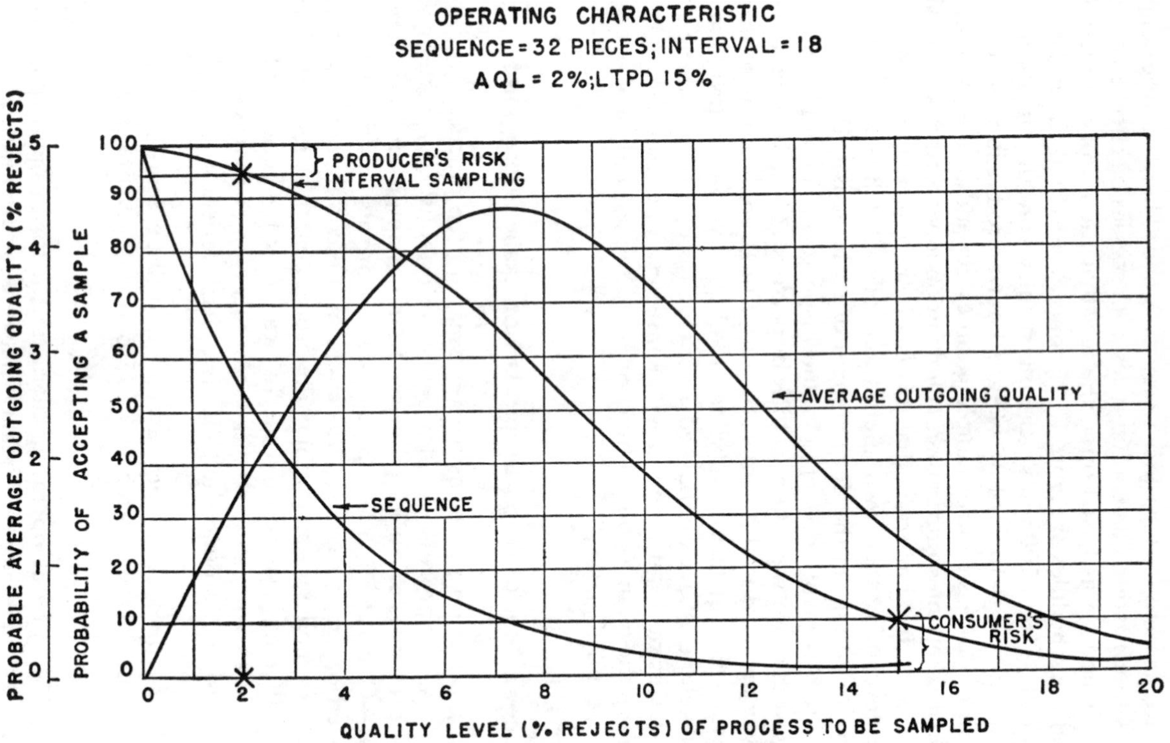
OPERATING CHARACTERISTIC
SEQUENCE = 32 PIECES; INTERVAL = 18
AQL = 2%; LTPD 15%
PRODUCER'S RISK
INTERVAL SAMPLING
AVERAGE OUTGOING QUALITY
SEQUENCE
CONSUMER'S RISK
PROBABLE AVERAGE OUTGOING QUALITY (% REJECTS)
PROBABILITY OF ACCEPTING A SAMPLE
0
1
2
3
4
5
0
10
20
30
40
50
60
70
80
90
100
0
2
4
6
8
10
12
14
16
18
20
QUALITY LEVEL (% REJECTS) OF PROCESS TO BE SAMPLED

FIG. 15.27

SAMPLING TABLES IN ACTION

15.30 The Relation of Process-Control Sampling to Acceptance Sampling

Whenever both process-control sampling and acceptance sampling plans are established in a factory, two questions almost inevitably arise:

1. Why bother with both types of sampling table—why not use only one? Are not the objectives of process control and acceptance sampling overlapping? Are not acceptance sampling tables fully as economical for process-control purposes as are process-control tables?
2. Is it not uneconomical duplication of effort to use successively both process control and acceptance sampling procedures on the parts produced within the same factory area by the same manufacturer?

These questions are now discussed in order:

1. In an abstract sense, of course, the objectives of process-control and acceptance sampling techniques are similar. They both aim to aid in the production of satisfactory parts and in the prevention of the production of unsatisfactory ones.

    From a practical point of view, however, the purpose served by process-control techniques is very different from that served by acceptance techniques. One is developed to aid in the control of the quality of material during the course of its production, the other to aid in determining the acceptability of lots of finished materials.

    Agreeing that the purpose served by the two techniques is different does not tell the complete story; the forms of the techniques themselves are considerably different, and they cannot be used interchangeably in every instance. It is often impractical and certainly frequently uneconomical to use acceptance sampling tables for process-control purposes. Lot sizes and sample sizes are often too high, and the required acceptance and rejection procedure is often inadequate.

    By the same token, process-control sampling tables are equally impractical and uneconomical for use in acceptance sampling. Both sample and lot sizes may be much too small for economy, and acceptance and rejection procedure will probably be inapplicable.

    There is a place for both process-control and acceptance sampling tables in a factory program of controlling the quality of its products; the place for one of these techniques cannot be usurped by the other without loss of economy and sampling effectiveness.
2. It is most certainly an uneconomical duplication of effort, in many instances, to use successively both process-control and acceptance sampling plans on parts from the sample production area.

There is justification for the use of both techniques when acceptance sampling tables are used as a check upon the effectiveness of newly established process-control plans. It is also justifiable to use acceptance procedures occasionally to audit the quality results in an area in which process-control sampling tables are in use.

These are, however, exceptions; in general, a manufacturer should find no need to follow up process-control techniques with acceptance sampling on the parts from the same factory area.

Acceptance sampling tables often enjoy maximum value in control over parts and materials received from sources external to the factory—over whose production the factory has a minimum of control. Process-control sampling tables enjoy their maximum value in use with the internally manufactured parts and materials over which the factory does have full control.

15.31 Some Practical Aspects of Sampling Tables

Perhaps the most typical practical problem encountered in the use of sampling tables is the tendency toward their misapplication. Acceptance plans are frequently used for process-control purposes; a plan established for a certain AQL and a given process condition is suddenly set up as "the" sampling plan for the entire factory; the existence of reduced sampling schedules may be discovered, and they may be applied to a wide variety of sampling conditions whether or not they are applicable.

In many plants there is a constant struggle to reduce sample sizes and to give "general adaptation" to sampling plans that have been established for certain specific purposes. This objective is both practical and necessary for factory purposes, but it takes a fine sense of judgment on the part of plant personnel to decide how far, if at all, it is possible and feasible to go with such "general adaptations."

It is very interesting to note that this misuse, or perhaps "overuse," of sampling tables is frequently encountered in those plants where the original introduction of scientific sampling encountered its greatest difficulty. It is possible that the problem of misapplication of the plans is at least partly due to the basis upon which the plans were originally "sold" to the factory. If, to overwhelm resistance, they were presented as general cure-alls, to be applied under any and all circumstances, the tendency on the part of the shop to apply them in such a fashion is only natural.

The most important cure for this problem of misapplication is, therefore, prevention—proper introduction of the plans and adequate education in their limitations. Sampling tables usually have sufficiently great advantages over existing spot-checking procedures so that their merits can be fairly presented without having to gloss over their limitations. It is equally important that the selection and approval of the sampling plans used be placed in the hands of an individual or individuals who are familiar with both the practical and statistical aspects of this tool.

Another problem frequently seen in connection with sampling plans is the attitude that the sampling job is adequately done when a sampling table has been developed or selected. The importance of proper measuring and gaging equipments to successful application of sampling plans seems so obvious as to be scarcely worthy of mention. Yet it is not uncommon to see a great deal of attention devoted in a plant to the development of sampling tables and supporting records, while allowing that sampling be done with worn, outmoded, cumbersome gages or measuring equipments. The proper selection of these quality information equipments is fully as important as the design of the sampling plan with which they will be used.

Also of importance is the proper training of the inspectors, testers, and operators in the use and meaning of sampling tables. This training is too often done superficially, resulting in improper use of the sampling plans.

That this situation may exist was brought forcibly home to an inspection supervisor in one factory. He had explained to his inspection force quite briefly —and, he thought, quite fully—the meaning of the double-sampling plan he had asked them to use in place of 100 percent inspection. Several days after this explanation, he was stopped by one usually conscientious inspector, who told the supervisor that he liked the sampling plan very well and that he could certainly see that it was aiding in his examining many more lots than he had previously been able to check under 100 percent inspection procedures. This inspector felt, however, that he had a suggestion whereby the double-sampling plan in use might be even more thoroughly streamlined.

The supervisor eagerly asked for the man's suggestion. He was told that the inspector just could not see the sense in always taking a second sample even though the first sample had shown the lot of material to be satisfactory. Therefore, suggested the inspector, why not make taking of the second sample dependent upon the results of the first sample?

The supervisor had thought that such a double-sampling fundamental as selection of a second sample only upon the basis of evidence from the first sample had been clearly explained to his inspection group. He was astounded by the lack of knowledge of double sampling expressed by his inspector's suggestion. Needless to say, the supervisor scheduled a series of additional meetings for the purpose of instructing his personnel in the fundamentals of modern sampling plans.

The supervisor should not have been so thoroughly surprised at the lack of insight exhibited by this inspector; no matter how simplified sampling plans may be made, for their effective application they must still be thoroughly explained to those who will use them. While the supervisor-inspector example cited is an extreme one, variations on it may be found in many factories whose personnel have not been satisfactorily grounded in the use of statistical sampling procedures.

Another matter whose importance is frequently overlooked in determining the overall economy of a given sampling plan is the adequacy of the drawing specification for the characteristic that is being sampled. This is particularly important in those instances where specifications have been "picked out of the air" and where they may not really be indicative of whether the part will be satisfactory for its particular application.

How substantial this problem may be can be illustrated as follows: Results of identical economy can be achieved by inspecting a part characteristic to a tolerance of ± 0.005 inch using a 1 percent AQL plan and by inspecting the characteristic to a tolerance of ± 0.004 inch using a 5 percent AQL plan. The difference in the AQL which is applicable when a change in tolerance of ± 0.001 inch has been made is startling to those who have not previously squarely faced this issue. It leads to this conclusion: Determination of the particular sampling plan most economical for a given situation is most effectively accomplished when the adequacy of the part specification involved is itself first critically examined before the sampling plan is chosen.

Other practical issues in the application of sampling plans—forms for recording sample results, techniques for the fullest employment of sampling tables—are discussed in Part 6, "Applying Quality Control in the Company."

15.32 Practical Applications of Sampling Tables

The variety of applications possible with sampling tables is almost unlimited. These sampling applications have ranged from standard uses of acceptance tables in the receiving of incoming material to the development of sampling plans for use by factory technical staffs in the product appraisal "life test" of units selected just previous to shipment.

The three examples that are discussed below cover three of the more usual of sampling plan applications:

1. Improving the effectiveness of the incoming-material inspection and test force (see Sec. 15.33).
2. Separating the vendors of products of satisfactory quality from those who sell products of spotty quality (see Sec. 15.34).
3. Reducing the number of rejects from factory processing operations (see Sec. 15.35).

15.33 Improving the Effectiveness of Incoming-Material Inspection and Test Force

Certain types of complex electronic equipments require for their assembly a wide variety of components. When these equipments are produced in large numbers, the problem of assurance that the quality of the many components purchased from outside vendors is of an acceptable level becomes a major one. Examination of each one of these parts can be both an expensive and an extremely lengthy procedure, requiring a very large staff of inspectors and testers.

The problem faced by a factory manufacturing these electronic equipments was, therefore, that of devising an economical system of determining whether incoming lots were of a quality level satisfactory for use in assembly operations so that the incoming-material inspection force might be reduced to a reasonable number.[36]

A decision was made to establish a type of sampling procedure which would be sufficiently general in scope to minimize the problem of its administration and yet sufficiently rigorous that only an acceptable percent nonconformance might be allowed to enter the assembly areas. These nonconforming parts would be detected during the course of test and assembly, so that the problem was one of internal factory economy rather than of running the danger of customer ill will by shipping equipments with defective component parts.

The quality-engineering component of the plant developed for this purpose a double-sampling table indexed by AQL. Based upon experience, a ¼ percent acceptable quality level was indicated for a number of the key components. Cost data were unavailable for most of the parts. Even if they had been available, the quality engineers reasoned, the operation would be better off to establish one value for AQL which would be generally applicable on an experience basis than to run the risk of administrative confusion by establishing a number of individual AQLs. There therefore was established the ¼ percent schedule in the table as the AQL for all incoming parts subject to inspection.

In connection with use of the plan, there was also developed a card for recording sampling results, the front and back of which are shown in Figure 15.28.

The sampling plan was first introduced on a small number of parts and then gradually expanded until it covered almost all electronic equipment components that were subject to inspection and test. Inspectors and testers were carefully instructed in the use and application of the sampling plan, and their efforts were carefully supervised during the early stages of the plan.

After several months of operation, the plant personnel unanimously agreed that the double-sampling plan had satisfactorily solved the incoming inspection and test problem on electronic equipment components. Many dollars in inspection and test expense had been saved, and the plant personnel concluded that the operation was actually obtaining better inspection with the ¼ percent AQL plan than under the old 100 percent system. At least two reasons for this conclusion were advanced by plant personnel:

1. The rigorous discipline attendant upon a sampling plan, including the maintenance of quality inspection plans and records, makes it easier for an inspector and tester to know what characteristics are really of greatest importance to the job of examining the parts in question. For example, the card in Figure 15.28 listed the critical dimensions to be checked on each part and so did not leave this selection in doubt by use of the sometimes vague "100 percent inspection required" statement.

INCOMING MATERIAL INSPECTION RECORD

¼%

SAMPLING TABLE   AQL = ¼%

LOT SIZE	n_1	n_2	c_1	c_2
UNDER 25	7	14	X	X
25 – 50	10	20	X	X
50 – 100	13	26	X	X
100 – 200	20	40	X	↓
200 – 300	25	50	↓	↓
300 – 500	35	70	↓	↓
500 – 800	50	100	↓	1
800 – 1300	75	150	0	1
1300 – 3200	100	200	0	2
3200 – 8000	150	300	1	2
8000 – 22000	200	400	1	3
22000 – 110000	300	600	1	5
110000 – 550000	500	1000	3	7
550000 & OVER	1000	2000	5	12

DRG. NO. X231132

PART _____ COIL

VENDORS

A – JONES COIL CO.

B – BROWN WIRE MFG'S.

C – SMITH PRODUCTS CO.

COMMENTS

FUNCTIONAL DIMENSIONS:

$X - \frac{1}{2}" \pm .005$ – I.D. OF HOLE

$Y - 2' \pm \frac{1}{32}"$ COIL HEIGHT

CHECKING FIXTURE :

24317

(X) USE SINGLE SAMPLING PLAN

(↓) USE FIRST SAMPLING PLAN BELOW ARROW

FRONT

NO.	VEN-DOR	DATE	LOT SIZE	NO. INSP.	NO.FD DEF.	DISPOSITION PASS	DISPOSITION REP.	DISPOSITION REJ.	INSPECTOR
1	B	1/10	5000	150	1 – Y / 0 – X	✓			A. B. C.
2	A	2/5	825	75	0 – Y / 0 – X	✓			A. B. C.
3	C	2/5	1000	225	2 – Y / 0 – X			✓	A. B. C.
4	B	2/5	1000	75	0 – Y / 0 – X	✓			M. A. D.
5	A	3/6	2000	300	2 – Y / 1 – X	✓			A. B. C.
6	C	3/8	1000	75	2 – Y / 0 – X			✓	M. A. D.
7	B	3/10	200	25	0 – Y / 0 – X	✓			M. A. D.
8									
9									
10									

BACK

FIG. 15.28

2. When operators are required to inspect only a small number of similar parts, the probability of error due to fatigue is much less than if they are required to inspect a large number of these parts. The caliber of the inspection test and job is, therefore, likely be be higher.

15.34 Location of Unsatisfactory Vendors of Small Castings

Even though apparatus may be produced on a job-lot basis, it is still perfectly possible that the component parts used on the apparatus may be purchased in sufficient quantity to make a sampling procedure useful. One such example is a large rotating apparatus, which uses a small casting called a brush holder. Each piece of apparatus uses a large number of brush holders, so the castings are purchased in quantity. While these brush holders are purchased in varying quantities and sizes, the characteristics that are important when the holder is assembled to the apparatus are quite similar in all types of the casting.[37]

The factory producing the rotating apparatus had been experiencing large manufacturing losses and other high quality costs because the brush holders were defective in use after assembly. It was felt that these losses were primarily caused by the poor condition in which the brush holders were received from the vendors. The factory was purchasing its brush holders from three different vendors, and although there was an incoming inspection procedure on these holders, records were not adequately clear as to which of the vendors were primarily responsible for the poor quality of the holders. Each vendor insisted that he was shipping consistently high quality.

It was decided to institute an acceptance sampling plan on the holders as they were received from the vendors and to record the results of the sampling on suitable record cards. A 2.5 percent AQL was decided upon to cover all characteristics of the brush holders. It was further decided that all brush-holder shipments that did not meet the sampling test would not be sorted but shipped back to the vendors, production warranting. The three vendors were so informed and agreed to the procedure.

The results of the sampling plan were soon forthcoming. Sampling record cards indicated that two of the three vendors were consistently meeting the 2.5 percent AQL sampling plan, and that one of the vendors was just as consistently not meeting the plan. The company purchasing representative discussed this situation quite pointedly with the vendor in question, who improved his processing techniques and came up to par with the quality of the shipments from the other vendors.

As soon as the holders from the unsatisfactory vendor were eliminated from the production stream because of the improvement in his process, the losses to the factory due to this cause dropped off sharply and have remained low. The 2.5 percent AQL sampling plan has been retained, however, because the factory was certain that it helped assure them of the quality of this important production component.

15.35 Reducing Rejects with Process Control

The machining section of a factory manufacturing electromechanical devices had, for some time, subjected its production parts to a 100 percent inspection after they had been completed. The factory was a new one, located in a region in which there had earlier been very little modern manufacturing. Factory operators, while conscientious, were entirely new to a manufacturing environment. Also, the machines, while new, were being placed into operation by newly trained manufacturing engineers, and the speeds, feeds, and tooling sometimes required changes and attention. Plant management therefore believed that this rigorous inspection was necessary to prevent any nonconforming parts from being received in the assembly area.

Yet nonconforming parts were received by the assembly area in spite of the large amount of inspection that was being applied to them. The decision was made, therefore, that the factory would institute an acceptance sampling plan for these parts so that the final inspection force might be reduced, permitting some inspectors to be freed for service as floor inspectors on the machines. It was felt that these floor inspectors would eliminate the rejects at their source by assisting both machine operators and machine setters.

A MIL-STD-105D acceptance plan was selected, and different values for AQL were applied to various parts. The sampling procedure was established so that those lots which were rejected under the sampling plan would be 100 percent sorted in the inspection area.

The acceptance plan resulted in some decrease in the final inspection force. But the decrease was not so great as desired, largely because the quality of the lots coming from the machining section remained poor. About 25 to 30 percent of the lots received failed to pass sampling inspection and so had to be 100 percent sorted. The parts were small, and there was no means for identifying the machine or operator that had performed the nonconforming operations—each part had an average of 10 different operations, and there simply was not room on the parts for identification marks for the source of each operation. As a result, corrective action in reducing the rejects on the floor was hampered because there were few positive guides to the actual source of the nonconforming parts.

While some inspectors had been released for duty on the floor, their effectiveness seemed open to question. Little change was noted in the number of rejected lots after these floor inspectors had been in action for several weeks. It was felt that this situation resulted, at least partly, from the hit-or-miss activity of these inspectors. Also, the very presence of these inspectors implied a "policing" action which seemed to reduce the quality motivation of machine operators.

It was therefore decided that the services of these inspectors might better be utilized if a process-control sampling plan were established for the machining area. A sampling plan was devised, very similar in its detail to that shown in Figure 15.25. The general policy was established for the machine floor that

1. There would be first-piece inspection to help machine operators and machine setters ensure that quality was satisfactory before a job was allowed to run.
2. The operators would, after this approval, deposit their output into a small tote box.
3. The floor inspector would visit each machine each hour and examine 10 pieces from the tote box.
4. If no rejects were found, the inspector would dispose of the contents of the tote box into a finished work tray. If one or more rejects were found, the operator and foreman would be notified; they would stop the machine if required, have the correction made, and have the parts in the tote box sorted.
5. When the machine was started again, the procedure in step 1 above would be repeated.

There were many initial problems establishing this plan, such as the temptation by all concerned to dispose of parts into the finished work tray whether or not they had been inspected. In a period of 6 weeks, however, the number of rejected lots in the final inspection cage had dropped from the 25 to 30 percent figure to a negligible value. It was later possible to omit entirely the acceptance sampling procedure that had been established earlier and to base assurance of the quality of the parts upon the process-control sampling routine.

The results of this program were a steep decline in the losses caused by rejected parts and a decrease in the overall amount of inspection required. As time went on, more and more of the process-control checks were made by operators themselves. The control approach was that the operators themselves had the basic control responsibility.

The factory concluded that these results were possible from process-control sampling as opposed to acceptance sampling for the following reason: Process sampling could detect and prevent the production of nonconforming work, whereas acceptance sampling could merely reject the parts some time after they had been completed and merely hope for corrective action by reporting these rejections back to the manufacturing floor.

Notes

[1]K. E. Ross has made an analysis of this popular example in an unpublished paper, "Out of the Darkness with Scientific Sampling," Fort Wayne, Ind. Figure 15.1 is after his analysis.

[2]This table is a modification of a portion of MIL-STD-105D, which is one of the most widely used standard statistical sampling tables. For an overview of the history and evolution of the present MIL-STD-105D, see Gordon J. Keefe, "Attribute Sampling—MIL-STD-105," *Industrial Quality Control*, April 1963.

[3]An important contribution to this improvement in the precision of sampling terminology is "Terms, Symbols and Definitions for Acceptance Sampling," *ANSI/ASQC A2-1978*, American National Standard. This document was prepared by the following Writing Committee: Richard A.

Freund, Chairman; Thomas W. Calvin, John W. Foster, John D. Hromi, J. Stuart Hunter, Norman L. Johnson, Jack V. Lavery, William M. Mead, Harrison M. Wadsworth, Jr. Several definitions in this chapter and book are in accordance with this document.

[4]Ibid., *ANSI/ASQC A2-1978,* p. 8.

[5]The term "operating characteristic curve" was probably first used by Col. H. H. Zornig of the Ballistics Research Laboratories at Aberdeen Proving Ground, Maryland, just before World War II. Its origins go back to the pioneering work in the Bell Telephone Laboratories in the 1920s, when the approach was termed "probability of acceptance curves."

[6]For the classic discussion of why OC curves for the lot-by-lot situation (type A OC curves in technical sampling terms) and OC curves for the continuous stream of lots situation (type B OC curves in technical sampling terms) may generally be computed in similar ways for practical purposes, see E. L. Grant, *Statistical Quality Control,* 2d ed., McGraw-Hill Book Company, New York, 1952, pp. 323 ff. See also Irving M. Burr, *Statistical Quality Control Methods,* Marcel Dekker, Inc., New York, 1976, p. 231.

[7]The discussion in this section is adapted from an unpublished note by J. W. Gross, Schenectady, N.Y.

[8]ANSI/ASQC Standard A2-1978, p. 6, recommends that the term "not-accept" be used in place of "reject" because of the inference that the latter term may convey unsafe or unusable products. This chapter uses this recommendation where possible. The term reject and rejection is integral to many widely used sampling tables, and, when reference to them and relevant company and plant examples is made, the terms in the tables and examples are employed to retain clarity and accuracy of reference.

[9]Harold Dodge and Harry F. Romig, *Sampling Inspection Tables,* 2d ed., John Wiley & Sons, Inc., New York, 1959.

[10]United States Department of Defense, "Military Standard, Sampling Procedures and Tables for Inspection by Attributes," MIL-STD-105D, U.S. Government Printing Office, Washington, D.C., Apr. 23, 1963; "Sampling Procedures and Tables for Inspection by Attributes," ANSI Z1.4 (1971), American National Standards Institute, New York. "Sampling Procedures and Tables for Inspection by Attributes," ISO 2859 (1974), International Organization for Standardization, Geneva.

[11]Abraham Wald, *Sequential Analysis,* John Wiley & Sons, Inc., New York, 1947, is the classic work.

[12]K. S. Stephens, "How to Perform Continuous Sampling," *ASQC Basic Reference Series,* American Society for Quality Control, Milwaukee, Wisc., 1979.

[13]K. S. Stephens, "How to Perform Skip-Lot and Chain Sampling," *ASQC Basic Reference Series,* American Society for Quality Control, Milwaukee, Wisc., 1979.

[14]H. A. Freeman, Milton Friedman, Frederick Mosteller, and H. Allen Wallis, *Sampling Inspection,* McGraw-Hill Book Company, New York, 1948.

[15]For a discussion of some graphical aspects of sequential analysis, see Donald W. Kroeber, "A Graphical Approach to the Design of Sequential Attribute Sampling," *Journal of Quality Technology,* vol. 12, no. 1, January 1980, pp. 36–39.

[16]The original discussions underlying CSP-1, 2, and 3 can be reviewed in the following references: "A Sampling Inspection Plan for Continuous Production," *Annals of Mathematical Statistics,* 14, 1943, pp. 264–279; "Sampling Plans for Continuous Production," *Industrial Quality Control,* vol. 4, no. 3, 1947, pp. 5–9; "Additional Continuous Sampling Inspection Plans," *Industrial Quality Control,* vol. 7, no. 5, 1951, pp. 7–12, from which the table in this discussion is drawn.

[17]G. J. Lieberman and H. Solomon, "Multi-Level Continuous Sampling Plans," *Annals of Mathematical Statistics,* 26, 1955, pp. 686–704.

[18]Military Standard MIL-STD-1235A, "Single and Multi-Level Continuous Sampling Procedures and Tables for Inspection by Attributes," is one of the widely available documents.

[19]H. F. Dodge, "Chain Sampling Inspection Plan," *Industrial Quality Control,* vol. 11, no. 4, 1955, pp. 10–13.

[20]H. F. Dodge, "Skip-Lot Sampling Plan," *Industrial Quality Control*, vol. 11, no. 5, 1955, pp. 3–5; and "A System of Skip-Lot Plans for Lot by Lot Inspection," *Annual Technical Conference Transactions*, American Society for Quality Control, 1971, pp. 469–477.

[21]For a classic discussion, see James R. Crawford, "Discovery Sampling," Lockheed Aircraft Corp., Burbank, Calif., 1952.

[22]For further information on the mechanics of discovery sampling, see Ervin F. Taylor, "Discovery Sampling," *National Convention Transactions*, American Society for Quality Control, Milwaukee, Wis., 1955, p. 315.

[23]For a further discussion of the use of the tightened and discontinuation features of MIL-STD-105D, see B. S. Liebesman, "The Use of MIL-STD-105D to Control Average Outgoing Quality," *Journal of Quality Technology*, vol. 11, no. 1, January 1979, pp. 36–43.

[24]For a discussion of a diagram for switching to tightened or reduced inspection, see P. R. B. Whittingham, "Visual Guide to Switching Rules for MIL-STD-105D," *Journal of Quality Technology*, vol. 9, no. 1, January 1977, pp. 33–37.

[25]This discussion is after Edward G. Schilling, "A Lot Sensitive Sampling Plan for Compliance Testing and Acceptance Inspection," *Journal of Quality Technology*, vol. 10, no. 2, April 1978.

[26]A. J. Duncan, "Addendum to Proposed Standard for Small Lot Sampling Plans Based on the Hypergeometric Probability Distribution," *The Reliability Commission Review*, vol. 2, no. 2, Summer 1977, p. 6. Professor Duncan has indicated "computations of producer's risks . . . reveal that . . . plans with zero acceptance numbers . . . can be hard on the producer unless most of his lots are perfect."

[27]This discussion has been largely influenced by an unpublished paper by J. W. Gross, Schenectady, N.Y.

[28]When a sample is tested on a pass-fail basis and is found to contain one or more nonconformities, a program may be instituted to improve the product. A method to determine the smallest sample of "improved" items necessary to demonstrate superiority over the original batch is described by the following papers: Milton Sirota, "Minimum Sample Sizes for Superiority Comparisons of Prior Tested Items," *Industrial Quality Control*, vol. 21, no. 12, June 1965, pp. 603–605; Lloyd S. Nelson, "Minimum Sample Sizes for Attribute Superiority Comparisons," *Journal of Quality Technology*, vol. 9, no. 2, April 1977.

[29]"Sampling Procedures and Tables for Inspection by Variables for Percent Defective," MIL-STD-414, U.S. Government Printing Office, Washington, D.C., 1957. These procedures are essentially similar also to "Sampling Procedures and Tables for Inspection by Variables for Percent Defective," ANSI Z1.9 (1972), American National Standards Institute, New York.

[30]For a further discussion of applications of MIL-STD-414, see August B, Mundel, "Acceptance by Variables for Percent Defective," *Quality Progress*, vol X, no. 2, February 1977, pp. 22–24.

[31]This discussion and Figs. 15.21 and 15.22 follow Peter R. Nelson, "A Computer Program for Military Standard 414: Sampling Procedures and Inspection by Variables for Percent Defective," *Journal of Quality Technology*, vol. 9, no. 2, April 1977.

[32]"Sampling Procedures and Tables for Inspection by Variables for Percent Non-Conforming," ANSI/ASQC Z1.9 (1980), American Society for Quality Control, Milwaukee, Wis. This is essentially similar to international standard ISO3951 (1980).

[33]The plans presented in the forerunner of MIL-STD-105D (MIL-STD-105A), and MIL-STD-414 were structured to match each other's protection. However, new tables and procedures were introduced in the MIL-STD-105D attributes acceptance plan without corresponding revisions in MIL-STD-414, somewhat limiting the ability of these standards to supplement each other. The need for revision was identified by a task group, with A. J. Duncan as chairman and A. J. Bender, Jr., F. E. Grubbs, G. J. Lieberman, and E. G. Schilling.

The standard was developed by a committee consisting of E. G. Schilling, Chairman; R. A. Abbott, Secretary; R. L. Griffith, L. I. Johnson, and R. N. Schmidt. The standard is discussed in "ANSI/ASQC Z1.9 (1980)—A Modernization of MIL-STD-414," E. G. Schilling, *Quality Progress*, March 1981, pp. 26–28, from which Fig. 15.23 is drawn.

[34]These steps have been noted by W. T. Short, Schenectady, N.Y., in an unpublished article.

[35]K. E. Ross, "Out of the Darkness with Scientific Sampling," unpublished paper, Fort Wayne, Ind.

[36]Adapted from an application carried on by H. C. Thompson and associates, Schenectady, N.Y.

[37]Adapted from a study by L. T. Stafford and associates, Schenectady, N.Y.

CHAPTER **16**

Special Methods

Will methods change A make a greater quality improvement in the production process than methods change B? Do engineers have to assume for their product designs that tolerances of mating parts "build up" arithmetically during production assembly of these parts? Can they take advantage of some more economical form of tolerance buildup?

Are there any graphical methods which simplify the analysis of data taken during investigations of technical quality problems? Do differences in testers' skills account for "significant differences" in the test readings of similar apparatus? Will design change 1, 2, or 3 solve the product-reliability problem?

Problems such as these arise almost inevitably in total-quality-control programs. Their solution is the objective of statistical special methods.

16.1 The Needs Satisfied by Special Methods

A factory may be experiencing quality difficulties on an operation for the heat treatment of castings. It may be suspected that the critical factor in casting quality at this operation is the temperature maintained in the heat-treat furnace.

The manufacturing engineer may run through the furnace a series of samples, each composed of several castings, to determine the effect of different temperatures on casting quality. One of the temperatures tried may seem to produce somewhat higher quality castings than other temperatures.

The manufacturing engineer may wonder if this quality improvement is "real"; is the difference between the effect of this temperature and all others "significant" as far as casting quality is concerned? Bitter previous experience may have convinced the engineer of the risks involved in coming to general conclusions from the results of tests using samples of small size. The engineer knows that such risks become particularly dangerous when there is involved, as in this case, the authorization of a substantial sum of money to make a process change which may not actually make any improvement in the quality of heat-treated castings on a production basis.

The manufacturing engineer may vaguely feel that there "must be" some statistical technique that will help him make a decision based upon "significance" of the results obtained from his samples of castings. Yet such standard methods as he may know of do not seem applicable to his problem. The frequency distribution does not appear to be useful, or the control chart or sampling tables.

The manufacturing engineer may even wonder if the very basis upon which he conducted his series of sampling tests has been sound. Was his effort to hold all factors constant except furnace temperature wise and reasonable? In effect, was his experiment properly designed?

The statistical technique for which the manufacturing engineer is looking is probably found among the variety of special methods that have gradually been hewn out of the mass of mathematical statistics for use in just such quality investigations as that of the castings. These special methods have demonstrated great effectiveness in analyses of a wide range of product-quality problems.

Special methods include techniques like "tests of significance" which would be helpful to the manufacturing engineer faced with the heat-treat problem. Special methods are also useful guides for establishing sampling test programs that will yield the maximum of information with the minimum of time and money, usually termed the *design of experiments;* for determining whether there is an observable relationship between variables—*regression*; and as an approach to the establishment of tolerances for parts and materials—*tolerance analysis.* Special methods also relate to the use of "probability paper" and other graphical techniques.

The mathematics attached to some of these methods is sometimes more complex than that associated with the statistical tools described in Chapters 13 to 15. This mathematics may, in many instances, be most effectively used by trained statisticians. Computer applications of these techniques can be particularly useful. But the point of view represented by special methods is probably more important than the technical methods themselves—and is essential in understanding the technical conditions being reflected in the computer program—and this point of view may be readily acquired and applied by those with little or no formal statistical training.

This chapter surveys the general nature of some of the more important special methods, with emphasis upon their point of view, and discusses in detail a few of the more powerful techniques.

16.2 The General Nature of Special Methods

Special methods may be broadly classified in two ways:

Graphical Special Methods—Descriptive Statistics

These consist of a variety of techniques which concentrate upon pictorial presentation of quality data in such a form that the picture itself is the basis for decision and action.

Graphical special methods—or descriptive statistics as they are sometimes termed—are essentially shorthand techniques. They consist of unique means for tabulating and plotting quality data. As such, their nature and applications are straightforward, and their use requires only an understanding of some relatively simple procedures. Several of these graphical methods have been used for many years in industry, and other methods are continually being developed. Sections 16.3 to 16.6 discuss this portion of special methods.

Analytical Special Methods—Mathematical Statistics

These consist of a variety of techniques which concentrate upon mathematical analysis of quality data.

Analytical special methods are built around what is basically a philosophy toward the analysis of data. The mathematics and other procedures associated with this portion of special methods may be of secondary importance in the factory to the philosophy that is used and developed by their application.

While they have been available for some time, the actual applications of these analytical techniques are still relatively new to most of industry. They fill a need in the design and analysis of quality data that had not previously been adequately met in industrial quality-control applications. Sections 16.7 to 16.12 discuss analytical special methods.

GRAPHICAL SPECIAL METHODS

16.3 Graphical Presentation of Frequency-Distribution Data

Frequency-distribution data are usually presented in the standard form shown in Figure 16.1. As was pointed out in Chapter 13, this method is normally used for pictorial presentation and also during the calculation of the measures of central tendency and spread of a frequency-distribution sample.

In place of this method of presentation, a somewhat different descriptive statistics treatment may be used during the determination of these measures. This graphical method often involves a simplification in computation. It consists of presenting the data in cumulative form, such that the percentage of values falling below a given value is plotted against the value.

The plots may be made on either standard rectangular or rectilinear graph

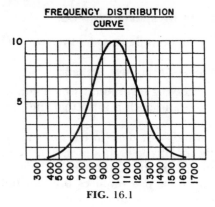

FIG. 16.1

paper or on graph paper known as *probability paper,* specially designed for this purpose. Thus, the data of Figure 16.1 can be plotted on rectangular coordinate paper, as in Figure 16.2, or on probability paper, as in Figure 16.3. Quite straightforward computer programs may be applied to either method, when appropriate.

Both the rectangular coordinate and the probability-paper presentations lend themselves to smoothing out sampling errors and enabling fair estimates to be made of measures of spread and central tendency. The rectangular

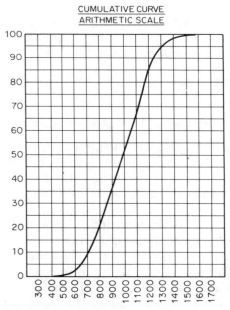

FIG. 16.2 **Cumulative curve—arithmetic scale.**

coordinate presentation is particularly useful in determining the median and estimating the average. Probability paper is often of more general utility, however, and it is discussed in Sections 16.4 and 16.5.

In analyzing skewed or nonsymmetrical frequency distributions which depart very widely from the shape of the normal curve, this graphical method may be more accurate and more meaningful than undiscriminating application of the more conventional methods applied to these skewed curves based upon normal-curve analysis.[1]

16.4 Probability-Paper Graphing

Probability-paper graphing is an extremely useful means for determining approximate values of the average, median, and standard deviation of a frequency-distribution sample. The data in this sample should, of course, be known to have come from a homogeneous source—articles made under the same manufacturing conditions, drawn from the same lot, and so on. A probability-paper graph also shows, at a glance, just how closely the frequency distribution in question approaches the shape of the normal curve. It is thus very useful in deciding whether a given sample of data can be used in a standardized computation which assumes a fairly close approach to normality in the data used.[2]

Probability-paper is a form of graph paper whose scales are so adjusted that a perfectly normal frequency distribution will plot as a straight line. One of the

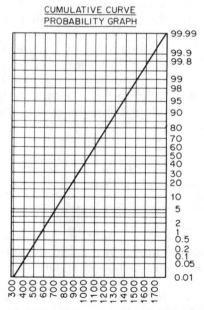

FIG. 16.3 **Cumulative curve—probability graph.**

two scales—it may be either the vertical or the horizontal—is laid out in the usual arithmetic fashion found on the standard graph-paper forms. On this scale are plotted the appropriate values for the cells of the frequency-distribution sample. In the case of both Figs. 16.2 and 16.3, this arithmetic scale is the horizontal. In some instances of probability-paper application, a logarithmic scale may be used here also.

The other probability-paper scale is so constructed that normal-curve data will develop a straight line on the graph. In the case of Fig. 16.2, the vertical scale, on which is plotted the percentage of readings falling below given cell values, has been established in the standard arithmetic fashion, and the resulting curve has taken a reversed-S shape. The vertical scale in Fig. 16.3—the probability graph—has been so established that this curve has been flattened into what is substantially a straight line.

Figure 16.4 illustrates one form of probability paper that is popular in industry. The percentage of readings is shown on the vertical axis on this paper. The individual cell values can be plotted on the horizontal axis. The 1-, 2-, and 3-sigma lines have been so designated on the graph.

Other forms of commercially available probability paper usually differ from Fig. 16.4 in only two major respects: The sigma lines may not be so designated, and the horizontal and vertical scales of Fig. 16.4 may be reversed. Figure 16.5 shows another form of probability paper, on which the various sigma lines can be established, by drawing them in at the required points.[3]

The steps to be taken in probability-paper graphing are as follows:

1. The particular quality characteristic to be plotted is selected, and sample size is decided. The regular procedure in setting up a frequency-distribution analysis is followed.
2. A form is prepared for tabulating the readings, preparatory to the probability plot. Suitable cell values are established. Cells of equal width are usually desirable. For a satisfactory probability graph, 12 to 20 of these cells are generally required. Any logical series of values can be used in establishing these cells. This tabulation usually includes six columns as follows:

Column no.	1	2	3	4	5	6
	Readings to be included in cell	Record as (cell boundary)	Tally	Tally total	Cumulative total	Cumulative % of total

3. Actual readings are made on the units in the sample. As the readings are taken, a tally is made of those which fall in the appropriate cells.
4. The tabulation of these readings is completed when all sample readings have been taken.
5. The suitable data from this tabulation are plotted on probability paper at the upper boundary of each cell.[4]

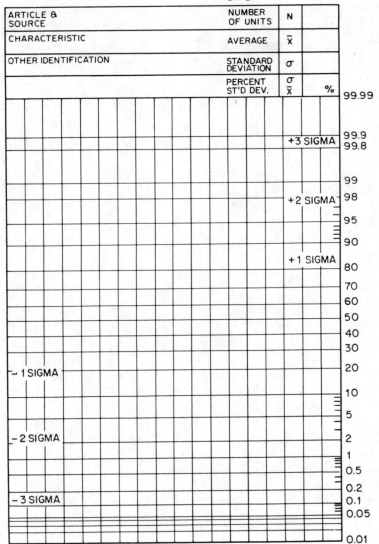

PROBABILITY CHART

FIG. 16.4 Probability chart.

PROBABILITY PAPER

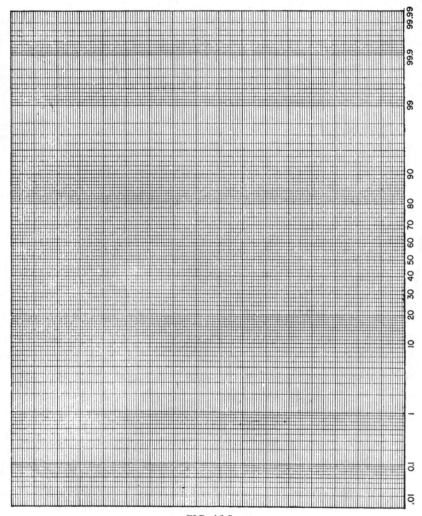

FIG. 16.5

6. The probability graph is examined to determine the
   a. Normality of the distribution
   b. Value of the average, or median
   c. Value of the standard deviation

The data may be taken, for example, on the resistance (measured in ohms) of a sample of 100 resistors. It is expected that the total range of the readings will be 145 ohms, or between 25 and 165 ohms. To determine for step 2 the appropriate number of cells and the steps between cells, it is first necessary to divide 145 ohms by 12 and by 20 because 12 and 20 represent the band of the desired number of cells.

This division operation indicates that the step between cells should be somewhere between the values of 7 and 12 ohms. The most convenient value in this range is 10 ohms, and it is this value which will be used as the step between cells. These cell limits are established at values of 30, 40, ..., 110, 120, ... ohms, and a tabular form is prepared as in step 2. As readings are made on the resistors, their values are plotted in the tabulation.

Let us assume that the first six readings have the following values: 32, 38, 41, 46, 54, and 67. If, for some reason, resistance readings for the rest of the 100-unit sample were discontinued, the six readings would result in the following tabulation.

Column no.	1		2	3	4	5	6
	From	To	Cell boundary	Tally	Total	Cumulative	Cumulative % of total
	30 ohms	39 ohms	39.5 ohms	11	2	2	33.3
	40 ohms	49 ohms	49.5 ohms	11	2	4	66.7
	50 ohms	59 ohms	59.5 ohms	1	1	5	83.3
	60 ohms	69 ohms	69.5 ohms	1	1	6	100.0

The fashion in which the individual readings are placed in their respective cells should again be noted. Column 2, cell boundary, represents the upper cell limits and the highest value of readings that will be included in that particular cell. This is unlike the typical practice in standard frequency-distribution plots of recording all readings in a cell against the middle value for the readings that are included in the cell in question.

16.5 A Typical Probability Graph Example

Suppose that it is desired to determine the value for the average and standard deviation of a 450-unit sample of a certain type of resistor. It is expected that there will be a range of about 1150 ohms in readings in this sample.

To determine the suitable step between cells, 1150 ohms may be divided by 12 to 20. The resulting values are shown to be 57 and 95 ohms. The intermediate step of 75 ohms would be less convenient for tabulation purposes than would steps of 50 or 100 ohms. Either 50 or 100 ohms could be selected, but the decision is made in favor of the 50-ohm step because it will enable the tabulation to reflect actual sample readings more accurately than would the 100-ohm step.

The 450 resistance readings are taken and tabulated as shown in Figure 16.6.[5] Thus steps 1 through 4 of Section 16.4 are accomplished. Note that this Figure 16.6 tabulation eliminates column 3 as shown in the tabulations of Section 16.4 because inclusion of this column would have made the table too bulky for presentation.

Probability-Paper Tabulation
Ohms Value of Resistors

1		2	4	5	6
From	To	Cell boundary	Total tally	Cumulative total	Cumulative % of total
400	449	449.5	1	1	0.22
450	499	499.5	. . .	1	0.22
500	549	549.5	1	2	0.44
550	599	599.5	2	4	0.89
600	649	649.5	4	8	1.78
650	699	699.5	7	15	3.33
700	749	749.5	13	28	6.22
750	799	799.5	19	47	10.44
800	849	849.5	27	74	16.44
850	899	899.5	36	110	24.44
900	949	949.5	42	152	33.78
950	999	999.5	48	200	44.44
1000	1049	1049.5	50	250	55.56
1050	1099	1099.5	47	297	66.00
1100	1149	1149.5	43	340	75.55
1150	1199	1199.5	35	375	83.33
1200	1249	1249.5	28	403	89.55
1250	1299	1299.5	20	423	94.00
1300	1349	1349.5	13	436	96.89
1350	1399	1399.5	6	442	98.22
1400	1449	1449.5	5	447	99.33
1450	1499	1499.5	2	449	99.78
1500	1549	1549.5	. . .	449	99.78
1550	1599	1599.5	1	450	100.00

FIG. 16.6

To carry out steps 5 and 6 of Section 16.4, the following procedure is followed:

Step 5: Plot the suitable data from the tabulation on probability paper. To plot the data of Figure 16.6 on the probability graph of Fig. 16.7, the steps are as follows:

a. Establish on the horizontal scale the various cell boundaries shown in column 2. On this particular graph there is only sufficient space to record these cells in steps of 100 ohms. It is usually good practice to record cell values both below and above those actually used in the tabulation; thus the values plotted on the horizontal scale run as low as 299.5 ohms and as high as 1699.5 ohms.

b. Plot the cumulative percentages shown in column 6 on the vertical scale of percentage of total against the appropriate values of column 2.

c. Fit a curve to the resulting plotted points. Note that the points between 599.5 and 1399.5 ohms arrange themselves in a straight line. The single point at 499.5 represents one reading, or 0.2 percent of the total. The single point at 1499.5 represents another 0.2 percent of the total. The point at 1549.5 is

PROBABILITY PLOT OF
OHMS VALUES OF RESISTORS

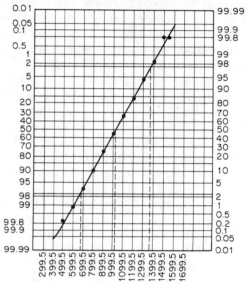

FIG. 16.7 **Probability plot of ohms values of resistors.**

plotted for completeness. There can be neither a 100 percent point nor a 0 percent point on normal probability paper, so cumulative percentages for 0 and 100 percent are never seen on these normal plots.

Step 6: Determine normality and values for the average and standard deviation. For these determinations, the steps are as follows:

a. Determine the "normality" of the distribution. In most practical cases, a reasonable conformance to a straight line between 2 and 98 percent of the cumulative readings is evidence that the distribution in question approaches quite closely the shape of the normal curve. Particularly when the number of readings in the distribution is small, close conformance to a straight line at each end of the plot is quite unusual. In such a case, a straight line between 5 and 95 percent of the total values is usually sufficient evidence of relatively normal distribution.

Thus the first decision that can be made from the picture of Figure 16.7 is that the straight-line plot indicates that the data represent a relatively normal frequency distribution.

b. Determine the value for the average. This average value can be obtained from the probability graph by striking it off at the 50 percent point on the vertical scale. On Figure 16.7, this is 1020 ohms. Actual arithmetic calculation of the average will be found to equal 984 ohms.[6] The graphical average will not, however, check closely with the arithmetic average in all cases; it is determined from a curve that has been fitted to the data rather than from the data themselves, as in the case of the arithmetic average. The relation between the graphical and arithmetic average depends, therefore, upon how closely the probability curve is fitted to the plotted data. Error in reading this graphical value can be minimized by its determination as the average of the actual values at which the curve crosses the $\pm$1-, or 2-, or 3-sigma lines. Thus, $+1$ sigma equals 1200, -1 sigma equals 840, and their sum, 2040, divided by the number of readings, 2, equals 1020 ohms.

   c. Determine the value for the standard deviation. The standard deviation can be determined graphically by reading the values between the point at which the probability curve crosses the 50 percent line and either the $+1\sigma$ or -1σ line. In the case of Figure 16.7, about 180 ohms are between the 50 percent point and $+1\sigma$. A more accurate determination can be obtained by taking the difference between the points at which the probability curve crosses the -2 σ and the $+2\sigma$ lines and then dividing by 4. In this case, the calculation becomes $1380-680/4 = 700/4 = 175$ ohms.

   Only when the line representing the probability plot is a straight one does the point at which the 50 percent line is crossed represent both the median and the average. When the line representing the probability plot is a line curving in one direction, the point at which the 50 percent line is crossed will represent only the median and not the average. A straight line drawn through the points at which this line crosses -1σ and $+1\sigma$ will cross the 50 percent line at approximately the average, and the standard deviation will be approximately one-half the difference between the $+1\sigma$ and -1σ points.

   Even extreme variations from the straight-line form of probability curve do not appreciably affect the rule that the average and standard deviation of a distribution can be determined with a fair degree of accuracy be drawing a straight line through the $+1\sigma$ and -1σ points.

   The accuracy of probability-paper graphing in estimating the average and the standard deviation is satisfactory for general purposes. It may not be satisfactory for precision purposes unless there is a large number of readings. For most industrial applications the accuracy is sufficient.

16.6 Graphical Regression for Two Variables

   The objective of regression is to determine the relationship, if any, existing among variables. These variables are often different quality characteristics of the same part or material.

   The regression technique may be divided into two parts:

1. Simple graphical regression, which is discussed in this section
2. Mathematical regression, which is discussed in Section 16.11

   For graphical regression, regular rectangular coordinate paper is generally used. One variable, usually the one assumed to be "independent," is laid out on the horizontal scale. The supposedly related "dependent" variable is laid out on the vertical scale. Readings of the two variables are then made on the parts in question. The values of these readings are plotted on the rectangular coordinate paper.

Effort is thereupon made to fit a curve to the plotted points. The sketched curve should divide the plotted points approximately in two groups; it should pass very close to the median values for the two variables, and the sum of the deviations from the sketched curve should approximately equal zero. This curve may take a very wide variety of forms: a straight line, a curve with one bend, a curve with two bends, a half circle.

When this curve has been sketched, the resulting graphical picture may be examined for the amount of deviation from the curve shown by the plotted points. If the amount of this deviation is quite small, the band within which the points fall may be sketched in and the regression may be said to represent a well-defined relationship. If the amount of this deviation is quite large, then there may be no reason to attempt to sketch in the band into which it falls and the regression may be said to represent a poorly defined relationship if, indeed, there be any relationship at all.

Figure 16.8 represents the condition of a well-defined relationship, and Figure 16.9 represents the condition of a poorly defined relationship.[7]

Thus a factory may be manufacturing small metal inserts for which the elongation under load is a critical characteristic. It may not be practical for the factory to apply load to each insert and to measure the resulting elongation.

It is desired, therefore, to determine if some other quality characteristic of the inserts, which can be determined in a nondestructive fashion, bears a very close relationship to elongation. This other quality characteristic could then be inspected in place of the destructive elongation checks.

Such a related characteristic is thought to exist in the hardness of the inserts. To check this relationship graphically, factory personnel would pursue the following sequence: Suitable cell values for elongation would be established

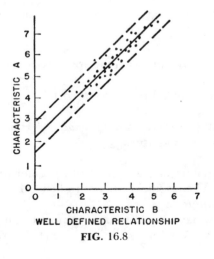

CHARACTERISTIC B
WELL DEFINED RELATIONSHIP
FIG. 16.8

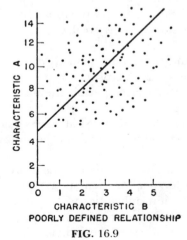

CHARACTERISTIC B
POORLY DEFINED RELATIONSHIP
FIG. 16.9

on the horizontal axis of a sheet of rectangular coordinate paper, and appropriate cell values for hardness would be established on the vertical axis.

A series of tests would then be made on sample inserts to determine elongation and hardness under given load. These data would be plotted on the rectangular coordinate paper, just as shown in Figure 16.8. If the resulting picture were similar to that of Figure 16.8, the conclusion would be drawn that hardness may be checked in place of elongation within the band of deviation shown. A corresponding statistical regression analysis would probably be carried out to determine actual numerical values for the regression relationship.

If the resulting picture were similar to Figure 16.9, the conclusion would be that little if any significant relationship can be said to exist between the hardness and the elongation of these inserts.

16.7 Analytical Special Methods

Of the several analytical special methods that have been used in industry, probably the following are among the most important:

1. Statistical tolerance analysis
2. Tests of significance
3. Design of experiments
4. Mathematics of regression
5. Sequential analysis

Each technique is briefly discussed in Sections 16.8 through 16.12.

16.8 Statistical Tolerance Analysis

Engineers designing products in which there are subassemblies made up of several mating parts are almost always faced with a common problem: How should the tolerance for the individual parts[8] be balanced off with the tolerance for their subassembly so that

1. The individual parts actually *do* mate when they reach the appropriate point in their manufacturing cycle
2. These tolerances permit the most economical production costs

Activity to achieve this balance is usually termed *"tolerance analysis."* Historically, it has often resulted in the following situations:

1. The sum of tolerances of the individual parts is allowed to be greater than the tolerance for their subassembly. The engineer "trusts to luck" that no production difficulties will be encountered.
2. The tolerance for the subassembly is made equal to the arithmetic sum of the tolerances of the individual parts. This forces the engineer to either

a. Establish extremely wide subassembly tolerances, with all the attendant problems of such a situation
b. Allow the high manufacturing costs which accompany the narrow individual part tolerances resulting in narrow subassembly tolerances

Situation 1 is probably the more usual. It has provided relatively so little manufacturing difficulty in many plants that it has become an accepted part of plant custom.

Situation 2, while accepted as not so economical in the short run, has found acceptance in some plants which "want to be sure" that they do not have production difficulties during subassembly and assembly.

Even though their approach seems the least logical, those shops which have lived with situation 1 may have chosen the more effective alternative. In trusting to luck, they have had a well-established law of probability working on their side, namely, that *under certain circumstances,* the overall tolerance of a group of mating parts equals the square root of the sum of the square of the individual part tolerances—a value less than that for the straight arithmetic sum of the individual tolerances. Expressed algebraically:[9]

$$T_t = \sqrt{T_1^2 + T_2^2 + T_3^2 + \cdots + T_n^2} \tag{38}$$

where
$$T_t = \text{overall tolerance}$$
$$T_1, T_2, \text{etc.} = \text{tolerances of individual mating parts}$$

Suppose that an engineer is faced with fixed tolerances for eight mating parts, as follows:

$T_1 = \pm 0.004$ inch $= 0.008$ inch	$T_5 = \pm 0.001$ inch $= 0.002$ inch
$T_2 = \pm 0.003$ inch $= 0.006$ inch	$T_6 = \pm 0.002$ inch $= 0.004$ inch
$T_3 = \pm 0.003$ inch $= 0.006$ inch	$T_7 = \pm 0.005$ inch $= 0.010$ inch
$T_4 = \pm 0.003$ inch $= 0.006$ inch	$T_8 = \pm 0.003$ inch $= 0.006$ inch

The question is: What tolerance should the engineer establish for the overall assembly of the mating parts? Use of the old custom of arithmetic addition of individual parts tolerances would force the engineer to set a total overall tolerance of ± 0.024 inch, or 48 mils in this case.

Using Formula (38), however, the engineer would develop the following computation (in mils):

$$T_t = \sqrt{8^2 + 6^2 + 6^2 + 6^2 + 2^2 + 4^2 + 10^2 + 6^2}$$
$$= \sqrt{64 + 36 + 36 + 36 + 4 + 16 + 100 + 36}$$
$$= \sqrt{328} = 18 \text{ mils}$$

or

$$T_t = 0.018 \text{ inch}$$

This overall tolerance of ± 0.009 inch, or 18 mils, represents a considerable improvement over the arithmetic total of 48 mils. It provides the engineer with a more realistic and, most likely, a more economical value for the overall tolerance.

The wide difference between the values of 18 and 48 mils probably represents no real surprise for experienced engineers. They have intuitively recognized this situation in product designs for many years, without the formal analytical apparatus provided by Formula (38).

Understanding Formula (38) is advantageous to engineers in the two typical situations that exist when tolerances are being established for a group of mating parts:

1. *When the overall tolerance is fixed and the individual parts tolerances must be adjusted.* It points the finger at those individual parts to which attention should be directed for reducing the overall tolerance of the subassembly. Thus, in the above example, reducing T_6 from ±0.002 to ±0.001 inch might be very expensive and would reduce $\sqrt{328}$ to only $\sqrt{316}$. Reducing T_7 from ±0.005 to ±0.004 inch might be less expensive and would have a much greater effect in reducing the overall tolerance because it would reduce $\sqrt{328}$ to $\sqrt{292}$.

   This problem of the actual reduction of these individual parts tolerances and how far it can proceed is discussed elsewhere in the book; see particularly Chapter 20.

2. *When the individual part tolerances are fixed and the overall tolerance must be adjusted.* This enables engineers to establish much more economical and realistic overall tolerance values if the individual parts tolerances are "frozen."

Note that the probability law discussed above stated that it has application *under certain circumstances.* The two most basic of these circumstances are as follows: (1) Practically all the mating parts in question should pass their individual part tolerances without requiring scrap or rework, or, in other words, the frequency distributions for each individual part should approach fairly closely the shape of the normal curve, with the nominal drawing values corresponding closely to the average value for the part frequency distribution; (2) each mating part must be drawn from essentially different sources.

In this latter connection, for example, is the case of assemblies consisting of parts made to the same drawing, clamped, welded, or riveted together. If the parts are punchings which are stacked together as they are produced so that all those in one assembly come from the same sheet of steel with relatively uniform thickness, the situation is particularly pronounced. For assemblies of this sort—alternating current solenoids are a case in point—it is not sound practice to depend upon Formula (38) for the determination of the overall tolerance. Here the number of punchings required to meet the drawing dimensions for overall thickness should be determined by weight or by a similar system.

Another common example is drift due to tool wear when there is little variation between parts at a given instant in time as compared with time-to-time variation.

Another limiting case is that of an assembly of parts made to the same drawing, where the frequency distribution for those parts used in each assembly may not approach sufficiently closely the shape of the normal curve. Here also Formula (38) should be bypassed in favor of the procedure of specifying an operation for machining the assembled parts to the required overall dimension or by controlling this dimension by varying the number of parts used in the assembly.

With these limiting conditions in mind, several factories have conducted investigations to determine how applicable Formula (38) is to their manufacturing conditions. Reports from these companies have indicated that the formula does have wide application in the tolerance analysis of many products and that the conditions for its use are frequently met in actual industrial circumstances. Tolerance analysis concepts are now widely used throughout a large number of industrial applications where part tolerances are critical to the output of a product design.

The tolerance analysis concept has also been extended to some applications —particularly complex equipment systems—where the uncertainties are not of tolerances as such but relate to the lack of clearly documented physical and other principles which determine product performance. Applications range from large-scale electronic environmental tracking systems to nuclear reactors. The term "uncertainty analysis" is more likely to be used for these applications. The work of this analysis involves determining the product-performance distribution resulting from the variables whose means are the nominal design values and whose variances are related to the tolerances. The probability functions of these variables are used to predict the variability of product performance.[10]

16.9 Tests of Significance

Statistical tests of significance tell whether the quality of a lot of material, the output of a given product type, or a batch of parts just received from a vendor differs "significantly" from a standard value or from the quality of a second or more lot or sources. These tests can be used to compare material from two or more sources or to determine which of a number of factors affect the quality of a process.

Collectively, the tests of significance may detect differences in percents defective, averages, spreads, and other measures. These tests have been evolved to meet the frequently encountered industrial problem that the difference between good- and poor-quality levels is often so slight that it is masked by random variations in small samples.[11] As quality- and process-control engineers have learned by long and bitter experience, it is difficult to evaluate such process changes without analytical techniques, a situation pointed up by the example cited in Section 16.1. The use of significance tests greatly reduces the chance of coming to incorrect conclusions in such cases.

The two most used significance tests are listed below, along with a description of their most useful application:

1. The t test, used to determine the significance of differences between measures of central tendency of two samples[12]
2. The F test, used to determine the significance of differences among the spread of samples[13]

For interested readers, useful presentations of these techniques are in the references in the footnotes.

16.10 Design of Experiments

The concept of statistical tests of significance has been used in the analysis of quality problems in industry in two patterns:

1. *Tests of significance are brought in at the end of the experiment.* When tests have been run, experiments completed, and all data taken, the analyst is presented with the results and asked to prepare and report accurate information from them. Under these circumstances, the analyst must try to use the appropriate tests of significance under the handicap that all required data may not be available or in proper form.
2. *The concept is used to guide the establishment of the experimental procedure.* The analyst is asked to suggest the type of experimental program that will provide the required data before any tests have been started or any data taken. The entire study may then be geared so that the data required for the analysis will be taken at minimum time and expense. The analyst designs the experimental procedure so that through what are called the a posteriori (i.e., after the experiment) tests of significance, the analysist can get *likelihood* answers to the questions that prompted the need for the experiment in the first place.

The advantages of pattern 2 over pattern 1 are obvious. The growth of total-quality-control programs in plants and companies is accompanied by corresponding growth in emphasis upon pattern 2. While there will be some circumstances when pattern 1 cannot be avoided, both economies in expense and increases in analytical accuracy are gained from pattern 2 under usual practice.

Tests of significance are also put to use on data taken under two somewhat different philosophies of experimentation.

1. *The philosophy that all factors except the one under study be held constant.* This is the approach that has been used in some factories for many years. While it has

resulted in some satisfactory results and must be used under certain conditions, it is subject to such circumstances as the following:

   a. Under the constantly changing conditions in the modern plant—such as bearing wear, tool use—it is difficult to be sure that "everything is constant." The experiment may thus be subject to error.
   b. Fallacious conclusions of cause and effect can be a result of this approach.
   c. A very large number of individual tests are required when several variables are being investigated.

2. *The philosophy of randomization, either of all factors or of all but a few which are deliberately varied.* This is the modern statistical approach, which permits the minimization of experimental error: of the fallacious reasoning to which the "all factors constant" philosophy may be subject and of the number of tests required to gain a given result.

The approach toward the use of significance tests in experimentation whereby statistical expertise is brought in at the start of the experiment and where randomization and/or deliberate variation is brought into use in the experimental framework is usually termed the "design of experiments."[14] A test program that has been designed around these techniques almost always yields better results both in reliability and economy than those conducted under hit-or-miss and "hold constant" circumstances. The economies made possible by the reduction in the number of tests required by designed experiments, as compared with older procedures, is startling in many cases.

Three of the most popular experimental design techniques are listed below, with one of their most useful applications noted. Design technique 1 is the general case of which techniques 2 and 3 are special adaptations:

1. *Analysis of variance table.* This experimental design permits the randomization of all factors. It uses the F test in a situation where the quality of a process is affected and where it is desired to study simultaneously the variation among several samples to determine whether a suspected cause of variation in a measured variable is real or merely attributable to chance.[15]

2. *Latin square.* This experimental design permits at least two factors other than the one being studied to be deliberately varied, while all others are randomized. It uses the F test in a case such as the following: It is desired to determine which of five springs of different pull characteristics has the best result in increasing the drop-out voltage of a certain relay. It is felt that test machines and test operators are also variables which might affect the drop-out voltage of the relays.

   With five spring types to be compared, the Latin-square arrangement requires five test machines and five operators. The machines and operators are allocated to spring A, spring B, and soon in such a way that the separate springs, test machines, and operators are associated in the same trio only once. The tabular arrangement for the analysis is shown in Figure 16.10, from which the use of the descriptive term Latin square can be readily appreciated.

3. *Graeco-Latin square.* This experimental design allows the deliberate variation of variables to permit obtaining the maximum of information about the effect of these variables from a minimum of tests. It uses the F test in a situation such as the following: It is known that some combination of fixed amounts of five different compounds provides the best protective coating for mechanical devices being shipped to the tropics. But how should the five compounds be mixed together in fixed amounts to achieve best results? If four amounts of each of the five compounds were tried under ordinary experimental procedure, 4^5 tests—1024 in all—would be required. By arranging each variable in groups that permit one and only one occurrence of each variable with all the others, the Graeco-Latin square design provides the same information from only 16 tests.

Figure 16.11 shows how, in this experimental design, each amount of each compound is given a deliberate association with all the others only once.[16] Useful presentations of these and many other experimental designs are in the references in the footnote.[17]

16.11 Mathematics of Regression

Section 16.6 pointed out the instances where, after a graphical regression plot has been made, it is desired to make a more precise determination as to the strength of the relationship between the variables involved. Three of the basic steps in the technique of mathematical regression analysis are listed on pages 561 and 562.

LATIN SQUARE

		TEST MACHINE				
		1	2	3	4	5
	1	SPRING E	SPRING B	SPRING D	SPRING A	SPRING C
	2	" C	" D	" B	" E	" A
TEST OPERATOR	3	" A	" C	" E	" B	" D
	4	" D	" E	" A	" C	" B
	5	" B	" A	" C	" D	" E

FIG. 16.10

GRAECO-LATIN SQUARE

	I	II	III	IV
A	1a ①	2b ②	3c ③	4d ④
B	2c ④	1d ③	4a ②	3b ①
C	3d ②	4c ①	1b ④	2a ③
D	4b ③	3a ④	2d ①	1c ②

4 X 4 SQUARE — 4 AMOUNTS OF 5 COMPOUNDS

WHERE

1, 2, 3, 4	—	DIFFERENT	AMOUNTS	OF	THE	SAME	COMPOUND
a, b, c, d	—	"	"	"	"	"	"
①, ②, ③, ④	—	"	"	"	"	"	"
I, II, III, IV	—	"	"	"	"	"	"
A, B, C, D	—	"	"	"	"	"	"

FIG. 16.11

1. The determination of the strength of the relationship in question by computation of the coefficient of determination r^2. Ideally, r^2 equals one (1), as in the case of the following two variables x and y:

x: 1, 2, 3, 4, 5   independent variable
y: 2, 4, 6, 8, 10   dependent variable

This type of perfect regression almost never occurs in industry, however, where r^2 is almost always a value between 0 and 1.

2. The establishment of a mathematical expression that can be used to forecast average values of the dependent variable from values of the independent variable. This is merely the mathematical expression of what Section 16.6 termed the "sketched line, or curve of best fit." Two important classifications of these curves of best fit, or curves of regression, as they are termed in mathematical regression, are listed below.

a. A linear relationship between the two variables, for example,

$$y = mx + b$$

This is termed a "linear regression."

b. Power curves of the form

$$y = a + bx + cx^2 + dx^3 + \cdots + nx^n$$

Curves of this form are generally termed "curvilinear regressions."

3. The establishment of limits within which it may be expected that the values obtained from the expression developed in step 2 will fall.[18]

16.12 Sequential Analysis

Section 15.11 discussed the use of sequential analysis as one of the techniques for the development of statistical sampling tables. Sequential analysis is not, however, limited to inspection in its application. It may also be extremely useful in the analysis of complex quality problems.

Sequential analysis may, for example, be used in testing for significant differences in averages or in the uniformity of product manufacture. Section 15.11 pointed out that the sequential approach calls for the establishment of two contingencies: an X_1 and X_2 factor and a Y_1 and Y_2 factor.

In applications cited, X_1 and X_2 become specific values for the differences in averages or uniformity of product manufacture. Y_1 and Y_2 are the associated risks taken in the analysis.

The classic text of Professor Abraham Wald on sequential analysis, together with other useful works, was referenced in Chapter 15.

SPECIAL METHODS IN ACTION

16.13 Practical Applications of Special Methods

Of the four quality-control jobs, special process studies is the one in which special methods find their widest application. Tests of significance, designed experiments, and correlation are among the special methods which have their chief use in special process studies.

Special methods also have varying amounts of practical application in the other quality-control jobs. Statistical tolerance analysis, analysis of variance, and probability paper are extensively used in new-design control, and other special methods have been used in incoming-material control and product control.

Three practical applications of these special methods are discussed below:

1. Analysis of a lot of questionable quality by graphical regression (see Sec. 16.14)
2. Study of a proposed methods change by tests of significance and probability-paper analysis (see Sec. 16.15)
3. Examination of a complex assembly temperature-compensation problem by use of a Graeco-Latin square variance analysis (see Sec. 16.16)

16.14 Analysis of a Lot of Questionable Quality: Graphical Regression

An interesting use of graphical regression discussed by Armstrong and Clarke[19] involves investigation of a lot of springs whose quality was in question. These small compression springs were being tested for their free length under a given pressure.

It was decided to make a regression study to analyze the quality of the springs. A sample was selected from the lot of springs. Each spring in the sample was tested for load, and its free length was measured.

The results of these tests, as number of occurrences, were plotted on rectangular coordinate paper, with free length on the vertical axis and pressure on the horizontal axis. Figure 16.12 shows this regression plot and indicates that *two* different patterns were present in one lot.

Further investigation disclosed that there were two different types of spring in the lot, differing in wire diameter. This situation was traced to the fact that some wire of slightly off-standard 0.0085-inch diameter had been inadvertently used on the production line in place of the standard 0.008-inch wire.

Because two different types of springs were mixed in the lot, it was found necessary to sort the entire lot by 100 percent testing and thus to separate the standard springs from substandard ones.

16.15 Study of a Proposed Methods Change: Tests of Significance and Probability Paper

The effective application of electronic tube technology has always been closely dependent upon systematic quality and reliability analysis. This has been true over a wide product range, from small units to power magnetrons and to the cathode ray tubes whose reliable operation is central to the "soft-readout" information in modern computer installations.

In an example of such analysis on one type of electronic tube, one electrical quality characteristic—*grid current*—was the cause of a high percentage of tubes found defective in final test. The specification limits for grid current were 25 to 55 milliamperes, and the rejections were largely caused by the excessive spread in production lots of the tubes.[20]

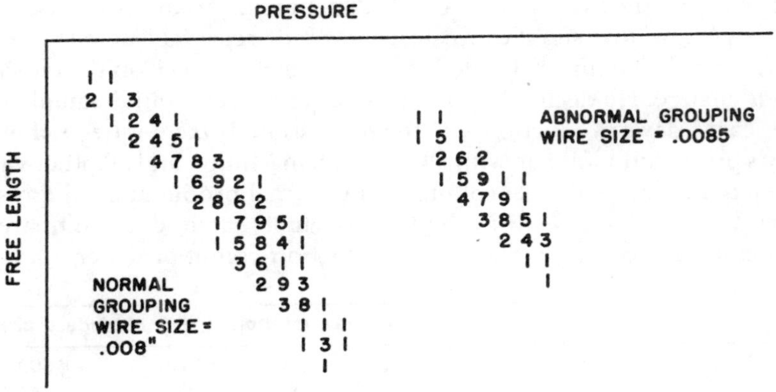

FIG. 16.12

To eliminate this rejection, the engineer in charge of the tube developed a change in the method of one phase of tube assembly. He hoped that this methods change would reduce the excessive spread in grid current.

Before authorizing the expenditure necessary to make the required change in the assembly methods, the engineer wished to investigate the actual effect of the change upon tube quality. He planned his study as follows: 100 standard production tubes would be used. These 100 tubes would be assembled under standard procedure, using the same regular materials, processing equipments, and operators. However, 50 of the tubes would be subjected to the new assembly method. The other 50 tubes, used as a "control" sample, would be assembled in the standard fashion.

The engineer felt that this experiment would permit the full and most effective utilization of tests of significance and gained agreement from the plant's statistical analyst that this was so under the conditions surrounding the tube type.

As a result, the proposed procedure was followed. The 100 tubes were put through the final test, and the following results were tabulated for the grid-current quality characteristic:

	Sample with new method	Control sample
Sample size (n)	50 tubes	50 tubes
Average ($\bar{X}$)	37.4 milliamperes	42.0 milliamperes
Standard deviation (σ)	4.2 milliamperes	7.1 milliamperes

Did the sample assembled by the new method show a reduction in spread that was significant? In other words, were these results statistically significant?

The t and F tests were used to determine the significance of the difference between averages and the difference in variability, respectively, as indicated by the two samples. The results showed that these differences were highly significant so it was safe to conclude that the change in method did have a highly non-chance effect on the average and a real reduction in variability for these tubes.

The application of significance tests was still relatively new to the plant, however, and the engineer decided to make a further check on the effect of the methods change. He decided to obtain a larger representative sample by running at least 1 day's production with the new assembly technique. In doing this, the day's production was run with all shifts, all machines, and all other variables completely randomized as encountered in normal production. The results in the final tests of the tubes with the new assembly method, as compared with those manufactured under standard production conditions, were:

	Sample with new method	Standard production
n......................	309	500
$\bar{X}$......................	36.8	44.1
σ	4.5	8.0
Percent defective	1.0	14.0

The comparison between the two groups was made graphically by probability paper. Figure 16.13 shows the comparison between the groups.

The engineer approved the new assembly method after examination of the probability plot. A considerable reduction in rejections, with a corresponding improvement in quality and reduction in cost, was obtained from subsequent production of the tube type while using the new method.

16.16 Examination of Temperature Compensation: Graeco-Latin Square

In aerospace equipment, which is likely to pass through a very wide range of different temperatures, it is essential that the design of these equipments —particularly instrumentation—provide suitable compensation for these temperature variants. For this reason a plant manufacturing indicators for certain aircraft applications was concerned about the temperature compensation of these assemblies. It was recognized that any analysis of temperature compensation involved the study of a number of combined factors. It was decided therefore that the required examination could be made most effectively by designing an experiment through use of the Graeco-Latin square technique.[21]

The plant took four steps in applying this technique:

1. Application of sound engineering principles to select the variables that appeared influential
2. Design of the experiment from which the data were to be obtained
3. The actual work of testing and recording the data
4. Mathematical treatment of the data to measure the relative importance of the separate factors on temperature compensation

In making this analysis, it was determined that four factors contributing to the problem being studied on the indicator assembly were (1) location of the compensator plate, (2) conductivity of the drag disk, (3) coefficient of conductivity of the disk material, and (4) thickness of the compensator plate.

Three values of these factors were chosen in the critical region for temperature compensation. They were applied to a 3×3 Graeco-Latin square, as shown in Figure 16.14. Each setup was duplicated for a measure of repeatability. Errors were tabulated at various temperature levels, and the analysis was aimed at finding the arrangement that would produce least error.

The data shown were read at $-22°C$; similar work was done at $+49, -37$, and $-56°C$. The final tabulation of results is shown in Figure 16.15.

From this analysis of temperature compensation, using only nine indicator assemblies, it was found that conductance values were a more critical parameter for locating the compensator plate properly than were thermal coefficients. A considerable saving in labor cost for adjusting the indicators in the plant was one result from this study.

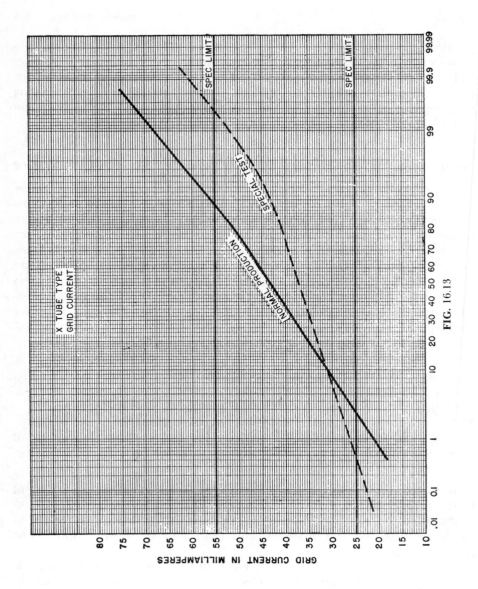

FIG. 16.13

3 X 3 SQUARE

	I	II	III
A	1 α	2 β	3 γ
B	2 γ	3 α	1 β
C	3 β	1 γ	2 α

LOCATION
$\begin{cases} I & II & III \\ .115 & .085 & .055 \end{cases}$

CONDUCTIVITY
$\begin{cases} A & B & C \\ 1600 & 1800 & 2000 \end{cases}$

COEFFICIENT
$\begin{cases} 1 & 2 & 3 \\ .025 & .040 & .060 \end{cases}$

THICKNESS
$\begin{cases} α & β & γ \\ .010 & .020 & .040 \end{cases}$

EXPERIMENTAL DATA

L	+ 1.603	+ .369	− 2.507
MEAN	+ 1.655	− .066	− 2.784
R	+ 1.706	− .502	− 3.062
L	+ 2.312	+ .958	− 1.212
MEAN	+ 1.470	+ 1.290	− .642
R	+ .627	+ 1.622	− .0707
L	+ 2.52	− .378	+ 2.47
MEAN	+ 2.51	− .003	+ 2.32
	+ 2.50	+ .372	+ 2.17

TEST SETUP

I	.115	II	.085	III	.055	LOCATION
A	1600	A	1600	A	1600	CONDUCTIVITY
1	.025	2	.040	3	.060	COEFFICIENT
α	.010	β	.020	γ	.040	THICKNESS

I	.115	II	.085	III	.055	LOCATION
B	1800	B	1800	B	1800	CONDUCTIVITY
2	.040	3	.060	1	.025	COEFFICIENT
γ	.040	α	.010	β	.020	THICKNESS

I	.115	II	.085	III	.055	LOCATION
C	2000	C	2000	C	2000	CONDUCTIVITY
3	.060	1	.025	2	.040	COEFFICIENT
β	.020	γ	.040	α	.010	THICKNESS

FIG. 16.14

Values of Statistic F and Critical Values for the Indicator

Factors	Sum of squares	Degrees of freedom	Mean square	F	Critical (1 %)
Location	15.63	2	7.815	22.10	8.02
Conductivity	12.13	2	6.065	17.30	8.02
Coefficient	3.28	2	1.640	4.65	8.02
Thickness	14.41	2	7.205	20.60	8.02
Residual	3.19	9	0.354		

FIG. 16.15

Notes

[1]For the reader interested in a discussion of a broad range of techniques for exploring data, including stem-and-leaf, box-and-whisker plots, smoothing methods and others, see John W. Tukey, *Exploratory Data Analysis*, Addison-Wesley Publishing Company, Inc., Reading, Mass., 1977.

[2]Much of this probability-paper analysis is adapted from the discussion by W. H. Abbott, Cleveland, Ohio, in an excellent paper "Use of Probability Charts in the Study of Distribution and the Determination of Sigma."

[3]The form of probability paper shown in Fig. 16.5 is well-suited to use for theoretical statistical purposes because of its vertical scale, which begins with 0.01 and goes upward to 99.99. All theoretical distribution functions must start from 0 and proceed to 1, hence this vertical scale provides the basis for such plots.

[4]This discussion is limited to plotting the percentage of values *less than* the curve in question. It is also possible to use probability paper in the fashion of plotting the percentage of values *more than* the curve in question, in which case data are plotted at the lower boundary of each cell.

[5]Data after Abbott, op. cit.

[6]This is performed in the usual fashion:

$$\overline{X} = \frac{\Sigma fx}{n}$$

[7]The band width should, of course, be compared with the commonly used range of the dependent variable. Thus, if the range of inquiry in Fig. 16.8 is from 5.0 to 6.0 in characteristic A, the curve is no more useful than Fig. 16.9 if the range of inquiry is 5.0 to 15.0.

[8]In this section it is assumed that the tolerance for each individual part fairly closely approximates its process capability. If this is not true, then process capabilities should be substituted to compute the overall tolerance for the subassembly.

[9]For additional information, see E. L. Grant, *Statistical Quality Control,* 5th ed., McGraw-Hill Book Company, New York.

[10]For a computer-based example of an application to nuclear reactor safety, see N. D. Cox, "Tolerance Analysis by Computer," *Journal of Quality Technology,* vol. II, no. 2, April 1979, pp. 80–87.

[11]When the difference among sample values can be shown so great as to make untenable the assumption of a common source for the lots in question, these differences are said to be statistically significant. An illustration of significance may be made briefly. Part 5 showed that different samples of the same part may well vary in their values of central tendency and spread. Section 13.18 showed that this will occur with samples drawn from the same lot or same source. When the difference in central tendency and spread is caused by this random variation in samples from the same source, the difference among sample values may be said to be statistically not significant. When the difference among the sample values can be shown to be caused by their having come from different lots or different sources, these differences may be said to be statistically significant.

[12]This test is sometimes also called "Student's t," after W. S. Gosset, whose work appeared under the pseudonym Student. For a comprehensive discussion, see Irving W. Burr, *Applied Statistical Methods,* Academic Press, Inc., New York, 1974, pp. 171–174.

[13]Burr, ibid., pp. 179–180, 225–228.

[14]There is now an effective body of literature for the reader interested in experimental design at various degrees of detail and complexity. For a basic reference, see W. G. Cochran and G. M. Cox, *Experimental Designs,* John Wiley & Sons, Inc., New York, 1957. See also Jerome L. Meyers, *Fundamentals of Experimental Design,* 2d ed , Allyn and Bacon, Inc., Boston, 1972; B. J. Winer, *Statistical Principles in Experimental Design,* 2d ed., McGraw-Hill Book Company, New York, 1971; M. H. Quenoville and J. A. John, *Experiments: Design and Analysis,* 2d ed., The Macmillan Company New York, 1977; and Gerald J. Hahn, "Some Things Engineers Should Know about Experimental Design," *Journal of Quality Technology,* vol. 9, no. 1, January 1977.

[15]For an excellent classic reference, which is somewhat complex, see R. A. Fisher, *Statistical Methods for Research Workers,* Oliver & Boyd Ltd., Edinburgh, 1948. For an interesting discussion, see also S. S. Shapiro and M. B. Wilk, "An Analysis of Variance Test for Normality (complete samples)," *Biometrika,* 52, pp. 591–611, 1965.

[16]See, for example, Maurice G. Kendall, *The Advanced Theory of Statistics,* vol. II, Charles Griffin & Company, Ltd., London, 1948, p. 261.

[17]For Graeco-Latin squares as well as other designs, see the classical text by the inventor of such designs: R. A. Fisher, *The Design of Experiments,* 5th ed., Hafner Publishing Company, Inc., New York, 1949; see also Kendall, ibid.; also M. G. Kendall and Alan Stuart, *The Advanced Theory of Statistics,* vols. 1 to 3, Hafner Publishing Company, Inc., New York, 1968–1973.

[18]The reader interested in detailed aspects of this methodological discipline may review such references as Frederick Mosteller and John W. Tukey, *Data Analysis and Regression,* Addison-Wesley Publishing Company, Inc., Reading, Mass., 1977; Allen L. Edwards, *Statistical Methods,* 2d ed., Holt, Rinehart and Winston, Inc., New York, 1967; John E. Freund, *Mathematical Statistics,* 2d ed.,

Prentice-Hall, Inc., Englewood Cliffs, N.J., 1971; M.G. Kendall, *Rank Correlation Methods*, 4th ed., Charles Griffin & Company, Ltd., London, 1970; and for a classic discussion, W. A. Shewhart, *Economic Control of Quality of Manufactured Product*, D. Van Nostrand Company, Inc., New York, 1931, pp. 214–229.

[19]Adapted from G. R. Armstrong and P. C. Clarke, *Statistical Methods in Quality Control.*

[20]This discussion is adapted from an analysis made by C. G. Donsbach and associates, Schenectady, N.Y.

[21]This discussion is adapted from an analysis made by P. E. Thompson, West Lynn, Mass.; it directly follows his exposition of the project.

CHAPTER 17

Product Reliability

A reliable product is one that will perform the function it is designed to perform when required to do so over its period of use. Reliability is a quality characteristic that represents one of today's principal buyer demands. A customer interviewed in a marketing survey put it very simply: "I want to buy products that work correctly day after day when I push the button."

Meeting reliability requirements has become one of the major demands upon modern product technology. Buyers who once concentrated their purchases upon products that were primarily innovative or attention-getting now concentrate upon such products which *also* operate reliably.

The reliability of products is one of the major areas of total-quality-control attention. This chapter considers the concepts underpinning the statistical and mathematical point of view toward reliability and reviews key activities for achieving and assuring reliability.

17.1 The Increasing Emphasis on Product Reliability

Certain products have always been marketed based upon their high level of reliability and their engineering and production have had this value as a primary objective. For example, fossil-fuel large steam turbines have long been sold with emphasis upon their reliability; an undue proportion of down time can mean both excessive costs for the electric utility and great difficulty for the community that uses the electricity being generated. Diesel road locomotives have been purchased or leased by railroads primarily for their anticipated reliability in long-haul freight operations. In consumer markets, household refrigerators have been bought by families in anticipation of the relatively high levels of reliability they have come to expect from the products' record over a number of years. Certain brands of consumer electronic products have come to dominate their marketplace because of published and word-of-mouth information concerning their reliable performance as compared to competitive appliances.

However, for many other products, in the past, companies too frequently concentrated on testing primarily for the start of product life t_0 (time t subscript zero) rather than also evaluating product performance at stages during product life (times $t_1, t_2, \ldots, t_n$). In many cases, the related life testing and environmental testing were cursory. Inevitably, increasingly major problems were experienced with these products when they were used by customers.

In recent years, there has as a result been both a great broadening of reliability attention across a very wide range of products and a greater formalization of reliability activity itself. This formalization has been strongly influenced by the development of complex, multicomponent equipments, especially in aerospace and electronics, where it was necessary very early to institutionalize reliability as a product objective in itself. As the importance of reliability also became recognized in a variety of products—industrial and consumer—emphasis has been placed upon quantitative measurements which help make reliability a number—a probability—that can be expressed very specifically. Such measurements make it possible, rather objectively, to evaluate product reliability; to predict it; to balance it objectively with other product-quality parameters such as maintainability; and to control it. They make possible the establishment of explicit programs to assure product reliability. These programs are an important activity throughout all four jobs of total quality control.

17.2 The Evolution of Formal Product Reliability

For a full understanding of the reliability activities of total quality control, it is important to recognize four basic steps that have been involved in the evolution of modern product reliability:

1. The first step, now several decades old, has had the objective of the *prediction* of product reliability and the *demonstration* that this reliability has been achieved. One of the key techniques, particularly in electronics and later extended to mechanical and other products, was the determination of parts failure rates. When these data were generalized, they showed that many types of parts had a high initial failure rate; a constant failure rate over a significant period of time that could be expressed mathematically; and another high failure rate as the part wore out.

    Straightforward mathematical and statistical models have been developed so that these established parts failure rates could be translated into failure rates for the products and equipments in which the parts were assembled. The basic assumption of these models has been a relatively constant failure rate with high initial-failure-rate components and products removed by the incoming-material job of total-quality-control inspection and failures due to wear out avoided by preventive maintenance programs provided by the product-control job of total quality control. Moreover, there have now also been developed more involved mathematical models that apply to very complex products which have several manners of operation, which may be maintained and repaired during operation, and which have numerous patterns of degradation other than constant.

With these techniques applied to certain well-established product designs, whose fully acceptable predicted time to failure was a relatively limited number of hours, it has been increasingly possible to readily provide the necessary assurance of reliability through product testing programs, supported by statistical evaluation, to demonstrate the continuing achievement and maintenance of product reliability.

2. However, for products whose design, manufacture, and use are complex, or where it may be necessary and required to have a long period of reliable and trouble-free operation, the second step in the evolution of product reliability has evolved: that is, the *improvement* of product reliability. A number of techniques of great importance have been developed in product design, product manufacture, and product service and maintenance.

In product design, some of these principal techniques are design margin, derating, redundancy, environmental stress control, failure mode effect and criticality analysis (FMECA), research in the physics of failure, human engineering design, packaging and transportation design, and many others. In manufacture, many areas of incoming-material control and product control are essential to assured reliability. In product service and maintenance, the entire area of maintainability, together with product-repair policy and maintenance documentation, are important.

3. Because of the growth of these several techniques, the third step in the evolution of product reliability became necessary. This has been to bring together in a coordinated way the series of activities whose objective is the establishment, achievement, and ongoing maintenance of reliability. What has come to be termed a reliability "program"[1] is basically a group of reliability activities together with their performance requirements.

4. The fourth step in product reliability's evolution has been to ensure fully effective and fully economic operation and utilization of these mathematical and statistical techniques and these reliability activities, not as ends in themselves, but as integral parts of the complete company program for quality.[2] These reliability activities are thus significant components of modern total quality systems which assure all aspects of customer quality satisfaction for a company.

17.3 Customer Requirements, Reliability, and Costs

In the final analysis, as with all quality characteristics, the reliability requirements of a product are determined by its customers' requirements in use.

There is a certain product-reliability level that provides the most economical device to meet customer needs. However, if this level is too low, actual total cost of use to the customer may be high because of excessive repair, maintenance, and out-of-use costs. If an unduly high reliability level is evolved, total cost may still be excessive to the customer because of the higher price caused partly by unique requirements for components and assemblies.

The importance of a proper determination of this level is reflected in what has come to be thought of as the "availability" of the product or service (Sec. 17.7). This relates to what in earlier years was often referred to as product "up time" or "down time."

There is an optimum product-reliability value—determined as overall costs —both to the purchaser and the manufacturer. Purchasers have increasingly emphasized that they expect this standard of product reliability without undue premiums in prices they pay to manufacturers. As one knowledgeable purchaser noted:

> We all recognize that increased effort in any area necessitates extra expenditure. Just as any other customer . . . [we] must be willing to pay for those specific costs incurred to improve reliability; however, we must separate the traditional and basic elements of good management and engineering from those unusual and justifiable expenditures for higher reliability achievement. We must insist that the term 'reliability' is not used as camouflage for additional charges for those functions which are an intrinsic part of an effective industrial operation.

The manufacturer may address the problem from a different perspective: "People are sometimes misled when they hear us say we're working to improve quality. It may cause them to think our quality has deteriorated. In fact, it hasn't. We are saying we must do our job even better as machines become more sophisticated . . . and methods for producing them, more technically demanding."[3] The reason for this is that acceptable levels of reliability are never fully fixed in any long-term sense because of the dynamic efforts of business—due to competitiveness and other factors—toward giving the customer progressively higher reliability without increasing product costs, or even while reducing product costs.

It is to assist in the circumstances discussed above—by stripping away the camouflage and identifying the areas in which attention is really required— that quality costs are broken down into their respective elements. Insofar as the reliability elements of quality cost are concerned, many segments of reliability-related costs and user and life cycle quality costs have been already considered in the discussion of overall quality costs thoroughly reviewed in Chapter 7.

> Certain reliability-related costs must be incurred to ensure that the required product reliability is attained: these are included as parts of prevention and appraisal costs.

- These costs must be balanced against failure costs to achieve the specified product reliability.
- The total costs of quality must be optimized to meet company quality objectives, including their reliability component.

DEFINITION AND MEASUREMENT OF RELIABILITY

17.4 What Is Product Reliability?

Product reliability is one of the qualities of a product. Quite simply, it is the quality which measures the probability that the product or device "will work." As a definition:

> Product reliability is the ability of a unit to perform a required function under stated conditions for a stated period of time.

And correspondingly, quantitative reliability, as a definition, is:[4]

> Quantitative reliability is the probability that a unit will perform a required function under stated conditions for a stated time.

Four of the significant elements in this concept of quantified and measured reliability are

1. Probability
2. Performance
3. Time
4. Conditions

1. The first element in reliability is the consideration of variation, discussed in Chapter 13, which makes of reliability a *probability*. Each individual unit of product will vary somewhat from other units; some may have a relatively short life and others a relatively long life. Furthermore, a group of units may have a certain average life. Thus it is possible to identify distributions of product failure which permit prediction of the life of units of product.

2. The second consideration contained in the definition is that reliability is a *performance* quality characteristic. For a product to be reliable, it must perform a certain function or do a certain job when called upon. For example, a heating pad must give the intended degree of heat when it is switched onto the Low setting and must do the same for the Medium and High settings.

    Implied in the phrase "performing its intended function" is that the device is intended for a certain application. In the case of the heating pad, the intended application is that of applying warmth to various areas of the human body. If, instead, the pad is used outdoors to keep a large container of coffee at a certain temperature, the heating pad might be inadequate because of changes in rate of heat transfer and greater volume to be heated as well as a change in environment.

3. The third element in the definition of reliability is *time.* Reliability, stated as a probability of the product's performing a function, must be identified for a stated period of time.

   An analogy is life insurance actuary tables. The probability of an individual's living through the next year is a different number than the probability of the person's living through the next decade. By the same token, a statement about the reliability of a product must be coupled to its intended life, whether 10 minutes or 10 years or whatever the life span is.

4. The fourth consideration in the definition is *conditions,* which include the application and operating circumstances under which the product is put to use. These factors establish the stresses that will be imposed upon the product. They need to be viewed broadly enough to include storage and transportation conditions because these also can have significant effects on product reliability.

The environment which a product "sees" will greatly affect its life span and performance. In the case of the heating pad, the outdoor environment of the container of coffee is quite different from the relatively dry environment of a room and would significantly alter reliability of the pad.

The term "inherent reliability" identifies the potential reliability that the designer conceptually creates with the design. This is presumed to be the highest reliability that the particular design will provide. When the design is actually produced in the form of "hardware," it normally has some reliability value always less than the inherent reliability. This is usually considered as the achieved reliability.

The "achieved reliability" of a device is the reliability *demonstrated* by the physical product. Hence, it includes the manufacturing effects on product reliability, which, in reality, are always present for a physical product.

To obtain "reliability improvement," the physical product is measured and analyzed to determine what effects may be causing the achieved reliability to fall short of the inherent reliability. This calls for a study of the failure mechanism for the product under consideration.

"Failure mechanism" may be defined as the chronological series of events which logically lead to product failure. An understanding of these events and the causes for them permits identification of reliability program activities directed to elimination of those factors responsible for low achieved reliability.

17.5 The Measurement of Reliability

Much of reliability analysis has been founded on statistical studies to identify, product by product and component by component, distinct patterns of failure versus time during the life cycle of products and components. In the context of reliability prediction, items have been generally considered components when they cannot be economically or practically repaired; items which can be repaired are considered "multicomponent products," or "equipment systems." As an example, molded capacitors and resistors in this context are components; automobiles, spacecraft, and refrigerators are products or equipment systems.[5]

An increasing amount of such reliability data is becoming available, as a result of studies by manufacturers, research institutes, and other agencies, for use by companies that are considering use of the product. Figure 17.1 illustrates an example of a structured approach to the development of such data.[6]

One pattern, for example, that seems basic for many electronic products is shown in Figure 17.2.[7] The life cycle consists of three distinct periods:

- The first period is termed the "infant mortality" period and is caused by early failure of weak components due principally to nonrandom "assignable causes." This period is typified by a fairly high failure rate which drops off rapidly in the case of some products.
- The second period is typified by a fairly constant rate of failure. Failures occur in the random manner associated with a constant-cause system.
- The third period is termed the "wear-out period," in which the failure rate starts to rise rapidly as the number of survivors approaches zero until all units have failed and no more are "left to die."[8]

The reason for establishing these patterns is similar to that discussed in Chapter 13 in connection with rather more simple frequency-distribution plots: When these patterns become known, they then permit the application to them of established mathematical probability distributions for measuring and predicting the failure rates of given products and components from sample data.

17.6 The Measurement of Reliability: Some Examples

Frequency Distribution of Life for 200 Switches

As an example, let us start with the frequency distribution in Figure 17.3 and show how it can be used to measure product reliability. This shows the lifetimes of 200 switches in terms of numbers of operations during the normal operating portion of switch life, i.e., after the infant mortality, or debugging, period and before the wear-out phase. This is the second period shown in Figure 17.2.

As shown in Figure 17.3, 20 switches failed during the first 1000 operations, 18 between 1000 and 2000 operations, and so on. By the time the switches had operated 8000 times, a total of 114 had failed—57 percent of those that started on the test.

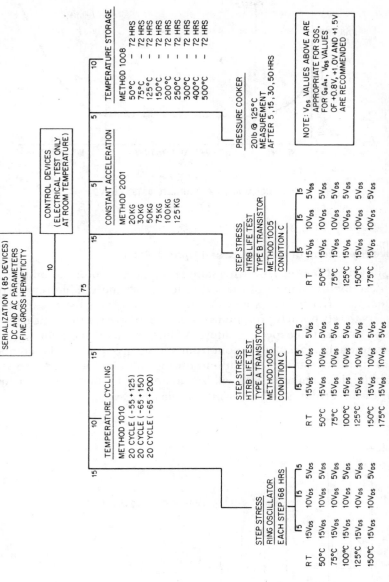

FIG. 17.1 From D. H. Phillips, "QA Aspects of Silicon-on-Sapphire and Gallium Arsenide Integrated Circuits Devices," *Quality Progress,* **vol. XIII, no. 11, November 1980.**

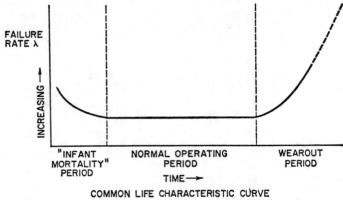

COMMON LIFE CHARACTERISTIC CURVE

FIG. 17.2

Relative Frequency of Failures Based Upon a Sample

As shown in Chapter 15, such a sample can give us information that permits us to describe the nature of the larger lot which the sample represents.

Where experience with a new design is limited, as is usually the case, it is necessary to rely upon representative samples to provide the logical basis upon which to predict the expected failures. Thus, in the observations of a sample of N components taken at random from a large group of similar components, if n_t of them have lifetimes that end during the time period t, the statistical probability that similar results will be obtained from the remainder (untested items) of the group is defined as the *relative frequency:*

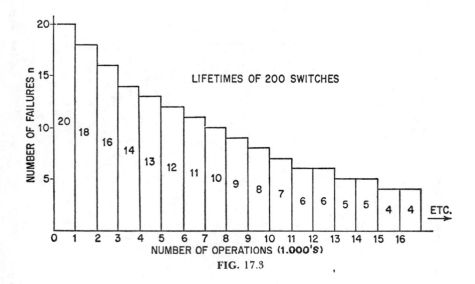

FIG. 17.3

$$P_t = \frac{n_t}{N} \tag{39}$$

where P_t = probability of failure during period t
$\quad\quad n_t$ = number of items having lifetimes ending during period t
$\quad\quad N$ = total number of items in sample

Applying Formula (39) to the data presented in Figure 17.3, the probability that a switch will fail after 5000 and before 6000 operations is $^{12}/_{200}$ = 0.06.

Confidence in this estimate increases with larger sample sizes. As the sample size approaches the total number of units produced, confidence in the parameters of this lot approaches certainty. Putting it another way, there is a greater chance that the ratio n_t/N, computed for each of two equal sample sizes taken from the same lot, will more closely agree with each other when the sample size is large rather than small. And this ratio, n_t/N, can be regarded as an experimental value of a constant P_t, related to the time period t and referred to as the *probability of occurrence for the period t.*

Reliability Related to Relative Frequency of Failure

In the definition of reliability given in Section 17.4, performance over intended life was one criterion. The intended or required life T can be measured in different ways; i.e., total elapsed time, energized time, number of operating cycles, and the like. To obtain a measurement for reliability, the actual life t must be compared to the required life T.

The relationship between the reliability of a unit and the frequency diagram of lifetimes can be illustrated by using Figure 17.3. If the area of the combined bars, assuming all 200 switches were run to destruction, is set equal to 1, then the probability, or relative frequency of a particular class of lifetimes—say, 5000 to 6000 operations—equals the area of the bar representing that class of lifetimes; in this case, the bar labeled 12. Note that this is equivalent to plotting relative frequency n_t/N rather than n_t along the ordinate of Figure 17.3. Also, the relative frequency of failures in the interval $0 \leq t \leq T$ is $(20 + 18 + 16 + 14 + 13 + 12)/200 = {}^{93}/_{200} = 0.465$ when T equals 6000 operations; thus the probability of a switch failure during the first 6000 operations is $P_{t=T} = 0.465$. Conversely, the probability that a switch will *survive* the first 6000 operations (i.e., its *reliability* R_T) is $1.00 - 0.465 = 0.535$, or symbolically,

$$R_T = 1 - P_{t=T} = 1.0 - \frac{1}{N} \Sigma_0^T n_t \tag{40}$$

The symbol Σ (Greek letter capital sigma) denotes arithmetic summation. Thus the term $\Sigma_0^T n_t$ in Formula (40) is read "the summation of the number of items having lifetimes ending during period t, (n_t), where t ranges from zero to the required life T."

Development of a Continuous (Smooth) Curve and Summing of Areas

If Figure 17.3 had presented data for 1000 rather than 200 switches, and if the abscissa were to be subdivided into hundreds of operations, 170 slender rectangles would result and their tops would approximate a smooth curve. The limiting form of the frequency diagram, as the fineness of divisions and the number of observations increased indefinitely, is generally a smooth curve like that shown in Figure 17.4. The relative frequency n_t/N is seen to be a function of time $f(t)$ so that

$$R_T = 1.0 - \int_0^T f(t)\, dt \tag{41}$$

As the number of observations increase indefinitely, the summation of a particular area under the curve, in this case from 0 to T, is computed by the *probability density function*, which the reader with a background in calculus recognizes as the definite integral over a specified interval on the independent variable axis, giving the area under the frequency distribution curve.

It is generally easier to measure the failure rate of a class of units than to measure its reliability directly by constructing frequency diagrams like the one in Figure 17.3. Less time is required, and fewer samples are destroyed. However, failure rate data are of little value unless judgment or theoretical considerations can be relied upon to indicate the general form of the frequency diagram that would be generated if sufficient data were available.

Constant Failure Rate Results from Exponential Probability Density Function

As discussed in Section 17.2 and generalized in Figure 17.2, a constant failure rate may be identified under certain conditions over a period of a unit's life for those units that are so complex as to offer failure mechanisms with different rates. If approximately the same *percentage* of units remaining at the start of each time interval fail during the interval, the failure rate is constant. For example, Figure 17.3 depicts a situation for a constant failure rate of

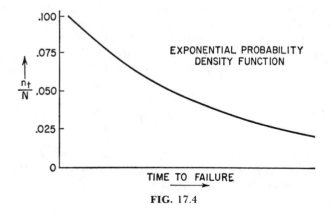

FIG. 17.4

approximately 10 percent. In the first cell, $^{20}/_{200} = 10$ percent; in the second cell $^{18}/_{180} = 10$ percent; in the third cell $^{16}/_{162} = 9.9$ percent; and so forth.

The exponential probability density function, which describes the constant-failure rate situation, results in a frequency curve as shown in Figure 17.4 and is represented by the formula

$$f(t) = \frac{1}{\theta} e^{-t/\theta} \tag{42}$$

If this function is substituted in Formula (41), the following results:

$$R_T = 1.0 - \int_0^T \frac{1}{\theta} e^{-t/\theta} \, dt = e^{-T/\theta} \tag{43}$$

where T = required life
θ = mean life or mean time to failure (MTTF), sometimes expressed as mean time to first failure (MTFF)
e = a constant (2.7183)[9]

Reliability Determined Directly from Failure Rate

The failure rate λ by definition is the reciprocal of the MTTF and can be substituted in Formula (43), giving

$$R_T = e^{-\lambda T} \tag{44}$$

In this example, the failure rate λ approximates 10 percent, or $\lambda \cong 0.10$. From Formula (44), the probability of a switch of the type described by Figure 17.3 surviving 6.0 (thousand) operations is

$$R_T \cong e^{(-0.10)(6.0)} \cong 0.55$$

which is in close agreement with 0.535, determined from the relative frequencies of the data given in Figure 17.3.

Note that in this case the required life T is expressed in thousands of operations because the data are in failures per thousand operations.

17.7 Other Reliability Patterns; Availability

Failure Rates, Other than Constant, Described by Other Density Functions

The example discussed here was one involving a constant failure rate which derives from the exponential probability density function.

Although this is a frequently encountered pattern of failure, there are other density functions which accommodate most of the patterns encountered in practice, including the following:[10]

1. Normal
2. Gamma
3. Weibull[11]

Figure 17.5 illustrates representations of these functions in practice.[12]

Measures of Reliability

Together with the measures discussed above of *mean time to failure* (MTTF) and *failure rate* (λ lambda), one of the basic measurements of the probability of the reliability of a unit—what might be considered its probability of survival —is that of *mean time between failures* (MTBF), often employed as an indicator of the average time between failures.

Some other measures are the following:

Time to Wear Out (L)

The longevity (L) period represents the time to wear out on the life characteristic curve. Longevity terminates when the failure rate life characteristic curve becomes twice the value of the reciprocal of the acceptable MTBF. Beyond this time, the MTBF will be different.

Time to Uniform Replacement (LR)

In complex equipments, parts with differing life characteristics may exhibit a multiple series of level failure rate plateaus following the longevity period. Consecutive major overhauls of the equipment will reveal life distribution patterns which collectively can exhibit a constant failure rate characteristic. The time in a complete life cycle required to establish this new constant failure rate is known as the *LR*.

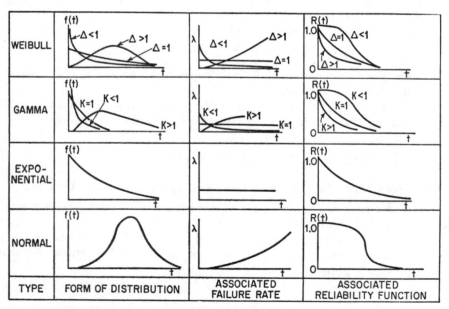

TYPES OF PROBABILITY DISTRIBUTIONS ENCOUNTERED IN RELIABILITY
AND THEIR ASSOCIATED FAILURE RATES AND RELIABILITY FUNCTIONS

FIG. 17.5

Mean Time between Replacement (MTBR)

This is the reciprocal of the average failure rate for an equipment during the period following its LR.

Mean Time between Maintenance (MTBM)

This is the average operating time of a system or equipment between mainte- nance to correct or prevent malfunction.

Mean Time to Repair (MTTR)

This is the average time of a system or equipment to be restored to a specified state in which it can perform its required function.

Selection of the proper survivability measurement will depend upon the design, manufacturing process, and end-use environment of the particular product or component. As an example, for the product which is expected to require defineable levels of maintenance and which can normally be readily repaired or adjusted when necessary, MTBF may be the measurement se- lected. MTTF (or the equivalent term MTFF) has been useful in many cases, including those where an equipment or subassembly will be installed where it may not be readily accessible for maintenance. At component level, MTTF is often used to measure survivability of a component employed in an extremely severe environment.

Need for Characterizing Failure Patterns

Although significant technical effort and substantial funds have been de- voted to reliability studies, great continuing effort is required to establish progressively more meaningful failure rate patterns because

1. Many more product tests are required than can be justified economically upon certain commercial components and products, so that these reliability parameters have frequently been analytical projections for which much more actual sampling evidence is still required.
2. Many extremely expensive components, particularly those used in research products, have not been extensively tested for reliability data because of the attendant destruction of the component.
3. In one- or few-of-a-kind products and components, failure rate patterns have necessarily been somewhat speculative.
4. Interaction of components, one on the other, has resulted in a reliability value for the system quite different from that which would be estimated on the basis of the components in the system.[13]

Combining Component Reliabilities to Get Product Reliability

Series combination. If a product is an assembly of m components, each with its own reliability R_{T_1}, and if failure of any component will cause failure of the product, then the product reliability will be predicted by the following:

$$R_T = R_{T_1} \times R_{T_2} \times R_{T_3} \times \cdots \times R_{T_m} \qquad (45)$$

Such a system is schematically illustrated by Figure 17.6.

If the components in Figure 17.6 fail in accordance with the exponential probability density function, then Formula (45) can be written as

$$R_T = \left(e^{-\lambda_1 T}\right)\left(e^{-\lambda_2 T}\right)\left(e^{-\lambda_3 T}\right) \cdots \left(e^{-\lambda_m T}\right) \tag{46}$$

or

$$R_T = e^{-T(\lambda_1 + \lambda_2 + \lambda_3 + \cdots + \lambda_m)} \tag{47}$$

in which λ_1, λ_2, λ_3, $\cdots$, λ_m are the failure rates of the M components as determined by component testing, reference to catalogs, or theoretical considerations.

For example, consider the problem of predicting the 10-hour reliability of a product containing the following components:

Component	No. in product (m)	Failure rate, λ per hour	Combined failure rate, $(m)(\lambda)$
Diode	52	120×10^{-6}	6.240×10^{-3}
Motor	3	100	0.300
Relay	18	145	2.610
Resistor	213	10	2.130
Potentiometer	26	70	1.820
Switch	82	25	2.050
Transformer	21	20	0.420
Soldered joint	341	18	6.138
			$\Sigma\lambda = 21.708 \times 10^{-3}$

The summation of the component failure rate is the predicted failure rate of the product for product failures per hour. The product failure rate is 21.708 $\times 10^{-3}$, and the 10-hour product reliability, using Formula (47), is

$$R_{10} = e^{-(10)(0.0217)} = e^{-0.217} = 0.805$$

Availability

Among the important considerations in the determination of the reliability pattern for a product is the ability of that product to be restored, within a given period of time, to the specified state in which it can perform its intended function.

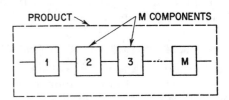

FIG. 17.6 Series arrangement of components.

Thus, a product which can be quickly and cheaply repaired—without discomfort and difficulty to the user—may have quite a different reliability requirement than a product without readily accessible or economic repair facilities—a communications satellite, for example. The satellite must be designed and manufactured with high reliability, including proper redundancy (further discussed in Sec. 17.14); the product that may be readily repaired (the subject of maintainability is discussed in Sec. 17.19) may, all other things being equal, be designed and manufactured with less demanding reliability objectives.

The identification of this *availability* of a product and service can be very important in reliability establishment and control. As a definition:

> Product availability is the ability of a unit to perform a required function at any point of time when used under stated conditions, where the time considered is operating time and active repair time.

And correspondingly, quantitative availability, as a definition, is as follows:

> Quantitative availability is the probability of a unit to perform a required function at any point of time when used under stated conditions, where the time considered is operating time and active repair time.

Availability may be represented as follows:

$$\text{Availability} = \frac{\text{mean time to failure (MTTF)}}{\text{MTTF} + \text{mean time to repair (MTTR)}}$$

Thus, if in a product MTTF is large and MTTR is small, the availability is near one or 100 percent.[14]

17.8 Reliability of Software

The widespread use of computers and microprocessors in today's products, processes, and management systems has placed increasing emphasis upon quantitative measurement of the reliability of programmed logic, or software—which can be fully as important in many applications as the reliability of the hardware itself.

Software reliability may be defined as

> The probability that a software system or component will operate without failure for a specified period of time in a specified environment.

In this context, a *failure* of software may be considered as an unacceptable departure of program operation from requirements.

It can thus be readily seen that, in approach, software reliability strongly resembles hardware reliability, the difference being that in software reliability the source of failure is primarily in design, as has been earlier reviewed in this book, while in hardware reliability the source of failure can also be physical, manufacturing, service, and other degradation. Indeed, the principles of software reliability measurement may in some cases be applicable to hardware design.[15]

If $R(t)$ represents the probability that failure will not occur in time (t), then

$$F(t) = 1 - R(t), \; R(t) = 1 - f(t) \tag{48}$$

represents the probability that failure will occur. The hazard rate $z(t)$ is defined as the instantaneous failure rate, or the failure rate given that a system or component has survived until now. Thus

$$z(t) = \frac{f(t)}{R(t)} \tag{49}$$

and

$$R(t) = \exp\left[-\int_0^t z(x) \, dx\right] \tag{50}$$

The MTTF is the expected value of $f(t)$, or:

$$\text{MTTF} = \int_0^\infty tf(t) \, dt$$
$$= \int_0^\infty R(t) \, dt \tag{51}$$

If the hazard rate is constant, the MTTF is shown to be its reciprocal.

A number of software reliability models have been developed, two of which are Musa's execution time models and Littlewood's models.[16] The principal objectives of such models is to predict behavior of the software in operation. Reliability or MTTF ordinarily increases as a function of accumulated execution time; since expected behavior changes rapidly, it can be tracked during program test and the accumulated data used to predict expected behavior in the field. A software reliability estimation execution time model is shown in Figure 17.7.

THE BASIC RELIABILITY PROGRAM ACTIVITIES IN THE FOUR QUALITY-CONTROL JOBS

17.9 Activities of Reliability

The activities of total quality programs that are geared to the establishment and control of a product's failure rate, as to the elements of probability, time, performance and conditions, represent important elements of work that are carried on in the four jobs of total quality control. These reliability activities can be grouped under six headings:

1. "Establishing the Product-Reliability Requirements," Section 17.10.
2. "Developing the Reliability Program to Meet the Requirements Including Product Design, Manufacturing Processes, and Transportation," Sections 17.11 through 17.19.
3. "Evaluation of Reliability Plans By Tests," Section 17.20.

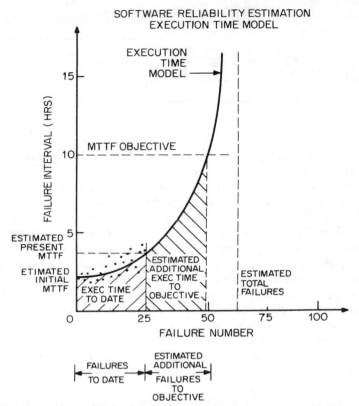

SOFTWARE RELIABILITY ESTIMATION
EXECUTION TIME MODEL

FIG. 17.7 From John D. Musa, "The Measurement and Management of Software Reliability," Proceedings of the IEEE, vol. 68, no. 9, September 1980.

4. "Reliability Growth," Section 17.21.
5. "Continuing Control of Reliability," Section 17.22.
6. "Continuing Reliability Analysis," Section 17.23.

Activities 1 to 4 and 6 are among the key activities in the new-design control job. Activity 3 is a very important activity also in incoming-material control. Activities 4 to 6 are vital portions of the product-control job.

Figure 17.8 shows the relationship among these six activities. The data drawn from continuing analysis of product reliability are fed back so that requirements are regularly reviewed with respect to adequacy of product design, process design, and the related control systems.

17.10 Establishing the Product-Reliability Requirements

The initial new-design control activity involves establishing the requirements for MTTF and whatever other reliability targets may be indicated to meet the reliability required for the product. As discussed in Section 17.3, the

ACTIVITIES OF PRODUCT RELIABILITY

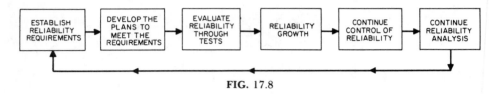

FIG. 17.8

cost of attaining an incremental increase in reliability must be balanced against the costs associated with not attaining it.

Since this overall balance is of primary interest to the customer, the selected reliability target should be a matter of agreement between the customer (or the customer's representative) and the manufacturer, in such areas as industrial products and military equipment.[17] In the case of consumer products, where the customer will not be present at the reliability review, every effort should be made by the manufacturer to represent the customer as realistically as possible, with due regard to the achievement of positive customer satisfaction through feedforward studies as earlier discussed in this book as well as with regard to the avoidance of product liability and recall hazards.

The selection of a reliability standard should be a practical matter rather than a speculative exercise. The standard must be chosen with due attention to the state of the technical art and with understanding of what it will take to extend this art beyond current limits. It must be obtainable within economic bounds.

Too often these elements have not been realistically considered when reliability standards have been created, and unrealistic reliability specifications and costs have been the result.

To be meaningful, the reliability targets must be within reach at a planned date. This means separation of the reliability analysis into two areas:

- Reliability considerations that can be currently established in relation to current capabilities
- Considerations that require further analysis, testing, and development before satisfactory data can be considered as established, i.e., new components, new use of old components, and so on

The reliability specified may thus require further technical advances before it can be attained. To accomplish these advances requires that the greatest effort be placed where it is needed. A careful analysis of the proposed product will reveal the components with the highest failure rates. These should be "split out" of the package for further research and development work.

Required reliability values may ultimately be realized only after the product has been placed in production. Some of the increase in reliability results from increased skill as a result of the learning process. Such reliability "growth" is further discussed in Section 17.21. A major portion, however, is afforded by basic refinements to both product design and process design, made possible by sufficient numbers of units and accompanying data on which fundamental decisions can be based for reliablity improvement.

Throughout it must be remembered that the objective is achieving the optimum value for the reliability parameter of product quality—rather than the establishment of any particular special means for this purpose. This means emphasis on simplicity to the extent possible. As an observer noted,

> The present trend toward complexity of equipment systems must be reversed before it becomes a limitation. Is it reasonable to expect reliability of an inverted pyramid of four gadgets to cure the bugs in two gadgets which are necessary because the original device was inadequate? How much better to use a simple well-thought-out design in the first place. We fear that many are so confused they think a clever fix is the equal of good design. Reliability unsupported by crutches, no matter how artistically they are carved, should always be the end in view.

17.11 Developing the Reliability Program to Meet the Requirements, Including Product Design, Manufacturing Processes, and Transportation

The plan by which the product-reliability requirements are to be attained involves the product engineering specification which establishes the equipment system, components, and configuration; the manufacturing-process specification by which the product is to be made; the techniques to assure reliability; the packaging and transportation specifications by which the product will be protected; the selection of the transportation by which it will be moved to the customer; and the maintenance and repair functions that will keep the product functioning according to the design intent.

Attention is first directed toward determination of product-reliability requirements and the design engineering considerations necessary in specifying a product to meet these requirements. It becomes the problem of the design engineer to specify the design, manufactured by a certain process, that will meet certain reliability requirements within the economic limitations involved.

Where does the design engineer start? Usually, the desired product function, on which a reliability requirement is placed, determines the reliability of the product that is to provide that function. The product, however, is composed of many individual components. Each component contributes its share to the reliability of the product, as was shown by the example near the end of Section 17.7.

The design engineer starts by considering the arrangement of components necessary to provide the supporting functions essential to the overall product function. The design engineer then evaluates the reliability of the product on the basis of the individual component reliabilities, utilizing various reliability-oriented techniques. If certain individual component reliabilities are unknown, it may be necessary to evaluate them by simulation tests. Where analysis shows that certain types of components have a critical effect upon the reliability of the product, it may be necessary to alter the design so less use of such critical components is made possible. Or it may be necessary to obtain components with a higher reliability, use components with higher ratings, or provide redundancy in the design. These alternatives are discussed in Sections 17.12 to 17.14.

When the optimum theoretical product design has been created on paper, it is prudent to build a prototype and test it, measuring its performance and thereby determining its reliability. Such tests show up the weak components, where additional reliability improvement is required. It is then possible to concentrate on these component types, thereby improving product reliability to the required standard of inherent reliability.

The larger the number of components in a product, the more serious the reliability problem becomes. If a product must have a reliability of 0.90 and is composed of 10 components, the reliability of each component must be approximately 0.99; however, if the product employed 1000 components, the reliability of each component would have to be 0.9999. When the reliability requirements get this high, as noted above, a very substantial amount of testing is required. A practical solution appears to be the designing of products with adequate design margins and suitable redundancies and the manufacturing of products with satisfactory precision and control.

Among the important considerations involved in the designing process and related to the product are:

1. "Design Margin," Section 17.12
2. "Derating," Section 17.13
3. "Redundancy," Section 17.14
4. "The Manufacturing Process: An Integral Part of the Reliability Program," Section 17.15
5. "Packaging and Transportation Planning: An Essential Part of the Reliability Program," Section 17.16

A number of other techniques can be utilized to determine reliability, including:

1. "Failure Mode, Effect and Criticality Analysis," Section 17.17
2. "Physics of Failure Research," Section 17.18
3. "Maintainability," Section 17.19
4. "Human Engineering Design," Section 17.19

Evaluation of the reliability planning resulting from all these considerations is accomplished by tests, discussed in Section 17.20. Section 17.21 considers the prediction of reliability improvement and growth. The continuing control of reliability is then discussed in Section 17.22, and continuing reliability analysis in Section 17.23.

17.12 Design Margin

One of the most important concepts in designing a reliable product is *"design margin."* This is comparable to the so-called factor of safety that civil engineers have been using for centuries. For example, if a bridge is designed with a factor of safety of 4, this simply means that the bridge is four times stronger in design approach than necessary to meet the ordinarily expected stresses. This has often been called the "ignorance factor." In other words, this factor of safety covered unknown stresses that might occur, variability in the strength of the materials used, variability due to workmanship, misuse, and so on. As knowledge increases and variability decreases, it is possible to use lower safety factors.

A better idea of how design margin relates to product strength variability[18] can be gained from Figure 17.9. As discussed in Chapter 13, product variability is measured in units of standard deviation (sigma). One recommended practice for designing certain electronic controls with adequate reliability, for example, is to allow a margin of 5 sigma between the lowest strength product item that will be encountered and the maximum stress imposed by the environment that the product will encounter. Thus, this 5-sigma margin becomes the *design margin.*

To design intelligently, using any specified margin, it is necessary to know the variability of product strengths and the maximum stresses imposed by the environment. Often neither are known with sufficient accuracy. This necessitates building the product and subjecting it to the environments it will encounter in service. In this way, the product weaknesses (lack of product strengths) are determined in relation to a given environment by a trial-and-error process. In this manner, the "weak links" in the chain are identified and strengthened to provide the required design margin.

Both product strength and environmental stress values can be affected, sometimes drastically, by what happens during manufacture. Much of the variability that the design engineer must work with is caused by the variability of manufacturing processes. It is the manufacturing process that causes variability in the strength of materials due to nonhomogeneity, variations in dimensions, and variation in composition.

The same can be said of the electronic characteristics of components. For example, the use of certain integrated circuits in designs does not become practical until manufacturing processes and techniques are developed to provide the required purity of material. A significant contribution to the reliability program comes from studying the effects of process capabilities and process stability so necessary process improvements can be made. A more detailed treatment of manufacturing effect on reliability is reserved for Section 17.15.

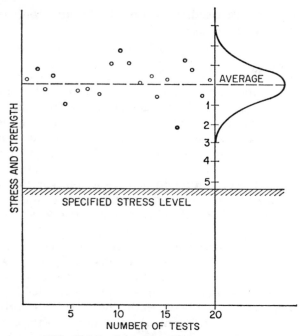

FIG. 17.9 **Product strength versus stress.**

17.13 Derating

One technique of design in providing a greater margin between design strengths and environmental stresses is to derate components. Derating simply means that the component is being assigned to a task somewhat less arduous than that for which it was originally designed. For example, a 3000-ohm resistor may have originally been rated at a standard of 70°C ambient temperature and a 1-watt power dissipation. If this resistor were selected for an application where the ambient temperature is 60°C and power dissipation ½ watt, it might be derated for both ambient temperature and wattage dissipation. The effect of such derating would be to put less stress on the part; hence one would expect less deviation of resistance values from the original resistance over a given period of time.

17.14 Redundancy

The reliability of products can be increased by providing a spare component that can be used if a component fails. The use of a spare tire on an automobile is a homely example of redundancy. In electronic systems design, provision is normally made to automatically switch the spare component into the circuit should the original component performing the specific desired function fail.

Redundancy is one of the key techniques in designing products for high reliability, particularly where the reliability of key product components cannot be grown to the necessary levels that will be required to assure necessary product function over the intended life. Similarly, where repair facilities are not readily accessible and the product cannot be readily restored after a malfunction, availability considerations also may place emphasis upon a redundancy approach to the product's engineering.

In the designing of the redundancy—such as of support circuitry, of standby mechanical subassemblies and backup devices—significant attention must be placed upon the tradeoffs among reliability, cost, safety, and other parameters of the product. Redundancy is a design approach that must be used carefully and selectively, with major orientation to those product subassemblies and components that have reliabilities which seriously reduce the total reliability of the system. In airborne equipment, redundancy increases weight; hence it is to be considered carefully in terms of tradeoffs. In any application, redundancy generally increases initial costs and maintenance costs. Care must also be taken to see that reliability is not itself adversely affected. This may happen as a result of the interaction between redundant components and other components of a system.

Experience across many high-reliability products shows, however, that redundancy, properly designed in equipment and services, can so increase the life cycle of some products that the additional initial cost of the redundant components is more than balanced by the longer life, improved availability, and other improved customer quality-satisfaction features of the product.

17.15 The Manufacturing Process: An Integral Part of the Reliability Program

If there is a "best product design," there has to be a related "best manufacturing process." There is always a manufacturing process present when a device is brought into being, be it a prototype or a production item. To determine what maximum reliability is possible from a given design, it is necessary at some point to build something and make it operate to see what it will do.

Achieved reliability thus must always be referred to a given product design and to the process used to produce it. A higher reliability value might be attained by changing the design or the process or both.

When this point of view is identified, it can be seen that the manufacturing function of a company has a major contribution to make in programming product reliability. Manufacturing people can take aggressive, dynamic action in pushing ahead the frontiers of knowledge in their specialty fields to improve product reliability.

One of the important contributions that manufacturing can make is the identification of process conditions as to their effects upon product reliability. For example, what fast-feed-solder temperature gives electronic connections on a printed circuit board the highest reliability? What are the effects of residual particle removal by certain solvents on dielectric strength of printed boards?

These are highly simple examples of the often complex kinds of questions to which answers must be found if desired product reliability is to be attained. This involves careful research and development of manufacturing processes and entails the use of scientific experimentation. Maximum information can be gained by making use of designs of experiments as discussed in Chapter 16.

17.16 Packaging and Transportation Planning: An Essential Part of the Reliability Program

The only product reliability that counts is what the customer can actually experience. There is not much point in having a device with a highly reliable design, carefully manufactured, if its reliability is seriously deteriorated because of poor protection and rough handling during shipping.

In many companies, the design of packaging is all too frequently regarded as a secondary matter, yet it can be essential to the achievement of the necessary levels of reliability. Even though the size of some companies cannot justify packaging specialists, the responsibility should be assigned to an organizational component with the required competence.

After packages have been designed, they should be evaluated. If simulated shipping tests are conducted by impact testers, vibration tables, compression testers, and so on, the parameters of the stresses that the packaged product will experience during shipment must be known.

If actual trial shipments are made, care must be used to see that they are representative of what may be encountered shipment upon shipment. A single shipment can hardly be expected to render conclusive results. Routes, method of transportation, and extremes of temperature and humidity should be represented in such tests.

OTHER RELIABILITY-ORIENTED TECHNIQUES

17.17 Failure Mode, Effect, and Criticality Analysis

The primary purpose of failure mode, effect, and criticality analysis (FMECA) is to identify potential product weaknesses.[19] Employment of this technique begins with the study of known failure modes for each component of a product. Then, using physical analyses or mathematical models, a determination is made of the effect of the part failure on a given component, subsystem, or complete operating system.

In turn, this analysis identifies conditions where the failure of a single part would cause the complete failure of the equipment system. When such failures—which are sometimes designated "single point failures"—are identified, a reliability program objective will be made to eliminate them through changes in design. If the failure cannot be eliminated through design modification, parts so identified are placed on a critical parts list and tagged to receive special quality-control attention. FMECA is more fully discussed in Section 18.20.

17.18 Physics of Failure Research

This technique involves the breakdown, dissection, and analysis of parts which have failed, with the aim of pinpointing the cause(s) of failure. Certain basic facilities are needed to perform such research, the complexity of which will of course depends upon the complexity and nature of the failed part. At the very least, appropriate tools for breakdown and disassembly will be required; for more complex equipment, the engineer will need access to such instruments as spectroscopes and electron microscopes.

17.19 Maintainability; Human Engineering Design

An important aspect of product reliability is the degree to which the product, in use, can be maintained economically and expeditiously.

The maintainability of a product can be expressed as a function of design and installation characteristics which influence scheduled or unscheduled maintenance under environmental operating conditions. As discussed in Section 17.7, mean time between maintenance (MTBM) is thus one of the basic measurements of the probability of reliability. [This measurement is sometimes also referred to as mean time to repair (MTTR).]

Defined more specifically, maintainability relates to:[20]

> Ability of a unit under stated conditions of use to be retained in, or restored to, within a given period of time, a specified state in which it can perform its required functions when maintenance is performed under stated conditions and while using prescribed procedures and resources.

Among the factors considered in quantifying maintainability are the work force, skills, technical data, test equipment, and support facilities required to keep a unit operational. One yardstick used to measure maintainability is the number of service calls per machine per month (SC/M/M).

Human Engineering Design

This technique is intended to eliminate from the design-manufacturing-delivery-customer use-service cycle potential sources of human-induced failures. Thus, in effect, human engineering design addresses issues similar to the technique known as maintainability, but from another viewpoint.

Human engineering design considerations include such product features as ease of disassembly and assembly for test; checkout and inspection; the safe and convenient use of hardware or software; and the degree to which the system is easily fabricated, handled, maintained, and operated with minimum hazard both to human safety and integrity of the equipment.

17.20 Evaluation of Reliability Plans by Tests

Whether the reliability planning be for product, process, or packaging designs, it should be tested at appropriate points during the reliability program. Early design proposals will be checked out by means of so-called breadboard tests. Proposed manufacturing processes will be tested by trial runs and further proved out by pilot runs. As discussed in Section 17.16, packaging may be proved by laboratory tests and trial shipments.

To obtain the most information from reliability tests, it is normally necessary to run the devices to failure. In this manner the failure mechanism can be determined, as well as the distribution of failures with time. This should be accomplished early in a product-development plan during the prototype stage.

Since such tests are destructive and usually expensive to conduct, the desire is to test as few samples as possible over as short a time as possible. As a consequence, such tests are often run under accelerated conditions obtained by increasing loading and environmental stresses and terminating the tests prior to failure. If accelerated tests are used, they must correlate reasonably well with actual operating experience in the field. An indication of the time involved in testing for moderately high reliability values is suggested in the following example:[21]

If it is desired to evaluate a product to a 0.990 reliability at a 90 percent confidence level, it is necessary to test 230 unit-minutes for each operational unit-minute without a failure. This means that if a device is to be operational over a period of 1 year, a sample of 230 units would have to operate over a year's time without a failure. Or using a tradeoff of number of devices with time, 460 units could be tested over a 6-month period. This assumes an exponential chance failure curve and must be well ahead of the device's wear-out portion of the life curve.

Indeed, the very great importance in reliability activity of the negative exponential density function, as earlier discussed in Section 17.6 and Formulas (42) to (44), is particularly demonstrated by its significance in failure testing. These formulas can be expressed for life-testing purposes as: $f(t) = e^{-\lambda t}$, $F(t) = 1 - e^{-\lambda t}$, and $R(t) = 1 - F(t) = \lambda e^{-\lambda t}$. Thus, in time t, the probability of no failures is $e^{-\lambda t}$; one failure is $\lambda e^{-\lambda t}$; two failures is $\lambda^2/2! \, e^{-\lambda t}$; and so on. As discussed in Section 17.6, this distribution has the advantage of a constant failure rate λ. Moreover, all other distributions in reliability theory may be transformed to this one.

Recognition and identification of the differences in reliability distributions, as they apply to different situations, are in fact especially essential in failure testing. For example, there are some reliability distributions that are both discrete and continuous, such as a missile which does not work when tried at time zero. This may mean that $R(0) = 0.25$, perhaps; and $R(t) = 0.75^{-\lambda t}$, $t > 0$.

Disciplined practice is therefore very important when testing to evaluate reliability plans. The area of life testing, for one example, has been guided by several program approaches. One of the most significant has been MIL-STD-781D (U.S. Printing Office, Washington, D.C.), whose application has been one of the indicators of the developing technique of modern testing programs.

General Life Tests

General life-test methods are used by some companies for new high-volume products. One approach incorporates a series of three tests beginning when the first prototype units are built and continuing for the production life span of the product. In abbreviated form, the test sequence also can be applied with good results for existing products when a reliability problem exists. These tests define the potential reliability of the product design, the reliability of the product as it is produced by the production process, and the life expectancy of parts likely to wear out first. The three tests are:

1. *Design maturity test.* A reliability demonstration to identify and correct design problems.

   The object of this test on the first prototype units is to demonstrate that the design, overlooking the way it was built and how much debugging was required, can meet the reliability requirement for that product. When such is not the case, the design must be improved during the test until it is qualified or until it is capable of meeting the specification requirements, including MTBF.

2. *Process maturity test.* Measurement of infant mortality to correct any existing incompatability between the design and the processes producing it and to determine the amount of testing necessary to achieve the specified reliability at shipment.

   The first production units are operated (burned in) for a given period of hours while their performance is closely monitored to measure their declining failure rate. Generally, this test provides sufficient test experience after the infancy effects have subsided to measure and verify the useful life reliability of the product for comparison to the results obtained during the design maturity test. The failures observed during infancy are analyzed to identify and solve problems.

   The duration of the burn-in period for a product is set from the observations in this test. It may be reduced only when subsequent valid data prove that the infancy has been reduced by better process control. Improvements in manufacturing and inspection processes should substantially reduce the burn-in period to several hours, but it is necessary to have test data which show that the product reaches its mature MTBF within a statistically valid shorter time period.

3. *Life test.* Measurement of the distribution of wear-out failures of components to eliminate any failure mechanisms that reduce life expectancy below the acceptable point.

   The time to failure is measured on a number of samples so that MTTF and the distribution of each observed failure mode can be determined. In this type of life testing, the following distinction is made between MTBF and the MTTF: MTBF is approached as the mean interarrival time between independent failures that occur randomly at an approximately constant rate during the useful life of a unit. MTTF is approached as the mean time to failure (for a particular mode) caused by wearout. When the parameters which determine the distribution of that particular wear-out mode are known, the life expectancy to various cumulative percent failures can be estimated. The life test ensures that wear out starts beyond a desired minimum life cycle time. The distribution of a specific failure mechanism can be analyzed to determine whether the mechanism is caused by infancy or wear out or is truly random.

By these three tests, key factors that influence and control the reliability of the product will be determined during the measurement process. Once these factors are known, the reliability of the product can be maintained at an acceptable level. Customer satisfaction, relatively trouble-free warranties, and low support and manufacturing costs result from acceptable reliability. By realizing and controlling the reliability of the product shipped, the product manager can realistically plan and control the future. Without such control, a major factor in the profitability of a product is left to chance.

Further discussion of reliability testing will take place in Chapter 18, "New Design Control."

17.21 Reliability Growth

As discussed in Section 17.10, the initial production of a new design involves a learning factor which varies with the complexity of the product and process together with the level of experience and training of personnel. Thus, a certain period of time will be required to develop the necessary proficiency to achieve and maintain targeted levels of reliability. The accurate prediction of this reliability growth period is a basic activity of the reliability program of the plant and company.

Using failure rate and service-call data supplied by Design, Production, and Field Engineering, predicted reliability development can be plotted graphically as a *reliability growth curve*.[22] Typically, the reliability growth curve for complex products assumes the shape illustrated in Figure 17.10—with the highest incidence of service requirements initially in the production cycle. Over time, with suitable reliability program actions, the curve gradually flattens, reflecting the rate of reliability improvement, and eventually levels off to a basic percentage of total units produced.

17.22 Continuing Control of Reliability

At the conclusion of new-design control work, the next activity in the reliability program is continuing control. The product-control job of total quality

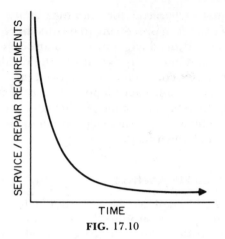

TIME

FIG. 17.10

control includes work in all areas that will affect product reliability: incoming components, process control, transportation, and so forth.

For example, when a manufacturing process is improved and a new standard of reliability is established, it needs to be "pegged" so there will be no slipping back to old standards.

How can this be accomplished? How can it be determined when the process is slipping? It was shown earlier that variation is inherent in any manufacturing process. How then can there be determined the difference between a slippage from the newly pegged standard and a normal variation from that standard? This is one of the areas in which the technique of process-control engineering contributes to product reliability.

It is possible statistically to determine the limiting values of the pattern that typifies the controlled state. This is the basis for the control chart discussed in Chapter 14. A controlled process is a predictable process, and an uncontrolled process is not predictable; hence, a controlled process is essential to achieving a product with a specific reliability. As has been noted: "A state of statistical control must be the goal of our entire effort—design, production and testing. This is the only known path to reliability. It is inescapable; it is incontrovertible."[23]

The process-control engineer, in endeavoring to bring about a state of control for a process critical to product reliability, should carefully consider the control function served by modern quality information equipment. Especially those processes that are subject to drift due to tool wear, exhaustion of chemicals, temperature effects, and other environmental influences can be automatically adjusted to compensate for such effects and kept in a state of statistical control. Becoming increasingly available are specialized process-control computers that can take measurement information, statistically analyze it, and automatically feed back information to adjust the process the required amount to maintain the subject quality characteristic within specified limits. Such systems were discussed more fully in Chapter 12.

Measurements of quality characteristics and their analyses by control charts or computers detect a change in processing that could have a decided influence upon the reliability of the product; however, a process-control engineer's responsibility does not end here. What would be the result if some important quality characteristic were completely overlooked and no measurements taken? The only safeguard against such a possibility is to actually measure the end result, specifically the reliability of the product after manufacture. This has to be done on a continuing basis with actual production units to protect against the intrusion of some unknown factor.

17.23 Continuing Reliability Analysis

Product reliability is seldom, if ever, a "one-shot" effort. Even in those cases where only a few prototypes are produced as part of a research and development program, intensive study and extensive reliability testing are continuously performed to gain knowledge that can be used for succeeding generations of similar products.

This sustained new-design control effort is made to increase reliability in the majority of cases because

1. State of the art may not yet have advanced to a point where the required reliability has been realized in the product in question.
2. The costs, because of low reliability, may be excessive because of too many premature product failures.
3. Maintenance and repair costs during the expected life of the product may be excessively high.
4. Consequences of product failure may be serious for lost life, property damage, lost income, or inconvenience.
5. Competitive products may be pushing to higher reliability values.
6. Customers may be dissatisfied and demanding higher reliability values.

Research and Development Programs for Reliability Improvement

In some cases, the value of a highly reliable product is so great as to justify multimillion-dollar research and development programs to gain an incremental increase in the reliability of a critical component or system. For most industrial and consumer products, improvement in reliability is the result of a sustained effort on the part of the technical and factory personnel normally assigned to the particular product under consideration. The efforts of such personnel are directed to a considerable extent by a continuing, thorough reliability analysis of the product.

Continual Testing to Evaluate Product Reliability

Continual testing is not only necessary for purposes of control, as discussed in Section 17.22; it is also necessary for providing exhaustive data upon which to base reliability-improvement programs. Such data eventually would accumulate as a result of field experience; however, for most products, elapsed time extends far beyond useful limits. The product might become obsolete before its reliability could be improved. Hence, it is necessary to intensify testing, not only by testing large samples of product as discussed in Section 17.20 but by crowding as many operating hours as possible into as short a time as possible. This may require operation under simulated field conditions.

As a very basic example of a product that requires such intensified testing, consider the electric hand iron. It is used only 4 hours per week in the average home. Under such conditions, it would take 10 years to determine its life. Certainly, such a lengthy wait for data is out of the question when an analysis is required for sustained product-reliability improvement.

An intensive test established in a hand laundry or shirt factory would log 16 hours per day, or 80 hours per week. This is 20-fold increase in energized time and gives an answer in 6 months instead of 10 years. Even 6 months is longer than is desirable, and the conditions encountered are not equivalent to those encountered in the home; e.g., the iron is not being turned off and on as frequently per operating hour. Weakness because of differential expansion and contraction of parts might not become as apparent. Conceivably, a simulated test might be established that could be run 24 hours per day with an arbitrary number of heat-up and cool-down cycles. Here the quality information equipment engineer can make an important contribution in simulating time cycles and duration of environmental stresses for equipment to evaluate product reliability.

Accelerated Tests for Obtaining Results Promptly

Accelerated tests are often used where the nature of the device permits it. This is done by increasing the environmental stress to show product weaknesses in the shortest period of time. In the case of the electric hand iron, this might be accomplished by operating it at 150 volts rather than the rated 120 volts. This would have the effect of making the heating element operate at a higher temperature; hence, it would tend to burn out more readily, thereby showing up defects affecting reliability in the shortest time, e.g., nicks in the resistance wire used in the heating element. The increased voltage would also require the thermostat to break higher current values, thereby increasing arcing and attrition of the contacts.

Accelerated life tests are of value only to the degree to which they correlate with actual-use life tests or intensive life tests. There is a definite limit to severity of conditions. Beyond this limit, other factors, quite different from those encountered in actual use, enter to give misleading and false evaluation of life. There are many devices that do not lend themselves to accelerated testing to any appreciable extent. Certain electron tubes are one such device.

Importance of Preserving Failure Mechanism

If the device being subjected to accelerated testing is fairly simple and its life depends on a simple failure mechanism that can be speeded up by increasing certain stresses, fairly good regression can be obtained. Capacitors and resistors lend themselves to accelerated testing. Many other components and assemblies, including certain cathode ray tubes, cannot be accelerated because the increased stresses create additional failure mechanisms rather than merely speeding up those that are present under normal operation. For example, if increased voltage causes arcing, the cathode ray tube is "killed." Under normal voltages, such arcing probably would not have occurred, and its life might well have been exceptionally long.

Importance of Regression

Whatever tests are used, they must be standardized as to conditions of environment, and the resultant mean time between failures can be referenced to some standard of reliability. The referencing must be done through use of a regression line that correlates the test-condition results with the actual-use-condition results. This is necessary to obtain meaningful data.

If it is found through experience that there is a poor regression between tests run under simulated conditions (or accelerated conditions) and actual end-use conditions, it will be necessary to change the standard test conditions until reasonably good regression is established.

Efficiency of Tests

Reliability testing is expensive. It requires elaborate test setups to simulate environmental conditions; testing extends over relatively long periods of time; the devices tested are usually consumed as a result of the test; power requirements are often high where high loads are necessary. Furthermore, when the testing is done to monitor the process and to discover where it can be improved, it must be done on a continuing basis. It is not a one-shot test, such as used when qualifying a design. It is in effect a matter of continually requalifying the design and the current process.

Because of the expense involved, it is important to get the maximum efficiency out of tests, i.e., the most information in the shortest time for the least expenditure of money. Full use should be made of statistical techniques in proving the specified reliability at the required confidence level.

Field Test Data

As pointed out earlier in this section, data resulting from use of the product in the field, while slow to accumulate, are essential for regression with accelerated tests to determine the latter's effectiveness. Field data, when available, are most valuable and certainly should not be ignored. Every effort should be made to see that they are accurately recorded and fed back to the plant for analysis on a continuing basis.

Data Collection and Analysis Sometimes a Contractual Requirement

In many contracts involving the production of complex equipment systems, the collection and analysis of field data for reliability improvement are made a contractual requirement. A complete log is kept on each system and follows the device throughout its life. Its complete history is recorded: transport, storage, tests, service, maintenance, and use. All data on all systems of a given type are brought to a data center, where they are processed and analyzed. Periodic reports are issued to the procurement agencies.

Reliability Improvement Is the Objective

Continual reliability testing, as discussed in this section, provides test data, the analysis of which shows where the technical effort must be placed to improve reliability. Certain components will show up as the "weak links" in the system. These must then be studied as to their failure mechanism. When the true failure mechanism has been identified, it is often possible to tell whether the answer to the problem involves a change in product design or manufacturing methods or simply better control of established manufacturing processes. A consistent upgrading of reliability through a series of effective design changes, method changes, and improved quality control generally provides an economic means for attaining required product-reliability goals.

The effectiveness of reliability work can be measured by quality-cost improvement in a number of areas. Among the most important are inspection and test of field stocks, spares' carrying costs, defect-cause investigations, and vendor failure analysis charges.

ACHIEVEMENT OF PRODUCT RELIABILITY THROUGH THE QUALITY SYSTEM

17.24 Total Quality Control and Its Reliability Process

Since reliability is one of the more important "qualities" of the product, it cannot be operationally or systematically separated from other product-quality considerations. The first chapters of this book quite thoroughly reviewed this total quality concept. This section further relates this concept and its reliability component.

As noted in Part 1, responsibilities for product quality thread throughout the entire company organization. This is true for reliability, just as it is for all components of quality, with specific assignments being made to appropriate positions.

Each of the four jobs of quality control includes important reliability activities. The first three jobs are used as illustrations of how the assurance of reliability results from operation of total quality control:

1. "New-Design Control," Section 17.25
2. "Incoming-Material Control," Section 17.26
3. "Product Control," Section 17.27

17.25 New-Design Control

This job involves such product-reliability activities as the following:

- Determining the standard of reliability required by the customer for the product
- Clearly identifying the environment the product will encounter
- Determining the economic balance between reliability and total costs to obtain it
- Optimizing the design to obtain the required product reliability
- Selecting processes and process parameters that contribute to high product reliability
- Proving by prototype and pilot-run tests that required reliability is attainable
- Eliminating from product design and process design, so far as possible, any threats to product reliability
- Review of guarantees and warranties with respect to product reliability and their equitable adjustment
- Reliability evaluations of competitive products

17.26 Incoming-Material Control

This job involves product-reliability activities of which the following are examples:

- Clear delineation of reliability requirements to vendors
- Evaluation of vendors' capabilities for producing products of the required reliability
- Evaluation of vendors' product reliability on a continuing basis
- Servicing of vendors for product-reliability improvement

17.27 Product Control

This job involves the following product-reliability activities:

- Control of product and process to assure reliability achievement
- Information flow from factory to field with reference to anticipated reliability problems and corrective action
- Information flow from field to factory with reference to reliability problems encountered and corrective action
- Certification of product reliability to the customer
- Audit of product reliability after shipment, during and after warehousing, after installation, and in use
- Reliability maintenance through adequate instructions concerning installation, maintenance, and use; serviceability of product; tools and techniques for repairs; quality cost and timeliness of field service
- Measuring of product-reliability performance in the field by costs and failure rates

17.28 Summary of Part 5

The statistical point of view toward industrial product quality may be briefly summarized: *variation* in product quality must be constantly studied within batches of product, on processing equipments, between different lots of the same article, on critical quality characteristics and standards, in regard to the pilot runs of a newly designed article. This variation may best be studied by the analysis of samples selected from the product lots or from units produced by the processing equipments.

There are five statistical tools which have been found useful in making practical application of this point of view in the four quality-control jobs:

1. Frequency distributions
2. Control charts
3. Sampling tables
4. Special methods
5. Reliability

These five tools, although highly useful in many cases, represent in the final analysis only one of the technologies that are used in an overall total-quality-control program for a company. These statistical tools were been discussed in detail in Part 5 primarily because they are one of the most used of the quality-control technologies.

A few applications of these statistical tools were presented in Part 5, but fuller discussion of their use, along with the other quality-control technical methods, is reserved for Part 6.

17.29 Glossary of Important Symbols and Terms Used in Part 5

X: an observed value of a quality characteristic. Specific observed values are designated X_1, X_2, X_3, and so on.

$\overline{X}$: the average, a measure of central tendency. The average of a set of n observed values is the sum of the observed values divided by n.

n: the number of observed values; the sample size, or number of units (articles, parts, specimens, and so forth) in the sample.

σ: the standard deviation of the population of observed values from their average.

s: the sample standard deviation.

R: the range, the difference between the largest observed value and the smallest observed value in a sample.

p: the fraction nonconforming or fraction defective, the ratio of the number of nonconforming or defective units (articles, parts, specimens, and so on) to the total number of units under consideration, sometimes referred to as the "proportion nonconforming or proportion defective." Also, the percent nonconforming or percent defective.

np: the number of nonconformances or defectives (nonconforming or defective units) in a sample of n units.

c: the number of defects or nonconformities, usually the number of nonconformities or defects in a sample of stated size.

$\overline{X}_0$, s_0, R_0, p_0, c_0, u_0: the standard values of $\overline{X}$, s, R, p, c, or u adopted for computing the center line and control limits for control charts—standard given.

Q: a constant related to the modified control limit.

$\overline{\overline{X}}$, $\overline{\sigma}$, $\overline{s}$, $\overline{R}$, $\overline{p}$, $\overline{np}$, $\overline{c}$: the average of a set of values of $\overline{X}$, σ, s, R, p, np, c.

N: lot size as used with sampling inspection tables.

d_2: a constant that varies with n, relating to the average range $\overline{R}$ for samples of n observed values each to the standard deviation of the population.

A, A_2, A_3, B_3, B_4, B_5, B_6, D_1, D_2, D_3, D_4, E_2: factors for computing control limits.

R_T: the reliability of a product having intended life T.

T: the intended life of product.

θ: the mean life or mean time to failure (the term θ is also used in an entirely different sense in computing the V mask of a cusum chart).

λ: the failure rate for items of product failing per unit time.

t: an interval of time; also, the present time.

Piece, part, unit: an object upon which a measurement or observation may be made.

Sample: one or more units of product (or a quantity of material) drawn from a specific lot or process for purposes of inspection to provide information that may be used for making a decision concerning acceptance of that lot or process.

Lot: a definite quantity of some product accumulated under conditions that are considered uniform for sampling purposes.

Defect: a departure of a quality characteristic from its intended level or state that occurs with a severity sufficient to cause an associated product or service to not satisfy intended, normal, or reasonable foreseeable usage requirements.

A defective: a defective unit (article, part, specimen, and so on), containing one or more defects or having several imperfections that in combination cause the unit to fail to satisfy intended, normal, or reasonably foreseeable usage requirements.

Nonconformity: a departure of a quality characteristic from its intended level or state that occurs with severity sufficient to cause an associated product or service to not meet a specification requirement.

Nonconforming unit: a unit of product or service containing at least one nonconformity.

Quality characteristic: a property of a unit, part, piece affecting performance or customer satisfaction, such as a dimension, weight, or viscosity, and which helps to differentiate among units of a given sample or population.

Reliability: the probability of a unit to perform a required function under stated conditions for a stated period of time.

Failure mechanism: the chronological series of events which logically lead to product failure.

17.30 Important Formulas Used in Part 5

Chapter 13: Frequency Distributions

Average:
$$\overline{X} = \frac{X_1 + X_2 + X_3 + \cdots + X_n}{n} \tag{1A}$$

$$= \frac{\Sigma fX}{n} \tag{2}$$

Grand average:
$$\overline{\overline{X}} = \frac{\overline{X}_1 + \overline{X}_2 + \cdots \overline{X}_r}{r} \tag{3A}$$

$$= \frac{n_1\overline{X}_1 + n_2\overline{X}_2 + \cdots n_r\overline{X}_r}{N} \tag{3B}$$

Sample standard deviation:

$$s = \sqrt{\frac{(X_1 - \overline{X})^2 + (X_2 - \overline{X})^2 + (X_3 - \overline{X})^2 + \cdots + (X_n - \overline{X})^2}{n - 1}} \tag{4A}$$

$$= \sqrt{\frac{\Sigma fX^2 - n\overline{X}^2}{n - 1}} \tag{4B}$$

Average sample standard deviation:

$$\bar{s} = \frac{s_1 + s_2 + \cdots + s_r}{r} \tag{5}$$

Range:
$$R = X_{\text{high}} - X_{\text{low}} \tag{6A}$$

Average range:
$$\overline{R} = \frac{R_1 + R_2 + \cdots + R_r}{r} \tag{6B}$$

Chapter 14: Control Charts

MEASUREMENTS CONTROL CHARTS

No Standard Given

When Range Is Used As Measure of Spread

Average: Lower limit $= \overline{\overline{X}} - A_2\overline{R}$ (13A)

$$\text{Center line} = \bar{\bar{X}}$$

$$\text{Upper limit} = \bar{\bar{X}} + A_2\bar{R} \tag{13B}$$

Range: Lower limit $= D_3\bar{R}$ (14A)

$$\text{Center line} = \bar{R}$$

$$\text{Upper limit} = D_4\bar{R} \tag{14B}$$

Process limits: Lower limit $= \bar{\bar{X}} - E_2\bar{R}$ (21A)

$$\text{Center line} = \bar{\bar{X}}$$

$$\text{Upper limit} = \bar{\bar{X}} + E_2\bar{R} \tag{21B}$$

When Standard Deviation Is Used As a Measure of Spread

Average: Lower limit $= \bar{\bar{X}} - A_3\bar{s}$ (15A)

$$\text{Center line} = \bar{\bar{X}}$$

$$\text{Upper limit} = \bar{\bar{X}} + A_3\bar{s} \tag{15B}$$

Standard deviation: Lower limit $= B_3\bar{s}$ (16A)

$$\text{Center line} = \bar{s}$$

$$\text{Upper control limit} = B_4\bar{s} \tag{16B}$$

Standard Given

When Range Is Used As Measure of Spread

Average: Lower limit $= \bar{X}_0 - A\sigma_0$ (17A)

$$\text{Center line} = \bar{X}_0$$

$$\text{Upper limit} = \bar{X}_0 + A\sigma_0 \tag{17B}$$

Range: Lower limit $= D_1\sigma_0$ (18A)

$$\text{Center line} = R_0 \text{ (or } d_2\sigma_0)$$

$$\text{Upper limit} = D_2\sigma_0 \tag{18B}$$

When Standard Deviation Is Used As a Measure of Spread

Average: Lower limit $= \bar{X}_0 - A\sigma_0$ (17A)

$$\text{Center line} = \bar{X}_0$$

$$\text{Upper limit} = \bar{X}_0 + A\sigma_0 \tag{17B}$$

Standard deviation: Lower limit $= B_5\sigma_0$ (19A)

$$\text{Center line} = s_0 \text{ (or } c_4\sigma_0)$$

$$\text{Upper control limit} = B_6\sigma_0 \tag{19B}$$

LIMITS IN RELATION TO SPECIFICATIONS

Process Capabilities

$$\text{Lower control limit} = \text{lower specification limit} + Q \tag{22A}$$

$$\text{Upper control limit} = \text{upper specification limit} - Q \tag{22B}$$

Acceptance Control

Acceptable process levels: $\text{UAPL} = \text{UTL} - z_{p1}\sigma$ (23A)

$$\text{LAPL} = \text{LTL} + z_{p1}\sigma \tag{23B}$$

Rejectable process levels: $\quad$ URPL $= $ UTL $- z_{p2}\sigma \qquad$ (24A)

$\qquad\qquad\qquad\qquad\quad$ LRPL $= $ LTL $+ z_{p2}\sigma \qquad$ (24B)

Acceptance control limits: $\quad$ UACL $= $ UAPL $+ \dfrac{z_\alpha\sigma}{\sqrt{n}} \qquad$ (25A)

$\qquad\qquad\qquad\qquad\quad$ LACL $= $ LAPL $- \dfrac{z_\alpha\sigma}{\sqrt{n}} \qquad$ (25B)

$\qquad\qquad\qquad\qquad$ or

$\qquad\qquad\qquad\qquad\quad$ UACL $= $ URPL $- \dfrac{z_\beta\sigma}{\sqrt{n}} \qquad$ (26A)

$\qquad\qquad\qquad\qquad\quad$ LACL $= $ LRPL $+ \dfrac{z_\beta\sigma}{\sqrt{n}} \qquad$ (26B)

INDIVIDUAL READINGS

$$\text{Lower control limit} = \overline{X} - E_2\overline{R} \qquad (27A)$$
$$\text{Center line} \qquad\quad = \overline{X}$$
$$\text{Upper control limit} = \overline{X} + E_2\overline{R} \qquad (27B)$$

GO AND NOT-GO LIMITS

No Standard Given

$$\text{Percent control limits} \qquad = \bar{p} \pm 3\sqrt{\frac{\bar{p}(100 - \bar{p})}{n}} \qquad (30)$$

$$\text{Fraction control limits} \qquad = \bar{p} \pm 3\sqrt{\frac{\bar{p}(1 - \bar{p})}{n}} \qquad (31)$$

$$\text{Number of units control limits} = n\bar{p} \pm 3\sqrt{n\bar{p}(1 - \bar{p})} \qquad (34)$$

$$(c) \text{ count control limits} \qquad = \bar{c} \pm 3\sqrt{\bar{c}} \qquad (35)$$

$$(u) \text{ count control limits} \qquad = \bar{u} \pm 3\sqrt{\bar{u}/n} \qquad (36)$$

Standard Given

$$\text{Percent control limits} \qquad = p_0 \pm 3\sqrt{\frac{p_0(100 - p_0)}{n}} \qquad (30A)$$

$$\text{Fraction control limits} \qquad = p_0 \pm 3\sqrt{\frac{p_0(1 - p_0)}{n}} \qquad (31A)$$

$$\text{Number of units control limits} = np_0 \pm 3\sqrt{np_0(1 - p_0)} \qquad (34A)$$

(c) count control limits $\qquad = c_0 \pm 3\sqrt{c_0}$ $\qquad$ (35A)

(u) count control limits $\qquad = u_0 \pm 3\sqrt{u_0/n}$ $\qquad$ (36A)

Other useful formulas for particular applications of go and not-go data are

Average, $\bar{p}$: $\qquad\qquad\qquad \bar{p} = \dfrac{\Sigma c}{\Sigma n} \times 100$ $\qquad$ (28)

Standard deviation of p: $\sigma_p = \sqrt{\dfrac{\bar{p}(100 - \bar{p})}{n}}$ $\qquad$ (29)

Chapter 16: Special Methods

Tolerance buildup: $T_t = \sqrt{T_1{}^2 + T_2{}^2 + T_3{}^2 + \cdots + T_n{}^2}$ $\qquad$ (38)

Chapter 17: Product Reliability

Reliability: $\qquad\qquad R_T = e^{-T/\theta}$ $\qquad$ (43)

$\qquad\qquad\qquad\quad R_T = e^{-\lambda T}$ $\qquad$ (44)

$\qquad\qquad\qquad\quad R_T = R_{T_1} \times R_{T_2} \times R_{T_3} \times \cdots R_{T_m}$ $\qquad$ (45)

$R_T = (e^{-\lambda_1 T})(e^{-\lambda_2 T})(e^{-\lambda_3 T}) \cdots (e^{-\lambda_m T})$ $\qquad$ (46)

$R_T = e^{-T(\lambda_1 + \lambda_2 + \lambda_3 + \cdots + \lambda_m)}$ $\qquad$ (47)

$F(t) = 1 - R(t), \quad R(t) = 1 - f(t)$ $\qquad$ (48)

$$z(t) = \frac{f(t)}{R(t)}$$ (49)

$$R(t) = \exp\left[-\int_0^t z(x)\, dx\right]$$ (50)

$\mathrm{MTTF} = \int_0^\infty tf(t)\, dt$

$\qquad\quad = \int_0^\infty R(t)\, dt$ $\qquad$ (51)

Notes

[1]There are a number of documented reliability programs in several industry areas and covering numerous product lines. It is useful to recognize that many of these documents have been influenced by, or are derivations of, certain original reliability program documents, including MIL-STD-785, NASA NHB 5300.4(1A), and MIL-STD-499, which dealt with integrating reliability into a complete systems engineering management process. For a discussion of the evolution of these program documents, see Leslie W. Ball, "Assuring Reliability Program Effectiveness," *Quality Progress*, September 1973.

[2]For introductory discussions of this, see A. V. Feigenbaum, "The Engineering and Management Approach to Product Quality," *Proceedings of the Ninth National Symposium on Reliability and Quality Control*, pp. 1–5; and "Quality and Reliability," *Proceedings of the Society of Automotive Engineers*, National Aeronautic Meeting and Production Forum, Washington, D.C., Apr. 12, 1965.

[3]"Caterpillar World," *Third Quarter*, 1977, p. 8.

[4]These definitions are in accordance with International Electrotechnical Commission (IEC) Standard 271-1974. Various areas of this definition may be adapted for particular product situations.

For example, "stated conditions" may involve "at a designated time" for products subject to noncontinuous usage or with regard to initial startup. Also, in some product situations, "a stated period of time" will require a definition such as, "at least for a stated period of time." Some reliability applications will define this "time" parameter in such terms as "a specified interval" when related to products involving stated numbers of operations or cycles.

[5]For a discussion, see John H.K. Kao, "Characteristic Life Patterns and Their Uses," in W. Grant Ireson (ed.), *Reliability Handbook,* McGraw-Hill Book Company, New York, 1966, sec. 2–3.

[6]A number of companies and government organizations have contributed to the development and utilization of SOS and GaAs integrated circuits an approach to the development of whose survivability limits are shown in Fig. 17.1. For a discussion, see D. H. Phillips, "QA Aspects of Silicon-on-Sapphire and Gallium Arsenide Integrated Circuits Devices," *Quality Progress,* vol XIII, no. 11, November 1980, pp. 32–34.

[7]This has come to be termed the "bathtub curve" in the reliability literature.

[8]Note the similarity between the terminology of reliability and that of actuarial practice.

[9]Naperian base used for natural logarithms.

[10]For a discussion, see G. Ronald Herd, "Some Statistical Concepts and Techniques for Reliability Analysis and Prediction," *Proceedings, Fifth National Symposium on Reliability and Quality Control,* Philadelphia, Pa., Jan. 12–14, 1959.

[11]Developed by W. Weibull, a Swedish analyst of the phenomena of metallic fatigue, in "A Statistical Representation of Fatigue Failure in Solids," Royal Institute of Stockholm, November 1959.

[12]For a discussion of various probability density functions relevant to reliability analysis, see O. B. Moan, "Application of Mathematics and Statistics to Reliability and Life Studies," in W. Grant Ireson (ed.), *Reliability Handbook,* McGraw-Hill Book Company, New York, 1966, secs. 4-9-4-27.

[13]Theoretically, the reliability of a system made of a series of components can be obtained by multiplying together all the individual reliability values for the various components discussed later in the section. This assumes no interaction. In practice it is difficult to simulate tests for components that represent the environment of the system under end-use conditions. Actual values in practice may depart from predicted values, in either direction, as much as 200 to 300 percent. For military items, for example, this could be due to the following facts: (1) Laboratory conditions and field conditions were not the same; (2) errors were made in testing in the laboratory, or errors were made in the field in handling the equipment; (3) personnel were not adequately trained; (4) errors were made in data reporting itself.

[14]For a further discussion of availability, see John G. Rau, "Optimization and Probability," in *Systems Engineering,* Van Nostrand Reinhold Company, New York, 1970.

[15]This discussion and Fig. 17.7 follow a paper by John D. Musa, "The Measurement and Management of Software Reliability," *Proceedings of the IEEE,* vol. 68, no. 9, September 1980.

[16]J. D. Musa, "A Theory of Software Reliability and Its Application," *IEEE Transactions: Software Engineering,* vol. SE-1, September 1975; B. Littlewood, "How to Measure Software Reliability and How Not To," *Proceedings, 3rd International Conference on Software Engineering,* Atlanta, May 1978.

[17]For a discussion, see L. P. Crawford, LCDR, USN, "Reliability Programs for Complex Systems," *Annual Technical Conference Transactions,* American Society for Quality Control, 1977, p. 105.

[18]The term "product strength" as used here refers to a quality of a product to endure against the stresses of its specific environment and use. It is a comparative term rather than absolute; i.e., the product strength of a footbridge might be greater than that of a railroad bridge, although the former is of lighter construction.

[19]For a discussion of FMECA examples, see Murray E. Liebman, "Design By Elimination of Modes of Failures," Presentation at 14th International Academy for Quality Control Meeting, Houston, May 1979.

[20]This basic definition is in accordance with "Quality Systems Terminology," ANSI/ASQC A3-1978, American Society for Quality Control, Milwaukee.

[21]E. L. Fritz, and J. S. Youtcheff, "Sequential Life Testing in Systems Development," Missile and Space Vehicles, General Electric Company.

[22]For a discussion, see Irving E. Willard, Sr., "Reliability Growth Curves," *33rd Annual Technical Conference Transactions,* American Society for Quality Control, Houston, 1979.

[23]Harold R. Kellogg, "Statistical Quality Control and Reliability," *Industrial Quality Control,* vol. XVI, no. 11, May 1960.

PART SIX

Applying Total Quality Control in the Company

CHAPTER **18**

New-Design Control

Quality control becomes real when it is continuously at work hour after hour, week after week, year after year throughout the plant or company. The basis for the effectiveness of a modern quality program is the effectiveness of the specific quality-control *applications* that take place systematically and consistently in all marketing product plans, all engineering designs, all equipments and processes, all employee relations, all production operations, all maintenance and service, and all other relevant company activities.

Earlier chapters broke up these overall applications into the following four classifications called quality-control jobs:

1. *New-design control,* which involves preproduction quality-control activities
2. *Incoming-material control,* which involves the activities carried on while vendor and other incoming parts and materials are purchased, received, and examined
3. *Product control,* which involves quality-control activities carried on during active production and field service
4. *Special process studies,* which involve the troubleshooting of quality problems

These four jobs give substance to the basic principle of total quality control, which recognizes that product quality is affected at all stages of the production process. The core of modern quality control is the positive organization by management of many separate activities into a companywide total quality program—upon which foundation successful quality-control application is based.

Part 1 discussed the way in which diverse company quality-control activities are integrated into an overall structure which operates from the time a product is marketed, designed, and manufactured to the time it is packaged, shipped, and received by a satisfied customer. Part 2 described the quality system within which the four jobs of total quality control are carried out and the quality-system economics by which they are measured. Part 3 detailed key management approaches to organizing and motivating for total quality control.

Part 4 then reviewed the engineering technology of quality: quality engineering, process-control engineering, and quality information equipment engineering—the disciplines that provide the technical tools used. Part 5 presented the statistical point of view, which provides a central analytical basis for work done in the four jobs of total quality control.

With this foundation established, Part 6 discusses the quality-control jobs successively in its four chapters. Each job is described in two ways:

Organizational Practices and Routines

It is people who, in the final analysis, build and maintain quality. The engineer who writes specifications and guarantees affects quality fully as much as does the inspector who examines the product for conformance to these specifications. The methods specialist who develops manufacturing facilities is similarly involved, as is the foreman, the production operator, the purchasing agent, or the reliability analyst. Effective quality control therefore requires effective human relations—including satisfactory organization planning and sound administrative practices and routines—as well as a genuine company-wide commitment to quality.[1]

Technological Practices

Many quality problems are extremely complex technically. Proper attitude, organization, and spirit among personnel—although extremely important—cannot alone solve these problems. There must be the support of modern quality-control techniques to aid them in this task.

Several of these tools have been used in industry for many years, often neither termed "quality-control techniques" nor recognized as part of the company activities in controlling quality. Others of the methods reflect evolving developments.

These two factors—organizational routines and technological practices—become merged in actual plant and company quality-control programs. For ease of presenting the fundamentals of total quality control, however, the ensuing discussion considers these factors both independently and together. Emphasis throughout is placed upon the systematic approach required for a total-quality-control program as well as upon details of individual actions used in quality-control jobs.

Whereas earlier discussion centered upon the concepts and principles underlying total quality control, Chapters 18 through 21 concentrate upon the actual application of overall quality-control procedures and quality-control techniques in the plant and company.[2] Additional techniques, the application of which is confined to particular segments of the quality-control jobs, are also discussed. It is assumed in Part 6 that organizing for quality has been done, that the time necessary for development to maturity of the quality-control jobs has elapsed, and that an active quality-control program is in place.

18.1 The Importance of the Control of New Designs

The assurance of customer quality satisfaction must begin during new product development. Whenever a new product is planned and a new design begun, fully as much as major new marketplace opportunity, there will be potential quality risk to the company. Because this is so, there must be a thoroughly structured series of activities to minimize this risk and to assure the quality of the new design to satisfy the customer in the marketplace.

Too often in the past the quality risk of new products—and the marketplace benefit from genuine new product-quality leadership—has been only casually identified in some companies and occasionally even ignored. Even when recognized, the related control activities have sometimes not been deep or complete or thorough enough for effective assurance. Yet industrial experience shows that customer acceptance of a new product depends very heavily upon the quality of the design. Indeed, the profitability and success of companies can ultimately be based upon the marketplace reaction to the design quality of their product offerings.

18.2 The Needs for New-Design Control

Every company has the example of a product whose quality has been continually troublesome to maintain. The quality problems resulting from manufacture of this product are often never solved because "it would be too expensive to do so."

Similarly universal is the conflict between production people and design engineers on those parts tolerances which production insists are far narrower than the use of the part requires. On these parts, engineers may privately admit that "we call for ± 0.002 inch only because it increases the likelihood of our getting ± 0.005 inch."

When a situation of this sort exists, it inevitably results in lack of respect for tolerances established on drawings and specification sheets. It is also accompanied by excessive expense in securing and using manufacturing facilities of unnecessarily high precision.

A somewhat different situation is the perennial case of the engineer who has carefully designed a product, rigorously tested two or three toolmakers' models—or "breadboard" circuits with electronic products—which perform satisfactorily, and then complains bitterly about the "factory's incompetence" when large percentages of the product fail to perform properly when produced in mass quantities. Yet this poor performance may have been inevitable owing to overly great tolerance buildups, to a statistically unsound testing program of the sort discussed in Section 13.6, or to unsatisfactory inherent product reliability.

Another situation is when engineers sometimes design by trial and error—out of necessity in some products, but simply out of choice or habit in other products. Without satisfactory proof testing and analytical calculations, there may later develop inherent design weakness; for example, some parts may be overstressed and others used in the wrong application. Moreover, even when design and development validation has been performed by engineers, but without suitable documentation—instead, with the information retained in the head of an engineer who has moved into other work—there may be major quality problems in verifying later design alterations or product-application changes.

A further area has been the sometimes frequent practice of engineering selection of parts and components based solely upon technical and functional performance—a new integrated circuit module and a new printed circuit board specified for a new small computer design, for example. Yet insufficient data may be available concerning the reliability of these components, and the new design may enter the market with an uncertain quality life cycle in spite of its high initial performance characteristics.

18.3 The Needs for New-Design Control—Influence During Product Planning

These situations are some of the more readily apparent illustrations of the need for a properly coordinated, regularly scheduled program directed toward analyzing newly designed products for possible quality troubles before active production is started. This type of program also tends to improve several less obvious situations that may have long existed in the factory without even being recognized as problems affecting the quality of new designs.

There may, for example, be no organized means for feeding back to the design engineer information from the laboratory specialists or the manufacturing engineers about new materials or processes. Mechanical inspection or electronic testing groups may be forced to wait for information about what they should inspect or test until production has actively started and many defective units have been scrapped. Parts tolerances may be selected with no knowledge of or reference to the accuracies that may be actually held in the plant's machine tools and processes.

Sales efforts in product planning and merchandising may work in directions opposed to the design actually being developed. Desirable cost standards for parts inspection sampling and bogeys for manufacturing losses may be established only after the design has been in active production for a considerable length of time.

In a somewhat different area, data on field tests and performance of units in the customer's plants may not be effectively reported by the field organization for use by the engineer in the design of products similar to the one under development. Guarantees and warranties may be established based upon the performance of a few specially made models rather than upon a sufficient quantity of actual production units. Company efforts toward standardization and product simplification may be thwarted if the new design calls for many new and special parts. Manufacturing employees may be considerably handicapped by the nonexistence of adequate quality specifications.

Again, the issue of what really are realistic reliability and maintainability requirements for a product or component is a continual concern to every company that deals with high-performance articles. Too frequently, meaningful part and product data are not available for the environmental conditions to be encountered, yet a decision must nonetheless be made about proposals to be placed before the prospective customer.

Under such circumstances, the company will be served neither by optimism nor pessimism based upon speculation. It can incur a long-term product hazard if it is loosely committed by an overly optimistic sales engineer who works on the assumption that "our company can provide any reliability requirement you want." Or it can lose the opportunity to obtain a sizable contract which provides an extremely favorable entry into a high-precision product market by accepting the overly pessimistic view of the development engineer who refuses to identify any range of reliability targets "unless years of exhaustive components tests have been concluded."

Only a systematic quality-control logic, backed by meaningful technical procedures, can serve here. It will provide alternatives as to how far the company may (1) firmly commit itself to reliability levels, reasonably attainable with current know-how about components, and (2) identify the developmental work required before new reliability and maintainability levels can be firmly committed.

18.4 The Scope of New-Design Control

Too often in the past these problems have been faced and solved in some plants and companies long after the product design has been frozen and a considerable investment has been made in inventory and processing equipment. The latitude of decisions affecting process improvements or inspection schedules after the actual design has been completed is obviously much more limited than it is during the development stage of the product.

Indeed, industrial experience demonstrates very clearly that *the fewer the design changes after production has begun, the better the product quality level will be.*

Thus it is essential to view the new-design control activity as being much more than merely seeing that a completed design is ready to manufacture. It must have its influence early in the product planning and product research stage, beginning in the marketplace, where information on customer quality requirements and customer maintenance-and-use habits with similar products will contribute to determining the necessary product-quality requirements. In cases where there may be no such specific quality requirements, nor a quality specification in the product plan, it will be up to the new-design control activity to ensure that they are defined.

Many quality-oriented areas must be considered, such as marketability, customer applications, warranties, certifications, safety and health and industry standards, legal requirements, service capabilities, and product life cycles in both foreign and domestic markets. Environmental effects such as energy use and pollution may also have to be explored. For foreign markets, national laws and cultural use patterns must be taken into account.

Moreover, the new-design control activity must ensure that suitable reliability and other data about components are made available and that a thorough preproduction and use testing program is established. It must ensure the availability of experience with previous similar products, which will be of great value in delineating the likes and dislikes of customers. Likewise, the new-design activity should help the design engineer's effort to "get around" quality problems that previous designs may have engendered, in either the factory or the field. It must create an awareness of such quality problems.

Moreover, new-design control activity—and total quality control itself—has a fundamental effect on the design engineering process itself. To assure quality of design, this process must include (1) the product systems design; (2) the determination of the acceptable range of the quality and reliability parameters of the components and sub-assemblies; and only then, (3) establishment of tolerances and final specification dimensions. In earlier, less demanding days, the quantification and disciplined approach to, for example, step 2, could sometimes be too quickly and casually passed from step 1 to step 3.

That considerations of this sort should be faced and solved has been recognized as a "good idea" for some time. But effective action on the good idea has frequently been lacking because no machinery has been developed to carry out the required program. The quality-control job called *new-design control* has been developed to provide this machinery.

18.5 Defining New-Design Control

As a definition:

> New-design control involves the establishment and specification of the
> necessary cost-quality, performance-quality, safety-quality, and
> reliability-quality for the product required for the intended customer
> satisfaction, including the elimination or location of possible sources of quality
> troubles before the start of formal production.

This quality job tool is a structured approach for balancing the quality costs of a new product design with the service that the new product must render if it is to fully satisfy the customer. New-design control procedures aim to minimize these costs and maximize customer satisfaction.

New-design control activity includes all the quality efforts on a new product while its marketable characteristics are being decided; while it is being designed, sold to the customer, planned for manufacture, and initially costed;

and while its quality standards are being specified and quality-control procedures are being established to maintain these standards. In the case of quantity production, new-design control activities end when pilot runs have proved satisfactory customer quality-oriented production performance. With job-shop production, the routine ends as work on manufacture of component parts is being started.

All three disciplines of the engineering technology of total quality control discussed in Part 4 have application in new-design control, as does the entire range of statistical technology. In particular, quality engineering (Chap. 10) and quality information equipment engineering (Chap. 12) are the engineering technologies used most intensively. "Frequency Distributions" (Chap. 13), "Special Methods" (Chap. 16), and "Product Reliability" (Chap. 17) are the statistical areas most often brought to use. The application of these techniques in a systematized, orderly fashion is provided through the planning of the new-design control routine.

Such planning, and the consistent and unvarying attention to the new-design control routines in a plant and a company, is essential to successfully achieve the quality of new product offerings. Indeed, the effectiveness of new-design control improves progressively as the organization's new-design control-oriented "learning curve" improves.

The very nature of new-design[3] control makes its application, in significant part, a matter of experience; and what might be thought of as "experience retention" is of great importance. The task of eliminating and predicting potential product-quality troubles is, in fact, subject to such sources of error as (1) that we human beings, with all our susceptibility to faults in judgment, carry on the work; and (2) that it is necessary to allocate available—and, in many cases, highly limited—resources as effectively as possible to the testing and evaluation that may be indicated during initial new-design control planning.

As a result, fine questions of selection and interpretation arise—decisions as to what quality characteristics are particularly critical and which tests can be eliminated and which must be made. It requires thorough background in making these decisions to assure personnel as to which tests and what specifications will be most useful.

Computer-oriented reliability and maintainability data base management is becoming progressively more useful in retaining this necessary experience in some companies. These data, coded by parts history and application, by product field failure rates, and by other categories that are similarly useful for design and quality engineers, are today an important tool for new-design control applications.

The effectiveness of new-design control tends, therefore, to considerably increase as those carrying on the activity in the company develop the art of its application. This increase in effectiveness applies generally throughout the technical groups of the company, owing to the formal nature of a new-design control program, as opposed to the increase in effectiveness for only a few individuals, as in the case of the uncoordinated, sprawling types of individual design-control activities. The younger members of the technical groups benefit particularly in the plant with a well-organized new-design control program, because the quality phases of their product-development experience may be greatly expedited.

18.6 Application of New-Design Control

Whether the product is a wide-bodied passenger jet aircraft, a new integrated-circuit-based computer design, an offshore oil drilling rig, a medical life-support device, a pollution-control device, a large electric motor, a solar radiator, a household refrigerator, a microwave cooking oven—or any of a wide variety of offerings of seemingly less complexity, there is a need for a structured new-design control procedure. The same basic fundamentals obtain in this activity throughout industry, no matter what type of production conditions are being faced.

The detailed new-design control approaches vary from company to company, depending upon such factors as product mix, plant size, qualifications of available personnel, and the economics of the particular situation. One major difference is the distinction between the approach used in the mass-production type of manufacture and that used in the job-shop type of production, where only one or a few of a given design are to be manufactured.

In the former case, new-design control activities may make extensive use of such tools as pilot runs and the development of sampling quality levels. Job-shop new-design control, on the other hand, must rely upon such techniques as the establishment of quality standards and analysis of the quality performance of previous designs similar to the one under development. New-design control is of particularly great importance to a company quality program under these job-shop conditions. When only one or a few units are to be produced, "make it right the first time" becomes more than a slogan—it becomes a necessity.

Product-control routines may "catch" a defective nuclear reactor shell whose design is such that a satisfactory shell is difficult to cast, but the expense of recasting the shell to new specifications may be extremely high. A special process study may discover that the cause of the malfunctioning of a truck diesel engine at final test is faulty specifications, but the loss of customer goodwill because of the need for additional time to rebuild the engine may be a genuine disaster. An adequate new-design control program is a quality-control "must" in the plants producing these products.

Another major difference in the application of new-design control is the distinction between the approach used in the research and development–oriented company and that for the company which concentrates upon products which essentially use existing engineering and manufacturing know-how.

In the former case, new-design control activities may make extensive use of such techniques as environmental testing and reliability analyses in their various forms as applied to new components or to new uses of old components.

In the latter case, the orientation may be more heavily toward such techniques as process-capability studies to assure compatibility between the existing production facilities and the new product and toward techniques for analysis of quality performance of similar products.

There is thus a considerable difference in the emphasis, the application, and the details of the investment that is required on a new-design control activity as between a newly designed communications satellite or a newly designed videodisk recorder, a new integrated circuit for early-warning radar and the new emission control device in an automobile, or the design of a home-heating furnace and the design of a continuous process furnace. These differences in degree are determined by the judgments of those in charge of the activity in a company; the objective of assuring a good quality of design is the same in all cases.

Indeed, the quality engineer who has become experienced in new-design control activity ultimately learns that the similarity in concept and technique among all such products is greater than the difference. For this reason, among many others, the quality engineer who is truly skilled in the technologies of total quality control can make a professional contribution to the new-design control activity of a very wide range of products.

The quality engineer's experience and specialized knowledge of the variability of materials and manufacturing processes and their effects upon product quality, of product weaknesses that lead to product failures, and of the manufacturing and testing environment and its effect upon product quality and reliability uniquely equip the engineer to contribute to effective new-design control. The engineer will be familiar with types of design features that may increase the odds against manufacturing to specifications; tests that discriminate satisfactory from unsatisfactory quality; effects upon product of packaging, storage, transportation, installation and maintenance; and, of ultimate importance, the behavior of customers in the use of the product.

The quality engineer is aware of those features of a product which make it difficult to avoid quality problems, such as the product design that calls for a "blind hole" which traps chips from the machining operation. These chips are difficult to remove, and if left behind, they may dislodge after the device is in service and excessively wear moving parts or short circuits. Another example is the part that can be assembled two ways: correctly and incorrectly. The new-design control activity will encourage a design, together with the supporting manufacturing engineering, that results in a part which can only be assembled correctly. In a host of such situations, the quality engineer will be of real service to the design engineer—together with the manufacturing engineer—as part of the new-design control activity.

18.7 Organizing for New-Design Control

For the new-design control activity of a company to be fully effective, a definite routine for it must be established and maintained within the framework of the quality system. Basic to the operation of this routine is the decision that must be made in the quality-system plan of the plant and company as to the classifications of new products which will be subject to the new-design control routine. Many plants include all their new products in such routines; others include only those products which are new in development concept, sufficiently costly, or produced in sufficiently large quantities.

The principal criteria for this classification are the risks of unfavorable consequences of design errors in terms of customer satisfaction—including product reliability, safety, and maintainability—as well as of quality cost— including potential product liability.

This classification decision is made according to customer use and the economic circumstances in each company, based upon answers to such questions as "Can we afford not to have a new-design control routine for this product?" and "How extensive a testing program can we afford in the new-design control routine for this article?"

In the special case of those products upon which safety of humans and property is dependent, a complete new-design control program will be required for all products, apart from immediate economic considerations.

Based upon these classifications, each new product that is subject to the new-design control routine must then be geared into the steps of the routine. The action should be an automatic one; it should not be necessary for members of the quality-control component to ferret out the existence of a new design or to hear of it after considerable time has passed.

Engineering is the key functional group in new-design control activities. As "quality planning," the activity is an important complement to the design engineer's main responsibility of developing the most useful and ingenious product possible. Marketing also has a significant role to play to help assure the proper marketplace orientation of the activity.

Also important in new-design control are other members of the company technical groups, such as laboratory engineers; manufacturing engineering people; service, purchasing, and materials specialists; and inspection and test personnel. Manufacturing supervision, production-control, and other groups act chiefly in a consultative capacity.

The quality function of the company—through its quality-engineering component—has the responsibility of ensuring the progress and integration of the new-design control activity as part of the quality program for the company. In many areas where quality-control equipment is, or will be, required, the quality information equipment engineering component has the responsibility to become directly involved.

As discussed in Chapter 8, there are several ways of assigning specific responsibility for new-design control to the quality-engineering unit. In the case of some companies with heavy research and development content in each new product, it may be most useful to make new-design control activity for all new products a specialized assignment; it may thus become the responsibility of one or more quality engineers. In other companies, the quality engineer in charge of the quality system for a product line or product grouping will also be assigned responsibility for the new-design work on the new products to be added to that line; thus there will be as many new-design control assignments as there are quality engineers. For small companies, new-design control may become the parttime responsibility of the single quality engineer, or of the Quality-Control Manager, if this person acts as the quality engineer. Similar alternatives are available for structuring quality information equipment engineering assignments.

However the activity is assigned within the quality-control component, the responsible quality engineer will join with the representatives of other company functional components to form a project team to carry out the new-design activity on a particular product.

Much valuable information is available in development and design engineering, manufacturing engineering, and marketing groups in a plant as a result of accumulated past product experience. Since the project team will be made up of representatives of these various groups, it can use their past experience to the benefit of the quality of the new product design.

18.8 Pattern for the New-Design Control Routine

The cycle for developing a new product that takes place in many companies is now summarized. Several steps may be consolidated in some companies; the order of steps may be interchanged in others.

1. A new market opportunity to serve customers is identified and a new design is contemplated.
2. Technical, production, customer-use, and marketing analyses are made of the marketplace and the design. Cost targets, production volume, and price levels are preliminarily established.
3. General specifications are written. They may be in the form of
   a. Sales propositions in the case of job-lot production.
   b. Rough functional specifications for products that will be manufactured in mass quantity.
   c. Broad identification of the coverage of the quality program for the product.
   d. Overall outline of product service and maintenance objectives, quality-performance requirements, product life cycle targets, and other related product goals.
4. Preliminary design is made.
5. First prototypes are made. An extensive program of testing the characteristics of this design is carried out, including the components and subassemblies to be used. For products with electronic computing modules, the software will be evaluated and testing begun.
6. Preliminary design review takes place. Preliminary classification of characteristics of the design proceeds (including components and subassemblies); test procedures are evaluated; manufacturing and assembly capa-

bility are assessed; cost targets are reviewed; quality levels are identified; design changes are defined and reviewed; process and manufacturing considerations are identified.

7. Intermediate design is made, including production drawings, and prototypes are built.

8. Tests are made on this intermediate design, and design review takes place. Action continues on classification of characteristics and upon manufacturing, assembly, and test requirements. Marketing and pricing estimates are reviewed. Design changes are defined and reviewed.

9. Final design is completed along with final specifications, standards, guarantees, quality planning, and production drawings. Life and performance tests are culminated before final design completion. Components, subassembly, and assembly specifications are completed; assembly inspection plans are developed; tool design and procurement are completed; and costing is finalized.

10. Sample production units are built.

11. Shipping and service procedures are defined.

12. Capability studies are made of new and current machines' equipment and processes.

13. Supervisors and production employees are trained. Pilot runs are made using samples composed of production units. The results of the tests of these samples are incorporated into the design and manufacturing specifications if and as required.

14. Final design is reviewed. Product, software when appropriate, equipment, processes, facilities, and development test results are analyzed by those functions which need to become familiar with the plans and which can make constructive inputs. The basic product cost targets and life cycle cost objectives are reviewed to assure the goal of "design to cost." Product qualification tests are satisfactorily completed. Release for manufacture of production tools and facilities is given, consistent with final design review approval and completion.

15. Marketing announcements are confirmed; product information manuals, service publications, and training aids are completed, all with thorough attention to quality considerations.

16. The unit is released for active production.

Some steps of this sequence are quite general for both job-lot and high-quantity production; a few steps apply chiefly to units produced in mass quantities.

18.9 Pattern for the New-Design Control Routine—The Fundamental Activities

The fundamental activities of new-design control routines within the total quality program mesh into this sequence. These activities are now summarized:

1. *Establishment of the quality requirements for the product.* This involves analyses that culminate in customer-satisfaction-oriented specifications and standards which incorporate performance, reliability, maintainability, and safety requirements and the cost-quality balance for the product and the components. It includes activation of that portion of the quality program which covers the preproduction evaluation and testing of the product.

2. *Design of a product which meets these requirements.* This involves the establishment of the detailed drawings for the product and the preparation of the related engineering instructions. It includes following the quality program for classifying product and process characteristics, for conducting product life and safety evaluations, and for the carrying on of environmental and other tests to determine the reliability of components and subassemblies and of software where necessary. It also includes field tests and performance studies of assembled prototypes or handmade samples. Simulation studies of product quality may be made where physical prototypes cannot be made available. Product cost and life cycle quality and cost goals are evaluated.

3. *Planning to assure maintenance of the required quality.* This involves the formal activation of the details of that portion of the quality program which covers the control of purchased material, the maintenance of quality during processing and production, and the assurance of quality during field installation and product servicing. It also includes the development of the final specifications for the quality information equipments which are required for incoming material, in-process control, and field testing and evaluation.

4. *Preproduction review of the new design and its manufacturing facilities; formal release for active production.* This involves the planned, formal evaluation of the designed product at several stages of the complete design process to assure its capability of meeting its warranties and guarantees under conditions of actual use. It also involves analyses of the capabilities of the processes which will be required to produce the product. A series of performance and product qualification tests will be conducted, in terms required by the quality program, to review the product in all important customer end-use aspects.

   Particular emphasis is placed upon components testing under conditions which simulate actual customer use. These reliability tests also couple components into subassemblies to evaluate the effect of different combinations upon quality.

These four elements are quite basic in new-design control programs of plants which produce such a wide variety of products as major electronic and mechanical products, fluids, textiles, detail parts, small components like semiconductors and bellows, permanent magnets, aerospace products, nuclear and energy equipments, consumer durables including automotive products, medical electronic units, many forms of chemicals, and complex equipment systems.

Because of the wide scope of the accompanying routines, the following discussion of new-design control concentrates upon procedures used in companies which manufacture complex assemblies; similar features apply, however, to the routines of the other product types.

Many of the engineering and statistical techniques, as discussed in Parts 4 and 5, are used in these new-design control routines as they have been determined appropriate to the quality program of individual plants and companies.

18.10 A Typical New-Design Control Routine

A company which markets, designs, makes, and services small precision electronic and electromechanical regulating and relaying products ties its new-design control program directly to the cycle of Section 18.8 and the activities of Section 18.9 with the following steps:

1. The company quality program has established the policy that all major new product designs must proceed through the new-design control routine. For the criteria of the consequences of design errors as discussed in Section 18.7, this policy has been based upon the thorough determination that these consequences can be significant for the company's products. This is because of their complexity and because their applications are invariably critical to the performance and reliability of the customer products in which they are used as a primary equipment component.[4]

   Within the new-design control routine policy, the company design engineering function advises other key functional heads involved in this routine concerning each major new design proceeding into the development process. Figure 18.1 shows a typical information letter on a new product. Included also are information sheets providing preliminary data on the new product. Figure 18.2 shows one of the sheets from a typical initial product summary.

Subject: New-Design Notification

To: Designated Functional Heads:

   Information is hereby provided on aircraft control relay, with new model number 4ZP96B3-12, now proceeding from concept to preliminary design. Detailed product data will be made available prior to the design control evaluation meeting, chaired by B. B. Smith, model design engineer, that has been scheduled by quality engineering.

J. Jones
Engineering Section Head

FIG. 18.1

2. When such a new-design initiation is identified, representatives of key functional groups of the company work together to begin examination and evaluation of design data to ensure that the new product concept will meet the intended quality requirements.

One step in this evaluation is the initial formal design review meeting on the product, for consideration of its concept, function, and preliminary design. The product design engineer chairs this meeting, with close participation by quality engineering. Also in attendance are representatives from marketing, production, manufacturing engineering, purchasing and production control, product service, and other key areas as indicated. A formal agenda is established to ensure the systematic operation of the review meeting. Where appropriate, outside technical experts are invited to participate in the review so as to add their specialized experience to particular areas and to continue to provide this experience in later phases of the design reviews.

The purposes of this review are to discover critical features of the proposed design for expected customer use; to anticipate troubles the factory may have producing the product or in product service in maintaining it; to consider make-or-buy and purchased material requirements as to quality criticality; to recommend any changes in the design that seem immediately required; and to consider the assembly, subassembly, and component tests and quality evaluation needed for reliability and safety assessment and customer application and life cycle demands.

Specific consideration is given to product-liability hazards, to environmental considerations, to what will be needed for configuration control and traceability. Distribution and product introduction factors are carefully reviewed in such areas as logistics and spare parts demands, advertising claims, regulatory and standards requirements, and similar factors. Documentation of the design itself, as well as the recommended corrective actions, are given thorough attention.

For effectiveness, this design review meeting is limited to a minimum grouping of participants to provide meaningful communication and thorough information interchange. Between the issuance of the information represented in Figures 18.1 and 18.2 and the actual review meeting, an adequate period of time is allowed so that the necessary data are fully absorbed.[5]

3. The engineers plan and carry out the necessary analyses and test programs aimed at finding answers to design-oriented questions generated in step 2, with close participation and support by quality engineering. Each of the other design control-oriented functional representatives initiate, as appropriate, the marketing, manufacturing, and service-oriented investigations that also result from step 2.

4. The findings from the analyses and tests are incorporated by the design engineer into the new model design, as appropriate. Classification of

New-Design Notification   FORM #XYZ   DATE   March

Section #   100

Model #   4ZP96B3-12

Brief Functional Description:

Aircraft control relay

_____

_____

_____

Is This Design Similar To Existing Equipment?

Specify: Similar in function to 4ZP83CZ but with longer life cycle and duty

demand requirement.

_____

_____

Expected Quantity   25,000*

Design Will be Completed Approx.   6 months

Production Is Expected To Start Approx.   9 months

Remarks: *This is of the order of magnitude but it may be 50%–75%

wrong.

_____

_____

J. Jones, *Engineering Section Head*

NAME, TITLE

FIG. 18.2

product, subassembly, and component characteristics is performed by design engineering. Preliminary production drawings and specifications are issued to Manufacturing. Detailed quality planning is initiated for all steps of the product quality-control program, including inspection and test routines and the establishment, where possible and desirable, of AQL or AOQL values for parts sampling.

5a. Manufacturing makes prototypes from these drawings and submits them to the design engineer for approval tests. If the performance of the models is not satisfactory, tests and design changes are made until difficulties are eliminated. These changes are incorporated into the drawings and specifications. Life and performance tests are begun, and quality-engineering product evaluations take place. Reliability assessment proceeds.

5b. While these tests are in progress, manufacturing engineers complete the planning for all processing equipments and tooling. Work proceeds by Marketing and Production Control to detail spare parts requirements. Purchasing, with close participation by quality engineering, proceeds with definition of vendor quality requirements and initiates vendor quality surveys.

5c. Intermediate design review takes place.

5d. The individual pieces of quality information equipment are specified. The various elements of the quality plan are brought together and finalized by quality engineering and suitably documented for later use by process-control engineering (including inspection and test).

6. When the production tools and processing equipments are received, manufacturing begins the output of component parts on production tools. A pilot assembly run is started.

7. Engineering, manufacturing, and quality control analyze the performance of the pilot runs. They also study the quality of parts and assemblies produced for the pilot run by the processes and tools that will be used for the new product. Final design review procedure is initiated.

8. Results of these analyses are incorporated by the designer into the final design specifications, standards, and guarantees. Capability studies on processes and tools are used to guide any appropriate action to change tooling, manufacturing, or the quality plan itself.

9. Final product qualification tests take place. All product documentation, configuration control, product service, advertising, and sales brochures are completed. Final design review is completed.

10. The product is approved for production and sale.

18.11 Operation of This New-Design Control Routine—Preliminary Design

The actual operation of the routine of this company may be illustrated by following through the new-design control program adapted from that for the new control relay, 4ZP96B3-12, which was reported in the form in Figure 18.2.

When the development for the new design starts, several product concept studies are conducted before writing the preliminary specifications of the product characteristics, and market-oriented quality requirements and customer-use patterns are defined. Performance reports are studied based on field data of products which the 4ZP96B3-12 is to replace or supplant. Data taken from internal factory and inspection reports on these similar products and from information about the best of competitive products are analyzed. Meetings are held with marketing and sales people so that their product planning and merchandising activities may be properly and adequately recognized in the development program under way for the new relay design.

Pertinent standards which contain requirements set down as the result of experience in attaining high-quality products are examined. Mandatory and voluntary standards—industry, regulatory, ANSI, and others—are reviewed. Also considered are data and reports from the company laboratory on new developments in processes, theories of operation, materials, and electronic and mechanical component reliability. Extensive use is made—by discussions, study of reports, and any other available means—of the wide background of experience accumulated in the company in previous development and new-design control activities. The five statistical tools discussed in Part 5 are very useful in these several studies.

Utilizing the information gathered in this product-concept development, the final decision is made on the economic and customer-use balance that must be reflected in the characteristics of the relay between cost and service that will be rendered by the device. Preliminary design of the control relay is then accomplished. These documented characteristics will become the basis for preliminary process planning for internally manufactured parts and assemblies and for assessing vendor capability to supply purchased items. The 4ZP96B3-12 is a production device to be manufactured in volume, so the limits in this cost balance are quite rigidly specified, and thus what is called "design-to-cost" becomes a primary goal in the product design. If the device were developmental, these cost limits might be much more flexible.

Since the new control relay replaces models already in production, the aim is to develop product characteristics which will give assurance of fully satisfying the use requirements necessary to completely replace the devices now in production. It is not desirable to fall into the all-too-usual trap of creating a product that is merely an addition to, rather than a replacement for, these other products.

When the design has reached this preliminary design stage, a preliminary design review is held. This session, chaired by Engineering with close participation by Quality Control, is attended by representatives from Production, Manufacturing Engineering, Marketing, Purchasing, and Product Service. The design engineer reviews the function, concept, and technology of the 4ZP96B3-12, describes its operation, and points out those subassemblies and component parts which are likely to be critical to proper operation. The plans projected for the reliability and maintainability program for the 4ZP96B3-12 are reviewed. Safety and product-liability considerations are examined and actions established to assess the product design for these factors. Product-quality-cost targets—including prevention, appraisal, internal failure, and external failure—are established and product life cycle costs are preliminarily reviewed.

Manufacturing representatives bring up their questions concerning tolerances and possible machining and assembly difficulties. They challenge tolerances that cannot be held with the present manufacturing facilities of the plant, as shown by the results of process-capability studies.

They raise such questions as "Can we make this part from phosphor bronze instead of beryllium copper?" "Can this blind tapped hole be changed to a through hole?" "A tolerance of ± 0.001 inch on this hole necessitates a reaming operation. How about calling for ± 0.003 inch so we can drill the hole?"

While these questions are being raised, the designer is also bringing up questions, such as "That spring carries current; will its resistance be too high if I make it from phosphor bronze?" "Will a through hole cut down my magnetic section too much?" "Will the pin fit be satisfactory with a ± 0.003-inch tolerance?"

The quality engineer and other technical members of the project team may raise an additional series of questions, such as "Will silver-contact tips of this configuration and composition actually have the required life if the relay is installed in an extremely hot climate?" "Can the manufacturers of the small-discharge capacitors that will be used actually maintain their guarantee of $\pm$ 1 percent performance over the production lot? No one has been able to do it before." "Since even small quantities of moisture will affect performance and life, is the case for the relay truly moisture- and humidity-proof?"

And the design engineers will be raising component reliability questions of their own as well as those that will affect maintainability and serviceability, such as "This beryllium-copper spring will perform millions of operations during the life of the relay. Are we safe enough, metallurgically, with this particular composition, and do we know enough about the special requirements of heat-treating?" "Are we completely safe in assuming that the relay will be installed where the customer has told us it will be? Is there any possibility of application where it will be much colder or much warmer, or where there will be much more possibility of electrical interference?"

18.12 Operation of This New-Design Control Routine—Testing and Reliability

To find answers to the questions raised, a testing program will be outlined using prototypes built by Manufacturing in accordance with the preliminary design. The design engineer has the key responsibility for assuring the carrying out of the testing program because it relates to the engineer's basic responsibility for establishing the final product design. The design engineer will be assisted by reliability specialists and closely and actively joined by the quality-control engineer. Other functional representatives of the new-design control project team, as indicated, may be called upon for help.

Many techniques are used in the tests. The engineers use one of them—the frequency distribution—to great advantage. One particular useful frequency-distribution application is the tests of the strength under torsion of one of the relay's assemblies. This subassembly consists of a knurled part forced into a hole in a plastic part with the minimum allowable interference (amount the knurled teeth must cut into the plastic molding).

Figure 18.3 shows the frequency-distribution analysis of this knurled part.[6] The analysis illustrates that the minimum force indicated to the design engineer is about 5 inches-pounds ($\overline{X} - 3\sigma$) and that the design engineer should expect an occasional reading lower than that. This information is used to adjust the engineer's design specification.

Extensive testing programs are undertaken to gain technical information that will enable the design engineer to assess and, if necessary, increase the reliability of the device. Some of these tests may be used later by the process-control engineer in evaluating the reliability of current product. Nondestructive tests that pinpoint the mode of failure are particularly useful in controlling the reliability of continuing production. Information from such tests also provides an important feedback to the design engineer so that designs can be continually improved. Figure 18.4 shows a page covering reliability tests for component types.[7]

This reliability testing is segmented into four primary areas: (1) the basic reliability of the product design, (2) the reliability of the product as manufactured by the production processes, (3) the reliability and early wear out of components, (4) the customer-application reliability and life cycle of the product in use.

During this preliminary design stage, design maturity tests—dealing with area (1)—are performed to measure product MTBF, as earlier defined and

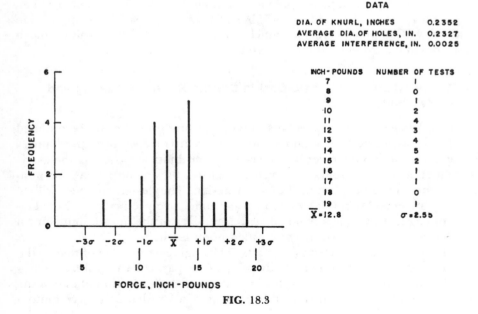

DATA

DIA. OF KNURL, INCHES	0.2352
AVERAGE DIA. OF HOLES, IN.	0.2327
AVERAGE INTERFERENCE, IN.	0.0025

INCH-POUNDS	NUMBER OF TESTS
7	1
8	0
9	1
10	2
11	4
12	3
13	4
14	5
15	2
16	1
17	1
18	0
19	1
$\overline{X}=12.8$	$\sigma=2.55$

FORCE, INCH-POUNDS

FIG. 18.3

Mechanisms of failure	Present nondestructive testing	Future nondestructive testing
Contact contamination	Contact resistance test	IR inspection of hot solenoid
Decomposition of organic films	Direct-voltage insulation check	Contact pressure measurement with piezoelectric crystal
Incorrect pull-in and drop-out	Contact pressure measurement with gram gage	
Contact wear and deformation		

Mechanisms of Failure: One manufacturer has indicated that contact contamination is the major reason for relay failure. This is particularly true when the relay finds application in a dry circuit (i.e., one where the current level is low). Even in hermetically sealed relays, the decomposition of organic matter within the unit causes films which cover up to 90 per cent of the contact face. The thickness of the contaminating film depends on the absorption characteristics of the contact material. Penetration of the preliminary thickness of a film is possible by the tunnel effect (i.e., electrons transmitted without energy loss through a barrier whose thickness is approximately equivalent to the electron wavelength). Thicker films can be punctured by field-strength voltage (i.e., coherer action). The latter, also known as *fritting*, occurs when the electric field within the film becomes large enough to form a minute metal bridge through the film. Oil, deeply embedded in the surfaces of metal parts, is the primary source of organic material which decomposes to form contaminating films. It has been found that activated carbon getters prevent failure due to films formed from organic decomposition.

The next major contribution to relay failure is insulation breakdown. Very fine wire is used to wind the solenoids which actuate the relay armature. It is very difficult to apply uniform coatings of insulation to this wire. The uneven coating breaks and causes hot spots and short circuits, which render the relay useless. Relays which do not meet specifications can be considered to have failed. An example of this is incorrect pull-in drop-out current or voltage. Pull-in current or voltage is the maximum current or voltage required to operate the relay. Drop-out current or voltage is the minimum current or voltage required to release the relay. Excessive contact pressure causes abnormal wear of the contact surface, greatly decreasing the reliable life of the relay. Arcs which burn during the recorded time of bouncing are sufficient to cause disturbances by transferring material. This latter effect causes pitting which deforms and weakens the contact surface. Enough pressure must be supplied to prevent excessive bouncing, but care must be taken not to increase the erosion rate.

FIG. 18.4

discussed in Chapter 17. Failure mode, effect, and criticality analysis (FMECA) tests are performed (Sec. 18.20) to examine all potential ways in which relay component failures can take place, so that compensatory design actions can take place or, if there is no other alternative, the inclusion of redundancy through backup components in the design. Figure 18.5 shows a section of the FMECA test conclusions on the 4ZP96B3-12 relay. Special attention during these tests is placed upon product-safety evaluation.

Significant attention is given to the estimate of the potential control relay product failure rate as a function of the collective component failure rates. To the fullest possible extent, component failure rates are obtained from the experience-retention data bank of the company, from component manufacturers, from user groups, and from handbooks. Since these individual data have been developed under different conditions, they must be normalized. The tradeoffs among component stresses, the necessary component-reliability improvement goals, and the overall control relay product failure rate then become the objectives of necessary design attention. The component-reliability area of the overall reliability testing program proceeds in this framework.

18.13 Operation of This New-Design Control Routine—Intermediate Design

The design engineer issues summary reports of this testing program, which are made available to the intermediate design review meeting among the key functional representatives. Figures 18.6 and 18.7 show the first two pages of such a report.[8]

Based upon information obtained from the program of investigatory tests, final production drawings are completed and issued. At this point,

1. Manufacturing builds several final design prototypes. "Several" may be 20 to 100 in the new-design control routine of the plant, depending upon the cost and complexity of the device and the statistical accuracy required in the analysis. Limitations of sizes lower than 50 are clearly recognized and are used only as applicable. For the 4ZP96B3-12, 25 models, manufactured in accordance with production drawings, are turned over to the design engineer, who tests them to determine whether they meet specifications. On those features of the models where performance is not satisfactory, Engineering makes changes and carries on tests until acceptable operation is obtained.
2. While activity 1 is going on, the manufacturing engineer completes the planning for all processing and tooling necessary for the job.
3. The quality engineer completes the quality planning, including the inspection and testing requirements and the operation guides, to control product quality: when the material will be received, when the product will be manufactured, and when it will be shipped, installed, and serviced. Figure 18.8 shows a section of the quality plan covering operator inspection of sealed relays.
4. The quality information equipment engineer either concludes a preliminary design or arranges with vendors for the procurement of the necessary

4ZP96B3-12 Control Relay
Failure Mode, Effect, and Criticality Analysis

PREPARED BY: R.T. Roe

DATE: May

APPROVED BY: B.B. Smith

DATE: May

Component	Possible failure	Cause of failure	P	D	S	Effect of failure	How can failure be eliminated or reduced
Printed circuit board module	Circuit Malfunction	Incorrect component insertion	3	2	4	Application malfunction	Failsafe assembly procedure
Primary control module	Connector fracture —connector distortion	Improper forming temperature; incorrect assembly	1	2	4	Loss of relay control	Process testing; consistent incoming inspection
Constructor module	Metals fatigue	Elbow stress buildup; incorrect metallurgical treatment	2	3	4	Loss of control	Adequate heat treat; process control
Energy module	Circuit failure	Connection failures through "cold solder"	3	2	3	No product function	Incoming mat'l control of electronic components solder proc. cont.
Base module	Plastic part purchase	Incorrect fabrication, incorrect material mixing	1	4	5	Safety of installation	Conformance to design specs

P = Probability of occurrence; D = likelihood of damage to surrounding components; S = seriousness of failure to the product and/or user.

1 = very low; 2 = low or minor; 3 = significant; 4 = high; 5 = very high or catastrophic

FIG. 18.5

637

4ZP96B3-12 – QUALITY CONTROL STUDY

CONTACTOR CALIBRATIONS AND ACTION

Purpose of Study

The purpose of this study is to anticipate difficulties in obtaining the desired calibrations and action of the contactor resulting from variations in dimensions or properties of parts, each of which is within the tolerances of the drawing but which accumulate to produce extreme effects. No such difficulties have been experienced with the handmade samples, twelve of which have been tested; but it is unlikely that all of the possible variations have existed or have been cumulative.

The principal factors to be studied are:

(1) Variation in deflection of the main spring when the relay is picked up.

(2) Variation in stiffness of the main spring and of the wipe spring.

(3) Variation in air gap at the junctions of various parts of the magnetic circuit.

(4) Variation in magnetic properties of the various portions of the magnetic circuit.

(5) Variation in coil resistance.

Only one adjustment is provided to compensate for all of the possible variations; this is the adjustment of the pole piece. The pole piece will be adjusted to provide the desired drop-out voltage, and all of the rest of the calibrations must come as they will.

The desired calibrations and action are as follows:

(1) Pick-up voltage (cold) – 15.0 volts or less.

(2) Seal-in voltage (cold) – less than pickup.

(3) Drop-out voltage (cold) – 4.8 to 3.2 volts.

(4) Air Gap – 0.015 in. or more.

(5) No hesitation during any part of the pick-up or drop-out stroke.

(6) No bouncing on pickup.

The pages of this report summarize tests made:

FIG. 18.6

quality-control equipment. Figure 18.9 shows a part of a specification for such quality information equipment.

When changes indicated by the tests on prototypes have been incorporated into the drawings and manufacturing planning and the necessary processing equipment has been secured, manufacturing begins output of a small number of parts on production tools. As soon as enough parts are available, a pilot assembly run is started.

18.14 Operation of This New-Design Control Routine—Final Design and Product Qualification

In the collection of information from this pilot run on the first production parts, the statistical tools of quality control are again used to good advantage.

4ZP96B3–12 – QUALITY CONTROL STUDY

CONTACTOR CALIBRATIONS AND ACTION

TEST RESULTS

Results:

The resistance of the coil was found to be 74.1 ohms at 24.0 C.

Table I shows the pick-up, drop-out, and seal-in voltages for various shim thickness and gaps at the end of the plunger in the picked up position. The voltages were calculated from the average values of current using a resistance of 74.1 ohms, and the gap was calculated from the angle through which the pole piece had to be turned to close the gap. As the table shows, the only point where "hang-up" occurred was during pick-up with zero shim thickness and a 21.2 mil gap; for this case, the seal-in value higher than the pick-up value.

TABLE I

Shim Thickness Mils	Gap Mils	Pick-up Volts	Seal-in Volts	Drop-out Volts
0	17.5	13.75	13.15	4.01
5	17.3	14.20	13.95	3.87
11	18.1	15.25	14.00	3.91
16	18.1	15.55	14.22	3.82
0	20.1	15.95	15.13	3.93
5	20.1	18.10	18.05	3.95
11	20.1	17.50	15.35	3.97
16	20.1	17.45	15.40	4.09
20	20.1	17.60	16.10	4.04
26	20.3	18.15	15.30	3.99
31	20.3	18.85	15.50	4.05
40	19.05	19.80	15.39	3.93
45	19.05	21.10	15.50	3.96
52	19.05	20.57	15.98	4.08
56	19.05	21.10	15.95	3.88
61	19.05	22.79	17.97	3.89
0	21.2	15.50	16.85	5.90
31	10.5	16.35	12.95	2.48
61	0	18.20	10.66	2.04

The results of contact-closing bounce tests are shown in Table II. These tests were made using an electronic bounce recorder. For these tests the gap at the poles was set to 0.020 in., and the coil was energized at 28.0 volts. The contact bar was 1/8 in. thick instead of 5/32 in. which it will be in the manufactured device.

TABLE II

Drum Speed	Shim Thickness	No Bounce	Number of Operations 1 Bounce	2 Bounces	3 Bounces
Fast	0	34	0	0	0
Fast	0.031 in.	2	33	5	
Slower	0.061 in.	0	30	7	11*

* It was almost impossible to tell whether there were 2 or 3 bounces, but it looked like 3.

FIG. 18.7

Frequency-distribution studies are made on the important dimensions of the critical parts in the assembly. Such distributions reveal whether the manufacturing processes, in their present condition, will produce parts within the specified tolerances.

Figures 18.10 to 18.12 illustrate statistical analyses on parts produced by three punch-press tools—drawings 934782, 934784, and 934787. These tools, developed specially for production of 4ZP96B3-12 mechanical components, are set up on presses in the plant tool room. Fifty parts are manufactured by each tool.

The frequency distribution of Fig. 18.10 illustrates that tool drawing 934782

GENERAL PROCEDURE FOR INSPECTION BY
"OPERATOR" OF SEALED RELAY ASSEMBLIES

I.   SUBASSEMBLY

Process instructions and/or other supplementary written instructions will exist at work stations describing such things as:

    A) Setup
    B) Method of test or inspection
    C) Number of samples and frequency of operator check
    D) Instructions as to action in the event of failure. One failure consti-
        tutes rejection unless otherwise specified
    E) A log and/or samples indicating time of operator and inspector check
        for purpose of "evidence of inspection"

II.   ASSEMBLY AND ADJUST OVERCHECK

Unless otherwise specified by check lists, the following inspections and/or
tests are made on each relay:

    A) Tip pressure
    B) Tip gap
    C) Pick up and drop out
    D) Hi-pot (after cover assembly)
    E) Contact resistance (after sealing)
    F) Leak test

III. AUDIT (ROVING) INSPECTION

Each relay line type will have at least one in-process inspector who will monitor each operation to ascertain "process in control" by:

    A) Sampling in accordance with the method described for the particular
        operation
    B) Examining evidence of operator inspection
    C) Stamping the log in the appropriate column, accept or reject
    D) Taking the necessary action in the event of reject by tagging operation,
        impounding material, continuing investigation beyond the particular
        work station to ascertain extent of "process out of control"

Immediately on rejection, notifying the manufacturing foreman and quality control
foreman, as required so that immediate corrective action can be instituted.

W. E. John
SUPERVISOR
QUALITY CONTROL

FIG. 18.8 A section of a quality plan.

will produce parts satisfactorily within tolerances. Figure 18.11 shows that
parts produced by tool drawing 934784 do not meet specification limits. The
frequency-distribution picture indicates that this tool must be repaired or
replaced before it is used for regular production.

Tool drawing 934787 also must be repaired or replaced but for a different
reason. Figure 18.12 shows that the tool produces parts within tolerance limits but that the parts thus produced are very close to the tolerance limit in

---

SPECIAL ASSEMBLY TESTER
A P C A T
SPECIFICATIONS

A.   Purpose

The purpose of this specification is to outline in general terms the requirements for an item of information equipment that will provide a static and/or dynamic functional test on all circuits of each printed circuit assembly manufactured by this company.

B.   General Specifications

I.   Power Supplies

a.   D. C. Voltage Power Supplies

This company has standardized on input D. C. voltage levels of 6 volt multiples; ie., 6, 12, 24, 48, and 18 VDC. The input voltages should be variable over a ra~   Ripple should be
readi~

~ the 250 cycle sine w~   ~ ≤500 ma.

II.   Input Power Program Requirements

a.   All D. C. input voltages should be capable of being programmed into the tester distributor over a range of ±20% full scale.

b.   The A. C. power supply shall be capable of being programmed into the tester distributor at 208 cyc., 250 cyc, and 312 cyc. ±5%

c.   The one shot step pulse input shall be capable of being programmed repetitively of from 1 to 10 pulses.

III.   Programmed Load Requirements

a.   M~

FIG. 18.9 **Quality information equipment specification.**

the direction of tool wear. If this tool were used during production in its present condition, it would have a much shorter life before a repair was necessary than would be economical and would soon begin to produce defective parts.

Quality Control is interested in frequency-distribution analyses of parts from several points of view: sampling inspection of outside-vendor die-cast parts, approval of molds, and so on. The design engineer's chief interest in these pilot-run analyses, rather than in such studies of individual parts, is measurements distributions of the overall functional performance of the device. Such performance characteristics as contact pickup voltage, motor starting current, switch actuator travel, and power supply voltage output are expressed by the design engineer frequency distributions.

Through the product reliability studies that have been made, as well as through such basic techniques as sketching specification limits on the frequency-distribution pictures, the engineer secures at a glance an indication as to whether the 4ZP96B3, as designed, will perform within specification limits and

b.   The following circuit must be connected to various output terminals to provide a clamp voltage at the gate outputs:

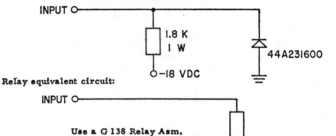

c.   Relay equivalent circuit:

Use a G 138 Relay Asm.

d.   Provisions should be made for adding equivalent load circuits at a future date (a minimum of 10).

IV.   Output Measurements

   a.   It shall be necessary to measure the following:

   1.   Output pulse rise and fall time of from .05 to 5u Sec. ±5%.

   2.   Steady state D. C. output voltage levels of either zero or +6 volts ±5%.

   3.   The duration of a pulse of from 1 micro-seconds to 5 milli-seconds ±2%-- pulse width.

   4.   The delay time between the leading edge of one pulse to the leading edge of a following pulse of from .1 micro seconds to 5 micro seconds.

   5.   In order to establish and verify the input pulse conditions, it shall be necessary to measure pulse frequencies up to 2 MC and pulse widths to .1 micro seconds. This can be done with an oscilloscope to set up the initial test conditions.

V.   Programmed Resistance Comparison

   a.   In order to test for the forward and reverse resistance of diodes mounted on a diode gate board, it will be required to program standard resistance values

(FIG. 18.9 continued)

whether the company can expect a minimum of rejects if specifications are followed throughout. In those cases where poor performance or a substantial number of rejects are forecast by the distribution, the engineer will wish to determine how the unsatisfactory conditions can be eliminated. Special methods may be used by the engineer in those instances where the solution of the problem is particularly complex.

When assembly of the mechanical and electronic components into the control relay final product takes place, the production-oriented area of the reliabil-

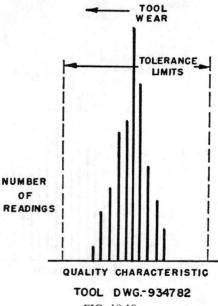

FIG. 18.10

ity program proceeds with the performance of process maturity tests. This ensures that the manufacturing processes are qualified to produce the necessary reliability for the product, whose design reliability was qualified by the earlier design maturity tests.

Together with process maturity tests, assemblies are tested within a customer-use environment, so that the reliability testing area of customer-application reliability and life cycle are evaluated.

In parallel with these tests, product-safety testing (Sec. 18.21) that was initiated during the earlier FMECA tests is completed for safety and product-liability assurance.

Final product qualification testing then takes place, in accordance with the established company quality program and the established qualification criteria. These complete product qualification tests are performed by engineering and quality control and require their joint endorsement of product qualification.

The conclusion of these new-design control activities is the formal release, after a final design review, of the 4ZP96B3-12 for active production. This step is taken as an indication that, if specifications and drawings are rigidly followed, satisfactory quality performance related to its guarantees can be expected from the new device in the field and a minimum of rejects may be expected on the production line.

Figure 18.13 shows the general sequence of the new-design control routine used by this company.

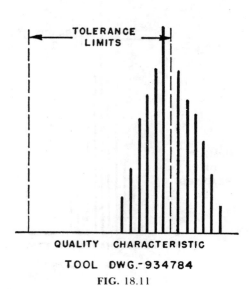

QUALITY   CHARACTERISTIC

TOOL DWG.-934784

FIG. 18.11

18.15 Quality-Control Function's Technical Participation in New-Design Control

As discussed in Chapter 8, the company and plant quality-control function has major quality-systems planning, quality-systems leadership, and quality-systems operation and maintenance responsibility in the new-design control routines.

Quality control, through use of the engineering technology and statistical disciplines of quality, also has major technical responsibilities in new-design control. Figure 18.14 summarizes one approach to structuring some key aspects of these responsibilities.[9]

18.16 Techniques Used in New-Design Control

A large number of technical methods are used in new-design control activities.[10] Many of these were reviewed in Parts 4 and 5. It may be worthwhile, however, to summarize some of the more significant methods that apply to new-design control activity:

Merchandising and Product Planning

The new-design control portion of these activities is carried on from the standpoint of establishing the most economic quality requirements for incorporation in a product which will sell well on the market and satisfy its customers.

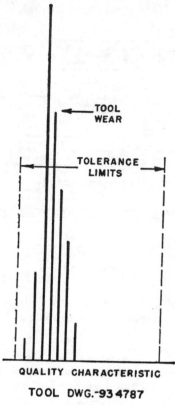

QUALITY CHARACTERISTIC

TOOL DWG.-93 4787

FIG. 18.12

Statistical Analysis of New Designs

Frequency distributions, special methods, and reliability studies are especially useful in answering such questions as "Have enough test runs been made?" "Is the variation to be expected from this product too great for manufacturing purposes?" "What performance can we guarantee for this product?"

Failure Mode, Effect, and Criticality Analysis

FMECA is a procedure for studying the causes and effects of potential component failures, in actual use or reasonable foreseeable misuse or abuse, to minimize the probability of failure and product liability.

Human-Factors Analysis

The target of this type of analysis views the product as to its adaptability to the attributes and capabilities of the human being who will use it. It is primarily

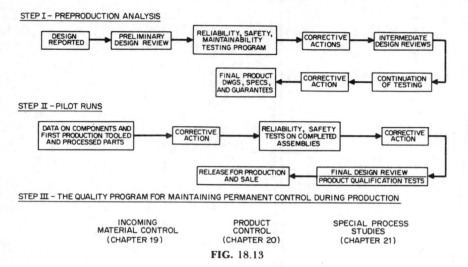

NEW DESIGN CONTROL SEQUENCE

STEP I – PREPRODUCTION ANALYSIS

STEP II – PILOT RUNS

STEP III – THE QUALITY PROGRAM FOR MAINTAINING PERMANENT CONTROL DURING PRODUCTION

| INCOMING MATERIAL CONTROL (CHAPTER 19) | PRODUCT CONTROL (CHAPTER 20) | SPECIAL PROCESS STUDIES (CHAPTER 21) |

FIG. 18.13

concerned with potential factors leading to anticipated use or misuse of a product, with subsequent liability implications.

Tradeoff Studies

These studies consider the product parameters and limitations in which tradeoffs are made among reliability, complexity, weight, cost, safety, performance, failure consequences, manufacturability, and other pertinent product and process factors.

Vendor and Purchasing Department Records

These records are used so as to employ in the new product only parts purchased from those vendors who are most reliable, most quality-minded, and most economical and so that costs for "quality extras" can be eliminated in material purchases.

Process-Capability Studies

Records of the accuracies that can be maintained with the factory manufacturing facilities are of great value in decisions as to the type of product design and parts tolerances to be established.

Data on Old and New Materials

Extensive use is made of the results of laboratory and research engineering's analyses of old methods and their experiments with new materials, processes, and theories of product operation.

QUALITY CONTROL'S PARTICIPATION

Commercial Products

Quality shall be an integral part of the product programming; Quality Control's involvement shall begin in the marketplace, where Quality Control shall gather information for use in defining the quality requirements; and Quality Control shall:

- Participate in market research to gain knowledge of consumer product preferences, consumer demands for quality, how the product will be used and maintained, quality competition among manufacturers.
- Research consumer complaints to define problems and resolve them during product design and development.
- Participate in the considerations that must be made in the development of a new product, such as marketability, consumer satisfaction, warranties, safety, and service system; participate in product considerations for foreign markets, such as cultures, national laws, and product life cycles; and gain knowledge therefrom with which to develop the required quality system.
- Participate in simulation techniques, field tests, and trial manufacturing to accumulate technical knowledge for finalizing the quality system for production.
- Develop quality requirements that are consumer-oriented and tailored to the product as an integral part of developing the product requirements.
- Prepare quality specifications, or quality program plans, or both as appropriate, reflecting the requirements of the engineering or product specifications; defining the quality requirements; establishing the scope and intent of the quality system to be used and its areas of application, such as design, procurement, and manufacturing; and translating any quality requirements specified by the consumer.
- Participate in contract and program-level planning for the product.
- Prepare quality planning to implement the quality system according to the quality program plan or specification; describing the degree and type of quality control required for each part, assembly, and the end product; and providing for the necessary facilities, inspection tools, and test equipment

Government Products

Quality shall be an integral part of the product programming; Quality Control's involvement shall begin with the customer's request for proposal (RFP), in which quality requirements are specified; and Quality Control shall:

- Prepare a quality program plan that is responsive to the RFP, coordinated with other program plans, in accord with the company's proposal philosophy, and submitted as a part of the proposal.
- Assist in pricing the proposal.
- Upon award of contract, participate in program-level planning.
- Prepare quality planning that is coordinated with overall program planning to implement the committed quality requirements according to the quality program plan and to ensure that facilities, tools, equipment, work force, and skills

FIG. 18.14

will be on hand when needed.
- Participate in management reviews of the program progress and status to update the quality programming as required

Design

Quality Control shall participate in design to the extent necessary to ensure that the required quality is designed into the product such that the manufacturing process can build the designed quality into the product and Quality Control shall:

- Establish the mechanics of the quality participation with engineering management in advance and obtain executive support.
- Assign to the design activity quality personnel who are technically competent, experienced, communicative, objective, constructive, and respected by the designers.
- Locate the quality personnel near the design function.
- Provide consultation to the designers and make sure that they understand the quality requirements, concepts, and techniques before the design activity begins.
- Prepare checklists which are suitable for the product for use in design review, including drawing and specification review.
- Participate in the choice of standard and nonstandard parts and in the selection of subcontractors and suppliers.
- Participate in formal and informal design reviews and product reviews.
- Review drawings and specifications and review engineering changes where cost effective.
- Where feasible, participate jointly with tooling or manufacturing engineering, procurement, and manufacturing in design review, including drawing and specification review.
- Evaluate the design for quality requirements, clarity (is understandable to inspection and manufacturing), processing requirements, inspection criteria, nondestructive testing requirements, accessibility for inspection, methods of verifying hardware requirements, controllability of the design (can be inspected, tested, measured, and evaluated, need for inspection tools and equipment, net technology, quality-cost effectiveness of the design (not too much or too little inspection), and quality problems.
- Work out any new methodology specified; acquire any required skills, tools, equipment, or facilities prior to need; and resolve any quality problems at the design stage.
- Document the quality design review and the review of drawings and specifications, showing results and actions taken and comments and resolution of comments as appropriate.
- Make reports on the progress and status of the quality design activity as may be required by the customer or the company management.

Design-to-Cost

Quality costs are an important part of the total product cost and shall be established in time for the allocation of requirements, targets, goals, or bogeys to the design functions prior to the beginning of design activity.

648   **(FIG. 18.14 continued)**

Life Cycle Costs

The quality necessary to meet life cycle cost requirements must be in the product at the time of delivery to the customer, or the product quality is lost to the cause of life cycle costs. To this end, Quality Control must become involved in programming and design as above.

(**FIG.** 18.14 **continued**)

Accumulated Past Product Experience

Examination is made of plant quality data on the actual production performance of earlier models of similar design.

Special Tests in the Plant on Production Units Similar to the New Design

This is particularly useful in new-design control activity under job-shop conditions because it replaces the mass-production type of pilot run.

Component-Reliability Experience Retention

This is necessary to provide a data base from which design and quality engineers can secure necessary parts reliability information.

Field Tests and Reports

This technique is a complement to that retention. Maximum use is made of data from field performance of similar designs. Special tests may be established for this purpose in the field where possible and practical.

Software Design Control

Where software is required in the computer operation of a product design, the design control of this software is essential, as earlier reviewed in Section 10.30.

Tolerance Analysis

Activity here is threefold: to establish the widest possible manufacturing tolerances, to be assured that the "buildup" of these tolerances will not be excessive for proper functioning of the device, and to ensure that the various components will fit together when assembled.

Shop-Practice Tolerance Sheets

These sheets furnish data on the dimensions that can be maintained on standard factory operations which may be called for in the new design.

Standards

Reference is made to plantwide, industrywide, national, and international standards for the product in question and its components. These standards are available in several areas—trade associations, professional societies, government and regulation agencies, ANSI—or by statute, as in the case of medical, nuclear, and many chemical products.

Safety Studies

These studies are designed to ensure that products are not hazardous to customers and users, to operating personnel, interrelated equipment or field engineering personnel; do not constitute an unacceptable product-liability exposure; and conform to requirements established by all applicable product regulatory and certification agencies.

Standardization and Simplification

Techniques for this purpose are used as an aid to the sound design of a new product and for the achievement of the most economical performance-cost balance.

Drawings

With the specifications of the preceding paragraph, drawings constitute the basic core of representing the new product, its tolerances and dimensions, materials, and so on.

Quality Guarantees, and Reports for Sales Purposes

These data highlight the important quality standards for the product; for advertising purposes, they may include how these standards will be controlled during production.

Pilot Runs

This procedure involves the production and testing of samples composed of units of the actual product. It is usually carried out with production parts and the use of production facilities. It helps to determine, before the start of active production, those process improvements or design changes which may be required to enable a minimum of quality difficulties during production.

Planned Inspection

Vitally important during new-design control is the documentation of the quality characteristics to be inspected, the measurement equipment to be used, and the physical location of inspection stations so that suitable guide cards can be prepared for the use and training of the inspection force.

Planned Packaging and Shipping

The choice of the proper container and the proper shipping routine is important for the receipt by the customer of a satisfactory product with a minimum of shifts in adjustment, scratches in finishes, or other quality defects. Provision should be made to make possible tracing of outgoing product in the event of future problems or recall.

Statistical Analyses of Tools and Facilities Specially Purchased for Manufacturing the New Product

The frequency-distribution and process-capability studies are most useful here.

Development of Statistical Sampling Quality Levels

AQL and AOQL values may be established for use on production parts in the planned inspection guide cards.

Maintenance and Retention of All Pertinent Quality Documentation

Quality procedures, blueprints, specifications (including any modifications and revisions) require systematic retention for effective quality program use.

Establishment of a Definite Time Schedule for the New-Design Control Routine

This administrative device is most useful under fast-moving, modern industrial conditions to minimize and eliminate the ever-present hazard of bypassing essential phases of the new-design control activity.

Several of these techniques have been the subject for intensive study both throughout industry and in the universities. The literature reflects much of this attention in such fields as the making and dimensioning of production drawings, the writing of specifications, and computer-aided product and process design (CAD).

Yet the fundamentals of these technical methods are quite straight-forward and relatively uniform in their applications throughout industry. Specific details of each technique are, of course, adapted to the needs of individual plants.

Several of these new-design control techniques were described in detail elsewhere in the book. Those readers interested in considerable detail on others may wish to refer to the literature in the fields in question.

For illustrative purposes, details of six of these new-design control techniques are described below, as follows: "Tolerance Analysis," Section 18.17; "Planned Inspection," Section 18.18; Statistical Analyses of Tools Specially Purchased for the New Product," Section 18.19; "Failure Mode, Effect, and Criticality Analysis," Section 18.20; and "Safety Studies," Section 18.21.

18.17 Tolerance Analysis

The technique of tolerance analysis takes many forms in various companies. The procedure used in an Atlantic area plant represents, however, the typical fundamentals. This procedure is listed below:[11]

1. A tolerance analysis is required on all new devices before they are placed in production.
2. The analysis must be recorded on a special drawing.

3. The reference number of this analysis drawing must be recorded on the device drawing.
4. The design engineer's signature must appear on the tolerance analysis drawing before it is completed.
5. The proper time in the new-design control routine for making the tolerance analysis is determined by the design engineer and the quality engineer.
6. In those unusual cases where the design engineer waives a tolerance analysis, the analysis drawing must be made out. The facts must be so stated on this drawing and a number assigned to it and recorded on the device drawing.
7. The analysis will be made by the person drafting the device, with the assistance of the design engineer.
8. An analysis will be made on old existing designs only when a problem arises in the factory requiring such an analysis.
9. The analysis will cover such points as:
    a. All important functional dimensions.
    b. All specified limits either on assembly drawings or in specifications.
    c. All parts which have to be assembled and which must fit together.
    d. All spring loads at various compression, tension, or torsional stages, depending upon the variations of the spring space available. If necessary, this analysis can be made on graph paper and assigned a number. This number must be cross-referenced on the tolerance analysis record drawing.
    e. Such other auxiliaries as bellows and bimetals must also be treated as outlined in step d.
10. All changes or additions made on detail drawings which will affect the analysis must be properly recorded on the analysis drawings.
11. Whenever possible, a single drawing number should be used for the analysis with the use of additional sheets where needed.

Figure 18.15 illustrates one example of such a tolerance record sheet.

The tolerance analysis made according to this routine may be developed in two ways:

1. Using the time-honored procedure where tolerances of parts are added together arithmetically.
2. Using the procedure of Formula (38), as discussed in Section 16.8.

Which of the two alternatives that will be chosen will depend upon the circumstances of each individual product. Where it is possible to run the risk of a certain percentage of assemblies which do not fit together and where the other limitations of Formula (38) can be observed, use of this formula proves practical and economical.

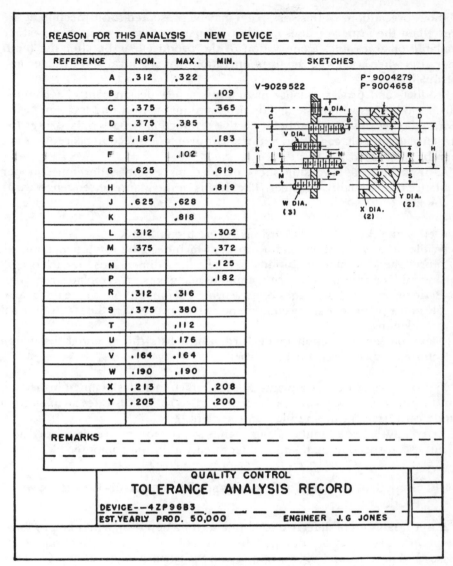

REFERENCE	NOM.	MAX.	MIN.
A	.312	.322	
B			.109
C	.375		.365
D	.375	.385	
E	.187		.183
F		.102	
G	.625		.619
H			.819
J	.625	.628	
K		.818	
L	.312		.302
M	.375		.372
N			.125
P			.182
R	.312	.316	
S	.375	.380	
T		.112	
U		.176	
V	.164	.164	
W	.190	.190	
X	.213		.208
Y	.205		.200

SKETCHES: V-9029522   P-9004279 P-9004658

REASON FOR THIS ANALYSIS   NEW DEVICE

REMARKS

QUALITY CONTROL
TOLERANCE ANALYSIS RECORD
DEVICE--4ZP96B3
EST.YEARLY PROD. 50,000   ENGINEER J.G JONES

FIG. 18.15

18.18 Planned Inspection

An important factor during the final development of the details of the new-design control portion of the quality program is the establishment of the kind and location of inspection that will be required during active production.

Without precautions of this sort, parts may be presented for inspection at the time when the inspector does not have proper measuring equipments either available or accessible. Examination of the product may be after the tenth operation when it may be the third operation that is critical and troublesome for quality.

Product- and process-quality planning is a new-design control technique which establishes within the quality program the quantity and location of the required types of inspection before active production is started. It assures the presence of suitable gages and fixtures. Hit-or-miss inspection procedures are thereby minimized.

As used in a metalworking shop, planned inspection is developed under guidance of the quality engineer. The details of the planning sequence are as follows:

1. Determine the critical dimensions for each operation.
2. While making out the planning sheets which describe in sequence the required metalworking operations, list the critical dimensions for each operation and specify the measuring equipments, gages, or templates required.
3. Place orders for those gages or measuring equipments which are not available in the plant so that the equipments will be present for the start of formal production.
4. Make out an inspection guide card, which lists the essential inspection information required for each part.

Figure 18.16 illustrates a planning card, which includes planned inspection for the punch-press work on a support.[12] Figure 18.17 illustrates an inspection guide card used for a yoke plate in the plant.[13]

As computerized manufacturing planning procedures are developed in a plant, this inspection planning is integrated within the computer planning.

18.19 Statistical Analysis of Tools Specially Purchased for the New Product

Large quantities of defective components for a new design may be produced before the inaccuracy of a new punch-press tool is discovered. Both high scrap losses and production holdups may result. Statistical analysis of new tools and processes is a new-design control method which aims to eliminate this condition by examining a sample of the parts produced by the tool or process as soon as it has been received from the outside vendor or from the toolroom of the plant.

A typical routine for accomplishing this objective is listed[14] below as it operates in actual practice.

All new tools shall be identified with yellow-colored metal disks and shall be subjected to the following routine before being used in regular production:

TITLE SUPPORT		IDEN. 6908866		PT.	GR.
DRAWING CHANGES		RATING			
PRICED	DATE	FIRST PLAN QTY.	CARD NO.	NO. OF CARDS	DISTR.
	BY				
PLANNED	DATE	PLAN CHGS	OPER. NO.		
			DATE		
	BY		SIGNED		

PT. NO.	MATERIAL SIZE	NO. OUT	SPECIFICATION	R ST. SN.
	.075 X 1"			
	B11-H16-A1			

OPER. NO.	OPERATION	PRICE	PER	RTG. SYM.	S/U	A.E.R.	WORK STATION NO	TOOLS	MACHINE
1	SLIT 1" WIDE						15-1		
2	PRC & BLK						15-1	DIE 6908865 .096" GAGE	
3	ANNEAL						TOOL ROOM	TOOLROOM TO CHECK FOR PROPER ANNEAL	
4	1 ST. FORM						15-1	DIE 6908865 GAGE FOR .218 ± .005 INSP. FOR SQ. BEND	
5	FINAL FORM						15-1	DIE 6908865 GAGE FOR .130 ± .005	
6	TRIM SHORT LEG						15-1	DIE 6908865 GAGE FOR .019 ± .002	
7	FINAL INSPECTION BEFORE SHIP'T								

FIG. 18.16

	__Yoke Plate__	INSPECTION INSTRUCTIONS
	__IMII__ CHECK	__IMII__ GAGES

Change No.	1. Ck frac. dims. ≠ 1/8" flat within SR tol.	1. 12" scale
	R2A	
	2. Square within SR tol. Check burrs	2. Scale & square hd.
	IMII	
Part No.	3. Check 2"dim. of cutout	3. Scale
	4. Check 3/8 R & 1/2"	4. Radius gage
	5. Check 1·9/16 & 154 hls.	5. #23 drill pin & scale
	R2B	
	6. After finding one conforming to dwg., by layout method, use this as template to ck. reaming plate	6. Layout tools and Instruments
Drg. 8647954 - 2	R2A	
	7. Check tap holes	7. 6-32 male thd. gage
	8. Check dia. of 9/32 drill holes	8. #12 drill pin

INSPECTION SCHEDULE

AVERAGE QUALITY LEVEL - 2 %   MAXIMUM DEFECTS PER LOT - 5 %

LOT SIZE	SIZE FIRST SAMPLE	ALLOWABLE DEFECTS SAMPLE #1	SIZE SECOND SAMPLE	ALLOWABLE DEFECTS SAMPLE I PLUS 2
1-15	ALL PIECES	—	—	—
16-109	10	0	20	1
110-179	15	0	30	1
180-299	25	1	50	2
300-499	35	1	70	3
500-799	50	2	100	4
800-1299	75	3	150	5
1300-3199	100	3	200	8
3200-8000	150	5	300	13

Note: Split Lots of Over 8000 Pieces

NO.	VENDOR	NO.	VENDOR
1		4	
2		5	
3		6	

FIG. 18.17

1. The tool section shall make 25 consecutive sample units using the new tools.
2. The person making the 25 units shall fill out two lavender tags, indicating drawing number of tool, one to be attached to the tool and the other to the 25 samples.
3. The 25 pieces shall be given to the inspection unit for checking. The tool shall remain in the tool section and not be used for production until proper approval on the 25 pieces is received from Inspection.

4. The inspection unit shall inspect all 25 pieces for their critical or functional dimensions as indicated on the planning card, using gages furnished. One of the pieces shall be inspected for all dimensions as called for on the drawing. If any dimensions are found wrong on the piece inspected, four additional pieces shall be inspected for the wrong dimension only. All data shall be recorded on a suitable tally card.

5. The tally card, after being filled in by the inspector in duplicate, shall be presented to the process-control engineer, who will make any calculations required.

6. The results of the calculations will be turned over to the tool section supervisor and the design engineer, who will accept, reject, or recommend further change in the tools.

7. If further change is necessary, the new-tool-approval routine shall be repeated until the tool is accepted for production.

8. After 25 tool-made parts have received approval, the inspector shall O.K. the lavender tag on the tool, which shall be filed in the tool crib. The lavender tag on the parts shall be filed in the inspector's office by the inspector.

18.20 Failure Mode, Effect, and Criticality Analysis

The frequency at which failures occur is the measure of an equipment's reliability. The higher the failure frequency, the more unreliable the equipment. Thus, failure rate is a frequency function; statistically it is relative to the number of failures that would be expected to occur over a large number of cycles, or a long period of time, or in a large number of items.[15]

Failure mode, effect, and criticality analysis (FMECA) normally is performed at the early stages of a new product design, preferably at the same time as the preliminary design review. In essence, it examines all the ways in which a component failure may occur—catastrophic failure, partial failure, or wear out of each component. It is then the basis for review of action already taken or planned to compensate for such events. The mode of failure (such as a switch jammed in the On position) and the degree of user negligence are also considered.

The first step is to identify critical components measured by the seriousness of potential failure to the product, to the user, or to bystanders, although many other factors can contribute to a critical designation. For example, the component failure may cause other components to fail, or the component may be a single source item—or a limited-life item—or one difficult to maintain or replace. The component may be used extensively throughout the product, or it may be one with no proven reliability history.

The analysis includes both the failure mechanism (the cause of failure) and the failure mode (the reaction of the component to the failure mechanism). It also includes the means by which failure is indicated and/or detected; the immediate effect as well as the ultimate effect of the component failure on the system performance; and the effect on production (i.e., must repair be immediate, or can it be done later in an off-duty cycle). It also identifies such things as the hardware items which must be removed to gain access to the failed component, the special tools needed to repair or replace it, and the estimated repair time.

The analysis is usually documented in tabulated form, with listings for each component. Figure 18.5, shown earlier, is an example. The first column lists only those components which meet the critical classification requirement. The possible failure mode and cause of failure is then entered in the second and third columns. The next three columns list the various weighting factors which will be assigned — P, for probability of occurrence; D, for likelihood of damage, and S, for seriousness of failure. In some FMECA analyses, when for a given item the product of $(P) \times (D) \times (S)$ is 9 or greater, the item is recognized as critical. The last two columns describe the effects of failure and how failure can be eliminated through suggested prevention and/or corrective action. This serves as a guide to minimize the number and impact of critical parts.

In cases where critical parts cannot be eliminated, Quality Engineering must establish in quality planning very stringent process control, inspection, and testing for such items. Where possible, a list of critical components by part number, with a description of each model, and a master list by part number in numerical order should be issued and kept current as required. Based on this list, provisions may be made for adequate means of traceability of all critical components in the event of necessity. (Discussion of a traceability program is given in Chap. 20.)

18.21 Safety Studies

In new-design control, the analysis of a product from a safety viewpoint will be geared to identify hazard sources and their possible interaction with users and the environment. This analysis permits an assessment of the frequency and severity of possible injuries, always taking into account intended product uses and reasonable misuses. It also permits the identification of alternative component or end-product designs which might reduce injury risks. The alternatives must be equally carefully evaluated, weighing the changes involved, including possible reduced performance features or convenience. When the latter are sacrificed, to a degree unacceptable by the consumer, inherently greater hazards sometimes result.

One typical approach for identifying and evaluating product hazards is diagrammed in Figure 18.18. Figure 18.19 then gives an abbreviated checklist of some common hazard cources and the associated hazards.[16]

Safety studies take many forms, depending upon the product and application situation—ranging from consumer product safety to aerospace safety stability studies. One large-scale example is the extraction of oil and gas on the Norwegian continental shelf, an activity in which safety considerations are paramount. For the protection of the several thousand persons working on mobile

APPROACH FOR IDENTIFYING AND EVALUATING PRODUCT HAZARDS

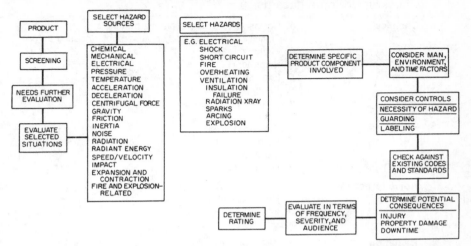

FIG. 18.18 **By permission M. F. Biancardi; reprinted in "Safety in the Marketplace--A Program for the Management of Product Safety," U.S. Government Printing Office, Washington, D.C.**

and fixed rigs in the North Sea, an offshore safety and preparedness program was developed by a number of oil companies, research institutions, engineering firms, and suppliers.[17]

The basic aim of the program has been to improve knowledge and understanding about the circumstances connected with petroleum activity so as to increase the total level of safety and emergency preparedness. In effect, the program has been designed to ensure that petroleum activities are carried out according to the same safety principles as are observed in other high-technology areas, such as the aerospace industry, nuclear power plants, and commercial aircraft.

The program addresses such matters as total risk assessment of offshore activities; human behavior and human relations in the offshore environment; specific technical solutions, including procedures, loading and control, and emergency preparedness. It is concerned with such specific safety considerations as diving and underwater operations, hazard source control, fire and explosions, transport of personnel, and drilling and production equipment as well as with assessment of the structures and foundations of the rigs themselves.

18.22 Some Practical Aspects of New-Design Control

Among the major benefits that a plant and company may gain from the new-design control routines discussed in this chapter are

---

Checklist of Some hazards

Chemical	1. Corrosive to animals, plants, materials
	2. Toxicity by inhalation, skin absorption, ingestion
	3. Flammable
	4. Pyrophoric
	5. Explosive
	6. Shock-sensitive
	7. Oxidizing
	8. Photoreactive
	9. Water-reactive
	10. Peroxide former
	11. Carcinogenic
	12. Decomposes
Noise (pressure)	1. High intensity
	2. High frequency
	3. Impulsive
	4. Vibration
Radiation	1. Alpha emitter
	2. Beta emitter
	3. X-ray emitter
	4. Gamma emitter
	5. Neutron emitter
Radiant energy (electromagnetic or nonionizing)	1. UV emission
	2. Visible light emission
	3. Infrared emission
	4. Microwave emission
	5. Radio wave emission

FIG. 18.19 **By permission M. F. Biancardi; reprinted in "Safety in the Marketplace—A Program for the Management of Product Safety," U.S. Government Printing Office, Washington, D.C.**

1. More effective administration of a coordinated quality program
2. More effective technical methods for use in controlling newly designed products

The first benefit is a matter of administration. It is, therefore, one whose value will take some time to prove. This circumstance is a major problem faced by quality program proponents who wish to institute new-design control in a plant.

These quality proponents, in describing and trying to "sell" company personnel on the ultimate results from the required new-design control procedures, may meet considerable passive resistance. This resistance may be typified by the statement "There's nothing new in that program—we've been doing the work all along. Our interest is in the new technical methods for accomplishing the new-design control objective."

In introducing new-design control under the quite common conditions of this sort, there is no substitute for practical results. Only these results will eliminate the passive resistance and bring home a basic fact to those who question the value of the program; new-design control *does* bring something new and necessary solely in its role of an administrative device which ties together already existing practices, entirely apart from its engineering and statistical methods, pilot runs, or tool and die program.

Quality-control proponents might fail to achieve their new-design control objective if they merely let these individual technical methods be added to the already large host of uncoordinated design-control activities in the factory. The purpose of new-design control—integrated quality planning and assurance for new products—can be accomplished through no other means than by the administrative integration of *all* the design-control activities in the plant. New technical methods can be added to this program as they are required *after* it has been organized.

Several other practical problems are generated because of the administrative objectives of new-design control. There is, for example, the very delicate organizational problem of minimizing friction among the participants in a well-operating program of new-design control. Technical personnel—design engineers, manufacturing engineers, laboratory technicians—will be the key individuals in the program because they have the direct responsibility for important elements of the new-design control program. Yet their activities in this regard are integrated by the quality-control component, which is responsible for integration of quality-control activities but not for the direct responsibilities of these technical people. Sound organization, skillful administration, and wise staff work by the quality engineers and managers are essential to achieving the teamwork required for proper performance under the necessary but delicate organizational plan for effective new-design control.

An administrative problem of a somewhat different sort may also be described. It is represented in the ever-present vigilance required of the quality-control people for maintenance of the company new-design control routine once it has been established.

Many new product designs are pushed through the factory under pressure; it is desired to place the product on the market as soon as possible. All possible shortcuts are taken and all possible obstacles eliminated to permit speedy production of the new articles. Always vulnerable in these drives for shortcuts are elements of the new-design control routine—reliability analysis, field tests, tests of prototype samples, tool and die control, and pilot runs.

Periodically, the quality-control organization may be requested to eliminate portions of this routine to help expedite a "really hot" product. The circumstances of the case may make possible the elimination of a few portions in the new-design control program for some products; circumstances may make such an elimination equally impossible for other products.

When the pressure for elimination still continues on these latter products, it may be necessary for the Quality Manager to refer the matter to company top management. Obviously the ultimate strength of the new-design control program will be directly dependent upon the support for the quality program by company top management.

Indeed, the quality-control component is making one of its fundamental contributions to the health of the company when it opposes the release of a product whose quality is not well enough established for actual production. Whether for industrial, consumer, or defense products, an effort to go to market with new features more quickly than competitors can always be present, and premature production releases have ruined the customer acceptance of several companies without adequate new-design procedures. However, as earlier discussed in this book, the primary, prevention-oriented objective of the new design-control routine must be to assist in the expeditious development of high-quality new designs which "beat" the market, rather than to delay the release of a new design because of poor quality.

On certain "very rush" new products, some plants provide a special routine which achieves the objective of quality planning but which involves a much more concentrated program of new-design control activities than that used under normal conditions. This routine is still an effective one, but it may involve relatively high expense. Both the quality-control component and company top management must approve the use of this routine for a given product, and it is used only in very special cases.

Special new-design control routines for a somewhat different purpose are also established in many companies. These plants have established satisfactory new-design control routines for all the new designs coming through the plant, and they wish to gain benefits from these activities in respect to old designs currently in production.

To accomplish this purpose, they use appropriate elements of the new-design control program for reviewing these old designs. Such new-design control techniques as reliability analysis often produce some extremely effective results in programs of this sort in helping to improve the quality of the old designs being reviewed.

Practical problems faced by quality-control personnel in a plant are not all confined to difficulties in establishing the administrative aspects of a new-design control program. Problems are also encountered in judging how far it is desirable to go in instituting additional design-control technical activities.

The issue is one of long-range economic considerations. New-design control activities should be established in a plant to the extent that the expense of their operation is justified by the value received in minimizing factory rejects, in maximizing customer acceptance of the quality of the product, in improving liaison among the plant functional groups. This value must be judged by the long-range influence of quality planning upon plant economics and not merely upon its effect on day-to-day cost data.

There are many companies wherein quality-control proponents can and should justify a wide extension of design-control activities. It must be recognized, however, that there are other plants where it may be uneconomic to concentrate much additional effort on new-design control; other quality-control jobs may warrant this attention.

There are plants, for example, in which a well-developed new-design control program has grown over the years out of sound company planning. This program may not have formally been recognized as a quality activity, nor can its routines be described in currently fashionable quality-control language. The individuals involved in the program may be reluctant to accept or show interest in either the administrative or technical method aspects of the proposed new-design control program.

This situation may be particularly true in those job shops which may have had to develop new-design control programs for sheer self-preservation in the early days of the plant. A great deal of prudence may be wise for quality-control proponents in situations such as these. Much of the publicity accorded new-design control has been devoted to programs on products produced in mass quantities. This publicity has included "success stories" about highly developed and highly specialized technical methods.

Less polished methods, on the other hand, may be perfectly satisfactory in accomplishing equally satisfactory quality objectives for the job shop. Here, rapid turnover of types of articles may make it overly expensive to develop sets of techniques as highly specialized as those often publicized in connection with mass production.

In plant situations such as these, quality-control proponents should assure themselves that they propose technical methods on the merits of these methods alone in accomplishing the new-design control objective, apart from the amount of "window dressing" that may accompany inauguration of these methods. The quality-control proponents should be certain that they are not promoting new technical methods simply because these methods seem to be necessary for a "completely well-seeming program of new-design control." In effect, therefore, quality-control proponents must be certain that the methods and techniques they propose are those which are best adapted to the needs of the particular plant, apart from those which may simply look good on paper.

Because new-design control programs throughout industry reflect this effort to adapt the type of routines used to the needs of individual plants, these programs take many forms. The activities accompanying them may be described in a wide variety of ways. Discussed below are five examples of new-design control activities of this sort as used in industry:

1. Section 18.23 discusses the application of an individual technical method —pilot runs—as part of a new-design control program.
2. Section 18.24 then documents, from an organizational and human relations point of view, an example of teamwork between design engineering and quality engineering in a vessel-detection project under government contract.
3. Section 18.25 describes qualification test procedures on telecommunications equipment.

4. Section 18.26 describes reliability testing on electromechanical equipment.
5. Section 18.27 describes the overall new-design control program established for planning the quality of a new electromechanical switch.

18.23 Pilot Run to Determine Spring Specification

Part of the program on the pilot run of a new mechanical product was to determine the specification that should be established for the tension of a main spring at the final preshipment test on the product. An upper limit for this spring tension was desired.

The design engineer wished to establish this upper limit during the pilot-run program on the new article. This pilot run was made on units manufactured by actual production facilities.

Data were taken on the spring tension of the first 100 assemblies that were put through the pilot run. All these units performed properly functionally. Figure 18.20 shows the frequency distribution of these data taken on spring tension of these satisfactory units.

From this information, the design engineer computed probability-paper plot, which is shown in Figure 18.21. From this plot and its accompanying calculations, the design engineer was able to establish an upper spring tension limit of 15 grams.

Experience during actual production of the new device indicated that this upper limit value helped the production of products of satisfactory quality.

18.24 An Example of Quality/Design Teamwork

A New England firm was awarded a Navy contract to develop an advanced array concept for seagoing vessel detection. The project presented some rather unique and difficult problems in design and assembly controls as well as stringent performance and reliability requirements—all within a tight 9-month delivery schedule and with a bare-bones budget. Management's first move in getting the project off the ground was to handpick a quality engineer as a permanent member of the plant design team.[18]

TENSION IN GRAMS	TALLY
7	X X X X
8	X X X X X X X X X X
9	X X X X X X X X X X X X X X X
10	X X X X X X X X X X X X X X X X X X X X X X X X X X X X X X X X X X X X X X X X
11	X X X X X X X X X X X X X X X
12	X X X X X X X X X
13	X X X X X X

FIG. 18.20

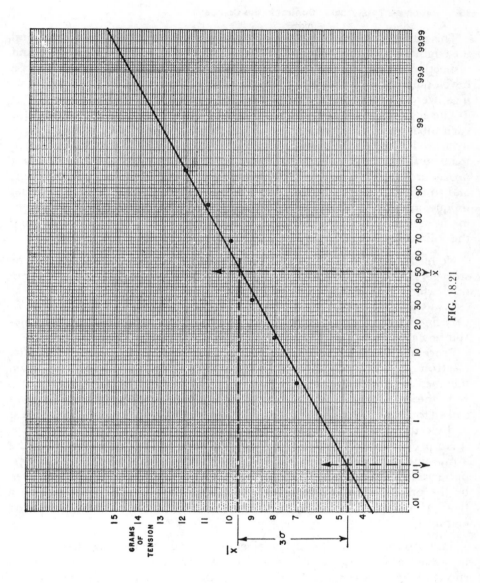

FIG. 18.21

This quality engineer's first responsibility was to generate a quality plan, and the engineer had to incorporate into it the in-process assembly, test steps, and inspection. Above all, the engineer had to remain flexible because this was a developmental program: For example, only photographs, rather than drawings, were available for certain lower-level assemblies.

The engineer's next responsibility was to prepare inspection instructions for each subassembly, including those to be assembled at the manufacturing facility as well as the engineering facility. Other normal quality functions also had to be performed: preparing instructions for receiving inspection, review of test procedures, witnessing test and quality surveillance of the engineering labs, and so on. As a team member, the quality engineer's position was somewhat unique; any corrective action requests for discrepant conditions the engineer might recognize were self-addressed. Among the problems encountered were the following:

No means existed to protect the complete array during assembly, transit, or storage. The quality engineer designed combination assembly/loading/tote trays which did the job.

It was difficult to split the array cable precisely because of a combination of very fine wire and extratough jacket. The engineer designed a special cable-splitting tool.

Process instructions were lacking in many operations of the array cable, the electronic boards, and other intricate assembly operations. The quality team member developed them.

As the date for sea test approached and schedules grew tighter, there was a need for someone to take responsibility for assembly and test of array harness and electronics. The engineer volunteered.

No procedure was available for the sequence and method of loading the arrays into their deployment tubes. What could have been a hit-or-miss type of operation was carefully procedurized by the quality engineer and approved by the project engineer. Several design problems—one of which caused a temporary setback—were resolved on recommendations made by the quality engineer.

The upshot of this quality involvement in an engineering development program was thoroughly satisfactory. The system was sea-tested on schedule, successfully deployed on the first try, and operated perfectly without any system failures. Plant management assesses these positive results as stemming from three key factors. First, the commitment came from the top and involved personnel were made aware of that fact. Second, the program manager helped enforce the controls established by quality control. Third, the quality engineer chosen for the team possessed not only the necessary skills but those personal qualities which made the engineer an especially effective team member.

18.25 Testing New Products

Quality control of new products at the completion of the development phase and before they are released to the field is a particularly important activity of the quality program. If not promptly identified and corrected, the quality problems which appear in any new product can quickly turn a manufacturer's budgeted profits into losses if units have to be recalled and refitted; and even when the situation is less extreme, there is the risk of a very real loss of customer goodwill. There is nothing new about this problem, but it has been intensified today by competitive pressures which reduce the time possible for new product development and price strictures which prevent overdesign and the use of generous safety margins.

To minimize these problems, a worldwide manufacturer of telecommunications products introduced a new procedure for testing the qualifications of a new product, electronic telephone exchanges, and a key subsystem, the computers that control them.[19] The purpose of the testing program was not to discover what was wrong with the product but to give assurance that the product was completely right—fundamentally a quite different approach. To this end, only those samples expected to pass were to be submitted for qualification testing by the development team.

Instituting and implementing the qualification test procedures were joint efforts of the firm's technical and quality staffs, who worked together on standards for qualification testing of several hundreds of products and then put the standards into action. An important part of the program was training technical and quality program managers and senior executives in qualification testing. These two courses were given to hundreds of executives and engineers.

Among the highlights of the qualification policies and procedures were the following:

1. It was made clear that qualification testing was not an "open-ended" investigation. In this application, its purpose was as a test for conformance to defined requirements. Technical personnel were required to formally issue a product specification and a qualification test specification.

2. While some of the tests could be performed by technical personnel, all these tests had to be audited by Quality Control for objectivity and conformance to specification. Quality Control wrote the formal qualification test reports to the general manager. Such reports were short, comprehensible, and definitive, giving the manager the assurance that testing has been properly performed.

3. No new product could be handed over to the customer until it has passed its product qualification.

18.26 Reliability Testing

To be fully effective, it is essential that the reliability program for a new design measure the reliability of the product at several steps in its development cycle. This makes it possible to know the potential reliability of the product design, the reliability of the product as it is produced by the production process, and the life expectancy of parts likely to wear out first in a product. Once the factors that control reliability are known, it is likely that the reliability of the product can subsequently be maintained at an acceptable level.

A manufacturer of data processing equipment meets this requirement by a program that involves design maturity testing, process maturity testing, and life testing.

These test schedules are set up well in advance so that the reliability improvements can be integrated with the achievement of high-volume shipments. Recognizing that the personnel needed to repair failed machines and find permanent corrective action far exceed the personnel needed to gather and analyze test data, there is heavy emphasis in this firm upon the latter.

Design Maturity Test

This test measures the mean time between failures (MTBF), as earlier discussed in Chapter 17, for a new product before it is committed to volume production. Generally, a failure is considered any malfunction that prohibits the product from performing according to its specification, particularly anything that would necessitate a field service call. The MTBF may be an indicator of the residual design problems remaining in a product design.

The test is usually conducted when the first prototypes have been completed and checked out to the design engineers' satisfaction. It is conducted by Reliability Engineering, whose responsibility is to operate the equipment and record and analyze the data. Product Engineering provides close technical support during the test.

The test is accomplished by functionally operating the test samples to simulate actual customer use for a prolonged period (typically 2 to 4 months). As failures are observed and recorded, they are classified by their similarity (i.e., symptom, failure mode, time, or environment cause). Similar failures are then ranked in groups in decreasing frequency of occurrences. This establishes a priority order for eliminating the causes. After the root cause of the failure is found and corrective action taken, the operation of the modified or repaired test samples provides true closed-loop evaluation of the effectiveness of the change. By iterating this sequence, the design or the test samples are improved until their measured MTBF meets the specification.

Test data are recorded in a way that provides a continuing narrative record of the sequence of events happening to each test sample, together with the environmental conditions and total running time of the test Figure 18.22 is an example of a failure report.

Failure Report Summary

Serial Number _____
Problem Number _____

When Failure Observed: Date _____   Time _____
When Failure Occurred: Date _____   Time _____
When Restarted: Date _____   Time _____

Failure Observations: _____

_____

_____

_____

Complete The Following Items, if Applicable: (*circle*)

1. Print head position	Left	Right	Col. # ____
2. Loss of position	Left	Right	
3. Fuse blown	Center	U. Left	U. Right
4. Motor condition	Hot	Warm	Cold
5. Paper jam	Left	Right	
6. Carriage binding	Yes		
7. Line feed status	Adjust		
8. Print quality	Bad		
9. Encoder: Checked	Good	Bad	
Adjusted			
10. Ribbon: Feeding	No		
Reversing	No		
Rivot Against Sensor	Left	Right	
Sensor Arm Binding	Yes		

Corrective Action: _____

_____

_____

_____

FIG. 18.22

Process Maturity Test

This test is a 96-hour burn-in of the first 120 production units. It is designed specifically to ensure that the product design which was qualified by the design maturity test and the process which is to produce it are now qualified. The data concerning observed failures are taken and analyzed according to an established procedure to produce a graphical presentation of the failure rate versus time. From this, an economic end of burn-in and the MTBF of the product at the ship point can be determined. A measured value for SHIP MTBF permits accurate projection of warranty and service costs. If the specified MTBF of the product is greater than 3000 hours, and as it and its process approach maturity, it may be necessary to conduct an additional short reliability demonstration to verify that the specified MTBF has been achieved.

The test is conducted at the start of production near the final test area. It is an extension of the normal scheduled product burn-in and is performed under the same conditions. Product Quality conducts the test, interacting with Design and Manufacturing, to make changes to improve the design of process. Reliability Engineering provides consultation.

Each unit in the test is operated with a diagnostic or exerciser program that reasonably simulates customer usage. Failures are recorded precisely during the prescribed time frames set up for the test. The average failure rate for each time frame is calculated and plotted to produce a graphical presentation of the front end of the bathtub curve. (See Chap. 17.) The length of burn-in required to produce units with an acceptably low failure rate is established from this infancy curve. The reciprocal of the failure rate reached at the end of the test provides the inferred MTBF of the product when shipped. Further analysis is conducted to fractionate the various types of failures into general categories and specific modes as a basis for corrective action.

Life Tests

This test measures the life expectancy of components of a unit. The time to failure is measured on a number of samples so that the MTBF and the distribution of each observed failure mode can be determined. In this life testing, a distinction is made between MTBF and MTTF, as earlier discussed in Chapter 17. When the parameters that determine the distribution of particular wear-out failure modes are known, the component life expectancy to various cumulative percent failures can be estimated.

Life testing is performed after the product has demonstrated that the design is reliable as it is manufactured. The product will have already successfully completed the design and process maturity tests and be in controlled production. At this point, the product will have accumulated more than 10,000 unit hours of testing with over 800 hours' operation on a number of samples. The product will have no obvious problems with early wear-out failure.

Life tests are conducted on relatively small sample lots (five to nine units each) selected at random from production that has proven reliable and is well-controlled. Engineering, Manufacturing, and Quality Control work together to perform the tests.

As the test data are analyzed, all failed parts and assemblies are retained. The smallest replaceable unit in which a failure occurred will be analyzed to determine whether the failure mechanism was random or time-dependent. Should a systematic design-related failure mechanism occur, it will be corrected by engineering change order. Autopsy of the failure provides the most reliable way of understanding various mechanisms so the failures can be separated into appropriate classes.

When all testing is completed, a final report is prepared, including all the data taken and analysis performed. It includes conclusions as to the minimum life expectancy of the product's components, identification of components requiring design changes to improve life expectancy, identification of most frequently used repair parts, periodic adjustment and maintenance required but not described in manuals, adjustments and maintenance that should be eliminated by design improvement, and projected maintenance costs based on test experience.

Reliability Results

Among the many beneficial effects realized by this firm as a result of its reliability program, management has counted the following as the most important:

1. Engineering change order activity has been minimized and concentrated at the start of the program.
2. Potential problems in the design and manufacturing process can be readily identified and avoided by advance planning.
3. Unit reliability is known and controlled from the start, eliminating the need for hurried reliability-improvement programs.
4. The transition from engineering to manufacturing is accomplished rapidly, minimizing engineering support so that engineers are free to be reassigned to new product development.
5. The processes involved in producing the product have become routine and well-understood, allowing concentration on efficiency.
6. Customers are receiving reliable units. Sales have increased.
7. Training, field service, and spare parts logistics have been improved.

The testing schedule is set up well in advance; if not scheduled from the start, the resulting needed improvements to the product will cause a delay in the anticipated achievement.

18.27 Overall New-Design Control Program on a New Electromechanical Switch

Facing the problem of designing a new electromechanical switch to better help the company meet competition from other manufacturers and to provide a high-quality product, an eastern factory drew great benefit from its new-design control routine.[20] The steps of this routine, as they were applied to the new switch, are listed below.

Establishing the Quality Requirements

The first step in establishing the quality standards for the new switch was a product evaluation. Existing switches were compared in regard to their mechanical and electrical characteristics, accessibility for repair, and ease of inspection and servicing. Mechanical and electrical life tests were run on several samples of each switch type used in the study, and careful analysis of other characteristics was made. The result was factual data on mechanical and electrical reliability and a tabulation of other desirable features for the quality required in the new switch.

The wide background of experience available in the company from previous new-design control activities was a second source of quality requirements. This know-how in the minds of the design engineers draws them away from designs that might later be subject to trouble. It correspondingly draws them toward new standards of quality derived from knowledge gained from past mistakes and troubles or gained from specialized experience in the application of other switch designs. A similar type of experience was available in the form of various standards. These standards contain many requirements set down as the result of experience in obtaining high-quality components, such as enclosures and contacts. They are generally expressed in the form of data such as temperature rises, ratings, or test requirements.

A third source of quality requirements was new developments in materials, processes, and understanding of the theory of electromechanical switch operation. These developments pointed the way to new quality standards. Many quality improvements incorporated in the new switch were made possible because of these new developments.

The accumulation of these quality requirements resulted in the writing of functional specifications for the new product. These specifications outlined the performance required.

Completing the New Design

The specifications that were thus written served as the bench mark for preliminary production drawings and prototypes of the new switch. The design engineers looked to these specifications for the required mechanical and electrical reliability, the standards to be followed, demands for corrosion protection, types of enclosures required for special conditions, voltage ranges, and special requirements.

While design of the new product proceeded, consultants and experts from the engineering group of the plant and from its laboratory were frequently called upon for advice in the selection and use of materials and processes. Working through the purchasing agent of the plant, the design engineers and planning people cooperated with outside vendors to determine the highest reliability parts available at acceptable cost.

Evaluating the New Design

After preliminary production drawings were prepared, prototype samples of the new switch were manufactured. These samples were critically analyzed and tested. The test program amounted to an audit of the new design by qualified persons. The original functional specifications were used as the criterion of performance.

The evaluation carried on during this test program consisted of three phases. The first was analysis of overall switch performance, having to do with such functional features as arc interruption, temperature rise, pickup voltage, and noise level. The second phase was materials examination by experts to evaluate whether proper use was made of materials in the new design. The third phase involved mechanical and load reliability tests on samples containing an ample number of switches. The objective here was to determine the life that could be expected from the new device under actual end-use environmental conditions. The three phases of this test program culminated in a report which was critically analyzed by a project team in a review of the design.

The results of these tests were incorporated into final production drawings. When actual production tools and facilities were available, a pilot run of production units was manufactured and a critical evaluation again made of all phases of switch performance. Any quality problems showing up in this pilot run were immediately analyzed, and the required corrections were made in the design of the new switch and in the plan for the quality system that would control the switch.

Groundwork for Maintaining Quality During Actual Manufacture

One of the most useful means for assuring the maintenance of quality during manufacture was the completion of a program of tolerance analysis of all major parts and assemblies. This analysis was made an integral part of the production drawing structure so that it could not be bypassed. Figure 18.23 shows an example of such a tolerance analysis.

The tolerance analysis program was also applied to many factors affecting operation of the device, such as the effect of coil turns and resistance on pickup voltage. The performance of the device throughout the possible mechanical variation of its components was thus established.

Early in the development of the new device, close liaison and a clear channel of communications were established among the design engineers, manufacturing engineers, quality engineers, and other concerned parties. As a result, the manufacturing organization understood why certain parts types were required and why it was necessary to set up to provide the required quality for these parts. On the other hand, Engineering was informed about potential difficulties in producing certain parts, about economies that could be effected by certain design changes, and so on.

To assist the manufacturing people, specifications were established by Engineering to cover many often overlooked shop details, such as screw-tightening torques, screw and lock-washer hardness, and hardness of the contact tips.

As part of the pilot-run procedure, samples of parts from the new production tools were carefully inspected for variations in their quality characteristics. Frequency-distribution analyses were made as required. Figure 18.24 illustrates some typical distributions made on important switch adjustments.

The plant summarized the benefits it received from this comprehensive new-design control program on its new electromechanical switch: "As a result

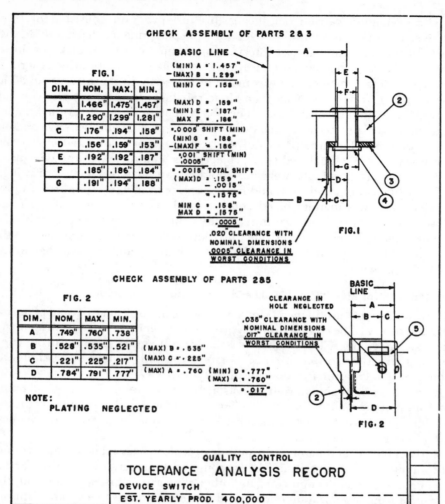

FIG. 18.23

of this work, we know that the new line of devices is technically the best on the market. We have, along with the basic design work, established many of the controls and data necessary to guarantee the maintenance of this high level of quality as production proceeds."

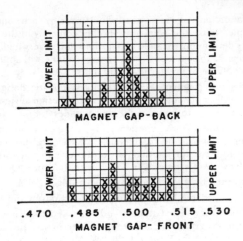

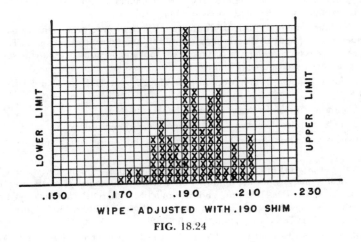

FIG. 18.24

Notes

[1]Chapter 8, Part 3, reviewed the principles underlying such planning, practices, and routines. It also emphasized that the application of these principles must be directed to particular company situations. Chapter 9, Part 3, discussed developing commitment to the point where the quality-control program is capable of carrying on the broad functions of the quality-control jobs.

[2]Some company installations of the individual quality-control jobs may incorporate only a portion of these procedures and techniques. The degree to which these procedures and techniques are used in any company situation depends, as pointed out in Chap. 6, upon the customer satisfaction and economy of that particular situation; these customer-oriented and economic decisions must be worked out for each case individually.

[3]The term "new design" as used in this chapter does not of course refer only to an entirely new product. It refers also to designs which are modifications of existing products.

[4]This policy determination must of course be carefully made by each company or plant for its own conditions. For example, unlike this company, another company in the industry producing products subject to far less demanding uses and applications and in very high volumes has determined that it is satisfactory that its formal new-design control routine will apply to new products which will be produced in a volume of greater than 500 units.

[5]Although not used by this company because of its systematic design-control routine, some companies develop checklists of subjects to be covered in design review—i.e., product function, component reliability, tooling—to improve the thoroughness of their review process.

[6]The relay example is adapted from experience in a composite of applications in new-design control activities, in order to provide completeness of technical presentation for teaching and demonstration. Figure 18.3 and the knurled part of this example are adapted from an article by W. H. Bloodworth, "How the Designer Can Tie in with Statistical Quality Control."

[7]Figure 18.4 is after a study by R. Warr and associates, Ithaca, N.Y.

[8]Figures 18.6 and 18.7 are adapted from a study by C. R. Mason and W. J. Warnock.

[9]Figure 18.14 is adapted from "Final Report and Proposed Doctrine of Principles in Quality Control's Involvement in Programming and Design," International Academy for Quality Project 9, Aug. 14, 1978. Project leader for Project 9 was J. Y. McClure, and project members were John L. Kidwell, Yoshio Kondo, Georges Borel, David S. Chambers, Philip Crosby, John M. Groocock, Masumasa Imiazumi, Masao Kogure, Noboru Yamaguchi.

[10]The term "technical methods" is used throughout to refer to the various individual techniques of the engineering and statistical technologies used in quality-control activities. Thus the term here refers not only to such mechanical techniques as tool and die control but to the several human relations approaches used in quality control.

[11]This discussion is adapted from a procedure developed by R. H. Schmitt and associates, Schenectady, N.Y.

[12]Adapted from a discussion by A. L. Fuller, Schenectady, N.Y.

[13]Adapted from a card developed by H. C. Thompson, Schenectady, N.Y.

[14]Adapted from a routine developed by W. T. Short, W. E. Polozie, and associates, Schenectady, N.Y.

[15]The principles of product reliability were reviewed in Chapter 17. For reviews of failure mode, effect, and criticality analysis, see the following on which this discussion is partly after: Irwin Gray, with Albert L. Bases, Charles H. Martin, and Alexander Sternberg, *Product Liability: A Management Response*, AMACON, New York, 1975; D. R. Earles and M. F. Eddins, "Reliability Physics (The Physics of Failure)," AVCO Corporation, March 1962.

[16]Figures 18.18 and 18.19 are the work of M. F. Biancardi, reprinted in "Safety in the Marketplace —a Program for the Management of Product Safety," U.S. Government Printing Office, Washington, D.C.

[17]After a report by Erik Jersin, "Some Aspects of Safety and Preparedness; Offshore Research in Norway," 1980.

[18]This discussion, which follows the experience of the Ocean Systems Division of Sanders Associates, Nashua, N.H., is described by Albert P. Chaparion, "Teammates: Design and Quality Engineers," *Quality Progress*, vol. X, no. 4, April 1977, p. 16.

[19]This section is after a paper by J. M. Groocock, "A Decade of Quality in a European Multinational Corporation," presented to the Institute of Quality Assurance, Great Britain, 1977.

[20]This discussion is adapted from a study made by A. W. Bedford, Jr., and associates, Schenectady, N.Y.

CHAPTER **19**

Incoming-Material Control

Many types of materials, components, and subassemblies are purchased by companies and contribute to the ultimate reliability and safety of the end product in use. These materials, parts, and assemblies run the gamut from steel sheet, castings, and forgings to machined parts, fluids, tapes, and hardware and an array of electronic devices such as integrated circuits, resistors, and printed circuit boards.

With today's increasingly complex products, the quality of these purchased materials[1] becomes increasingly important. That a safety problem in the field was caused by a part or component made by someone else is of little comfort to the producer faced with mounting customer complaints, profit-eroding warranty expenses, or the obligation to trace and recall large numbers of products to the factory. Activities for assuring the consistent high quality of purchased materials are therefore basic to programs for total quality control.

In the past, approaches to controlling the quality of incoming materials have ranged widely—from the very informal to the excessively rigid. At one extreme, there have been companies whose "control" of purchased materials has largely depended upon what might be thought of as blind trust in the quality standards and performance of their suppliers. At the other extreme, some companies have virtually inspected their incoming materials "to death," spending more time and money than are necessary to gain adequate control of material quality. Neither approach is satisfactory in today's fast-moving marketplace. The high price of the latter extreme is prohibitive, while the former extreme can increase the safety/liability risk beyond reasonable bounds. The objective is to establish and maintain close and positive purchaser-vendor relationships which reflect the reality that each person's success is dependent upon the other's.

The second quality-control job, incoming-material control, deals with techniques for achieving the objective of control while avoiding these extremes and establishing what might be thought of as a purchaser-vendor partnership. After new-design control activity has resulted in the specification of a well-designed product, incoming-material control techniques take over the task of seeing that materials of the proper quality will be available for use during actual manufacture of the new product. These techniques, which provide assurance that all purchased materials have been produced, controlled, inspected, and tested in accordance with quality program requirements, are discussed in this chapter.

19.1 The Needs for Incoming-Material Control

Visualize the following situation: An integrated group of automatic machine tools has started to machine a lot of casting bodies. Tools start to break; castings fail to "clean up." The machineshop supervisor reports to the superintendent that the entire lot is defective because of "hard spots." Since these are the only casting bodies available in the factory, the assembly line on which they are to be used must shut down until new castings can be secured from the foundry. Production stops; employees on the assembly line are sent home.

Visualize an additional situation involving castings: Precision machining is performed at high cost on a pump casting. At the twelfth machining operation, blowholes and porosity show up. These defects cause the scrapping of the casting and the loss of the effort spent on the previous 11 operations.

In both instances, ineffective control over incoming castings was the direct cause of the manufacturing difficulties.

Here is still another case: a small cross-shaped flat spring is carefully inspected for critical dimensions as it is produced by a battery of punch presses. The material specified for this spring is beryllium copper. After they are punched out, the springs are assembled to small electrical devices and serve as a mechanical counterbalance to the electrical force in the coil.

When the devices have been completely assembled, they are tested. After several weeks of satisfactory production-line performance, the devices suddenly begin to fail to meet specifications at this test.

After considerable time, expense, and a long production holdup, the cause of these failures is discovered. A batch of the cross-shaped springs has been punched from phosphor bronze instead of beryllium copper; when assembled to the electrical device, the phosphor bronze springs are unable to provide the proper mechanical counterbalancing force.

The entire production holdup on the device was caused by ineffective material-control activities. An incoming lot was accepted as beryllium copper simply because the material in the lot was "reddish brown and shiny"—a characteristic common to phosphor bronze as well as to beryllium copper.

These are failures detected before shipment. Many similar situations could be cited involving quality troubles in the field. This is one example: Bearings on a certain motor type begin to fail prematurely after only 1 year of operation in the plant of the customer who purchased the motors. The failures are finally traced to low-quality materials that were originally manufactured into the bearing linings.

Since no adequate reliability preshipment test had been performed on the motors, quality depended only on the control of incoming bearing lining materials. An unsatisfactory incoming control routine resulted in the considerable customer dissatisfaction developing from these bearing failures.

Control over incoming material and components may also suffer because of inadequacy of quality information equipment in the plant or careless maintenance of this equipment. Incoming inspectors may lack proper training or sufficient understanding of inspection objectives. They may not be provided with satisfactory specifications for judging conformance of materials.

Modern statistical acceptance sampling tables may be inadequately utilized. Incoming material may be damaged by poor handling during its receipt and travel through the plant. Certain materials which are placed on the shelf after incoming acceptance—insulating strips, delicate electronic components, bellows that require "aging"—may be harmed owing to improper storage facilities. Ineffective means for tagging and disposing materials found defective may result in occasional lots of the material finding their way into active production.

These instances illustrate the first of the three aspects in which the incoming-material practices of many companies have been unsatisfactory in assisting plant management to achieve its quality-product goal: These incoming-material procedures have too often permitted nonconforming materials to be accepted by the plant for use on its production lines.

The second aspect in which these incoming control practices have been inadequate is more directly related to economics. In some plants, the purchasing practice of selecting vendors almost entirely on price—with little attention to quality and delivery capability of the vendor—has resulted in low purchase prices but high ongoing material costs. This has occurred because of the additional expenses created by vendor rejects and by the need to expedite vendor corrective action as well as vendor shipments in the case of what is often called the "low initial price-high support cost" vendor. Such a vendor is likely to contribute to increases in plant quality costs.

Another aspect of economic problems in the incoming-material control of many plants is that incoming-material routines have been unnecessarily cumbersome and drawn out. Too much time and money have been spent to achieve the amount of control that is required for the materials and parts received.

A case of this sort may be briefly described: One manufacturer discovered that his inspection force had been 100 percent inspecting all incoming brass rod for its outer-diameter dimensions. The inspection force kept several charts and incoming-material inspection records on this brass rod; these charts showed the quality performance of the vendor in considerable detail.

The inspection force was quite proud of its extensive control routine for this material. Yet for 14 months there had not been a single reject of brass rod at incoming-material inspection. Obviously, the 100 percent inspection as well as the very considerable charting and recording routine was unnecessarily expensive.

Situations could also be cited illustrating uneconomical material purchase prices that result from an inadequate program of material control. In too many instances, components and materials have been bought at prices which reflect excessive costs for unnecessary quality extras or for special tests and inspections. These special requirements may have been required for applications of these materials at one time; they may, however, have been retained in purchase specifications long after the need for them has passed.

The purchasing group may consider that plant quality-control activities are concerned exclusively with internal factory quality problems and so may fail to gain contributions from these activities. Long-range purchasing efforts to establish "approved supplier" lists may suffer because of inadequate plant records on the quality of shipments by various vendors.

Company relations with respected vendors may be strained in several ways: Purchasing, Engineering, even Manufacturing may make independent, inconsistent contacts with one vendor on a single quality problem. Another vendor may complain bitterly about the rejection of thousands of his parts because of defective finish; he may insist that, according to the standards of his own plant, he has met the purchase specification requirement which states only that "fine finish is required." Still another vendor may embarrass a multidivision plant by pointing out that there is a completely nonuniform interpretation of specifications on the same material among the divisions of the plant.

The third aspect in which companies' incoming-material control practices have been unsatisfactory has been the lack of clearly established relationships between the vendor and the purchaser with regard to quality. One principal cause of this has been insufficient quality documentation covering the necessary quality requirements and quality controls. This has frequently resulted in the incorrect estimate by the purchaser of vendor quality and delivery capability, and the incorrect estimate by the vendor of purchaser quality requirements and quality controls. It has led to different vendor and purchaser understanding in such areas as suitable inspection and test practices, appropriate calculation procedures for quality information equipment, and the qualifications and responsibilities of quality program personnel.

However, even with quality documentation made available, some vendors with limited organizations may not fully familiarize themselves with this necessary information, particularly the information printed on the back of standard purchase orders but sometimes also the information that may be provided for particular supplier situations. Unclear relationships have contributed to such poor communications and delays in necessary quality actions. The end result has been mutually unsatisfactory vendor-purchaser incoming-material performance. Incoming-material control procedures provide the mechanism required to eliminate from company activities these aspects in which earlier control procedures have been unsatisfactory.

19.2 Defining Incoming-Material Control

As a definition:

Incoming-material control involves the receiving and stocking, at the most economical levels of quality, of only those parts whose quality conforms to the specification requirements, with emphasis upon the fullest practical vendor responsibility.

All three technologies of total quality control have application in incoming-material control, as does the statistical point of view in all its aspects. The planning techniques of quality engineering (Chap. 10) and the equipment techniques of quality information engineering (Chap. 12) are extensively used to establish the foundation for incoming-material control activity in the company. It is, however, the actual day-to-day control techniques of process-control engineering (Chap. 11) which are most intensively used in the second job of total quality control.

Among the analytical tools of statistics, it is the sampling tables (Chap. 15) that are most actively employed.

There are two phases in incoming-material control:

1. Control on materials and parts received from outside sources
2. Control on parts processed by other plants of the same company or other divisions of the plant

The scope of incoming-material control routines covers all quality-control activities carried on while material and component purchase contracts and prices are being arranged and these materials and components are being received, inspected, and stocked by the purchaser plant. Incoming-material control involves purchasing, process-control engineering, laboratory, and materials handling techniques as well as techniques in other functional fields. It concerns relations with vendors as far as quality is concerned. It applies to all parts and materials received by the factory for use in production; in some plants it also includes control over materials used in such plant-service activities as maintenance and plant protection. Its importance to a soundly operating, companywide quality-control program is very great under any type of manufacturing condition; under some conditions—chemical batch manufacture, for example—control of incoming material may be the single most important quality-control activity in the plant.

Early material-control routines concentrated most heavily upon incoming inspection procedures. Large areas lined with inspection equipment and peopled with an extensive inspection force were taken as representative of sound control programs.

Present-day incoming-material control technique is not so directed. It recognizes that widespread incoming inspection does not, of itself, relate to the preventive approach of total quality control. Modern incoming-material control activities place strong emphasis upon control of material at its source—in effect, upon close product-quality relationships between the vendor and the purchaser.

Receiving inspection, although recognized as very important, is used as an adjunct to this relationship rather than as the whole of incoming-material control. To further streamline this incoming inspection, statistical acceptance sampling tables are used as widely as possible in place of 100 percent, spot-check, or no inspection.[2]

The vendor whose material is being controlled may be another plant or division of the same company. In these cases, and with a strong companywide total-quality-control program, incoming control procedures may be far less extensive than when the vendor is an outside source.

With outside-source vendors, the objective of close vendor-purchaser relations imposes a definite set of administrative problems upon the company quality-control program. These problems differ in one important respect from those in the other three quality-control jobs: Vendor contacts in incoming-material control involve product-quality relationships by plant quality control with individuals and groups who, except as is provided in contractual relationships, are fully independent of the purchaser plant and who represent a sovereign legal unit. Obligations of these individuals to top management of the purchaser plant may be nothing more than those required by the ethics of business practice.

19.3 Principles of Vendor-Purchaser Relations in Quality

It is therefore essential that the purchaser establish a well-delineated structure—clear to both vendors and the purchaser organization—which guides and governs all key aspects of vendor-purchaser quality relations and administration. Among the principles that must be specifically identified here are that the purchaser will:

- Deal only with vendors whose quality standards and quality results fully and consistently meet purchaser requirements.
- Provide vendors both with adequate data on quality requirements and a means for being informed about the significance of these requirements including, for just one example, guidance concerning the purchaser's practice regarding classification of characteristics.
- Select vendors with important attention to evaluation of their quality capabilities, their ability to understand the purchaser quality requirements, and the willingness and the motivation consistently to meet these requirements.
- Place the burden of quality proof upon the vendor, and the fullest possible and practical emphasis upon utilization of the vendor's own quality-control program.

- Perform receiving inspection and test as part of an integrated incoming-material control program—with attention to the development of vendor quality information and without uneconomical duplication of vendor-based quality-control procedures.
- Measure vendor quality results for clear and mutually understood purchaser-vendor criteria.
- Identify quickly any needed areas of vendor material quality improvement.
- Assume and expect immediate and permanent vendor corrective action where required.
- Audit vendor quality programs where and when appropriate.
- Assist vendors in the development and improvement of their quality-control program, where mutually economical and appropriate.
- Regularly maintain clear, well-communicated, and mutually acceptable close working relationships with vendors on quality matters, not merely in response to problem situations.

It is of prime importance that plant and company quality control implement this structure by developing friendly yet firm relations with vendors in respect to product quality and modern means for its control. Wise vendors will soon come to recognize the commercial advantage of these relationships.

The contacts may take many forms. At the one extreme, with some vendors there may be the occasional interchange of correspondence. At the other extreme, there may be almost daily visits by the purchaser plant quality-control component to the vendor's plant to assist in its efforts to develop a total-quality-control program and, in some cases, the stationing of a purchaser plant employee in the vendor plant to help assure quality results. There is never any substitute for close, direct relationships between purchaser and vendor as a major contributor to effective quality assurance.

19.4 Organizing for Incoming-Material Control

The effectiveness of incoming control activity in a plant is directly dependent upon the caliber of the plan established.

The application of the various techniques of quality control is structured in that segment of the quality activity which relates to incoming material. This program is generally developed by the company quality-engineering unit, in close collaboration with the process-control-engineering unit (also including inspection and testing), which must make the program work. Collaboration in the development of the program is also sought from Purchasing, Engineering, and other concerned functional groups. Objective of the program planning is to ensure that all materials received in the plant will be controlled to the extent required for their satisfactory use in production.

The amount of control required for each type of material received will vary from plant to plant and among the materials received by any given plant. In establishing control procedures for material, consideration must be given to such factors as the size of the inspection force that should most economically be available, the laboratory testing facilities in the plant, and the quality variations allowed by material specifications. The routines must allow flexibility in such matters as inspection sampling schedules so that economical adjustments can readily be made for different incoming-material situations.

The key groups for incoming-material control organization are Design Engineering, the plant laboratory, Purchasing, and Process-Control Engineering.

Design Engineering's role in incoming-material control is the provision of designs and specifications which clearly delineate vendor quality requirements, including the classification of characteristics in accordance with the company new-design control routine.

Laboratory people enter into the incoming-material control picture by maintaining adequate quality specifications for basic raw materials and carrying on some of the detailed tests specified by the quality program for acceptance of complex incoming materials and parts.

Since it is Purchasing's responsibility to establish and maintain direct relations with vendors, purchasing activity is central to plant and company incoming-material control.

Purchasing's responsibility is to work as part of the plant quality-control team so that materials which are of the proper quality and which reflect the right cost so far as quality is concerned are ordered. To develop approved supplier lists, Purchasing must ensure that a close check is maintained to determine the quality performance of vendors once these orders have been placed and shipments have begun.

Purchasing, together with Quality Control, must also ensure that this vendor quality information is maintained as an integral part of the company purchasing management information system and, when this is computerized, that quality is suitably structured in computer software packages. This permits quick quality information retrieval similar to that provided for all other elements of purchase information. Where the plant operates by materials requirement planning (MRP) procurement and production planning and control practices, vendor quality information must be included in the software structure for the MRP computer program.

Purchasing must therefore be closely integrated with vendor quality appraisals and surveys, incoming-material inspection, and all other vendor quality information sources in the plant.

Through this quality-control activity, Purchasing is better enabled, where appropriate, to review purchase requirements established by plant technical groups, to question prices quoted by vendors in meeting the quality requirements, to keep these prices flexible in line with changing quality needs, and to ensure that adequate contacts are being maintained on vendor quality relationships.

The process-control-engineering unit of the company quality-control component is responsible for ensuring the progress and integration of the company's incoming-material control activity. It must work with the program developed by quality engineering and must make use of the equipment provided by the quality information equipment engineers.

Chapter 8 discussed the principal responsibilities of the process-control-engineering unit, pointing out that quality liaison between the company and its vendors, to ensure that the burden of quality proof rests with the vendor, is a major assignment. For one example, problems the vendor has understanding and meeting company quality requirements may, at the suggestion of the company's purchasing component, be reviewed by a process-control engineer and necessary assistance provided the vendor. Typical of other important process-control engineering activities in incoming-material control is to take a major role in vendor quality surveys and appraisals; to assure full vendor compliance with quality requirements; to take a significant part in postcontract award discussions with vendors; to establish any causes of variability in vendor quality and take leadership in reducing them; to assure effective nonconforming materials control; and to help establish and maintain clear vendor performance ratings.

As discussed in Chapter 8, there are several ways of assigning specific responsibilities for incoming-material control to the process-control-engineering unit. In the case of those companies where the receiving and acceptance of incoming materials are a major elements in the business, particularly in companies which are predominantly assemblers of purchased components, it may be most useful to make incoming-material control a specialized activity. It may thus become the responsibility of one or more process-control engineers. In other companies, where incoming-material receiving is a less significant factor, it may be added to the in-process and final-product control responsibilities of a process-control engineer who is assigned to a particular group of products and processes; thus there will be as many incoming-material control assignments as there are process-control engineers with product responsibilities.

Chapter 8 noted that the people who perform routine incoming-materials inspection may also be assigned in several ways. They may be assigned to the process-control-engineering unit itself, when this inspection has not yet been satisfactorily routinized and where technical judgments play a significant part in decisions. This is particularly true in rapidly expanding companies with new products for which quality programs have not yet been adequately defined.

Where incoming inspection has been routinized but where it is still a major factor in incoming-material control because adequate vendor-relations practices have not yet been established, the inspection unit may report through a supervisor directly to the manager of the company quality-control component. Here, process-control engineering audits the adequacy of incoming inspection and is able to concentrate on the technical aspects of vendor-company quality relations.

Where these relations have developed to the point where incoming inspection has been significantly reduced and is highly routinized, the inspectors may be assigned to the appropriate plant manager of Shop Operations. Process-

Control Engineering carefully audits the adequacy and performance of this inspection.

However these activities may be assigned within the process-control-engineering unit of a particular plant, the appropriate process-control engineers will join with the other functional groups to assure the establishment and maintenance of a sound, thorough, and economical program which will provide the right quality material for the plant.

19.5 Pattern for the Incoming-Material Control Routine

Summarized below are important areas in the cycle used by many plants for ordering, accepting, and controlling parts and materials from vendors:

1. Requirements having been defined, materials and parts are requested—generally by company or plant materials management in establishing production schedules.

2. Specifications, drawings, and all necessary materials identification data are secured or developed. All necessary quality information—including quality requirements, quality levels, reliability requirements, relevant quality plans, quality information equipment uses, certification procedures, if any, and similar elements—are secured or developed. Material that has criticality as to safety—including so-called safety parts—is identified and specified.

3. A purchase analysis is initiated to determine the most suitable vendor or, in the numerous cases where company policy requires multiple sources, the most suitable group of vendors. In all cases where a suitable "make-or-buy" evaluation of the material has not been made by Manufacturing Engineering, with the support of Design Engineering and Quality Control, this evaluation is made a part of the purchase analysis.

4. Purchase inquiries are sent to, or invited from, several vendors. The procurement package provided to potential vendors will include a complete package of the relevant quality information. With large procurements, and where appropriate, precontract award meetings are scheduled with suppliers to delineate all purchase requirements, including strong emphasis upon quality requirements.

5. Vendor bids and offers are received from the interested suppliers and reviewed by purchasing with involvement by all functions participating in the plant incoming-material control routine. Vendor capacity to meet quality requirements is thoroughly considered. Existing vendor rating and vendor performance rating data are reviewed to the full degree of their relevance and availability. Vendor sample materials and parts are evaluated, and reliability is confirmed, as appropriate.

6. Surveys of vendor quality capabilities are made at vendor plant sites in those instances where it is desirable and appropriate. This will take place

with major vendor contracts; or with consideration of a new supplier; or where review of the vendor bid and information about quality capabilities are not in themselves sufficient.

7. Vendors are selected and contracts established or orders placed. Vendor quality-assurance requirements are made an integral part of these contracts and orders as appropriate. With major contracts and new suppliers, post-contract award meetings are scheduled with suppliers to confirm mutual understanding of all purchase requirements. Vendor quality-assurance procedures are approved.

8. Contacts are maintained with vendors while they are in the process of producing or securing the material. Quality assistance is provided to the vendor when it is economical and appropriate. Preproduction samples are approved if required.

9. Production material is received by the purchaser plant. It is properly tagged, identified for traceability purposes, and routed.

10. Material is examined for conformance to specifications in accordance with the incoming-material quality plan.

11. Material is disposed—to the production line if satisfactory, for corrective action if unsatisfactory.

12. Appropriate records are kept, including vendor performance rating documentation and material traceability.

13. Information about the material being received is routed back to the concerned plant technical and purchasing people.

14. The records kept are used regularly to review inspection and purchasing practices on the material and to maintain vendor rating and vendor performance rating data.

15. Vendor relations are maintained during the course of shipments by the supplier, including strong emphasis upon close quality communications and the taking of corrective actions as needed.

16. Ongoing vendor surveillance and vendor audit activities are maintained.

Quality-control activity on incoming material correlates directly with this cycle. The activity falls in eight fundamental steps within the total quality program, common to the incoming-material control routines of most plants. Quality-control work is carried on during

1. Material request and material specification (areas 1 and 2, above)
2. Purchase analysis (areas 3 through 6)
3. Vendor selection and order placement (areas 7 and 8)
4. Material receipt (area 9)
5. Material examination (area 10)
6. Material disposal (area 11)
7. Record keeping and follow-through (areas 12 through 14)
8. Vendor relations and vendor surveillance (areas 15 and 16)

19.6 An Example of an Incoming-Material Control Routine

A plant incoming-material control routine can be described which illustrates some details of these eight steps. The routine applies to all materials purchased from outside sources for use in active production.[3]

The plant is a major facility of a large company and produces a broad mix of industrial products which use a wide variety of mechanical, electrical, electronic, plastic, chemical, and other materials. The products are shipped to other plants of the company, to other companies for use in their own products on an original-equipment-manufacturer (OEM) basis, and on an end-user basis to a number of industrial customers.

These materials range from steels, castings, and fluids to detail mechanical parts, electronic components, and electrical and electronic subassemblies. They are received in the plant in quantities ranging from one to two forgings of a certain type to hundreds of thousands of items of hardware.

Material Request and Material Specification

Before Purchasing can act on requests by the plant production-control people for placement of orders for a certain material, it must have adequate specifications for the material. Some of these specifications are made available to Purchasing directly from the company and plant new-design control routine; others are developed as one of the initial steps of the incoming-material control routine. One objective is to ensure that a complete quality information package will be available to be provided to potential vendors as part of the procurement package for preliminary vendor inquiries.

Among the classifications of materials and parts required by the plant are (1) those for new products, (2) those called for in reorders on old products currently in production, and (3) those required in orders of basic raw materials —copper, lubricants—which are needed for all products of the plant and which are ordered in large quantities for economy purposes.

The total quality program in this plant is relatively new. One of the first steps in its establishment involved the development of effective new-design control. Specifications for material of classification 1—new-product parts—become available to Purchasing as one of the results of this new-design control routine.

Material of classification 2—old-product parts—are not, however, available with equal adequacy because new-design control procedures had not been in operation when these parts were first designed. Adequate specifications for basic raw materials are also not fully available, even in the case of those required for new products on which new-design control procedures have operated.

An essential step taken in establishing the incoming-material control routine of this plant, therefore, was to make one of its activities the development of the specifications required for old-product parts and for basic raw materials. A large quantity of these specifications was involved. As a result, priorities were established for their development.

Parts for old designs were specified based upon the reorders for these parts; projects for establishing these specifications were set up when reorders for these parts were in prospect. The parts specifications were developed through the use of a modified form of new-design control routine, in which the design engineer assigned to the product acted as the key individual, in accordance with a routine similar to that discussed in Chapter 18.

In the case of basic raw materials, which are used quite generally in all products, priorities were similarly assigned. These raw materials are purchased in bulk to specifications which apply to requirements for a wide variety of these products. Thus, in contrast to specifications for old parts, this work was organized as a continuing project; as discussed above, the plant recognized that all new basic raw materials would not be specified quickly enough during new-design control activity which concentrates upon individual products.

The raw material specifications are developed by plant laboratory personnel in cooperation with design engineering. Among these laboratory people are experts in such fields as welding, surface finishes, lubricants, chemical testing, and magnetic and radiographic work. The specifications developed by the people include such quality requirements for materials as chemical composition, necessary physical properties, surface finishes, allowable variations in dimensions, and storage and shelf life parameters and safety requirements.

The quality-control component advises the laboratory people in determining some of the elements for these specifications: sampling levels required; critical quality characteristics; reliability considerations, including environmental demands; physical form in which the product should be shipped to the plant for inspection and testing; preproduction samples that may be required; types of tagging, color coding, or other designations necessary to identify the material and keep it segregated; the procedures under which vendor's certification of inspection and test will be accepted at the plant without requiring further inspection; and traceability requirements. When materials or parts require some form of approval by government service agencies, procedures to gain this approval may also be included in the specifications.

While old parts or basic raw materials are being specified as a part of incoming-material control activity, quality-planning studies are conducted just as they are in the normal new-design control routine of the plant. Regular quality-planning cards are prepared, which indicate such details as the dimensions and features to be inspected; the reliability evaluation, if required; the quality information equipment and gages to be used, the type of stamp to be used to denote inspection approval, and the location of this inspection stamp on the material.

These planning cards also identify so-called A materials—those which cannot properly be inspected with standard receiving inspection and testing facilities but which must be submitted to the plant laboratory for tests or for approval of vendors' certificates of inspection and test.

19.7 An Example of an Incoming-Material Control Routine (Cont'd.)— Purchase Analysis

After specifications have been made available to Purchasing, a study is initiated to determine where the material should be placed to permit most economical purchase prices, proper quality, acceptable delivery cycles, and other requirements.

Inquiries are solicited from vendors, who are provided with a procurement package upon which to base their response. This procurement package follows a standard format to clarify requirements for prospective vendors and to ensure that all vendors receive equal and fair treatment.

An essential portion of this vendor information is that which deals with quality. The quality information package for the vendor is made available to Purchasing by Quality Control from all relevant aspects of incoming-material quality planning. Together with the drawings, specifications, delivery requirements, and other procurement information provided by Purchasing, this quality information package includes all quality requirements that will apply to the material. This covers, as they are relevant, such areas as the following:

- Applicable quality standards, including physical, chemical, radiographic, visual, and other standards.
- Applicable classification of characteristics information.
- Applicable safety requirements.
- Quality levels, including AQLs that apply to various characteristics of the material. Figure 19.1 shows a basic form similar to the approach used in this documentation.
- Inspections and tests that are required, including both those to take place in the vendor's facility prior to shipment and those that will be performed by the purchaser when the material is received.
- Quality data to be included with material shipped.
- Quality measurement and method practices to be followed in material inspection and test.
- Reliability test information and records to be provided.
- Material identification requirements, including traceability data.
- Quality requirements to be applied to material packing and packaging, how package and shipping tests are to take place, and in-shipment material preservation requirements.
- Quality reports to be provided on an ongoing basis.
- Process-control limits applicable during production of the material.
- Vendor requirements for advising the purchaser about quality deviations that have been discovered which may apply to the supplied material, and vendor requirements for corrective action and material rework and resupply.

ITEM NO.	TEST REQUIREMENTS	CODE	CRITICAL CHARACTERISTICS	AQL	MAJOR CHARACTERISTICS	AQL

PART NAME   DWG. NO.   SPEC. NO.

QUALITY CONTROL INSPECTION PLAN   PER STANDING INSTRUCTION   SEC.

DIVISION   WORKS

ISSUED BY: SUPERSEDES: EFFECT. DATE:

CHARACTERISTICS AND ACCEPTABLE QUALITY LEVELS (AQL)

CODE LETTERS FOR TEST AND AQL'S ARE FOR PURCHASER'S INTERNAL USE ONLY.

ALL PARTS SHOULD BE TO DRAWING SPECIFICATION IN ALL RESPECTS. THE MOST IMPORTANT CHARACTERISTICS TO BE CHECKED WITH THEIR ACCEPTABLE QUALITY LEVELS ARE LISTED ABOVE. INSPECTION BY THE PURCHASER MAY BE MADE BY RECOGNIZED SAMPLING METHODS. LOTS EXCEEDING THE AQL PER CENT DEFECTIVE AS INDICATED BY THE SAMPLE INSPECTION WILL BE REJECTED AND RETURNED TO THE VENDOR OR, IF NECESSARY TO MAINTAIN PRODUCTION, WILL BE SORTED OR REWORKED AT THE VENDOR'S EXPENSE. THE REQUIREMENTS OF THIS INSPECTION PLAN ARE A PART OF EACH PURCHASE ORDER.

FIG. 19.1

In the case of certain large procurement contracts—such as for high-volume castings, mechanical parts, and electronic components—and of orders for special requirement/high-value material such as control assemblies and safety parts, Purchasing conducts what it terms Preaward Supplier Conferences. These conferences review the material procurement requirements with a group of invited prospective vendors, particularly with vendors with whose material the plant has no well-documented previous experience, to assure full mutual understanding. Quality Control discusses the quality requirements in great detail, including emphasis upon the expected quality relations with the vendors.

As vendor responses and bids are received, they are carefully reviewed by Purchasing, with close participation as appropriate by all members of the plant incoming-material control routine: Manufacturing Engineering, Engineering, Production, and Quality Control.

Quality Control examines the vendor proposal with relation to how it conforms to quality requirements and the quality information package that had been a guide to the vendor response. Attention is also given to the following:

· The plant vendor rating concerning this supplier, if the vendor has served the plant previously. The plant has a very complete computerized vendor rating program, maintained in the plant management information data base for both purchasing and quality-control use. The plant incoming-material control routine requires review of this vendor rating as a condition for all material purchase analyses.
· Vendor quality-cost information, if available or, if appropriate, as it can be estimated within ranges of high probability.
· Vendor rating data on the supplier that are maintained by other plants of the company.
· Vendor data on the supplier that are maintained by other outside sources.
· Discussions with the vendor requesting further information about the vendor's quality capabilities, which may be followed up by a short visit; and the careful examination and corroboration of this information. Figure 19.2 shows a segment of the initial pages of the supplier Quality Capability Information Request sent to those vendors from whom more detailed information is required. Subareas, rather than the full request, will be used as appropriate with some vendors. Some vendors with less clear organizations may not be able to provide information in the fully structured form; this is not negative in itself but indicates that the necessary information about vendor operations must be made clear.

Where available information concerning vendor capability is not sufficient to provide confidence, and particularly with large procurements and in the case of critical material, Quality Control may recommend to Purchasing that a vendor survey be performed. This will involve a thorough on-site review of vendor capabilities. Where necessary, a team from the plant, usually including representatives from Quality Control, Manufacturing Engineering, Purchasing, and other functions as required makes the survey. All vendor surveys are made in accordance with the specific plant procedures for this purpose. Figure 19.3 shows a segment of the Supplier Plant and Equipment Survey outline structure which guides the work of the team. This is supplemented by a Supplier Quality-Control Survey performed during the review as required.

SUPPLIER QUALITY INFORMATION REQUEST
Provided with regard to
Purchase Information Request No. <u>A3798-1</u>

Quality-Control Functional Capability Section

1. Please attach the detailed organization chart for the quality-control function, showing both reporting relations with upper management and internal quality-control departmentalization.

2. Please attach detailed representative position guides for the quality-engineering personnel that are shown on the quality-control organization chart.

3. Please attach detailed representative position guides for the reliability engineering personnel that are shown on the quality-control organization chart.

4. If reliability engineering does not report to quality control, please attach the detailed organization chart showing their reporting relationships and attach representative reliability position guides.

5. Please attach detailed position guides for the inspection and testing supervisory personnel that are shown on the quality-control organization chart.

6. If inspection and testing do not report to quality control, please attach the detailed organizational chart showing their reporting relationship and attach the position guides for inspection and testing supervision.

7. Please fill in the appropriate spaces
   a. The numbers of personnel in the following activities:
   Inspection _____
   Testing _____
   Quality Engineering _____
   Reliability Engineering _____
   Quality-Control Equipment Engineering _____
   b. Please fill in the following ratios:
   Inspection personnel to production workers _____
   Testing personnel to production workers _____

8. Please answer "yes" or "no" in the following and provide a brief description:

   Is there materials failure reporting?

   yes ____   no ____

   Are data maintained on reliability testing and analysis of material failure?

   yes ____   no ____

   Is customer agreement requested concerning design or other changes that impact reliability?

   yes ____   no ____

FIG. 19.2

Is reliability activity performed in accordance with documented procedures?

yes _____   no _____

9. Please attach the applicable sections of plant procedures covering the following:

Disposition of nonconforming material, and its segregation and control.

Tool and gage maintenance and calibration.

Test equipment maintenance and calibration.

10. **a.** Please identify below the quality and reliability records that (1) are available, and (2) may be reviewed by the purchaser, upon request.

B. Please identify below the quality and reliability records that will be provided to the purchaser with each shipment of material.

〜〜〜〜〜〜〜〜〜〜〜〜〜〜〜〜〜〜〜〜〜〜〜〜〜〜〜〜〜〜〜

〜〜〜〜〜〜〜〜〜〜〜〜〜〜〜〜〜〜〜〜〜〜〜〜〜〜〜〜〜〜〜

The above information has been prepared by:

_____

NAME

_____

ORGANIZATION TITLE

_____

DATE

FIG. 19.2 **(Continued)**

In other cases, such as where the vendor-related questions are primarily with respect to quality, the Quality-Control function may make the survey as the representative of the other plant functions, with primary concentration upon quality areas.

A significant area of the purchase analysis activity—with certain material-mechanical subassemblies, electronic parts, and assemblies—is the careful examination in the plant of samples of the material. Engineering examines material function, and together with Quality Control considers the relevant reliability data and safety assurance in accordance with practices discussed in Chapter 17, "Product Reliability," and Chapter 18, "New-Design Control." Manufacturing Engineering reviews the manufacturability—in machining, printed card assembly, or conveyorized production flow terms—of the actual material submitted by the vendor.

Until this incoming-material control routine for the plant had been established, purchase orders based upon study of only one or two vendor samples

SUPPLIER PLANT AND EQUIPMENT SURVEY

Performed in reference to Purchase Order No. <u>A4662-1</u>

Supplier Identification Information
 Supplier number _____

 Purchase material _____

 Supplier Location, Company Affiliation, Products made at Location _____

 _____

 Other Information _____

Supplier Plant Information
 Plant Size _____

 Plant Age _____

 Plant General Information:
  Physical Appearance _____

  Cleanliness and Housekeeping _____

  Support Facilities—Air Flow, Lighting, Heating _____

  _____

  Work Flow _____

  _____

  Production Capacity _____

  _____

  Development Facilities—Product and Process _____

  _____

  Other Information _____

  _____

Supplier Equipment Information
 Types of Equipment _____

_____

FIG. 19.3

Ages of Equipment _____

_____

Equipment Maintenance _____

Plant Layout _____

_____

Supplier Quality-Control Equipment Information (to be supplemented by Supplier Quality-Control Survey)

Receiving Inspection _____

_____

Laboratory Facilities _____

_____

Reliability Testing _____

_____

In-Process Inspection _____

_____

Final Inspection and Test _____

_____

Inspection and Test Calibration and Maintenance _____

_____

Environmental Test _____

_____

Other Information _____

_____

Supplier Data Processing Information

Equipment _____

_____

FIG. 19.3 (Continued)

Software _____

_____

Applications in Use _____

_____

Supplier Personnel Information
Number of Personnel _____

Types of Occupations _____

_____

Industrial Relations Status _____

_____

Regional Labor Supply Situation _____

_____

〰〰〰〰〰〰〰〰〰〰〰〰〰〰〰〰〰〰〰〰〰〰〰〰〰〰〰〰

〰〰〰〰〰〰〰〰〰〰〰〰〰〰〰〰〰〰〰〰〰〰〰〰〰〰〰〰

SURVEY PERFORMED BY   _____   **MFG. ENG.**

_____   **QUALITY CONTROL**

_____   **PURCHASING**

_____   **DEPARTMENT**

_____   _____   **DEPARTMENT**
DATE

FIG. 19.3 **(Continued)**

could have been placed for tens of thousands of parts. With the present routine in effect, the quality-control component has the opportunity to recommend that a more adequate sample be required from the vendor; the incoming-material troubles resulting from the older practice of inadequate sample size are thus minimized.

For parts and materials whose specifications have become relatively old, members of the quality-control component help investigate possible "water" in the prices bid by vendors caused by no-longer-necessary quality extras in the specification. These investigations may take the form of studies of the tolerances being demanded by the specification. The statistical tools discussed in Part 5 may be especially useful in these studies.

Before the purchase analysis is considered complete, an important area of purchase analysis in this plant is to ensure that purchase-oriented attention has taken place with regard to make-or-buy—that is, to decide whether the part or material should be placed with an outside vendor or reconsidered for internal manufacture. Make-or-buy considerations are basic in the new-design control routine and the product- and manufacturing-development program of the plant.

Thus, the parts and materials that flow to purchasing have already been identified as buy candidates by these routines and programs—looked at for such factors as available plant capacity, plant cost levels, and plant quality levels. However, a few of these parts and materials will nonetheless also become make candidates as a result of purchase analysis review of available vendor capacity to supply this material—or lack of this capacity—and as a result of vendor price—which may in some cases be much higher than full internal costs for parts produced on a make basis—and, above all, as a result of vendor capability to provide the necessary quality—or lack of this capability as compared to what the plant itself can do. These materials are so identified and referred to plant Manufacturing Engineering and other functions for further consideration, even though some immediate production needs may be temporarily met by purchasing.

19.8 An Example of an Incoming-Material Control Routine (Cont'd.)—Vendor Selection and Order Placement

Based upon the purchase analysis activity which has identified the best qualified vendor or vendors, Purchasing initiates the placement of the contract and purchase order to the vendor or vendors who have been selected. Full quality requirements, as appropriate and in accordance with the quality planning that has been developed by the plant for the material, are made a part of the purchase contract—or are referenced in it.

For reasons of purchasing practice, certain actual material orders may require the translation of plant specifications into standard commercial nomenclature. However, the plant specification, including the quality requirements package, will usually be sent to the vendor with an attention-gaining sticker, as shown in Figure 19.4

The vendor is informed in detail of all aspects of the quality requirements package that apply to the material the vendor will be supplying. The AQL area is one example of the establishment and communications of these requirements. This plant uses an MIL-STD-105D-type AQL acceptance sampling table to cover its receiving inspection sampling. Determination will be made with the vendor, as the order is closed, of the AQL to be required of a specific part or material. Agreement will also be made with the vendor upon sampling

```
┌─────────────────────────────────────┐
│ ┌─────────────────────────────────┐ │
│ │           ATTENTION             │ │
│ │                                 │ │
│ │   THIS PART MUST CONFORM TO     │ │
│ │   CERTAIN DETAILED PURCHASER    │ │
│ │   SPECIFICATIONS.               │ │
│ │   DO NOT PERFORM WORK OR        │ │
│ │   APPLY MATERIALS FOR THIS JOB  │ │
│ │   BEFORE FAMILIARIZING YOURSELF │ │
│ │   WITH APPLICABLE PORTIONS OF   │ │
│ │   SPECIFICATION (MATERIAL) -    │ │
│ │   NO. 8732.                     │ │
│ └─────────────────────────────────┘ │
└─────────────────────────────────────┘
```

FIG. 19.4

procedure and policy for disposing rejected lots. The vendor will, for example, be informed of the conditions under which the vendor's certificates of test or inspection will be expected and accepted.

The plant Purchasing Function convenes what it terms Postaward Vendor Conferences, to which the selected vendor or vendors are invited, in such situations as those in which the supplied material is critical to product safety, where the contract is particularly large or with special requirements, or where there are unique vendor needs that must be clarified. Plant experience has been that purchase analysis, including vendor surveys, shows what vendors *can* supply but not invariably what *will* be supplied. Postaward meetings place special emphasis upon quality and the detailed procedures that will be involved in control procedures. Particular attention is placed upon the compatibility of quality-measuring equipment as between the plant and the vendor—including all aspects of the relevant quality information equipment and standards to be used both in the vendor facility and the plant.

These practices, coupled with giving similar details in as many purchasing inquiries as practical, have helped the plant to largely eliminate unpleasant frictions experienced in earlier years with vendors. These frictions resulted from complaints by vendors who insisted that they were not told of certain details of the technical quality standards of the plant until they were informed of the rejections of their material based upon failure to conform with these details.

The policy of clarifying acceptance procedures and quality specifications to vendors has been particularly valuable for those materials to be used on products sold for government use. These materials may require preshipment inspection at the vendor's plant by government service personnel. Clear, mutually understood specifications act as a powerful agent to minimize misinterpretations of quality requirements at this inspection.

When the purchase order is placed with the vendor or vendors finally chosen, particularly with raw-material suppliers, the character of the vendor's business is noted on the plant receiving inspection planning. Raw materials may be purchased from primary sources, where the manufacturer itself sells the material and where the quality may be quite directly identified. They may also be purchased from secondary sources, where the actual manufacturing origin of the material may not be quite so clear because the vendor merely purchases from manufacturers and carries on no production. Knowledge of the character of the vendor's business may be useful at incoming inspection of raw material to help develop appropriate acceptance procedures.

For a variety of reasons—the plant policy to provide some contracts to small suppliers or to newly organized companies which provide employment or to firms in certain geographic regions—or for reasons of excellent past relationships or possibly the unavailability of other sources—a vendor seriously considered for contract selection, whose ability to produce and control satisfactory material quality is in question owing to inadequate procedures or know-how, may be seriously considered. Members of the quality-control component may visit the vendor's plant in such cases and help the vendor establish adequate quality-control activities which will make it possible for the plant to select the vendor for a contract award.

After orders have been placed, vendors may require additional interpretation of the specifications while they are setting up to produce the materials. Where orders have been placed with several small vendors, these suppliers may require some technical assistance from plant quality-control people.

In a number of plant purchase contracts, there is a requirement for the vendor to provide preproduction samples to be approved before deliveries are permitted. Purchase contracts on certain materials call for approval of a sample composed of a specified number of preproduction units. When they have been produced by the vendor, these units—castings or forgings, for example—are shipped to the plant for approval. Radiographs may be required with castings; vendors may be required to make fluorescent-penetrant or magnetic particle tests on forgings; die forgings may require cross sectioning and etching for study. On those fabricated parts where welding is involved, an adequate sample of test specimens will be required of the vendor.

The units in these preproduction samples are carefully analyzed, often in frequency-distribution form, by process-control-engineering personnel. Results of these analyses may be examined by the concerned design engineers.

For electronic components and assemblies, reliability verification will be required with certain orders. With safety parts, very thorough test and inspection performance data must be submitted.

When the vendor's preproduction sample is found satisfactory, the vendor receives approval to start active production. When the sample is unsatisfactory, the vendor is informed of details about its defects. Technical assistance may be given the vendor by process-control engineers or other appropriate plant personnel. The vendor must then submit another sample for approval.

With materials like castings and forgings, experience with preproduction samples may cause considerable revision of the quality requirements on quality planning cards. The types and amounts of radiographic evidence required for approval of castings may, for example, be adjusted to conform with the assurance of casting quality evidenced by a preproduction sample.

19.9 An Example of an Incoming-Material Control Routine (Cont'd.)— Material Receipt, Material Examination

When all preliminary approvals have been given, the next step in incoming-material control takes place when the first shipments are received from the vendor. These lots are identified and then tagged so that they will be routed properly and provide proper traceability. Lots will usually be routed to the incoming inspection area; some designated A material will require the plant laboratory to make chemical or physical tests or to corroborate the vendor's certificate of test and inspection or reliability and safety. In all cases, the concerned process-control engineer will carefully audit the validity of the conclusions.

This plant, being fairly new and well laid out for material flow, has only one major incoming-material acceptance area to which the parts are routed. It has been possible to centralize all incoming inspection and testing equipments and records. Older plants of the same company are not so fortunate; owing to scattered material flow, some of these plants must carry on incoming accept-ance at several areas.

Handling of the materials is carried on rapidly but carefully as they are transported to the appropriate inspection and testing areas. In the case of a tank car of lubricant or a hopper filled with a ceramic base, a sample of specified size may be transported directly to the plant laboratory. The entire carload may be held for release until the results of the laboratory test become known.

Material Examination

Material-examination procedures in the incoming inspection and testing area are generally more rigid on first lots shipped by a vendor on a new order than they are on lots of the material received after this "starting inspection" has been completed. Inspection planning and test planning for each type of material will be available and will act as a guide to the policy that should be used by the inspectors and testers assigned to this material.

Some planning will apply to those parts—hardware, for example—where sampling may be started on these first lots received. Other planning will apply to critical parts where 100 percent inspection is required on first lots to gain a picture of vendor quality; the AQL specified on the inspection planning may be used in sampling of subsequent lots. Still other planning will apply to that minimum of parts on which 100 percent inspection must continually be per-formed on all shipments received during the life of the order.[4]

Figure 19.5 shows the sequence followed on those parts where 100 percent inspection of first lots is followed by AQL sampling on subsequent lots. If the 100 percent inspection shows that the vendor's quality is poorer than required, this sampling may not be started economically. The vendor will immediately be informed of the results of the 100 percent inspection and requested to improve the quality.

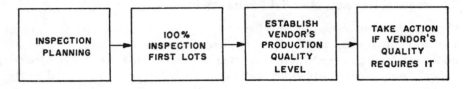

STEP I-100% INSPECTION ON FIRST LOTS

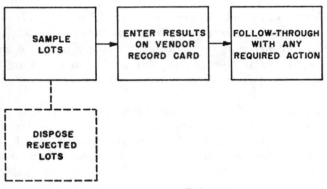

STEP II-SAMPLE INSPECT SUBSEQUENT LOTS

FIG. 19.5

The MIL-STD-105D-type acceptance table used by this plant for all its incoming inspection sampling is similar to that shown in Figure 15.11. Various AQL levels have been established for materials received by the plant.

The incoming sampling procedure provides an automatic routine for going to a reduced-sampling table, similar to the table shown in Figure 15.13, when a sufficient number of successive lots have been approved by normal sampling.

In so far as it can be worked out with the vendor, even these reduced-sampling schedules may later be replaced by a vendor's certification of test and inspection on the vendor's shipments or reports of certified reliability testing performance. These certificates take various forms with different materials. They may consist of a certified statement of the chemical and physical composition of a lot of metal; they may consist of a vendor filling in a form supplied by the plant, a typical example shown in Figure 19.6; they may be merely frequency-distribution pictures on the results of the vendor's inspection of the shipped lot, of which Figure 19.7 shows a picture on incoming springs.[5]

Acceptance sampling checks are made only occasionally on lots thus certified unless there is evidence of quality difficulties with the material on production lines.

An important element in the procedure of this plant for material acceptance

VENDOR CERTIFICATION OF QUALITY		REPORT NO._____ ORDER NO._____ DATE SHIPPED_____ QUANTITY_____	

PART NAME :_____ DWG. NO. _____
VENDOR :_____ ADDRESS :_____

SPECIFICATION	NO. CHECKED	RESULTS	REMARKS

SIGNED _____
TITLE _____

FIG. 19.6

is the training and orientation of the inspection testing and reliability and safety-evaluation people who carry on this sampling. Every effort is taken by Process-Control Engineering to make all required information available to them so that interpretation of material specifications will be uniform and correspond to the original intent of those writing the specifications.

Strong emphasis is also placed upon the securing and maintenance of adequate quality information equipments for use in acceptance inspection, test, and reliability evaluation. A complete routine for the regular examination and replacement of such gages as threads and plugs is also carried out through use of a gage color-coding program, each color representing a replacement date.

When material is accepted through these procedures, it is stamped, tagged, and made available for transportation out of the inspection area.

Materials like steels, lubricants, and ceramics—the so-called A materials—follow a somewhat different procedure from that required by the standard detail parts. These A materials may require special tests—chemical composition or hardness—which cannot be performed adequately with equipment in the inspection area. The A tests must be made in the plant laboratory.

PRODUCT __COMPRESSION SPRING__   PART NO. __1816320__
CHARACTERISTIC __TEST LOAD__   VENDOR __MC__
METHOD OF TEST __TESTER Y__   ORDER NO. __RT-8216__
SPECIFIED LIMITS __1.8# TO 2.4# @.281"__   QUANTITY OF LOT __75,000__
RECORDED BY __J.G. BROWN__   QUANTITY OF SAMPLE __80__
DATE __1-17__   DISPOSITION __PASSED__

LBS. LOAD	FREQUENCY TALLY	f
1.80		
1.83		
1.86		
1.89		
1.92		
1.95		
1.98		
2.01		
2.04		
2.07	IIIII II	7
2.10	IIIII IIIII IIIII	15
2.13	IIIII IIIII IIIII IIIII IIII	24
2.16	IIIII IIIII IIIII IIII	19
2.19	IIIII III	8
2.22	IIIII I	6
2.25	I	1
2.28		
2.31		
2.34		
2.37		
2.40		
	TOTAL	80

L I M I T S

VENDOR CERTIFICATION
FREQUENCY DISTRIBUTION FORM
FIG. 19.7

Many of these tests—those on chemical composition, for example—may be destructive in nature and so make sampling a necessity. This type of sampling is usually carried out on a variables basis.[6] Sample size is sometimes determined statistically; in other instances, where the physical form of the material is a limiting factor, past laboratory experience with the material determines the sampling details.

A case in point is that of a 6-foot 4-inch bar of purchased metal stock, to be machined and processed into a shaft about 6 feet long. If a destructive test were required here, the sample must obviously be restricted to one of the ends of the bar; to cut up the bar to produce several pieces for the sample would destroy its value.

A material of this sort usually remains physically in the inspection area where dimensional checks can be made after the sample is taken and sent to the laboratory.

Vendors' certificates of test, coupons of conformity, or statements of compliance with specification are widely used with A materials. These certificates are sent from the incoming inspection area to the laboratory for its approval.

The laboratory will consult the inspection planning for the material and note any statements on it about the vendor's quality history and whether the vendor is primary or secondary. The material specification will be briefly reviewed to determine the critical nature of the requirements. With many vendors, laboratory personnel may also draw upon their past contacts with the vendor and their experience with the vendor's shipments.

Laboratory approval of this material will take into account all these considerations, although with well-known materials from well-known vendors they will be consolidated into a very brief review. Approval may be made directly based upon vendor certification without further tests, or it may involve specific checks of such characteristics as physical properties or surface finishes.

Material approved by the laboratory is inspection stamped and tagged; material found nonconforming is appropriately tagged with that classification.

Other Divisions or Plants of the Same Company

Because of the companywide total quality program, a minimum of material-examination activity is required for those parts and materials processed by other plants of the same company. Except in unusual situations—an experimental part, a lot of material never before used—the purchaser plant does no incoming inspection on this material; the inspection stamp of the other plant is accepted as evidence of material quality. When, as in unusual times, this procedure results in the acceptance of some material of poor quality, temporary sorting activities may be undertaken by the purchaser plant. At the same time, however, corrective action at the vendor plant is demanded by the Manager–Quality Control at the company central office. Double inspection—examination at both the vendor and the purchaser plants—is recognized by this company as extremely uneconomical under usual incoming-material situations.

Were the plant discussed in this example one of several divisions of the same factory rather than a separate geographic entity, company policy would insist that the same philosophy of minimizing incoming-material control activity be followed. It would insist that these other divisions make more effective use of their product-control routines if defective materials were received from them. Costs for sorting the nonconforming materials and for the manufacturing losses caused by these materials would be billed by the purchaser division to the vendor divisions.

19.10 An Example of an Incoming-Material Control Routine (Cont'd.)—Material Disposal

Material accepted by incoming inspection or incoming test or the plant laboratory is carefully but quickly transported to suitable locations in the production areas for planned use in accordance with the plant material flow requirements. Some material may not be immediately required for use on production lines. This material accepted, however, is again carefully but quickly transported from the incoming inspection area to a storage area so that the material turnover in the inspection and test area will be maximum with a minimum of floor space and that approved material will not be disturbed in any way.

It is of course desirable from the point of view of inventory control as well as quality control that this material be stored for as short a time as possible. During its storage period, material is placed in areas actually set aside for this purpose, where temperature and humidity are such that possible damage is minimized and where there will be no deterioration in quality.

Material found nonconforming is also moved rapidly. In this plant, a special caged-in area is used for temporary storage of this material; exceptions are those materials where physical bulk or possibly dangerous inflammables make this practice impossible. A special orange tag, which means to all plant personnel Do Not Move This Material, is attached to the nonconforming materials in the cage.

Where disposition of nonconforming materials is at issue, a materials review board acts as the quality-control agency to make or coordinate the making of the required decisions. This board is composed of a concerned process-control engineer, representatives of Design Engineering, Purchasing, and, on material used on products for purchase by government service, the resident government inspector. Available to this board in making a decision about a specific lot of material are five major alternatives:

1. Reject the entire lot, and return it to the vendor.
2. 100 percent sort the lot, and return the nonconforming units to the vendor. The vendor bears the cost of the sorting inspection.
3. 100 percent sort the lot at vendor's expense, and repair the nonconformances right at the purchaser plant. The vendor pays the cost of these repairs.
4. Accept the entire lot, based upon a special disposition which temporarily relaxes specification requirements.
5. Alternatives 2 or 3, except that the purchaser plant bears part or all of the extra inspection and repair costs.

In addition to the major governing factor of effect on product quality, among the considerations governing the material review board's choice among these alternatives are

1. *Cost to the vendor.* Every effort is made to take, if possible, that action which is most economical for the vendor. To small vendors, blanket rejection of an entire lot could mean financial disaster.
2. *Plant production requirements.* Tightness of production schedules on a certain

part may make it necessary to accept, by sorting, if possible, some material to keep production lines in operation.

3. *History of the rejected lot.* Account must be taken of possible agreements with the vendor at the time of order placement in respect to how rejected lots would be disposed. Also out of fairness to the vendor, account must be taken of the rejection cause—for example, was the present specification the result of a revision made *after* the vendor had produced the lot.

Decisions are made rapidly by the materials review board, and the orange-tagged material in the cage is correspondingly disposed of at once. This permits the use of a relatively small area for the cage, and it reduces the danger of orange-tagged material "drifting into" the production lines.

19.11 An Example of an Incoming-Material Control Routine (Cont'd.)—Record Keeping and Follow-Through; Vendor Relations and Vendor Surveillance

Record Keeping and Follow-Through

Vendor records are kept on all materials and parts which pass through incoming-material control. There is a record for each material type or part number. Among the data shown by these records are dates of the various shipments, vendors' names, delivery dates, lot sizes, inspection test and reliability results, and the disposition of each lot examined. Lots accepted by vendor's certificate are so noted.

Vendors are immediately and directly notified as soon as shipments of unsatisfactory quality are identified. Complaint reports on these shipments will be similar to the rejection recorded in Figure 19.8. Visits to their plant by the best qualified plant personnel are required for some of these contacts.

The process-control engineer works closely with the other plants of the company to assure uniform relations with a single vendor by all plants of the company with respect to such matters as sampling procedures and specification interpretation.

In addition, purchase requirements for material quality are regularly reviewed. As more and more information is gained about production and field performance of a new product, quality specifications for its purchased parts and materials may be radically altered to improve customer quality results.

These data on incoming-material results provide significant information for the plant vendor rating and the plant vendor performance rating programs. These ratings are computerized, and their data are coordinated and are part of the data base in the plant management information program.

The plant vendor rating program's objective is to compare vendors of the high purchase-value materials—those which represent the great majority of material cost. Other forms of vendor comparison are maintained on the lower

INSPECTOR'S COMPLAINT ON NONCONFORMING MATERIAL

DATE 8/4

PAT. NO._____ DR. NO. 721832

{ WE HAVE RECEIVED_____ 570 GASKETS
        AND   (QUANTITY)   (NAME OF ARTICLE)
  I HAVE INSPECTED_____50_____SAMPLE__GASKETS
                        (QUANTITY)   (NAME OF ARTICLE)

FOR____BRAKE XR32_____
        (KIND OF MACHINE)   (KIND OF MATERIAL)
FROM__BROWN CO._____REQ'N Z-3218PI
        (NAME OF MFR.)

AND FIND____FOR ALL UNITS IN THE SAMPLE (50)

_____THE 1/16" DIM. IS O.K.

_____THE 6-7/8" ID IS +.009" OVER TOLERANCE

_____THE 4-1/4" OD IS +.010" OVER TOLERANCE

DISPOSITION RETURN LOT TO VENDOR

WHEN DID WE MAKE A SIMILAR COMPLAINT AGAINST THIS VENDOR ? 6/24

SIGNED J. R. WHITE

FIG. 19.8

purchase-value materials, to provide vendor comparisons of these materials.

The vendor rating program, which is maintained by Purchasing, includes the various categories of major purchased materials—functional subassemblies, precision mechanical parts, integrated circuits, capacitors, and similar material. Vendor rating is based upon an index which incoming-material control personnel have developed and which has a maximum rating of 100. This index is developed for each vendor and integrated from three primary factors: vendor quality, vendor price, and vendor service—measured for vendor deliveries. Any unacceptably low rating in each of these three input unit criteria is also identified.

Approximately 400 vendors are included in this rating. It is formally published quarterly but is continuously updated with new vendor result inputs. The computer software structure makes it possible for Purchasing, Quality Control, Design Engineering, and other groups to continually query the rating program to determine the status of vendors. Figure 19.9 shows a representation of a segment of the rating for vendors supplying a functional hydraulic subassembly.

Vendor Rating

Material:			Rating Period:
Hydraulic subassembly Dwg. 928740-1			3rd Quarter
Vendor code	Integrated index	Unit indicator	Indicator
HS-421	84.1	Low quality	CQ
HS-422	93.2		AB
FA-32	95.4		AA
FA-18	87.5		BA
HS-420	75.2	Low Quality, service	CQD

Indicator Legend:
AA = preferred vendor; *AB* = preferred second source vendor; *BA* = acceptable vendor; *CQD* = currently unacceptable vendor—quality, service; *CQ* = currently unacceptable vendor—quality.

FIG. 19.9

This rating is a major guide to Purchasing for ongoing order maintenance and future order placement.

Quality Control maintains the vendor performance rating, whose data are an input to and coordinated with the vendor rating. The vendor performance rating measures the results of key vendors for two primary factors: quality of incoming lots and delivery dates of these lots. Quality is measured as to the percent nonconforming of lots, and delivery is measured for on-time or days-late of deliveries. While immediate vendor contact is made upon delivery of unsatisfactory lots, continuing vendor contact proceeds, as required, for these ratings, and necessary corrective action is initiated and closely tracked. What is called in the plant the "must-do-better letter" to vendors is initiated as soon as the vendor performance rating so requires, and, as appropriate, process-control engineering visits are made to the vendor plant. Figure 19.10 shows a representation of the performance rating for a vendor supplying an electronic component.

This vendor performance rating provides the information to Quality Control, Production, Design Engineering, Manufacturing Engineering, and other plant groups concerned with current vendor results.

Vendor Relations and Vendor Surveillance

Through all activities of this incoming-material control routine, the plant places close and direct attention to clear vendor communications and well-organized ongoing vendor relations. The objective is to assist and encour-

Vendor Performance Rating

Vendor code: *EC-23*
Material: Component spec.: *CAP42530C*
Rating period: *Month 8*

| Date lot rcvd. | Quantity | Quality % nonconf. | Delivery | | Lot performance |
			On time	Days late	
8/5	4050	0	. . .	4	I–*e*
8/10	3522	0	. . .	3	I–*d*
8/15	5200	0.75	1	. . .	III–*a*
8/25	4522	0.35	. . .	3	II–*d*

Rating code:

Quality—% nonconforming:	*Delivery—days late:*
I—0	*a*—on time
II—0 –0.5	*b*—0–1 days late
III—0.5–1.0	*c*—1–2 days late
IV—1.0–2	*d*—2–3 days late
V—2 –3	*e*—3–4 days late
VI—3 –4	*f*—4–5 days late
VII—4 –5	*g*—over 5 days late
VIII—Over 5	

FIG. 19.10

age vendors to maintain high performance results. The principle of emphasis upon control by the vendor himself is implemented to the fullest extent—a principle that the plant terms its program of "vendor source control."

Heavy concentration is placed upon material shipments from vendors that have been found to need corrective action. While communications with vendors is direct and immediate on discrepant material, careful focus is placed upon assurance that the necessary effort and time have been taken to ensure that the *causes* of the discrepancy have been removed and that the corrective action is, in fact, permanent. This follow-through is tracked by records, of which Figure 19.11 is a representation, which both carefully define the discrepancies and then report and evaluate the actual steps taken and their effectiveness.

However, attention is given to all suppliers, the great majority of whom consistently provide material which fully meets quality requirements. Periodic communications are scheduled on an organized basis with all major suppliers. This takes several forms, such as the following:

MATERIAL DISCREPANCY REPORT

PURCHASE ORDER NUMBER: _____

A. Discrepant Material Detail

Part Number: _____ Description: _____

Qty. Received: ___ Qty. Inspected: ___ Qty. Found Nonconforming: ___

Reference Our Discrepancy Report Number: _____ Disposition: _____

Description of Discrepancies (*show details*):

Vendor Code: _____ Vendor Informed on: _____ (*show date*)

Process Quality Engineer: _____ Date: _____

B. Discrepant Material Correction

Corrective Action Taken:

 (*show details*)

By Whom Taken:

Effectiveness of Corrective Action Taken by Vendor: _____

Process Quality Engineer: _____ Date: _____

FIG. 19.11

· Vendors whose performance rating is consistently high are identified as High Performance Vendors, and this so-called HPV classification is much prized.
· Vendor conferences are scheduled with groups of suppliers of key com-

modities—such as finishes and paints—which are important to customer quality satisfaction and plant cost and from whom the plant expects consistent quality and delivery results.

· Surveillance of the performance results of all key suppliers is maintained in an organized fashion, and, where indicated, special studies of vendor lots take place by process-control engineering to contribute to further consistency of vendor performance.

· Vendor audits are performed in the case of certain suppliers of critical materials.

· Quality-engineering assistance is provided to suppliers—particularly smaller firms which have specialized and needed technical and production skills but which have not fully developed all necessary quality capability.

The result for the plant of this incoming-material control routine has been assurance of receiving material of the proper quality at the most economical cost levels. Substantial reductions in material purchase prices and in inspection and test expense on many materials have been achieved.

Extensive as it is, establishment of this incoming-control routine was accompanied by a decrease for the plant in general expenditures and in overhead. Several incoming control activities had been carried on previous to the establishment of the formal routine; they had been carried on in an individual, relatively ineffective, uncoordinated fashion whose duplications and overlaps were eliminated by incoming-material control. As a result, overall plant quality costs were reduced significantly.

19.12 Techniques Used in Incoming-Material Control

Parts 4 and 5 discussed a wide range of technological and analytical techniques, many of which find application to incoming-material control as reviewed in this chapter. It may be worthwhile, therefore, to summarize some of the more significant techniques used in the second job of total quality control.

Several techniques are used in incoming-material control activities. Major among these is sound inspection and test practice, details of which are well known and whose procedures are effectively discussed in the literature. Other technical methods include such tools as statistical acceptance sampling tables, materials specifications, vendor records and contact, statistical analyses of purchased parts, and proper materials handling. Some of the more important of these techniques are summarized below.

Material Receiving

Receiving inspection and test facilities, which provide adequate floor space and which are well laid out, are a basic requirement for effective incoming-material control.

Raw-Material Specifications

Components required by individual product designs will be specified and developed in the plant's new-design control routine. Basic raw materials which apply quite generally throughout the operations of the plant—steels, insulating materials—may have overly long "lead times" for such specifications prepared in new-design control. These specifications are therefore developed as part of the incoming-material control routine.

Proper Materials Handling

Inspection activity in assuring conformance will be wasted if the materials received are later damaged, scraped, or battered while being transported through the plant to production lines. It is essential that proper material-handling equipment be available for transporting these materials.

Acceptance Sampling Tables

Chapter 15 discussed in some detail acceptance sampling tables which have wide application in incoming-material inspection. These tables assist both in assuring quality and in enabling its maintenance at low inspection cost.

Proper Storage Facilities

Some materials received by the plant may be shelved for a period after their incoming inspection. If this storage space is inadequate—if it is excessively damp and thus ruins insulating materials or too unprotected from passing battery trucks and thus risks damage to bellows "being aged" or to electronic components being "burned in"—then the incoming-material control objective will not be achieved. Proper storage facilities are essential to adequate maintenance of incoming-material quality.

Vendor Quality Procurement Information

A complete package of quality requirements information—drawings, specifications, quality plans, and other necessary data—is established to provide vendors with an adequate basis for responding both to initial purchaser requests for quotations and to ongoing quality maintenance after order placement.

Vendor Surveys and Audits

Organized evaluations of vendor capabilities to furnish materials of the necessary quality and quantity are an important basis for initial vendor selection and ongoing vendor surveillance.

Vendor Material Qualification

Specific approval of vendor parts, subassemblies, and other material is a basic technique for initial supplier selection and for acceptance of the first samples of vendor production.

Quality Measurement Compatibility

The establishment of uniform measurement procedures and standards between the vendor and the purchaser are a necessary incoming control technique to assure common quality evaluation practices.

Quality Information Equipment

The increasing complexity of parts and materials purchased under modern material specifications makes it essential that the inspection, test and reliability evaluation of these materials be carried on with modern quality information equipments. The selection and location of these equipments are important incoming control techniques.

Equipment and Gage Maintenance

It is inevitable that delicate measuring equipments will go out of adjustment. It is essential therefore that these equipments and gages be properly maintained and their accuracy rigidly controlled.

Inspection Training and Education

The quality of materials being released to the shop floor depends to an important degree upon how well incoming inspectors have done their job. To help them better perform this task, inspection training is a fundamental requirement. Inspectors may attend training classes developed for their use and are given inspection manuals and inspection guide cards. They are qualified through specific criteria to assure full capability to perform all inspection tasks.

Vendor Support

Quality-engineering assistance to selected vendors is a technique to develop within suppliers the capability to provide consistent quality of shipments and to improve supplier quality performance in areas where technical corrective action must take place.

Material Quality Identification

Clear marking of inspections and tests performed is an essential portion of material identification to confirm the quality status of parts and assemblies that have proceeded through receiving inspection and testing.

Vendor Corrective Action

Expeditious action to eliminate the causes of nonconforming vendor material requires careful monitoring of incoming-lot quality performance and close working relationships and communications with vendors to assure permanent correction of quality problems.

Disposal of Nonconforming Materials

Nonconforming materials discovered in incoming inspection must be disposed of rapidly. Otherwise, some of this nonconforming material may seep into the production lines, may take up available floor space, or may remain in the purchaser plant for so long a time that the vendor will not or may no longer be obligated to accept it back. Proper tagging, adequate disposal areas, and effective material review routines are essential tools for use here.

Statistical Analysis of Incoming Material

The statistical methods discussed in Part 5 may be used to good advantage in analyzing data on materials received by the plant. The frequency distribution is probably most useful for this purpose.

Vendor Quality Costs

The operating quality costs of suppliers, included in the material purchase price, are a very major economic factor both for the vendor and the purchaser. As discussed in Section 7.13, vendor quality-cost control is a very important incoming-material control technique.

Measures of Inspection and Test Performance

Periodic checks on the effectiveness of inspection in maintaining adequate quality of incoming material are essential. The actual details of the techniques used for this purpose will depend upon conditions in individual plants. Work sampling is particularly useful here.

Vendor Quality Data Processing

Vendor quality information is structured for computerized data handling as part of the plant management information system to the extent that it is cost-effective and balanced with manual vendor information handling where appropriate.

Vendor Certificates

Certification by a vendor of the quality of the material results in both commercial advantage for the vendor and minimum incoming inspection for the purchaser. Techniques for this purpose are important incoming-material control methods. Documentation is provided by the supplier, demonstrating in the necessary detail that quality-control practices have been performed which ensure that the material provided is of the required quality.

Purchase Contracts Embodying Quality-Control Fundamentals

An important influence upon the effectiveness of incoming-material control is the character of the initial purchase inquiry—the extent to which it informs vendors of the quality requirements that will be provided in the procurement package, for example—and the effectiveness of the provisions bearing upon quality in the final purchase contract made with the vendor.

Control of Vendor "Drop Ship" Materials

Incoming-material control routines are applied to all materials—including products and spare parts—shipped directly to customers or placed in spare parts inventories. The details of these methods naturally vary from company to company, but there is enough uniformity among them to allow concrete discussion of their basic fundamentals.

Several incoming-material control techniques are described in detail elsewhere in this book. Those readers interested in considerable detail on others may wish to refer to the literature in the fields in question.

The following discussion gives examples of four technical methods: "Vendor Relations," Section 19.13; "Vendor Records and Information Processing," Section 19.14; "Vendor Ratings," Section 19.15; and "Incoming Inspection Gage Control," Section 19.16.

19.13 Vendor Relations

The art of sound vendor relations in incoming-material control consists much more of a philosophy of buyer-seller contacts than it does of any single technique or group of techniques. Basic to this philosophy is the general ethics of courteous business practice; there are, however, certain features of the relationship which are distinct to quality control.

First, there should be assurance that the vendor is informed about the acceptance procedures of the purchaser plant for the material the vendor ships. Under most desirable conditions, the vendor is a party to the establishment of such procedures as quality levels, types of tests made and the importance of these tests, and the character of the inspection on the part.

Much of this information should be interchanged while the purchase contract is being concluded, particularly that which will apply to policies for the return of rejected material. Other practices—assurance that the vendor's inspection and test procedures and equipment are similar to those of the purchaser plant, for example—must be reviewed both before shipments have started and after they have begun and as experience has accumulated.

The vendor should not be confused by a variety of inconsistent, uncoordinated quality contacts from the purchaser plant. It is essential to sound incoming-material control that these contacts be made as part of the overall plant quality-control program. All visits to the vendor by the process-control engineer should, for example, be coordinated and/or arranged by plant Purchasing.

The issue of suggesting that a respected vendor, with an excellent quality reputation, should improve quality-control activities because of progressively tightening quality demands may be a particularly ticklish vendor relations problem for the purchaser plant process-control engineer. Efforts in this direction will be successful to the extent that the process-control engineer convinces the vendor that the quality-control organization is a support to the vendor as well as to its own employer.

Frequently very effective in this connection is a visit or a series of visits through the vendor's factory, where the complete operation is reviewed. If the vendor can be encouraged to discuss the trouble spots, the process-control engineer may be able to make suggestions regarding technical quality-control methods that may usefully be applied.

Effort toward improved vendor relations in incoming-material control certainly has no effect toward minimizing the obligation of the vendor for the production and shipment of material of specified quality. It does, however, involve realistic recognition by the purchaser-plant quality-control program that its own quality performance and costs may be improved in direct proportion to the improvement in the vendor's quality practices and that aid to the vendor in this direction not only is friendly business courtesy but involves intelligent self-interest.

19.14 Vendor Records and Information Processing

The importance is unquestioned to incoming-material control of adequate records on the quality of shipments from vendors. These records must, however, be maintained with a minimum of paperwork and clerical effort. In the past, too often vendor records were stored in cumbersome filing systems, with the result that additional expenses were incurred to maintain unduly extensive records.

To provide necessary vendor record information in a cost-effective manner, the total quality approach to incoming-material control is as follows:

1. Vendor quality results data are structured in modern information processing flow patterns to assure expeditious data acquisition and recording with elimination of unnecessary and overlapping reports. Quality Control is assisted in the establishment of these flow patterns by the specialized help and guidance of the company and plant information processing component. This detailed information structuring is essential because it identifies the actual vendor results facts that are being dealt with so that, with the degree of computerization which is practical and economic, Quality Control is aware of this vendor data in more than only computer "black box" and "hard copy printout" sheets or "soft copy" cathode ray tube displays.

2. All aspects of vendor records information are established for this information flow pattern so that they can be handled manually—if necessary—practically and economically. Most plants historically have evolved their vendor records in manual form, and these are fitted into the flow pattern, with necessary improvements, together with additional records that may be required. This manual identification gives support to full understanding by Quality Control of what might be thought of as the "physical reality" of this vendor information. It also provides the necessary redundancy backup for computer applications when the computer temporarily "crashes" and is out of operation.

3. The economy and effectiveness of computer application are evaluated for some or all aspects of the vendor records information flow. This is done

with regard to both use of the plant and company's central mainframe computer installation and use of minicomputers and microcomputers for the specific objective of incoming-material control. Where the smaller computers are selected, they are maintained on a distributed data basis and integrated, as appropriate, with the company mainframe computers when they cover the plant and company management information systems and its purchasing components.

4. This vendor quality records program is maintained and operated by Quality Control, with the help of the information processing component, and with close working relationships with Purchasing, Design Engineering, Manufacturing Engineering, and Production.
5. The usual form taken by this vendor quality data is records established for each key incoming part, assembly, and other material and provides the quality information pertinent to the material. The records are physically maintained in the incoming inspection and test area. Ongoing data are recorded as a regular part of the routine for disposing of incoming lots.

One approach to vendor records that has proved popular serves both as an inspection procedure sheet and inspection record sheet. Figure 19.12 shows the manual form of this record.[7] The data instruction for filling in the form to initiate the procedure and set up the record is also shown, as Figure 19.13. The numbers in the instruction correspond to the numbered spaces on the form. A review of the form and accompanying instruction shows the completeness of the information given with respect to the instruction. The method of recording inspection results by quality characteristic and the record of the disposition provide a complete historical record by attributes for a given part from a given vendor.

There are other types of cards which provide space for plotting a graph of inspection measurements for certain quality characteristics on the part in question.

Vendor records supply an invaluable reference library for determination of vendor quality performance, as an input to vendor ratings, and for analysis of difficulties being experienced with given parts and materials. By standardizing the data-recording procedure for incoming parts and materials, they tend to raise the caliber of the hour-by-hour and day-by-day incoming inspection activity.

When all blank spaces on vendor records have been filled in, the data are retained on file for a period of time which varies among plants, depending upon such circumstances as the provisions of the purchase contract and the length of the manufacturing cycle. Data may be retained for a long time period in a long-manufacturing-cycle plant such as turbines or in an automotive plant where the traceability of safety parts is essential; they may be retained in a short-cycle plant for only a short time. Before discarding individual data records on expensive parts and materials, some plants which require such information summarize their results on master computer or manual records.

19.15 Vendor Ratings

There have been a considerable number of incoming-material rating plans designed by various companies to measure vendor performance with respect to the quality of the material delivered. However, not all these plans have followed the vendor rating and vendor performance rating principles discussed in Section 11.13. Some shortcomings of these rating plans have been the following:

1. Vendors have complained about the fairness of plans which compare one vendor against another when the two vendors are receiving ratings on a different "mix" of parts or materials. For example, the vendor that took the tough-to-make parts might receive a poor rating compared to a vendor making a simple, noncritical part.
2. The plan may not take into account the number of shipments or number of items on which the rating is based. Or it may not count a nonconforming item defective unless it is returned to the vendor.
3. Some plans measure the performance of the vendor on only "quality" and neglect two other practical measurements, namely, "price" and "service."

FIG. 19.12
(Front)

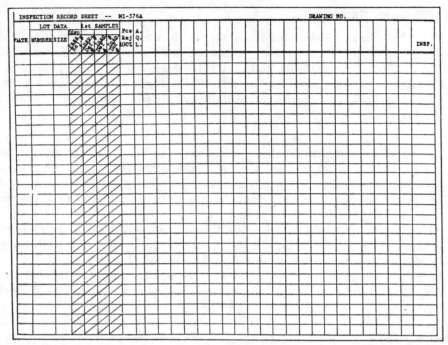

FIG. 19.12
(Reverse)

4. Some plans are not consistently maintained. They are emphasized when there is a "vendor quality improvement drive" and then are allowed to disintegrate gradually until the next "drive."
5. The rating criteria for some plans are vague and ambiguous and not clear to vendors and sometimes not to plant personnel themselves.
6. Some plans are not strongly managed. The reports are very late and therefore neither current nor accurate. Correspondingly, the information exists only in a computer memory or in a manual file and is not actively used.

Company experience over a period of years has shown that vendor rating plans, to be effective and useful, must be established in regards to the following six characteristics. The plan must be

1. Clearly defined and clearly communicable
2. Inclusive of only necessary information
3. Economical to operate
4. Practical in its coverage of materials and parts
5. Maintainable
6. Auditable so that its efficiency can be periodically evaluated

Instruction and Procedure for Originating Inspection Procedure Sheet

1. Drawing number, group or part number, and revision letter or number for card identification.
2. Drawing number, group or part number, and revision number or letter.
3. Name of part as designated on drawing.
4. Area where inspection is performed and type of inspection.
5. Outside vendor supplying parts or internal manufacturing area; use one form for each.
6. AQLs in use.
6a. N, T, or R for normal, tightened, or reduced inspection for each supplier.
7. Name of planner or foreman setting up inspection procedure sheet.
8. Date inspection procedure sheet is originated.
9. Signature of inspector.
10. Signature of foreman or general foreman approving inspection procedure sheet for inspection.
10a. Customer's signature as required.
11. Same as 6.
12. AQL for each characteristic or 100 percent.
13. Characteristics being checked in order of checking. This also includes tests being performed as a separate group.
13a. Setup checks will be listed and the check number of the setup inspector posted in block 18A as required.
14. List inspection equipment or method used.

Instruction and Procedure for Sampling and Recording Results of Inspection on Inspection Procedure Sheet

15. Date.
16. Lot size.
17. Actual sample size inspected.
18. For O.K. characteristics, place inspector's stamp in box. For nonconformances, divide box with diagonal and indicate number over tolerance in upper part and number under tolerance in lower part of box.
18a. Setup inspector's check number opposite setup checks.
19. Total number of nonconformances for each AQL.
20. Total number of nonconformances found in 100 percent inspection.
21. Black in appropriate space for disposition of lot.
22. For internal, laboratory number or serial number; for external, vendor's name and order number.
23. Check number or stamp of inspector completing final check listed.
24. Use sampling tables supplied by Quality-Control Engineering.
    a. Select enough pieces for largest sample size required.
    b. Samples to be selected at random from all sections of container or lot.
    c. If several containers constitute lot, divide the sample size by the number of containers and take an equal amount from each container at random.

FIG. 19.13

There are many different types of vendor ratings which meet the requirements of these characteristics to fit the varying needs of plants and companies. A principal difference among these plans is the factors they include in the vendor ratings. However, there are three key factors that experience shows are essentials in vendor ratings:

1. Vendor quality
2. Vendor price
3. Vendor service

A basic vendor rating plan that has been widely used is based upon the foundation of these factors. It weighs these factors as follows:

Quality	40 points
Price	35 points
Service	25 points
Total	100 points

This weighting should be flexible from one type of business to another and may be varied to fit a given type of business. The use of this plan is as follows:

1. Its *quality* rating is based upon the fraction of total lots received that are acceptable for a given part. For example, if supplier A had 54 lots accepted out of a total of 60 lots delivered, $54/60$, or 90 percent, of the lots were accepted. The quality rating would be 0.90×40 (weighting factor) $= 36$ points.
2. On *price*, the vendor with the lowest net price receives the full 35 points (or whatever weighting factor was chosen for price). If, for example, supplier B had the lowest net price of 93 cents per 100 pieces, the rating on price would be 35 points. If A's price was $1.16, then supplier A's rating would be

$$\frac{0.93}{1.16} \times 35 = (0.80)(35) = 28 \text{ points}$$

3. The *service* rating can be based upon the percentage of promises kept. If supplier A kept 90 percent of his promises, his service rating would be $(0.90)(25) = 22.5$ points.
4. Supplier A's total rating would therefore be:

Quality	36.0 points
Price	28.0 points
Service	22.5 points
Total	86.5 points

This rating can be compared with comparable vendors on the basis of single-part number or catalog number. These comparisons are then a basis for company-purchasing action in placing future purchase orders.

This basic rating may be expanded to include further specific vendor quality results information, as required by the particular plant and company needs. Examples of this expansion are as follows:

· *With regard to quality:* The rating may include indicators of the detailed percent nonconformities found in the lots received. The vendor rating example discussed in Section 19.11 and Figure 19.9 provides an example of this by having the backup of the data in Figure 19.10. Other inclusions may be indicators of the criticality of the lot nonconformities, particularly safety deficiencies; latent nonconformities in incoming material which are found in production and in the field; nonconforming lot trends and trend projections; and vendor certification.

· *With regard to service:* The rating may include indicators of the specific days late deliveries have been received. It may also include indicators of vendor cooperation in such areas as surveys, corrective action, and providing advance notification of lot defectives.

Measurements themselves may be reported either in terms of points achieved by vendors—the positive-performance-oriented approach as shown above—or demerits incurred by vendors—the approach that makes clear that there are deficiencies. Plants have different philosophies on these measurement concepts and both approaches are widely and effectively used.

The operation of vendor ratings in manual and computer terms follows the same sequence as that discussed in Section 19.14. This includes (1) structuring rating data flow in information flow patterns; (2) establishing an economical and practical manual basis for vendor rating; (3) establishing computer application for vendor rating, which will normally be an integral part of the plant purchasing information system; (4) maintaining the vendor rating by the functional component most directly affected—normally Purchasing—with strong Quality-Control cooperation; (5) maintaining records for key suppliers and key materials, with data inputs from receiving inspection.

Many practical manual aids are also useful in vendor rating. One that has had very long-term usefulness, in simple calculation of the rating pattern for a given vendor, is a circular calculator.

Figure 19.14 shows this circular slide rule designed with scales and windows that give the rating directly for each of the three factors when using the weightings shown in this example.

19.16 Incoming Inspection Gage Control

To maintain adequate control over incoming materials, it is first necessary to be able to measure the quality characteristics of this material. It is frequently necessary to make these measurements through the medium of quality information equipment devices designed especially for this measurements purpose.

These devices range from the relatively simple plug gage to much more complex quality information equipment such as radiographic equipment or supersonic testing devices and a wide variety of reliability testers. They also

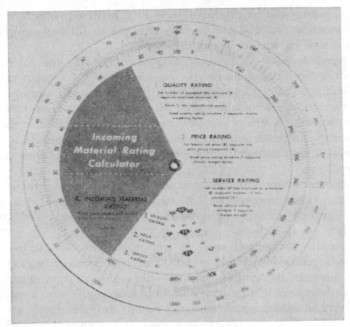

FIG. 19.14 **Incoming-material rating calculator.**

include such basic inspection and test aids as surface plates, gage blocks, angle plates, plug and snap gages, thread gages, optical gages, air-pressure gages, gear gages, micrometers, pin gages, profilometers, and many others.

A number of these mechanical gages will be used in the control of incoming material; like other electronic or mechanical equipments subject to wear, it is essential there be assurance that (1) the indication given by the gage is accurate before the gage is used at all, (2) the gage be designed so as to permit its efficient use by personnel, and (3) the gage be maintained so that the indication given is accurate throughout its useful life.

To give this assurance in a plant incoming-material program is the task of gage-control procedures. These may consist in

1. A procedure for approving all new gages before they are used in the factory at all. In large plants, this approval may be obtained by checking the gage with high-precision-measuring equipments which may be located in the plant laboratory or in a special gage-approval area. Small plants may use for this purpose commercial laboratories or government bureaus.
2. A procedure for the periodic recheck of all gages after they have been in use in the factory and for making whatever adjustments or repairs that may be required to enable the gage to be returned to use. This is accomplished through a preventive maintenance program very similar in concept to that

used for production machine tools and processes. "Check times" vary, depending upon the type of gage that is being maintained, the amount of usage it receives, and so on.

A gage-control procedure for expensive thread gages that check critical tapped holes may be cited as an example: On all new thread gages being checked in the plant laboratory for initial approval, a "pickup card" is made out. Data on this card include type of gage, its serial or drawing number if there is one, its size, the location where the gage is to be used, its particular usage, and any other pertinent information.

When the gage has been given this initial approval, it is then stamped with a special indelible ink whose color dates the gage for its first maintenance check. A definite scheme of colors is used which will show at a glance to incoming inspection personnel the month, week, and even day—in the case of those gages which require such close check—that the gage should be returned to the laboratory for its maintenance checkup.

As a cross-check to ensure that gages are actually picked up for this check and that the color coding has not been somehow overlooked on the inspection floor, the pickup card for each gage has a color tab clipped to it. The pickup card is then filed in a cabinet along with similar cards, which are regularly reviewed.

During this review, those cards whose tabs call for gage pickup will be pulled from the file and a check made to ensure that the gage is actually returned to the plant laboratory for proper examination. Where the gage to be picked up has regular production usage, it is necessary with this system to have spare gages which may be placed out on the floor while the regular gage is being checked.[8]

19.17 Study of Rejects on Incoming Plastic Cases

The actual factory operation of both organizational and technical aspects of incoming-material control can best be summarized by a review of six typical case examples. Sections 19.18 to 19.22 discuss five such cases; this section presents the first example, that of a joint vendor-purchaser effort to determine the cause of inferior quality of shipments.

A northeastern factory noted an excessive number of rejected lots at incoming inspection of molded plastic cases. These cases were used on one of the assemblies manufactured by the plant. The molded case was produced by the vendor in a multicavity mold, and cases produced by all the cavities were mingled together in each shipment. There was no means of identifying cases produced by an individual cavity.

It was suggested that there might be an appreciable variation in the quality of cases produced by the different cavities. It was decided, therefore, to undertake a joint investigation with the vendor to determine the influence of the several cavities upon quality.

Figure 19.15 illustrates the results of this analysis as it applied to cavities 17 and 18. As can be seen from Figure 19.15, cavity 18 was producing out-of-limits cases.

The vendor repaired cavity 18 based upon the results of this analysis. The vendor's future shipments reflected a great improvement of quality because of this action.

A further result of this analysis may also be cited. On all multicavity molds thereafter produced for use by this plant, a small number were manufactured into each cavity. Since these numbers were thereafter molded into all plastic cases produced, they enabled ready identification of the cavity from which an individual case had been manufactured.

19.18 Integrated Vendor-Purchaser Control of Paint Treatments

A manufacturer of conversion coating chemicals used by automotive companies for metals which will be painted maintains high standards in the finished product through a cooperative effort with its customers. Because the type and method of application of even the most ideal coating chemical will affect the surface finish, the whole chain of events in assuring quality is of great importance.[9]

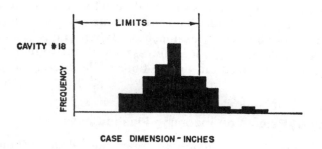

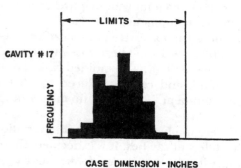

FIG. 19.15

In the vendor's plant, control of quality begins with a careful check of the ingredients for each batch. These are proprietary formulations using ingredients supplied by other chemical manufacturers. In-process controls vary with the formulation; included can be tests for viscosity, acidity or specific gravity, and visual checks for off-standard conditions such as color, clarity, or packing density in the case of powders. The shop order is a detailed directive to the chemical operator for the manufacture of the material, including special customer identification on containers and mandatory color coding indicating the corrosive, oxidizing, or flammable nature of the product.

At the end of production, but while the product is still in the batch tank, a sample is taken for laboratory testing. A sample of each production batch is kept for a year after shipment so that it can be further analyzed in the event of any problem in use.

Most automotive plants accept the chemicals without further chemical testing, emphasizing instead the performance of the material. Further chemical testing is carried on by the vendor, however, after the product has been delivered. Using test panels typical of automotive body stock, purchased from the automotive company, the vendor's salesperson visits the customer plant each month to conduct in-process tests. A special rack permits the panels to pass through each pretreatment and treatment line, after which they are returned to the laboratory for analysis. The salesperson also regularly checks those aspects of plant operation and equipment which bear upon proper application of the coating chemical and periodically inspects equipment during scheduled down time. In some cases, the vendor helps the automotive manufacturer in the design of pretreatment equipment.

Together with the automotive manufacturer's own checks on panels which have been painted after coating, the information gained by this on-going vendor control has been a prime factor in the standard of end quality of the finished product.

19.19 Control of Purchased Springs

A plant manufacturing large electrical assemblies purchased a great quantity of springs for use in these assemblies. The plant was dissatisfied with its incoming control procedures on these springs for several reasons:

1. Many lots of springs, rejected at incoming inspection for failure to meet specifications on dimensional accuracy or load limits, were later accepted by the material review procedure for rejected material of the plant.
2. Occasional troubles in assembly and test led to the observation that the plant's go and not-go acceptance sampling routine for springs did not always detect lot variation outside the specification limits.
3. Quality relations between the plant and its spring vendors were not so close as was felt desirable.

4. Purchase prices for some springs were felt to reflect unnecessary, unrealistic, or outmoded spring specification requirements.

Among the steps taken by plant Quality Control to improve these incoming-material situations were three major projects:

1. Establishment of an acceptance sampling procedure by the variables method for springs
2. Review of spring specifications to assure their mirroring up-to-date quality requirements
3. Establishment of a procedure for vendor certification of the quality of lots of springs so as to reduce the need for acceptance sampling at the plant

Each of these three projects is now discussed.[10]

Variables Sampling Procedure

The first project initiated was that of replacing the go and not-go acceptance sampling procedure with one by the variables method. A new spring tester was obtained to make possible the recording of the individual measurements on springs. This tester was used in the following procedure.

A frequency-distribution tally was made by incoming inspection on a sample of springs from each incoming lot. Actual spring readings were plotted on this tally, an example of which is shown in Figure 19.16. No definite sample size was specified to the process-control inspector for these tallies; the picture of the buildup of the sample distribution, with respect to the specification limits, indicated to the inspector the number of springs to check from each lot. Those lots were passed, the sample distributions of which were properly located in relation to the specification limits. The lot represented by Figure 19.16 was rejected on this basis.

The tally reports thus made were forwarded to Purchasing for comparison of the performance of various vendors and for the action shown necessary by this comparison. When lot variations were outside specification limits, as in the case of Figure 19.16, Purchasing and Quality Control reviewed this report with the vendor for corrective action.

Among the advantages obtained from this variables sampling plan are the following:

1. It reflects, at a glance, both the amount of variation in the lot and the relation of the average value to the specification limits. Far more effective data than mere go and not-go information are therefore available for consideration on rejected lots which enter the plant's materials-review procedure.
2. It provides a ready comparison between vendors, helps individual vendors make decisions on disposition of rejected lots, and decreases the amount

PRODUCT: Extension Spring	PART NO.: 6172583
CHARACTERISTIC: Test Load	VENDOR: "B"
METHOD OF TEST: Tester 732	ORDER NO.: SP-697146-B
SPECIFIED LIMITS: .357# to .535# @1.232"	QUANTITY OF LOT: 2,250
RECORDED BY: T.Green	QUANTITY OF SAMPLE: 88
DATE: 12-19	DISPOSITION: Rejected

Lbs. Load	FREQUENCY TALLY	f
.355		
.365		
.375		
.385		
.395		
.405		
.415		
.425		
.435		
.445		
.455		
.465		
.475		
.485		
.495		
.505		
.515		
.525	II	2
.535	IIIII II	7
.545	IIIII IIIII I	11
.555	IIIII IIIII IIIII III	18
.565	IIIII IIIII IIIII IIIII	20
.575	IIIII IIIII IIIII	15
.585	IIIII IIII	9
.595	IIIII	5
.605	I	1
.615	TOTAL	88

(LIMITS: .355 to .535)

FIG. 19.16

of incoming inspection time as compared with the previous sampling method.

3. It gives vendors more detailed information on causes for rejection, tends to encourage the use of this tally sheet practice by vendors, and provides design engineers establishing tolerances for new designs with a useful reference library on the amount of variation to be expected in lots of purchased springs.

Review of Spring Specifications

The distributions made on these incoming lots of springs highlighted several areas in which the spring specifications of the plant were unsatisfactory. Only one of these instances will be cited: those specifications which called for acceptance limits much narrower than could be met by the normal manufacturing variation in the vendors' processes. Springs of this sort had to be 100 percent sorted by the vendors or 100 percent tested by the purchaser—either step adding to the spring cost.

It was suspected that some of these specifications were the result of outmoded formulas for calculating spring limits rather than the result of actual assembly quality requirements. Subsequent analysis proved that this was so in a number of cases, and specifications were consequently adapted. New formulas, reflecting modern spring-manufacturing technique, were made available to the plant's design engineers. Many cost improvements on springs were a result of these steps.

Vendor Certification

A number of acceptance inspection distribution tallies were made on lots of springs purchased from one vendor. Process-Control Engineering and Purchasing discussed the results of the tallies with this vendor, who made such tallies for his own record on every lot of springs shipped to this purchaser.

An arrangement was later made for the vendor to document this tally for each lot and to forward this documentation to the plant. The plant was soon able to minimize its own acceptance inspection in favor of this form of vendor certification. Only periodic sampling checks are now made on lots shipped by this vendor.

The purchaser plant has summarized the benefits it has received from this incoming control procedure:

1. Improved spring test facilities and more effective incoming inspection methods
2. Realistic revision of spring specifications, better understanding of spring materials and characteristics, and improvement of spring quality
3. Better purchaser-vendor relations and closer quality comparison among vendors
4. Reduction in lost time in assembly because of poor-quality springs and reduction in spring costs by reducing the former 100 percent testing and by receipt of vendor certificates of test
5. Reduction in purchased price of many springs as produced by the vendor

The following excerpt from a letter concerning a single spring type by the vendor to the purchaser plant may be of interest in this connection: ". . . these changes, which were in accordance with your new standards, eliminated the gaging and adjusting operations which had previously been necessary. The savings to your plant on this order amounts to $4000. In looking back over previous purchases on this spring, we find that the savings due to the use of your new specifications will amount to over $89,000 per year at the present purchase rate."

19.20 Control of Printed Circuit Requirements

A manufacturer of electronic keyboards is a large purchaser of printed circuit boards (PCBs) used both in keyboards and photoelectric and proximity switch lines. This company has emphasized reliability largely through stringent computerized testing of incoming materials.[11]

Noting an excessive number of nonconforming lots of purchased PCBs, a program was undertaken to reduce the overall percentage of defects and at the same time increase vendors' awareness of the problem.

To determine the dollar effect of nonconforming lots, an analysis was made of the five printed circuit board vendors compared to almost 800 vendors supplying purchased parts to the company. The report showed that the five PCB/vendors averaged 98 nonconforming lots each, or approximately 52 times more nonconforming lots than the overall average vendor, who supplied 1.9 nonconforming lots. The average additional cost to process nonconforming lots from the five PCB vendors was $18 per lot, or more than 450 percent the cost of processing nonconforming lots from the average vendor.

A flowchart was made of the keyboard processes pertaining to the PCBs, which gave an overall picture of exactly what was affected by the quality of the boards from the vendor through the company's final inspection. It was determined that problems directly related to the boards appeared to be minimal once the boards had been cleared through Receiving Inspection. A Pareto analysis (Fig. 19.17) was made of the nonconformances from the five vendors for an 11-month period. Nine, or one-third, of the sequences resulted in over 80 percent of the defects. The two top defects, hole size and board dimensions, were accepted to "use as is." Deviations were then requested for a total of 868 nonconforming characteristics: 526, or approximately 61 percent, were accepted with no sort or rework required.

Thus, it was concluded that the product definition—or what was specified versus what was accepted—varied to such a degree that it was virtually impossible for any of the five PCB vendors to achieve credibility.

Accordingly, prints and/or specifications were reviewed and revised to reflect what the company actually had been using 61 percent of the time. Substantial changes were made in such areas as increased hole size tolerance range, increased board dimensions tolerance range, and reduced gold thickness requirements. The company also investigated the use of electrical testing of PCBs to cull for shorts and voids.

The final step in the program called for visits to vendor facilities to evaluate manufacturing systems, process controls, and gaging compatibility. Vendors' past quality records were reviewed, and vendors informed that, because of revised specifications, defects would no longer be accepted.

As a result of this program, the company now sorts or reworks only the minimal amount of boards to meet immediate production needs; the balance of nonconforming product is returned for the vendor's action. The vendor's production and quality personnel are aware of the volume of rejected material, and vendor management is aware of the dollar credits which must be issued on this material, with resulting effective corrective action.

Specification	Pareto distribution			Accept/dev.	
	No. of defects	% defective	Accumu- lative %	No. accept	% accept
Hole size	165	19.0	19.0	150	90.9
Board dim.	110	12.7	31.7	96	87.3
Cond. defects	79	9.1	40.8	23	29.1
Gold thickness	69	8.0	48.8	31	44.9
Plating visual	66	7.6	56.4	31	50.8
Gold visual	61	7.0	63.4	27	44.3
HTH thickness	61	7.0	70.4	10	16.4
Hole location	56	6.5	76.9	54	96.4
PTH visual	29	3.3	80.2	16	55.2
Bevel	29	3.3	83.5	11	37.9
Solder mask	29	3.3	86.8	15	51.7
PN and artwork	21	2.4	89.2	20	95.2
Hole registration	18	2.1	91.3	10	55.6
Gold adhesion	17	2.0	93.3	1	5.9
Laminate defects	13	1.5	94.8	5	38.5
Solderability	10	1.2	96.0	6	60.0
Vendor ID and U/L	9	1.0	97.0	5	55.6
Warpage	6	0.7	97.7	5	83.3
Plating adhesion	6	0.7	98.4	0	0.0
Key slot location	6	0.7	99.1	3	50.0
Packaging	5	0.6	99.7	4	80.0
Material thickness	1	0.1	99.8	1	100.0
Material identification	1	0.1	99.9	1	100.0
Cu and resist removal	1	0.1	100.0	1	100.0
Pattern registration	0	0.0	100.0	0	0.0
Scratches	0	0.0	100.0	0	0.0
Missing circuitry	0	0.0	100.0	0	0.0
	868			526	60.6

FIG. 19.17 From Virgil L. Bowers, "Procurement Quality Assurance of PC Boards," 32nd Annual Conference Transactions, American Society for Quality Control.

19.21 Instituting Improved Control over Incoming Material in a Going Business

A heavy-equipment manufacturer was able for many years to control the quality of incoming materials through, in part, the medium of very light incoming inspection. Recently, however, some degree of change in the character of the business forced the manufacturer to buy widely from vendors with whom he had had little previous experience.

The quality produced by these vendors was so spotty that it soon became evident that the manufacturer required a more rigid form of incoming inspection routine. To meet this need, Quality Control developed a formal incoming acceptance procedure through use of a MIL-STD-105D-type acceptance sampling table.

The steps taken to establish this routine were

1. Thorough analysis of the purchased material arriving in the plant
2. Provision of adequate inspection equipments for this material
3. Establishment of an appropriate inspection routine
4. Selection of the most useful acceptance sampling table

Steps 2 and 4 were carried on jointly. For discussion purposes, however, each step is now discussed independently.[12]

Analysis of Incoming Material

Several incoming-material analyses were made of the type of materials accepted at the incoming stations, of the lot sizes in which this material was received, and of those incoming lots which were causing the gravest quality difficulties on the production lines. It was found that material was being received and inspected at five different locations in the plant; in some cases, the same type of material was received at two different locations because of nearness of these stations to the various assembly points.

Results of these analyses indicated that a concentration of incoming inspection effort should be placed at one station, which could be adequately laid out and provided with proper equipment. The parts which were most critical to quality were to be funneled through this one location. The five incoming inspection stations should be reduced to a total of three—one for critical materials and the other two for general materials which could satisfactorily be accepted close to their point of use.

The analysis also pointed up the relatively small size of the typical incoming lot. It was found that these lots were generally 1000 pieces or under, calling for a sampling procedure which would be most useful at these lot sizes. Relatively few parts and materials were found to be received in large lot quantities.

Provision of Inspection Equipment

The parts and materials received by this plant are widely varied. They include castings, bar stock, terminal screws, fabricated parts, complicated die-cast gear cases, sand-cast cams, and frames.

Inspection of materials of this character requires for a basic inspection kit such tools as surface plates, gage blocks, sine bars, and plug and snap gages; specialized gages are also required for those high-production parts which are critical.

Where they had not been previously available, the required tools were secured. Specialized gages were developed to the extent that they would be required by high-production parts. Inspection planning procedures were applied to those parts where they were appropriate.

Inspection Routine

Critical parts, formerly routed among the five original inspection stations, were rerouted to the single acceptance station for parts of this nature. The routine was established so that all incoming parts were accompanied by both a copy of the original material requisition and a receiving notice.

A vendor-record procedure was established, based upon drawing numbers of parts and materials. A file based upon vendor codes was also established for those parts received from several vendors.

Acceptance Sampling Table

Because of the wide variety of types of lots received by the plant, a very comprehensive MIL-STD-105D-type acceptance sampling table was chosen, similar to that shown in Figure 15.11. This table provided 16 AQLs, ranging from 0.015 to 10 percent.

In the case of some individual materials and parts, various AQLs are applied. For the great majority of incoming lots, however, a 2.5 percent AQL is used. Break-even-point analysis, based upon experience, showed that this 2.5 percent AQL is generally appropriate for the type of materials received; the single AQL greatly simplifies the sampling procedure required for incoming material in the factory.

Company Quality Control has summarized the results from this program:

1. Far better quality is being received from vendors.
2. Quality troubles on assembly lines have been reduced.
3. Purchasing has obtained better information about vendor's quality shipments.
4. Vendors have developed a far better sense of their quality responsibility.

19.22 Vendor Rating Through Data Processing

The vendor rating program of a semiconductor manufacturer has been computerized according to the following practices:

Each incoming lot of components is inspected and quality identified in accordance with purchasing procurement specifications as critical, major, or minor. A quality demerit rating system is then applied, based upon a minimum of 3 months' performance. Defects in the critical parameter are awarded three demerits; major defects, two demerits; minor defects, one demerit. Thus, a particular lot may be given a maximum of six demerits for failing all three defect classifications per sample plan specified. If no defect classification appears on the drawing, or if material is bought to a corporate material specification, a rejected lot is given six demerits.

When a lot has rejects in excess of the number permitted, the shipment is rejected and subject to return to the vendor. This applies to any defect classification. The inspection log or sheet at the receiving station then becomes the initial data source for scheduled computer input and analysis. Information appearing on the vendor rating summary includes the vendor's name, date of inspection, part number, pass/fail rating for each defect classification, delivery report, and date received.[13]

The computerized system permits early retrieval and analysis of data regarding a vendor's quality rating so that an immediate determination of the existence of a vendor problem can be made. In addition, upon request the computer can also provide a monthly report on each vendor, a cumulative report on each vendor for any desired period, retrieval features by vendor or individual part number—or by vendor and part number—and a notation to alert a vendor of poor rating so that the vendor can initiate corrective action. Records pertaining to 500 vendors are maintained and upgraded by one quality-control engineer and one secretary, each of whom expends only a brief time each month feeding data into the computer.

Stored data become the latest data source for the current monthly computer analysis and retrieval. Any time a pattern of failures begins to appear, the quality engineer can determine the cumulative rating of a vendor by simply requesting a cumulative vendor rating report. Monthly ratings of vendors are circulated to the purchasing department, the quality manager, the receiving-inspection department, and the quality engineer. The monthly data retrieval can be in the form of listings by vendors, in which part numbers, lots, number of failures, and ratings are printed out, or it may be in the form of a histogram. This way all pertinent division personnel have a running record of each vendor's performance.

A quarterly report is evaluating particular performance for quality, the percentage of defective lots received, and the percentage of on-time deliveries sent to each vendor. Files on vendors are maintained for 1 year, and information pertaining to a vendor's performance for any given period can be retrieved from the computer in the form of a graph. Each vendor's monthly rating is revealed on a scale from 0 to 6. The company has instituted a Vendor of the Year award in recognition of superior performance.

Notes

[1]The term "material" is used to indicate all material, parts, and assemblies.

[2]Chapter 15 discussed quite extensively the comparison of acceptance sampling tables with 100 percent, spot-check, and other forms of inspection.

[3]This incoming-material control example is adapted from experience in a composite of applications in order to provide completeness of technical presentation for teaching and demonstration.

[4]Considerations involved in properly carrying out acceptance sampling are extensively discussed in Chap. 15.

[5]Figure 19.6 is after a form developed by C. D. Ferris and associates, Bridgeport, Conn.

[6]Section 15.20 discussed several aspects of variables sampling.

[7]The form appearing as Fig. 19.12 was developed by Norman Cheever and associates of Everett, Mass.

[8]This color-coding procedure follows a system developed by L. W. Macomber, H. Richards, and associates, Lynn, Mass.

[9]After a discussion by E. A. Stockbower, "Consumer-Supplier: An Advantageous Relationship," *Quality Progress*, vol. XI, no. 1, January 1978; pp. 34–35.

[10]Adapted from a study by R. S. Inglis and W. J. Masser, Philadelphia, Pa.

[11]After a discussion by Virgil L. Bowers, "Procurement Quality Assurance of PC Boards," *32nd Annual Technical Conference Transactions,* American Society for Quality Control, Chicago, 1978.

[12]This discussion is adapted from a study made by A. J. Showler and associates, Erie, Pa.

[13]After a discussion by Vincent A. Falvo, "A Computerized Rating System," *Quality Progress,* vol. X, no. 6, June 1977, p. 20.

CHAPTER **20**

Product Control

The acid test of the adequacy of a quality-control program comes during actual product manufacture. The total-quality-control job termed Product Control provides the mechanism for this phase of quality activity.

Product control has often been publicized for its technical aspects—control charts, quality audits, electronic subassembly reliability testing, tool and jig control. The vitally important human relations activity that must be involved in successful product control has frequently been minimized in these discussions. Without high plant morale and motivation, without a genuine desire throughout the company and its service sectors to produce and maintain products of high quality—including safety and reliability—without adequate communication of quality objectives throughout the plant, the more technical product-control methods can have few lasting results. This very important companywide commitment to quality which is basic to programs for total quality control was discussed in Chapter 9.

The importance of the human as well as the technological influences on product quality was brought forcibly home to a young quality engineer who had established an elaborate control charting procedure for a very critical lathe operation on pump fan blades. The frequency-distribution analysis, which had preceded establishment of the control charts, had convinced the quality engineer that the lathe could maintain the ± 0.0005-inch tolerance required by the blade job; regular review of the charts themselves indicated that the job was a stable one and that the blades produced were well "in control."

One Monday morning, however, the control charts made it clear that the blade job was no longer stable or in control. The variation on blades had increased to several thousandths of an inch.

The veteran operator who had operated the lathe for many years had retired at the end of the previous week. Investigation into causes of the out-of-control operation finally disclosed that the lathe had a very definite taper in its ways; the veteran operator had known the machine well enough to be able to "nurse it along" in the production of satisfactory blades, and the new operator was simply unable to match the performance of the veteran.

The result of this analysis was location of the job on another machine. Several changes were made in its tooling. In establishing a control chart procedure for the new machine, the young quality engineer was much more humble in making conclusions, based upon purely technical factors, from statistical analyses without further judgment.

Modern product-control activities take full cognizance of this overwhelming influence that human beings exert upon the results from technical methods for controlling quality. This influence is reflected in the nature of the techniques and organizational methods of the third of the quality-control jobs. This chapter discusses these product-control techniques.

20.1 The Needs for Product Control

The percentage of internal failure costs to total planned direct labor cost reflects, for many plants, startling evidence of the effect of inadequate control of product quality during manufacture. These manufacturing losses—composed of such elements as costs for scrapping and/or reworking material of unsatisfactory quality—represent a ratio of as high as 20 to 40 percent and much more in some plants.

High costs for the inspection of manufactured parts and materials may be another evidence of inadequate control. These high appraisal costs were once justified in some quarters as a reflection of good control of product quality. Modern industrial thinking now recognizes that these costs in some plants may, on the contrary, result because control has been poor. Satisfactory quality may not have been built into the products *before* they were presented for inspection. This modern thinking recognizes that high appraisal costs may be merely a different side of the high-internal-failure coin, with both types of expenditure directly traceable to unsatisfactory control over plant quality.

Yet high appraisal costs and high internal failure costs may indicate that some portion of control has been exercised over quality, namely, that unsatisfactory parts and materials are being "caught" before they are shipped to customers. Even more distressing for many plants are the problems which develop when this unsatisfactory material is actually shipped to customers. Arising from these situations are the numerous customer complaints, the high external failure costs for which result either from the need for completely replacing the complainant's material or from the need for repairing or servicing it.

The immediate financial loss due to complaints is only part of this particular problem. While less tangible to a company in the short run, the loss of customer goodwill from these complaints will ultimately have a direct bearing upon the marketing position of the company.[1] Every reader has heard a purchaser—either industrial or consumer—comment about a manufacturer that "You can't depend upon that company's products." Such statements may presage a serious decline in the company's commercial position.

Another aspect of the complaint situation relates to those products upon whose proper performance human safety and comfort depend. Poor quality of these products may raise much more serious and immediate issues than long-term decline in the company's commercial position. It may result in costly recall of large numbers of products from the field and, in some cases, heavy legal liability penalties. In these cases, one poor-quality lot received by customers may be all that is required to put a firm out of business. This is especially true in companies heavily committed to research and development, which may produce "one of a kind" items or limited numbers of high-technology products.[2]

Poor control over quality during active production may cause financial problems of a more subtle form than that of losses or complaints or liability expenses. It may be reflected in increases in planned cost on a part to allow for second operations like finish tapping or grinding "just to be safe." It may be reflected in unbalanced inventory conditions because of periodic rejections of lots of parts, which force production holdups while additional lots are being manufactured. It may be reflected in machine overruns or in the informal procedure of order clerks to "order a few percent more just to allow for possible rejections." It may cause parts shortages which create down time in later operations. It may necessitate overtime scheduling or even purchase of added production facilities.

These cost situations broadly tend to indicate the needs of a plant for adequate control of products. Other, somewhat more specific, factors may also be cited:

There may, for example, be inadequate maintenance of the condition of processing equipments, assembly robots, soldering baths, heating ovens, numerically controlled machining programs, and other tools—or lack of knowledge of the capabilities of these processing equipments. There may be ineffective utilization in the plant of such quality-control technical methods as station control or the control chart or quality-level control or the process-sampling table. There may be imperfect use of engineering specifications or data developed by the company new-design control routine. There may be little use of modern quality information equipment or computer-based data flow.

There may be lack of quality-mindedness among plant employees. There may be lack of truly high quality-performance targets—reflected in very low defect rate objectives. This failure in attitude may revolve in a vicious circle, with such conditions as poor housekeeping and loose inspection performance. There may be failure to keep operators informed of plant quality objectives or to go over with them nonconforming work they have produced. In plants which have extensive report systems covering such elements as car loadings and labor take-home records, there may not even be the crudest attempt at informing management of the quality index of the manufacturing operations of the plant.

Solutions of problems of this sort may be most effectively achieved in those plants which operate a total-quality-control program. Their solution depends upon a foundation of satisfactory new-design and incoming-material control activities; in particular, it depends upon a broadly conceived and efficiently operating series of product-control routines.

20.2 Defining Product Control

As a definition:

> Product control involves the control of products at the source of production and through field service so that departures from the quality specification can be corrected before defective or nonconforming products are manufactured and the proper service can be maintained in the field to assure full provision of the intended customer quality.

This tool includes all quality-control activity on a product from the time it is approved for production and its materials and components are received to the time it is packaged, shipped, and received by a customer who remains satisfied with it.

The emphasis upon prevention and control at the source of production may be readily appreciated. The product whose quality is poor during manufacture faces the strong likelihood of high manufacturing losses, high inspection and test costs, and high complaint expense in the field. For the sake of example, such an article can be termed product A.

Another article—product B—whose quality is high during manufacture will represent a better situation. The likelihood is that this article will experience a good loss, cost, and complaint record.

Figure 20.1 reflects this situation from the statistical point of view. The quality of product B has been controlled at the source, and the frequency distribution shown is that of the product as it is presented for inspection.

Product A is an article without effective control at the source. Its inspection costs have been very high. They have, however, never resulted in sufficiently dependable activities to erase the high complaint expense due to articles which have "slipped through" inspection or those whose characteristics have "drifted" after inspection. Internal failure costs have also remained at correspondingly high levels.

The product-control concept itself, as noted in the definition, is expressed in widely differing details of application among varying types of manufacturing conditions. Chemical processes, as contrasted to those for mechanical products, may be cited as an example. Electronic process control, with its need for high component quality, may be cited as another example.[3]

Indeed, product-control objectives are increasingly and necessarily moving to very low parts nonconforming and defective levels as essential quality needs.

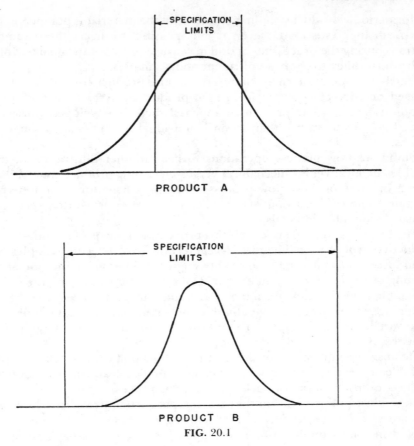

PRODUCT A

PRODUCT B
FIG. 20.1

The objective of a very small number of nonconforming parts per million—which is increasingly termed the "ppm" approach in such products as volume electronic assemblies—is today being identified as quality requirements for certain product lines, as introduced at the beginning of Chapter 11.

Product control of quality at the source may, for one of its phases, be very effectively operated in a machine shop or on an assembly conveyor belt by selecting periodic samples during the progress of product manufacture. By showing trends of tool wear or of increasingly less satisfactory operator skill, these samples may "red-flag" potential causes of defects before rejections occur.

In contrast, selection of comparable samples from a batch chemical process may be an ineffective means of control. Selection of samples may be both physically difficult and of questionable practical value.

After the components of the chemical have been measured and the vat valves set for the manufacture of a large batch of material, there may be little opportunity for periodic product sampling checks until the material is pumped in final form from the system. And even if it is possible to select these samples, reactions during the processing period may cause results at the final test of the batch which differ from those of the periodic samples.

Some batch operations may, therefore, require product-control activity that is based on corrective action from final product analyses rather than from periodic sampling. The preventive approach here is developed toward the *overall batch process* rather than toward individual lots passing through this process.

Continuous-flow process operations furnish another illustration of these possible chemical versus mechanical versus electronic product-control differences.[4] In some of these flow processes, chemists have for some time been selecting samples consisting of a single unit of product—often selected at regularly scheduled intervals.

Before unquestioningly rejecting this procedure in favor of including in the product-control routine the more typical technique of selecting samples composed of several units, the wise quality engineer determines the operational meaning of such a several-unit sample. Does the variation among the units of the sample have the same meaning in a continuous-flow process as it has in a machining process where a several-unit sample is generally a requirement? Are those variations which appear in the flow process sample due largely to the influence of the testing device alone?

The answer to questions of this sort may show that a single-unit sample is desirable in several instances for the most practical and most economical product-control routine for such a continuous process.

These illustrations point up the fact that product-control procedures must be tailored for the particular manufacturing situation at hand rather than adapted in total from a routine developed for a so-called similar situation. While the basic emphasis upon prevention is fundamental to product control among all these manufacturing situations, the technical details of the application of the principle will vary widely from plant to plant.

It cannot be overemphasized that the purpose of a product-control procedure is tangible results in quality maintenance and improvement; the individual techniques employed to produce these results are only means to an end —they are not ends in themselves. Quality-control specialists must continually guard themselves against concentration upon these individual product-control techniques lest the specialists' perspective be narrowed in regard to the overall plant quality-control program.

20.3 Organizing for Product Control

Key individuals in the quality-control practices for product control are the men and women who actually produce the product—machinists, electronic assemblers, testers—together with product supervisors and foremen. All practices are built around these employees and managers because it is of and through them that the great bulk of product-control activities must be carried on. Also involved in a very important degree are mechanical inspection and electrical/electronic test activities.

Detailed planning of that segment of the quality program which relates to product and process control is accomplished by the quality engineer assigned for the particular product line. In establishing the planned activities, the quality engineer may consult Product Engineering, Manufacturing Engineering, Production Control, Cost Accounting, and Shop Operations.

As much quality checking as is practicable is made the responsibility of the production operators who are generating the quality characteristics. This technique has been called "source control" in some contexts, or more recently, "station control." Quality characteristics are measured at those points in the product flow which are the economic and strategic "stations" for control of product and process. At other "stations," an independent quality audit may be conducted by Process-Control Engineering personnel.[5]

Implementation of the product and process quality-control program is the responsibility of the process-control engineer. This individual may be said to be the key quality-control person in this third job of total quality control. If for any reason the established quality program cannot be applied, the process-control engineer does the necessary emergency planning to permit continuation of production at required quality levels. If the situation that necessitated emergency planning is more than transitory, the process-control engineer requests that essential changes be made in the established program by the quality engineer. The process-control engineer also keeps process-capability studies up to date and analyzes quality problems as they arise day to day. The process-control engineer may request help of the quality engineer or bring other functional specialists to work on the problem.

It is of prime importance that the knowledge gained by the process-control engineer is fed back to those responsible for quality planning, quality information equipment design, and process and product design and that it is used directly to develop appropriate control methods and effectively implement quality planning. Some shortcomings in quality planning and equipment design can be traced directly to failure to properly determine process-quality ability and feed it back to other engineers. Note in this discussion of organization that product-control activities are inevitably bound up with the work of the other management programs used by a plant in its manufacturing operations.

If a plant has ineffective personnel policies and is willing to hire low-caliber employees and then spend little time training them; if its production-control scheduling and routing procedures impair shop morale by imposing a maximum of red tape and a minimum of orderly material flow through the factory; if materials handling is still in a primitive stage, if production and quality data processing remain on a "back of notepaper" basis; then the effect and nature of product-control procedures will themselves be strongly influenced.

Whether product control will exert a tug on these other functions sufficiently strong to raise their effectiveness or will be dragged down to their level will depend upon the particular plant situation and the strength of the personalities and policies involved. Certainly it is a basic error to suppose that the mere establishment of a product-control procedure will automatically solve shop quality problems that have been generated by misuse of other management programs.

As a corollary, it must be noted that it is equally erroneous to suppose that a weak product-control procedure will suffice simply because some other management programs are strong. The answer here is a matter of balance a plant must be assured both that it has adequate product-control procedure and that its other management programs include satisfactory practices that may influence these product-control procedures

20.4 The Role of Process-Control Engineering in Product Control

As discussed in Chapter 8, the Process-Control Engineering component has a major contribution to product quality. Process-Control Engineering is responsible in the production phase to ensure that personnel, methods, materials, and equipment are being employed according to quality plan and that the quality procedures are being followed by those performing quality measurements. One of its primary goals is to determine an ongoing cause-and-effect relationship between the product and the preceding processes.

Definite procedures are operated by members of the process-control unit to ensure that the product-control activities are an integral part of plant practice. These procedures are established within the total quality program by the quality-engineering unit assisted by the production supervisor and the concerned functional people. Because of the wide variety of manufacturing activities that may exist even within one plant, the procedures must cover a number of different control conditions that can be grouped under two general headings:

1. Control of machining or processing of components
2. Control of assemblies and packaging and on batches

Procedures required for these control conditions on the factory floor may cover control of work passing through the machine shop, materials being processed through welders or furnaces, assemblies being built up from component and electronic subassemblies, assemblies being produced by robotized equipments, chemicals being produced in a batch process, and wire being coated in a continuous-flow process. The procedures may involve control of tools, jigs, fixtures, and numerical control machining software programs; preventive maintenance; utilization of process-capability studies; means for improving operator quality-mindedness; application of control chart and process sampling plans; strategic placement of mechanical inspection and electrical/electronic test stations and nondestructive evaluations (NDE); development of product-quality indices.[6]

These procedures will depend upon proper material flow and sound plant layout for as large a degree as possible of "built-in quality" through the basic manufacturing plan. They will emphasize rigid procedures for disposal of defective parts and for establishing proper reject analyses.

The procedures depend upon good factory supervision as much as upon sound technical methods. They require adequate product-control organization throughout the factory and genuine acceptance throughout the plant of the point of view of total quality control. They are built around procedures which enable corrective action when such action is required; they involve taking of data only to the extent that they may be a basis for action.

BUILDING THE PRODUCT-CONTROL ACTIVITIES

20.5 The Pattern

Product-control activities may cover the entire cycle of actual manufacture, where raw materials and purchased components are, through one process or another, converted into a finished product. They may cover only the components-processing portion of this cycle—as in the case of a processing plant or processing division of a large plant. The procedures may cover only the assembly portion of the cycle.

Whatever coverage is taken by the procedures, they will gear into a flow of manufactured parts and materials which, for many manufacturing floors, often pursues at least seven identifiable steps:

1. Receipt of order for the part, material, or assembly in the manufacturing area.
2. Examination of the requirements of the order and taking the steps required to make the order ready for production, including product and process classification, correct assignment of all necessary equipment and controls.
3. Release of order for production.
4. Control of material while in process of manufacture.
5. Approval of product.
6. Quality audit with specific reference to safety and reliability considerations, and evaluation of results.
7. Packaging and shipment. If a component, the product may merely be transported to the area where it will be used in assembly.

Product-control activities which carry through these seven steps may be considered in two major divisions:

1. Setting and maintaining standards (carried on during steps 1 through 3).
2. Control of material during actual manufacture (carried on during steps 4 through 7).

Sections 20.6 and 20.7 discuss factors that must be taken into account while developing practices involving each of these two divisions.

20.6 Standards

In building the standards portions of product-control activities, the quality-control organization must first take into account such factors as

1. *Product requirements.* The article's specifications, its guarantees, and tolerances.
2. *How it is to be made.* The quality factors in planning for manufacture, determination of processing equipments upon which the article may be produced, and selection of required tools, jigs, fixtures, software programs, and other guides for numerical control.
3. *What is important on article.* Classification of characteristics; inspection and test requirements; point of inspection or test; quality levels for sampling.
4. *How quality is to be assured.* Quality information equipments to be used; reliability testing to be performed; automatic inspection and testing practices; computer-aided quality practices that are integrated with computer-aided design and manufacture.

When the product has been subject to new-design control activity, information about these four factors will have been sent to the manufacturing area along with the order in the form of such media as the quality planning for the article. In a newly installed total-quality-control program, where new-design control activity has not yet proceeded to cover all products, the overall product-control procedure must incorporate an abbreviated form of this activity to produce comparable information.

Note that it is not best practice for product-control procedures to thus attempt to backtrack over these required new-design control steps for an article. Particularly in the development of specifications and guarantees and in the establishment of inspection and test requirements and quality levels, such a backtrack is both less economical and less satisfactory technically than a straightforward new-design control program would be. The "design trail" of the article may already have gone cold, and the design engineers concerned may no longer be readily available for consultation. Proper equipment may not be available for making the required tests; tight production requirements may permit no time for adequate analyses.

There are, of course, certain conditions which make it inevitable that such a necessarily sketchy new-design control program be incorporated into product-control procedures. The plant which has recently initiated new-design control activities will be forced for some time to cover such activities in its product-control procedures which apply to existing articles.

Also, there is the quite typical situation of the plant which does only the machining or assembly of articles designed or specified in another plant. Similar is the case of the so-called contributing divisions (printed circuit cards, screw machines, punch presses, and so on) of a large plant. These plants or divisions may merely receive drawings or sketches of the part or possibly simply a written order for it, from which they must establish manufacturing, material-ordering, and quality procedures.

There is nothing unique about the techniques used in this so-called new-design phase of product control. The techniques are simply those regular procedures discussed in Chapter 18 adapted to particular situations as needed.

Process-capability studies are particularly widely applied in this work. In the often-encountered plant which has just initiated new-design control, tabulations of the results of these process studies are generally used by the plant engineers during the growth of their formal design-control activities.

20.7 Manufacturing Control

When these standards for the article have been incorporated into the procedure, actual production-control activities may then be developed. Typical factors that must be evaluated during this consideration are the following:

1. *Type of manufacturing process.* Is it an assembly being built up on a conveyor? A part being worked at several successive machine tools? An electronic subassembly being produced by single operators at single stations? Material being processed as individual batches? An assembly being built by robotized operation? Numerically controlled machining and processing being accomplished?

2. *Manufacturing quantities.* Are there high quantities, same material day after day? Job lots, different parts always? High quantities but short runs of different parts?

3. *Type of shop personnel.* Skilled workers, each a quality-conscious person? Relatively unskilled operators, each performing a repetitive operation? Experienced, competent factory foremen? Newly appointed, inexperienced supervisors?

4. *Type of product.* Is it a precision machined part? Intricate assembly? Material with loose quality requirements? Electronic component of widely variable yields? Safety-oriented subassembly?

5. *Product-control procedures on other processes in the shop.* Can the controls for this process be easily integrated with those in effect on other processes, with corresponding simplicity of administration and minimum of expense? If they cannot be thus integrated, will the control procedure conflict with these other instructions, resulting in confusion?

6. *Acceptance of product control.* Is there acceptance among the concerned personnel of the value of total quality control? How can the details of the product-control activity employ to the greatest possible extent the language and practice best understood in the factory? How can the principles of the product-control activity best be sold to production personnel?

If the article is to be produced as a relatively small element in the overall production of a large machine shop, a semiconductor production facility, or an extensive assembly area, it is likely that its control procedure will merely be absorbed into the standard, overall product-control procedure for the area, as suggested in factor 5 above. Such overall procedures, which incorporate the same control principles for all parts, may be both practical and economical when properly established. They are particularly useful in those areas where quality requirements are relatively uniform even though production consists in a wide variety of types of articles.

The article may, however, be produced as a major element of overall production, perhaps in an area devoted largely or exclusively to its manufacture. In cases of this sort, individual control activities will be developed for sole application to the product.

This discussion of factors involved in developing control activities cannot be concluded without emphasis upon factor 6 above, relating to factory acceptance. A product-control procedure which is excellent technically but either is not or cannot be sold to the personnel who must work with has little positive value and may actually be detrimental.

20.8 High Quantities Versus Job Lots

It may be emphasized that the two divisions discussed above—standards and manufacturing controls—are quite generally applicable as the basis for product-control activities. This is true whether production is job lot or high quantity, whether output takes the form of individual parts or intricate assemblies, whether production time required is several days or only a few minutes.

Section 4.12 summarized its general review of this job-lot–high-quantity issue in the following conclusion:

> In mass-production manufacturing, quality-control activities center on the *product and process,* while job-lot manufacturing is a matter of controlling the *process.* For example, in the mass-production manufacture of coils, the emphasis of quality-control activities is on the coil type itself—its dimensions, fiber wrappings, and so on. But where varying types and sizes of coils are produced on a job-lot basis, the quality-control activities center on the common manufacturing process for producing the coils.

This conclusion may be paraphrased in the language developed in this chapter: When production is high-quantity and will run for a sufficient length of time, techniques may be used in the product-control activity both for setting and maintaining standards and controlling parts during manufacture. When production is job-lot or of short duration, the techniques used may concentrate almost entirely upon setting and maintaining standards. The process and processing equipment is thus controlled rather than the parts themselves.

If a screw machine is set up for a production run which will involve thousands of parts over a several-day period, it may be useful and effective both to set and maintain standards—through such means as tool and die control or process-capability studies—and to establish manufacturing controls—through such means as patrol inspection, process sampling, or control charts. If an assembly process is established for a long continuous run with components being automatically fed into robot assembly equipments at a pace of hundreds of units per three shift operations over a several-week period, the operation of this full range of controls will be similarly effective. However, if a punch press is set for a production run which will involve 300 to 400 parts but which will be completed in less than an hour, it may be impractical and uneconomical to concentrate upon any techniques other than proper standards setting. If a large shaft is being slowly turned and faced, control chart technique may be very inappropriate and the setting of standards may again be the indicated product-control technique.

The details of the various individual standards and manufacturing control techniques used in the accompanying product-control routines are discussed in Section 20.14.

TYPICAL PRODUCT-CONTROL ACTIVITIES

The actual forms taken by product-control activities vary much more widely throughout industry than the forms taken by procedures of any of the other quality-control jobs. This situation is probably because of the very wide variety of manufacturing situations involved. It is therefore most useful to discuss typical product-control activities in relation to actual industrial cases rather than to more abstract, generalized examples.

Five actual examples are discussed below, covering major situations encountered in the overall product-control activity: (1) "Job-Lot Machine Shop," Section 20.9; (2) "Process Sampling in a Machine Shop," Section 20.10; (3) "Characteristics Approach to Numerical Control," Section 20.11; (4) "High-Quantity, High-Reliability Subassembly," Section 20.12; (5) "Assembly," Section 20.13.

20.9 Job-Lot Machine Shop[7]

The production machine shop in a middle Atlantic area factory includes sensitive drill presses, radial drill presses, milling machines, lathes, screw machines, punch presses, grinders, welders, and brazing and burning equipment. From 100 to 150 jobs go through this shop daily, with average lot sizes of less than 100 pieces. A large proportion of these jobs are nonrepetitive; they may not pass through the shop again for a period of from 6 months to 2 years.

Each job lot passing through the shop requires several operations before completion. A typical part may require not only turning but milling and drilling.

The importance for control purposes of adequate standards setting and maintenance activity under conditions of this sort is recognized in this shop in several ways. One is its emphasis upon the utilization of the results of process-capability studies. Insofar as possible, jobs are planned for and placed upon processing equipments known through these studies to be capable of maintaining the required dimensions.

A preventive maintenance program is actively followed to keep these processing equipments in proper condition. Tools, numerical control programs, dies, jigs, and fixtures are closely controlled so that they will be in adequate shape to assist in producing work of the quality called for in new-design control specifications.

Were this standards activity the only element in the product-control procedure for this plant, the shop would suffer from the occurrence of such nonconformances as

1. An undersized or an oversized hole when all that was required was the proper-sized drill
2. A radius being ground on the wrong side
3. A hole being drilled out of location
4. The wrong side being milled
5. A missed operation
6. Holes countersunk on the wrong side or not deep enough
7. Defective burring
8. Damage during processing

To eliminate defects of this sort, the shop complements its standards activity with an effective procedure for control during manufacture. This procedure embraces five major elements:[8]

1. First-piece inspection. Operators make their own process checks thereafter, and gages are provided them for this purpose.
2. Acceptance sampling inspection of completed lots.
3. Control through data from final inspection.
4. Quality audit by process-control engineer.
5. Follow-through to gain corrective action from final inspection-control data and quality audits.

Note that these five elements do not include process sampling or patrol inspection, which often characterize the preventive approach in a machine shop. Both analyses and experience have shown this type of sampling to be uneconomical and relatively impractical in this shop. Production quantities are very small, runs are short, jobs may be completed and shipped between inspection checks, and it has been found practical in this shop to place responsibility for periodic checks upon the operators themselves.

Emphasis is therefore upon one interpretation of the job-lot product-control approach discussed in Section 20.8. *Control is set up for the entire production shop, the "process" in this particular case.* It is not based upon an individual part or job.

With this fundamental established, each of the five steps in the machine-shop control may be briefly reviewed:

First-Piece Inspection

All jobs receive a first-piece inspection. If the inspector approves the first piece, the job is allowed to run and the operator will thereafter periodically check this work.

All jobs receive a first-piece inspection at each operation. It is therefore possible for one lot to receive three, four, or five such inspections.

Acceptance Sampling of Completed Lots

Completed lots are routed to a final inspection area, well-stocked with measuring equipments. Here the lots are sampled through use of a MIL-STD-105D-type acceptance sampling table.

It has been found practical and economical to use a single AQL for the great majority of lots entering the final inspection area. The quality level used was determined through use of the type of analysis discussed in Chapter 15.

Figure 20.2 illustrates graphically the inspection sequence followed in this acceptance procedure.

Control Through Data from Final Inspection

Data are taken on each lot passing through final inspection. For corrective action and to reduce record keeping to the required minimum, detailed data are kept only on the jobs found nonconforming.

Figure 20.3 presents the form on which this record is kept. It is made out

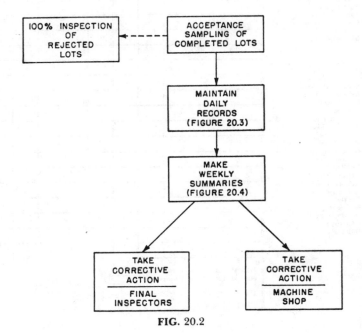

FIG. 20.2

daily by the final inspectors. These inspectors record the total number of jobs accepted and rejected, and the total number of first-piece inspections and rejections. For all nonconforming lots, they record the drawing number, lot size, quantity inspected, quantity rejected, the operation responsible for the nonconformity, the type of nonconformity, and the disposition of the lot.

The operation responsible for the nonconformity and the type of nonconformity are, of course, the most important items on the form. The various types of operations are listed by numbers, and the various types of nonconformities are listed by letters. For example, reference to Figure 20.3 shows that, for a lot rejected owing to an undersize dimension on a milling operation, the inspector would record 11 (milling operation) and T (undersize).

Date_____

OPERATIONS	Jobs Passed_____				Jobs Rejected_____		
1 – Brazing/Burning 2 – Broaching 3 – Engineering Errors 4 – Drilling "Sen." 5 – Drilling "Rad." 6 – File Bench 7 – Forming (brake) 8 – Grinding 9 – Lathe 10 – Layout & Brush Gr. 11 – Milling 12 – Other Divisions 13 – Production Errors 14 – Punch Press 15 – Sawing 16 – Steel Fabrication 17 – Welding 18 – Screw Mach. 19 – 20 –	DRAWING NO.	JOB QUAN.	QUAN. INSP.	QUAN. NON-CONF.	OPERATION & NONCONF.	DISPOSITION	
						REJ.	PASSED
NONCONFORMITIES							
A – Compound Group B – Countersinking C – Def. Burring D – Def. Material E – Def. Threads F – Def. Radius G – Finish too rough H – Missed Operations J – Mixed Parts K – No Job Tag L – No Print M – Other Faults N – Out of Location O – Oversize P – Plating Q – Reaming R – Rough Handling S – Shortage T – Undersize U – V – X –							

No. of 1st piece Inspections_____
No. of 1st piece Rejections_____   Inspector_____

FIG. 20.3

The record kept on the form of lot size, quantity inspected, and quantity rejected provides primarily the opportunity for a check by the process-control engineer to determine if the acceptance sampling table is strictly adhered to. The data also furnish the basis for gaining some degree of indication of the percent nonconforming in the lot. These data provide the manual foundation for computer analysis.[9]

The record kept of drawing numbers is of value in a frequency-of-occurrence analysis. Corrective action—whether change in engineering design or in manu-facturing method—may then be requested by the process-control engineer.

The daily record form of Figure 20.3 is summarized weekly. Figure 20.4 shows the manual form of the record used, one particularly useful for weekly process-control-engineering reviews to determine the basis for corrective ac-tion.

Quality Audit

The process-control engineer, as part of the job of implementing the quality program, monitors the quality-control procedures being used throughout the shop.

In addition to this activity, the process-control engineer periodically con-ducts an audit to evaluate the quality that is being shipped from the machine shop. This is a customer-centered audit, the process-control engineer playing the role of the assembly supervisors who must use the machined parts. These periodic evaluations provide a continuous monitoring of the machine shop's quality plan. Any weakness discovered in the parts call for a review of the plan and necessary changes in the planning by the quality engineer to assure the desired parts quality.[10]

Follow-Through to Gain Corrective Action

Whether discrepancies in parts quality are noted on the daily inspection records or as a result of the quality audits, it is essential that prompt investiga-tion be made and proper corrective action taken. Data from the record sheets usually show in this shop that two or three operations and two or three types of nonconformities are responsible for 75 to 85 percent of all rejections. These data are reviewed weekly by the process-control engineer. Decisions upon corrective action represent the essence of the work because the futility of record keeping without corresponding action is recognized. This action may take such forms as the following:

1. The supervisors will notify their instructors or leaders to concentrate upon the operations found to be nonconforming.
2. Manufacturing Engineering may start to design foolproof jigs or fixtures on these operations.
3. In the rare case of epidemics, patrol inspection may be temporarily estab-lished for the troublesome processing operation.
4. Nonconforming work is returned for the instruction of the operators who

produced it. These operators are correspondingly provided with further guidance and training.

A number of steps are taken in this plant to improve the quality-consciousness and quality-mindedness of all employees. In addition to such factors as operator training, good supervision, and quality campaigns, the quality-control personnel make several specific moves which are integrated with the data-recording activity at final inspection. The results of the weekly analyses of Fig. 20.4 are posted prominently in the plant in the form of two charts. One chart shows the percentage of effective jobs for each operation. The second chart shows the percent nonconforming trend of all jobs passing through final inspection.

In addition, particularly troublesome parts scrapped at final inspection are displayed each week. Cards attached to these parts explain the defects, show the amount of money lost owing to the nonconformities and may indicate any information as to business lost owing to the scrappage.

The plant using this product-control activity recognizes that it does not employ some of the more highly publicized techniques whose value has been analyzed and found uneconomical for this particular situation. Plant personnel feel that they have gained considerable advantage from the activities tailor-made to their job-lot machine shop. Among these advantages the plant lists

1. Ease and economy of the operation of the activity
2. Its complete analysis of shop quality
3. Its provision for continually monitoring the output of the quality plan by the process-control engineer
4. Its red-flagging of needs for corrective action
5. Its indication of the effects of corrective action
6. The fashion in which the activities point out those individuals—operators, inspectors, or others—who require further instruction
7. The reductions in losses and increases in output that have accompanied operation of the activities
8. The reductions in inspection time that have resulted from quality improvements developing from operation of the procedures

20.10 Process Sampling in a Machine Shop

A product-control procedure which utilizes several different techniques from those discussed in the preceding section operates very successfully for the machine shop of a New York State factory. This machine shop includes milling machines, numerically controlled equipments, drill presses, lathes, and other similar tools. Work passing through the shop requires only a fair degree of precision, ranging from tolerances of plus or minus two- or three-thousands of an inch to tolerances expressed in fractional terms:

Production quantities range from job lots to high-quantity runs. Many lots

Week Ending_____

SUMMARY SHEET

	Jobs Passed	Jobs Rej.	Jobs. Insp.	% Nonconf.
Monday				
Tuesday				
Wednes.				
Thursday				
Friday				
Saturday				
TOTAL				

Row labels:
1- Brazing/Burning
2- Broaching
3- Engineering Errors
4- Drilling "Sen."
5- Drilling "Rad."
6- File Bench
7- Forming (Brake)
8- Grinding
9- Lathe
10- Layout & Brush Group
11- Milling
12- Other Divisions
13- Production Errors
14- Punch Press
15- Sawing
16- Steel Fabrication
17- Welding
18- Screw Machine
19-
20-
21-
TOTAL

Column labels:
TOTAL
W-
V-
U-
T- Undersize
S- Shortage
R- Rough Handling
Q- Reaming
P- Plating
O- Oversize
N- Out of Location
M- Other Faults
L- No Print
K- No Job Tag
J- Mixed Parts
H- Missed Operation
G- Finish Too Rough
F- Def. Radius
E- Def. Threads
D- Def. Material
C- Def. Burring
B- Counter sinking
A- Compound Group

FIG. 20.4

are nonrepetitive: others are processed regularly. Work passing through the shop consists chiefly of relatively small parts, each of comparatively low cost. As many as a dozen individual operations may be performed on these parts.

Shop employees are well-trained in the operation of the machine tool to which they are assigned. Most of the men and women operating the machines are not, however, skilled mechanics.

This shop carries on some standards-setting and -maintenance activity. This consists largely of the same techniques as those noted in Section 20.9—preventive maintenance, process-capability studies, tool and die control, and so on.

Because of the character of this machine shop, its primary quality emphasis is placed upon the control of parts during processing. After a dozen operations have been performed and the parts have been degreased and cleaned, it is virtually impossible at a final inspection to do more than sort the bad parts from the good. There is, for example, no room on the small parts for operators' identification stamps.

Both experience and analytical studies have shown the management of this shop that it is most practical and economical to carry out its control of parts through process sampling. This process-sampling activity covers all parts manufactured in the machine shop. A process-sampling table is used similar to that discussed in Section 15.24 and shown in Figure 15.25. A single AQL has been determined to apply to all parts, and a single shopwide patrol inspection schedule is operated.

The process-sampling procedure used in this shop has four major steps:

1. The setup for a job is made by the operator or setup person. When this individual is satisfied that it is correct, first-piece inspection is made by the process inspector. When the piece is approved, the inspector punches a record card which is hung at each machine and the operator starts the production run.
2. The operator checks the work at regular intervals. If a defect is discovered, the process is corrected. The new setup must thereupon be approved by the process inspector.
3. At the intervals specified by the process-sampling table, the patrol inspector checks the required number of parts. These parts may be chosen consecutively or at random, depending upon the job circumstances.[11] If no rejects are found, the inspector segregates work that has been processed since the last check, punches the record card "O.K.," and production continues.
4. If defects are found by the process inspector, the proper authority is notified to get the process corrected immediately. The parts that have accumulated since the last inspection are set aside for sorting. The inspector punches the reason for rejection on the record card. When the process is corrected, approval by the process inspector must be obtained before production is allowed to continue.

Except for an occasional final acceptance sampling check on lots periodically to audit the continued effectiveness of the process-sampling procedure, no final inspection is required in this shop. Process sampling has been proved so satisfactory that lots are merely transported to the assembly area after their completion.

In addition to the immediate follow-through gained through this process-sampling procedure, the process-control engineer regularly reviews the record cards taken from the machines. Corrective action is decided upon, and responsibilities are assigned to appropriate positions. Special process studies (see

Chap. 21) may be initiated in particularly troublesome problem situations. Figure 20.5 shows the sequence followed in this procedure.

The value the factory has gained from this procedure is due not only to these sampling techniques but to the extensive program of quality education carried on in the plant. Employee participation in "better quality" committees, periodic slogan and poster campaigns in the plant newspaper, and both preliminary and refresher training of operators are examples of this educational activity.

20.11 Characteristics Approach to Numerical Control

The process characteristics generated by machine tools are important contributors to the overall quality of the finished product. This is particularly true in the case of numerically controlled machine tool equipment. In a New England plant, such NC tools are widely used because of their high repeatability performance. Recognizing that the repeatability of NC equipment is directly related to the dimensions of the machined parts, the company decided to review its inspection criteria for NC machined parts to determine if this relationship could be used to reduce inspection.[12]

The following technique was employed: First, the dimensions generated by

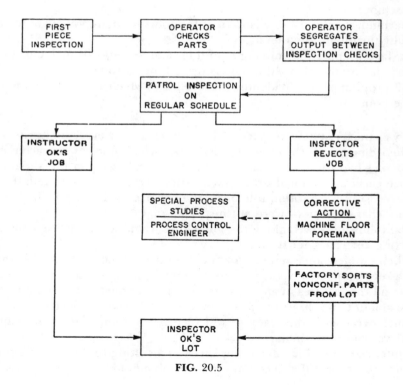

FIG. 20.5

each cutting tool were determined, and other process variables evaluated; then certain "key characteristics" were selected as process indicators. In other words, if a cutting tool generated several dimensions, only those dimensions which were representative of the total performance of that tool were selected for inspection. All other characteristics were considered secondary, with acceptance based on the actual inspection readings of the key characteristics.

Review of Process Variables: To assure optimum selection of key characteristics, several major process variables were reviewed:

1. Fixture design—for compliance to part drawing definition and position with respect to the machine axis.
2. Cutting tool design—to determine size, length and tolerance requirements. (Excessive tool overhang can result in tool whip, introducing taper into machined surfaces.)
3. Past history—to utilize earlier nonconformity reports in determining key characteristics.
4. Machine capability—to reveal peculiarities which affect characteristic selection.
5. Product design—to determine part tolerance and cross-sectional changes; whether surfaces are dimensioned from a common feature or from other machined features.
6. Machining method—to ensure that the tools used are adequate to consistently maintain the tolerances.
7. Surface preparation (milling, spotting, and so on)—to maintain location and size requirements if a hole is drilled into a rough surface.
8. NC programming—to identify those features which are not programmed to the nominal.

Key characteristics were selected from each axis for every tool generating a finished dimension. (In other words, a tool which finishes characteristics in three axes had three key characteristics.) Depending upon the variables described earlier, additional key characteristics might also be selected. If the key characteristics were within tolerance, the balance of the dimensions—or secondary characteristics—were not inspected.

The following were among the guidelines found useful by the company in selecting key characteristics.

When a dimension is not programmed to the nominal, it is desirable to select it as a key characteristic *in addition* to a nominally programmed feature. In cases where all the features in any axis are not programmed to the nominal by the same amount and direction, a key characteristic may be selected in the usual manner because all the readings will vary by the same amount providing all other variables are similar.

Quite frequently Manufacturing specifies a cutting tool which will produce a hole size toward the maximum limit to obtain added positional tolerance where true position tolerancing is used. The difference between the minimum hole size and the actual drilled hole size can be added to the true positional tolerance. Similarly drilled, bored, reamed, or threaded holes in a pattern or combination of patterns thus may be checked randomly for size, depth, and location, with a predetermined sample of features taken rather than inspecting every diameter or location for each part.

Likewise, on milled surfaces, a random selection may be made where variables are similar, when selection has been determined on the basis of the length of cut (to indicate tool wear).

Key Characteristics List: In this company, a key characteristics list was compiled for Quality Engineering for both key and secondary characteristics in a column format headed by respective tools. All characteristics were preceded by an abbreviated tool description to help relate key characteristics to secondary characteristics. Operational work instructions were changed and a special note added to identify it as a key characteristic operation. In the event a key characteristic was found to be nonconforming, the special note instructed the inspector to identify the nonconformity report in the same manner. After reviewing the nonconformity report, the quality engineer would use the key characteristic list and the knowledge of the process to determine the need for inspection of secondary characteristics.

Advantages of the NC Key Characteristics Approach: Before implementation of the key characteristic system, the average NC machined part required inspection of 53 characteristics; with the system, the average was 22 characteristics. It was possible to apply the key characteristic approach to between 30 and 40 percent of all NC machining operations; for these operations, characteristics inspected were reduced by 60 percent. Inspection audits have confirmed that product-quality level is unchanged with the new system. Management estimates that the key characteristic system was directly responsible for major reductions in inspection and machine down-time costs as well as significant savings in systems improvements associated with the key characteristics program.

20.12 High-Quantity Subassembly

An electronic component factory manufactures, as one of its major products, a small component which consists essentially of a series of windings enclosed in a leakproof, canlike case.[13] This component—termed here a *subassembly*—is both shipped directly to customers and used as a subassembly for other products manufactured by the plant.

Applications of the subassembly require 2.5% final AQL results. While total production quantities of the article are large, a number of different types are manufactured each week. All articles, however, pass through essentially the same manufacturing cycle involving the same operations and processes.

Product control on this article was initiated by a quality-control engineer, whose responsibilities include

1. Integration of all product-control activities carried out on the subassembly by the various functional groups concerned
2. Initiation, approval, and organization of all product-control procedures
3. Issuance of quality-control instructions covering product-control routines in inspection, test, reliability, quality-maintenance, and quality-auditing procedures
4. Initiation and revision of the quality reports required
5. Assigning of projects, as required, to appropriate positions for investigation and action

An approach to the manufacturing-control aspects of the overall product-control procedure for the subassembly, as developed by the quality engineer, is shown in Figure 20.6, which shows a product flowchart indicating both the several processing operations and the eight individual control stations that are the keys in the product-control activity.

A quality-control instruction has been written for each of these eight stations, clearly specifying the product-control techniques to be used. Shown in these instructions is such information as the sampling tables to be used and the quality levels to be applied. Also shown are the inspection- and test-planning data that were developed during new-design–reliability-control activity on the subassembly.

Figure 20.7 illustrates one of these quality-control instructions. It covers the product-control procedures for control station 4 and is self-explanatory.

Of particular interest in product control for this subassembly is control station 7. It involves a final quality audit of the outgoing product and consists of checks over and above the normal factory inspection and tests. Acceptance of the day's production depends upon the outcome of this audit.

The quality-audit procedure includes selection of a random sample of the day's production and subjection of these units to three groups of acceptance tests, which are comparable to regular production tests previously made. These tests include the following:

1. Mechanical inspection
2. Electrical test
3. Oven leak test

Each test is conducted and judged to a 0.65 percent AQL. Records of the tests are made on conventional percent nonconforming control charts. These charts are used to determine the amount of sampling required on future lots.

The charts are analyzed in the following fashion to determine the amount of sampling: If the quality level shown by previous audits is running less than ¼ percent, a reduced sampling plan is employed. If the quality level is between

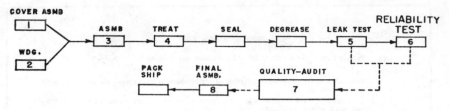

NOTE: EACH NUMBER (1,2, ETC.)
REFERS TO AN INDIVIDUAL
CONTROL STATION

DESCRIPTION OF CONTROL STATIONS:

1. PATROL INSPECTION.

   ELECTRICAL TEST (100%).
   FINAL LOT SAMPLING CHECK (1% A.Q.L.).

2. DRY TEST (100%) OPEN CIRCUITS.

3. LOT SAMPLING CHECK (1% A.Q.L.)

   SPLIT LIGHT TEST FOR SHORTS AND GROUNDS (100%)

4. POWER FACTOR AND OTHER ELECTRICAL SAMPLE CHECKS ON THE
   QUALITY OF THE TREATING OPERATION.

5. LEAK TEST (100%)

6. ELECTRICAL TEST (100%)----- ANALYSIS OF ELECTRICAL AND
   ELECTRONIC EXCEEDING EXPECTED %

7. QUALITY-AUDIT---- FINAL PRODUCTION SAMPLE TEST PERFORMED
   IN A SEPARATE ROOM DESIGNED ESPECIALLY
   FOR THIS PURPOSE

8. FINAL SAMPLING INSPECTION (0.65% A.Q.L.)

PRODUCT CONTROL

HIGH QUANTITY SUB-ASSEMBLY

FIG. 20.6

¼ percent and the upper limit on the control chart, a normal sampling plan is used. If the quality level exceeds the upper control limit, a more rigid sampling plan is used.[14]

When a sample is rejected as a result of this audit, the manufacturing group is required to sort out all of that type of subassembly for the specified defect before the lot can be released.

The quality-audit procedure has been particularly useful for this subassembly, which is a relatively precise component whose characteristics make it impossible by regular production 100 percent testing to weed out all articles which may become nonconforming early in actual operation. This is particularly true of possible borderline cases, where a second test is all that is required to show up the defect.

The value of the audit is further illustrated in Figure 20.8, which compares

Subject: Product Control Tests – Class 7321-7322 Sub-assembly Treating.

Purpose:

1. To detect unsatisfactory sub-assembly characteristics caused by faulty operation of the sub-assembly treating system.

2. To detect such characteristics as soon after treat as possible, before the doubtful sub-assemblies become mixed with previously treated sub-assemblies.

General: These instructions apply to all Class 7321-7322 sub-assemblies treated with any of the treating materials and in any of the treating processes covered by Laboratory and Engineering Instructions.

Procedure: Each day, three sub-assemblies, all of the same catalog number, shall be taken from each treating tank unloaded between 8:00 AM and 5:00 PM. These sub-assemblies shall be selected after the baskets are turned over for unloading, where baskets are loaded on their sides, but shall be taken before actual unloading begins. Sub-assemblies shall be taken from the center of one of the top baskets.

Over a period of days, all catalog numbers of Class 7321 and 7322 sub-assemblies being built in quantity shall be sampled.

The samples selected shall be immediately sealed, degreased, and placed in a forced circulation oven operating at 70° C, with a minimum of elapsed time between selection of samples and placing them in the oven. Sub-assemblies shall remain in the oven long enough to bring their dielectric temperatures within the range of $65^{\circ} - 75^{\circ}$ C after which they shall be measured for power factor and capacity at either rated 60-cycle volts, or at a 60-cycle voltage in accordance with the following table if sub-assemblies are rated for DC voltage.

DC Rated Volts	60-cycle Test Volts	DC Rated Volts	60-cycle Test Volts
400	220	1500	660
600	330	2000	880
1000	440	Over 2000	35% of DC rating

In the event the desired test voltage exceeds the maximum rated voltage of the bridge, measurements may be taken at the maximum voltage available.

If the power factors obtained exceed those given in the tabulation given below for the applicable case style, voltage rating and treating material, the tank load of sub-assemblies represented by the sample shall be removed from the production flow and an additional sample shall be taken and measured. Results of tests on both samples shall be referred to the Engineering Department for decision as to disposition of the tank load in question.

If elevated temperature power factors are satisfactory, the samples shall be cooled to a dielectric temperature of 20°-30° C and the power factor and capacity measurements repeated at the same voltage as was used for the previous measurements.

$65^{\circ} - 75^{\circ}$ C POWER-FACTOR LIMITS

Case Style and Size	*Rated AC Volts	Max % P.F. 1476	1436	Oil
All round cans	660 and below	.50	.50	.30
All round cans	Above 660	.40	.40	.25
2 in. x 2-1/2 in. oval	660 and below	.50	.50	.30
1-3/4 in. x 2-1/2 in. oval	Above 660	.40	.40	.25
All other oval	All	.40	.40	.25
All rectangular	660 and below	.50	.50	.30
All rectangular	Above 660	.40	.40	.25
Bathtubs	All	.60	.60	.30
AVDG	All	.60	.60	.30

* For DC sub-assemblies - consider 1500 V DC equivalent to 660 V AC.

Records: A permanent record of all measurements shall be kept in the office of the Quality Control Manager. Each week the over-all Quality Performance report for Class 7321-7322 sub-assemblies shall include a record of the number of tanks sampled and the number of tanks whose samples had high power factors.

A. R. JONES
Eng. Department

APPROVED:

B. F. SMITH   Mfg. Superintendent

T. D. GREEN   Mgr. - Q. C.

R. M. BROWN   Eng. Department

FIG. 20.7

the results of the regular production 100 percent leak test with the quality-audit samples. During the latter part of February, a sharp decline is shown in the percentage of leaks found by operators at the regular production test. Simultaneously, an increase in leaks is shown in the quality-audit sample results.

Investigation of this situation was initiated because of these dissimilar results. It revealed faulty operations of process ovens such that many of the

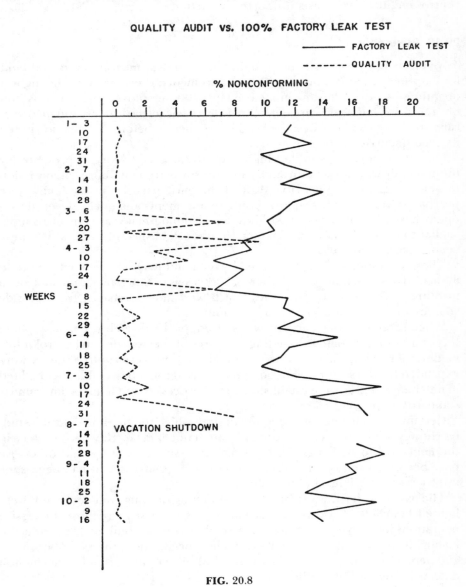

FIG. 20.8

subassemblies were not receiving the heat treatment required to reveal a leaky unit. Had not the quality audit both rejected the defective lots before shipment and highlighted the need for corrective action, no steps might have been taken until floods of complaints began pouring in from customers.

Figure 20.9 shows a typical quality-performance report, which presents a regular picture of subassembly quality result. This report shows a quality index for each of the eight control stations. It is reviewed periodically by the process-control engineer as a basis for corrective action.

20.13 Assembly

An electronic assembly, composed of a number of intricate parts and built for extremely rigid customer quality requirements, is produced in the highest quantities of any product manufactured in a 4000-employee plant. The assembly, requiring low rejection rates at final electronic/electrical test and mechanical inspection, had been designed and in production before the plant instituted its total-quality-control program.

One of the first steps in developing an overall quality-control program for the assembly was carrying through a necessarily extremely abbreviated version of new-design control activity. Most of the parts used in the assembly were purchased from outside vendors. Using requirements and quality levels developed during the new-design studies, an incoming-material control routine, similar to those discussed in Chapter 19, was established through which these vendor parts would pass.

Those component parts processed by the plant itself were manufactured in a small-parts machine shop, where a process-sampling program had been instituted. The few subassemblies which were not purchased from outside sources were also subject to process sampling.

When product-control activity was started for the assembly, its initial phase was utilization for standards-setting purposes of the new-design control information. Several assembly fixtures were altered, process-control checks were expanded for the several robot equipments used for subassemblies, expedited maintenance checks were established for all processes and fixtures, and similar standards steps were taken.

Certain basic changes affecting the design, which the brief new-design studies showed would reduce rejections although not affect quality performance in the field, had to be bypassed, however. Excessive expense would otherwise have been incurred on an assembly where a large investment had been sunk in processing facilities and inventory.

The assembly itself was manufactured rapidly on long well-equipped, well-lighted benches, at which several employees were seated whose successive operations in applying parts and subassemblies quickly built up the product to its final form. Because of the critical quality specification, the assemblies were 100 percent tested for performance and 100 percent inspected for mechanical defects at the end of the bench.

QUALITY PERFORMANCE—CLASS 6241 SUB-ASSEMBLIES

W/E 1-16

COVERS	QTY.	%	
ASSEMBLED	74,306		
MECHANICAL REJECTS	309	.42	B
COVERS 100% ELEC. TESTED	1,806		
NO. FAILURES	13	.72	B

WINDING			
ROLL PRODUCTION	113,226		
PARTIAL ROLL LOSS	5,672	5.	B
TEST LOSS	1,523	1.3	B

TREATING 70° P.F. CHECK			
LOTS CHECKED	10		
LOTS REJECTED	0	0	

BASE DEFLECTION LEAK TEST		
TESTED		
REJECTED	NONE	

OVEN LEAK TEST			
TESTED	8,526 *		
REJECTED	538	6.3	A

FINAL ELECTRICAL TEST			
TESTED	64,625		
REJECTED	2,556	4.	A B
% ACT. SCRAP — YR. TO DATE		4.7	B

B.D. ELIMINATION			
LOTS TESTED	9		
LOTS REJECTED	0		
PROCESS AVERAGE	1/1085	.09	A

FINAL PRODUCTION SAMPLING TEST			
MECHANICAL — INSPECTION (0.65% AQL)			
LOTS CHECKED	35		
LOTS REJECTED	0		
PROCESS AVERAGE	20/3960	.51	A
ELECTRICAL TEST (0.65% AQL)			
LOTS CHECKED	35		
LOTS REJECTED	2		
PROCESS AVERAGE	29/4395	.66	A
LEAK TEST (0.65% AQL)			
LOTS CHECKED	27		
LOTS REJECTED	0		
PROCESS AVERAGE	5/3055	.16	

A---REPAIRED   B---SCRAPPED
* THIS SIZE PROD. SAMPLE TAKEN TO OBTAIN %

FIG. 20.9

Together with the equipment quality improvement steps that had been taken and the actions to assure high reliability component inputs, very great emphasis was placed upon more effective quality training of operators and supervisors and the development of quality commitment programs, as discussed in Chapter 9. Process-Control Engineering's patrol checks on the assembly lines provided an important quality technical aid. Many assists to operator quality were instituted, ranging from clear visual standards established at each work station to color coding assemblies through a colored dot label easily removed at the end of assembly to identify the station at which the work was performed.

At the end-of-line control points of final inspection and final test stations, go and not-go control charts were plotted, both charts for major individual quality characteristics and a single chart for all inspection and test nonconformances combined. These control charts were directly tied in with daily reject breakdowns which, with the charts, were reviewed each morning as the basis for corrective action by the process-control engineer. Even more rapid hour-by-hour corrective action was initiated by the shop foreman based upon reject analyses provided him.

Frequency distributions on major performance characteristics were plotted semiweekly by the test organization, using random samples, each composed of 50 assemblies. Each week, a quality audit sample of several units was selected from assemblies being packed for shipment; this sample was sent to the plant laboratory for rigorous test and examination. Data from these laboratory investigations were used for review by the Manager–Quality Control.

Figures 20.10 to 20.12 illustrate one aspect of this overall program. These figures show the "all nonconformities combined" control chart plotted after final inspection and test and directly posted on the manufacturing floor. Figure 20.10 pictures the reject situation for the month of January, a situation that had existed on the assembly for the several-month period since it had reached its full weekly production rate. Rejects were running about 1.4 percent nonconforming—approximately 1.4 nonconforming units per 100.

Figure 20.11 pictures the March reject report, showing the gradual effect of the newly initiated quality-control program—fast corrective action initiated by process-control engineering on individual reject problems, the psychological improvement of operator motivation, better equipment adjustment, and other factors. Nonconforming units per 100 had dropped to approximately 1.1.

Figure 20.12 illustrates the situation for the month of May, the first month for which a control limit was plotted for shop view.[15] The rejection rate had dropped to approximately 0.7 units per 100 units produced. While this improvement of almost one-half was a step in the right direction, company management continued to emphasize this product-control program to obtain much further quality improvement which ranged at approximately 0.35 to 0.45 rejected units per 100. It was recognized, however, that significant design and processing changes suggested by the new-design studies would have to be made before this reject level could be made very low.

This control situation was thereafter maintained for the assembly until its order commitments had been satisfied and production was ended in favor of a new model upon which extensive new-design control activity had been conducted and whose design features permitted sharp further reduction to significantly small rejection rates.

QUALITY CONTROL CHART NUMBER X-1

PRODUCT Electronic Assembly   **MONTH** January

STATION Final Inspection & Test   **CHARACTERISTIC** All Nonconf.

PERCENT NONCONFORMING

DATE	INSP.	NONCONF.	%
1/1	205	2	.9
1/2	355	4	1.3
1/3	210	2	1.0
1/4	254	2	1.0
1/5	291	3	1.0
1/6	180		.2
	1495	15	1.0
1/8	405	5	1.4
1/9	224	3	1.7
1/10	203	3	1.5
1/11	300	3	1.0
1/12	391	3	1.1
1/13	293	4	1.4
	1716	23	1.4
1/15	469	8	1.9
1/16	403	5	1.2
1/17	271	2	.8
1/18	456	7	1.6
1/19	374	6	1.7
1/20	290	3	1.1
	2263	33	1.5
1/22	459	5	1.2
1/23	315	4	1.5
1/24	443	6	1.3
1/25	349	5	1.6
1/26	432	6	1.4
1/27	592	8	1.4
	2590	37	1.4
1/29	473	11	2.3
1/30	446	6	1.5
1/31	312	3	1.1
2/1	514	7	1.4
2/2	184	2	1.3
2/3	428	5	1.2
	2 357	36	1.4

1WK	1495	15	1.0
2WK	1716	23	1.4
3WK	2263	33	1.5
4WK	2590	37	1.4
5WK	2 357	36	1.4

MO	10421	144	1.4

FIG. 20.10

QUALITY CONTROL CHART NUMBER ___X-2___

PRODUCT _Electronic Assembly_   MONTH _March_

STATION _Final Inspection and Test_   CHARACTERISTIC _All Nonconformities_

PERCENT CONFORMING

DATE	INSP.	NONCONF.	%
3/5	472	6	1.3
3/6	359	5	1.6
3/7	303	3	1.3
3/8	381	4	1.1
3/9	429	5	1.3
3/10	443	5	1.3
	2387	30	1.3
3/12	445	4	1.0
3/13	328	4	1.5
3/14	190	3	1.7
3/15	469	5	1.1
3/16	527	4	.8
3/17	504	5	1.1
	2373	27	1.1
3/19	379	4	1.1
3/20	380	5	1.5
3/21	371	3	1.0
3/22	329	4	1.4
3/23	465	6	1.4
3/24	436	3	.7
	2360	27	1.1
3/26	393	4	1.0
3/27	472	3	.8
3/28	356	2	1.1
3/29	291	1	.8
3/30	393	4	1.1
3/31	362	2	1.1
	2267	18	.8

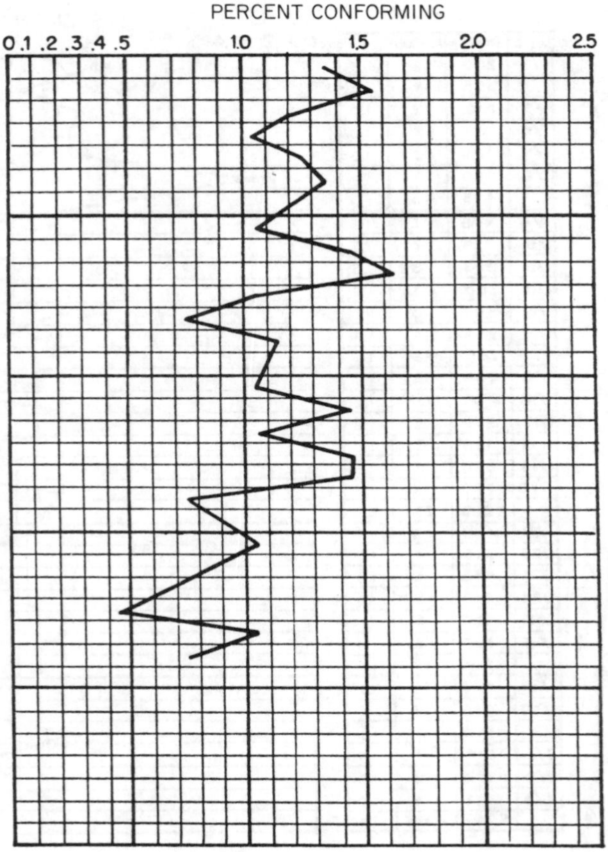

Scale: 0 .1 .2 .3 .4 .5 ... 1.0 ... 1.5 ... 2.0 ... 2.5

	INSP.	NONCONF.	%
1 WK	2387	30	1.3
2 WK	2373	27	1.2
3 WK	2360	27	1.2
4 WK	2267	18	.8
5 WK			

	INSP.	NONCONF.	%
MO	9387	104	1.1

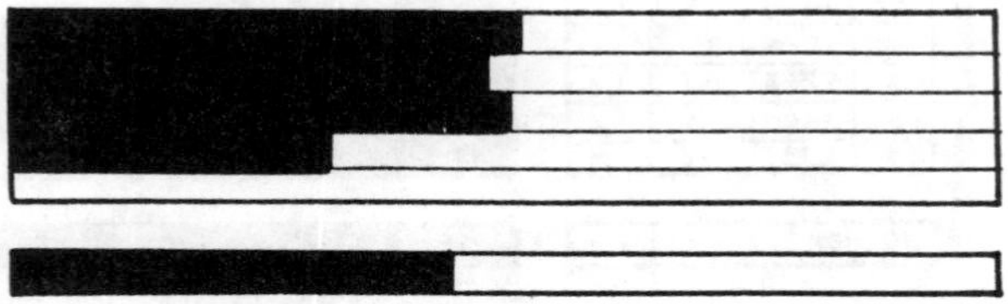

FIG. 20.11

768

PRODUCT Electronic Assembly   **MONTH** May

STATION Final Inspection and Test   **CHARACTERISTIC** All Nonconformities

PERCENT NON CONFORMING

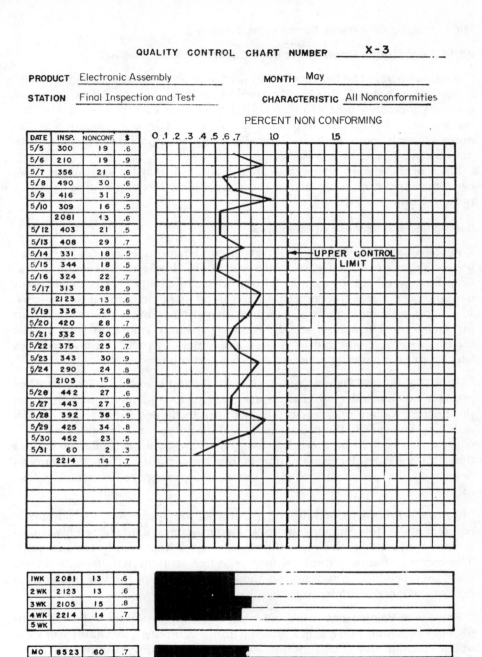

DATE	INSP.	NONCONF.	%
5/5	300	19	.6
5/6	210	19	.9
5/7	356	21	.6
5/8	490	30	.6
5/9	416	31	.9
5/10	309	16	.5
	2081	13	.6
5/12	403	21	.5
5/13	408	29	.7
5/14	331	18	.5
5/15	344	18	.5
5/16	324	22	.7
5/17	313	28	.9
	2123	13	.6
5/19	336	26	.8
5/20	420	28	.7
5/21	332	20	.6
5/22	375	25	.7
5/23	343	30	.9
5/24	290	24	.8
	2105	15	.8
5/26	442	27	.6
5/27	443	27	.6
5/28	392	36	.9
5/29	425	34	.8
5/30	452	23	.5
5/31	60	2	.3
	2214	14	.7

IWK	2081	13	.6
2 WK	2123	13	.6
3 WK	2105	15	.8
4 WK	2214	14	.7
5 WK			

MO	8523	60	.7

FIG. 20.12

20.14 Techniques Used in Product Control

As demonstrated by the procedures discussed above, there are a great many individual techniques that can be used in product control. These technical methods include a host of elements ranging from such readily identifiable quality-control techniques as process sampling and effective inspection procedures to such more general factors as adequate floor area, good factory housekeeping, and air conditioning.

Many of these were reviewed in Parts 4 and 5. It may be worthwhile, however, to summarize some of the more significant techniques that apply to product-control activity.

Setting and Maintenance of Standards

Process-Capability Studies: With given combinations of materials, speeds, feeds, temperatures, flows, coolants, and so on, almost all processing operations have an inherent variation. This process "capability" is largely independent of specification tolerances for parts to be manufactured on the process. It is necessarily important to determine these capabilities as fundamental to product-control standards setting. Process-capability studies provide a basis for this determination and its related assignment of parts to those facilities which can economically maintain the required tolerances.

Tool, Die, Jig, and Fixture Control: Proper tooling is essential for control of product quality under all circumstances: With low-quantity, short-duration production, tooling is a basic product-control technique. New design control activities may specify the proper tools and dies: it is a fundamental product-control necessity to be thereafter assured of the continued effectiveness of these tools by regular examination before and/or after production runs to determine the desirability of adjustment, sharpening, replacement and so forth.

Software Program Control: The control of the programs for automatic equipment—robots, numerically controlled machines, digital assembly equipments—is essential to product control under modern manufacture conditions. The control of such software is most effective at its design stage; however, program reproduction and careless handling and machine tending make ongoing maintenance also important.

Preventive Maintenance: Machine tools, soldering processes, robots, assembly machines, and other major manufacturing equipment inevitably will wear under constant use. The resulting loose bearings and worn pins may cause poor-quality products. A program of preventive maintenance is an important quality-control technique because it enables a regularly scheduled examination of processing facilities before they break down.

Accounting Standards on Quality Cost: Quality cost data concerning inspection and test requirements, quality levels, and other quality cost factors are the most effective information available to accountants for the determination of the quality-cost elements to be included in standard costs. Quality-cost goals can similarly be determined from these data. Such accounting determinations are a quality-control essential because they are the economic basis for much of a plant quality-control program.

Process-Quality Design Review: The quality compatibility of processes with product and part manufacturing is an essential area for product control. When new-design control design review techniques have not yet covered new processes to be used in older product and part applications, this important technique should be utilized to assure stable, consistent, and controllable operation of new processes.[16]

System Planning for Calibration and Maintenance of Equipment: Calibration and maintenance can be scheduled in several different ways. Probably the most common is at fixed time intervals regardless of actual equipment usage, but many firms plan such work according to an elapsed-time meter installed on all electrically operated equipment. A far more efficient method is used in large operations with access to a computer data base. In this method items are checked in and out via the terminal keyboard, utilizing an "equipment pool." The computer totals the "days out" and signals a calibration requirement only when actual usage has amounted to the prescribed interval. Such a system can be programmed to pinpoint for corrective action any equipment that falls below a predetermined acceptance level, and the interval may be shortened if the problem becomes generic. When called for, it can be used in tandem with sophisticated measuring devices, such as a laser interferometer.

Computer control of maintenance, both scheduled and unscheduled, is another advantage of such a system. Key data such as causes of malfunction, mean time between failure, down time, and repair costs are stored in the computer and recalled only when necessary.

Control During Manufacture

Shop Personnel Quality-Mindedness: Selection of employees with the proper aptitudes, training of these individuals in operating skills and sound attitudes toward both the importance of product quality and their jobs in general, continued stimulation of the quality interests of these operators through their direct participation in plant quality activity and refresher training if required, the return to and review with operators of the nonconforming parts they have produced, regular physical examinations of employees to determine the need for such physical aids as glasses, competent supervision to provide the leadership needed on the manufacturing floor for quality-mindedness—all are basic to product control.

Proper Material Flow: Quality can be economically and consistently built in material only if the factory floor layout permits proper routing of material accompanied by efficient materials handling which, at the very minimum, eliminates damage to parts in transit. Similarly important are satisfactory balances of inventory so that a lot of one type of part need not be subject to damage and deterioration on a stock-room shelf while its release to the assembly floor awaits a matching lot of another type of part.

Planning for Mechanical Inspection and Electrical Test Procedures: Well-trained inspection and test personnel, supplied with the right quality information equipments and placed at strategic locations in the production process, provide one of the most important elements of the manufacturing-control aspects of product control. The types of inspection or test that can be used vary all the way from first-piece checks and reliability evaluations to rigid 100 percent examination—the choice being dependent upon the particular quality situation.

Nondestructive Evaluation: As discussed in Chapter 11, certain parts and components can be inspected only by methods which cause no change or deformation in their structure. Nondestructive evaluation techniques important in product control include such areas as fluorescent-penetrant testing, eddy current testing, x-ray, magnetic particle testing, and many others.

Control Charts: The control chart, by red-flagging potential causes of non-conformities before they result in rejections, is the most useful statistical method in product control. With machine-shop and electronic component parts this complement to inspection effectiveness usually appears in the form of a measurements control chart, and its usual adaptation for assemblies is as a go and not-go chart.

Process-Sampling Tables: Statistical process-sampling methods are an efficient foundation for process-control activities. Process sampling is especially useful in component part processing, frequently in instances where the control chart is not readily applicable. Process sampling is also valuable in control of subassembly manufacturing operations. This sampling may take the form of the regular selection of the same number of units every period. Or it may be a continuous sampling plan—CSP-1, CSP-2, CSP-3, and others—of the sort discussed in Section 15.11.

Process-Drift and Tool-Wear Studies: Reliable knowledge on the wear of tools and the drift of processes is valuable information for many production decisions as well as for product-control considerations involving matters like process-sampling frequencies. Measurements-control charts are an excellent medium for studying wear, as illustrated by the wear pattern in Figure 20.13. This figure illustrates one of the several tool-wear patterns; the tool literally seems to "cave in."

Acceptance Sampling Tables: Lots of parts may require a final sampling check before shipment. Acceptance sampling tables are generally used during this type of inspection.

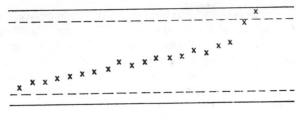

MEASUREMENTS
CONTROL CHART
SHOWING
TOOL WEAR
FIG. 20.13

Other Statistical Techniques: Mathematical analytical techniques may also be used, such as analysis of variance, cusum charts, and designed experiments.

Quality Audit: Experience has shown the usefulness of selecting a small sample from the production output after all other regular inspections and tests have been performed. This quality audit takes various forms under various circumstances: It may or may not be the basis for the release for shipment of the lot sampled: it may or may not be conducted more vigorously than the regular inspections or tests: it may or may not provide the data for a quality index for the product. Most quality audits point toward corrective action relating to equipment performance, inspection efficiency, operator skill, and so on.

Quality Level Index: Of prime importance as a mirror of the effectiveness of a quality-control program on a product is maintenance of a regular index of the quality of that product. Such an index may be compiled from results of sampling from 100 percent inspection data, from quality-audit information. It may be developed by giving equal weight to all nonconformities or by varying these weights.[17] The quality level index is reported to management on the same basis as the information received by management on production output, average labor take-home earnings, and other elements of the business.

Final Inspection Data: Cumulative data on rejection and reinspection reject rates are reported to management as a summary of production quality levels. The same data, coded to include a listing of characteristics which resulted in rejects, are used by Manufacturing to improve quality levels.

Process-Control Computing Devices: Small, specialized computers will calculate $\overline{X}$ (X-bar) and σ (sigma) for a given set of data. Chapter 12 discusses some techniques used for designing such quality information equipment. Some equipments are included in closed-loop arrangements whereby the manufacturing process is directly controled by the feedback of quality information.

Disposing of Non-conforming Parts: Because of the danger that rejected parts may, without approval, find their way back into the production process, it is important that procedures be available for rapid disposition of such parts. These procedures will involve a rigid system of tagging, "holding for disposition," and routing. They will include a quality-control–component-sponsored review for disposition of those parts which have been rejected but which may be approved for repair. They will include a similar review of those rejects which may be approved for use "as is" in such special cases as when the cause for rejection is not critical to quality.

Major-Part Record Forms: Particularly with expensive parts that are produced individually or in job lots for ultimate manufacture in an assembly, data forms may be maintained for control and record purposes. Figure 20.14 shows a portion of a typical form developed in connection with a shaft type.

Complaint Analyses: Records and analyses of customer complaint reports from the field furnish useful product-control information. While usually a considerable time lag exists between these reports and current production, they nonetheless both reflect the effectiveness of control programs and highlight those nonconformities upon which more aggressive corrective action must be initiated. Complaint reports on individual articles may also be the basis for intensification of product-control activity on similar articles.

Regular Quality Performance or Reject Breakdown Reports: A much more immediate indication than complaint reports of the adequacy of control measures is a quality performance record. Such a record, often in the form of a reject breakdown report, is frequently posted every hour, day, or week in conspicuous view of the manufacturing area. Figure 20.15 shows such a form for an armature assembly—a breakdown by individual charts on each of the major quality characteristics on which inspections and tests are made.

Control of Quality in Packaging and Shipping: A common quality danger for all products is damage during shipment. With intricate, finely adjusted assemblies that are improperly packaged, a severe jar during transportation may cause a shift in quality characteristics; with certain chemicals, a change in temperature during transit may cause product ruin. Great importance rests, therefore, upon adequate quality activity both during the design of the product container and during actual placement by shipping employees of the article in its container. The mode of transportation, climate and temperature, etc., must all be considered during this important phase of product control.

Control of Field Service: Although control of quality during manufacture of a product may have been excellent, there remain subsequent points for control. The importance of packing and shipping were discussed. The next important point occurs at time of installation. For certain products this may be a very critical stage requiring experienced services. The installation of central air conditioning systems falls in this category. Any dirt entering the piping for the refrigerant can ruin the compressor, completely negating the precision machining done at the factory. If moisture is allowed to enter the system, the system's effectiveness is greatly diminished.

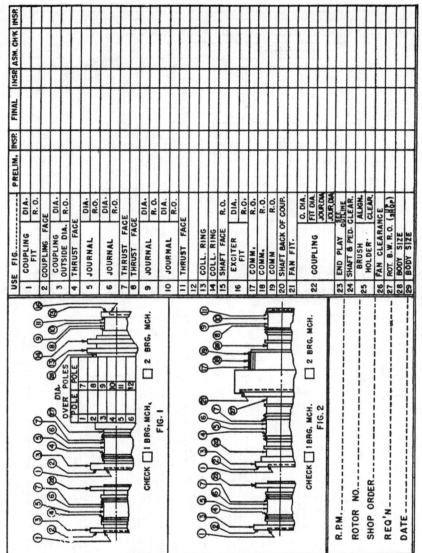

USE FIG.		PRELIM.	INSP.	FINAL	INSR	ASM.	CH'K	INSR
1	COUPLING FIT	DIA.						
		R.O.						
2	COUPLING FACE							
3	COUPLING OUTSIDE DIA.	DIA.						
		R.O.						
4	THRUST FACE							
5	JOURNAL	DIA.						
		R.O.						
6	JOURNAL	DIA.						
		R.O.						
7	THRUST FACE							
8	THRUST FACE	DIA.						
9	JOURNAL	R.O.						
		DIA.						
10	JOURNAL	R.O.						
11	THRUST FACE							
12								
13	COLL. RING							
14	COLL. RING							
15	SHAFT FACE	R.O.						
16	EXCITER FIT	DIA.						
		R.O.						
17	COMM.	DIA.						
18	COMM.	R.O.						
19	COMM	R.O.						
20	SHAFT BACK OF COUP.							
21	FAN FIT.							
22	COUPLING	O. DIA.						
		FIT DIA.						
		JOUR.DIA.						
		JOUR.DIA.						
23	END PLAY	SEE OUTLINE						
24	SHAFT & PED. CLEAR.							
25	BRUSH HOLDER'	ALIGN.						
		CLEAR.						
26	FAN CLEARANCE							
27	ROT. B.W.R.O. (SHOP)							
28	BODY SIZE							
29	BODY SIZE							

DIA. OVER POLES

POLE | POLE

1	7
2	8
3	9
4	10
5	11
6	12

CHECK ☐ 1 BRG. MCH.   ☐ 2 BRG. MCH.

FIG. 1

CHECK ☐ 1 BRG. MCH.   ☐ 2 BRG. MCH.

FIG. 2

R.P.M. ------------

ROTOR NO. ------------

SHOP ORDER ------------

REQ'N ------------

DATE ------------

FIG. 20.14

775

ARMATURE CHARTS

WEEK ENDING

WINDING

PRE-BALANCE

FINAL ELECTRICAL TEST

ELECTRICAL TEST AFTER LEAD CLEANING

PREVIOUS WEEK

BOGEY

NAME

M — NUMBER REJECTS / NUMBER STARTED / % DEFECTIVE
T — NUMBER REJECTS / NUMBER STARTED / % DEFECTIVE
W — NUMBER REJECTS / NUMBER STARTED / % DEFECTIVE
T — NUMBER REJECTS / NUMBER STARTED / % DEFECTIVE
F — NUMBER REJECTS / NUMBER STARTED / % DEFECTIVE
S — NUMBER REJECTS / NUMBER STARTED / % DEFECTIVE

DAYS

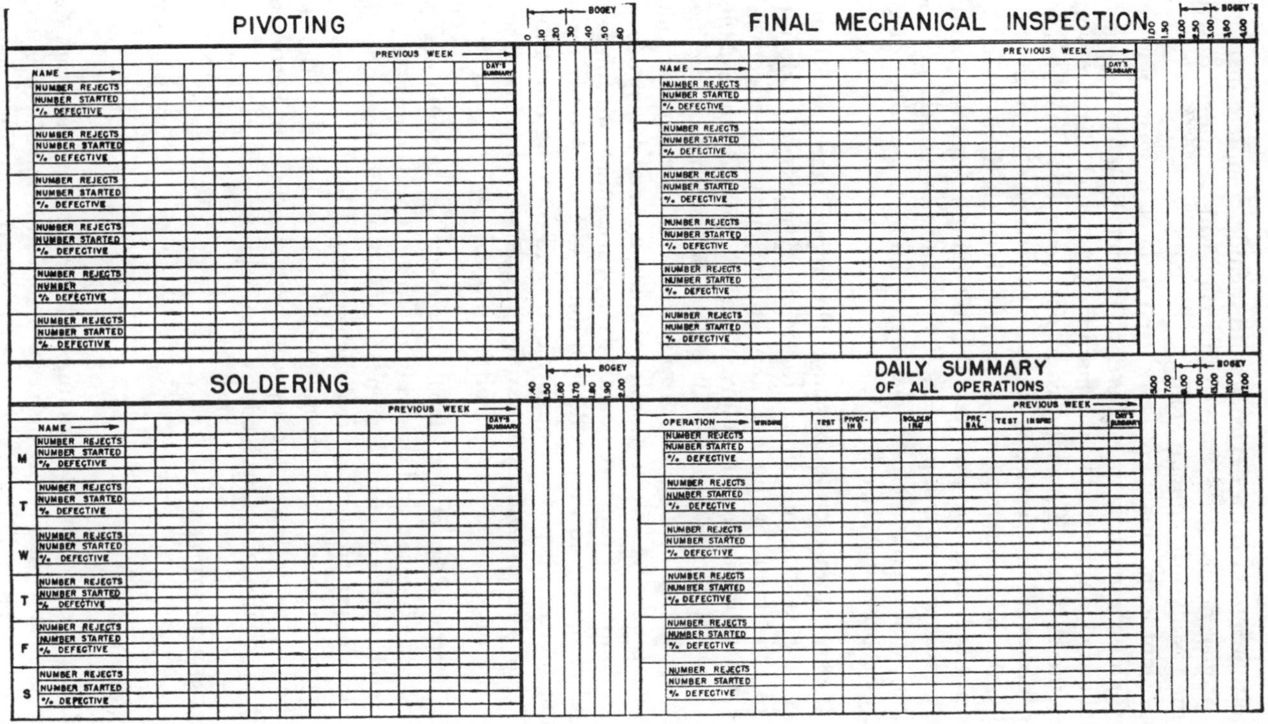
PIVOTING
FINAL MECHANICAL INSPECTION
SOLDERING
DAILY SUMMARY OF ALL OPERATIONS
BOGEY
PREVIOUS WEEK
DAY'S SUMMARY
NAME
OPERATION
NUMBER REJECTS
NUMBER STARTED
% DEFECTIVE
M
T
W
T
F
S
WINDING
TEST
PIVOTING
SOLDERING
PRE-BAL.
TEST
INSPEC

FIG. 20.15

The quality program for a device should include complete installation instructions prepared with great care so that they will be understood and followed by the installer of average ability.

Also important is the quality of work used in later servicing and repairing of a device. This is especially true where the product requires service because of some deficiency on the part of the manufacturer. Such deficiency might be forgiven by the customer if prompt, courteous service is available at little or no cost. If, however, the service is slow, or expensive, or requires repeated service calls, the customer becomes not only dissatisfied but irate. The customer may not only refuse to purchase the offending company's products but may actively condemn the company and its products to associates. The value of an efficient, well-trained field service organization as a builder of goodwill can scarcely be overemphasized.

Product Quality Information Processing: The importance of efficient quality information flow has become central to the effectiveness of modern production. The establishment of this data flow in the most cost-effective fashion requires its structuring in modern information flow patterns; the establishment of efficient manual procedures for all data flow to establish the necessary systems foundation, to provide a backup in the event of computer failure and a realistic basis for the relative economics of computerized data processing; the economic evaluation of product quality data processing both for use of the plant central computer and for dedicated mini- and microcomputer installations for the specific purpose of quality data; and ongoing operation of the integrated quality information processing program—both manual and computerized—as a major product-control technique.

Predicting Warranty Costs and Liability Claims: Data on outgoing product quality, warranty expenses, and customer complaints and claims are projected to predict trends in these sensitive areas. Feedback and analysis of such information are important product-control techniques.

Details of two representative examples of these technical methods are be discussed below, as follows: process-capability studies in Sections 20.15 through 20.18, quality audit in Sections 20.19 through 20.21.

PROCESS-CAPABILITY STUDIES

20.15 Background

The facilities selected for manufacture of a part are an important determinant of the cost and quality of the resulting production. If the processing equipment selected is sufficiently accurate to meet the quality target as established by drawing tolerances, reasonable costs and acceptable quality can be expected. If the processing equipment cannot consistently meet the quality target, high costs, scrap, and reworked materials are inevitable outcomes.

In some companies, experienced manufacturing engineers, operators, and foremen have learned from long experience that "Machine 27 can handle the close turning work up to ±0.002 inch and machine 33 is better for the work from ±0.003 to ±0.006 inch." Not all plants are so fortunate as to possess this experience however. Even in the plants where a great deal is known about the capabilities of processing equipments, it is sometimes rare to have this information in such a form that it can be shared with designing engineers, planners, and methods engineers.

Since such knowledge about the performance capability of processing equipment is essential to the proper functioning of a quality-control program, many plants have made scientific investigation of these capabilities a keystone of their entire product- and process-control program. In so doing, they were forced to develop techniques for this investigation which were more effective for quality-control purposes than the old rule-of-thumb techniques that had prevailed for many years. One of the most useful of the techniques developed for this work is the process-capability study.

The process-capability study consists essentially of determining the capability of a single process operation, often in relation to the individual quality characteristic of a part. It is discussed in some detail below.

20.16 Concepts of Capability Studies

Process capability is a measurement with respect to the inherent precision of a manufacturing process. As a definition:

> Process capability is quality-performance capability of the process with given factors and under normal, in-control conditions.

Two significant elements in this concept of process capability are

1. Process *factors*
2. Process *conditions*

1. The first consideration necessary to the concept of process capability is that a process is made up of a number of distinct factors. These factors include raw material, machine or equipment, the operator's skill, measuring devices, and the measurer's skill. A change in one or more of these factors may change the process capability. Hence, to be meaningful, a process capability must be stated with respect to a given set of specifically listed process factors.
2. The second element contained in the definition is that involving process conditions. For a process-capability study to be meaningful, the process being analyzed should be one that has measurements *normally distributed and in a state of statistical control.* As shown in Chapter 13, normality is essential to the identification of a process pattern and determination of how that pattern relates to the specification requirement. Chapter 14 discussed statistical control and showed that only a controlled process is a predictable process. To be useful, a process-capability value must have an established pattern that is consistent over time.

Mathematically, the process capability is defined as six standard deviation units (6σ). As developed in Chapter 13, 99.73 percent of all the readings for a normal distribution fall within the area bounded by ± 3 standard deviation units from the mean. So, a process capability study, mathematically, is merely a well-organized, carefully disciplined frequency distribution analysis of the appropriate process data. The formula for the process capability is, therefore, Chapter 13's (4A), adapted for σ multiplied by 6. It is

$$\text{Process capability} = 6\sigma = 6\sqrt{\frac{\Sigma(X - \bar{X})^2}{n - 1}}$$

where
$$\sigma = \text{standard deviation of sample population}$$
$$X_1, X_2, \ldots, X_n = \text{individual measurements}$$
$$\bar{X} = \text{arithmetic mean of individual measurements}$$
$$n = \text{number of individual measurements}$$

Section 13.11 discussed the distinction between s, the sample standard deviation and σ, the population standard deviation, which is used in this process-capability calculation for the process conditions that have been required—emphasizing statistical control over time.

Discipline of the Study. There are three phases to making a capability study: planning the study, taking the data, and analyzing the data. The first step must be the selection of the output characteristics to be investigated. A process may generate several characteristics, each of which will have its own pattern of variation. For an example, a cutting tool in a lathe can generate size, concentricity, finish, and taper. To study the variation in each of these generated characteristics, a separate set of data is needed to make possible an individual analysis. Each characteristic can be measured on one production run, however, as long as each is recorded on an individual data sheet. In most cases, it is impractical to make a study on *all* characteristics because many have only a minor effect on product quality and quality costs and thus the expense and time are not justified.

The number of studies to be made on any particular operation will vary with the amount of knowledge and experience available for the process. When a process is new, or when a new type of operation is being introduced on an old process, or if studies have not been made previously on the machine, a more complete study may be required, but as capability information is built up on similar operations, this information can be used as a guide for selecting which studies should be made.

The setup and running conditions must be completely recorded so that the computed process capability can be identified with the actual test conditions For example, in a capability study on a lathe, the following might be the conditions which should be identified because a change in any one of the conditions could change the capability of the lathe operation being studied:

MATERIAL TYPE: composition, hardness, grain structure

MATERIAL SIZE

TOOLHOLDER: knee tool, four-way post, back-tool post, box tool, adjustable toolholder

TOOL LOCATION: turret, cross slide

TOOL GRIND

TOOL MATERIAL

TOOL SIZE

TOOL SETTING: the amount of tool overhang in the holder or the length of a drill, reamer, or boring tool

TYPE OF CHUCKING: collets, 2-, 3-, or 4-jaw chuck, holding fixture

STEADY RESTS: type used and location

LENGTH OF CUT

DEPTH OF CUT

DISTANCE FROM CHUCKING DEVICE

TYPE OF STOP USED

TYPE OF CUT: plunge cut or continuous cut

SPEED

FEED

COOLANT

OPERATOR

TEMPERATURE

MACHINE CONDITION: parallelism of ways, tightness of ways, and so on

AMOUNT OF MACHINE WARMUP

Other machine tools may be affected by many of the same variations, but each will have a set of variables which are peculiar to that machine and must be identified for each process-capability study.

The physical characteristics of the material (such as thickness, hardness, flatness, or chemical composition) which is input to the process must be determined and recorded. Also, the variations in characteristics generated by preceding operations must be measured and recorded, when these characteristics affect the operation being studied. The measuring equipment used for the study must be accurate and repeatable and its capability known.

Conducting the Study: A process-capability study should be conducted under normal operating conditions with a single set of factors making up the manufacturing process. For example, a study should use a single batch of raw material, a single operator, and a single measurer throughout the period during which data are being collected. The operator should avoid feeding "corrections" into the process or making adjustments during the study.

Recalibration of the measuring equipment during this period should be avoided unless it is "normally" calibrated at frequent intervals. All these separate factors are subject to variation over long periods of time, so it is advisable to make several separate studies at widely separated intervals to determine the effects of normally varying factors on the process capability.

The capability study should contain a sufficient number of measurement readings so that a representative sample is obtained. For most operations, a minimum of 50 readings should be adequate.

The order of the readings should be preserved. It is advisable to tag items with a numbered tag as they come off the process; their identity is then retained. If some question arises later with regard to the accuracy of measurement, a recheck can be made. Caution should be exercised in making rechecks to take into account possible changes that might occur with time, i.e., change in dimension due to a part dropping in temperature, decrease in moisture content, and so forth.

Inspectors or process technicians are often well-qualified for taking the data because of their training in measuring and data recording.

If the recorded readings are plotted in order of production on an ordinary graph, it is often possible to gain further information about the process than if the readings were merely accumulated into a frequency distribution. This simple technique often reveals short, erratic periods in the process. Since such erratic periods are not predictable, they need to be eliminated and controlled before a meaningful process-capability study can be made.

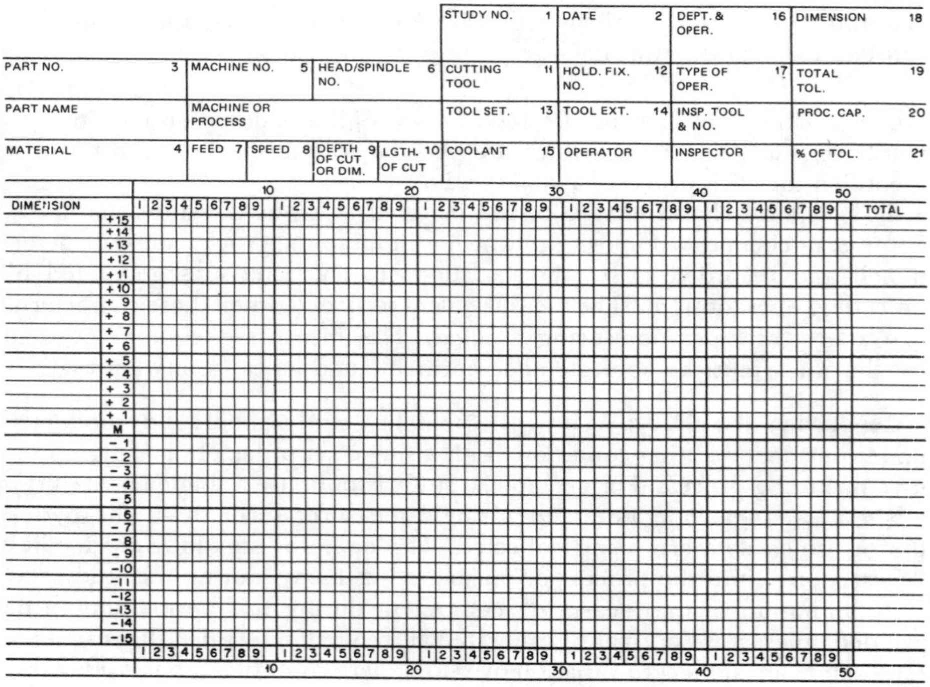

					STUDY NO. 1	DATE 2	DEPT. & OPER. 16	DIMENSION 18
PART NO. 3	MACHINE NO. 5	HEAD/SPINDLE NO. 6			CUTTING TOOL 11	HOLD. FIX. NO. 12	TYPE OF OPER. 17	TOTAL TOL. 19
PART NAME	MACHINE OR PROCESS				TOOL SET. 13	TOOL EXT. 14	INSP. TOOL & NO.	PROC. CAP. 20
MATERIAL 4	FEED 7	SPEED 8	DEPTH OF CUT OR DIM. 9	LGTH. OF CUT 10	COOLANT 15	OPERATOR	INSPECTOR	% OF TOL. 21

DIMENSION grid (columns 10, 20, 30, 40, 50; subdivisions 1 2 3 4 5 6 7 8 9):

Rows: +15, +14, +13, +12, +11, +10, +9, +8, +7, +6, +5, +4, +3, +2, +1, M, −1, −2, −3, −4, −5, −6, −7, −8, −9, −10, −11, −12, −13, −14, −15 | TOTAL

FIG. 20.16

A well-designed form is an important tool for making a process-capability study and helps ensure that the complete information is recorded at the time the study is made. Figure 20.16 is a typical example of such a form. With measurements recorded in this manner, there is both a ready comparison between the measurements made and the design tolerances and a picture of any apparent out-of-control conditions or nonchance cause variations.

20.17 Calculation of the Process Capability

There are several ways of calculating the capability of a process. As was earlier discussed, both computer application and electronic calculators may be widely and effectively used for routine process-capability evaluation. It is, however, essential to understand the "physical reality" fundamentals of these studies; hence the discussion below emphasizes these fundamentals.

One method of calculation is to go through the rather cumbersome procedure of using Formula (4A).

A rather rapid method for calculating a process capability is discussed here. This method involves the use of a process-capability worksheet used in conjunction with a nomograph. It uses a variation of Formula (4B), adapted for practical factory use and simplification (involving what the statistically minded reader will recognize as "rounding" with n's in the two denominators in place

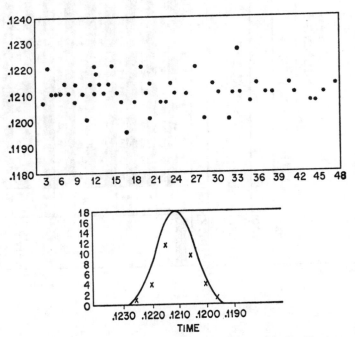

FIG. 20.17 Measurements in sequence and frequency distribution.

PROCESS CAPABILITY STUDY

MACHINE OR PROCESS ___ MILLING #3 ___

DATE ___ 11/20/59 FIRST SHIFT ___

TOOLS _____

CYCLE TIME ___ 2.4 MINUTES ___

PROCESS CAPABILITY VALUE ___ .0037" ___

MATERIAL ___ STAINLESS STEEL ___

OPERATION ___ #35 ___

SIGNED _____

THICKNESS

Frequency - f

Variation from Nominal / ACTUAL SIZE	1	2	3	4	5	6	7	8	9	10	11	12	13	14	15	16	17	18	19	20	21	22	23	24	25	White	Black
◆ 10	10	20	30	40	50	60	70	80	90	100	110	120	130	140	150	160	170	180	190	200	211	220	230	240	250		
	100	200	300	400	500	600	700	800	900	1000	1100	1200	1300	1400	1500	1600	1700	1800	1900	2000	2100	2200	2300	2400	2500		
◆ 9	9	18	27	36	45	54	63	72	81	90	99	108	117	126	135	144	153	162	171	180	189	198	207	216	225		
	81	162	243	324	405	486	567	648	729	810	891	972	1053	1134	1215	1296	1377	1458	1539	1620	1701	1782	1863	1944	2025		
◆ 8	8	16	24	32	40	48	56	64	72	80	88	96	104	112	120	128	136	144	152	160	168	176	184	192	200		
	64	128	192	256	320	384	448	512	576	640	704	768	832	896	960	1024	1088	1152	1216	1280	1344	1408	1472	1536	1600		
◆ 7	7	14	21	28	35	42	49	56	63	70	77	84	91	98	105	112	119	126	133	140	147	154	161	168	175		
	49	98	147	196	245	294	343	392	441	490	539	588	637	686	735	784	833	882	931	980	1029	1078	1127	1176	1225		
◆ 6	6	12	18	24	30	36	42	48	54	60	66	72	78	84	90	96	102	108	114	120	126	132	138	144	150		
	36	72	108	144	180	216	252	288	324	360	396	432	468	504	540	576	612	648	684	720	756	792	828	864	900		
◆ 5	5	10	15	20	25	30	35	40	45	50	55	60	65	70	75	80	85	90	95	100	105	110	115	120	125		
	25	50	75	100	125	150	175	200	225	250	275	300	325	350	375	400	425	450	475	500	525	550	575	600	625		
◆ 4	4	8	12	16	20	24	28	32	36	40	44	48	52	56	60	64	68	72	76	80	84	88	92	96	100		
	16	32	48	64	80	96	112	128	144	160	176	192	208	224	240	256	272	288	304	320	336	352	368	384	400		
◆ 3	3	6	9	12	15	18	21	24	27	30	33	36	39	42	45	48	51	54	57	60	63	66	69	72	75	3	9
	9	18	27	36	45	54	63	72	81	90	99	108	117	126	135	144	153	162	171	180	189	198	207	216	225		
◆ 2	2	4	6	8	10	12	14	16	18	20	22	24	26	28	30	32	34	36	38	40	42	44	46	48	50	10	20
	4	8	12	16	20	24	28	32	36	40	44	48	52	56	60	64	68	72	76	80	84	88	92	96	100		
◆ 1	1	2	3	4	5	6	7	8	9	10	11	12	13	14	15	16	17	18	19	20	21	22	23	24	25	11	11
	1	2	3	4	5	6	7	8	9	10	11	12	13	14	15	16	17	18	19	20	21	22	23	24	25		

.1225"
.1220
.1215

Process-capability computation / tally sheet

	1	2	3	4	5	6	7	8	9	10	11	12	13	14	15	16	17	18	19	20	21	22	23	24	25
-1	1	2	3	4	5	6	7	8	9	10	11	12	13	14	15	16	17	18	19	20	21	22	23	24	25
-2	2	4	6	8	10	12	14	16	18	20	22	24	26	28	30	32	34	36	38	40	42	44	46	48	50
-3	3	6	9	12	15	18	21	24	27	30	33	36	39	42	45	48	51	54	57	60	63	66	69	72	75
-4	4	8	12	16	20	24	28	32	36	40	44	48	52	56	60	64	68	72	76	80	84	88	92	96	100
	16	32	48	64	80	96	112	128	144	160	176	192	208	224	240	256	272	288	304	320	336	352	368	384	400
-5	5	10	15	20	25	30	35	40	45	50	55	60	65	70	75	80	85	90	95	100	105	110	115	120	125
	25	50	75	100	125	150	175	200	225	250	275	300	325	350	375	400	425	450	475	500	525	550	575	600	625
-6	6	12	18	24	30	36	42	48	54	60	66	72	78	84	90	96	102	108	114	120	126	132	138	144	150
	36	72	108	144	180	216	253	288	324	360	396	432	468	504	540	576	612	648	684	720	756	792	828	864	900
-7	7	14	21	28	35	42	49	56	63	70	77	84	91	98	105	112	119	126	133	140	147	154	161	168	175
	49	98	147	196	245	294	343	392	441	490	539	588	637	686	735	784	833	882	931	980	1029	1078	1127	1176	1225
-8	8	16	24	32	40	48	56	64	72	80	88	96	104	112	120	128	136	144	152	160	168	176	184	192	200
	64	128	192	256	320	384	448	512	576	640	704	768	832	896	960	1024	1088	1152	1216	1280	1344	1408	1472	1536	1600
-9	9	18	27	36	45	54	63	72	81	90	99	108	117	126	135	144	153	162	171	180	189	198	207	216	225
	81	162	243	324	405	486	567	648	729	810	891	972	1053	1134	1215	1296	1377	1458	1539	1620	1701	1782	1863	1944	2025
-10	10	20	30	40	50	60	70	80	90	100	110	120	130	140	150	160	170	180	190	200	210	220	230	240	250
0	100	200	300	400	500	600	700	800	900	1000	1100	1200	1300	1400	1500	1600	1700	1800	1900	2000	2100	2200	2300	2400	2500

Measurement tally column (left): .1210, .1205, .1200, .1195

Column totals (carried): −9 → 9; −10 → 20; −3 → 9

Totals White & Black: +2 | 78

INSTRUCTIONS

1. Sample size must be 25 or 50 pieces. These should be the first 25 or 50 pieces produced after the machine or process has been set up and properly adjusted.

2. Measurement should be done with accurate gages, i.e., micrometers, electro-limit gages, etc.

3. The tally of the pieces checked can be accomplished by circling the red and black number combination which corresponds to the proper frequency (f) and the proper variation from nominal.

4. After the tally has been completed, the largest value circled for each individual variation should be carried to the proper column at the right of the table.

    a. The White numbers should be placed in the White column and the black numbers in the Black column.

    b. The White column must be added algebraically and the total placed in the box marked Total White.

    c. The Black column must be added arithmetically and the total placed in the box marked Total Black.

5. These totals White and Black can now be transferred to the process-capability nomograph to obtain process capability value.

6. The unit probability value will depend on the unit assigned to the sample, i.e., .0001", .001", etc.

FIG. 20.18 Process-capability sheet.

785

of a single $n - 1$). A worksheet, shown in Figure 20.18, assists in computing the two factors Σfd and Σfd^2 in this formula:

$$\sigma = i \sqrt{\frac{\Sigma fd^2}{n} - \left(\frac{\Sigma fd}{n}\right)^2} \qquad (39)$$

The white-on-black numbers (hereafter called white numbers) are the fd values, and the black-on-white numbers (hereafter called black numbers) are the fd^2 values. The sheet (Fig. 20.18) is arranged so that the vertical scale is the quality characteristic under investigation and the horizontal scale is the frequency with which the various sizes of the characteristic are encountered in the sample taken.

To illustrate its use, a process capability will be calculated for a process used for milling stainless steel bars to a thickness of $0.12 \pm .003$ inch. A capability study was run on milling machine #3 during the first shift with stainless steel on operation #35. Measurements in inches were:

1	0.1220	11	0.1200	21	0.1205	31	0.1210	41	0.1205
2	0.1205	12	0.1215	22	0.1200	32	0.1220	42	0.1200
3	0.1210	13	0.1210	23	0.1220	33	0.1200	43	0.1210
4	0.1210	14	0.1220	24	0.1205	34	0.1215	44	0.1210
5	0.1210	15	0.1210	25	0.1210	35	0.1210	45	0.1215
6	0.1215	16	0.1215	26	0.1215	36	0.1200	46	0.1210
7	0.1210	17	0.1215	27	0.1205	37	0.1225	47	0.1205
8	0.1215	18	0.1220	28	0.1205	38	0.1210	48	0.1205
9	0.1205	19	0.1210	29	0.1215	39	0.1210	49	0.1210
10	0.1210	20	0.1195	30	0.1210	40	0.1215	50	0.1215

In Figure 20.17, these readings are plotted in the order which they were produced over time and also are cumulated into a frequency distribution.

The steps in calculating the process capability based upon these readings are:

1. Average the first five measurements. This average (0.1211) shows that the distribution is tending to center around 0.1210.
2. Establish this (0.1210) as the nominal point (zero) in the "variation from nominal column" (Fig. 20.18).

   If some other value, such as 0.1215 or 0.1205, were chosen, this would not affect the result. The objective is to center the distribution so there will be an adequate number of cells on both sides of the mean to accommodate all the data.
3. Assign appropriate "coded" values to each cell and write these in the column headed Actual Size opposite respective cells. In this example, the measurements are in 0.0005-inch increments. If 0.1210 is chosen as the 0 cell, 0.1215 is written opposite the $+1$ cell, 0.1205 opposite the -1 cell, and so on.

4. Circle the single set of white and black numbers in the frequency (f) column that corresponds to the frequency of occurrence in each respective cell.
5. Transcribe white and black numbers to their respective columns on the extreme right-hand edge of the worksheet. These columns are added. Note that the "white" column contains both positive and negative numbers and must be added algebraically. The white sum corresponds to Σfd and the black sum to Σfd^2 values computed by the longhand method of calculation shown in Section 13.15.
6. The white and black numbers' totals, 2 and 78, are then entered in columns A and B, respectively, on the process-capability nomograph shown in Figure 20.19. A straight line is passed through these points on columns A and B to intersect column C. At this point, the coded process capability is read in column C, which in this case is 7.5.
7. "Decode" the process-capability value read in column C by multiplying it by the incremental value represented by one cell width, in this case, 0.0005 inch. The result is the process capability of 0.0037 inch.

Slide rules have been developed that accomplish the same purpose as the nomograph. Figure 20.20 shows such a slide rule. The worksheet could have been used independently of the nomograph by substituting the white and black numbers' totals into the equation:

$$\text{Process capability} = 6\sigma = 6i\sqrt{\frac{\Sigma fd^2}{n} + \left(\frac{\Sigma fd}{n}\right)^2}$$

$$= 6(0.0005 \text{ inch})\sqrt{\frac{78}{50} + \left(\frac{2}{50}\right)^2}$$

$$= 0.0037 \text{ inch}$$

20.18 Use of Process-Capability Studies

Now that methods for computing process capability have been demonstrated, the application of the results is considered.

The applications considered here include

1. Information to facilitate the design of the product
2. Acceptance of a new or reconditioned piece of equipment
3. Scheduling work to machines
4. Selection of operators
5. Setting up the machine for a production run
6. Establishing control limits for equipment that has a narrow process capability in comparison with the allowable tolerance band
7. Determining the economic nominal around which to operate when the process capability exceeds the tolerance

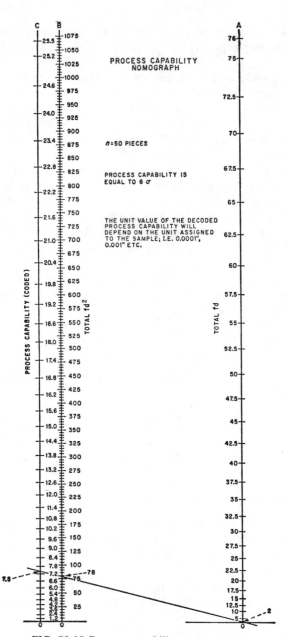

FIG. 20.19 **Process-capability nomograph.**

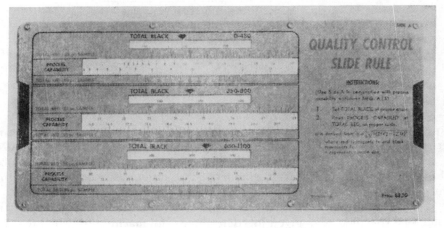

FIG. 20.20 **Process-capability slide rule.**

The last three techniques have been put in the form of nomographs.

1. Information to Facilitate the Design of the Product

When a product is being designed, an important area to be considered is the machines' available to manufacture such a product. Process-capability values for the available machines and the corresponding quality characteristics provide the designer with a realistic approach to the work. New equipment needs will be highlighted when the present machines are not capable of producing the tolerances required by the design. Designing products both to fit existing equipment capabilities and to highlight new equipment needs will help in quality planning. Furthermore, reduced losses, smoother conversion to the new design, and faster scheduling will result.

2. Acceptance of a New or Reconditioned Piece of Equipment

The new equipment needs that were mentioned above must be fulfilled and must be capable of producing the dimension required. Before accepting the new piece of equipment, process-capability studies should be conducted for assurance that the machine is adequate for the job to be performed. Process-capability studies can also be used by a manufacturer before shipping a piece of equipment to ensure that it meets its guaranteed performance.

3. Scheduling Work to Machines

Different machines that create the same type of characteristics may have different process capabilities because of such factors as make, size, age, model, and the like. Various product designs, scheduled through the manufacturing, may have different tolerances for the same type of characteristics to be generated. By knowing the capabilities of the machines, these products can be so scheduled to minimize or eliminate rework and scrap costs. To illustrate this,

	Process-capability value	
Lathe	Soft brass	Stainless steel
A	0.001 inch	0.003 inch
B	0.002 inch	0.004 inch
C	0.005 inch	0.007 inch

consider a machine shop with three lathes of different makes. The characteristic that they are creating is the turned diameter of the parts produced. After a series of process-capability studies, the results are tabulated (see table above). It not only is found that the lathes are different in capability but that they will vary according to the material used.

With this information in hand, it is possible to assign work such that the tolerance specified on a given job determines the machine to which that job is assigned. For example, if a turned diameter of soft brass were specified as 0.969 ± 0.002 inch, the total tolerance band is 0.004 inch. This job would necessarily have to be assigned to either lathe B or lathe A because these are the only lathes in the shop capable of producing that class of work. If there is a possibility that parts with a tighter tolerance than this might be scheduled during this time, in all probability lathe B would be used for this particular job.

It is advisable, whenever possible, that the process-capability value not exceed 75 percent of the total tolerance.

4. Selection of Operators

It should be pointed out that process-capability studies can be run where no machine is involved. Take one case that was studied, namely, the adjustment of thermostats. These were adjusted by an adjusting screw which was turned until an indicator light came on. The only tool involved was a knob which had no influence upon the process. Twelve operators were involved, and the thermostats were all of the same design and went to the operators randomly from the fabrication process. The effectiveness of the adjusting process was measured by the temperature at which the thermostat closed under operating conditions.

Some very interesting results were obtained. As might be expected, the process-capability value was large when an operator first started on the job and generally narrowed appreciably with experience. However, there were two operators who showed no improvement. They were finally placed in other jobs because they were incapable of adjusting thermostats. On the other hand, there was one operator who exhibited outstanding skill, having a process-capability value (6σ) of approximately half the average operators. Figure 20.21 shows schematically how the process-capability value changed with time for each operator. Here is a good example of how a process-capability study enabled a foreman to select operators best fitted for a certain exacting operation.

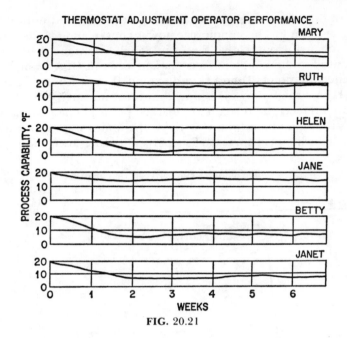

FIG. 20.21

5. Setting Up a Machine for a Production Run

When readying a piece of equipment for a production run, it is necessary to ensure that the machine will be set up to produce parts that are within the engineering tolerance. This is done by measuring some of the first parts produced, and based upon what is found, the machine is either accepted for that production run or readjusted and other parts subsequently checked. The questions raised are (1) "How many measurements need to be made?" (2) "Between what limits should these measurements fall to ensure that the machine is properly set?" (3) "The measurements falling outside of what limits indicate that the machine needs to be readjusted?" To answer these questions, one must first know the process capability of the machine and the acceptable quality level of the characteristic created.

With this information, the above questions can then be answered. A nomograph has been developed for easy calculation of this information. To illustrate the use of the nomograph shown in Figure 20.22, consider the example just used and presented in the preceding section. In this example, a turned diameter of soft brass was specified as $0.969 \pm .002$ inch, for a total tolerance band of 0.004 inch. This job was assigned to lathe B, which had a process capability of 0.002 inch for soft brass. So the process capability of the lathe expressed as a percent of the tolerance is 0.002 inch/0.004 inch = 50 percent. This point is so marked in Figure 20.22 and labeled point D. The quality level (AQL) for this dimension is 2.5 percent and is marked point E in Figure 20.22. A straight line (1) is drawn connecting points D and E and extended until it intersects pivot line 2 at point F. The sample size now is chosen and marked on the scale labeled Number of Consecutive Pieces in Sample. Assume that only a single piece is desired in the sample; this is marked as point G. A straight line (2) is drawn connecting points D and G and extended until it intersects pivot line 1 at point H. A straight line (3) is now drawn connecting points F and H and extended to intersect the reject limit, marked point J. The point at which this line bisects the setup limit (point K) yields the limit within which the setup is acceptable. This limit is expressed as a percent of tolerance and is pictured in

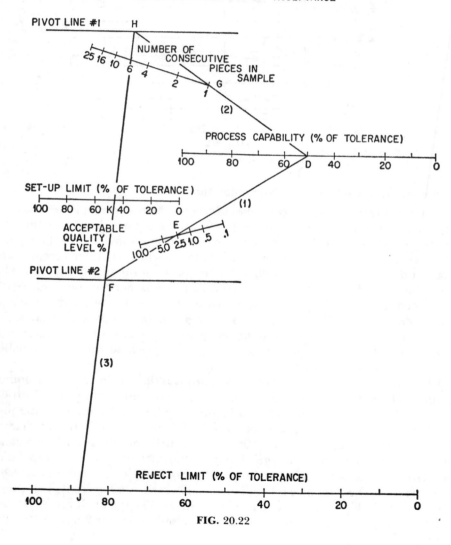

FIG. 20.22

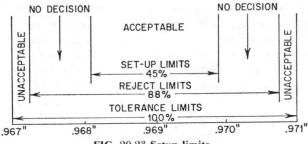

FIG. 20.23 **Setup limits.**

Figure 20.23. The point at which this line intersects the reject limit (point J) yields the limit outside of which the setup needs to be adjusted. Once again, this limit is expressed as a percent of tolerance and is pictured in Figure 20.23. The area between these limits is an indecision area and can be reduced by increasing the sample size.

The setup limits for this example would be 0.969 $\pm$ (0.45) 0.002 inch = 0.9681 inch and 0.9699 inch. A single piece sample value between these two limits indicates the setup is proper. The reject limits are 0.969 $\pm$ (0.88) (0.002 inch) = 0.9672 inch and 0.9708 inch.

If the single sample is less than 0.9672 inch or greater than 0.9709 inch, the setup should be readjusted.

6. Establishing Control Limits for Equipment That Has a Narrow Process Capability in Comparison to the Allowable Tolerance Band

In many types of operations, the process capability of the equipment used is narrow in comparison to the tolerance band of the parts it is producing. When such is the case, it may be desirable to take advantage of the entire allowable tolerance band. Such a case would be a process that has an inherent drift in the dimensional setting. Such drift usually occurs in processes when the tool used to generate the characteristic is subject to wear or degradation. Examples of such types of processes are lathes, screw machines, jig borers, drill presses, and grinders. Normally, the process capability of such equipment is small in relation to the total allowable tolerance, and the setting can drift within tolerances. Such a condition is shown in Figure 20.24.

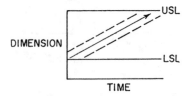

FIG. 20.24 **Tool-wear rate.**

The problem that arises in such cases is to set control limits that will allow one to take full advantage of the tolerance band and yet have assurance that an excessive number of parts out of tolerance are not being produced.

A nomograph has been derived to assist in determining the proper control limits. This is shown in Fig. 20.25 and consists of four variables. Once two of these variables are chosen, the other two are fixed. These variables are

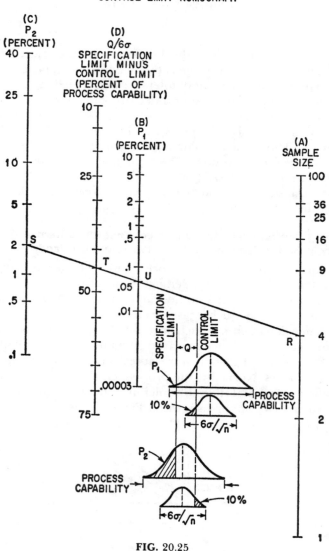

FIG. 20.25

1. The sample size used (n). This is column A.
2. p_1 percent (column B). This is the minimum percent of parts out of tolerance that one could expect if the average of the sample fell directly on the control limit.
3. p_2 percent (column C). This is the maximum percent of parts out of tolerance one could expect if the average of the sample fell directly on the control limit.
4. The distance the control limit is inside the specification limit and expressed as a percent of the process capability (column D).

For instance, consider the example used previously where a turned diameter of soft brass was specified as 0.969 ± 0.002 inch for a tolerance band of 0.004 inch.

Previously, this job was assigned to lathe B with a process capability of 0.002 inch, but for this example, it is assigned to lathe A with a process capability of 0.001 inch. Here the process capability is small in comparison to the total allowable tolerance (25 percent). A sample size of 4 is taken periodically. This is marked as point R on Fig. 20.25. Further, a maximum of 2 percent parts out of limits at any time is established. This is marked as point S on Fig. 20.25. A straight line (1) is drawn between points R and S. This establishes the distance between the control limit and the specification limit to be 45 percent of the capability (point T), and the minimum percent out of tolerance, for a sample falling on this control limit to be 0.05 percent (point U).

7. Determining the Economic Nominal around Which to Operate When the Process Capability Exceeds the Tolerance

Many dimensions are so set that an undersize part will result in scrap and an oversize part can be reworked. The cost of scrap may be greater than that for rework, or it may be that the rework cost is greater than the scrap cost. If the process capability of such a process for some reason exceeds the tolerance band, it may be necessary to continue the operation until such time as the process capability can be improved. However, during that time nonconforming parts have been made, resulting in scrap and rework dollars. Rather than minimize the percent nonconforming produced, a shift of the nominal toward the lesser cost side of the tolerance may be desirable to reduce the total nonconforming quality dollars to a minimum.

A nomograph has been derived to assist in computing the amount to shift the average from nominal to realize the lowest cost situation. This consists in four variables and is shown in Figure 20.26. These variables are

1. Tolerance band. This is the width of the tolerance band beyond which the parts produced will result in either scrap or rework (column 1).
2. Process capability *at the time being studied* (column 2).
3. The cost ratio. This is the ratio of the greater cost divided by the lesser cost (column 3).

NOMOGRAPH FOR DETERMINING MINIMUM SCRAP AND REWORK COST

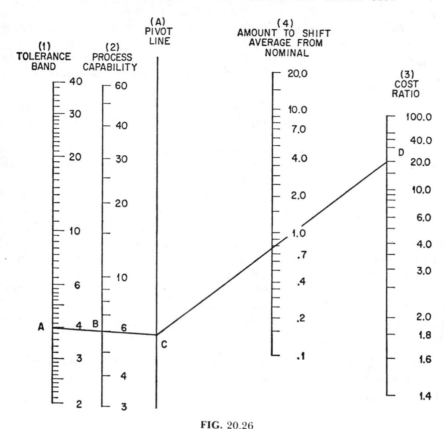

FIG. 20.26

4. The amount to shift the average from nominal. This shift is always toward the tolerance limit with the lesser associated cost (column 4).

To illustrate the use of this nomograph, consider once again the example given near the beginning of this section. If the turned diameter of 0.969 $\pm$ 0.002 inch is too small, the shaft is scrapped at a cost of $10. However, if the turned diameter is oversize, it can be reworked at a cost of 50 cents per shaft. Lathe B's capability normally is 0.002 inch but suddenly changes to 0.006 inch, and replacement parts for the lathe are temporarily unavailable. The shaft order is necessary to maintain production, so it is decided to keep producing despite the scrap and rework cost. If the present nominal is maintained, the nonconforming quality cost will be ($10) (0.023) + $0.50 (0.023) = $0.246 per piece.[18] Using the nomograph with a tolerance band of 4 mils (point A) and a process capability of 6 mils (point B) will yield point C on the pivot line when connected with a straight line. The cost ratio is $10/$0.50 = 20 and is marked point D. Connecting points C and D with a straight line shows that a shift of approximately 0.75 mils will minimize the total nonconforming quality dollars. The nominal is shifted to 0.9697 inch, with a resultant 10.6 percent of the parts reworked and .3 percent of the parts scrapped. So the total nonconforming quality cost now is $(0.106 \times \$0.50) + (0.003 \times \$10) = \$0.083$ per piece, or a two-thirds reduction.

Summary: The process-capability study is a powerful tool. Not only can it be easily computed, but its uses are many. All possible applications were not covered here, nor was this attempted. Only some were discussed, to give a flavor of the types of possible applications for which it can be used.

Through use of the process-capability study, savings can be realized in losses caused by inadequate processes, poor tool maintenance, unskilled operators, and the like. It can help assure optimum programming of machines and operators in making the product to specification at a minimum cost.

QUALITY AUDIT

20.19 Background

The basic evaluation of a quality-control program must be made from appraisal of the satisfaction gained by customers in the articles they purchase from the plant. In a very important sense the customer is the final "control station" for factory product-control activity.

Customer satisfaction will eventually be mirrored by the number and seriousness of customer complaints. But the delay between time of actual production and customer reports on satisfaction with the articles thus produced is often long; as control data, complaint reports are valuable chiefly for picturing long-run quality trends. More immediate data on customer satisfaction are necessary as a guide to required corrective action because thousands of articles may have been produced with a certain defect before customer complaints are received on the first such defective article shipped.

Since it provides customer-viewpoint data of the sort thus required, the quality audit has assumed increasing importance as a product-control technique with the major audit activity being provided by Process-Control Engineering, with other involved plant functional components. The principles of audit were discussed in Sections 11.23 through 11.27 as to the product, procedures, system, and other audit categories. For the product-control job of total quality control, the following audit areas are reviewed: *product audits,* discussed in this section; *procedures audits, systems audits,* and *measurements audits* in Section 20.20; and a service-quality audit example, "Audit of Quality of Research and Development Work," Section 20.21.

Product Audit: Product audits usually take place on the following basis:

1. Selection of a sample of units of product from a lot upon which all operations, tests, and inspections have been performed and which awaits shipment. Size of this sample is usually relatively small and may include as few

as 10 or 15 units, although a 50-unit sample is desirable when such a sample size is economical.

2. The units in the sample are examined by the process-control engineer from the viewpoint of a critical customer. This examination in some cases uses the same standards as those for the regular production inspection and tests. In many instances, it uses much more rigorous standards than those used for regular production, including accelerated life tests and product tear-downs.

3. Results from this examination are used as the basis for action of various sorts:

   a. In some instances, the quality audit must result in approval of the sample before the lot from which it was drawn may be released for shipment.

   b. In most instances, release does not await the quality-audit results. These results are, however, used by the process-control engineer to show trends and to guide corrective action that may be required.

4. The frequency of quality audits varies widely from plant to plant, depending upon economic and quality requirements. Some plants require a quality audit of each lot shipped, others require an audit periodically—each day, each week, each month.

5. Quality-audit results are published as a significant quality index for the product studied for the period covered by the audit.

The product-quality audit is *customer-centered* and pays special attention to those characteristics that are of greatest importance to the customer, especially including those that may be most frequently troublesome to him or her. The audit includes weighing factors depending upon whether the characteristics are of critical, major, minor, or incidental nature to the customer. The audit may then provide a weighed number, or index, to be used to evaluate product-quality continuously and relative to time. This index number also is an indicator of how well the product-quality program is actually operating.

To the extent possible, the index number should correlate with customer complaints and the customer's reaction to the quality of the product. This correlation requires that the proper time lapse between the date of manufacture and the date of use of the product be factored in. Therefore, the audit can be used to forecast the magnitude, number, and cost of future complaints.

The magnitude can be forecast by extending the weighed index number on a per unit basis. The higher the index number, the lower the magnitude of potential complaints. The cost can be forecast by relating each characteristic to its potential complaint cost if it were to reach the customer in a substandard condition. This cost-weighed type of index number then becomes a weighed potential dollar loss number. The number of complaints can be forecast by trends, per time, as indicated by the index.

In a very broad sense, a product-quality audit provides verification of the quality of the product. Since this type of audit is not designed to accept or reject product, an indication of low quality means that immediate and thorough analysis must be initiated. This analysis includes a thorough study of the substandard indication to determine both acceptability of product and the cause of this substandard condition. In addition, corrective action should be immediately taken to eliminate or control the substandard condition.

Whenever the index number shows this trend toward lower quality—or when a poor index number is itself determined—a very fast feedback of this information is essential. This may indicate that an individual equipment or an entire process has not been maintained properly or is out of control; that gage, instrument, or equipment control programs have not been properly maintained; or the quality procedures have not been followed or the quality planning itself is not adequate. If any one of these causes is present, then several lots of product may already have been affected and losses can be minimized only by an accurate analysis and commensurate corrective action.

Audit samples are most easily selected where the product is small and units can be easily handled. The same approach has been applied to larger apparatus, however, often through the medium of selecting important subassemblies or critical components.

In substance, therefore, this technique is just what its title states—an audit of product quality—and is directly comparable in need and principle to the more widely known accounting audit. The product-quality audit is not a control measure in the short-term preventive sense because the articles examined by the process-control engineer have already been manufactured along with the lot from which they have been drawn. However, its longer term effects are very significant. It is also an extremely useful and economically productive overcheck on the effectiveness of the regular day-by-day plant routines for controlling quality—involving inspection skill, test performance, operator care, and so on. It may also provide a ready customer-viewpoint quality barometer.

20.20 Product-Control Audits of Procedures, Systems, and Measurements

Procedures Audit: The procedures-oriented form of product-control audits is used to verify the adherence of practices to established procedures within the quality program. A simple and widely used index of the results of this audit compares the percentage of procedures that are being systematically followed to the total number sampled. A high incidence of nonconformance may indicate a number of different conditions, but primarily either that the procedures are not adequately being followed in the plant—which requires immediate management attention—or that the procedures may not be effective or understood, or even available—all of which require a different type of action.

Thus, conditions which are carefully examined in the audit include the supervision of quality actions, the clarity of communications, and adequacy of follow-through on the part of operator, inspector, or tester. Whenever discrepancies between practice and procedure are identified, suitable corrective action must be brought into agreement with the prescribed procedure, or in instances where it is required, the procedure should be improved to permit effective quality operation and quality compliance.

Systems Audit: This form of product-control audit is directed to an evaluation both of adherence to the quality system and the effectiveness of the quality system in meeting the plant and company quality objectives of customer satisfaction. Section 11.26 reviewed an example of this form of audit.

Measurements Audit: This type of audit verifies the quality and accuracy of the measurements taken by inspectors, testers, and shop operators. It is similar, in some respects, to supervisors checking or testing their own operations. The measurement under study should be verified using an alternate method of measuring whenever practicable. This technique points out operators who are not measuring properly. It also locates measuring instruments that are improperly planned for the job, tools that are out of calibration, and it will minimize differences in measuring techniques from distorting the audit results.

Practices involved in measurement audit are the following:

1. Randomly select several lots of product. (These lots can be selected by using a random number table by matching up the last three digits from the table.)
2. Take a 5- or 10-piece sample from each lot.
3. Measure and compare with the inspector's results. The number of lots selected and the desired frequency of repeating this audit are based upon the degree of need exhibited by the index number.

An index based upon the percentage of measurements that are found to be accurate is a most widely used indicator here. This is a simple index, easily understood and interpreted throughout the factory.

20.21 Audit of Quality of Research and Development Work

Research and development, while a very important activity in many companies, is also sometimes a very difficult area to quantify. A large multidivisional company headquartered in the midwest allots millions of dollars for research and development work to upgrade the state of the art for the markets it serves. While direct responsibility for conducting the development work rests with the Director of Research and Operating Division Managers, top management has ultimate responsibility for determining that development projects and programs are well-planned and executed as well as cost-effective.[19]

Executive concerns lie in areas such as potential duplication of development activities within the operating divisions, prudent deployment of resources, and the value of the results of development expenditures. As a measure of how effectively the various research and development activities were being carried out, the company's chief executive directed that an audit be performed. While the concept of auditing is in no way unusual, the unusual nature of the quality area being audited presented some unique problems which were addressed in a rather unorthodox way.

The audit team, consisting of three individuals independent of any of the divisions or activities being audited, worked out a plan calculated to reduce dramatically the audit work hours normally involved in this type of audit: The auditees (the divisions that were to be audited) were given an active partnership role in the audit itself. This participative approach to problem solving reflects the involvement and the quality-circle techniques discussed in Chapter 9.

The audit team first compiled standards against which to measure. This was accomplished by researching available literature, from discussions with other engineers and scientists, and from the company's own procedure and policies for R&D. The data gathered resulted in approximately 40 standards. Because they would be dealing with managers and executives, the audit team decided to place the standards within a framework that took a management viewpoint; thus, each was listed under one of four generally accepted functions of management: planning, organizing, directing, and controlling. This management-oriented approach helped establish a climate which permitted a productive relationship to flourish.

Having decided upon the approach, the audit team next addressed the question of the preliminary survey which, in audits of complex activities not previously audited, may be a key function of the examination upon which all the subsequent auditing activities are based. The importance of the preliminary survey is substantial, but it can be fraught with difficulties. The auditor must talk with people in the midst of their work and ask many questions, trusting that the questions are understood, that they are correctly answered, that the auditor will understand the answers and be able to place them in proper perspective. Unless the person is a first-rate auditor with considerable experience, it is more than likely that information so gathered will not truly focus on what is needed and that recorded information will be full of gaps that need clarifying and augmenting. If the initial questions have not already made the auditees defensive, repeated return visits for additional information almost certainly will.

The participative approach provided a way around these difficulties. The technique called for a series of questions (under the headings of Planning, Organizing, Directing, and Controlling) which were counterparts of the standards previously generated. The questionnaire had to be answered in writing by auditee personnel and documented with appropriate records, procedures, forms, and reports. In effect, the preliminary survey was to be carried out by those most knowledgeable of the activity—the R&D people themselves.

When the questionnaire was returned, the team reviewed the replies and took stock of their position, which was to have accumulated, with far less time and effort than would normally be the case, the essential information and records. In addition, a subtler benefit accrued from the participative approach:

The questionnaire became a self-audit for development department managers, permitting them to take a good, hard look at themselves while answering pertinent questions about their activities.

Analysis of the questionnaire brought to the surface those areas where in-depth study was indicated, and these were the focus of the actual audit. Thus, objective, knowledgeable, professional assurances were provided to executive management as to those activities which were working effectively as well as substantial recommendations for improvement in certain other areas. The latter encompasses a broad range of subjects, from consideration of long-term plans and reducing objectives and goals to writing, to developing consistent policies and procedures and tightening management control over development projects.

In some audit environments these recommendations might have resulted in antagonism, hostility, or even refusal of the auditee to take action. Under the participative approach, division management more readily accepted the findings which auditors were amply able to demonstrate, and prompt corrective action ensued.

OTHER AREAS FOR PRODUCT-CONTROL ACTIVITIES

20.22 Product Traceability

An important product-quality technique which involves documentation of the engineering, manufacturing, and distribution "history" of products is necessary to track product in the field so that quality trends may be considered and rapid action can be taken in such extremes as product recall.

Traceability activities identify the location of a unit of a specified configuration, and the date of manufacture, at any desired point within a production sequence. The unit may be a part, a subassembly, or a product. It should be expeditiously located at any point from incoming-materials inspection through all the manufacturing processes, the point of shipment to customers, and with the customers themselves—rapidly and at minimum cost.

To trace units efficiently, a methodical program must be established for identification, product configuration, record keeping, and dissemination. The desired degree of traceability must be established, usually based upon the criticality of the unit and the economics of the situation—such conditions balanced against the likelihood of future product-quality change by the product or, in cases of customer notification or refund, recall of product from the field. Among the factors that must be weighed in such a decision are the costs of backtracking through all processes, sifting all records, sorting all components at various stages of completion, reviewing all shipping records, and locating all faulty products which might be in company or customer warehouses or in actual use. Traceability of 100 percent can be costly, and companies will adapt the program to product lines as practically required to maintain marketplace customer satisfaction.

As an example, the approach of some companies is to maintain a traceability program in which critical components are identified through failure mode, effect, and criticality analysis performed by Engineering and Quality-Control personnel in conjunction with preliminary product design or preproduction review. This analysis results in a critical components master list issued and maintained by Quality Control with the cooperation of Production Control and Shipping, which is used to identify critical components either at Receiving or at appropriate manufacturing and assembly points. A Tracing Code is assigned at the beginning of the material flow, and a traceability flowchart is established. The major activity levels of the flowchart include:

1. Critical component selection and listing by part number.
2. Vendor part coding (recording vendor name and date of receipt).
3. Coding internally manufactured parts, subassembly, assembly, and storage in a daily tally. At the end of the assembly line, each shipping container is date coded. This sequential coding procedure provides sufficient data to tie in critical components to specific dates of receiving inspection, manufacturing, and final assembly.
4. Computerized shipping records, including date codes, customer name, and destination. Correlation of these data with tracing code numbers results in very effective traceability of critical components.

20.23 Software Product Control

Testing, verification, and validation of software modules and systems are basic to modern programs for total quality control. Product-control activities in the area of software include techniques for configuring (arranging the software, hardware, personnel and logistics for the test); conditioning (bringing the system to the initial state for testing); introducing actual or simulated data; initiating and synchronizing the test; collecting data; and displaying and analyzing results.[20]

One representative approach involves qualification testing of both hardware and the "support" software. The qualification test includes a documentation audit and an audit of conformance to design rules, followed by functional testing through environmental simulation. Defect measurement and reporting provides information which will enable preventive corrective action to reduce the number of software nonconformances. Standards are established to define nonconforming categories, to establish the stages at which nonconformance levels will be measured, and to define percent nonconformance using a base suitably oriented to nonconformances present in a software item the first time it is linked.

20.24 Quality Information Processing and Flow

A manufacturer of nuclear fuel kept inventory of more than 100,000 items of in-plant nuclear material by means of an automatic keypunch and batch processing system until new regulations stipulated more stringent precautionary inventory procedures, including in-process records and source and disposition records of all special nuclear materials. The nuclear safeguard problem faced by this manufacturer, while seemingly highly specialized, sums up the general basic production-quality need for more accurate means of lot and serial number tracking, a fundamental element in quality information processing.[21]

To gear up for the increased accuracy and audit requirements, plant management converted to an on-line transaction processing system which would verify all shop inputs as they were made and whose on-line data base would contain enough information to expedite physical inventory without extended delays in plant operations. The system also included necessary quality- and production-control logic and data to support production monitoring, process yields, material release, material traceability, and product certification.

The information processing hardware configuration consisted of dual mini-computers, connected to a common communication multiplexer for 70 factory and 10 office terminals. The software supported a multiprogrammed transaction processing system. It was necessary to gear the program to operate when only one of the computer systems was available as well as when both were functioning.

The two halves of the system operate in a primary-secondary mode, where the primary machine acts as the controller of the pair of machines; the secondary machine follows the processing in the first machine. The primary machine communicates with the factory floor terminals and processes transactions in a multiprogramming mode, while the secondary machine receives its inputs from the primary machine. As each transaction is finished processing on the primary machine, its input data are sent to the secondary machine and the terminal is released for the next transaction. Transactions are reprocessed serially in the secondary machine in the order of completion in the primary machine. Only transactions which successfully update the data base are sent to the secondary for processing; inquiry and aborted transactions are not sent.

Advantages of Information Processing: Plant management estimates that a 20 percent reduction in the manufacturing cycle was achieved by the system and its associated shop loading and quality systems as the result of improved management visibility and corrective-action potential. In addition, plant down time for physical inventories was reduced from 2 weeks to 3 days, and the work force needed to accomplish inventories was reduced by almost two-thirds.

The quality status information on each container of fissionable material in the plant has been used for increasingly complex consistency checking when material in containers is moved into processing stations. Quality and production needs have been optimally combined through conditional material releases subject to exception recall. This whole control process has resulted in both higher process yields and reduced scrap.

Notes

[1] Intangible quality costs and liability exposure costs were discussed in Sec. 7.14.

[2] For a discussion of such production, see Harry N. Lange, "QA for Small Programs in a Large Industry," *32nd Annual Technical Conference Transactions*, American Society for Quality Control, Chicago, 1978.

[3] For just one instance, in the manufacture of integrated circuits (ICs), very low field failure rates are necessary.

[4] For a discussion which continues to have long-term value, see Charles A. Bicking, "Quality Control in the Chemical Industry, I," *Industrial Quality Control*, vol. III, no. 4.

[5] Depending upon the size of the plant, there may be as many as 700 to 1000 so-called stations, or as few as 10 to 30. The purpose of station control is to maintain economical and consistently acceptable output quality, regardless of the location of the station—whether in new product and process introduction, process control, or in the areas of quality planning and quality effectiveness.

[6] Process-capability determinations are discussed in Secs. 20.15 through 20.18.

[7] This discussion largely follows an unpublished paper, "Quality Control Applied to Job Shop Production," W. J. Masser and R. S. Inglis, Philadelphia, Pa.

[8] A somewhat different approach to machining control, where there is a foundation of computer-aided design and computer-aided manufacturing—together with computer-aided quality assisted by such quality information equipments as coordinate measuring machines—was discussed in Sec. 12.9.

[9] For a discussion of an inspection data computer program for a similar analysis, see Fred Krannig, "A Quality Assurance Information System," *31st Annual Technical Conference Transactions*, American Society for Quality Control, 1977, p. 40.

[10] Quality audit is discussed in more detail in Secs. 20.19 through 20.21.

[11] For a discussion of this matter, see particularly Sec. 15.25.

[12] This follows a discussion by Larry R. Lavoie, "The Key to Control of N/C," *Quality*, November 1977, pp. 42–45, with permission from Mr. Lavoie and *Quality*.

[13] This discussion is adapted from an unpublished paper by D. A. Gensheimer, Pittsfield, Mass.

[14] Reduced, normal, and more rigid sampling plans were reviewed in Sec. 15.12.

[15] The example in this Section 20.13 is adapted from a composite of data from experience in trends in several product control installations oriented to the establishment of improved rejection rates in complex assemblies where great emphasis must be placed upon low nonconformity rates in component parts. The data are adapted to the utilization of control charts, Figures 20.10–20.12, which are similar, for consistency of teaching and demonstration, to assembly control charts employed in the 2d edition of this book. Figures 20.10–20.12 are similar to the control chart whose technical background was amplified in Sec. 14.27.

[16] For a discussion of process optimization, see Carl Mentch, "Manufacturing Process Optimization Studies—Theory and Use," *32nd Annual Technical Conference Transactions*, American Society for Quality Control, Chicago, 1978, pp. 268–272.

[17] Section 14.23 discusses such indices.

[18] 0.023 is the area on one side under the normal curve beyond 2σ. In this example, after the change in the process capability, the tolerance band only includes $\pm2\sigma$ of the process distribution.

[19] After a paper by R. Wachniak, "Participative Audit—a New Management Tool."

[20] For a discussion of software product control, see John B. Goodenough and Clement L. McGowan, "Software Quality Assurance: Testing and Validation," *Proceedings of the Institute of Electrical and Electronic Engineers*, September 1980.

[21] This discussion is after a paper by G. D. Detelfsen, R. H. Kerr, and A. S. Norton, "Two Generations of Transaction Processing Systems for Factory Control," presented at IEEE COMPCON, Washington, September 1976.

CHAPTER 21
Special Process Studies

For any plant or company, there may develop design, production, or service quality problems which, if not dealt with effectively and quickly, will jeopardize customer satisfaction in the marketplace. The competitive advantage for those companies with strong total-quality-control programs is that they have in place the mechanisms to deal with such problems in a systematic, timely, and permanent way—not merely as a temporary and uncertain "patch up," hopefully geared to getting the product to market.

Where such a mechanism is not available, an epidemic of production-line quality failures or a sudden avalanche of customer complaints may sound the starting gun for a host of independent, uncoordinated approaches to what is hoped to be rapid elimination of the causes of the trouble.

These approaches are often conflicting and overlapping; sometimes they are actually directed to contradictory interpretations of the problem to be faced. Too frequently they cause a slow rather than a fast solution; the answer finally decided upon may be one that does not really solve but merely transfers the problem elsewhere. The "solutions" are incomplete and so they may "work" for a time; however, they may involve the basic risk of later and greater problems which may end in costly liability exposure or even recall of product from the field.

In plants which enjoy total-quality-control activity, these critical quality problems generally are identified in parallel with product-control operations. To provide a channel for carrying through the major project effort required to deal with them, special process studies have been established as the fourth of the quality-control jobs.

These process studies provide the total-quality-control medium through which basic product-quality problems can be effectively faced and rapidly solved. They are geared to permanent corrective action. This chapter briefly reviews special process studies.

21.1 Defining Special Process Studies

As a definition:

> Special process studies involve investigations and tests to locate the causes of nonconforming products, to determine the possibility of improving quality characteristics, and to ensure that improvement and corrective action are permanent and complete.

These studies are directed to major, usually nonrepetitive quality problems requiring activity from more than one group in the company organization. There may, for example, be the sudden appearance at final assembly of high rejects which cannot be eliminated by readily available methods, a controversy between Design Engineering and Manufacturing Supervision as to whether a new and tightened tolerance is required for a high-quality expensive part, or the need for making a long-range study of the cause of a field complaint.

As noted in the definition, by no means all the problems passing through the special studies activity are those generated by factory quality troubles. These studies are also used for many of the major investigations initiated by Product Engineering, Manufacturing Engineering, Field Service Engineering, and other groups to determine the feasibility of improving quality standards on existing products or facilities.

Experience has taught plant management that basic problems demanding major project effort should be faced by a total quality activity organized of and by itself. Before the institution of the special process studies job, consolidation of these nonrepetitive projects with the product-control routines designed to deal with regular, repetitive quality issues too often resulted in disservice both to the regular procedures and the nonrepetitive projects.

21.2 The Elements of Special Process Studies

Fundamental to all special process studies are two elements:

1. *Coordination of company effort* so as to utilize all resources in an integrated approach to the problem and to ensure the institution of permanent improvements.
2. *Employment of the best technical methods* both to enable a sound technological attack on the problem and to encourage a solution whose reliability or lack of it is quite precisely understood.

For many special studies, coordination of effort and the taking of rapid and simple action are all that are required when the problem under consideration has been analyzed. Indicated steps may be a drawing change by Engineering, a process adaptation by Manufacturing Engineering, an increase in care by Shop Operations; all may be readily dovetailed together to eliminate the causes of the trouble.

In contrast, determination of the causes and solutions of other quality problems may be technologically very complex. Every plant has experienced the case of product failures which seemed to have been caused by "mysterious" and "unidentifiable" factors.

A situation in point is that of the assembly plant whose mechanical-device quality was so poor that, on occasional days, more units were rejected than were shipped. There were so many variables which "could" cause the rejections that company personnel found it difficult to make even a satisfactory start on the problem of isolating the possible causes.

Operators might have been at fault, test stands might have been defective, materials might have been unsatisfactory, design specifications might have been unsound. And when some process change was made which temporarily seemed to improve quality, company personnel were faced with the question of how much confidence could be placed in the long-term value of the apparent problem solution.

In knotty cases of this sort, extensive utilization of quality-control technical methods must supplement special process studies coordination activity. Sound understanding of the philosophy of scientific industrial experimentation is essential as the foundation upon which effective applications of these technical methods may be built.

The statistical point of view is especially useful here. Special methods in particular find their widest value with special process studies in analyzing problems, examining causes, and suggesting solutions of given statistical reliability.

The technical methods used in process studies are merely adaptations of the quality-control methods already listed in Chapters 10 to 17. The statistical point of view has itself been reviewed in Part 5. Especially to be emphasized for consideration in relation to special process studies are the sections in Chapter 16 which review the fundamental philosophy of the design of experiments as well as those which cover such techniques as regression, tests of significance, and analysis of variance.

21.3 Organizing for Special Process Studies

Involved in special process studies organization are the regular members of the company quality-control component together with key individuals in the other functional groups integrated in the company total quality program—Design Engineering, Manufacturing Engineering, Production, Purchasing, Service Engineering, and others. When a major quality problem arises which demands a special study, the problem is immediately discussed and analyzed as far as possible by process-control engineers and quality engineers.

Responsibilities are assigned for carrying out the various individual steps required for the investigation. As soon as the results of these individual analyses become known, they are tied into a problem solution.

Corrective steps that must be taken to bring this solution to reality are assigned to appropriate personnel. In the cases of shop-quality problems, these corrective steps also include assurance that a control is built into the solution such that the quality problem will not recur.

Very often, the key position in the organization for special process studies is the process-control engineer, who acts in a role comparable to that of a football quarterback in ensuring that the problem is handed to the proper individuals and groups. The process-control engineer is usually fully grounded in the application of quality-control technical methods and particularly in statistics and is therefore well-qualified to integrate special study projects.

Procedures established by plants for this activity are usually very simple in nature. These procedures merely assure identification of such factors as

1. *Types of problems to be entered in the special process studies channel.* The major distinctions between problems which may and those which may not be entered are cost and customer quality satisfaction and safety assurance; problems are carried through the channel only when they are sufficiently important economically and in customer satisfaction terms to balance the cost of the required investigation.
2. *Specification of the procedure for rapidly bringing these problems to the attention of the process-control engineer.* Most of the special process studies involving factory quality troubles are initiated by report of the factory supervisor—as key individual in the product-control routine through which most of these issues arise—about problems which the supervisor and the group cannot solve alone.
3. *Outline of the general steps that must be taken for final problem solutions by the appropriate individuals and components.* Such procedures frequently require that case reports be placed upon file after completion of the corrective action resulting, as appropriate, from a special study. A file of these reports thus provides a store of know-how for approaching similar problems which may arise.

Figures 21.1 and 21.2 illustrate essential portions of a case report filed after solution of a problem involving electrical devices which would not meet a specification at final test. The problem typically involved multiple causes—incorrect specifications, poor quality material, wrong operating methods—as well as integrated multiple solutions—correct test specifications, improved methods, elimination of poor quality material.

SPECIAL PROCESS STUDIES EXAMPLES

21.4 Thermometal

Section 21.2 emphasized that the approach to process studies is characterized by two elements fundamental to all such investigations: (1) coordination of effort to ensure permanent improvement and (2) employment of the best technical methods. After this basic approach has been established, the detailed

SPECIAL PROCESS STUDIES CASE # 112

PROBLEM 72E4 Relays, which had been adjusted and tested in Preliminary

Test, were out of limits in Final Test on the Pick-up Volts

Quality Characteristic.

LOCATION −72E4 Line

PRESENTED BY Test   **DATE** 7/15

✳✳✳✳

PAST DATA ON PROBLEM See Condition I on FIGURE 21.2

✳✳✳✳

CONTROL DATA TO BE TAKEN (1) Distribution data on pickup voltage and

dropout current for 50 relays at Final Test.

       (2) Trend data for 14 consecutive days on 10

relays.

ACTION TAKEN (1) Test limits were corrected from .4−.5 to .35−.65 for

pickup volts.

       (2) Constant current hereafter to be held in main contactor coil

during test of differential element.

       (3) Phosphor bronze springs, which had gotten on the line

by mistake, were scrapped.

RESULTS See present condition on FIGURE 21.2

R. F. Johnson

DATE 8/15   PROCESS CONTROL ENGINEER

FIG. 21.1

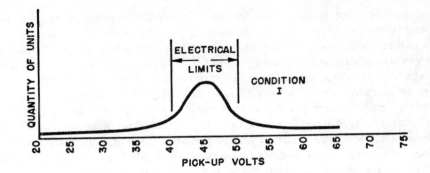

CONCLUSION: LIMITS – BOTH NOMINAL AND SPREAD INCORRECT AND COULD NOT BE MET WITHOUT HIGH REJECTS; LIMITS THAT WERE REQUIRED FOR CUSTOMER SATISFACTION WERE CALCULATED, NEED FOR IMPROVEMENT IN METHODS AND OPERATION REPORTED, AND CORRECTIVE ACTION STEPS ESTABLISHED.

STEPS TAKEN: METHODS IMPROVED; CORRECT LIMITS ESTABLISHED; OUT-OF-SPECIFICATION SPRING MATERIAL FOUND AND ELIMINATED.

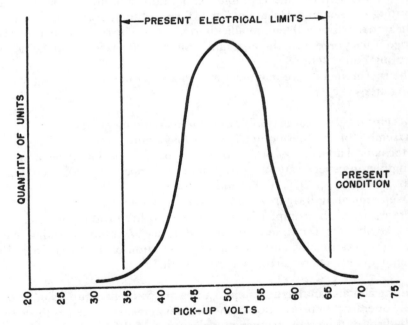

CONCLUSION: NEW LIMITS MADE POSSIBLE; QUALITY SPREAD ACCEPT-ABLE FOR CUSTOMER SATISFACTION; NECESSITY FOR IMPROVING OPERATING CHARACTERISTICS IDENTIFIED, WHICH WORK IS NOW COMPLETE'

FIG. 21.2

development of an analysis may demand—particularly on complex processes —comprehensive knowledge of the related process technology.

Active participation in special studies may, therefore, be required from plant process specialists and technologists—in electroplating when unsatisfactorily uneven finish thicknesses are being experienced, in drilling and reaming when there is excessive variation in distances between hole centers, in integrated circuit assembly when parting in connected joints persists, in casting when quality is spotty on steel motor casings, in porcelain glazing when cracks appear after heat treatment of bushings. The following examples are concerned with two distinctive types of process technology where specialists' assistance was required for successful completion of the study: adjustment of thermometal strip subassemblies (discussed in this section), and castings of sintered metal blocks (discussed in Sec. 21.5).

Because the purpose of this chapter is application of quality-control techniques, discussion of these examples will be concentrated primarily upon the various quality-control techniques employed; in spite of its importance to the solution, the appropriate process know-how will be reviewed only to a necessary minimum.[1]

Thermometal subassemblies act as the tripping mechanism for protective devices which control unacceptable temperature buildup in a wide variety of operating equipments. Unsafe or other forms of temperature increase generate heat that activates the bimetallic thermo strip. The protective device is then tripped, thus preventing the heat and temperature hazard from damaging the operating equipment.[2]

The thermometals are manufactured in a sequence with essentially the following steps:

1. Receipt on the production line of the metallic elements.
2. Assembly of the thermometal strip subassembly.
3. Mechanical adjustment of the strip for proper operation in accordance with engineering specifications. Adjustment tolerance is ± 0.005 inch, but strips are set at the specification nominal value.
4. Oven annealing heat treatment of the subassembly.
5. Transport of the completed subassembly to the production line, where it is assembled to a completed protective-device assembly. This device is later tested operationally, and the tripping operation of the thermometal is the major quality characteristic checked by this test.

During actual manufacture, steps 3 and 4 are combined into a single job held by one operator. In production of the thermometal assembled as the activating mechanism in the 403A protective device, two of these combination stations are in operation, each with an adjusting fixture and an operator and each using a common heat-treat oven.

On this 403A device, rejections at the final test in step 5 amounted, before a special study on the process, to 75 percent. The distribution shown in Figure

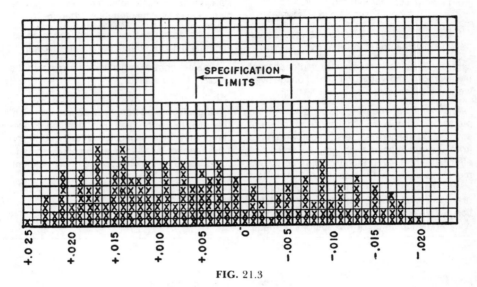

BI-METAL ASSEMBLY
AFTER I HOUR ANNEAL
TOLERANCE ± .005

FIG. 21.3

21.3 pictures the adjustment-setting values on thermometals in a nonconforming lot of 403A devices from which the thermometal had been disassembled and its adjusted setting checked.

This figure illustrates the very large proportion of strips that were found to be out of limits. Yet the two operators at the adjust stations were known to be conscientious, quality-conscious employees who insisted that the adjustments had been at the specification nominal when the subassemblies had left the adjust fixtures.

After considerable effort toward solving this problem of high rejects at final operational test caused by out-of-limits thermometal subassemblies, the concerned shop supervisor called for assistance from the process-control engineer. The engineer initiated a special process studies project, which had the final result of reducing the rejection rate on the thermometal subassembly from 75 percent to an acceptable figure of 1 percent.

In bringing this special study to a successful conclusion, the following activities were carried through:

Preliminary Analysis and Action

A preliminary analysis by the process-control engineer concerned initiated a series of investigations which disclosed four faulty process features, corrected as follows:

Faulty feature	Corrective action
Each of the two adjusting fixtures permitted inaccurate and discrepant settings because of worn mechanical parts in the fixtures.	Fixtures were repaired, and their settings were correlated one against the other. Fixtures were made subject to regular review through the plant preventive maintenance program.
Excessive variation in temperatures was experienced within the heat-treat oven.	Temperature variation was reduced to an acceptable amount by installation of a blower.
Errors in establishment and maintenance of the average temperature value held on the oven were experienced.	A master control switch which eliminated the problem was installed.
The metallic elements received for use on the production line were coming from different sources. Materials from each source differed from the other sources in trip characteristics after heat-treat, even though the same adjustment had been made throughout. Figure 21.4 shows the two-peaked distribution curve of one of these mixed thermometal lots. This distribution picture gave the first indication of the presence and importance of two sources of metal.	Material received from each source was identified before use on the production line. Procedures were established for differences in the adjustment of metal from each source so as to compensate for the effect of the heat treatment.

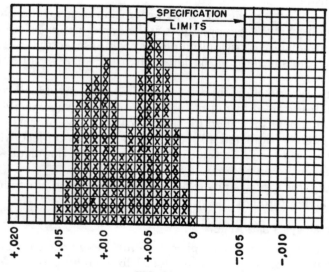

FIG. 21.4

After this activity, the process-control engineer ran a sample lot of thermometal subassemblies through the production sequence. The final operational test results on this sample showed that 30 percent rejects were still being experienced. Frequency-distribution analysis of the adjustment setting of the thermometal strips in the sample assemblies showed that the average strip setting was still several thousandths of an inch on the "high side" of the specification nominal value.

Further Analysis and Action

Further action in reducing rejects was obviously indicated. Several sample lots of thermometal strips were therefore sent through the production sequence. Distributions were plotted on the samples after units had been adjusted and again after the same units had been heat-treated but before they had been assembled to relays.

These same plots showed that the trip settings of thermometal strips drawn from the same source had a very definite and discernible tendency to "drift" after heat-treat.

A sample lot was then sent through the process adjusted and heat-treated as usual. Its distribution plot is shown in Figure 21.5. This distribution was analyzed for its average value, which was shown to be 0.004 inch above the specification nominal value.

A second lot, with thermometal drawn from the same source, was then sent through the process, with the initial adjustment 0.004 inch *below* the specification nominal value. Figure 21.6 pictures the resulting distribution, showing the first lot of thermometals whose quality was satisfactory after heat treatment.

Final Action and Control

Satisfied that the thermometal setting had an inherent tendency to drift as a result of heat-treat, the process-control engineer established a procedure whereby this quality hazard would be eliminated. Operators at the adjust and heat-treat stations were first furnished masters for the thermometal settings. They were then asked to follow a very simple procedure:

1. When a new batch of metallic elements was received, operators were to assemble and adjust a sample of the thermometal subassembly, heat-treat the sample, then check the adjustment settings, and plot them in tally form.
2. Operators were then to compensate for the drift tendency as shown by the average value for this sample by adjusting strips from that lot the required amount above or below the specification nominal.
3. Operators finally had the responsibility for periodically sampling the resulting subassemblies after heat-treat. Whatever adjustment compensations seemed indicated could be made by operators on the subsequent lots.

Figure 21.7 shows the tally form used by operators for the purpose outlined in step 3.

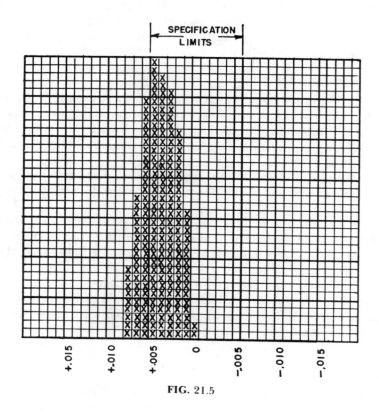

FIG. 21.5

Soon after this procedure was instituted, the following results could be seen:

Rejects at final operational test of the 403A device stabilized at about 1 percent.

The adjust operators were highly satisfied with a simple procedure which removed from them the onus of poor workmanship.

The shop supervisor was able to get out device production without being forced to pass back and forth lot after lot of devices for readjustment of the thermometal.

In the file report on the completion of this study, the process-control engineer included the following summary comments:

"If the investigation had ended after fixtures, furnace, and source of supply were corrected, the factory would still have had 30 percent rejections. From the results obtained in reducing this figure to 1 percent, it is obvious that the

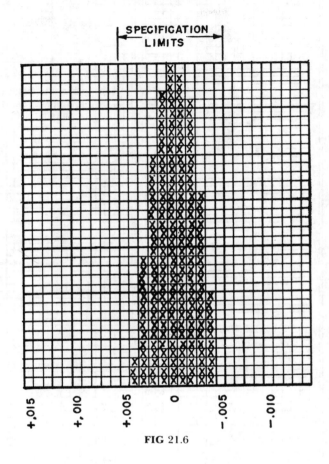

BI-METAL ASSEMBLY
AFTER I HOUR ANNEAL
TOLERANCE ± .005

FIG 21.6

use of these quality-control techniques aids greatly in solving factory quality problems on a permanent basis."

21.5 Casting of Sintered Blocks

Sintered metal blocks are produced in a process whose basic steps are shown in Figure 21.8. One type of these blocks possesses magnetic properties.

Output of this block was subject to 25 percent rejections at the test of its magnetic properties. To reduce these rejections and the attendant manufactur-

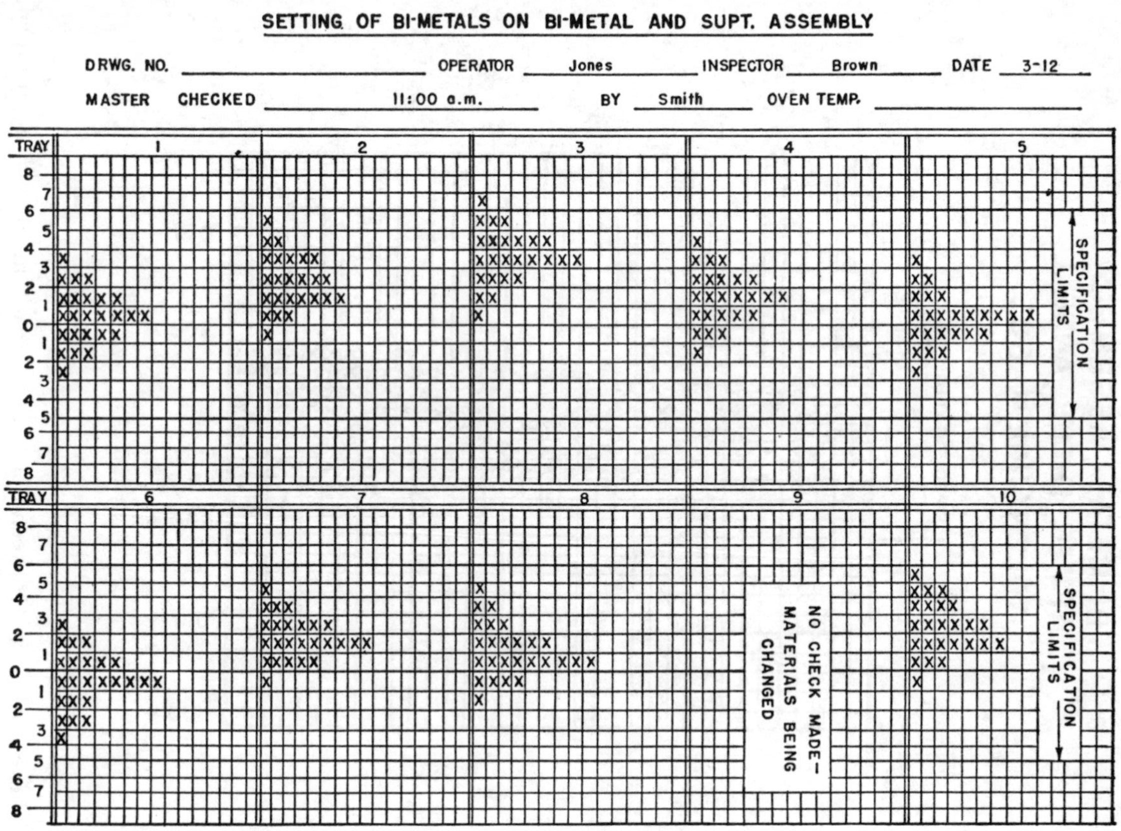
SETTING OF BI-METALS ON BI-METAL AND SUPT. ASSEMBLY
DRWG. NO.
OPERATOR Jones
INSPECTOR Brown
DATE 3-12
MASTER CHECKED 11:00 a.m.
BY Smith
OVEN TEMP.
TRAY
1
2
3
4
5
6
7
8
9
10
SPECIFICATION LIMITS
NO CHECK MADE—MATERIALS BEING CHANGED

FIG. 21.7

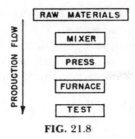

FIG. 21.8

ing losses, a special process studies investigation was begun on the entire process of casting sintered magnetic blocks.[3]

The casting process is rather intricate, with many possible variables. There would consequently be a great deal of difficulty in making a step-by-step analysis of the process unless some indication was available of the type of variable for which to watch.

It was decided, therefore, that the process study would be begun by analysis of the quality of blocks received at final test; potential reject causes would then be traced back from that point. As first step in the investigation, a sample of 150 blocks was sent through the regular production process.

Each block in the sample remained untouched until the final test, at which point the magnetic properties of each was recorded in the distribution shown in Figure 21.9.

The two-peaked distribution in this figure pointed to the possibility of two influential source factors affecting magnetic quality. Hypothesizing that two such factors operating at the same point in the process were at work, the production sequence was analyzed for their possible location.

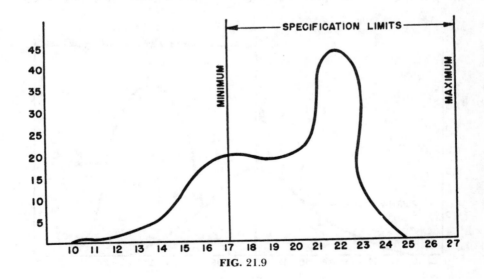

FIG. 21.9

After a step-by-step study, evidence began to point to possible major discrepancies between blocks produced by two sintering furnaces, called here furnace 1 and furnace 2. To explore the effect of these furnaces, a sample lot was sent through the regular process, with a portion of the blocks passing through sintering furnace 1 and the remaining blocks passing through sintering furnace 2.

The blocks passing through each furnace were so identified. After the rest of the processing period had been completed, test results on each block were recorded as shown in Figure 21.10.

This figure showed that furnace 1 was producing blocks of acceptable quality. Both the average and spread were satisfactory for the distribution plotted for blocks which had passed through this furnace.

On the other hand, furnace 2 was producing blocks which were approximately 50 percent nonconforming. Both the average and spread were unsatisfactory for its distribution.

Owing to this analysis, furnace 2 was made subject to a searching methods study. It was found that there was an uneven heat distribution internally which set up hot and cold zones within the furnace. Changes were at once made in furnace structure, which resulted in a much more even internal heat distribution.

With furnace 2 repaired, rejects at final test dropped sharply from the 25 percent level. To help maintain the much improved quality level, a procedure for periodic sampling of sintering furnace output was made a part of the plant product-control procedure.

21.6 Summary of Part 6

Quality is affected at all major stages of the production process. Effective control of quality must, therefore, involve quality-control activities which start

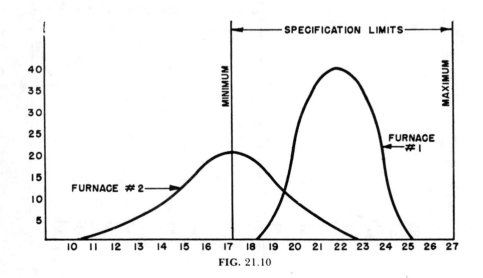

FIG. 21.10

while a product is being sold and designed and end only when the product is received by a fully satisfied customer.

These activities fall into four natural classifications termed the jobs of quality control, which are:

1. New-design control
2. Incoming-material control
3. Product control
4. Special process studies

Part 6 discussed each job, with emphasis upon the two major phases involved in each: (1) organizational practices and (2) technological routines. While organization practices are relatively uniform for all four jobs, there are a variety of technical routines unique to each.

These jobs of total quality control are founded upon what might be thought of as the principles of total quality control. The final part of this book, which follows, summarizes certain key areas of these principles.

Notes

[1]For a discussion on analyses of technically highly complex problems in whose solution special methods played a major part, see Secs. 16.15 and 16.16.

[2]This discussion is adapted from a study made by W. T. Short and associates, Schenectady, N.Y.

[3]This discussion is adapted from a study by G. S. Berge and associates, New York, N.Y.

PART SEVEN

The Total Quality Imperative for the 1990s

CHAPTER **22**

The Total Quality
Imperative

Eight out of ten consumer and industrial buyers in major international markets of the 1990s now make quality equal to or more important than price in their purchase decisions. A decade ago, only three to four customers out of ten thought this way and bought this way. This doubling of buyer emphasis on quality is one of the most significant trends in modern marketplace history.

Summarizing the reason very simply, the lifestyles of consumers and the work processes of companies now depend almost completely upon the reliable, predictable operation of products and services with little tolerance for the time and cost of any failures—something quite different from the past.

What good is a warranty to a mother of three on a Monday morning with four loads of laundry and a defective washing machine? How can a small telemarketing company remain in business when its state-of-the-art telephone system breaks down every other day? Warranty or no warranty, an unreliable product breeds an unsatisfied customer.

The old "we'll fix or replace it for you" policy of many companies, while honorable and important, is a traditional after-sales service approach—what can best be described as a failure-driven policy instead of one reflecting quality leadership. For some companies, thirty percent of all resolved customer complaints requiring product service leave a dissatisfied buyer who is looking for another seller.

Quality competition has now gone global. In the 1980s, it was concentrated in the Pacific Basin, primarily the United States and Japan with the so-called Four Dragon regions of South Korea, Taiwan, Hong Kong and Singapore. Now in the 1990s each of the major European nations is driven by the quality demands of the integration of Europe. This is also developing in South American countries where the total quality emphasis is increasingly strong. Moreover, both Soviet Union and Eastern Europe will inevitably enter the quality arena in this decade.

All of this means that to protect its position in its domestic market, a company must be able to design, build, and sell its major product lines today with the potential also for supremacy in the international marketplace—even though there isn't yet much import competition or interest in exporting. Murphy's Law, internationalized, says that if a company can get foreign competition today, it will get it. Operating in international quality leadership terms is the only way today for a business to grow with Murphy rather than be eroded by him.

As a result of this, some of the world's strongest companies are now building their growth around a necessary but very tough-to-execute new business quality strategy that fits this increasingly competitive world marketplace.

The strategy is that, to have both market share and profitability strength in the 1990s, quality has become the most powerful corporate leverage point for simultaneously achieving total customer satisfaction, human resource leadership, and lower costs.

This recognizes that basic changes in the marketplace, in the motivation of workers, and in the complexity of business operations have been the primary factors for fueling the quality revolution. It recognizes that the lighted match was increasing customer expectations—not Japan. The buyer has always demanded significantly higher quality when confronted with the significantly higher prices that have characterized consumer markets for both products and services over the past several years.

The quality revolution also recognizes that, during the past decade, care in buying—the art of purchasing—has improved more rapidly than any other commercial skill for both business firms and consumers.

In the 1970s and early 1980s, the prevailing business attitude in many areas of America, Europe, and some parts of the Far East was that the way for a company to succeed was to make products and deliver services quicker and cheaper, sell them hard, and finance them cleverly. Business processes were structured to accomplish this, managers were trained to insist on it, and were promoted if they did, and employees were encouraged to work this way. Some national purchasing programs seemed to be oriented this way, and educational institutions, including many engineering universities and most higher management and business administration schools, treated quality as a footnote, if they treated it at all.

In the 1990s, international business has recognized that while making products quicker and cheaper remains a competitive necessity, making them better is the best way to make and sell them cheaper and quicker. But the business processes and attitudes and training of the past can still be there, pushing in the wrong direction away from quality.

Leading an organization from a make-it-quicker-and-cheaper past to a make-it-better future in a competitively acceptable period of time can be the single most demanding task before many managers today. It requires not only quality awareness but, of perhaps much greater importance, personal, managerial know-how for leading in quality improvement with the same sureness of touch that the managers have in the areas of technology, sales, and finance.

This is because quality, approached as first-time customer satisfaction rather than quicker responsiveness in fixing customer quality problems, will mean basic changes in the fundamental business processes themselves, perhaps in sales, in how manufacturing is structured, and in supplier relations. It means emphasizing very high quality performance in the development and introduction of new products. And it surely means planning automation and robotics so as to improve quality rather than merely to produce more poor products quicker than before.

The acceleration of quality improvement is just as important in service operations—financial intermediaries, government bodies, hospitality providers, and health care, to name a few—as in products. In some service processes, only one work product out of ten goes through error-free. While much of the widely publicized increase in service employment has come about through market growth, some has been created by these do-the-job-over quality problems. They are a principal reason for the minimal productivity increase in services.

While it is not yet widely apparent, without significant quality improvement, some service operations have the same vulnerability to foreign competition that affected manufacturing long ago. Our experience in the quality processes of financial service companies is an example. A telecommunications satellite is indifferent to whether service operations of a financial institution or of a data processing organization are located in New York, London, Tokyo, Paris, or Frankfurt so long as the operations are quality-effective.

For all these reasons, accelerating the rate of quality improvement is the single most important competitive task facing companies. In today's market, when a customer is satisfied with quality, he tells eight people; when he's dissatisfied, he tells twenty-two. That's the hard arithmetic of quality's effect on sales growth in the marketplace. Moreover, the General Systems Company experience in the installation of total quality control in hundreds of companies throughout the world is that quality leadership can give companies a five-cents-on-the-dollar competitive advantage, as much as ten cents in some cases. For many companies, this can be their key opportunity for improved profitability and return on investment in the 1990s, one that our experience shows will pay off early, with a sustained and growing return.

There are basic benchmarks of total quality control that are central to achieving this result. Chapter 23 reviews these benchmarks.

Ten Benchmarks of Total Quality Control for the 1990s

Fundamental to total quality control are ten benchmarks that are the keys to its successful application in the 1990s. These are the following:

1. *Quality is a company-wide process.* Quality is not a technical function nor a department nor an awareness program but instead a systemic customer-connected process that must be totally and rigorously implemented throughout the company and integrated with suppliers.
2. *Quality is what the customer says it is.* It is not what an engineer or marketeer or merchant says it is. If you want to find out about your quality, go out and ask your customer—nobody can compress in a market research statistic the buyer frustration from a water leak in a new car.
3. *Quality and cost are a sum not a difference.* They are partners, not adversaries, and the best way to make products and offer services quicker and cheaper is to make them better. Quality is a fundamental business strategy and an outstanding opportunity for high return on investment, for which careful quality cost identification is an essential guideline.
4. *Quality requires both individual and teamwork zealotry.* Quality is everybody's job but it will become nobody's job without a clear infrastructure that supports both the quality work of individuals as well as the quality team-work among departments. The biggest problem of many quality programs is that they are quality improvement islands without bridges.
5. *Quality is a way of managing.* Good management used to be thought of as getting the ideas out of the boss's head into the hands of the workers. Today we know better. Good management means personal leadership in

empowering the quality knowledge, skills, and attitudes of everyone in the organization to recognize that making quality right makes everything else in the company right. The belief that quality travels under some exclusive national passport, or has some unique geographic or cultural identity, is a myth.

6. *Quality and innovation are mutually dependent.* The key to successful new product launches is to make quality the partner of product development from the beginning—not the sweep-up-after mechanism for development problems. It is essential to include early on the determination of buyer attitudes toward the new product or service because the customer can't seriously tell you his likes and dislikes until he sees and uses the product —paper studies don't do it.

7. *Quality is an ethic.* The pursuit of excellence—deep recognition that what you are doing is right—is the strongest human emotional motivator in any organization and it's the basic driver in true quality leadership. Quality programs based solely on charts and graphics are never enough.

8. *Quality requires continuous improvement.* Quality is a constantly upward mov-ing target. Continuous improvement is an in-line, integral component of a quality program, not a separate activity, and is achieved only through help, participation, and involvement from all the men and women in the company and its suppliers. It can be thought of as the jogging and fitness discipline for company quality leadership.

9. *Quality is the most cost-effective, least capital-intensive route to productivity.* Some of the world's strongest companies have blindsided their competition by concentrating on elimination of their hidden plant—that part of the orga-nization which exists because of bad work. They've done it by changing their productivity concept from the old Frederick Taylor four-letter word —M-O-R-E—and added on the quality leadership four-letter word—G-O-O-D, into the more good quality productivity concept. They've backed this up with the informed application of a wide range of new and existing quality technology—used within the company quality process rather than as an end in itself.

10. *Quality is implemented with a total system connected with customers and suppliers.* This is what makes quality leadership real in a company—the relentless application of the systematic methodology that makes it possible for a company to manage its quality rather than just have it happen. Technical capability isn't the principal quality problem for companies today. What differentiates the quality leaders from the quality followers is quality disci-pline and clear quality work processes that men and women throughout the organization understand, believe in, and are a part of.

These are the Ten Benchmarks of Total Quality Control for the demanding decade of the 1990s. They make quality a way of totally focusing the company on the customer—whether it be the end user or the man and woman at the next desk or work station.

There are some fine examples of companies with excellent total quality programs built in terms of these benchmarks. However, the quality programs of some other companies have traveled at best only fifteen to twenty percent of the hard road to meeting these benchmarks for achieving the demands of total customer satisfaction. In these companies, quality still is not a board room interest, still is thought of as primarily a specialist's job operating at secondary levels of organization. Quality is still not a mainline activity in development and engineering, where innovation is thought of as the basic drumbeat for technology and quality work a much less challenging task.

Nor is quality a mainline activity in the finance communities of these companies—even though accounting miscodes and billing mistakes create more customer ill will than product returns. Nor is it mainline in marketing—where quality is thought of as what you have to sell to the customer even though the engineers and production people may not be doing it right.

In today's markets, quality excellence is a total-value demand that includes not only expectations for good intrinsic product function but also for good extrinsic product-support and service features coordinated for the buyer from all these parts of the company. This is why advanced product technology of and by itself hasn't produced sales for the small computer companies in the business market. It's why some airline companies with a rather narrow approach to their function have tended not to succeed in a market that expects "getting there" to mean getting there in a way that includes relatively comfortable and smooth passage through airports, and to and from the city. The point is that the buyer total-value quality demands call for not only a reduction in things gone wrong—the old quality control approach—but also an increase in things gone right—our total quality approach.

It takes relentlessly consistent and disciplined management leadership and methodology to convert all of this to a company quality program that leads the quality requirements of customers—which is the essence of competitive advantage—rather than merely reacting to these requirements. Key management principles for accomplishing this are reviewed in Chapter 24.

CHAPTER **24**

Four Management Fundamentals
of Total Quality

Four basic management fundamentals of competitive quality leadership are essential in implementing the benchmarks of total quality control.

The *first,* is that there's no such thing a permanent quality level. One of the flaws in traditional quality control programs has been that they establish a single right quality level and then target all effort to meeting and maintaining that level. Today, when this so-called "right" quality level has been attained, international quality leadership demands more and more upgraded quality levels. This is what customers will demand and what competition will call for because quality is a rapidly upward moving target in today's markets.

For example, a very successful components company has moved itself from the marginal supplier in a major segment of the aircraft and computer electronics market to the preferred supplier. It has moved from processing several hundred defective high-technology components per million, that had to be reworked during final testing, to processing a very few per million today. Quality costs have been reduced by two-thirds. Is this company now immune from quality competition? Not on your life! Certain competitive processors are looking to improving component processing to a low defects per billion quality performance. That's why, more than ever today, the only way to compete with quality is with more quality.

The *second* fundamental is that a hallmark of good management is personal leadership in mobilizing the quality knowledge, skill, and positive attitudes of everyone in the organization to recognize that what you do to make quality better helps to make everything else in the organization better.

For example, the all-important activity of employee participation in quality improvement contributes significantly only when it is an basic part of in-line quality activity and is supported by effective quality actions. Too often, what

831

has been called participation has been merely an off-line exercise in motivation without much visible operational support. Moreover, the evolution toward genuine employee quality empowerment comes about only where quality improvement becomes an integral rather than an incidental part of every job.

When this fundamental is not understood it is the reason why long-service employees in some organizations will tell you that they are now going through the seventh or eighth quality improvement crusade in their careers, all the earlier ones having quietly died and been buried without autopsy. These employees want to know what is solid and different about the new program that will really make it stick.

The answer is that, to be effective, the emphasis must always be on in-line involvements, on job-related quality improvement activities that take place at the employee's work station in plant or office. Only there can the involvement be real, and only from there can the quality improvement be passed on directly from job performance to product reliability to customer satisfaction, often through employee work teams.

Effective company-wide quality education is not a department nor training course but a continuous, management-led process that is a fundamental part of all aspects of company operations. The key is job-related implementation of the processes for the involvement, training, recognition and empowerment of all men and women in the organization for making quality a fundamental way of life in all jobs throughout the organization. The company-quality culture, which is so strongly influenced by it, isn't a matter of words, but, instead, a composite of the company-quality actions.

This is why total quality programs are the single most powerful change agent for company improvement today and bring as much as ten times more hands on attention to such improvements.

This depends heavily on front-line supervisors and the support they receive —an area that has been too often overlooked in some quality programs. It is they who must provide the employees with the leadership, technical guidance, and persistent inculcation of the quality ethic on which the success of the entire program rides. The supervisors, for their part, will need the time and tools to do the job, including relief from excessive paperwork.

In total quality control, supervisors spend much more time in teaching and leading both individual employees and employee work teams on quality, productivity and related matters. Employee participation becomes institutionalized in the quality effort as a sustained in-line program, and front-line supervision in both plant and office becomes, as it should, a principal center of the company's quality aspirations and activities. What is too often overlooked as a hidden strength of total quality applied at middle management level is that over 25 percent of supervisory time is directly oriented to improvement.

The *third* fundamental is that quality is essential for successful innovation. There are two reasons:

The *first* is the greatly increased speed of new product development. The television set took twenty years to mature as a product; the personal computer four years; many new integrated circuit devices now no more than twelve months.

The *second* reason is that, when a product design is likely to be manufactured in several countries and where international suppliers must be involved very early, the entire development process must be clearly and visibly structured. The total quality approach to this has four steps.

1. Make quality a full and equal partner with innovation from the inception of product development.
2. Emphasize getting high quality product design and process matches up-stream—not after manufacturing planning has already frozen the alternatives.
3. Make full service suppliers a quality partner at the beginning of design rather than a quality surveillance problem later.
4. Make the acceleration of new product introduction—not its slowing down —a primary measure of the effectiveness of a company's quality program.

Experience demonstrates that this will not only assure that new product quality will be very high, but also that product development cycles will be reduced by one-third or more. This is because of the clear, up-front connection with the customer and the consequent reduction of continuous and frequently very late engineering changes for quality reasons. At least 20 percent—and often much more—of total product development costs can be created by this quality recycling. The systematic partnership of quality and innovation dramatically lowers both these upstream costs and their impact on creating much higher downstream manufacturing costs than had been originally anticipated in the company's product plan.

The *fourth* fundamental is that quality and cost are complementary not conflicting business objectives. For many years, the managements of some companies routinely operated on the basis that a choice had to be made between quality and cost—the so-called trade-off decision—because better quality was thought to mean "goldplating" and inevitably would somehow cost more and make production more difficult. Experience throughout the world has shown that this simply is not true; on the contrary, good quality fundamentally leads to good resource utilization—of the workforce, of equipment, of materials—and consequently means good productivity and very low quality costs. Management must make clear throughout the company that what is expected is both *quality* and *cost.* Management thus does not give any opportunity for the old myth, that good quality is, in some ways, more expensive, to become a self-fulfilling prophecy within the organization.

These fundamentals make clear that quality leadership is now the key to business success for companies and, aggregatively for national economies. Correspondingly, national and regional initiatives are becoming of increasing importance in fostering quality leadership.

Japan's quality prize structure has been very effective. In the United States, the Malcolm Baldrige National Quality award program is for the first time a statement of America's national will for quality leadership. It provides for the first time, guidelines for American manufacturing and service organizations which define the total quality basis of this leadership; and it for the first time provides an increasingly organized way through which American organizations can share and exchange quality improvement experience and know-how on a national scale—both for those companies that apply for the Baldrige Award and those that do not. Similar initiatives are evolving in Europe and in Latin America.

Moreover, such international standards as the ISO 9000 series, while minimum total quality entry level in concept, nonetheless point toward a broad and systematic, rather than narrow, approach to quality achievement.

Taken together, all of this places emphasis upon the fact that quality has become, in its essence, a way of managing—a way based upon:

- A clear understanding of domestic and international markets and of how people buy in these markets.
- A thorough grasp of the kind of total quality strategy that provides the business foundation for satisfying these customers.
- A hands-on management that has the know-how for creating the necessary company environment for quality and for establishing the stretch goals and detailed implementation programs needed for quality leadership.

These are the keys to making quality today's best investment in corporate competitiveness.

The Principles of
Total Quality Control:
A Summary

A series of "principles" continues to simmer out of industry's experience with the management of quality and total quality control.

An interpretation of these principles is presented below. It is offered as a summary of the "total quality management" approach which regards the quality of products and services as a primary business strategy and a fundamental determinant for business health, growth, and economic viability.

1. Total quality control may be defined as

> An effective system for integrating the quality-development, quality-maintenance, and quality-improvement efforts of the various groups in an organization so as to enable marketing, engineering, production, and service at the most economical levels which allow for full customer satisfaction.

2. In the phrase "quality control," the word "quality" does not have the popular meaning of "best" in any absolute sense. It means "best for certain customer requirements." These requirements are the (a) actual use and (b) selling price of the product.

3. In the phrase "quality control," the word "control" represents a management tool with four steps:
    a. Setting quality standards
    b. Appraising conformance to these standards

    c. Acting when the standards are exceeded
    d. Planning for improvements in the standards

4. Several quality-control methods have been carried on in industry for many years. What is new in the modern approach to quality control is (*a*) the integration of these often uncoordinated activities and an engineered, operating systems framework which places the responsibility for customer-oriented quality efforts across all the main-line activities of an enterprise, giving quality *organizationwide impact,* and (*b*) the addition to the time-tested methods used of the new quality-control technologies which have been found useful in dealing with and thinking about the increased emphasis upon reliability in product design and precision in parts manufacture.

5. As a major new business strategic area, quality is explicitly structured to contribute to business profitability and positive cash flow. Total-quality-control programs are highly cost-effective because of their results in improved levels of customer satisfaction, reduced operating costs, reduced operating losses and field service costs, and improved utilization of resources.

6. The need for such programs is underscored by changing buyer-producer relationships and major marketplace demands for quality. These are reflected in mounting product and service liability trends and consumer pressures which impact strongly upon producers. In addition, there are new social and economic demands for more effective materials use and production processes to turn out increasingly technologically based products, new working patterns in factories and offices, and a growing trend toward internationalization of markets.

7. The factors affecting product quality can be divided into two major groupings: (*a*) the technological, that is, machines, materials, and processes; (*b*) the human, that is, operators, foremen, and other company personnel. Of these two factors, the human is of greater importance by far.

8. Total quality control is an important aid to the good engineering designs, good manufacturing methods, and conscientious product service activity that have always been required for the delivery of high-quality articles.

9. The fundamentals of quality control are basic to any manufacturing process, whether the product is a nuclear reactor, a space vehicle, a consumer durable, or bakery, drug, or brewery products. They are equally basic to so-called service industries, where the product may be an intangible, such as medical care, hotel accommodations, or telephone communications.

    Although the approach is somewhat different if the production is job shop rather than large quantity or small components rather than large apparatus, the same fundamentals still obtain. This difference in approach can be readily summarized: In mass-production manufacturing, quality-control activities center on the *product,* whereas in job-lot manufacturing, they are a matter of controlling the *process.*

10. Quality control enters into all phases of the industrial production process, starting with the customer's specification and the sale to the customer through design engineering and assembly to shipment of the product and installation and field service for a customer who remains satisfied with the product.

11. Effective control over the factors affecting quality demands controls at all important stages of the production and service processes. These controls can be termed the *jobs of quality control,* and they fall into four natural classifications:

   a. New-design control
   b. Incoming-material control
   c. Product control
   d. Special process studies

12. New-design control involves the establishment and specification of the desirable cost-quality, performance-quality, safety-quality, and reliability-quality standards for the product, including the elimination or location of possible sources of quality troubles before the start of formal production.

13. Incoming-material control involves the receiving and stocking, at the most economical levels of quality, of only those parts, materials, and components whose quality conforms to the specification requirements.

14. Product control involves the control of products at the source of production and through field service so that departures from the quality specification can be corrected before defective products are manufactured and proper product service can be maintained in the field.

15. Special process studies involve investigations and tests to locate the causes of defective products so as to improve quality characteristics and implement permanent corrective action.

16. A total quality system may be defined as

> The agreed companywide and plantwide operating work structure, documented in effective, integrated technical and managerial procedures, for guiding the coordinated actions of the people, the machines, and the information of the company and plant in the best and most practical ways to assure customer quality satisfaction and economical costs of quality.

The quality system provides integrated and continuous control to all key activities, making it truly organizationwide in scope.

17. The details for each quality-control program must be tailored to fit the needs of individual plants, but certain basic areas of attention are common to most programs for total quality control.

18. The target of the quality program attention is to control product quality

throughout the process of design, manufacture, shipment, and service so as to *prevent* the occurrence of unsatisfactory quality.

19. Benefits often resulting from total quality programs are improvements in product quality and design, reductions in operating costs and losses, improvement in employee morale, and reduction of production-line bottlenecks. By-product benefits are improved inspection and test methods, sounder setting of time standards for labor, definite schedules for preventative maintenance, the availability of powerful data for use in company advertising, and the furnishing of a factual basis for cost-accounting standards for scrap, rework, and inspection.

20. Quality costs are a means for measuring and optimizing total-quality-control activities.

21. Operating quality costs are divided into four different classifications:
   a. Prevention costs, which include quality planning and other costs associated with preventing nonconformances and defects.
   b. Appraisal costs, or the costs incurred in evaluating product quality to maintain established quality levels.
   c. Internal failure costs, caused by defective and nonconforming materials and products that do not meet company quality specifications. These include scrap, rework, and spoilage.
   d. External failure costs, caused by defective and nonconforming products reaching the customer. They include complaints and in-warranty product service costs, costs of product recall, court costs, and liability penalties.

22. Cost reductions—particularly reductions in operating quality costs—result from total quality control for two reasons:
   a. Industry has often lacked effective, customer-oriented quality standards. It has, therefore, often unrealistically tilted the scales in the balance between the cost of quality in a product and the service that the product is to render.
   b. An expenditure in the area of prevention can have a severalfold advantage in reducing costs in the areas of internal failure and external failure. A saving of many dollars for each dollar spent in *prevention* is often experienced.

23. Organizationwise, total quality control is management's tool for delegating authority and responsibility for product quality, thus relieving itself of unnecessary detail while retaining the means of assuring that quality results will be satisfactory. There are two basic concepts important in organizing for quality control.

   The first is that *quality is everybody's job.* Every component has quality-related responsibility, e.g., Marketing for determining customers' quality preferences, Engineering for specifying product quality specifications, and Shop Supervision for building quality into the product.

   The second concept is that *because quality is everybody's job, it may become nobody's job.* Management must recognize that the many individual responsibilities for quality will be exercised most effectively when they are buttressed and serviced by a well-organized, full-time, genuinely modern management function whose only area of operation is in the quality-control jobs.

24. While the general manager must, in principle, become the chief designer of the quality program, the general manager and the other major company functions are assisted by an effective, modern, quality-control function.

25. This quality-control organizational component has twin objectives: *(a)* to provide quality assurance for the company's product, i.e., simply to be sure that the products shipped are right, and *(b)* to assist in assuring optimum quality costs for those products. It fulfills these objectives through its three subfunctions: *quality engineering, process-control engineering,* and *quality information equipment engineering.* These quality-control subfunctions provide basic engineering technologies that are applicable to any product for assuring its right quality at optimum quality cost.

26. *Quality engineering* contributes to the quality planning which is fundamental to the entire quality-control program for the company.

27. *Process-control engineering* monitors the application of this quality-control program on the production floor and thus gradually supplants the older policing inspection activity.

28. *Quality information equipment engineering* designs and develops the inspection and testing equipment for obtaining the necessary quality measurements and controls. Where justified, this equipment is combined with production to provide automatic feedback of results for control of the process. All pertinent results are then analyzed as a basis for adjustment and corrective action on the process.

29. From the human relations point of view, quality-control organization is both a

   a. *Channel of communication* for product-quality information among all concerned employees and groups.

   b. *Means of participation* in the overall quality-control program by these employees and groups.

   Quality-control organization is a means of breaking down the attitude sometimes held by factory operators and functional specialists that "our quality responsibility is so small a part of the whole that we're really not a part of the plant quality-control program nor are we important to it."

30. Total-quality-control programs should be developed carefully within a given company. It is often wise to select one or two quality areas, to achieve successful results in attacking them, and to let the program grow step by step in this fashion.

31. Necessary to the success of the quality program in a plant is the very intangible but extremely important spirit of *quality-mindedness,* extending from top management right to the men and women at the bench.

32. Whatever may be new about the total-quality-control program for a plant must be closely coupled throughout the entire plant organization so as to obtain willing acceptance and cooperation.

33. A quality-control program must have the complete support of top management. With lukewarm management support, no amount of selling to the rest of the organization can be genuinely effective.

34. Management must recognize at the outset of its total-quality-control program that this program is not a temporary quality improvement or quality cost-reduction project. Only when the major problems represented by the initial quality improvements and cost reductions are out of the way can the quality-control program take over its long-range role of the management *control* over quality.

35. Statistics are used in an overall quality-control program whenever and wherever they may be useful, but statistics are only one part of the total-quality-control pattern; they are not the pattern itself. The five statistical tools that have come to be used in quality-control activities are
   a. Frequency distributions
   b. Control charts
   c. Sampling tables
   d. Special methods
   e. Product reliability
   The point of view represented by these statistical methods has, however, had a profound effect upon the entire area of total quality control.

36. The statistical point of view in total quality control resolves essentially into this: Variation in product quality must be constantly studied—within batches of product, on processing equipments, between different lots of the same article, on critical quality characteristics and standards. This variation may best be studied by the analysis of samples selected from the lots of product or from units produced by the processing equipments. The development of advanced electronic and mechanical test equipment has provided basic improvement in the approach to this task.

37. The demands of total quality control are increased by automation of the manufacturing process. With automatic equipment, higher quality levels for parts sometimes are necessary for trouble-free operation. In fact, until higher quality levels are attained, excessive down time may make operation of the automated process uneconomic. Rapid detection of out-of-control conditions, feedback for process adjustment, and quick response of the process to correction are essential to low defect and nonconformance rates.

38. An important feature of a total quality program is that it controls quality at the source. An example is its positive effect in stimulating and building up operator responsibility for, and interest in, product quality through measurements taken by the operator at the station.

39. Product reliability is, in effect, "product function over the product life expectancy (time)." It is a part of the balanced total product-quality requirement—just as are appearance, maintainability, serviceability, supportability, and so on—and hence cannot be treated separately from total quality control.

40. The total quality program provides the discipline, methodology, and

techniques to assure consistently high product quality in the four basic jobs of

a. New-design control
b. Incoming-material control
c. Product control
d. Special process studies

It coordinates the efforts of the people, the machines, and the information which are basic to total quality control to provide high customer quality satisfaction which brings competitive advantage to the company.

Quality is, in its essence, a way of managing. And total quality control's organizationwide impact involves the managerial and technical implementation of customer-oriented quality activities as a prime responsibility of general management and of the mainline operations of marketing, engineering, production, industrial relations, finance, and service as well as of the quality-control function itself at the most economical levels which provide full customer satisfaction.

Good Management in the 1990s

The Ten Benchmarks for the application of these principles in the 1990s show that what good management is all about is achieving competitive leadership in customer satisfaction. The total quality way of managing encourages everyone in the organization to focus almost obsessively upon serving the customer—whether it is the end user or the man or woman a desk away. The company culture, so strongly influenced by these principles, is not made of words, but of company-wide quality actions. This means:

- Making quality the strategic center of the organization's business planning with stretch goals directed to competitive quality leadership.
- Encouraging the evolution toward genuine employee empowerment where quality improvement becomes an integral rather than an incidental part of every job by establishing quality work and teamwork processes that men and women throughout the organization understand, believe in, and are part of.
- Recognizing the crucial role of front-line supervisors through work structures which enhance their leadership of quality improvement instead of overwhelming them with meetings and bureaucratic paperwork.
- Relating and integrating quality education and job training with the development and establishment of the work processes in which the training will be used through a continuous management-led activity, which becomes a fundamental part of all aspects of company operations.
- Emphasizing that total quality results from long-term implementation oriented toward continuous improvement, based—not on episodic projects or lectures—but upon systematic total quality methodology that is relentlessly applied.

Index

About the Author

DR. ARMAND V. FEIGENBAUM is the originator of total quality control, an approach to quality and productivity that has profoundly influenced the competition for world markets in the United States, Japan, and throughout the industrialized world. He is president of General Systems Company, Inc., Pittsfield, Mass., an international engineering firm that designs and installs integrated operational systems for major corporations here and abroad. Earlier, he was manager for ten years of worldwide manufacturing operations and quality control at the General Electric Company. He was the founding chairman of the International Academy for Quality and is a past president of the American Society for Quality Control, which has presented him its Edwards Medal and Lancaster Award for his international contributions to quality and productivity. He lectures widely. His articles have appeared in the *Harvard Business Review*, *International Management*, and other publications. He was still a doctoral student at the Massachusetts Institute of Technology when he completed the first edition of *Total Quality Control*.